Date Due

SOCIAL THOUGHT
FROM LORE TO SCIENCE

In Three Volumes. Volume I.
A History and Interpretation of Man's Ideas about
Life with His Fellows to Times
when Change and Progress Deeply Concern Him

Third Edition

by HOWARD BECKER

Late Professor of Sociology, University of Wisconsin;
President, 1959-1960, American Sociological Association

and HARRY ELMER BARNES *with the assistance*
of Émile Benoît-Smullyan and Others

With an introductory note by Merle Curti, prefaces to all three editions,
1960 addenda for all chapters, a terminological commentary, a 1937-1960
appendix on contemporary sociology; 1960 bibliographies,
notes and subject indexes.

Dover Publications, Inc., New York

Published in Canada by General Publishing Com-
pany, Ltd., 30 Lesmill Road, Don Mills, Toronto,
Ontario.
Published in the United Kingdom by Constable
and Company, Ltd., 10 Orange Street, London
WC 2.

This Dover edition, first published in 1961, is an
expanded and revised version of the second (1952)
edition of the work originally published by D. C.
Heath and Company in 1938.

The work has been previously published in two
volumes, but the present edition is published in
three volumes. Volumes One and Two of this Dover
edition comprise the original Volume One, whereas
Volume Three of this Dover edition comprises
Volume Two of previous editions.

Professor Howard Becker's articles from the
various issues of the *Britannica Book of the Year*
are reprinted through the courtesy of Encyclopaedia, Britannica, Inc.

Standard Book Number: 486-20901-6
Library of Congress Catalog Card Number: 61-4323

Manufactured in the United States of America
Dover Publications, Inc.
180 Varick Street
New York, N.Y. 10014

To
Those Who Share the Age-Old Hope
that
Man's Inhumanity to Man
Can Be Diminished

Introductory Note, 1960

I N GRANTING WITH THE UTMOST pleasure the request of Dover Publications, Inc., for appropriate comment on the third edition of what has clearly become a standard work in its field, enthusiastic reiteration of the remarks that appeared eight years ago seems to be indicated:

In his witty and sprightly statement, "Fourteen Years After," Howard Becker clearly sets forth all that anyone needs to know about the new material added to the present reprinting of *Social Thought from Lore to Science*. It would be superfluous to repeat what he has said so authoritatively and so well.

Charming though Professor Becker's reference to the "resurrection" of this book is, I must enter a disclaimer. For like Joe Hill, *Social Thought from Lore to Science* never died. It was, to be sure, difficult of access after the edition ran out and the plates were destroyed. Even the most resourceful second-hand dealers often failed to find a copy for an eager scholar. But it continued to live in private and public libraries, in academic lectures that drew heavily upon it, and in writings that borrowed from it. Now, fortunately, it has turned up again like an old and valued friend who has been hard to find. And it turns up in a new and attractive outfit, thoroughly up to date. For as the added preface explains, the present edition contains Professor Becker's illuminating "1951 Commentary on Value-System Terminology" and his informed and thoughtful "1937-1950 Appendix on Sociological Trends." I speak for many scholars and teachers in welcoming again *Social Thought from Lore to Science*.

To the sociologists, anthropologists, psychologists, philosophers, and historians who have known this remarkable work, no further comment is needed. But perhaps a historian may be permitted to recall the reception that the volumes had on their appearance in 1938. Admiration, discriminating praise, and a deep sense of gratitude characterized the reviews in both the journals of opinion and in the learned periodicals. Indeed, on reading the reviews one is struck by the frequent recurrence of such phrases in notice after notice as "impressive accuracy, competence, and discrimination," or "reliable information, pertinent criticism, and historical perspective," or "a huge enterprise carried out with courage and ability." Few if any reviewers took exception to the prevailing view, as attested by comment from literally all over the world, that this was the best single treatise in any language on the history of social thought. The wonder is, in view of the impressive reception of the book and the place it so quickly assumed in the literature of social science, that it was permitted to go out of print and that so long a time has passed before its reissue.

On re-reading the book with the perspective of fourteen years, one may with some certainty maintain that the basic decisions made by Becker and Barnes in planning and executing the work over a twenty-year period were both sound and unusually forward-looking. Especially the inclusion of the social reflections of preliterate peoples and the social thought of non-Western cultures; the combined topical, chronological, and regional approaches; and the superb bibliographical guides that invited the reader to further intellectual adventures. Most of all, however, one is now impressed by the amazingly early adoption of the methods of the sociology of knowledge for the study of social thought. This involved, of course, search for the interactions of social ideas and other factors in the culture, or in other words, the treatment of social thought as process rather than as a series of mere topics. It further involved, and this was especially remarkable in view of the prestige of relativism at the time, a sustained effort to analyze and synthesize the data in such a way as to transcend the barriers of nations, classes, and historical epochs, and thus to approximate theoretical generalizations of more than mere relative validity.

This work will beckon new readers hitherto unfamiliar with it. Whatever their major interests, whether sociology, anthropology, philosophy, psychology, or the history of society and civilization, they will be deeply grateful to the publishers, to Harry Elmer Barnes for initiating the project, and especially to Howard Becker for his significant part in the original edition and for all that he has done to give the present one even greater usefulness to scholars, teachers, and general readers of our own time.

Thus ran the 1952 remarks. The present edition, with supplements for every chapter and updating of the appendix on contemporary sociology, merits even more hearty approval.

MERLE CURTI

Madison, Wisconsin
January, 1960

Twenty-Two Years After

PREFACE TO THE THIRD EDITION

FROM TIME TO TIME, when more than ordinarily bored by what Parkinson has christened "Blahmanism, Confusionism, and Comitology," and by other routines of the academic life, I take down from my shelves a collection of the essays of Finley Peter Dunne, disguised as the observations, opinions, philosophy, and what-will-you-have of that peerless saloon proprietor, Mr. Dooley. Sipping discreetly of the dew thus dispensed, my boredom vanishes, and I again face life—even the academic life—with serenity if not courage. Indeed, I am sometimes so rejuvenated that I then turn to the swashbuckling romances of Dumas and find that they manifest all the fascination exercised upon me in my now so distant youth; I become Athos, Porthos, Aramis, and D'Artagnan all rolled into one. This happened just the other day, and I sprang with alacrity to write this preface, for it had occurred to me that "Twenty-Two Years After" might be as stirring in the writing as *Twenty Years After* is in the reading. But then Mr. Dooley intervened again, and this time in a way not customary with him; he chilled my elation by remarking, ". . . if ye got at th' rale feelin' iv three-meal-a-day men about writin', ye'd find they classed it with . . . playactin', dancin', an' lace-wurruk. . . . An' do I objict to th' pursuit iv lithrachoor? Oh, faith, no. As a pursuit 'tis fine, but it may be bad f'r anny wan that catches it." After exposure to such congealing comment, I retained just enough strength to proceed with what was now my irksome prefatory chore; I could spring only an inch or two, and not with alacrity.

Let me then proceed soberly and sedately to tell you how this third edition has taken shape. After undergoing many and various vicissitudes, the first and second editions went out of print. Then, three or four years ago, Mr. Hayward Cirker, President of Dover Publications, Inc. suggested that we plan on a third edition in three paperback volumes. At first this seemed to me a fantastic notion, but the more I thought

about it the more sensible it began to appear. Finally, an arrangement was made in accordance with which not only
Social Thought from Lore to Science but also my old augmented adaptation of an important German treatise,
abridged and under the revised title of *Systematic Sociology
as Based on Wiese,* would be issued in paperback form.

Other obligations—teaching, research, conferences, outside lectures, field work abroad, publication, functioning as
President-Elect and President of the American Sociological
Association, departmental busywork — seriously hindered
both projects, but today I have at least been able to wind up
the revision of *Social Thought from Lore to Science,* and in
a few months *Systematic Sociology* should also be ready for
the press.

In revising what students at the University of Wisconsin
irreverently call "Stiflits," the only way that I could see to
avoid excessive costs was to leave the text of the second edition unaltered except for correction of minor errors. Comment qualifying and extending the earlier treatment was then
added, in smaller type, at the end of each chapter and at the
end of the commentary on value-system terminology. Further, the bibliography was brought up to date, and the appendix on contemporary sociological trends was extended to
include the period from the end of 1950 to the beginning of
1960.

It will be noted that at many points in the end-of-chapter
comments, the bibliography, and the appendix I have referred to writings in which I myself have had a part as editor, co-author, or author. This is not because these writings
are viewed by me as possessing extraordinary merit, but
merely because, knowing them well, I could refer to them in
qualification or expansion of the text without doing a great
deal of digging in the library for publication details, page
numbers, and the like, of other books and articles, many of
them quite as relevant and more authoritative, but not so intimately familiar. As sufficient punishment, *faber compedes,
quas fecit ipse, gestet.*

To Merle Curti, who since the days of his Pulitzer Prize
has had many more honors deservedly heaped upon him, particularly that of being elected President of the American
Historical Association, I wish to express my heartiest appreciation of his Introductory Note. Combining the old and the
new in a graceful way, it thereby dispels some of the doubts

that inevitably have arisen in my mind with regard to a revision that itself combines the old and the new. Naturally, I should have liked to have rewritten everything, but although the reading by Mr. Dooley and similar worthies occasionally rejuvenates me for an hour or two, I do not yet suffer from delusions of lasting rejuvenation.

To the various publishers who have waived any claims that they might have had, due acknowledgment of their courtesy; to Harry Elmer Barnes, who has once again renounced all proprietary rights, my sincerest thanks.

To the indexers and compilers who now and again confuse me with Howard S. Becker, a younger sociologist now located at Kansas City, Missouri, and whose achievements I esteem, I should like to confide the fact that my middle initial, P., which I use only for signing checks and other worthless documents, stands for Paul. The practice of transmuting Paul into Saul reverses all sound Biblical tradition, and is to be deplored accordingly.

HOWARD BECKER

Madison, Wisconsin
February 1, 1960

Fourteen Years After

PREFACE TO THE SECOND EDITION

THE PREACHER PUT IT WELL: "Of the making of books there is no end, . . . much study is a weariness of the flesh," and "a living dog is better than a dead lion." The presses buzz and whir and clank, and the "definitive treatises" of yesterday are soon knocked over by and buried under the "never-to-be-superseded masterpieces" of today. Finally volumes that once were sprightly become cadavers for dissection or surreptitious cannibalizing, and at the end wither into twisted shapes that only a fond parent could recognize.

But the Preacher, with his Old Testament outlook, knew nothing of the promise of resurrection eventually to be set forth in the New. Books seemingly dead reappear, once more to be seen of men, and great is the rejoicing among the faithful.

Social Thought from Lore to Science has been out of print for many years—eight for Volume One, twelve for Volume Two. Now, thanks to the zeal of the new publisher and the loving-kindness of the former publishers and of the *Encyclopaedia Britannica,* it again sees the light of day, not merely as it once was, but with a new Revelation.

Unto Volume One has been added a commentary dealing with certain value-system terms that must be rightly divided if the truth of the text is to have full force and effect. Volume Two brings the glad tidings of sociology and its kindred studies throughout the world up to Anno Domini 1951, not only by means of a lengthy 1937-1950 record based on all of the present writer's *Britannica Book of the Year* and *Ten Eventful Years* articles, but also through a selected bibliography containing several important 1951 items, not least among them being other bibliographies. Filling the cup so that it runneth over is the new introductory note by Merle Curti, the well-known historian, winner of the 1944 Pulitzer prize for his *Growth of American Thought.*

Seeing the glory of this resurrection, one might almost dare to think that the present treatise, in its first and mortal body short-lived and hence sown in weakness, has today been raised in power; "Death is swallowed up in victory."

And in language less exalted, it may also be noted that the reprinting of a book that came out just before the Hitler war will perhaps help to re-establish that continuity of intellectual endeavor which is so needful but often so sadly absent. General readers and even specialized students are sometimes led to believe that sociology and related disciplines suddenly became "scientific" or "interpersonal" or "functional" or "empirical" or "systematic" or "value-oriented" or "interactional" or "small-groupal" or "structural" about 1945 or thereafter.

This impression, natural enough when a world-shaking crisis has called forth a "start-all-over-again" mood, also has apparently been deliberately fostered by certain recent writers—unless we assume that they belong among the fairly numerous variety of those who are merely hasty, superficial, ignorant, or inclined to forget where their ideas came from. Readers who now encounter *Social Thought from Lore to Science* for the first time will perhaps be startled when they discover that several of today's social scientists are flaunting attire that, to put it discreetly, seems to have been borrowed from writers discussed in Volume Two—and borrowed without adequate acknowledgment.

If the discovery is disillusioning, it is well to remember that by far the greater number of social scientists have been and are scrupulously and even pedantically honest in giving credit to predecessors and contemporaries; Diogenes would not have to wander among us long. Further, it should be borne in mind that some writers quite sincerely believe that frequent citation or quotation is superfluous in certain contexts; they intentionally place upon the reader the task of recognizing the sources of their "winged words" (by no means all of the Biblical allusions in this Preface, for example, are set off by quotation marks). If the reader is not up to his task, ludicrous misattribution may result. Either the writer gets for his "originality" credit that he does not deserve and does not want, or, quite as frequently, the source is held to be some other author with whom the reader happens to be conversant, whereas in actuality the quotation or paraphrase is from a source that perhaps should be widely known but unfortunately is not.

May this be pointed up by anecdote? Assuming permission, the story goes that a clergyman from Edinburgh was enjoying a holiday among the green hills of Yarrow. Being old-fashioned, he was given to quoting liberally from the metrical Psalms and Biblical paraphrases once the sole vehicles for congregational singing in the Church of Scotland. Take, for instance, "I will lift up mine eyes unto the hills, from whence cometh my help" (Psalm 121: 1). In the metrical version this goes, "I to the hills will lift mine eyes, from whence my help doth come." Well, the clergyman was enjoying a morning's ramble along a low ridge when he met a shepherd who seldom attended the kirk but was an avid reader of Scotland's best-known folk poet. The shepherd respectfully touched his bonnet and said, "Hoo are ye likin' yer holiday, sir?" The clergyman replied—it is to be feared, a bit unctuously, as sometimes happens with "thae frae Embro' "—"Oh, it is indeed wonderfully restful in this secluded spot. 'I to the hills will lift mine eyes, from whence my help doth come.' " "Aye," said the shepherd with enthusiasm, "he's a gr-rea-at mon, Rabbie Burns!" . . .

Volumes One and Two of the present book of social-scientific Salvation *can* be used separately; each has its own notes, indexes, and table of contents. It must be made clear, however, that many thinkers are dealt with in *both* volumes —Ward, Tönnies, Marx, Hobhouse, Max Weber, Durkheim, Pareto, and scores of others. The same is true of many topics, such as dialectical materialism, secularization, sociology of knowledge, and so on and on. Hence the wisest course would ordinarily be to treat the two volumes as a unit; maximum benefit from one cannot be secured without due heed to the other—although it is freely granted that special needs or circumstances may occasionally make it advisable to concentrate on a single volume.

The 1938 Preface makes the distinction between the history of social thought and the history of sociology reasonably plain; nothing more will be said here. In view of surviving practices in American sociological instruction, however, attention must be given to the difference between historical treatment of value-systems and theor*ies* having sociological relevance, on the one hand, and substantive sociological theory, on the other. The present treatise is organized about a framework of the latter type, set forth at length elsewhere in the writer's *Through Values to Social Interpretation* (Durham, N. C.: Duke University Press,

1950) and in many of his earlier books and articles. But although this organizing framework is in evidence at many points, the treatise now before the reader makes no claim to be anything other than a historical treatment of value-systems and theor*ies*. Such treatment, the writer feels, is highly valuable and should form part of the program required of every undergraduate major in the social sciences, at least where Volume One is concerned. Both Volumes One and Two might well be included in the program of the undergraduate major in sociology, but they can never substitute for works of substantive character such as those by Davis, Hiller, MacIver and Page, Martindale and Monachesi, Merton, Parsons, Wiese-Becker, Znaniecki, *et al.* To analogize, a book on the history of mathematics is not the same as a book on higher algebra. What we are now looking at is the history.

The main text of this treatise is photographically reproduced from the 1938 version with only about twenty minor changes, hence errors and corrections need not be listed. Moreover, all the additions are separate and easily noted. This being the case, the question may arise: "What would be done if a complete revision were undertaken?" The writer of this 1951 Preface can speak only for himself, but inasmuch as he has now assumed full responsibility for the treatise and has made all the additions, etc. (which accounts for the reversal in the original order of authors' names), what he says may be thought to be of interest.

Naturally, the text would be revised in the light of the commentary, *plus* a good deal that is not there set forth (but contained in the *Through Values,* etc., book above mentioned). The 1937-1950 appendix, considerably expanded where countries other than the United States are concerned, would be absorbed in the text. Further, there would be proper attention to current research in the history of ideas, sociology of knowledge, and the like; some of the more general statements as well as the evidential details would now and again be changed. Nevertheless, it would still be recognizably the same treatise, both in frame of reference and content. (Where particular chapters are concerned it would be possible to be more specific, but unfortunately space does not permit. A full-page list, omitted at the last moment here, may be secured by anyone interested by addressing a request to the present writer.)

In this task of revision, a number of the books listed in the new selected bibliographies at the end of Volume Two would be used intensively (which means that the bibliographies *they* contain would also receive much attention). Moreover, the practice of securing special research papers from co-workers who permit the alteration and rewriting of their contributions would be continued. Again, proper emphasis on the history and contemporary range of social- and cultural-anthropological theories would be secured, it is hoped, through similar reinforcement coming from leading writers. Once more, several younger social scientists not yet widely known—Don Martindale, René König, Jean Stoetzel, Jacques Maquet, and Charles Madge, to mention a few—would be invited to collaborate, not only as research-paper contributors but as general advisers. In this advisory capacity, clearly enough, older co-workers of wide reputation and experience would be indispensable. Not only would Barnes be called on again, but in addition the Macedonian cry would go out to a group of the present writer's former professors. In particular, Wiese's systematic gifts and knowledge of the literature—strikingly evident in the "Historical Postscript" of the present writer's *Systematic Sociology on the Basis of the* Bezichungslehre *and* Gebildelehre *of Leopold von Wiese*—would be of great aid, as would also Paul Honigsheim's linguistic facility, amazing industry, tremendous range, and incredibly accurate memory. Among colleagues at the University of Wisconsin who have strong historical interests and on whose counsel and ready relief for the heavy-laden reliance would be placed would certainly be included Merle Curti, Robert Reynolds, Merritt Y. Hughes, Helen White, W. R. Agard, Selig Perlman, C. M. W. Hart, Edmund Zawacki, Gian Orsini, Charles Léveque, George Urdang, Erwin Acker-knecht, J. H. Herriott, and last but by no means least, the erudite H. H. Gerth.

This is an imposing array, and may be thought to point toward an encyclopedia rather than a mere two-volume treatise, but the writer may perhaps be permitted to invoke the popular query, "I can dream, can't I?" even though there are no present plans for making the dream an actuality.

This account of an unlooked-for Resurrection and a faintly-hoped-for Assumption is now really at an end, but another admonitory anecdote might be viewed with indulgence. In spite of additions, and in spite of revisions as yet imaginary, the belief is cherished that the text as it stands today should be read by all those hoping for social-scientific Salvation. If it is not read, the consequences may be as dire as was the neglect of the wise and sober words of the good parish minister of Kilmarnock. He had been much irritated by the fact that although "the pulpit caught fire, the pews failed to ignite," and he resolved to preach a sermon that would put an end to spiritual lethargy. And thus went the sermon:

"My text for the Sabbath is from Joel, 2:28—'Your old men shall dream dreams . . .' And I hae dreamed a dream. In my dream I went to Heaven, and there I was welcomed at the pairly gates by guid Saint Peter, and he tuk me throughoot a' the precincts o' Heaven, and at last ushered me intae the awfu' presence o' the great Laird Almichty. And in His infinite maircy and compassion the great Laird Almichty tuk me oot tae the ramparts o' Heaven, and there we looked doon intae the mirk, black pit, where, I grieve tae say, I saw mony members o' the parish o' Kilmarnock.

"And then, writhin' and groanin' and gnashin' their teeth, and puttin' oot their tongues tae get a wee drap o' water tae quench their burnin' thirst, they cried oot, 'Oh, guid Laird Almichty, what hae we done that we should suffer here throughoot a' Eternity?' In His infinite maircy and compassion, with me, a' unworthy that I am, stan'in' by His side, the great Laird Almichty said tae thae puir sinners, 'Hadna ye heard, didna ye ken, that didna ye listen tae the wise and sober words o' the guid parish minister o' Kilmarnock that ye'd be here throughoot a' Eternity, writhin' and groanin' and gnashin' yer teeth, and puttin' oot yer tongues tae get a wee drap o' water tae quench yer burnin' thirst?'

"Thae puir members o' the parish o' Kilmarnock looked up tae where stood the great Laird Almichty, in His infinite maircy and compassion, and with me, a' unworthy that I am, stan'in' by His side, and they yelloched in muckle pain, 'Oh, guid Laird Almichty, we hadna heard, we didna ken.' Then said the great Laird Almichty, 'Aweel, ye ken it noo.' "

Thus endeth the story of the good parish minister of Kilmarnock, and thus endeth this 1951 Preface to the resurrected book of social-scientific Salvation. But—we have forgotten that we began by quoting Ecclesiastes, where among other things the Preacher said, "He that increaseth knowledge increaseth sorrow. . . ."

HOWARD BECKER

Drafted at the home of
John Scott, shepherd of Brockhope
Ettrick, Selkirk, Scotland
July, 1951, shortly before
The Gathering of the Clans at Edinburgh

Finished at Madison, Wisconsin
November 1, 1951

Preface to the First Edition

I

STEVENSON was undeniably right when he said that the world is full of a number of things, but we cannot be quite so sure of his inference from this; namely, that we should all be as happy as kings. To begin with, mankind has long known that kings are not always happy — but let that pass. More important is the fact that many of the things of which the world is full jangle and clash with one another, and the resulting discord brings unhappiness to many of us. Perhaps the most prolific source of harsh and jarring din is man's apparent inability or unwillingness to get along with his fellows — does not the horrendous clangor of " man's inhumanity to man " beat upon our ears in even this Century of Progress? It is cold consolation to be assured that the end is not yet, that things must become much worse before they can grow better. We want to know why and how we have come to such a pass, and whether we can avoid a " successful " operation that may result in the death of the patient.

But these cravings for solutions of, or at least insights into, the problems raised by man's strife with man are by no means new. Long before social philosophers and scientists began to sit in judgment, answers of all sorts were set forth by tribal elders, seers, priests, wandering traders, speculative sages, and what not. Lores were proclaimed that in their times and places gave satisfying replies to queries such as " What is a good social life? Why is it good? How can it be safeguarded or attained? " The history of man's life with his fellows reveals numerous attempts to produce or to prophesy harmony from the dissonant strains issuing out of " old, unhappy, far-off things, and battles long ago."

These attempts are surveyed with reasonable fullness in Volume One of *Social Thought from Lore to Science*. Social thought in the broadest sense of the term " thought " is dealt with; for example, even when man has not yet found words to express his inchoate ideas, we try to infer, from the evidence provided by folklore, moral practices, and general social and cultural organization, something specific about his vague ponderings. For this reason the subtitle of Volume One is " A History *and Interpretation* of Man's Ideas about Life with His Fellows." When the art of writing has developed, we are less dependent on inference, but in all cases our stress on interpretation is strong. Relatively little space is granted to direct quotation, and much to description and analysis of the social and cultural situations within which the different types of social thought, explicit or implicit, should be interpreted.

A broad meaning also attaches to the term " social " in Volume One, especially in the earlier chapters. We attempt to sort out from the mass of mores, proverbs, sacred writings, and discourses on what would now be called ethics, politics, economics, history, geography, or biology, those portions which deal with general modes of social conduct that underlie the more specific expressions. That is to say, we hold that the contributions of many thinkers to general social thought are separable from their ethical, theological, or political contributions, and we attempt to separate them and set them forth here.

Such separation, however, can at best be but partially achieved. For example, the history of social thought is almost inextricably bound up with the history of political thought as traditionally received. The reason for this lies in the fact that there has been a general failure, down to relatively recent times, to distinguish clearly between the state and society. Consequently much of the relevant speculation about social processes, structures, and the social aspects of personality — i.e., speculation about social or interhuman conduct as such — has been the work of men who believed that they were dealing exclusively with the state. Ethics also provides an instance: all the early sages and many of the later philosophers paid quite as much attention to man as he is as they did to man as he ought to be, with the result that their precepts and codes are rich source material for the study of everyday social life and thought.

Volume One, therefore, is primarily a history of numerous types of thought from which, as it were, a social essence can be distilled; only in its final stages does this first division deal directly with the more systematic and precise methods of studying human conduct. To these methods we apply the term " science," but only in the older, well-attested, broader sense of *Wissenschaft* or *scientia,* not in the newer, narrower sense of " natural " science. In our usage, any systematic, rationally communicable, secular analysis of a determinate body of empirical data, " subjective " or

" objective," is a science; e.g., Classical philology or introspective psychology equally with chemistry or physics. " Lore," on the other hand, always has sacred connotations in this treatise; an emotional halo, an aura of the ineffable, is an essential characteristic. " From Lore to Science " therefore might be paraphrased as " From Sacred to Secular " without much loss of meaning.

In saying that the study of lores will engage much of our attention in Volume One, we by no means intend to belittle the earlier writers or the effort to study them more thoroughly than has hitherto been the case. Two errors are especially frequent in contemporary American social science : one is the error of attributing originality to methods and conclusions that are hoary with age; the other is the error of confusing new points of view and new results with old doctrines to which they have a merely superficial resemblance. Both could be avoided if a serious effort were made to place all social theories in their full social and cultural contexts, to apply what has been called the method of " the substantive sociology of knowledge." In thus making use of *Wissenssoziologie* we might learn to understand fully " what thoughts of old the wise have entertained." This would have its values, for in multitude of counsel there are often some bits of wisdom that place problems in a new or at least a different light. The sages of the lores were not scientists, obviously enough; we can expect from them only suggestion, not hypothesis. Suggestion, however, may be worth while; as Barrie ironically puts it, " There were great men before William K. Smith."

The present writers have therefore attempted to select and set forth the more important doctrines concerning problems such as the factors making for association and dissociation, the more important social structures and institutions, and the nature of the processes which weave the web of relations we call " society." Faced by an overwhelming mass of material, one of the most serious difficulties in executing such a study has been that of selection; we can only hope that no irrelevant topics or writers have been included.

The procedure followed in Volume One has been to combine the historical and *wissenssoziologische* mode of exposition with the topical. Roughly speaking, we first make an effort to present the general social and cultural situations with which the social thought of each of the periods described is related. There then follows a general sketch of the development of social thought in the particular era under discussion, and in many cases there is added to this an intensive study of the most characteristic social-theoretical problem of the age. In earlier periods, when lores are dominant, it is of course difficult to isolate much that can be called " social-theoretical," but we do our best even though our remote great-*n*-grandsires probably did not draw bow at Hastings.

So much for Volume One. In Volume Two, carrying the sub-title " Sociological Trends throughout the World," our problem is considerably simpler. Lores of many kinds still plague us here and there, to be sure, but we are usually able to devote the greater part of the available space to relatively recent developments (since Herbert Spencer's time, let us say) in sociology, the social science that provides the basic generalizations upon which its sister specialisms erect their imposing structures. We should like to stress the fact that, in calling sociology the basic social science, we do not intend to assert its supremacy over economics, govern-ment, and kindred disciplines. Grammatical structure is basic to verbal communication, for example, and in this sense compara-tive grammar, as a branch of general linguistics, is the basic philo-logical science — but no one would say that a man must be a great comparative grammarian in order to be a great Greek scholar. So it is with sociology; in one sense it is basic to all the other social sciences, and yet in another it is merely a specialism coördinate with other specialisms. " Sociology is here regarded neither as the mistress nor as the handmaid of the other social sciences, but as their sister."

Having thus stated the meaning we attach to " sociological " in the subtitle of Volume Two, we can now turn to " trends " and " throughout the world." We try to indicate what seems to us the desirable course of theoretical development if sociology is adequately to fulfill its function as " the grammar of the social sciences," but we cannot and do not ignore lines of growth that do not agree with our prepossessions. Not only do we turn our gaze on Britain, France, Germany, and the United States — coun-tries where sociology has enjoyed greatest prominence — but we also survey Russia, Italy, Holland, Japan. Turkey, and a dozen other lands. Current trends in each of these are traced, and we trust that we have justified, so far as in us lies, the claims of our subtitle.

Manifestly, we have utilized secondary sources in numerous instances, feeling, with Mark Twain, that " old, second-hand dia-monds are better than none at all." Or, to change the figure, some-one must rush in where angels fear to tread, and we have rushed — cautiously. Oftentimes we have " looked problems boldly in the face and passed on," feeling certain that the specialist who is

kindly disposed toward our venture will give us the benefit of the
doubt. Others, to be sure, will not. May we therefore conclude
this section of our Preface with an apt *apologia* from another
foreword, written by a scholar far more profound than either of
ourselves?

I can therefore only remind all these [specialists] of the virtues of
patience and charity, begging them to remember that in contrast to its
parts, a whole is at once less easily circumscribed and more easily punc-
tured. No doubt a little knowledge is a dangerous thing, but it is also true
that where nothing is risked nothing is won.

Since, then, honesty as well as modesty forbids me to wish the reader
a safe voyage, may I at least wish him storms instead of fog! (Edward
M. Pickman, *The Mind of Latin Christendom*, p. vii).

II

Our next task is that of indicating adequately the authorship
of various sections and chapters of this treatise, for it is in a certain sense a composite. As is later noted, the Table of Contents
provides a detailed analysis, but a general statement of " sources "
seems advisable here. In order to avoid excessive repetition of
names, we have decided to speak of A and E; A is bArnes and
E is bEcker.

To the writer of the A source we owe the original inspiration
for and plan of our treatise. He it was who conceived the idea of
a combined chronological and topical method of presentation in
Volume One, followed by arrangement on the basis of country
and language in Volume Two. From 1916 onward he had been
writing on the history of social thought for the learned journals,
so that he had collected a mass of material ready to be worked up.
Interesting editor and publisher in his project early in 1927, he
at once began the task of revising his earlier articles, writing sections and chapters to supply continuity, securing unpublished
theses and like fugitive aids, and having translations of otherwise
inaccessible articles and excerpts made. In 1928 the enterprise
came to a standstill because A ceased systematic academic instruction and engaged in new and engrossing activities that left little
opportunity for research and writing of the type needed to bring
both volumes to successful completion. He then began to look for
a collaborator, and late in 1930 the writer of the E source agreed
to finish the work. Is it permissible to point out that A may therefore be taken as a symbol for *Anfang,* and E for *Ende?*

Except for a few interruptions, the most important of which

was caused by research abroad on the " sociology of knowledge " in 1934–'35, E labored as steadily as his professional duties permitted. He edited and revised A's contributions, made minor changes in the original framework, adapted some of his own articles on the history of social thought to the altered plan, and wrote numerous sections and chapters not provided by A. Certain gaps that E lacked time to fill were taken care of by Émile Benoît-Smullyan and other specialists working under E's direction; these are indicated in the Notes, the Table of Contents, and the portion of this Preface (III) dealing with acknowledgments.

The task of introducing some semblance of unity into the composite fell to E, and he attempted to achieve it by making use of several organizing conceptions and modes of analysis: sacred and secular societal types, individuation, mental mobility and immobility, release, secularization, the distinction between organismic and organic, ideal-typical method, the sociology of knowledge, and the like. Had E become acquainted with the minutiae of *Wissenssoziologie* at an earlier stage in the preparation of the treatise, more consistent interpretation would have been attempted, but as it is, only the first four chapters measurably conform to his present standards.

The full results of these intricate interrelations cannot be adequately set forth here, and we have consequently given a full Table of Contents in which the authorship of every chapter and section is indicated by * (A), † (E), ‡ (joint A and E), and § (others). At this point we shall merely say (1) that E alone is responsible for the Preface, the Epilogue, the first three and the last five chapters, and two sandwiched in between, (2) that from A's pen come most of the framework and nearly all of the content of eleven chapters ranging through the middle of the work, and (3) that eight chapters containing many sections by A, some by E, a few by A and E jointly, and several fairly large clusters by others make up the remainder. E has supplied all titles and captions, done all the editing, and seen both volumes through the press.

Although the foregoing paragraphs dispose of the question of Genesis, the reader will have to go to the text itself for the Revelation. (We sincerely trust that the Apocrypha have been omitted.)

III

We now turn to the pleasant task of expressing our thanks for the assistance we have so generously received.

First of all come those scholars who have contributed directly, by writing, research, or translation, to the content of our treatise. Émile Benoît-Smullyan has written sections on primitivism and the normative conception of nature, on DeBonald and DeMaistre, and on numerous sociologists dealt with in the chapter on Sociology in the French Language. George Selleck wrote, under E's supervision, large portions of the chapter on Christian Social Philosophy to Thomas Aquinas, and also contributed to one or two other parts of the treatise through special research. Richard Hays Williams contributed several sections on Ibn Khaldūn in the chapter on The Meeting of East and West. Dorothy Wolff Douglas provided a paper on DeGreef that was of much help in certain sections dealing with Belgian sociology. Rex Crawford made available papers on Pareto, Vaccaro, Loria, and Gini on which we leaned heavily in the chapter on Sociology in Italy. Ephraim Fischoff wrote a paper on Alfred Weber that was of much use in the chapter on The Deflation of Social Evolutionism. Frances Bennett Becker wrote much of the chapter on New Gospels: Revolutionary Socialism and the Winds of Doctrine. Research papers on Yugoslavia came from Mirko M. Kosić; on France from Célestin Bouglé and Robert K. Merton; on Greece from Panajotis Kanellopoulos; on Roumania from G. Vladesco-Racoassa; on India from Haridas Muzumdar and Radhakamal Mukerjee; on Japan from Junichiro Matsumoto, Kanrei Inoue, and Yoshihiko Yamada; on China from Leonard S. Hsü; on Spain from John Lord; on Holland and on Othmar Spann from Barth. Landheer; on social case work by Philip Klein; on social and cultural dynamics by Pitirim Sorokin; on Dilthey by George Morgan; on Wundt, Dilthey, and Rickert by Alexander Goldenweiser; and on Max Scheler by his widow, Marit Scheler. Translations of articles on Polish, Ukrainian, and Czech sociology came from Antonín Obrdlík; and on various writers and countries from other scholars mentioned in the Notes. Mrs. J. P. Shalloo verified a large proportion of A's citations and quotations, and Mrs. Karl Schafer checked the dates of many of A's and E's references.

Indirect assistance, in the form of reading and comment, may be classified as follows: Chapter One, Gladys Bryson, Frank H. Hankins, Talcott Parsons, Alexander Goldenweiser, Read Bain, E. A. Ross, Carle C. Zimmerman, Paul Lieder, and Edward Smith. Two, Walter Barnes, Hans Kohn, Otto Kraushaar, Kurt Koffka, and William Allan Neilson. Three, Frank H. Hankins, Gilbert Ross, Edward Smith, and Read Bain. Four, William Gray, Amy Barbour, Maurice Halbwachs, Alfred Weber, and

Gustave Glotz. Five to Nine, inclusive, Read Bain. Twenty-one, W. Y. Elliott, Twenty-two, Daniel Warnotte. Twenty-three, Thorsten Sellin. Twenty-four, Read Bain, Kimball Young, and L. L. Bernard. Twenty-five, Michele Cantarella. Twenty-six and Twenty-seven, Pitirim Sorokin. Twenty-eight, L. L. Bernard. Twenty-nine, Junichiro Matsumoto. Preface and Epilogue, J. L. Gillin, E. A. Ross, and Kimball Young.

We of course bear full responsibility for our respective contributions, and for those of our collaborators as well.

Much help has come through institutes, foundations, libraries, and the like. The fellowship for study of the sociology of knowledge granted by the Social Science Research Council figures most largely here; although it will later bear fruit in more specific researches, its influence on the present treatise should not be minimized. In this conjunction mention should be made of Donald Young, American fellowship secretary when the grant was made, and of Tracy B. Kittredge, European administrator of Rockefeller assistance in the social sciences. The *École normale supérieure* and its genial leader, Célestin Bouglé, should not be overlooked, nor should the Paris branch of the *Institut des recherches sociales* and its director (until 1936), Paul Honigsheim. Research facilities were also made available by the *Institut de sociologie Solvay,* the sociological seminar of the University of Cologne, and the libraries of the University of Pennsylvania and of Smith College. Special reference should be made to the generous grant for the purchase of research materials provided by the Board of Trustees of Smith College through the sponsorship of its Chairman, President William Allan Neilson.

The indices of Volume One were prepared by Ruth Hill; of Volume Two by Frances Bennett Becker.

Finally, heartfelt thanks are also due to our silent partners, those patient students who have listened to us " think out loud " on the crucial issues of social thought.

HARRY ELMER BARNES and HOWARD BECKER
Auburn, N. Y.   Madison, Wis.

Jan. 1, 1938

CONTENTS

Authorship and editorial responsibility for each chapter and section is indicated by the following marks:

When chapter is not marked, see the section markings; when section is not marked, see the chapter marking.

III. Social Thought of the Ancient Near East.†

IV. The Mobile Background of the Greco-Roman World and Its Effects on Social Thought

V. Classical Theories of the Origin of Society and the State.*

VI. Christian Social Philosophy to Thomas Aquinas

VII. THE MEETING OF EAST AND WEST AND THE ADVANCE OF SECULARISM

VIII. THE EXPANSION OF EUROPE, HUMANISM, AND THE PROTESTANT REVOLT

CONTENTS

A History and Interpretation
of
Man's Ideas about Life with His Fellows
to Times when
Change and Progress Deeply Concern Him

CHAPTER I

Social Thought of Preliterate Peoples

FOLK WITHOUT WRITING. — Off the bleak coast of northern
Scotland, to the west of the spray where the headland of
ultima Thule justifies its name of Cape Wrath, lie some
jagged splinters of rock with patches of treeless moorland between
their wild mountains and lochs. Only four hundred years ago —
close up in the foreground of the long perspective of history — the
crofters who tilled the fertile corners of the remoter Hebrides
had virtually no written records.[1] More, there had never been a
time in their tradition when the art of writing had been effectively practiced; they were not simply illiterate but preliterate.
Among the scattered islets of simple folk voyaged the legend, the
ballad, and the proverb — little coracles far too frail even to
carry all the exploits of the Lords of the Isles and other valorous
doings of " them of old time," to say nothing of those of lesser
mortals. But frail or not, the busy craft of folklore transported
the ever-dwindling fragments of long centuries that passed as a
tale that is told. Fresh from Burns and Maclaren and Barrie, we
sometimes think of the Scottish peasant as one who stood between the handles of his plow and quoted to the passing wayfarer
the fruits of his long winter's reading in the Good Book or —
publish it not abroad! — the writings of Davie Hume. Here,
however, were Scotsmen who knew nothing of their own past except as old men and women relived the bygone drama in their
hearing. Among the farthest Hebrides the ear was still the gateway to the realms of old.

In the North Island of New Zealand dwell the vanquished
remnants of a once warlike people, the Maori. On the bronze
faces of a few of the aged warriors are delicate intertwining
traceries, blue lines that remind one of Caesar's description of
the ancient Britons, " stained blue with woad." Secret dyes and
piercing needles in hand, ritually adept tattooers once lavished
the mysteries of their craft on the highborn tribesmen. After
months and years of pain patiently endured, the Maori nobles became the background for arabesque designs that a Haroun-al-
Raschid might have coveted for the illuminated margin of his

Koran. These Maori had once been great seafarers: centuries ago — perhaps when Caesar first stared at the cliffs of Dover or Agricola's lookout dimly descried the haze of *ultima Thule* — the " skeely skippers " of the southern Vikings voyaged afar. One day an intrepid company, forerunners of many later bands, swung gleaming paddles aloft and, in those long-boats that look so flimsy but are so stout, forever left behind the eastern Polynesian region that had been their home. Chanting in unison, they thrust the richly carved prows of their canoes across the heaving expanse of the South Pacific,

Where the sea-egg flames on the coral, and the long-backed breakers croon
Their endless ocean legends to the lazy, locked lagoon.

Journeying by the stars and winds alone, fighting epic battles, they eventually reached the land of Aotearoa that was to be theirs by right of conquest until the manifest destiny of another seafaring people wrenched it from them. But of all that tale of hardihood, of sublime confidence, of superb seamanship, of victories won before the British came, no word was set down. " The old men say " — and that is all. A splendidly endowed folk, among whom flourished the subtle arts of star-gazing, labyrinthine tattoo, and fantastic, incredibly intricate ornamental carving, never hit upon the comparatively simple device of writing, of crystallized speech.[2] Preliterate.

And so we might go on, listing the peasant peoples of remoter regions the wide world over and the so-called " wild men " of the Seven Seas and beyond, but we have said enough to show that we need not confine our discussion of preliterate social thought to the racially different peoples. Folk without writing are not always members of the lesser tribes without the law. In addition to the Hottentots, Winnebagos, and Tarahumares whom we carelessly lump under the ambiguous and misleading terms " primitive," " savage," and what not, there are European and American folk-fragments [3] that for all practical purposes are preliterate. True, they are scarce and are rapidly becoming scarcer, but they are still to be found.[4] Moreover, many of them have already been analyzed thoroughly enough by students of folklore to permit us to compare their traits with those of the " treacherous aborigines," " ye beastlie heathen," and to discover fundamental similarities. Such preliterate folk, obviously enough, are almost without exception inhabitants of districts " back beyond the backwoods," utterly out of touch with the great streams of traffic.

In spite of their biological kinship with city dwellers of the same country, their ways of thought are more like those of similarly isolated " nature peoples " widely different from them in race.[5] The crofter of Heisgier in the Hebrides is more like the native hillsman in the remote interior of New Zealand, so far as the essentials of social action and mentality are concerned, than either the preliterate Scotsman or his Maori counterpart is like the citified denizen of Glasgow or Auckland.[6] (As the remainder of this chapter will show, inclusion of the peasant under the preliterate category does not commit us to the tracing of " survivals " à la Tylor and Frazer, or to the other methodological errors of nineteenth-century ethnology.) [7]

Hereafter, therefore, we shall use " preliterate " to denote peoples lacking a certain cultural characteristic — namely, written language [8] — regardless of their race or geographical habitat. White, black, yellow, red, or brown, dwellers in the frozen North or the sweltering South — their social thought, as expressed in proverbs and other epitomized experience, is sufficiently similar to be labeled with the same headings. Under many of these we shall have a good deal to say about the fixity of such thought, and although we point out in several places that this characteristic, taken by itself, gives us no warrant for assuming that " primitives " are " inferior " to " civilized man," it is well to guard against misinterpretation at the very outset. Hence the following:

Growth is possible . . . only when we have intelligently and actively absorbed the past. For this there is no opportunity if each generation can preserve this heritage only by bodily and mechanically repeating it lest it be forgotten. The invention of writing freed us from the necessity of doing only this. How concerned nonliterate man is that the past of his fathers and his grandfathers should not be forgotten, everyone who has had any contact with aboriginal peoples can testify. Faced with the alternative of preserving this or embarking upon something new, he has quite sensibly chosen the former. *It is thus erroneous to imagine that he is innately any more conservative than civilized man.* He is simply more insistent upon preserving the continuity of his culture, under unfavorable circumstances, in the only fashion possible.[9]

The social thought of preliterates, therefore, must be considered on its own merits or the lack thereof, without resort to the facile assumption that " they think as they do because they're more like monkeys."

Vicinal Isolation and Mental Immobility. — But before we can deal with social thought as such, certain implications of the preliterate phase of culture must be made plain. If a peasant community, for example, remains preliterate in the midst of the almost all-pervasive hum of communication, written and otherwise, in the modern world, it means that such a community has lived behind the barrier of isolation. In some way it has been kept out of effective contact with outside peoples; little genuine communication has taken place.[10] This relative absence of communication may be a cause of the preliterate condition, or it may be an effect, but the two are rarely found apart.[11]

The first point to be clarified in any discussion of isolation is the difference between geographical and vicinal isolation. The term "vicinage," or rather an adjectival variant in the phrase "vicinal location" (or position), was chosen by Semple as a translation of Ratzel's *Lage,* and was differentiated from geographical location as follows:

A people has . . . a twofold location, an immediate one, based upon their actual territory, and a mediate or vicinal one, growing out of its relations to the countries nearest them. The first is a question of the land under their feet; the other of the neighbors about them.[12]

In other words, a hypothetical human being who had never had any contacts with other human beings except those involved in the birth process, like Mowgli of Jungle Book fame, would have geographical location, but he would not have vicinal position, for the latter implies relations with other human beings. Vicinal position cannot exist without geographical location as a substratum, so to speak, but geographical location may be greatly changed with relatively little alteration in vicinal position, and conversely. It goes almost without saying that the earlier social theorists did not discriminate between geographical and vicinal isolation; the two are inextricably intermingled in all their discussions. As a matter of fact, only with the advent of Bagehot's *Physics and Politics* did the concept of isolation receive adequate attention:

. . . the "protected" regions of the world — the interior continents like Africa, outlying islands like Australia or New Zealand — are of necessity backward.[13]

One need not focus his attention on preliterate or prehistoric peoples, however; the same phenomena are found in early and modern historic times:

When the scope of culture contacts is limited, intellectual impoverishment is unavoidable even when the wealth of ideas is apparently inexhaustible.

We find this to be true, for example, of the peoples who gave birth to our classical literature; "they knew and recognized only themselves" (Saint-Beuve). The mental isolation, the cramped imagination is evidenced in the use of ever-repeated metaphors and images from nature, history and mythology — novelty is virtually unknown, and even new combinations are rare.[14]

It is now time that we raise the question, in Ogburn's phrase, "as to whether human nature predominantly resists change or is essentially change-loving." [15] An answer would in a sense be an answer to the general problem of social change; the most we can do in this chapter is to compare the opinions of a few authorities.

Bagehot insists on the rarity of cultural advance, and says categorically that "a stationary state is by far the most frequent condition of man. . . . When history begins to record, she finds most of the races . . . arrested, unprogressive, and pretty much where they are now." [16] The available data certainly show that many preliterate and semi-literate peoples retain their old culture traits and complexes with the utmost persistence, that they manifest a high degree of *mental immobility*.

From such data Vidal de La Blache concludes that in isolated cultures a certain amount of advance may take place, but after a time "there comes a certain impotence." Unless intrusive factors break the vicious circle, stagnation reigns supreme. This is quite true, but it seems a bit rash to conclude from this that "man is sluggish by nature." [17] As Ogburn has properly pointed out, "in some situations human beings want to change and in others they do not"; [18] the one most unfavorable to change is vicinal isolation, but a situation can hardly be considered part of man's "original nature," no matter how frequently we may find it on the simpler levels of culture. In the more complex stages there is sometimes a premium upon change in the material culture.[19] Further, as the writer just mentioned has said, the difficulties of adopting new culture traits and complexes may be greater than the outsider imagines.[20] In short, cultural inertia and its closely related mental immobility are not results of "human nature," but issue from a particular situation very frequently found among preliterate groups and in the earlier stages of man's history; *this situation is vicinal isolation.*

Further, the type of personality found in an isolated, static culture area is not a cause of cultural inertia, but a result.[21] Habit, custom, and routine dominate everything because no intrusive factors disrupt the orderly sequence of events. When cultures are extremely disorganized in many segments, the force of habit is relatively slight.[22] Modern American urban culture is sufficiently disorganized in some areas to permit of a minimum of traditional and habitual responses, but this mental mobility should not be exaggerated; the willingness of modern civilization to experiment, fortunately enough, is half-hearted. Habits and other entrenched characteristics still play a large part because intrusive factors affect only particular segments of our complex culture — indeed, a culture must be very simple before a migration, a great natural catastrophe, or a new invention can markedly affect many parts of it.

As many ethnologists have indicated, the relatively high degree of disorganization with which intrusive factors threaten simple cultures perhaps accounts in part for the reluctance to change their bearers so frequently manifest. The modern man is seldom or never called upon to make so great and sudden modifications in his way of life, for example, as the introduction of English-woven cotton cloth has entailed upon the natives of India — hence the symbolic power of the *charkal* or spinning wheel. Boas has pointed out that the opposition to change correlated with such isolation often roots in emotional resistance to disturbance of any deep-rooted habit, any automatic reaction — " To witness an act contrary to our automatic behavior excites at once intense attention and the strongest resistances must be overcome if we are required to perform such an action." [23] At any rate, the peoples living in such isolated, simple cultures rarely evince any desire for change; they are the examples *par excellence* of mental immobility.

Interpreted in the light of modern theory, and with a few qualifications, then, generalizations about the hampering effect of vicinal isolation seem valid. Now, just how is this effect exerted?

Some recent answers have been about as follows : Vicinal isolation is favorable to the development of rigid social control, and when the latter is once established, cultural fixity follows. Recent answers are not the only ones, however, as we shall see; Plato, for example, saw the effect of isolation during his visit to Sparta, and became so enamored of " Dorian " mental immobility in contrast to the mental mobility of " Ionian " Athens that he apotheosized the former in the *Republic,* and in order to maintain it proposed the vicinal and social isolation of the ideal commonwealth. " Come ye out from among them and be ye separate " seems to have been the slogan governing his speculations. Other less speculative and more active advocates of fixity actually instituted a vigorous policy of isolation for the purpose of preventing change. The Spartan *xenelasia,* or prohibition of strangers, probably was due to some such considerations as those which led to the regulations above noted.

In the case of Sparta, however, there were undoubtedly other reasons; e.g., the danger of a slave revolt and of invasion. Vidal de La Blache has commented on the latter aspect of isolation:

> In certain remote countries isolation has become a systematic policy. Those enjoying the benefits of the soil have tried to maintain their isolation by artificial means, for the frontier notion is . . . deeply rooted. . . . This is why the jungle savages of Africa lay snares at approaches to their villages, why mountain tribes such as Circassians (Cherkess), Kurds, and Kafirs intrench themselves in the least accessible places; why even Tibetans have relegated their national holy of holies to the most distant valley.[24]

But we unduly anticipate later chapters and succeeding sections of this one. At this point let us simply say, therefore, that as a consequence of vicinal isolation virtually all preliterates are marked by extreme *mental immobility,* by unwillingness or inability, or both, to change their ways of acting. and thinking.[25] This does not mean that they are inherently backward or conservative; it merely means that long isolation has permitted the growth of fixed habits that lead to great resistance to change. Quoting again:

> . . . it is important to understand the reasons that bring about fixity of type . . . the variations are confined within the limits established by the fixed motor habits of the people. . . . The more fundamental the motor habits . . . the less likely will be a deviation from the customary type.
>
> . . . the mind becomes so thoroughly adjusted to the use of definite motor habits, and to certain types of association between sense impressions and definite activities that a resistance to change appears as the most natural of mental attitudes; if for no other reason, because it requires the effort of learning and unlearning.
>
> The familiarity established through long . . . [habituation] may readily lead to an emotional attachment that finds expression in permanence of form, and in the refusal to accept [the] new and unfamiliar . . . an emotional resistance to change that may be variously expressed — as a feeling of impropriety of certain forms, of a particular social or religious value, or of superstitious fear of change.[26]

This is the same tendency to regard the old and familiar as *sacred* that Schiller noted:

For of the wholly common is man made,
And custom is his nurse! Woe then to them
That lay irreverent hands upon his old
House furniture, the dear inheritance
From his forefathers! For time consecrates;
And what is gray with age becomes the sacred.

For these and like reasons practically all preliterate communities may be called sacred communities — i.e., communities in which a sort of emotional halo encircles the ways of the fathers and thereby prevents their profanation by change.[27]

Kinship Organization and Mental Immobility. — Another aspect of the preliterate phase of cultural development is the frequent prevalence of kinship organization. The stronger social bonds are predominantly kinship bonds, for the wider contacts that would make the establishment of other relationships possible are cut off by isolation. Such bonds make for mental immobility; the kinship group, the tradition-transmitting unit, strongly influences the character of the child, thus laying the basis for adult uniformity and conformity. The child is one with the kindred, and the breaking of the bond, if deviation occurs, is almost like the severing of the navel cord, for biological adaptations count for more in the unity of the kinship organization than in any other kind of social group. For example, sex contrast, with its accompanying sex appetite, acts as a strong cohesive force. Men and women are drawn together and held together; no matter how frequently partners are changed, or how many there are, the two sexes are always present, and their permutations and combinations are never on a basis of pure chance. Another unifying factor is the great difference between the ages of parents and children in human society; adult life has become fairly well stabilized before its patterns are stamped upon the younger generation, thus aiding the rigid impress of father upon son, mother upon daughter. A corollary of this is the long period of human infancy; there is plenty of time for the elders to mold the young in their image, while at the same time the former must maintain sufficient continuity in their own lives to ensure the survival of the children. When we remember that in many preliterate groups breastfeeding extends into the third or even fourth year of life, it is obvious that the bonds between husband and wife, mother and child, are vital. The interdependence of all these biological factors makes the kinship organization a type of structure that is exceedingly powerful in the production of fundamental character; the influence exercised is effective because it is literally inseparable from human life itself in virtually every preliterate culture of which we have knowledge [28] (not that the biological family and the kin group are here considered identical).

Further, this biological pattern is overlaid and modified by the social experiences of the kindred in such a way that control is even more firmly established; through the subtle processes of sociation the experiences of the more mature members dominate and fuse with those of the immature, thus begetting the attitudes, sentiments, social ritual, and traditions of the kinship group — the social nature of the children is primarily elicited and shaped by their parents and other kin (who of course need not necessarily be actual blood relatives). No other types of preliterate grouping afford such a powerful means of welding human beings into a homogeneous structure and of forging them into a considerable degree of similarity.[29] So long as kinship units remain relatively isolated, the likelihood that marked deviations from the sacred pattern will occur is almost negligible. And let it again be emphasized that the early preliterate community is virtually without exception an isolated community; the mental immobility engendered by kinship influence has every chance to perpetuate itself.

Social Control and the Elders. — It can thus be readily seen that kinship organization is peculiarly favorable to that type of social control exerted by the older members of the group (sometimes called gerontocracy). Moreover, this control need not be couched in the form of definite commands or prohibitions. Perhaps the most effective social control is that which is not noticed; which is not overt or formal; which is, as it were, " closer to us than breathing, nearer than hands or feet." [30] The power of the elders need never be exerted directly; the part they play in drawing forth and molding the character and life-policy of every younger person in the kinship group makes the necessity for direct control much less frequent in isolated cultures than in more accessible communities. Partially or wholly unverbalized avoidances, taboos, rites, sanctified methods of work — in short, standards (mores) and institutions — exercise the dominant influence in many cases.

Moreover, the fact that these isolated kinship organizations are also preliterate, the fact that personal observation and the absorption of tradition through the spoken word are the only sources of knowledge and wisdom, gives the elders a tremendous advantage, as Goldenweiser has pointed out.[31] A man who has passed through the various crises of life; who has been a bachelor, a married man, a father, and a father-in-law; who as an elder has taken part in the deliberations that decide the fate of the group; who has experienced the tragic emergencies of defeat and flight; and above all, who has had time and opportunity to talk with his own elders and to absorb whatever knowledge they themselves possessed — such a man comes to be an impersonation of the preliterate culture itself. He is a dictionary, an almanac, a history, an all-round handicraftsman, a general, a statesman, and a presbyter, *multum in parvo*. He is admired and respected; he is the source of advice in doubt, perplexity, and peril.

> And still they gazed, and still the wonder grew
> That one small head could carry all he knew.

And so it is that in isolated preliterate groups united by the bonds of prolonged interaction and kinship the elders usually rule the roast. Their generation is the prop and mainstay of the *status quo;* there prevails an established routine, a circumspect eschewing of the untried and novel; a shrewd management of the younger generation — for were not the elders similarly trained and are they not grateful to those departed wise men who gave them all that anyone can possibly know?[32] Who can be so impious and thankless as to break with the sacred community the ancients established in glory and in power?

With these and like phenomena in view, it has been noted that authoritative rule of the *traditional* type is frequently found in preliterate cultures — that is to say, a kind of rule which derives its legitimacy in the eyes of all concerned from belief in the sacredness of orders and powers of rulers by virtue of their having " always " existed.[33] In contrast with the state of affairs found in secular cultures, the relations between the ruler and his staff on the one hand and the subjects on the other are personal and based on piety toward the ruler. Moreover, the members of whatever administrative staff may exist are not " officials " but servants, and the ruled are not " members " but are either " colleagues " or subjects. They give their allegiance not to impersonal norms but to the ruler himself. Needless to say, no specifically new norms are issued, and innovations, should they perchance arise, are explained as having always existed. Arbitrariness and irrationality have wide scope in traditional authoritative rule, which we shall frequently term " traditional domination."

Five definite sub-types (not all of them preliterate) have been distinguished: (1) gerontocracies; (2) patriarchies; (3) patrimonies and sultanates; (4) " estatism," [34] and (5) feudalism.

The first two are characterized by the absence of an administrative staff: the elders, who transmit the sacred lore, rule in the gerontocracies, and both the elders and the patriarchs stand in direct relation with their " colleagues "; i.e., with their fellows of the sacred community. In patrimonial, " estatal," and feudal types of rule the position of the administrative staff is very important: it is chosen by the ruler either (1) patrimonially, from among his own clan, slaves, clients, or household; or (2) extrapatrimonially, from recruited confidants, favorites, and like persons who join his authoritative group. (Max Weber, to whom we owe these distinctions, held that modern bureaucracies such as those of France and Germany had their origin in this extrapatrimonial type of administration, and were in the beginning but recruited servants of the ruler.) [35] Here we are most concerned with gerontocracy and patriarchy, for the emergence of the other forms is usually conditioned by a degree of cultural complexity that involves at least the simpler kinds of writing; scribes are almost a necessity.

In general, we may say that traditional rule is characterized by a dutiful, pious obedience on the part of the ruled, and that this facilitates the preservation of mental immobility.

Isolation and Aversion to Strangers. — Another aspect of the mental immobility of preliterates is the distrust of strangers that is frequently manifested. There is an old saying to the effect that " Whoever speaks two languages is a rascal " and, like many another proverb, this correctly represents the feeling of preliterate communities when the sudden intrusion of new thoughts and disturbing examples breaks down the entrenched tyranny of the single sacred code, and leaves pliant, impressible, mentally mobile man — for such he then is — to follow his unbridled, irreverent will without guidance by traditional morality and traditional religion. The old oligarchies, such as Sparta, were wise in prohibiting journeys abroad and visits by strangers; they wanted to keep their type intact, and they knew that culture contact would inevitably bring personal and social disorganization into their sacred community.

Even when no such barriers are set up, and when no formal prohibition of strangers exists, there is frequently a general air of dislike, hostility, and even hatred that is unmistakable.[36] It should not be assumed, however, that aversion to strangers is part of " human nature "; in certain situations they may be welcomed as bearers of news or traders. When suspicion and antipathy are especially evident, they are frequently due to disagreeable past experiences, religious fanaticism, or infraction of the sacred code by the stranger. This last is probably a fruitful cause of antagonism, for when preliterates have followed certain practices for centuries, they are not likely to greet with acclaim the man who calmly disregards the most elementary injunctions of the sacred community. To quote Boas again:

Intolerance is often, if not always, based on the strength of automatic reactions and upon the feeling of intense displeasure felt in acts opposed to our own automatism. The apparent fanaticism exhibited in the persecution of heretics must be explained in this manner . . . Its psychological basis was . . . the impossibility of changing a habit of thought that had become automatic, and the consequent impossibility of following new lines of thought, which, for this very reason, seemed anti-social; that is, criminal.[37]

In view of the multiplicity of taboos and restrictions governing even the minute details of the institutional life of many preliterate groups, it is easy to see how the most amiable of strangers might commit sacrilege every time he turned around; only long training by some preliterate friend combining the rôles of Emily Post and Cardinal Hayes could save him from the deadly social-religious blunder.

A further corroboration of the thesis that the aversion is not to the stranger as such, but to the stranger offending against the sacred code of the " in-group," is found in the fact that social control also weighs heavily on the occasional local deviate who has the itch for innovation, and not merely upon the stranger. New found that among the Wanika a villager who improved the style of his hut, who made a larger doorway than ordinary, who wore a finer or different dress than his fellows, was instantly fined; Tylor has made classical the case of the Dyaks who were severely punished for felling trees by V-shaped cuttings in the European fashion instead of the much less efficient method sanctified by custom; the tremendous, conservative influence of religious practices in ancient Greek and Roman society is virtually the sole theme of Coulanges's well-known book, La Cité antique; and Keane refers to conservative cannibals in Africa who argued that abolition of the custom of killing and eating enemies would ruin the community. Regardless of altered theories about the causes of aversion to any change that involves a break with the ancient ways, there is no doubt whatever among modern social scientists that such aversion is a widespread phenomenon. Preliterate culture and mental immobility are often closely related.

Even apparent exceptions confirm this thesis. In Samoa, for instance, where *minor* variations in the culture are not only tolerated but encouraged, there is nevertheless so much active disapproval of all who would copy the innovator and so much hostility to change in the *major* phases of Samoan life that fixity is inevitable. As Mead puts it:

> The whole flexibility of Samoan culture, which at first blush looks so favorable to the display of individuality, so pliant to the molding hand, is also a powerful conservative force. It possesses all the strength of the tough willows, which bend and swing to every passing breeze but never break.[38]

Social Thought Usually Implicit or Proverbial. — Now that we have distinctly before us this general background of reluctance or inability to change, we can turn our attention to the details of the preliterate picture. The theme of this chapter is social thought, but, as has been evident in the foregoing discussion, *we must give a very wide interpretation to the term when dealing with mentally immobile peoples* — a large part of their thought is not expressed in words, much less in systematic theories, and even when they do give verbal expression to their social insights, proverbs rather than more thoroughly generalized abstractions are the rule.[39] In short, their social thought must often be inferred from their conduct; it is usually concrete and implicit rather than abstract and explicit. Even when it is explicit, it takes the form of pithy sayings arising from circumscribed experience rather than condensed formulas of universal applicability. Instances: "The face of a wife shows what her husband is; the shirt of a husband shows what his wife is," as contrasted with "The pair always behaves otherwise than either member would if alone, or at the very least, in cases where one partner is overwhelmingly dominant, than the passive member if left to himself would behave." [40] Concrete *versus* abstract with a vengeance!

The disinclination to think in any other than a concrete way is of course part and parcel of the mental immobility engendered by and engendering isolation. The typical member of a preliterate group is not given to highly abstract, rational thought [41] (although there are of course preliterate "intellectuals" who indulge in cosmogonical speculation and the like). If our typical preliterate is a herdsman, he knows individually and personally every one of his charges; Crumple and Spot are not just so much meat. If he tills the soil, he becomes with the passage of time so attached to the particular plot over which he labors that transposition to another, upon which he has not grown up and with which he has not the same familiar relation, causes a severe wrench — and indeed, the disturbance of deep-set motor habits does bring with it a feeling of uneasiness or even distress. " For such a man, the neighboring valley, or even the strip of land at the other end of the village, is in a certain sense alien territory." [42] That is to say, immobile, stable persons are held to the concrete and personal because nothing else comes within their ken. The moment effective contacts with the outside world are established, forces set at work that tend to depersonalize the relationships of the sacred community; the concrete begins to become abstract, sentiments to become interests, the emotional to become rational, the sacred to become secular. When this occurs, social thought not only becomes explicit but also tends toward a high degree of generality; when it does not, the implicit or the proverbial holds sway.

In thus calling attention to differences between the thought of the great majority of preliterates and that of modern man in his more rational moments, we do not necessarily assert that the former are generally inferior in any biological sense, as we have already pointed out — and neither do we dogmatically assert *die Gleichheit alles dessen, was Menschenantlitz trägt*. The whole question of biological difference in mental capacity is exceedingly controversial and, in spite (or because) of the contentions of extreme cultural determinists on the one hand and rigid biological determinists on the other, is far from solution. Our present knowledge is not sufficient, and the possibilities of controlled experiment are still too far away, to hope for a final answer in the foreseeable future. Nevertheless, we do maintain that there are *differences* between preliterate and modern. Many recent ethnographical field-workers are over-eager to defend peoples with whom they have identified themselves against charges of *innate* incapacity for abstract thought.[43] Although they are probably right in their defense, their unduly sweeping countercharges have led to an error almost as serious as that perpetrated by earlier social scientists who thought that preliterates were "primitives." This error is that there is no discoverable difference between the thinking of the mentally immobile member of an isolated, sacred society and the mentally mobile resident of an accessible, secular society such as the modern urban world affords. In other words, it is gratuitously assumed that the most advanced preliterate and the most advanced modern think in the same way — an assumption that, to say the least, is mistaken. There most certainly is a difference rooting in the very categories of thought, and it should not be minimized. In spite of the fact that writers representing the dominant trend in present-day psychology and sociology maintain (rightly or wrongly) that this difference is socially acquired rather than biologically inherited, it is exceedingly important however caused, and cannot be denied without flouting a vast body of evidence. Let us therefore proceed with our examination of the implicit and proverbial aspects of preliterate social thought.

Ethnocentrism. — Aversion to the stranger offending against the sacred ways has already been noted; closely allied with this is the opinion that one's own group or people, one's *ethnos,* is the center about which all else revolves, is overwhelmingly more important than any other.[44]

Such naïve conceit has its favorable side; the so-called savage, for example, is not so savage within his familiar community.[45] Offenses against standards are not often deliberately punished by physical force unless gross sacrilege is involved; toward the members of one's own group the weapons used in social control are often merely moral indignation, "jabbering," ostracism, or more or less spontaneous physical chastisement. The preliterate thinks too much in terms of "we," so far as his intimate associates are concerned, to be lastingly vindictive, and he makes relatively few attempts to enforce the Guilt = Punishment equation upon his closer kindred or people.[46]

It is where outside peoples are concerned — and "outside peoples" may dwell very near by or bear only a slightly different name — that the unfavorable aspects of ethnocentrism become obvious. Here the savage is truly savage; no bonds of sympathy or fellow-feeling link him with the despised "they-group"; its members are beyond the pale.[47] Torture, slaughter, fire, and rapine are dispensed as freely by the preliterate as if he were a modern patriot bombing and gassing the cities of the foe. In many languages the words for "man" and "our people" are the same; conversely, "stranger" and "enemy" are often identical terms.[48] The limited world-views linked with such culture traits are well illustrated by Westermarck:

According to Eskimo beliefs, the first man, though made by the Great Being, was a failure, and was consequently cast aside and called *kob-lu-na,* which means "white man"; but a second attempt of the Great Being resulted in the formation of a perfect man, and he was called *In-nu,* the name which the Eskimo give to themselves. . . . When anything foolish is done, the Chippewas use an expression which means "as stupid as a white man." . . . A Fijian . . . having been to the United States,

was ordered by his chiefs to say whether the country of the white man
was better than Fiji, and in what respects. He had not, however, gone
very far in telling the truth, when one cried out, " He is a prating fellow "; another, " He is impudent "; and some said, " Kill him." . . .
Even the miserable Veddah of Ceylon has a very high opinion of himself,
and regards his civilized neighbors with contempt. . . . When a Greenlander saw a foreigner of gentle and modest manners, his usual remark
was, " He is almost as well-bred as we," or, " He begins to be a man,"
that is, a Greenlander. The savage regarded his people as *the* people, as
the root of all others, and as occupying the middle of the earth. The
Hottentots love to call themselves " the men of men." . . . The aborigines of Hayti believed that their island was the first of all things, that
the sun and moon issued from one of its caverns, and men from another.
Each Australian tribe regards its country as the centre of the earth, which
in most cases is believed not to extend more than a couple of hundred
miles or so in any direction.[49]

  · But we need not restrict our exhibit of ethnocentrism to the
simpler preliterates alone; groups having more complex cultures, and even some in the early stages of literacy, manifest an
outlook equally narrow. Thus Westermarck continues:

  We meet with similar feelings and ideas among the nations of archaic
culture. The Chinese are taught to think themselves superior to all other
peoples. . . . According to Japanese ideas, Nippon was the first country
created, and the centre of the world. The ancient Egyptians considered
themselves as the peculiar people, especially loved by the gods. . . . To
the Hebrews their own land was " an exceeding good land," " flowing
with milk and honey," " the glory of all lands "; and its inhabitants were
a holy people which the Lord had chosen " to be a special people unto
Himself above all people that are upon the face of the earth." . . . The
Greeks called Delphi — or rather the round stone in the Delphic temple
— " the navel " or " the middle point of the earth "; and they considered
the natural relation between themselves and barbarians to be that between master and slave.[50]

  Proverbs are replete with the same exalted, naïve belief in
the superiority of the native land or race: " Among flowers the
cherry-blossom; among men the Samurai " (Japanese) ; " The
Englishman bawls, the Irishman sleeps, but the Scotsman goes
till he gets it " (Scottish) ; " The Italian is wise when he under-
takes a thing, the German while he is doing it, and the Frenchman when it is over " (Italian) ; " The difference between Arabs
and Persians is the same as that between a date and its stone "
(Arabian) — and so on and so on; ethnocentrism is omnipresent
in all groups with limited horizons.

  Age Discrimination. — Some attention has already been paid
to the fact that the absence of written records gives a great ad-

vantage to the older members of preliterate groups, as well as to the fact that kinship organization provides an excellent opportunity for the old to stamp the young with their image. This state of affairs is well manifested in the prevalence of initiation ceremonies,[51] ordeals, confirmations, and similar "rites of passage"[52] that afford to the elders awe-inspiring occasions upon which to impress the immature with the great importance of age.[53] The graybeard is venerated, yes, but not infrequently he also sees to it, consciously or unconsciously, that he gets the perquisites due the venerable. Here again proverbs supply instances: " 'Tis a bad house that has not an old man in it " (Italian) ; " If young men had wit and old men strength, everything might be well done " (Spanish) ; " In clothes we value novelty; in men old age " (Chinese) ; " Where the elders are not heard, there God does not help " (Yugo-Slavian) ; et cetera. The social thought dominant in the sacred community cannot be fathomed unless we are aware of the dominance that threescore years and ten may exercise.

Sex Discrimination. — A well-marked trait of most preliterate societies is the sharp division of social conduct into male and female categories. True, modern societies also set up standards of " man's work " and " woman's work," but the definitions have been becoming more and more vague, and in the short space of half a century sweeping changes have taken place that make it at least formally possible for woman to be man's competitor in many fields once in his exclusive possession. We may bewail this, or we may jubilate over it, but it is undeniable.

Now the preliterate has very definite notions of what is proper to the respective sexes. Of course, there is great variation as between groups in the functions exercised by women — in one culture they alone may till the soil, in another they may never touch any agricultural implement — but within any given society the sphere of female activity is laid out along fairly clear lines; individual, seasonal, or similar exceptions are — exceptions. Inasmuch as these preliterate societies are relatively isolated, there is very little opportunity for comparison with others in which female functions cover a different field, and hence the initial division of labor is perpetuated until it has become hallowed by time and almost unshakeably fixed.

One of the accompaniments of such fixation is the institution of specifically male and specifically female taboos. Men must not eat certain foods; women must not so much as taste others. The doughty warrior must never tell his lady-love the secrets of the men's masked dance; the woman skilled in midwifery must sedulously refrain from referring to the mysteries of her art in the presence of husband or father or brother. These and countless other taboos testify to the firmness with which the belief in radical difference between the sexes as regards practically all physical and mental traits is held by many a preliterate social thinker.

And after all he has many reasons for his belief — reasons that also pass current in very complex cultures. For one thing, he cannot but be struck by the mysterious phenomenon of menstruation; taboos with regard to menstruating women are legion. "The issue of blood," that fluid of magical potency, is rarely regarded lightly, and the being in whom it regularly recurs, for no apparent cause, is thought of almost as a being of a different order. Again, the part played by the female in reproduction is superficially more important and probably more difficult to understand (*contra* Malinowski) [54] than is the male's. When to this is added the even greater set of riddles posed by anomalies such as miscarriages, premature deliveries, and the birth of freaks and monsters, we can readily comprehend why the preliterate often draws a sharp line between the earthly realms proper to man and woman, and we are also able to appreciate, if not to approve, the frequent extension of this division into the next world. Preliterates often assert that women will not have any part in the life to come, for they have no souls; and, even if there is a belief that females may partake of immortality, a separate heaven or hell is frequently reserved for them.

But in spite of belief in woman's inferiority so deep-seated that this world and the next are thus cleft in twain by many preliterates, we must not assume that woman is always and everywhere relegated to a lower plane. There have been matriarchal cultures in which the peculiar powers of the female secured for her a privileged or even dominant position. Let us hastily add, however — in spite of the counterclaims of Bachofen and Briffault [55] — that such societies are by no means common. With but few exceptions, mostly among the simpler preliterates, it may be said that preliterate social thought and action not only place woman in a separate category, but also consign her to the status of an inferior, as witness the following proverbs: " Man without woman is head without body; woman without man is body without head " (German) ; " A woman is a very perfect devil " (French) ; " A man of straw is worth a woman of gold " (French) ; " Those with a female leader perish " (Hindu) ; " A woman's thoughts are after-thoughts" (Japanese); "It is as great pity to see a woman weep as to see a goose go barefoot" (English); "Woman has long hair but short brains" (Yugo-Slavian); "The hen should not crow like the cock" (Russian); and "A husband is father of his wife" (Russian). When these and hundreds more like them are cast in the balance, they far outweigh the occasional proverb (such as "It is sometimes well to obey a sensible wife" [Yugo-Slavian]) that grants woman a rung in the social ladder within reaching distance of man's.

Population Policies. — Not only does preliterate social thought frequently place the female far below the male, but in some simple societies she is exterminated at birth if the struggle for existence is severe. Chinese peasants, for example, have been known to kill girl babies because they may be hindrances rather than helps, whereas sons, who may greatly aid the family, are eagerly desired. (Other factors are operative, to be sure, but are not relevant here.)

Such limitation of population is not always carried out at the cost of the female alone, however; isolated societies the world over often restrict their numbers, and either sex may be sacrificed. Preliterates frequently see to it that the "natural" increase of population is checked; instead of resorting to mass migration when resources threaten to grow scanty, they reduce the drain on those resources. This policy is one of the clearest examples of foresighted action that early societies afford; the belief that "When God sends a mouth he sends food to fill it" is rare in simple cultures. Apparently some of the elders, long before Malthus, were vaguely aware of certain implications of two of his fundamental propositions. These propositions run thus: "Population is necessarily limited by the means of subsistence"; and "Population always increases when the means of subsistence increase." The implications dimly apprehended by the elders may be formulated thus: "Since population is necessarily limited by the means of subsistence, in *normal, stable* conditions it should remain stationary."

The reasons for giving the elders credit for some theoretical insight of this kind are many. For example, we have already seen that the usual state of affairs among simple human groups united by the kinship bond is stability; the isolated, sacred community does not change in appreciable degree. Alterations in the methods of obtaining subsistence are generally quite slow; the food supply is definitely limited by the technique available. The size of the group is in turn limited by the food supply, either directly or indirectly. That is, the group either starves out sufficiently to ensure adequate nourishment for the remaining members, or means are taken to limit increase in accordance with the resources available. As noted above, the latter is by no means uncommon; the use of crude contraceptives or abortifacients [56] and the practice of infanticide by exposure or actual slaughter (strangling, smothering, drowning) [57] were and are widespread among preliterates. In the animal world the organism wins or loses the struggle for existence on its own vital merits or defects; among preliterate peoples, on the other hand, the most vigorous infant may be killed if the elders decide that the drain on the food supply is becoming too great. The child's chances for survival are therefore arbitrarily limited by the sacred community as represented by the elders; the group does not grow at any threatening speed. Hence there were Malthusians and Neo-Malthusians among preliterate social thinkers; the warning of " Standing room only " is by no means new.

Charismatic Leadership. — Thus far we have confined our attention to a type of preliterate leadership (we shall not attempt to discriminate between leadership and domination here) that may be called traditional; although the elders frequently acquire prestige from other sources, their stronghold is their function of applying and transmitting the lore of the past.

Another kind of leadership that not infrequently appears in the more complex preliterate societies, and sometimes even in very simple ones, may be called charismatic (from the Greek word *charisma,* a divine or spiritual gift). Such leadership finds its source in " extraordinary devotion to the holiness or heroism or exemplariness of a person and of the regulations which he reveals or creates." [58] A recent treatise states it in this way:

Charismatic domination is established through the extraordinary qualities (real or supposed) of the leader. The recognition which he first receives is reinforced at times by striking coincidences or other " verifications " of his remarkable qualities, and is thus rendered relatively permanent. Nevertheless, he must continually arouse enthusiasm, be " a present help in time of trouble," and provide a warrant for " the hope that fails not." . . . Law is not the source of his authority; on the contrary, he proclaims new laws on the basis of revelation, oracular utterance, and inspiration.[59]

The terminology of this quotation might easily give rise to the assumption that the charismatic leader is always a religious leader, but this is by no means the case. He may exercise his sway, for example, almost exclusively in the political field — the extraordinary endurance, agility, or strength of a warrior may elevate him to the rank of charismatic chieftain.

But note that we have said " *almost* exclusively." There is an element of charismatic leadership that does involve supernatural religious notions, even though the religious aspect may not be in the foreground. This element is found in the fact that the charismatic leader is often thought to be in possession of or filled with a sort of mysterious impersonal power, variously called *hike, manitou, orenda, wakan, hasina,* or *mana,* that is responsible for his extraordinary qualities. Thus the chieftain is not chieftain primarily because of his endurance, agility, or strength, but because these qualities attest his possession of what we shall henceforth term mana. Belief in this uncanny impersonal power is not universal among preliterates, but it is very common. Mana differs from magic in that it is much more general; magical power is usually restricted and definitely localized, and is relatively personal.

The concept of mana as a mysterious power akin to a potent fluid or quality that can be poured into the designated person or object, together with its implication of negative power or taboo, has influenced preliterate social thought in many ways, but particularly in notions of leadership, kingship, and so forth. As already noted, the chieftain is not necessarily the priest, but the former is often identified, because of his mana, with the control of weather, crops, and processes of nature. Sometimes he is killed in order that his extraordinary powers may pass unimpaired into a successful rival and the fertility of the soil thereby be maintained. In other groups, lack of success is evidence of loss of mana, and speedy elimination is the result. Because of the belief in the chieftain's or king's mana as a force controlling the weather, food supplies, or healing processes, preliterate leaders receive offerings in return for mana imparted through the laying on of hands, embracing, and similar acts. This is mana in its positive form. If we accept the speculations of some scholars, the offerings finally became tributes, and eventually developed into royal revenue.[60] (Inasmuch as this revenue became increasingly devoted to works of public utility, it offers some analogies with taxation in the modern sense.)

Mana also has negative implications; a king may be so highly charged with it, so to speak, that it causes instant death or illness if the subject but touch the royal person or his possessions.[61] When this belief is thoroughly embedded in preliterate social thought, it obviously is a powerful agent of social control; it takes the place of bolts, bars, policemen, and soldiers, or at least makes the protection of the leader's property less difficult.

When one finds the idea that mana is inherited, which is in some respects a blend of traditional and charismatic conceptions, one may then see the cruder phases of a belief that has been exceedingly influential in the social thought not only of preliterates but also of members of complex literate cultures — the theory of the divine right of kings. In Madagascar, for instance, *hasina* (the local term for mana) is the power or virtue that makes a thing unusually good or effective, and it belongs in high degree to the king, inasmuch as " he is born in a family that has it, and is strengthened by the ceremonies of people having it, such as sorcerers and his own relatives." [62] This crude theory has of course been greatly refined by modern exponents of divine right doctrine, as witness the following excerpt:

The monarch is not in person divine, but he does enjoy and exercise a personal right to rule in virtue of his birth alone, and not of his office, a right based not merely upon national and customary law but founded in the law of God and Nature. Under it no king de facto can have any legitimate authority; all true kings must be kings de jure; under the law of God and the law of Nature they succeed by heredity alone to the rights of their ancestors, who in the beginning were divinely appointed to rule. They are never the creatures of the people; their authority does not come from the people's law, and their powers are not derived from their predecessors in the royal office, but from their ancestors alone.[63]

The tracing of parallels, to say nothing of survivals, is always dangerous, but we may nevertheless venture the assertion that there is some similarity here to the concept of mana. The king himself is not divine, but he exercises divine power. Could we present all the evidence here, we might go a long way toward showing that the power of mana is still believed to exist by advocates of the doctrine set forth in the above quotation; it has merely been restricted to a hereditary office and defined by law and custom (although such restriction and definition of course brings in a strong traditional element). The mysterious impersonal fluid, force, or stuff called mana by some preliterates has been identified with God and Nature by thinkers participating in the literate culture of the Western world. And, as we shall later see, this doctrine, for all its apparent crudity, has played a fateful part in the history of social thought.

Retracing our steps, let us now survey aspects of charismatic domination other than the strictly supernaturalistic. We have already said, in effect, that the minimum definition of charisma is that it is an extraordinary (*ausseralltäglich*) quality of an individual which commands the obedience of others. The most pressing problem of a charismatic ruler is to verify and perpetuate his charisma, whether through miracles, the cult of hero-worship, feats that regenerate trust in his leadership, or by otherwise gratifying the impulses of his subjects. When the ruler can no longer provide verification of his charisma this type of rule changes to other forms.

While it endures, the relation between ruler and ruled is a personal one based on belief and confidence in " extraordinariness." A leader or ruler having this quality needs no officialdom, no rational or even patrimonial administrative staff, relying as he does entirely on his band of personal disciples or henchmen who are held together by their belief in his charisma. Hence the rational, technical, methodical execution of legal norms is lacking (a point to which we shall later refer).

In contrast with both traditional and legal types of rule, therefore, charismatic domination is not only extraordinary but also, in its implications at least, revolutionary. " Ye have it said by them of old time . . . but I say unto you," the famous formula of Jesus, is cited by Weber as typifying the revolutionary character of charismatic authority.[64] " Charisma is the great revolutionary power in traditionally engulfed epochs." [65]

Obviously charisma is not something that can be acquired by systematic preparation alone. Even when there is a correlated belief in mana, the perpetuation of charismatic domination is always a difficult task; in its relatively unmixed forms it is seldom of long duration. Usually traditionalism comes to its aid or it develops into more secular types of rule. In many cases this secularization of the sacred is brought about by the pressure of the material interests of the immediate supporters and confidants of the charismatic ruler, or by the needs of his subjects. He finds it necessary, once he has power, to satisfy the demands of " the world."

When the bearer of the charisma dies or fails to prove the charismatic character of his powers by continual " extraordinariness," the grave problem of succession arises, and according to the way it is solved this or that new type of charismatic domination comes into being. One of these is the inheritable charisma already mentioned in connection with the kingly *hasina* of Madagascar; it is believed to be biologically transmitted. Domination of this type frequently evolves, ideal-typically speaking, into the tribal state (*Geschlechterstaat*) of which ancient Attica before the age of Peisistratus provides an example; one clan or group of clans alone is thought to be endowed with the charisma of leader-ship. Another variety is the charisma of the *office* of priest or king, noted above when discussing the modern versions of the divine right of kings doctrine; unworthy priests or feeble-minded kings maintain their positions by virtue of their office, but do so partly because tradition has reinforced charisma. The problem of succession may be solved in another way by designation or the devising of a method of naming the successor; Weber's example of this type is the transmission of the papacy, and here again there is obviously a mixture, not pure charisma.

Notions of Social Origins. — The traditional and charismatic modes of domination probably bear a close relation to the folk-tales and myths current among many preliterate peoples concern-ing the establishment of society and the state. For example, one occasionally finds the belief that some wise old man induced his fel-lows to band together against attack from without and dissension within, thus setting up a harmonious social order where previously only the rule of " dog eat dog " had prevailed. In addition to or independent of this traditional element there is usually a charis-matic factor: whether old or not, the founder of society is almost invariably believed to have been endowed with extraordinary qualities of some kind, and in many cases to have had a portion of mana so generous that he is godlike.

In other words, a " culture hero " deriving his powers in vary-ing proportion from both traditional and charismatic sources is frequently regarded as solely responsible for the body of customs and standards that the preliterate community in question has slowly accumulated over a period of centuries; the consequence is a sort of " great man " theory of social origins. Wissler, re-ferring primarily to the American Indian, puts it thus:

> The culture hero is not necessarily the creator of the world and of life, but is usually a human sort of god who established the present order of life. If one inquires as to how it is that women cook the food and dress the skins, the answer will be that So-and-so ordered it that way, and the name of the originator in each case will be that of a mythical character, to whom a series of narratives refer.[66]

Although these culture heroes are almost indistinguishable from gods or other supernatural beings among many peoples, they bear a larger number of human traits than spirits or deities *per se* commonly carry. Instance the fact that occasionally stories are to be found that make the culture hero a sort of Prometheus, a defender of mankind against the tyranny of the heavenly host, or that he is frequently cast in the rôle of trickster, stooping low to vulgarity and deceit in spite of his part as " founding father." [67]

Exceedingly common, of course, is the myth of the great law-giver: among the historical peoples the names of Moses, Lycur-gus, and many others may be cited. The " great man " theory antedates Carlyle.

Embryonic Law. — The mention of law suggests another type of domination that reaches its full fruition only in literate so-cieties, especially those in which the state is highly developed, but which may be traced in preliterate groups as well. This is termed rational domination, and has been analyzed as follows:

> Rational domination . . . in most instances derives its claims from ex-plicitly formulated principles, i.e., law. Rule and norms being thus techni-cally fixed, the dominant person has the status of a superior official; he issues his commands as the representative of an impersonal order.[68]

Other traits of this kind of authoritative rule, in its ideal-typical form, are the following: (1) new laws or norms may be issued from time to time, calling for obedience from all those within the sphere of jurisdiction; (2) the ruler is himself bound by the norms which he executes; (3) the ruled are not subjects of the ruler but are his " colleagues," fellow-members or fellow-citizens in a society, church, or state, and they do not obey him but obey the laws or norms; (4) in the execution of the law the administrator is restricted in his application of compulsion by a constitution, rules, or the like; (5) the execution of norms under rational or legal rule calls for a rational, ordered manner of administration, a " bureaucracy." [69]

Domination of this sort, with its elaborate hierarchy of scribes, legal experts, enforcing officers, and similar functionaries, is of course found in full flower only in complex cultures, and indeed does not reach its zenith until recent times in Western Europe and America. If, however, we center on one trait only and ignore the rest for the time being, we may say that rational rule is not wholly absent from preliterate societies, for embryonic or even half-fledged law is present in practically all of them. Such a state-ment runs counter to many opinions formerly held by ethnologists, for they believed that the preliterate is so completely submerged by tradition, the ties of kinship, and the opinions of his fellows that he spontaneously obeys all the norms and prescriptions of his group without even so much as feeling an impulse to go his own unfettered way. Indeed, earlier writers made much of what they called "primitive communism" or "tribal socialism" — they asserted that a vague sort of "group spirit" or "unwitting and intuitive obedience"[70] characterized all preliterate societies.

Such theories are entirely erroneous. In spite of the fact that in this chapter much attention has been paid to mental immobility, the sway of the elders, and similar forces tending toward the development and perpetuation of conformity, no one would be warranted in drawing the conclusion that any theories of "primitive communism" or the like have here been voiced. The preliterate feels some of the taboos or other restrictions laid upon him to be irksome; he does not "automatically" submit through sheer psychic inertia, and he at times evades his duty when he can do so without loss of prestige or prospective gain.[71] We can therefore agree in part with Malinowski:

> The force of habit, the awe of traditional command and a sentimental attachment to it, the desire to satisfy public opinion — all combine to make custom be obeyed for its own sake. In this the "savages" do not differ from the members of any self-contained community with a limited horizon, whether this be an Eastern European ghetto, an Oxford college, or a Fundamentalist Middle West community. But love of tradition, conformism and the sway of custom account but to a very partial extent for obedience to rule among dons, savages, peasants, or Junkers.[72]

For example, the preliterate may and often does share his wealth with his needy fellows in time of crisis, but he frequently does so because life would be intolerable for him if he did not. He would be looked at askance, insulted, scolded, or even expelled from the group; he could not gratify a large proportion of his fundamental human impulses. His "generosity" often does not spring from sheer amiability, but from considerations basically much like those that account for many varieties of good behavior in more complex cultures. Moreover, the ostracism and other forms of censure would not be "automatic" on the part of his fellows; in many if not most preliterate societies there exists a definite body of norms, rules, and reciprocities that determines exactly what shall be done in cases of tort or crime. In other words, there is a body of custom that is sufficiently explicit, binding, and adaptable to varying circumstances to be called *embryonic* civil and criminal law.

So much for agreement with Malinowski. At the same time, we should greatly exaggerate the importance of such codes, as Malinowski tends to do, if we were to assert that they are vastly more significant in preliterate life than the power of tradition, age, charismatic leadership, and mental immobility. After all, even the behavior of modern urban dwellers, for all their possible anonymity and range of contact, is not controlled by law to any-thing like the same extent that it is patterned by custom. There are laws against indecent exposure, for example, but no one who has watched subway denizens sweltering in their coats and collars believes that they are all restrained from wanton exhibitionism only by John Law on the beat overhead. How much more is the preliterate quietly pushed and pulled by notions of propriety, and what not, living as he does among persons who have known him since childhood — and before — and from whom he cannot escape by passing through the turnstile! [73] True enough, pre-literates do not always follow custom spontaneously or with en-thusiasm; they often have to be ridiculed by their fellows,[74] hec-tored by relatives, held up to scorn by elders, insulted by the opposite sex — but they *can* be hectored, contemned, and insulted. They cannot easily slip their moorings and set sail to acquire prestige in some other society; they cannot comfort themselves with the thought that posterity will read their books and regard them as martyred heroes; they cannot quickly salve their wounded feelings by setting up standards of value that reverse the judg-ment visited upon them. Hence we may say that law simply as law does not play a large part in the social thought of the pre-literate,[75] however certain we may be that it does have more of a rôle than earlier social scientists were willing to grant it.

Moreover, it should be recalled that we have consistently re-ferred to *embryonic* law; no matter how explicit or detailed the customary code may be, it usually if not always lacks one dis-tinguishing characteristic of positive law. In referring to groups on a very simple level of culture, Hobhouse has indicated what this distinguishing characteristic is: ". . . if we mean by law a body of rules enforced by an authority independent of personal ties of kinship and friendship, such an institution is not compatible with their social organization." [76] Even when preliterate cultures are complex enough to have a sort of impartial go-between to reconcile conflicts between kinship or similar groups (as is the case with the Ifugao, for instance), *enforcement* of decisions by a central authority whose acts are felt to be impersonal is certainly not common.[77] We are therefore justified in saying that rational domination and its corollary, law in its *precise* meaning, are rarely if ever found among simple preliterate groups.

Although we do not necessarily subscribe to the more sweeping

conclusions of the extreme " conflict school," it should be pointed
out here that a number of social scientists, of whom the most
prominent contemporary is Franz Oppenheimer, hold that law
in the strict sense is found only where one group has conquered
another and remains in the territory of the conquered as a dominant caste or class. The resulting social stratification is then rationalized, the inferior group is subjected to punishment for any
infringement of the interests of their superiors, and thus formal
law comes into being. Other theorists, such as MacLeod, maintain
that law is a product of complex differentiation *within* groups and
that conquest is not a necessary antecedent.[78] Master and servant
castes develop as a result of minor innate differences magnified by
social selection, and eventually the resulting social strata have so
little in common that the superiors regulate and punish the inferiors quite as if the latter were members of an " out-group " or
" they-group." (See under " Ethnocentrism.") In all these cases,
let it be noted, the groups in question are quite complex; consequently we may provisionally admit the contentions of either
Oppenheimer or MacLeod (which will be analyzed in detail in
another chapter) and still say that among very simple preliterate
groups law is seldom if ever more than embryonic; rational domination and formal law are functions only of a much higher degree
of cultural complexity and social stratification.

Property. — Let us now return to consider, in the light of this
conclusion, the " primitive communism " to which we have already referred. The historical school of ethnology has exposed
the completely misleading nature of theories that place " the
primitive horde," with its supposed communism of goods and
social relations, at the lower end of an evolutionary chain.[79] Depending on the quirks of the particular writer, this chain is supposed to lead from sexual promiscuity to nineteenth-century monogamy, or " from the homogeneous to the heterogeneous," or
from primitive communism through capitalistic individualism on
to transitional state socialism and ultimately to that perfect an-
archism, the apogee of Marxian communism, which results from
" the withering away of the state." All such unilinear, genetically
determined sequences are out of court. To restrict ourselves to
economic institutions: in virtually all forms of preliterate society
of which we have knowledge, personal and even private property
has been explicitly recognized in every case where such ownership
would in any important way advance the interests and efficiency of
the group or the welfare of the individual. A considerable proportion of the stock of customary norms, regulations, and reciproci-

ties functioning in the place of definite law among preliterates is devoted to property rights.

Preliterate theories and practices relating to property are extremely complex and diverse. Among simple peoples whose industrial activities are limited to hunting and fishing, not only is it common for groups as a whole to have the exclusive right to hunt and fish in certain areas, but specific persons or families are often accorded special rights within these areas. Among pastoral peoples a very common situation is that of communal or collective ownership of the land with sub-group or individual property in the livestock. Among agriculturists communal ownership of waste land and pasture land is often associated with individual or family ownership of the cultivated lands. There are likewise well-developed conceptions of individual ownership of movable chattels, such as women, slaves, pottery, tools, and animals. Indeed, preliterates even have crude personal forms of what are supposed to be very modern and sophisticated notions of property, such as the incorporeal property rights residing in patents and copyrights — preliterate songs, liturgies, and so on often belong in a peculiarly personal way to the composer thereof, inasmuch as he alone is permitted to utter them.

The same lack of uniformity holds with respect to inheritance: group inheritance, primogeniture, ultimogeniture, and multiple inheritance are all to be found among preliterates.

Moreover, some preliterate societies are stratified on the basis of wealth — the more blankets, the more coppers, the more cattle a tribesman has, the more prestige he enjoys, the more eagerly his offspring are sought in marriage, and the more power over community opinion he exercises. All the mental traits that go with this state of affairs in our own society are also to be found among preliterates: we stand in awe before the man who has a fleet of cars larger than he can possibly use, or who otherwise indulges in conspicuous waste and pecuniary emulation; the Indian of the northern Pacific coast renders homage to the man who can publicly burn more blankets or destroy more precious metal than anyone else.[80] The notion that the possession of wealth involves the possession of other praiseworthy characteristics is not by any means confined to modern social thought; similarly, the idea that the possession of wealth is in and of itself the supreme praiseworthiness is also to be found among preliterates.

Here again, however, we must be on our guard; it is possible to react too strongly against the earlier theorists. In spite of the great variety in the forms of property and inheritance listed above, there can be no doubt that collective property, however defined, is much more frequent and the right of making a will more limited than in our own society. Moreover, the homage paid to the possessor of great amounts of personal property by some preliterates should not blind us to the fact that, in times of crisis or general need, many if not most preliterates share their possessions to a very much greater degree than is the case in civilized societies. There is also general recognition of the principle that so far as one's own community or kinship group is concerned, property should be held for use (although the " use " to which it is put may differ vastly from our conception of what is proper) and not for profit. Hence, if we define private property as exclusive ownership of the means of production for the purpose of reaping profit through their use by others, and establish a separate category for personal property, held for exclusive use but not for profit, we are able to say that strictly private property is by no means common among preliterates. To recur to the example of incorporeal property rights: the fact that a preliterate composer has the exclusive right to perform his own songs does not mean that he holds them as private property, for he does not make a profit by selling the right to others. It is strictly personal and strictly inalienable. Hence we go much too far if we call such prerogatives anything more than crude *personal* forms of copyright or patent; we cannot find exact parallels with highly developed modern notions of private property. Everything that we have said about the limiting effects of isolation and mental immobility, traditional domination, charismatic leadership, taboo, and ethnocentrism with regard to law also applies to preliterate social thought on the subject of property.[81]

Religion. — The reader has perhaps wondered why up to this point there has been so little reference to religion as that word is commonly understood. The reason is that it is all too easy to exaggerate the rôle of the religious element in human behavior, and particularly in preliterate behavior.[82] Almost everything the preliterate does has religious or magical adjuncts, to be sure, but in some cases these adjuncts are not taken as seriously as some of our earlier observers, many of them missionaries, were inclined to believe.

Having surveyed other phases of preliterate social thought, however, we are not in grave danger of distorting the general picture if we give full recognition to the importance of religion. Let us begin by trying to discover just what it is.

A serious difficulty at once arises: it is impossible to define religion as a single unified body of practice and thought. Indeed, Goldenweiser contends that religious experience falls into at least three major phases: (1) the emotional basis, which arises from the thrill of the extraordinary or mysterious; (2) the ritualistic aspect, which embodies man's reaction to the stimulus of the emotional thrill; and (3) the conceptual or doctrinal aspect, which embodies man's rationalization of the meaning and value of the religious thrill and of his subsequent behavior in response to that thrill.[83]

A number of theories have been offered to explain the origins and nature of this emotional thrill and of the supernaturalism linked with it. Earlier ethnologists based their explanations on propitiation of and reverence for natural forces, and on the belief in personal souls and spirits called animism [84] (most strikingly involved in the phenomenon of ghost-fear and the more limited practice of ancestor-worship). Somewhat later, other ethnologists advanced the theory of animatism; they assigned the origin of the religious thrill to experiences linked with vague notions of an animating force; i.e., of mana, that mysterious impersonal power to which we have already referred.[85] As Shotwell expresses it, man believed that he apprehended some all-pervading, all-animating influence in the universe, but did not comprehend its real meaning, thus leaving in his mind a thrill-provoking mystery.[86] Durkheim, famous French sociologist, suggested a sociological explanation of the religious thrill on the ground that when preliterates come together in crowds to carry out their religious rites and festivities, they are thrilled and stimulated to an unwonted degree because of the heightened suggestibility engendered in the crowd situation.[87] Inasmuch as preliterates are not experts in the social psychology and sociology of the crowd, they do not recognize the real source of their surging emotions and increased sense of power; these phenomena are believed to be due to the intervention of the gods or spirits which are being worshiped or placated by the crowd. Another explanation of the religious thrill has recently been attempted by the so-called dynamic psychologists, of whom Martin provides a good example.[88] Such writers call attention to the tendency of the child to build into his attitudes toward the supernatural world the emotions and sentiments of fear, trust, awe, and dependence elicited by his elders, particularly by his parents. The mother tells the child that God " made " things, and then explains that God is " our Father in Heaven "; in this way the attitudes clustering about the family become intertwined with the thrills of a supernatural world peopled by heavenly fathers and mothers and brothers and sisters. Persuasive as Martin's theory is, however, it applies primarily to the more complex cultures; it may well be doubted whether it touches the root of the problem of religious origins.

We have now considered a number of theories focusing on the emotional side of religion; let us now turn to the activational side. This falls into two categories: magic and worship. A number of the earlier ethnologists, notably Frazer, were inclined sharply to distinguish magic from religion and to represent magic as crude science.[89] No reputable scholar now maintains this view of the matter.[90] Magic is that phase of preliterate religious behavior which is devoted chiefly to coercing the gods according to a definite ritualistic contract which the gods have supposedly revealed and which they have agreed to observe. If the mystic formulas are accurately set forth and complied with in every respect, then, as the theory of magic has it, the gods will hand over the desired results to the practitioners. Worship, in contrast to this, is the ritualistic and ceremonial expression of man's awe, reverence, humility, and gratitude toward the supernatural world and its dominating powers. The reason for rejecting doctrines which, like Frazer's, maintain that magic and religion are sharply differentiated in preliterate thought is simply that in both early and modern religious behavior magic and worship are often closely interwined rather than widely separated. Some recent writers even regard magic as the technique of preliterate religion.

The conceptual side of religion, or man's rational explanations of his emotional experiences and his religious behavior, has passed from the animism and animatism of the preliterate to scholastic theology, from scholastic theology to such writings as Paley's *Natural Theology* more than a century ago, and from Paley to the latest apologetics of the modernist theologian. Only of very recent years, in the works of the ethnologists, sociologists, and cultural historians, have we begun to secure non-theological analyses of the origins and nature of religious beliefs and practices. What the final outcome of these inroads of the naturalistic viewpoint will be is speculative, but there can be no doubt that the conceptual content of religion has already been greatly modified by the advances of science, and that it will be modified still further.

The future does not greatly concern us here, however; our problem is the past. What can we discern regarding the development of religion, particularly of its conceptual phase? Earlier writers thought that there was a period in which there was no animism, no notion of individual spirits or gods, a period in which

animatism, with its vague feeling or notion of mana, held exclusive sway. We now know that there is no proof that animatism
preceded animism; the former seems to be a somewhat simpler
form of belief than the latter, but that is the most we can say, and
that is certainly no proof of priority.

But however and whenever the belief in individualized and personified spirits — that is to say, animism — came about, there is
fairly good evidence for the assertion that the more complex
forms of religious belief found in it more fertile soil than in
animatism. Most preliterates firmly hold to a comprehensive doctrine of supernatural causation, and where the animistic form of
this doctrine is strong, there is also present, in most instances, a
belief that all good things happen as a result of the benevolent
aid of good spirits and that all disasters come about because of
the malicious activity of evil spirits. When all events are thus
strongly infused with a personal element, there is an opportunity
for a further degree of complexity in religious belief : the preliterate is accustomed to social situations in which traditional, charismatic, and semi-rational domination hold sway, and he tends
to project the visible earthly hierarchy into the imagined world.
Consequently there come to be leaders, social ranks and grades,
domination and submission, and countless other social phenomena
in the realm of gods and spirits. Under certain circumstances
there results a still more complex type of animistic religion :
a hierarchy of good spirits confronts one made up of evil spirits,
each having as its head a spirit embodying the principles of good
and of evil respectively. Sometimes the good spirits have virtues strangely like the group believing in them, whereas the evil
spirits oftentimes bear the stigmata of enemy peoples or oppressors.

From these and like phenomena it is plain that preliterate
religion is markedly affected by its social setting. Nevertheless,
it is exceedingly important in its own right, and is perhaps even
more important in the influence it exerts on virtually every other
aspect of life. For example, religious beliefs furnish the chief
framework of preliterate cosmology and technics. Again, few if
any forms of preliterate economic endeavor are ever thoroughly
secularized; everything must be done under the proper religious
auspices. In fact, many preliterates spend quite as much time in
religious exercises related to economic undertakings as they do
in the undertakings themselves. Once more, there is a great deal
of evidence to show that many if not most preliterate religious and
political practices are linked with the assumption that leadership

requires qualities so extraordinary as to be possible only to those having a divine gift or possessing divine aid and approval; what has been said about domination of all kinds, but particularly about the charismatic variety, should be recalled at this point. Further, the embryonic jurisprudence discussed in connection with rational domination is closely bound up with theories of supernatural intervention and control; nothing really approaching the sharp separation of supernatural and secular law peculiar to our own culture is found in preliterate life. Still further, preliterate education is vitally linked with supernatural sanctions; a great part of it is simply inculcation of religious beliefs and social practices supposedly enjoined by or derived from supernatural sources. Again, many aspects of preliterate ceremonial life are strongly conditioned by one or another form of religious activity. All in all, it may be said with considerable assurance that there is no phase of preliterate life unaffected by supernaturalistic or religious factors, and in numerous instances these factors are more important than any others.

At the risk of seeming to take away with one hand what we give with the other we must insist, however, that the rôle of *explicit* supernaturalism in preliterate life has often been exaggerated.*This has been largely a result of the prevalent failure of sociologists to discriminate between the realms of the sacred and the supernatural. As we have seen, the isolation characteristic of an overwhelming proportion of preliterate societies engenders extreme mental immobility, gives rise to great unwillingness or inability, or both, to change established ways of acting and thinking. A sort of emotional halo envelops the ways of the community and thereby prevents their profanation by change — they become *sacred*. This mental immobility and its emotional overtones may be quite as effective in checking the rise of innovations as explicit taboos backed up by threats of supernatural terrors, but it is not in and of itself supernaturalistic. That there is almost always a close connection between the sacred and the supernatural cannot be denied, but in many such cases the supernaturalistic doctrine — animism, animatism, or what not — is used to rationalize one or another kind of mental immobility primarily bound up with sacred factors. To be sure, once supernaturalistic doctrines have become an integral part of the culture of a group, they play a tremendously important rôle in generating mental immobility and its attendant set of social attitudes. Nevertheless, the sacred and the supernatural are not the same, and much of the importance of the latter is qualified, to say the least, when due attention is paid to

* Here and elsewhere in book an antihesis between the "supernaturalistic" and the "sacred" is set up, whereas proper usage deals with the "supernaturalistic" as a sub-variety of the more general term "sacred." The latter *includes* the holy (supernaturalistic), ritualistic, loyalistic, intimate, commemorative, moralistic, fitting, and appropriate. See 1951 Commentary on Value-System Terminology.

the significance of the sacred — as we have tried to do in the earlier sections of this chapter.

By thus giving heed to sacredness we have in a way anticipated our present section on religion, for there can be no doubt that religion, properly defined, includes both supernaturalistic and sacred elements. Indeed, if much value could be granted such evidence, the word's etymologies alone might even lead to the conclusion that the sacred was a more important element than the supernatural in lending it meaning. Cicero's old etymology, for example, derives the Latin *religio* of which our word is an off-shoot from *religere,* to execute painstakingly by means of repeated effort. Can we help recalling Boas's analysis of the sacred society in this connection? " The more fundamental the motor habits . . . the less likely will be a deviation from the customary type. . . . The familiarity established through long . . . [habituation] may readily lead to an emotional attachment that finds expression in permanence of form, and in the refusal to accept [the] new and unfamiliar. . . ." And when we turn to the etymology given by the " Christian Cicero," Lactantius, what do we find? He derives *religio* from *religare,* to bind, and from what we know of the binding force exercised by mental immobility and its " emotional halo," the resulting emphasis on the sacred phase of religion does not seem misplaced. These etymologies are not at present in good standing, however; what is the result when more modern researches are drawn upon? Well, one authority says that the root word is not Latin, but Greek, ἀλέγειν, and that it means to heed or have a care; its antithesis is neglect. Here again the relation to the sacred clearly outweighs the relation to the supernatural; the very essence of conduct in many isolated preliterate societies is religious, in the sense that the most anxious care is taken to preserve the sacred ways even when no supernaturalistic doctrine specifically enjoining such preservation has been formulated. Few aspects of daily life are too insignificant to be neglected; the preliterate " heeds " or " has a care " for many phases of conduct that are left to inclination or chance in less religious societies. Hence it may be said that in spite of divergent etymologies and the general shakiness of such evidence, the analysis of language lends support to or at least does not conflict with our contention that although the word " religion " comprises them both, the supernatural and the sacred are not the same.

The extent to which attitudes toward these phases of religion may differ is clearly shown by the contrasting attitudes found within the same society. Radin furnishes some excellent examples.

First, we have at one extreme the successful defiance of *super-natural* powers:

> Among the Winnebago there exists a delightful story of a man who dared to state that he disbelieved in the powers of the most terrifying and holiest of the Winnebago deities, and who in public expressed his contempt for him. A short time later, the deity in question appeared to the skeptic and pointed his finger at him, an action that was supposed to bring immediate death. The man stood his ground and did not budge and the deity — Disease-Giver was his name — begged the man to die lest the people make fun of him! [91]

Next, we have in direct antithesis an assertion by the same author that the preliterate rarely if ever issues a fundamental challenge to the *sacred* aspects of his culture:

> We have nothing even remotely comparable to primitive man's sense of an objective social world. . . . Like the external world it is never static. . . . Yet in spite of this . . . *it is always the same, a unique and unalterable social world.* An individual may sin against varying parts of it without incurring dangerous consequences, but if he sins against any fundamental aspect he must be prepared either to dissociate himself entirely from this world or die.

> Possibly we have here one of the reasons for *the absence of consistent skeptics or unbelievers and for the nonexistence of revolts against the real structure of society.* [92]

In other words, it may on occasion be far easier to defy the supreme supernatural being than to break the sacred code regulating everyday, commonplace conduct. Here, certainly, is excellent warrant for the statement that the supernatural and the sacred are not the same. Although the latter term will frequently be used to cover both aspects of religion, the distinction between the two is of some importance in the present volume, inasmuch as we shall occasionally refer to processes of secularization initiated by migration, communication, and other modes of culture contact. [93] In using the term " secularization " the reference will be *primarily* (but not exclusively) to those kinds of social change that disrupt the sacred aspects of the societies in question; alterations in supernaturalistic doctrines are often involved, of course, but these are not the sole objects of interest. In a highly secular society the power of religion as a means of social control is weak, but so are all other means of non-political social control; conversely, religion in its supernaturalistic phases is by no means the only agency of social control in a sacred society. The more remote implications of the terms " sacred society," " secular society," and " secularization " will only gradually become apparent, however; it is merely hoped that some idea has been given of preliterate sacred societies and of the implicit or explicit social thought generated in them.

Abstract Epitome of Chapter. — Most of this chapter has not been too forbiddingly abstract, and the reader can easily provide his own summary. It seems advisable, however, to set forth an abstract frame of reference that will more closely relate what has been said here to succeeding pages and to the general background of systematic sociology. Such a frame of reference is not a summary (in the strictest sense), for it is both retrospective and prospective, and in addition is an ideal-typical [94] construct based on *selected phases* instead of a concrete recapitulation. If it proves helpful to the novice in sociology, so much the better; if not, he can safely disregard it for the time being. The graduate student and the professional sociologist will probably wish to assimilate it at this stage:

The isolated sacred society is isolated in three ways: vicinally,[95] socially, and mentally. Vicinal isolation leads, among other things, to the fixation of motor habits and intense opposition to change; social isolation leads to habitual relations of withdrawal and the fixation of attitudes toward the in-group and out-group (ethnocentrism); mental isolation . . . is usually associated with social isolation, and leads to similar results. . . .

In addition to being isolated this society is completely sacred (in the special sense here given the latter term). No comparison, classification, analysis, and abstraction, habitual or otherwise, is practiced; everything is unique, concrete, and personal, for all contacts are primary. The organism is so thoroughly adjusted to definite motor habits, attitudes inculcated in childhood [etc.] . . . that there arises " a feeling of impropriety of certain forms, of a particular social or religious value, or of superstitious fear of change." [96] Tradition and ceremonial play a large part in the life of the society, and . . . [most situations] are defined in customary and sacred terms; Tarde's " custom-imitation " prevails. The folkways and mores rule; there is a minimum of rationalistic criticism, and of individuation a similar minimum. Even the maintenance folkways and the material objects associated with them are under the sacred sanction. . . . In other words, rational and utilitarian considerations do not have wide scope even in one of the most organically " utilitarian " of all activities, that of gaining a livelihood. This dominance of sacred sanctions is facilitated by the fact that the isolated sacred society is economically self-sufficient; there is no foreign trade or any other opportunity for the intrusion of pecuniary valuation and the development of detached economic attitudes. Inasmuch as there is no trade, the division of labor is simple; further, no strangers, with detached, critical attitudes leading to disregard of or contempt for sacred matters are tolerated. What is sacred is kept sacred; isolation has a powerful ally in the emotional resistance to change it engenders. The form of the kinship group is that of the large family, the *Grossfamilie*, the *genos*, and is completely under the control of sacred sanctions. . . . There is . . . a minimum of social control by physical force, and even of overt control; offences against the mores are punished by general aversion, indignation, and traditional and spontaneous verbal or corporal chastisement, and not by attempts at the Guilt=Punishment equation. . . . Verbal or even tacit "understanding" prevails instead of formal, written contract; when unusually binding obligations are entered into, the promise given in the presence of the whole society or of its traditionally delegated, especially sacred representatives is the method followed. The home or familiar domestic environment, as well as the *milieu natal* or place of birth and upbringing, are closely linked with fixed motor habits lending them a strongly sacred character; pecuniary valuation is altogether excluded, and change of such environment is attended by marked emotional resistance. The function of training the children is completely under sacred control; parenthood is a cultural far more than a biological fact. Irrationalism and supernaturalism, whether traditionally religious in derivation or otherwise . . . [tend to be] dominant; rationalism and scepticism [in sacred matters] are only potentially present. Rational science is unknown.[97]

This ideal-typical description serves well enough as an epitome of some phases of this chapter, but it seems necessary to complement it by another ideal-typical construct that serves as its methodological counterpart: namely, the accessible secular society (best exemplified by the large city). Only by setting forth the content of this concept can we lend meaning to "secularization" and allied terms that will frequently occur in later chapters.

The accessible secular society . . . is accessible in three ways: vicinally, socially, and mentally. Its vicinal accessibility is the result of geographical location that furthers to the utmost limit all the cultural factors leading to such accessibility: terrestrial, maritime, and atmospheric conditions make possible the fullest utilization of all the devices of rapid transportation. In this way the fixation of any dominant percentage of motor habits is rendered practically impossible among a large proportion of the population; there is a premium upon change of every kind, and Tarde's "mode-imitation" prevails. The social accessibility of this secular society is the result of the complete absence of occupational, professional, class, caste, racial, religious, or moral barriers; there is nothing whatever to hinder social circulation. Competition is consequently unrestricted, for there are no non-competing groups, and the free movement made possible by vicinal accessibility facilitates the spatial allocation of the members of such a society in strict accordance with their economic status. Topographical irregularities being "ideally" absent, zones of population distribution arise that in their spatial patterning reflect closely the competitive order. The mental accessibility of this society is the result of common basic education, complete literacy and lack of language barriers, popularized science and scholarship, a press or similar agency that distributes uniform news to all, etc. As an ideal type the accessible secular society has all of these characteristics to the nth degree.

In addition to its accessibility this society is completely secular (in the special sense here given the latter term). Every relationship is treated as a means to an elusive end, " happiness " as defined in terms of the strictly egoistic wishes of the individual, and never as an end in itself. Comparison, analysis, classification and abstraction are habitually practised; the unique, concrete, and personal are . . . set aside. Nothing is sacred, for the lack of fixed motor habits and the continual contact with new sensual values puts a premium upon change; instead of inability to respond to the new there is inability to refrain from responding to the new — one aspect of mental mobility. Tradition and ceremonial play no part in the life of such a society, and every situation is defined in rationalistic and secular terms. The readily perceivable folkways and mores give ground to rational constructs; there is a maximum of rationalistic criticism, and of individuation a similar maximum. The maintenance folkways are subjected to rational analysis, and are changed with whatever frequency and completeness such analysis shows to be necessary . . . The dominance of secular standards is reinforced by reason of the fact that the accessible secular society is highly differentiated economically; it has a complex metropolitan economy, with a territorial as well as an occupational division of labor . . . The stranger is free to come and go as he will; inasmuch as everyone is more or less a stranger, cosmopolitanism acquires prestige value and becomes a further aid to the detachment characteristic of the stranger. Not only *ubi bene ibi patria,* but also, " wherever my *economic* good is found, there is my country "; not only *homo sum, humani nihil a me alienum puto,* but also " I am an *economic* man; I deem nothing that relates to man a matter *economically* foreign to me." The kinship group is reduced to the particularistic family, and all the production and almost if not all the consumption functions of the latter are taken over by the metropolitan economy. Property is entirely free of collective and sacred consideration; rights of testation are unlimited, and the individual can " do what he will with his own." There is a minimum of informal social control; offences against the laws frequently involve no social ostracism, and the Guilt $=$ Punishment equation has full sway. Inasmuch as the metropolitan economy with its anonymity and differentiation prevails, social control in the form of gossip has little or no power. . . . Formal, secular, rational, legal contracts are the rule; even the marriage relationship is cast in the form of a secular contract between two individuals. . . . The home has no sacred character, but is a secular stopping-place changed without emotional reluctance — indeed, with gratification. The function of training the children is under the complete control of secular agencies. Irrationalism and supernaturalism of *traditionally* religious derivation are not found; rationalism and naturalism have prestige value, and all irrationalism and supernaturalism must seem to be their opposite, i.e., " scientific." Genuine science has great power and wide range.[98]

Now that we have before us these *ideal* types, of which the remote peasant village on the one hand and the teeming cosmopolitan metropolis on the other — i.e., folk society and urban society — afford good *empirical* examples, we possess a guiding strand that will be of some aid in threading the mazes of the chapter just concluded and of chapters still to come. Let us not forget, however, that " the isolated sacred society " and " the accessible secular society " are merely ideal types; let us not miss the living fullness of social life and social thought in following schematism that at best is only a means to an end.

Since this chapter was first written, Becker has altered and developed further the organizing conceptions and modes of analysis mentioned in the Preface to the First Edition. Here the following may be noted:

"Sacred" and "secular" have been more precisely handled: the 1951 Commentary on Value-System Terminology, included in the present edition, gives some indication of this. After the latter date, however, further efforts toward precision were made, especially in Howard Becker and Alvin Boskoff, eds., *Modern Sociological Theory in Continuity and Change* (New York: Dryden Press, 1957), chap. vi, "Current Sacred-Secular Theory and Its Development," pp. 133-85. Even this treatment has been slightly modified in a definition written by Becker for the forthcoming UNESCO dictionary of the social sciences (exact title not yet available) dealing with "sacred society"; in particular, the terms designating points along a sacred-secular continuum have been reduced to holy, loyalistic, intimate, moralistic, conventional, pursuant, consequent, comfortable, and thrilling, with ceremonial cutting across the first five or six much more definitely than across the succeeding three. Moreover, ritual is treated explicitly as the religious subvariety of ceremonial, and as that only. In addition, the societal types incorporating the value-orientations above listed have been designated as proverbial, prescriptive, principial, and pronormless; sacred society has proved somewhat too general a term for many analytic purposes.

"Ideal type" is now used by Becker only to apply to Max Weber's relevant work; where his own efforts are concerned, he consistently refers to constructed type or construct. The differentiation roots in the distinction between the objectively possible and the objectively probable, between the logically devised and empirically demonstrable, between the pure idea, if you will, and the concept planfully constructed out of the stuff of evidence at least potentially available to every informed investigator. Here see Becker's *Through Values to Social Interpretation* (Durham, N. C.: Duke University Press, 1950), the Becker and Boskoff volume above noted, using indexes, and Becker's article, "Culture Case Study and Greek History: Comparison Viewed Sociologically," *ASR,* vol. xxiii, 5 (Oct., 1958), pp. 489-504, with special reference to the footnote citations and quotations.

CHAPTER II

Social Thought of the Ancient Far East

WHY WEST SHOULD GO EAST. — In presenting certain phases of thought in ancient China and India, we repeat the disavowal set forth in the preface: we make no claim to competence in many of the fields which the demands of a résumé such as this compel us to glean, and in particular, no pretense of working exclusively with primary sources is made — indeed, for a number of chapters we are chiefly if not wholly dependent on secondary aids. This is especially true here; the ground to be covered is so vast and so unfamiliar to all but the most erudite of specialists that the most we can hope for is a reasonably accurate condensation of what these specialists have said. Any notion of using translations of the original sources unassisted by commentaries telling what such translations really mean could be entertained only by those who rush in where angels fear to tread. Here more than anywhere else in this book we are dependent on our guides; if they cannot stay on the true path, we also fall into the ditch.

Until fairly recent times most general treatments of the history of social thought began with the Greeks. Now, we hold the Hellenic genius in high regard, as later chapters will show; nevertheless, to ignore the thinkers of the Far East is nothing short of willful blindness, as Sorokin, among others, has pointed out.[1] To be sure, we must not commit the error of reading into their terse sayings the whole content of modern social science, but that error, egregious though it may sometimes be, is perhaps less mentally dwarfing than the all-too-common assumption that we have nothing to learn from the experience of past generations and alien cultures. We shall not, however, devote much space to direct quotation. The task of *interpreting* social thought as well as merely giving its history imposes upon us a mode of presentation quite different from that followed, for example, by Hertzler, *Social Thought of the Ancient Civilizations*. (This book, by the way, is a useful complement of our volume — at least, of the first three chapters.)

Chinese Beginnings. — No one at all familiar with the imposing history of Chinese culture could doubt its significance for the
modern world. When the ancestors of present-day Europeans and
Americans were still at a cultural level little higher than that of
the Australian black-fellow, which is to say more than thirty
centuries before the year of our Lord, the inhabitants of the valley of the Yellow River had developed a civilization at least as
complex as that of the Europe of the Middle Ages.[2]

Obviously, such a culture did not develop overnight; it seems
clear, in spite of numerous migration theories,[3] that the valley of
the Yellow River has been inhabited for many thousands of years
by a people in all respects similar to those who dwell there today.[4]
There also seems rather good evidence for the belief that Chinese
culture, indigenous from a very early period as it was, remained
relatively indigenous throughout the thousands of years during
which its main outlines were becoming fixed. Isolation is of course
never absolute,[5] but even when we grant this we must assert that
ancient China (a unit less than one-twentieth as large as the
sprawling mass called China in modern times) was isolated from
the rest of the world to a degree that is almost unique in the
historical record. " Desert, mountain, and sea had conspired together and presented an almost insurmountable barrier to human
intercourse." [6] This geographical situation had its very definite
mental counterpart. Indeed, one might even contend that ancient
India, the Mesopotamian civilizations, the Mediterranean world,
and Europe shared (within the widest limits of variation) one
system of human thought, while ancient China presents us with
another.[7]

These Chinese who " from the first day of their known history
appear as an agricultural people " [8] developed a form of village
life, based on agriculture, which seems to have been the archetype
from which the entire Chinese conception of the world and even
of the cosmos grew. Sacred society and mentality were closely
bound together; hence the importance of a clear understanding
of the former if we are to understand Chinese social thought.

The Chinese Village as Sacred Society. — Fundamental to the
more rarefied conceptions of the sacred that later appeared in
Chinese thought seem to have been the five household " awesome
places " — the outer door, the inner door, the hearth, the well,
the atrium [9] — and the communal " sacred place," a mound representing the earth. The word for " awesome places " (*shên*) is
almost the same as that for " sacred place " (*shê*), and several
authorities link them together closely, on the assumption that,

however differentiated they may later have become, they were at the beginning parts of a naïve agricultural cult, rooted in the soil — literally. That is to say, the cult was earth-bound, chthonian, devoted to the obscure powers that make man's life as a settled village dweller and agriculturist possible.[10] Sacrifices were made to these vague entities, and they eventually came to be spoken of in much the same way as the Roman *lares* and *penates,* but they never became so sharply defined as to make the terms " god " or " spirit " in their Western senses strictly applicable.

The mound or " sacred place " just mentioned appears to have been the center of the life of the village, which typically did not comprise more than about twenty-five families, thus following the minute pattern of virtually all early groups. The family solidarity that developed in this sacred society was most intense; [11] even to this day the strength of the bonds of kinship among the members of the Chinese " large family " has no parallels in the West, with the possible exception of the Southeast-European *zadruga.*

Other sacred aspects of the life of the village dweller were linked with the succession of the seasons, so vitally important to agriculture.[12] Millet and rice were the two great crops, and with both the year falls into two sharply divided seasons in which almost every phase of the agriculturist's existence is drastically altered.[13] One is the planting, growing, and harvest season, the other is the time of cold and darkness. During the first the whole family went to the fields and lived in little huts near the scene of their labors, where the men carried on the arduous tillage and the women and children merely prepared the food and brought it to them. Masculinity, sunlight, and vigorous activity formed one dominant configuration — *yang.* After the harvest was gathered the mode of life changed; the whole group went back to the village home to wait for spring. This was the season when women did a large share of the work: grinding meal, making clothing, and the like.[14] Femininity, darkness, and sedentary " passivity " (as judged by the male) formed a second configuration — *yin.*

Spring and autumn were consequently times of great importance, for they marked the relaxation of the efforts of one sex and the intensification of those of the other. Again, spring was marked by anxiety for the fate of the common crop of which so much seed, useful for food, was being risked, as well as by rejoicing at the return of vegetation; autumn was attended by the emotions of joy for the harvest and fear of the hardships of the impending winter. These times of emotional duality and tension found release in the two great festivals of the ancient Chinese, which came approximately at the equinoxes. The division of the sexes played its part in another way: at the spring festival, ceremonies were celebrated near the sacred mound in which young men and young women danced opposite each other (apparently oriented north-south) singing ceremonial songs. This practice parallels the spring festival of many of the simpler peoples elsewhere, for the ceremonial dancing finally culminated in a general pairing-off, followed by copulation on or near the sacred mound. In the case of the Chinese, marriage seems frequently to have followed at the autumn festival if pregnancy had resulted from the earlier celebration.

The interrelation of season, sex, and sacred mound in this ancient agricultural life is of particular importance because it probably had much to do with the peculiar nature of the *yang* and *yin* conceptions, for these originally were merely ways of cataloguing objects in general in relation to the symbolic attributes of male and female. When we later discuss Sinism we shall have something more to say of *yang* and *yin;* they are mentioned here only because division along sex lines seems to have been one of the most important sources, if not the most important, of these philosophical " emblems."

Still another way in which the life of the early agricultural village was important to Chinese social thought we have already discussed in general terms when dealing with the problem of mental immobility in Chapter One. Vicinal isolation, close-knit kinship organization, domination by the elders, and other factors to which we have attributed great importance in the genesis of mental immobility were all present in well-marked form in ancient China. For example, the notion of *li,* which is usually translated " propriety," may ultimately be traced to the body of sacred customs or mores according to which it was necessary to live in order to gain social approval and prosperity and to avoid disturbing the cosmic order. The joining together of propriety and the regularity of the cosmos seems odd until it is recalled that many of the simpler peoples believe that their religious rites " keep the stars in their courses and the seasons in their appointed places." Nor is it at all unusual to encounter the belief that conformity or non-conformity with the traditional code of conduct has spectacular cosmic consequences: Sodom and Gomorrah are not the only examples. The Chinese merely developed this conception of the relatedness of the moral and physical universes to an extreme, until finally nearly every calamity in the catalogue was referred to the failure of some person or persons — usually the emperor

— to live up to the *li* for all time established. Associated with *li* is the idea of *h'u,* meaning harmony, union, concord, agreement. *H'u* is the normal, beneficial thing which results from *li* (and, of course, *vice versa*). Men must follow the sacred ways in order to maintain both social solidarity and cosmic harmony. When the times are out of joint it is because men have failed to keep them right.[15] This body of beliefs we shall henceforth term " social monism."

The Sacred Leaves Little Room for the Supernatural. — Thus far we have paid very little attention to ideas of which much has been made by scholars determined to reconcile Chinese history and religion with Genesis; namely, *T'ien* and *Shang Ti* — respectively translated as " heaven " or " sky " and as " upper ruler " (probably another form of " heaven "). No apology need be made for this seeming neglect, for in early Chinese thought " heaven " plays an altogether subordinate part; the " awesome places " and the sacred mound are of the earth earthy. Only when the emperor became " the Son of Heaven " and the sacred writings were edited by his appointees, say some writers, did *T'ien* and *Shang Ti* receive any measure of popular notice. But however this may be, it seems clear that the Chinese peasant played his part, here as elsewhere, in shaping the notion. It is from the sky that rain comes and the sun sends his beams. To the agriculturist it becomes a symbol of the orderly rotation of the seasons, and thereby is bound up with his loved harmony and propriety. Moreover, heaven is all-seeing, and is therefore linked with justice and government, the attributes of the earthly ruler projected upon the heavenly. Once more, the sky is active; it sends driving rain and piercing sunlight upon the earth passively harboring grain that does not germinate until the sun, " the great *yang,*" endows it with life. Quite naturally, the male *yang,* the active, came to have its seat in heaven, while the female *yin,* the passive, was of the earth. Pastoral people have their sky gods, their *Dyaus pitar,* but agriculturists are by no means indifferent to the powers above, even though they may not at first yield them a place as important as that assigned the more familiar and intimate *lares* and *penates.* For the Western peoples, ever since the Greeks cast aside the chthonian cults and wailed, " Great Pan is dead! " the sky has been most closely associated with the supernatural. The heavenly spirit descends, the transfigured savior ascends, and the faithful are taken up into the New Jerusalem. For the Chinese, however, no comparable supremacy of the powers above was ever established. In the first place, the dualism involved was foreign to their mentality — but more of this later. Second, the persistence of Sinism, that social monism engendered in the agricultural community, made it impossible to eliminate the sacred or even to shake its dominance over the supernatural.[16] To justify what is said in the foregoing sentences, however, involves a discussion of Chinese mentality, and before launching upon this, it seems advisable to pay some attention to the more tangible aspects of Chinese cultural history.

The Main Stream of Chinese History. — Although those writers who leave without definite dates all events in Chinese history before 842 B.C. are probably correct, this does not mean that everything prior to that period is in the realm of pure conjecture. About five thousand years ago the Chinese dwelling along the lower reaches of the Yellow River in what are now the modern provinces of Honan, Hopei, and Shantung began to develop some measure of political organization. The peasants lived in little hamlets placed on the heights overlooking the cultivated land, and in the spring they came down from these winter refuges and tilled their fields. Harvest in and autumn ended, they began their preparations for winter by reëstablishing themselves in their upland dwellings. These were more than shelters against cold; feud and foray ravaged the countryside. In spite of defenses, however, the scattered agriculturists slowly yielded to force judiciously applied, and became components of little domains ruled over by confraternities of marauders which later took the feudal form of hereditary chieftains and their subordinate nobility. Thus supplied with masters and protectors, the peasants undertook innumerable tasks of drainage and irrigation, rendering their cut-up country more amenable to agriculture.[17]

Northward, southward, and westward of this clump of feudal domains the land was inhabited by " barbarians " inferior in culture but apparently identical in race. Gradually pushing away from the Yellow River valley, adding to their acres by bartering grain and utensils for land, the more civilized valley dwellers extended their influence so far that they finally occupied all of the great plain lying between the lower reaches of the Yellow River and the sea. The barbarians were not wholly ousted by the occupation; many little enclaves centering in marshes and other places difficult of access were formed, and for centuries raiding and counter-raiding were frequent. The states which were soonest consolidated were those on the borders; they could take into their service the great masses of barbarians spread over the steppes, the mountains, and the marshy districts.

The overlords who organized the peasants for this task of consolidation do not clearly emerge into the light of authentic history
until a very late date; before that time, mythical sage-kings (culture heroes) whose combined reigns constituted a golden age of
peace and virtue, and dynasties like the Hsia and Shang, flutter
like bats in the dense blackness of tradition. Some light pierces the
gloom toward the end of the Shang dynasty (about 1100 B.C.),
but it does not enable us to discern a great deal. Nevertheless, we
can say that the culture was fairly complex: e.g., writing on ivory,
bronze, tortoise-shell, and bamboo; numerous domesticated animals; a well-organized army. Agriculture was still the basis of
all social life, but the rural cult in which there was no priestly
class was beginning to yield to cults more closely connected with
the chieftain, his town, and mountains, rivers and the like with
which his cosmic bond was particularly close. The mana of the
" awesome places " and the sacred mound began to flow in the
direction of altars where differentiated entities rather than un-
defined holy forces were honored. Nevertheless, the efficacy of
the sacred places of the peasantry reappears intact in the localities
especially evocative of the chieftain's virtue. The mountains and
rivers, that like the chieftain regulate the social as well as the
natural order, are endowed with the mana which flows through
him as well. Ruling over nature as he rules over his followers, the
power possessed by the chieftain is held in partnership with
the sacred places of his country. " In them he sees, as it were, the
exteriorized principle of his own power." [18] Moreover, the social
monism characteristic of the rural cult is an integral part of the
rites honoring heaven and the Son of Heaven. The power of
the chieftain and of his sacred place have, as Granet puts it, " the
same duration, the same extent, the same quality, the same nature." [19] That is to say, they are indistinguishable; the feudal
hero and his sacred place are aspects of each other; it is by his
virtue, like that of the mythical sage-king Yü the Great, that the
sacred rivers flow and the foundations of the everlasting hills are
laid. And by the same token, it is only because the chieftain incorporates the mana of these manifestations of all-pervading
cosmic unity that he *is* a chieftain.[20]

From all this it is clear that the traditional domination formerly
exercised by the elders of the peasant community finally yielded
to a type of charismatic domination in which the chieftain shared
his quality of " extraordinariness " with one or another phase of
the natural order with which he was identified. One of his chief
functions was the utilization of his charisma in divination; only

the oracular deliverances of the Son of Heaven, interpreted by the soothsayers, could allay fears and chart the true course.[21]

It is worth noting that this function of divination, probably transmitted at first through the elders, did not depend solely upon mana that was, so to speak, acquired through being the recipient of sacred lore; the chieftain had to have mana in his own right to be able to foretell the future. If he failed, that was *prima facie* evidence that mana was lacking, and hence that he had become evil. In such cases, a new chieftain possessed of the powers of charismatic leadership soon took the place of the old, and the peasants and subordinate aristocrats again felt themselves under the guidance of a true Son of Heaven.

The Process of Dynastic Succession. — But how could a new chieftain " take " the place of the old? The sacred character of the chieftainship would seem to make revolution impossible. This might perhaps be true if the nature of the chieftain's sacredness had not changed. We saw that he came to be identified with the sacred place that eventually took on the character of his ancestral center, and that the principle of hereditary mana slowly established itself, thereby legitimating dynastic rule. Curiously enough, however, the notions of social monism derived from China's remotest antiquity were not vanquished by this establishment of the principle of the divine right of kings. The Son of Heaven and the offspring of his loins are not removed from the vicissitudes of nature; even as rivers change their courses and mountains level toward the plains, so do all things human change. The mana of every dynasty passes through a time of growth and fullness, then declines, and after an ephemeral resurrection becomes exhausted. The dynasty ought then to be set aside, for it is no longer united with heaven, and heaven ceases to treat its erstwhile chieftains like sons; " the Great Happiness does not come twice." [22] Every dynasty which retains power when its time has passed retains it only *de facto*: *de jure,* it is merely a usurper. Some vassal upon whom the favor of heaven has descended should then rise in revolt, and by his victory prove that heaven has entrusted its mandate to him.[23] Legend has it that the Hsia lost their hold in this way, and that their successors, the Shang, similarly passed into oblivion.

The Priest-King. — Then came the Chou. The war-hardened frontier vassal, Duke Fa of Chou, who overthrew his decadent Shang ruler, must have been wise and powerful, but he lacked either the wisdom or the power to put an end to the feudal system through which he gained the ascendancy but which ultimately de-

stroyed his own dynasty.[24] Indeed, the characteristic relations of
the feudal period reached their fullest expression under the Chou.
The king was only the highest of the chieftains, and he could
never be indifferent to the feudatories who governed the principalities and dukedoms clustering about the little central kingdom.
At the same time, his religious function gave him a lever of great
power; he remained the Son of Heaven. The ancestral temple had
for a great while existed as an indispensable companion of the
palace, but opposite the ancestors still stood the sanctuary of
earth, reminiscent of the sacred mound of the ancient rural cult.

   In addition to secreting efficacy, as it were, in the religious and
political realms, the Chou monarchs, like their predecessors, had
also the duty of maintaining the order of nature. This they did by
the performance of sacrifices appropriate to the changing seasons,
and inasmuch as the maintenance of *h'u* or harmony between
earth and heaven depended not only upon the sacrifices as such
but also upon their exact timing, an accurate calendar fixing all
the necessary dates was established. It will be recalled that the
early sacred societies of the peasants made much of the spring
and autumn festivals, and this rural influence passed over into the
calendar, but this was not all:

   At the time when rituals were edited, the observations of the peasants
served to illustrate learned calendars on an astronomic basis: they were
represented as emanating from the princely wisdom. It was even acknowledged that the " good luck of the husbandmen " was an effect of
the virtue of the overlord.[25]

Thus one more phase of the early rural culture eventually became
concentrated in the person of the chieftain.
   This feudal figure had other than religious functions; high
priest and sovereign were combined. In the exercise of rational
domination he was apparently assisted [26] by an elaborate bureaucracy divided into six boards, each presided over by a minister.[27]
Above the six boards was placed a prime minister, the king's
" other self " and often, in the case of feeble monarchs, his real
master. This description is primarily applicable to the central
government, but even the minor feudatories modeled their régimes
on that of the Son of Heaven, and were subject to his inspection
and control. Eventually the most rigid ceremonials held the daily
life of the king, the governmental officials, and the feudal lords
in a veritable strait-jacket; every act was performed by " the superior man " with appropriate ceremonies having prescribed
dress, speech, and posture — *li* to the *n*th degree.

" The People of Naught." — Far below the nobles were the peasants, " the people of naught," who had neither family names nor ancestral sacrifices, were not qualified to hold office or to receive fiefs, and whose marriages were without religious significance. Except as beneficiaries of the *h'u,* the celestial harmony secreted in and through the ritual observances of their rulers, the peasants as a class had no part in the affairs of the kingdom. They were divided into nine ranks according to the value of their services to the state, then as ever basically agrarian. In the first rank were the producers of grain, and in the last the class of beggars, vagrants, defectives, and miscellaneous groups having no fixed occupation.

The agricultural population held the land as tenants of their feudal lords, and delivered to them a percentage of the product proportionate to the fertility of the soil. The amount to be delivered was determined by the Director of the Multitudes, whose staff also instructed the peasants in the nature of the grains best adapted to their skill and resources, and fixed the time for tilling, sowing, irrigating, and harvesting.

The Great Happiness and Its Passing. — With Li, the tenth sovereign of the Chou dynasty, we arrive at the first date upon which all Chinese sources are in agreement, and which therefore may be accepted as presumably reliable — 842 B.C. At this time the power of the government was so great that it could extend its sway over virtually every activity of its subjects, but nevertheless Li was driven from his capital by a palace revolution. The chronicles record this and many similar upheavals, but at the same time insist that between the age of the rural chieftainships and the epoch of the tyrannies (beginning about the fifth century B.C.), there was a long era during which China was stable and happy. Now the chances are great, as Granet points out, that at all times the feudal order had been singularly unstable. True it is, however, that the Son of Heaven no longer attempted conquest of the aboriginal enclaves and barbarian border states by military means; rather, he proceeded to civilize and win over his erstwhile foes by conferring titles on their princes and by exhibiting to them the manifold superiorities of his own system of administration. Thus, " the ideal which inspired the feudalists and guided the chroniclers in their attempts at historic reconstruction is not altogether of their own invention." [28] It was believed that tranquillity, feudalism, and formalism had once held unquestioned sway, and despite all evidences to the contrary, the belief in the Great Happiness, the golden age, long persisted.

Such persistence was not a result of the peaceful expansion of Chinese civilization alone; a code of values that caused men to feel that those values *must* have demonstrated their efficacy in the historical process also played a significant part. This code took shape very early — perhaps in the time of the rural chieftains or the first feudal overlords. From the way of life followed by these aristocrats at court or in the army and from their domestic manners was derived a system of morals which was later to be espoused by the ruling classes of China as a whole. It was the code of " superior men " or " decent men " leading a life entirely dominated by the worship of honor and etiquette at the feudal court.

This feudal system, in spite of dissensions, maintained itself for a long time. But " nothing is changeless but change," and as time went on the frontier states grew restive. They were in close contact with the wind-swept northern plateau where lie the great battlefields commemorating the endless strife between the agricultural Chinese and the ancient ancestors of Attila's Huns, the Hsiungnu Tartars. The frontiersmen became stronger than the vassals of the central kingdom and learned more of the art of war. The king became a lay figure, encased within the walls of his palace and controlled by this or that powerful noble or minister in the belief, sincere or spurious, that his mana had to be conserved:

The august force which informs the chief is a mystical force whose tension is extreme and which is strangely contagious. As a rule, it acts by simple radiation, but to this end it must be kept concentrated and pure. On exceptional occasions it must operate with its full vigour, and for this reason it is advisable to preserve it from any diminution through lapse of time.The overlord leads an isolated and passive life in the midst of his court. The vassals " form a barrier." . . . The court labours to keep the overlord in a sort of splendid quarantine radiating glory. . . .

The prince, sheltered from every contamination . . . by a court governed by a meticulous etiquette, himself submits to an etiquette which is even more minutely regulated. He lives surrounded by his whole court, and each of his followers must at the least breach recall him to order. . . .

. . . the overlord reigns only on condition of remaining passive, of ordering nothing in detail, and of not directing an administration. He acts only through the simple efficacy of his prestige. The real activity is carried on by the vassals. Princely power is founded upon the possession of a Virtue of religious and magical essence. It is less a power of command than a power of inspiration. The overlord is the chief of a hierarchy and not a Chief of State.[29]

And lacking a chief of state, the decentralized feudal system lost all traces of celestial harmony; at the beginning of the fifth century B.C. there occurred a collapse that was followed by more than three centuries of almost continual war and disorder. This is commonly referred to by Chinese historians as the Age of the Warring Kingdoms, during which there emerged most of the great schools of thought that, together with their basic Sinism, thereafter dominated the Chinese mind.

Sinic Language and Thought. — Here and there throughout the foregoing sections we have referred to *yin, yang, h'u, li,* and related " emblems " — as Granet calls them, believing them too full of content to be termed concepts — but we must now get some coherent ideas about " basic Sinism."

That language and thought are closely related is almost a truism,[30] hence we need waste no space in justifying the following discussion. In spite of the multiplicity of spoken dialects, China has long had a written language (since about 1800 B.C.). It is monosyllabic, of limited phonetic scope, and dependent on word order for clarity and pitch for diversity when spoken. There are no parts of speech in our sense, and none of the grammatical apparatus of accidence and syntax. These and other traits make it a very poor medium in which to express abstract thought; instead of furnishing an array of colorless concepts it provides highly concrete emblems that are derived from and directed toward action. It is virtually impossible to use a word without expressing emotion, implying judgments as to proper or improper conduct, and assigning whatever is symbolized by the word to a definite niche in the social order.[31] The ideographic writing intensifies these characteristics, for at bottom Chinese signs, even of the simpler types, partake of the nature of the rebus. The reader must actively interpret; unless he is so steeped in the culture that he can immediately assign to the written emblems the proper emotional weighting and value-judgments, he cannot reconstitute the configuration which originally imparted to them their full meaning. It is literally impossible, says Granet, to understand the Chinese classics if one cannot actively " post-live " through what they relate.[32]

Chinese style takes full advantage of these characteristics and adds others essentially akin. Rhythm, allusion, subtle variation on a standard theme — all are utilized to the full. The well-known brevity of Chinese poems finds here its *raison d'être.* A few emblems are enough to conjure up images, moods, and implicit actions that would have to be laboriously set forth in one-two-three order in languages less concrete.[33]

The Concreteness of the Chinese Categories. — Small wonder, then, that the clank of exact definition and the whir of syllogism are not heard in the Chinese intellectual realm. Moreover, our abstract ideas of time, space, and number are present, if at all, only in strangely altered guise. Time takes its meaning from an order of seasons and epochs; it is inseparable from the notions of the calendar and dynastic succession. As abstract past, present, and future, or as the mere addition of quantitatively equal and qualitatively indistinguishable units, time is a distinctly Western category, not a Chinese one. To be sure, the Chinese type may bear concealed within it the Western, but if this is the case the latter is well hidden.

Space is also lacking in abstractness. Instead of extension as such it is square, and its four limits are the four oceans, near which live the animal-like barbarians. In its most intensely actual form, space is a concretion of sacred sites emanating from the localized activity of the chieftain. About this square are grouped those belonging to his vassals, who transmit his space-forming efficacy as far as the domains of the barbarians, who live in a sort of potential space outside of historic time.

Not only are the Chinese notions of time and space as such preëminently social, but their relation is also of this social character. An ancient custom required that each sovereign make a tour of the empire at certain seasonal intervals, following the path of the sun in order to connect time and space and thus ensure celestial and social harmony.[34]

Number also shares this peculiarly concrete nature. Mere ordinal succession and quantity play almost no part in Chinese thought apart from mundane trade and technics. True, the sages paid great heed to numbers, but as means of cataloguing things, actions, and persons in a hierarchy of essential character or worth. This hierarchy (or hierarchies) was ultimately based upon the ranks of the feudal system and the power allotted to the chieftain, and hence was fundamentally influenced by social considerations.[35]

From all of this it is apparent that the principles of efficacy, rhythm, and order, cultural or even social in origin, play the leading rôles in Chinese thought. This is not to say, however, that these principles are ever explicit; the dominant impression is that of a complex of customs, never taken apart and analyzed, woven about some value traceable to socio-cultural life.[36]

The Dialectic Interplay of Yang *and* Yin. — Perhaps by giving some conception of the specifically Chinese categories, greater definiteness can be achieved. Let us begin with *yang* and *yin*. It will be recalled that in all probability these were primarily emblems of configurations of male and female " attributes." If we also recall the interrelation of season, sex, direction, and sacred place in the ancient rural societies, astonishment at the following collection of " attributes " can be held within bounds:

Yang. (n.) The male or positive principle in nature. The sun. The south of a hill. The north of a river. Penis. (adj.) Male; masculine. Sunny; light; brilliant.
Yin. (n.) A shadow; shade. The south of a river. The female or negative principle in nature. The [female] . . . genitals. (adj.) Shady; dark; cloudy; gloomy. Cold. Mysterious; secret. Female; feminine.[37]

These conglomerations of meanings, so bizarre to the Westerner, provide vivid illustrations of the fact that *yang* and *yin,* like so many other Chinese " emblems," are not principles of classification in our abstract sense — not even of gender. Their stress is upon concrete qualification and differentiation. It may be thought, however, that inasmuch as *yang* and *yin* are two principles which when in harmony rule the world, they bear some resemblance to our classificatory concepts. How mistaken this is becomes apparent when we note that *yang* in its extreme form becomes *yin,* and *vice versa.*[38]

Other differentiating and qualifying notions are those of the five colors and the five elements. These groupings by fives go back to the space-time system with its four directions and four seasons plus the central or harmony-maintaining rôle of the chieftain. There are also the eight winds, left and right, and many minor attributes of like character that function in the same way as cataloguing emblems. The Chinese are indefatigable cataloguers, but abstract classification is unknown.[39]

Tao, *the All-Encompassing.* — Embracing all the symbols we have mentioned and yet in some way transcending them is the notion of *tao.* One of the earliest statements concerning it can be translated thus: " All *yin* and all *yang* are *tao.*" Literally *tao* means way, path, or road, but an examination of the classics shows that its deeper meanings are always those of social and cosmic order, totality, responsibility, and efficacy. In some contexts it bears a striking resemblance to mana; when we discussed the " virtue " of the chieftain in an earlier section it was his *tao* to which we referred. But inasmuch as a chieftain having this " virtue " secretes order and harmony, as it were, *tao* is also used in these senses. Basically, however, it is indescribable because, although it regulates and includes all other efficacies, it is above them, not of them, and therefore cannot be defined in " lower " terms. It is a concrete totalistic conception, not a first principle or axiom. *Tao* is always entire and the same. Its secret laws can be found in the rhythm of time and space at all occasions and sites. Moreover, possession of *tao* or participation in it ensures action in harmony with *li* — the body of mores or sacred customs. *Tao* may therefore be thought of as the etiquette of the universe, natural and social. The only way of learning this etiquette is by study of the classics; once they are thoroughly known the world order, with its eleven thousand five hundred and twenty special situations of which the *tao* must be known, is revealed to the sage.

Once more the essentially social character of these Chinese symbols is evident. *Tao* is simply a concretion of the notions having to do with the chieftain, his domain, the feudal hierarchy, the harmonious course of nature and society, and the like. It is the supreme emblem of social monism, the ultimate assertion of man's oneness with nature.[40]

The rôle of man in Sinism is that of microcosm. He is the epitome of the universe — the perfect chieftain had square feet and his head was round even as the bowl of heaven is round. There is no distinction between nature and convention; man's social arrangements, ritual, and etiquette express the all-pervading *tao* in exactly the same way as does a snake casting its skin or a rock falling from a cliff. Consequently the ideal physician, for example, is the man trained in etiquette, for etiquette is the omni-science. To know the *tao* of anything is to know the *tao* of everything.[41]

The Age of the Warring Kingdoms. — We have said more than enough to make it plain that Chinese mentality is quite different from ours. For the Chinese there is nothing absolute, nothing unrelated, nothing abstract, and nothing isolated. With the possible exception of the Legists, to whom we shall later refer, none of the schools of Chinese thought, however extreme, really represents a fundamental departure from Sinism. *Tao* is never questioned; schools arise only when the way to find it and the way to teach it give rise to differences of opinion.[42] Until the shattering impact of the West was felt the Sinistic system and its sacred hierarchies, religious and political, remained essentially the same. Only during the Age of the Warring Kingdoms (*c*. 500–200 B.C.) were the differences between the schools so great as to bring with them the danger of lasting sectarian cleavages, and these were finally overcome. It is significant that this period of mental mobility, known to early Chinese historians as a time of disorder and anarchy, should be known to historians of today as the climax of Chinese intellectual effort:

> It was as though the decay which was spreading through the land had liberated an all the more radiant spiritual power. . . . The clashing of the various civilizations and philosophies existing at that time on Chinese soil produced an awakening of the human consciousness which stands out clearly alongside the other great blossomings of culture sprung from similar clashings of competing civilizations — compare, for instance, the Greek philosophy born in the Ægean, on the borderland between Europe and Asia.[43]

The Master of the Old Sinism: Confucius. — Chief exponent of Sinism was Confucius (551–479 B.C.). Early left an orphan, he received little formal education, studying the ancient writings and traditions for himself. Of great native intelligence, he worked his way up in the government of Lu, a small feudal unit ruled over by a " marquis," until he became one of its chief ministers. As a protest against breaches of the *tao* by his chieftain he resigned, as the code of Chinese patrimonial officialdom required, at the height of his career, and thereafter wandered from one state to another seeking a permanent post which he never found. While engaged in this search he gathered a circle of disciples about him, and finally settled down in their company to teaching and writing.[44]

Confucius is a much misunderstood figure. In spite of his explicit assertions that he was merely a codifier and interpreter of tradition, he has been regarded as the originator of Sinism in its most stereotyped, rigid form. Nothing could be further from the truth; in so far as he allows his personal preferences to intrude, he figures as a rationalizer and humanizer of the old formulas:

> The Master said, " High station filled without indulgent generosity; ceremonies performed without reverence; mourning conducted without sorrow; — wherewith should I contemplate such ways? "[45]

Many other statements in the same vein might be quoted: their total drift is to show that it is his greatness of character — not exceeded, as Creel says, by any other figure in history — that constitutes his overwhelming significance in Chinese social thought.[46] He was charitable, just, modest, kindly, earnest, sincere, and courageous. As we have seen, he lived at a time when all the old standards were breaking down, and he resolutely set himself to the task of saving the good they contained for posterity.[47] The system of thought to which he adhered had been expounded by many men before him, but by the example of his personality he was able to kindle the imaginations of his contemporaries and, through his disciples, eventually to reinstate the old Sinism so that it endured, in only slightly modified forms, for more than twenty-four centuries after his death.

Filial Piety and the Rectification of Names. — Most Westerners are likely to think of Confucius chiefly in relation to " filial piety." This is no error. Sinism, it will be remembered, had as one of its integral parts the arrangement of society in a series of graded ramifications from the center, i.e., from the chieftain or king. Moreover, the emblems providing the complex image of the kingdom were in part magnifications of the emblems of the village. This rural organization was a family or a group of families, and the kingdom was conceived on the same pattern. Confucius was therefore entirely consistent in putting the family relations and virtues at the center of his social thought: justice between father and son; prudent reserve between husband and wife; respect between elder brother and younger brother; sincerity between elders and juniors (or, as some versions have it, between friend and friend) ; and loyalty between ruler and minister. Three of these ties are specifically within the smaller family, and all five are included within the empire regarded as a large family. The preservation of the family virtues and relations where they are still intact, and their restoration where they are not, is the essence of Confucius's program of social reconstruction.

One of his specific reconstructive measures was the " rectification of names." Many interpreters hold that Confucius clearly meant to reinforce the bonds of social stability by judiciously distributing praise and blame through the use of terms exactly descriptive of the conduct in question. If a son, for example, did not fulfill the duties which filial piety as embodied in the prevailing mores laid down, he either was no more to be called a son, or had to make good his claim to his " name " by returning to the fold of tradition. Similarly, the ruler, the wife, and all others in the network of the five relationships were to be subjected to social control through the precise apportioning of approval and disapproval. Indeed, it is held that when Confucius edited some of the ancient classics he did so in such a way as to make the most trivial clause carry a moral lesson – sometimes through the ironical use of a kinship term or the like which had been rendered grotesquely unfit by incest or parricide, and sometimes by withholding an honorific term traditionally applied and thus by implication meting out blame. (On the positive side, of course, praise was always given where praise was due.)[48]

There can be little doubt that the actual social effectiveness of the program for the " rectification of names," as applied by Confucius and his followers, makes such interpretation at least partially valid. But another school of interpreters maintains that all this is but the shallowest rationalism. When Confucius ejaculated: " Father [be a] father! Son [be a] son! " [49] he perhaps intended to influence in the ordinary way those whom he addressed by his words, say the critics, but it is also evident that in the Sinism of Confucius's time the act of naming anything was supposed to endow it with the individuality to which its true existence was due. " In the beginning was the Word." In short, these critics assert that magical realism (of the Sinistic kind with which we are already familiar) in which the name is the essence of the object lies at the root of the program for the " rectification of names." Confucius's seeming innovation is simply a convincing demonstration of his Sinistic orthodoxy.[50] It is not within our province to attempt to decide a dispute in which the contending parties are so evenly matched; nevertheless, we may perhaps hazard the conjecture that from what we know of Sinism in general it is quite unlikely that Confucius could have wholly avoided some trace of magical realism, however faint, in his social thought.

It must nevertheless be granted that this influence, if it existed, was not of a character that would promote a " superstition " that Westerners commonly associate with magical beliefs; namely, propitiation of " spirits." Confucius was not a complete sceptic as to their existence, but he declared unequivocally that the wise man should " keep aloof from them." [51] He was not a rationalist, but neither was the reverencing of ancestors which he advocated " animistic " as we ordinarily interpret that term (which means that the application of the phrase " ancestor-*worship* " to the practice introduces too many false connotations to be tolerated). After all, Sinism is close-knit social monism; the dualism involved in animistic belief can exist only at its fringes, not at its center.

The Goodness of Human Nature and the Superior Man. — The Sinistic orthodoxy of Confucius is still further demonstrated in his ideas about human nature. He held that human nature is originally good — and this the only position consistent with pure Sinism. The time when the whole cosmos, natural and social, was in accord with the principles of its being, i.e., in harmony with *tao,* was the time of the Great Happiness, the pristine golden age. Violations of the *tao* are simply perversions. To the Westerner, whose tradition incorporates the " problem of evil," it is natural to ask whence this perversion came, but there is no evidence that

Sinistic thinkers of Confucius's type ever tried to give a direct answer. Their interest was in practical statesmanship and social engineering, and they took no delight in discussing insoluble problems. Confucius's only relevant statement indicates that he traced the origin of evil to a gradual deviation from the original path of rectitude:

The Master said: " Extravagance leads to insubordination, and parsimony to meanness. It is better to be mean [and orderly] than insubordinate " [and disorderly].⁵²

Confucius was a member of the guild of *literati* who in happier times had enjoyed positions of great authority as encyclopedias of etiquette at the courts of the chieftain and his vassals. These *literati* or mandarins necessarily upheld the code of the " superior man," but by the time of Confucius they had modified it almost beyond recognition. Where once the " superior man " in the full sense could be none other than the seignorial aristocrat, he finally came to be any man, however humble his origin, who possessed the virtues upheld and represented by the scholars forming the recruited bureaucracies; namely, by the *literati* themselves.⁵³ (Even at the present time what Westerners call " Confucian ethics " is termed by the Chinese *ju kiao,* " the teachings of the *literati.*") ⁵⁴ Not the least of the reasons for the fame of Confucius was the trenchant utterance he gave to this essentially democratic doctrine of the possibility of becoming a " superior man " without benefit of lineage. The channels of upward social circulation were kept open, and the humblest peasant might aspire to become the counsellor of emperors.⁵⁵

Much more might be said about Confucius, but this must suffice. A man of the highest character, desperately concerned to save his country and his people when evil days had come upon them, he takes rank with the world's greatest.

Mystic and Philosophic Anarchist: Lao Tse. — An older contemporary of Confucius was Lao Tse (*c.* 604?–514? B.C.), " the old sage." He gave the *tao* so very prominent a place in his teaching that he is frequently called the founder of " philosophic Taoism " ⁵⁶ (as distinct from the " vulgar Taoism " that came later).⁵⁷ We have already seen, however, that the notion of *tao* is fundamental to Sinism of all types, not to " philosophic Taoism " alone, and we shall therefore follow Creel in using the term " Laoism " to refer to the thought represented by Lao Tse.⁵⁸

We have seen that Confucius maintained that the best means of restoring the natural and social universe to its state of original goodness is to find, by examination of tradition, the rules by which men acted in the time of the Great Happiness, and then to apply them as closely as common sense and humanity allow. This conclusion seems warranted, but the one drawn by Lao Tse is also plausible: if the world contains a natural tendency toward perfection, toward *h'u,* why meddle with it? *Wu wei, "* not striving," will ensure the return to the golden age. Thus did the exponents of social control and of *laissez faire* confront each other.

Some scholars would have it that Laoism, which flourished in the south of China, is an importation of the teaching of the Indian *Upanishads,* but several of the most recent authorities regard it as chiefly if not wholly indigenous, and in the absence of more conclusive evidence for the importation theory we choose the other.[59]

Lao Tse was the keeper of the imperial archives in the state of Chou. Living at the same time as Confucius, he too witnessed the upheavals that accompanied the breakup of the old feudal system and the establishment of the tyrannies. Lao Tse also was one of the *literati,* a man of the subtlest intellect, deeply distressed by the evils of his day and holding in especial detestation the wars of mutual extermination which the Chinese were then carrying on. Feeling his impotence deeply, he decided that the only thing for him to do was to leave the world altogether, so he set out for the West. (At least, so the legends have it.) Stopped at the border just before plunging into the timeless and spaceless chaos of the barbarians, he was asked by a guard to write down his wisdom before it perished with him. Lao Tse did so, and gave to the world *The Book of the Tao and Its Efficacy (Tao-Tê-King).*[60]

Laoism as Primitivism. — Totalling scarcely five thousand words, this collection of aphorisms contains much that is quite unintelligible. The fundamental notions, however, are fairly clear. Taking the Sinistic *tao* as " given," he altered its meaning slightly. One of his duties as keeper of the archives was to enter in the books of divination all natural phenomena of an unusual character — that is to say, he recorded omens and portents. The consequence was, says Haydon,[61] that cosmic processes came to assume an importance in his thinking even greater than that which they possessed for the ordinary Sinist. Confucius, at one time counsellor of a " marquis " and always concerned with affairs of state, interpreted the *tao* as the etiquette of the entire cosmos, natural and human, whereas Lao Tse held it to be independent of the artificialities of a man-made world. (Laoism, by the way, is a good example of one type of primitivism discussed in our chapter on " Theories of the Natural State of Man.") He even went so far as to proclaim that filial piety and the five family virtues and relations, so dear to the heart of Confucius, were never heard of until the world had fallen into disorder; the only way to regain that natural harmony which is mankind's only hope is to dispense with the inculcation of these " artificialities." [62]

To these Rousseau-like utterances Lao Tse added others even more drastic. His technique for political control, for example, was to " empty the minds and fill the stomachs, weaken the initiative and strengthen the backs " of men, to keep them " in ignorance and apathy." The Laoist sage, in case he should become counsellor of the chieftain, should allow all beings to function according to their nature without restraint, except that he is to repress such harmful excesses as wealth, power, and ambition! [63]

The departure from the principle of " not striving," interpreted as pure passivity, indicated by the repressive program just noted becomes still more evident when Lao Tse tells us what he would do " if I were king." First of all, intellectuals would be kept out of office, for they only use their intelligence to spoil things. Next, all travel would be prevented; subjects must be made so fearful of accidents and death that they dare not so much as set foot in boat or carriage. Again, all use of arms would be prohibited, all writing and learning swept away, the system of records reduced to the ancient knotted cords, and isolation made so thorough that although his people could hear " the crowing of cocks and the barking of dogs " in nearby villages, they would pass through life without knowing anything more of their neighbors, and thus would be kept healthy and peaceful.[64]

From this it is plain that for Lao Tse " not striving " (in any way contrary to nature) meant in practice a great deal of striving. In fact, his program would have established a despotism far more rigid than anything envisaged by even the most formalistic of the real disciples of Confucius.

The Strange Powers of the Ascetic Vacuum. — Yet it would be a mistake to judge Laoism solely in the light of this *reductio ad absurdum*. The fact that it was a genuine naturalistic quietism is clearly shown by the large part played in even its earliest manifestations by recipes for longevity. In addition to being a social program, " not striving " was also an elaborate ascetic technique for conserving the *tao* of the adept, who thereby acquired, among other things, powers of self-levitation like those of the sages of old time. Granet maintains that Laoism is closely linked with the tradition of the prehistoric Chinese sorcerers, who in their turn were heirs of ancient Chinese shamanism.[65] Be this as it may, there can be no doubt that *The Book of the Tao and Its Efficacy* here and there deals with states of mystic ecstasy produced by meditation on the *tao* that show some resemblance to shamanistic trances. Granet also points out that the asceticism enjoined by Lao Tse was not for the purpose of mortifying the flesh but of vivifying it, of restoring to it the powers it possessed in the golden age.[66]

That this is a correct interpretation becomes evident when we take account of Lao Tse's favorite analogy. " Not striving " is likened to a vacuum, and only in the vacuum lies the truly essential, e.g., the reality of a room consists in the vacant space enclosed by the walls, the reality of a pitcher in the emptiness that accommodates the water, and so on. The Laoist adept who can make of himself a vacuum through *wu wei* thereby renders it possible for others to enter into him freely, and hence becomes master of all situations — even as the pitcher controls the water it contains. It is plain, then, that Lao Tse's quietistic asceticism was practiced for the sake of its positive results.[67]

The founder of Laoism was undoubtedly an original thinker of high rank, and in quoting Creel's interesting psycho-sociological " explanation of Lao Tse " we do not intend to deny him the right to eminence:

Education in China, from ancient times until very recently, has meant almost entirely, education for governmental office. . . . The result has been a great over-supply of men trained only to govern, . . . but " out of work." . . . The only proper and dignified course for such a scholar was to retire from the world, and to live a life bordering on that of a recluse, if he did not, in fact (as many did), become a veritable hermit.

. . . it was the glory of Lao Tse to have the supreme intellectual daring to turn this debit into an asset. He had the genius to declare not only that inaction was the only proper course for the disappointed man, but that it was the only proper course for every person whatsoever — indeed, the recluse, apparently impotent, was actually the most effective man in the empire.

. . . certain passages of the Tao Tê King reveal Lao Tse's purpose of self-justification to have been central in his thinking. It will be recalled that he was keeper of the imperial archives. This was a position which gave him little, if any, opportunity to have a hand in the control of affairs. . . . His impotence to alter the situation [especially the fratricidal strife of the time] must have hurt him keenly. . . .[68]

The story of his retirement from the world and his writing of the *Tao-Té-King* we have already told. Creel discusses what he regards as the " defense mechanism " and " compensation " in Lao Tse's masterpiece as follows:

. . . he tells us that the Sages of old (of whom he considers himself a modern representative) were subtle, abstruse, and profound to a degree which language is powerless to describe. Those who follow the way which Lao Tse prescribes are always successful, even if they seem otherwise. To know oneself able to accomplish anything, but to hold oneself down to an inferior place, voluntarily to seem, indeed, the least important being in the empire — this proves that one really preserves within himself the primary virtue of the totality of the universe [the *tao*].

Very few, Lao Tse declares, recognize his worth, and few understand him. Therein lies his glory. He is mistreated because he is a sage, and misunderstood by the rabble who cannot see through his unpolished manner to the precious stones which fill his bosom. . . .[69]

Tradition has it that Lao Tse and Confucius once met, and that the latter soon thereafter said to his disciples that Lao Tse could be likened only to a dragon, i.e., to something powerful that cannot be understood because it soars above ordinary human experience.[70] By Western standards this might be taken as a confession of inferiority on the part of Confucius, but we must remember what this intensely practical old gentleman had to say about certain other transcendent or " spiritual " phenomena; namely, that the wise man should " keep aloof from them." In any case, the further fact should be borne in mind that the story of the meeting of the two sages is told by a disciple of Lao Tse.

The Following of " The Old Philosopher." — Lao Tse had a personal disciple called Yang Chu, who applied in a somewhat surprising way the master's ideas about letting things alone. If the thing to do is to be natural, argued Yang Chu, why not satisfy one's desires as they arise and live for the day only? He is usually described as a fatalist, an " Epicurean," and an egoist, which gives us a rather clear idea of how he impressed his contemporaries.[71] Space limitations prevent our dwelling further on Yang Chu, more especially as he is distinctly secondary to the most famous of Lao Tse's disciples, Chuang Tse. Concerning this great champion of Laoism very little is known, perhaps because of his success in following the master's injunction to live in obscurity.[72] Preferring, as he said, " to waggle his tail in the mud " like a retiring tortoise,[73] he devoted himself to the task of elucidating the teachings of *The Book of the Tao and Its Efficacy* and of continually rebutting Confucian arguments. He is sometimes referred to as the St. Paul of the Laoist movement, but this considerably exaggerates the degree of activity which his rôle involved.

Second only in importance to the writings of Chuang Tse as expositions of Laoism are those incorporated in the *Lieh Tse,* a composite book ascribed to a somewhat apocryphal thinker bearing the same name.[74] It is upon this collection and the recorded utterances of Chuang Tse that some scholars base their assertion that Laoism is fundamentally Hindu in origin, for the writings in question bear definite traces of *yoga* technique, i.e., of the physiological and psychic gymnastics of certain Indian ascetics. But the *Lieh Tse* assumed its final form, says Wilhelm, no earlier than the fourth century after Christ, and by that time Buddhism had been in China for over two centuries.[75] It therefore seems safe to follow Granet and Creel in concluding that, whatever *later* influences may have been, the origins of Laoism, as represented in *The Book of the Tao and Its Efficacy* of the fifth century B.C., are in all probability of Chinese mold and substance alone.

Laoism entered as an essential ingredient into the hodgepodge of folk beliefs, debased Buddhism, and the like, that eventually fermented into " vulgar Taoism," but this too, as we said when discussing the term Laoism, came much later. Moreover, it has little significance for the history of social thought, and we shall therefore content ourselves with this passing reference to its fundamental difference from what we here call Laoism.[76]

Mencius and Mo Tse: Confucianists Both. — Confucius attracted a much more brilliant galaxy of followers. Chief among them was Meng Tse or Mencius (372–289 B.C.), who is said to have received his training from the only grandson of Confucius. His relation to his great predecessor is much like that of his contemporary Chuang Tse to Lao Tse — in fact, Chuang Tse is sometimes called the Mencius of Laoism.[77]

In Mencius's day the sanguinary strife that had so appalled the earlier sages became even more widespread and intense. The towns of the warring feudal " kings " and their ilk were increasing in importance and splendor, and in the courts they harbored it was becoming fashionable to maintain retinues of itinerant scholars somewhat like the Cameralists of seventeenth-century Germany or, in some cases, like the Greek Sophists. These itinerant scholars, valued primarily for the immediate practical utility of their teachings in the maintenance of the established order, had much to say about " recipes for government." [78] Mencius stood forth as the champion of strong family control and its attendant subordination of the individual to the ends of the feudal state considered as a large family. He chose as his chief antagonists the egoistic Laoist Yang Chu, and the altruistic Confucianist Mo Tse.

Mo Tse, who was active in the latter half of the fifth century B.C., has been called a pessimistic conservative. He based his doctrines directly on the old peasant *ethôs* of neighborly mutual aid,[79] from which Confucius may have derived his maxim of "reciprocity" (the so-called Silver Rule).[80] Mo Tse bravely attacked the forces of anarchy and clannishness, themselves opposed to each other, surrounding him on every side. He has been called a teacher of "universal love," and the forces of both Christianity and Socialism have claimed him as a forerunner.[81] Other tags for Mo Tse are "utilitarian," "pragmatist," "sectarian," "monastic," and "pacifist." [82] At bottom, it seems plain that he simply pushed some of the Confucian conceptions to their logical conclusion; Mencius does him an injustice in treating him as an apostate.[83]

The Minor Heresies of Mencius. — In fact, Mo Tse's deviations from the Sinism of Confucius, striking as they appeared to later generations, were not as numerous as those of Mencius himself,[84] who is commonly regarded as one of the founders of Confucian orthodoxy. In his ideas of government, for example, Mencius was revolutionary whereas Confucius had been conservative. Instead of turning his gaze fondly backward to the splendors of the early Chou monarchs and longing for a revival of the kingly authority in the hands of their offspring, Mencius looked hopefully forward to the establishment of a new and more vigorous line of sovereigns. Moreover, he was revolutionary in the significance which he attached to the people. To him they were not only the most important part of society; they were also the true source (or its earthly reflection) of all political power: " Heaven sees as the people see, heaven hears as the people hear." [85] This comes fairly close to the democratic slogan of *vox populi, vox Dei,* and upon it many popular uprisings have been grounded. Confucius, to be sure, declared that a degenerate monarch should be overthrown, but by a noble whose success would attest his possession of *tao* — not by the people. Again, Mencius went so far as to approve the appointment as minister of a scholar who was neither vigorous, wise, nor sufficiently conversant with the *li*. Questioned, Mencius declared that " the love of what is good is more than a sufficient qualification for the government of the kingdom." [86]

Had Confucius been alive he would have been scandalized by such an utterance, for although he insisted on correct motivation he also laid stress on the necessity of knowing and practicing the *li* and thereby entering into and maintaining the harmony of the universe. In short, for Confucius one actually had to follow the *tao* to have it; the " outward signs of inward grace " should never fail.[87] By casting doubt on this fundamental precept, Mencius in some measure undermined the teachings of his master.

The Orthodoxy of Mencius: Man's Innate Goodness. — Mencius was in essential agreement, however, with Confucius's doctrine of the goodness of human nature, although this occupies a more prominent place in the thought of the disciple than in that of the master. Mencius's chief claim to originality perhaps lies in the theory of natural sympathy he developed in support of the " goodness " belief:

> If men suddenly see a child about to fall into a well, they will all without exception experience a feeling of alarm and distress. They will feel so not as a ground on which they may gain the favor of the child's parents, nor as a ground on which they may seek the praise of their neighbors and friends, nor from a dislike to the reputation of *having been unmoved by* such a thing.[88]

On the basis of this theory Mencius built a system of ethics which clearly shows that he held human nature to be not only innately good but also innately social,[89] thus paralleling his great contemporary, Aristotle. Orthodox Confucianism, including the Neo-Confucianism that developed after 1000 A.D., placed this conception of the social nature of man and its related theory of rule by benevolence at the very center of its system of thought.[90]

Hsün Tse the Apostate: Man's Evil Nature. — But not all who called themselves Confucians were orthodox. Hsün Tse (*c.* 315–235 B.C.) was acclaimed by the men of his time as a great follower of Confucius,[91] and he himself apparently thought that he correctly understood the ancient sage, but in reality his teaching marks a wide departure from that of Confucius. He set out to " modernize " and " interpret " the master, but like expounders of the " symbolic scriptures " and the " esoteric tradition " elsewhere, really introduced a new type of social thought.[92] He was basically empirical, naturalistic, and pragmatic; for example, he declared that natural catastrophes are not the result of the moral turpitude of the ruler; that the only reason for following tradition is that it has in experience proved useful; that heaven has nothing to do with the tenure of kings; and that law and the rules of propriety are merely strait-jackets devised by the ancient sages to control man's initially *evil* nature.[93] This is startling enough, but Hsün Tse went on to draw the following conclusions: (1) inasmuch as men often act in " good ways," it follows that this has been due to some change in their evil natures, and that change is the result of environmental influences (" All is the influence of association ") ; (2) these are chiefly from the social environment, and in the social environment the teaching of the rituals (*li*) and the restraint of the penal laws are most important; (3) history continually repeats itself, and there is nothing that can be called social progress, although individuals may and do frequently change from evil to good; (4) this change is effectively shown when the *literati* of the oncoming generation have perfectly absorbed the teachings and restraints of their predecessors and in turn act as the teachers of a new generation; (5) the essence of good conduct is therefore the unfailing repetition of tradition.[94]

Strangely " modern " in some ways and rigidly authoritarian in others, Hsün Tse is one of the most paradoxical figures in Chinese social thought, but he represents the first sweeping departure from the old Sinism,[95] and it is hardly to be expected that he could be entirely consistent. The most active part of his life fell in the period immediately prior to the establishment of the empire under Shih Huang Ti (*regnebat* 221–210 B.C.), the mighty Ch'in tyrant who unified China and completed the Great Wall.[96] Hsün Tse constantly saw before him horrible scenes of bloodshed and ruin. The "warring kingdoms " had once numbered fifty-five, but by his time ten larger fish had swallowed all the smaller, and among these ten the struggle for supremacy went on more savagely than ever before. As Creel puts it, " His day was one of slaughter, license, and sophistry." [97] By the time Hsün Tse had reached middle age the state of Ch'in had vanquished and annexed so many of its rivals that the era of the Empire was clearly foreshadowed. Witnessing the growing sway of organized force, he became increasingly sceptical of the Confucian doctrine of benevolent rule and human goodness, and took up the study of penal law. It is perhaps as a result of this train of events that his social thought assumed its peculiar form, so readily adaptable to the needs of an absolutistic government.[98]

Despotism and the Legists. — And adapted it was. Han Fei Tse, for a time one of the favorite *literati* of Shih Huang Ti, the " First Emperor," and Li Ssu, chief minister of the same emperor,[99] instituted a comprehensive system of formalized control, for " a single law, enforced by severe penalties, is worth more for the maintenance of order than all the words of all the sages." [100] Three principles guided these Legists: (1) man is evil by nature; (2) he seeks pleasure and avoids pain; (3) the absolute state as personified in the emperor is the source and purpose of all law.[101] On this basis an extensive system of objective punishments and privileges was set up. Wilhelm has the following comment:

> The great advantage of this school of thought, which made it acceptable to the people, was the objectivity of its doctrines. This way of administering the law provided a great and universally attainable standard of action, to which all must conform. But the unscrupulous methods it recommended, the Machiavellian way in which the profit of the state was insisted upon as the end justifying all means, endowed its theories with a narrow harshness which finally rendered them intolerable.[102]

Shortly after the death of Shih Huang Ti a revolution broke out, and with the resulting overthrow of the Ch'in dynasty the school of the Legists that had helped to assert its sway similarly passed off the scene, and the old Sinism, changed but still recognizable, once again played the leading rôle.[103]

In the Han and the later dynasties that succeeded the Ch'in many social thinkers appeared, but none of them loom as large in the history of Chinese thought prior to the nineteenth century as those we have so briefly noted. We shall merely mention Tung Chung Shu, creator of Confucian orthodoxy under the Han dynasty, Wang Mang, Wang Chung, Han Yü, Wang Yang Ming, and Chu Hsi, the great Neo-Confucianist, among the swarm that might fill our pages.[104]

China and India: Comparisons and Contrasts.[105] — From the Yellow River to the Ganges is a long stride, geographically and culturally, and we might well devote separate chapters to the social thought of China and India respectively. Categories of convenience there must be, however, and we therefore group them both under the colorless caption of " Far East."

But perhaps we can justify their juxtaposition by a certain amount of preliminary comparison that will show, among other things, why we are forced to use widely differing methods of presenting Chinese and Indian social thought. To begin with, we can say even less about the early cultural background of India than we did of China. The earliest Indian civilization was probably contemporaneous with or perhaps prior to its Chinese companion, but the reliable record of Indian antiquity cannot be traced so far back as that of Chinese (the earliest precise date in Indian history is the invasion of Alexander the Great, 326 B.C.). Moreover, there are many more gaps, both archaeological and historical, as yet unfilled. These facts, together with the absence of a satisfactory system of chronology, impose extreme caution as well as brevity.[106]

From what has been said of the feudal chaos, the " Age of the Warring Kingdoms," and the tyrannies that eventually engendered the Empire in China, it might be supposed that no other country could match the tale of " kites and crows " and the " jostling of iron and earthen pots " thereby offered. But where one Chinese tyrant slew his thousands there were a dozen Indian potentates and invaders each of whom slew his tens of thousands. This goes far to explain the tremendous gaps in the Indian records; sackings and burnings are not good for the archives. Another factor making for formlessness, or at least confusion, is the great size of India. It is not as large as modern China, of course, but when ancient India is compared with the eighteen provinces of ancient China, the Indian elephant far out-bulks the Chinese dragon.[107] This elephantine land-mass, almost a continent, is in addition sharply split into a number of geographical fragments that only the British have succeeded in thoroughly uniting. The highlands and deserts of Rajputana sunder the valley of the Indus (where the independent early culture of Punjab-Sind appeared) from that of the Ganges, and the Deccan plateau, with its jungle valleys and forbidding gorges, tapers off into the even more tropical southern tip where the dark-skinned aborigines and marginal Dravidians, splintered driftwood of the " pre-Aryan " population, have been left to molder.[108]

Race and Caste. — With this mention of race we encounter still another reason for the vast difference between Indian and Chinese cultural development. China expanded outward from an indigenous nucleus, intermingling the blood of various breeds in the process, and eventually attained a relatively high degree of racial homogeneity. In India, on the other hand, there have been continual mass migrations, primarily from the northeast where swarmed the " Aryan " pastoral nomads of the grasslands, that have resulted in the heterogeneous piling of layer upon layer. It is significant that the four *varnas* providing the main scaffolding of Indian caste structure mean the four " colors." The castes shade from light to dark, with the priestly Brahmans, purest-blooded and most jealously endogamous descendants of the " Aryan " invaders of about 3000 B.C. and thereafter, at the highest and lightest part of the framework. Only slightly lower down are the Kshatriyas, erstwhile warriors; beneath them are the Vaisyas, merchants and farmers; and at the bottom are the Sudras, slaves and serfs. Outside the caste structure altogether are the abject Chandalas and other " untouchables " upon whom even the lowliest Sudra looks down. Reference to race in conjunction with caste should not, however, be taken to mean more than a remote connection in the majority of cases, for intermarriage, economic status, vocation, and many other criteria play their part. The consequence is that Indian society is divided into some three to four thousand groups, each with its own *dharma* or code of conduct, and each maintaining relative separateness in its way of life (although of course functional interdependence — e.g., the *jajmani* system — is the rule).[109] We shall later have more to say about this peculiarly Indian institution (peoples other than the Indo-Aryans have had similar divisions without having developed anything even remotely resembling castes) ; [110] here we shall merely point out that the complexity introduced by the various caste *dharmas* makes detailed treatment within present limits quite impossible. The democratic Chinese ethic, on the other hand, considerably simplifies the task of analysis.

The Bulk of Indian Sacred Lore. — Finally, there is a tremendous difference between the sacred lores of China and India. The complexity of the Chinese characters, which were carved on the bones, stones, and wooden or bamboo staves used to record the divinations and sayings of the early sages, imposed extreme brevity.[111] By contrast, the esoteric and remarkably exact oral transmission [112] of the manifold Hindu groups, many of which cherished lores peculiarly their own, put a premium upon diffuseness. Indians boast the longest poem in the world, the *Mahabharata;* in addition, they might well lay claim to the most compendious conglomeration of sacred literature, and in this mass much of their social thought is embedded. Further, their secular writings are also voluminous.[113] Moreover, the Chinese *literati,* enmeshed in tradition though they were, did not go in for the practice of writing commentaries on other commentaries on other commentaries on cryptic half-sentences (*sutras*) from the earliest sacred lore, the *Vedas.*[114] As Dasgupta says:

It is . . . not possible to write any history of successive philosophies of India, but it is necessary that each system should be studied and interpreted in all the growth it has acquired through the successive ages of history from its conflicts with the rival systems as one whole.[115]

An exception is offered by the teachings of Buddha — perhaps because they became virtually extinct in India proper after A.D. 1000 or thereabouts. Taking one thing with another, however, it proves impossible to deal with Indian thinkers as we did with Lao Tse or Confucius, i.e., as individuals.

Hinduism, the Substratum. — Following our previous practice of seeking the postulates common to all types of thought within a given culture, we shall try to discover what lies beneath Brahmanism, Buddhism, and Jainism; namely, Hinduism.[116] (This is sometimes treated as the equivalent of modern syncretic Brahmanism, or even of *Bhakti* and the so-called monotheisms, but we shall use it in the sense mentioned above.) [117]

The most essential elements in Hinduism are probably the notions of *karma* and *samsara* (destiny and reincarnation or rebirth). The good and bad actions of men leave behind them residues that cluster about the self, soul, or soul-substitute,[118] as a result of which it is reborn, after the death of its whilom bearer, to a higher or lower plane of existence. (Only the fruits of those actions which are extremely wicked or extremely virtuous can be reaped in this life.) If the stored-up potencies of past actions prepare the soul for experiences that can be realized only in the life of a goat, let us say, so will *karma* ordain. On the other hand, the soul within an exceptionally meritorious goat may be reborn as a priest, although in general the passage from lower to higher planes, and *vice versa,* takes place by minute gradations. When the soul, after treading the wheel of reincarnation throughout the infinite past, is finally enshrined within the sage who has reached the pinnacle of contemplation and thereby annihilated all *karma,* the liberated soul achieves the state of *mukti* or emancipation. If all things that lead to actions, feelings, and ideas can be purged away, in other words, man finds within him the actionless self which neither suffers nor enjoys, neither strives nor undergoes rebirth.

This doctrine of *mukti* or emancipation is one of the chief connecting links between Brahmanism, Buddhism, and Jainism. Not only this: it lends an optimistic tinge to the otherwise unrelievedly world-negating, pessimistic *Weltanschauung* of Hinduism. If men by whatever means — *yoga* mortification, the Eight-Fold Path of Buddhism, the non-violent *ahimsa* of Jainism, or other practices — can pierce through the veil of *maya,* the illusions of the senses, "the play of magic shadow-shapes that come and go," the *karma* of sorrow and suffering will eventually lose its power and the emancipated soul will either blissfully merge with the all-encompassing Brahma (neuter) the world-soul, or achieve that final dissolution called *Nirvana*.[119]

Brahmanism and the Brahman Caste. — Brahmanism, which incorporates more of Hinduism than any other branch of Indian thought, can best be examined, for our purposes, by gaining some idea of the nature of the Brahman caste. First of all, it must be understood that the Brahmans are not exponents of a religion in the narrow Western sense of the latter term, viz., as the equivalent of a code of dogmas. It is quite possible to " worship " the gods of other faiths while remaining a zealous practitioner of one's own *dharma*; the ritualistic, etc., overshadows the holy. Many Brahmans belong to sects and worship their own special deities associated with one or the other phases of the Brahman *Trimurti* or trinity — Brahma (masculine) the creator, Vishnu the preserver, and Siva the destroyer — but readily accommodate themselves to Christianity or Buddhism.[120] Even the *dharmas* or ritual duties vary from caste to caste, as we have already noted, and in addition may undergo considerable change. For all its efficacy in social control, the system is very flexible.

The Sacred Writings, Sources of Brahman Prestige. — The *Vedas,* the Brahman holy books, are in reality only a prelude to the developed system, and give very little idea of its content. For example, the *Vedas* make no mention of the *Trimurti* or trinity, virtually denounce the ritual duties, ignore the sacredness of the cow, make reference to a hell and a heaven, are life-affirming and optimistic rather than life-denying and pessimistic, accept external phenomena as real and not as mere *maya* or illusion, and are absolutely silent on two of the most fundamental teachings of Hinduism, destiny and rebirth (*karma* and *samsara*).[121] It may seem odd that acceptance of the *Vedas* is complete among the followers of the Brahmans, but we must not forget that these sacred writings by implication sanction the position at the apex of Indian society which the Brahmans themselves now occupy.[122] In other words, the *Vedas* are a means of traditional domination for a charismatic caste which assumed its supreme status only about a thousand years before our era.[123]

The Brahmans, then, were not always at the top of the heap — at least not in their primary function as intellectuals and traditional bearers of a ritualistic charisma. In the earliest phases of the " Aryan " invasion, the " horse-herding " warrior chieftains were supreme, both by virtue of sheer physical force and through the charisma of virility and skill.[124] No one knows just how the Brahmans managed to relegate the Kshatriyas to lower rank. But their rôles as controllers of the magic of *soma*-drinking, the horse-sacrifice, and like rituals probably lent them their initial importance,[125] and they reaped usury on their capital. Once established they probably had a great deal to do with the solidification of caste.[126] Smith thus indicates what the process may have been:

> [They] . . . gradually framed extremely strict rules to guard their own ceremonial purity against defilement through unholy food or undesirable marriages. The enforcement of such rules on themselves by the most respected members of the Indo-Aryan community naturally attracted the admiration of the more worldly classes of society, who sought to emulate and imitate the virtuous self-restraint of the Brahmans. It being clearly impossible that ordinary soldiers, business men, peasants, and servants could afford to be as scrupulous as the saintly or at least professedly religious Brahmans, a separate standard of *dharma* (law) for each section of society necessarily grew up by degrees. Kings, for instance, might properly and must do things which subjects could not do without sin and so on. The long-continued conflict with the aboriginal Indians, who held quite different ideals of conduct, made both the Brahmans and their imitators more and more eager to assert their superiority and exclusiveness by ever-increasing scrupulosity concerning both diet and marriage.[127]

Brahman Pride, Place, and Power. — The prestige of the Brahmans is indeed great, and as a result they have been able to interpret the *Vedas* in almost any way they see fit. For example, the *Atharva-Veda* is in the main a book of spells and incantations appealing to the daimon world, and teems with notions about witchcraft current among the lower levels of the population,[128] but many intellectual Brahmans interpret this as exoteric teaching designed solely for purposes of social control, and in their quasi-esoteric speculations fearlessly question the very existence of the *Trimurti*. Not only has their religious power been virtually unchallenged, but they have in addition held great secular power throughout most of Indian history. This combination makes them distinctly different from the Chinese mandarins on the one hand and the prophets of Israel on the other. Kings and princes accepted the Brahmans as priests, teachers, and advisers, and in addition endowed them with landed property, probably because the Brahmans gave the social order, including the material interests of the rulers, an unsurpassable sacred sanction — to say nothing of the aid rendered by their learning and administrative ability.[129] The Brahmans, on the other hand, have usually been content to leave the actual rule to others, and in

India proper have consistently remained aloof from struggle for
political power as such, contenting themselves with a sort of cat's-
paw tactics.[130]

Supernaturalism and Brahman Teachings. — The Brahman
thinkers finally overcame the essential polytheism of the traditional lore and developed the pantheistic idea of a single, impersonal entity, Brahma, to whose all-in-oneness the evanescent
world of matter forms a counterpart.[131] In accordance with the
doctrines of destiny and rebirth, the Indian follower of the Brahmans tries to better his position at his next reincarnation through
good deeds and the painstaking fulfillment of his caste *dharma*
under his Brahman or Brahman-controlled director (the *guru,*
who is often revered as a "human god" in a distinctly anthro-
polatrous way).[132] In contrast to the Buddhists and Jainists, the
Brahmans hold fast to an idea of the soul that has a somewhat
animistic character.[133] Yet it must be granted that the Brahman
theory that the self is an integral part of the all-encompassing
whole or Brahma, as embodied in the famous dictum "*Tat twam
asi*" ("That also art thou"),[134] is not in line with the animism
of the usual Western type, in which souls are regarded as entities
eternally separate and distinct.

The Essence of the Sacred: Dharma. — Most of the Brahman
notions we have thus far discussed relate to what we have elsewhere termed the supernatural. Of chief importance among the
exceptions is the idea of *dharma,* which is primarily sacred in
character (although, as we shall later see, it has important
secular aspects). *Dharma* is variously translated as law, ritual,
justice, virtue, duty, sacred conduct,[135] and "practice of hereditary function in the social organism."[136] At this point it is not
necessary that we choose between these translations; let us first
see what *dharma* is.

Weber says that *dharma* rituals make up the most important
part of the religio-social life of the masses.[137] The specific practices are the outgrowth of magical norms bound up with sacred
ways of action laid down in past ages. *Dharma* is therefore a
peculiarly potent form of tradition; ideas of salvation may
change, but *dharma* remains eternal. Each caste has its own particular *dharma.* This may develop or become specialized through
the differentiation of castes, but to the Indian mind it remains
always the same. The decisive question is not "What do you believe?" but "What is your *dharma?*"[138] Those who overstep
its bounds automatically recede into a lower caste or even become
outcaste. *Dharma* therefore imposes terrific penalties on its trans-

gressors. In most cases the Brahman determines when transgression has taken place. Glasenapp characterizes the Indian conception of *dharma* as follows:

. . . the whole cosmos is completely dominated by one eternal law, the Law of Dharma. In the natural world this apportions to every thing and creature its appropriate attributes and activities; in the moral world it prescribes for all creatures the functions and actions they must fulfill, and inexorably determines their destinies in agreement with the way in which these prescribed deeds are carried out.[139]

For present purposes, "sacred law" seems to be the best translation of *dharma* [140] (in a later section we shall consider it as "law" only). These sacred laws and their attendant rituals created or at least accentuated the clefts between the castes, and provide for the believer an objective test of the course of his destiny and his status at his next rebirth.

In addition to the obvious consequences of the sacred laws, there may be traced a number of others that are somewhat less apparent. For example, the sanctions they lend to the caste system have prevented any development analogous to the Occidental bourgeois class and its struggle for political and legal power. Theories of natural rights to "life, liberty, and the pursuit of happiness," common to all men as men, are of course quite out of the question.[141] The idea of personality, so strong in the individualistic societies of the West, has no positive role in Indian thought *per se*. The sacred laws make competition in many of its forms virtually impossible, for they prevent change of social function and position through the control they exercise over the most minute details of the lives of caste members.[142] And so on.

Secular Social Thought: the Shastras. — We have now surveyed, albeit hastily and imperfectly, the main conceptions of Hinduism and Brahmanism. Buddhism and Jainism differ considerably from Brahmanism in their religio-social implications, but inasmuch as the former is now virtually extinct in India proper and the latter is confined to a small commercial sect, we shall not discuss them further except to say that neither succeeded in breaking the sway of *dharma* and the caste system.[143] It now seems well to turn to the more secular aspects of Indian thought. In fact, the attention we have already paid its more strictly sacred and supernaturalistic aspects has laid us open to the charge currently leveled at nearly all Western writers; namely, that Indian thought has been largely misunderstood because the secular literature embodied in the *shastras* and similar writings has been ignored.[144] *Shastra* means a systematic description and analysis of secular knowledge — in short, a *Wissenschaft* or " science " in the old meaning of *scientia*.[145] The famous Laws of Manu fall in this class, although they are considerably more sacred in content than some of the other *shastras,* notably those dealing with *smriti* or tradition, *artha* or human interests (" desired objects "), and *niti* or social behavior.[146] Some of the famous *shastra* writers, real or apocryphal, are Manu, Kamandaka, Shukra, and especially Kautilya (*floruit circa* 300 B.C.), the chief minister of the " Indian Alexander," Chandragupta Maurya. In the sections that follow we shall discuss the theories of these writers, but in order to avoid confusion will mention them by name in the text as little as possible. The theories are those dealing with: (1) the original nature of man; (2) the origin of the state; (3) the rôle of coercion in social life; (4) the relations of ruler and ruled; and (5) the notion of the social organism.

Eden, the Fall, and the " Logic of the Fish." — Anticipating the Hebrew story of Eden by several centuries, some unknown bard sings in the *Mahabharata* that " The people used to protect one another through innate righteousness (*dharma*) and sense of justice." [147] But alas, man seems to have fallen not once but many times, for the Hebrew story of the Fall also finds its homologue in the same poem:

Then foolishness or stupidity seized their minds. Their intelligence being thus eclipsed, the sense of justice was lost. Cupidity or temptation overpowered them next. Thus arose the desire for possessing things not yet possessed. And this led to their being subjugated by an affection under which they began to ignore the distinction between what should and what should not be done. Consequently there appeared sexual license, libertinism in speech and diet, and indifference to morals. When such a revolution set in among man *Brahman* disappeared, and with it law.[148]

The *shastra* writers echo this traditional teaching, saying that men are by nature passionate and covetous, given to usurping the places of others, and perpetually violating the moral code through lying, sexual promiscuity, theft, murder, and like conduct.[149] The *Mahabharata* also says that left to itself the " whole world would be in a mess " like a " devil's workshop." Man's nature after the Fall causes him to behave like " the creatures that cannot see one another when the sun and moon do not shine," or the " fishes in shallow waters," or the " birds in places safe from molestation where they can fly at each other's throats in a suicidal strife."

In short, fallen men follow only the *matsyanyaya*, " the logic of the fish," i.e., the big ones eat the little ones.[150]

Secular Salvation in Positive Law. — This Hobbes-like assertion of " the war of each against all " carries with it the conclusion at which Hobbes also arrived; namely, that if men are to live at peace with each other, restraint is necessary. This is found in *danda*, which is to say in sanction, coercion, punishment. *Danda* constitutes the essence of stable societal relations; social life is possible only because it is organized in the form of the state.[151] These drastic pronouncements of the epic poets, echoed by the *shastra* writers, show how nakedly secular Indian political life has been from the earliest times onward; in spite of the binding power of *dharma* as sacred law, *dharma* is also conceived as positive law in the strict sense, viz., rules of conduct imposed by a central authority through sanctions ultimately relying on physical force as the *ultima ratio*. In other words, law is identified with rational domination; it is sacred *dharma* plus secular *danda*.[152]

It should not be assumed, however, that in Indian thought coercion through force is morally neutral, a mere means to an end. *Danda* cuts both ways, for through fear of punishment men not only cease to follow " the logic of the fish " but become virtuous — the cruel, mild; the wicked, upright; and the malicious gossip, kind. All created beings are kept to their respective duties, thus causing coöperation for the happiness of mankind. The whole world is rectified by *danda,* and even the gods and demigods are subject to its beneficent authority. It is the very principle of omnipotence, comparable to the *majestas* of Bodin or the *summa potestas* of Grotius; it is absolute, with jurisdiction over all.[153]

" Uneasy Lies the Head . . ." — This exaltation of positive law as the essence of sovereignty has far-reaching consequences for the relations of rulers and ruled. The ruler in office personifies *danda,* but the ruler as person is himself subject to it. Hence the inevitable dilemma of kingship in the Indian theory of the state: only by wielding the weapon of *danda* can the king hold righteous sway, but it carries with it its own nemesis if it is misused. *Danda* smites the king who deviates from his duty; he may rightfully be put to death. Even the Laws of Manu calmly envisage regicide as necessary for the protection of the people: " The King who through foolishness arbitrarily tyrannizes over his own state is very soon deprived of his kingdom and life, together with his kith and kin." [154]

The right of revolution implicitly set forth in this and many other monarchomachic pronouncements derives from the Indian conception of the governmental compact, which is in turn connected with the theory of public finance: when the king is chosen by the people he takes an oath that he will protect them, and they reciprocate by promising to help him with the " root of the army," i.e., by paying taxes.[155] If the revenues exacted are ever unjust and the compact thereby violated, the people may legitimately revolt, for when the state does not guarantee the security of property from its own unjust officers, it is no longer the state but simply " the logic of the fish." [156]

This sounds radical enough, but even more drastic utterances are to be found in the *shastra* writings of Shukra: " Does not even the dog look like a king when it has ascended a royal conveyance? Is not the king justly regarded as a dog by the poets? . . . The ruler has been made by Brahma a servant of the people. His revenue is the remuneration for his services." [157]

Leviathan Upsurges: the Organismic Conception. — Here the link between ruler and ruled would seem to be simply the cash nexus, but the *shastra* writers do not carry this doctrine to extremes. In fact, virtually all of them accept the traditional notion of the state as an organism; Hobbes's *Leviathan* lived long ago.[158] In Brahman thought the four castes of society are regarded as having sprung from the four parts of Brahma's body, and the analogy thereby furnished naturally leads to the use of the term " limb-like " when discussing the rôles of the traditional seven elements of sovereignty: king, minister, territory, fort, treasury, army, and ally.[159] Other writers put it thus: " Sovereignty does not flourish if it is deficient even in a single limb ";[160] " Among these [elements of sovereignty] the king is declared to be the head, the minister is the eye, the ally the ear, the treasury the mouth, while the fort and the territory are the two arms and legs." [161] With the king thus regarded as the head, it might be assumed that the matter-of-fact attitude taken toward him by the *shastra* writers is thereby called in question, but in the Laws of Manu we read:

> Yet in a kingdom containing seven constituent parts, which is upheld like the triple staff [of an ascetic], there is no [single part] more important [than the others], by reason of the importance of the qualities of each for the others. For each part is particularly qualified for [the accomplishment of] certain objects, [and thus] each is declared to be the most important for that particular purpose which is effected by its means.[162]

In short, the king is only a part of the social organism.

By now it should be rather plain that by holding themselves aloof from direct participation in the political struggle while at the same time effectively preventing any doctrine of the divine right of kings that would make revolution difficult, the Brahman intellectuals buttressed their own power. India has never seen a theocracy in the sense of actual assumption of direct rule by a sacerdotal group, but no ruler could have maintained his sway for even a short time if faced by united Brahman opposition.[163] Proclamation of the secular nature of the head of the state was in India a means admirably adapted to controlling the political processes in the interests of the sacerdotal caste, the Brahmans.

We might say much more about the social thought of India. For example, the relations of *ego* and *alter*, of self and other, have been shrewdly analyzed in spite of the pervasive influence of the " all-in-oneness " idea. Similarly, concrete forms of social organization such as the *sangha* or village community, the *mahajan.* or guild, the *panchayat* or village council, and the *jajmani* system or reciprocal economic functioning of castes, are worthy of lengthy description and analysis.[164] For the ends we now have in view, however, we must here conclude.

Summary of the Chapter. — Chinese social thought is characterized by social monism; the laws of nature and the laws of man go hand in hand. This monism was probably engendered in the Chinese village community, and the rural cult was taken over by chieftains who later became kings and emperors. The identification of the natural and the social led to a great emphasis on ceremonial as an all-sufficient technique of control. The chieftain, incorporating the magical efficacies first stressed by the rural cult, became a lay figure dominated by court etiquette, in accordance with the teachings of Chinese social monism.

This social monism may be called Sinism. Its central emblems are *tao, yang, yin,* and the like. The outstanding representative of Sinism was Confucius, who regarded himself merely as an interpreter of the sacred tradition. He did, however, rationalize and humanize the old formulas to a considerable degree. Chief among his teachings were the necessity of filial piety, the rectification of names, the goodness of human nature, and the possibility for the humblest to become a " superior man." Lao Tse was a contemporary of Confucius, and interpreted the *tao* in a quite different way. Preacher of the return to nature, he also advocated a kind of ascetic mysticism based on his maxim of " not striving." Both Confucius and Lao Tse were *literati* who never succeeded in finding government posts worthy of their talents.

Only Lao Tse, however, seems to have rationalized his disappointment. The disciples of Lao Tse were less numerous and effective than those of Confucius. Mencius and Hsün Tse are outstanding among the followers of Confucius: the first for his stress on the doctrine of man's innate goodness, and the second for his apostasy in roundly declaring man's nature to be evil. Hsün Tse was the forerunner of the school of the Legists, who maintained that etiquette is vastly inferior to penal law as a means of social control.

Indian social thought is strikingly different from that of China; it is either dualistic or, when monistic, it reverses the Chinese belief by holding that the supra-sensible world alone is real. Hinduism, as the common denominator of Buddhism, Brahmanism, and Jainism, centers in the doctrines of destiny and rebirth. Closely allied to these is the conception of *dharma* or sacred law which regulates all caste activities and hence the greater part of Indian social life. Brahmanism stresses *dharma* strongly and adds the important notions of the identity of the self with the rest of the universe and of the " all-in-oneness " of Brahma. Indian thinkers also deal with *dharma* as secular or positive law, and have a theory of social origins in which an initial " war of each against all " is transformed into society politically organized, i.e., the state, through the use of coercion and punishment. Rulers of the state are themselves under the sway of the laws they enforce, and their subjects may rightfully revolt if *dharma* is violated. There is also a well-developed conception of the state as a social organism in which the ruler occupies the chief place but is dependent on all the other " members." The secular character of Indian political processes and structures greatly helped the Brahmans to utilize them in their own interests.[165]

Since 1938, when Becker first wrote this chapter, Max Weber's monographs on sociology of religion have appeared in translation by H. H. Gerth and by Gerth and Don Martindale. Obviously, Becker drew heavily on Weber, but where China is concerned, even more heavily on the writings of Marcel Granet, the more relevant of which are unfortunately not yet available in translation. See the notes at the end of this volume.

CHAPTER III

Social Thought of the Ancient Near East

THE INDIAN LINK. — "An elephantine land-mass" is a phrase applied to India in Chapter Two, where attention is called to the fact that this near-continent is split along natural planes of cleavage into a number of fragments. The valley of the Indus, for example, is sundered from the other discrete regions comprised in "India the geographical expression" by desert and mountain barriers. Here, in Punjab-Sind (territories through which the Indus flows), there flourished in the third millennium before Christ a complex civilization fully equal to those found in China, Sumeria, or Egypt of the same era, and its antecedents seem at least as old. Moreover, amulets and like objects already unearthed show such a striking resemblance to those still in use by many Hindu popular cults that strong connections with certain aspects of what we have called "basic Hinduism" may be inferred. These aspects are of course pre-"Aryan" and perhaps pre-Dravidian; if a strict chronological sequence were a desideratum in this book, our previous discussion of Indian thought should have been introduced by what has just been said about the Indus civilization. For us, however, the special significance of this culture, and the reason for its mention here, lies in the fact that it represents a sort of transitional zone between the ancient Far East and the ancient Near East.[1]

The Five Lands. — Indeed, Punjab-Sind has recently been linked with the other civilizations conventionally considered as those of the Near East proper — Mesopotamia, coastal Arabia, Egypt, and Syria — in the illuminating expression "the Five Lands." [2] It is now definitely known that in these areas numerous important improvements in material culture took place during the Neolithic period, but we do not know whether they arose independently in each country, or whether they spread from one to the others, or, if the latter view is true, which was the pioneer. Some advocates of the priority of the Indus civilization would have it that the domestication of animals such as sheep and cattle was first practiced there; enthusiasts for the cause of Sumeria assign to it the potter's wheel (although this claim is contested by proponents of Elam) ; coastal Arabia, particularly the region now called Yemen, is sometimes given credit for the first deep-sea vessels; and the earliest metal tools are thought to have been smelted from the ores of Mount Sinai by peoples of the Egyptian fringe.

These " firsts " are conjectural; we know only that the Five Lands all represent regions that escaped desiccation after the last great recession of the northern ice cap. The northward shift of the Atlantic winds following that recession turned into desert the once well-watered belt that had stretched all the way across the Sahara, central Arabia, and the Iranian uplands. Only in river valleys or coastal strips out of the reach of drought could man lead a settled existence conducive to the development of a complex civilization.[3] For three of these regions — Mesopotamia, Egypt, and Syria — we already possess information sufficient to enable us to say something about the social thought prevailing in each. For the other two — coastal Arabia and Punjab-Sind — modern archaeology is only now collecting data, and nothing of any decisive significance about their social thought has yet come to light.

Sumeria, Mesopotamian Model. — The first rulers of the Mesopotamian cities whose records have been discovered were called Sumerians. Almost certainly they were invaders, but no one yet knows whence they came. Some hold that central Asia was their earliest home, and for other possible points of origin, notably the western uplands of Iran, there are defenders, but the legends of the Sumerians themselves say that they entered Mesopotamia by way of the Persian Gulf, " the Sea of the Sunrise." The fact that some Sumerians wore their hair in a topknot like the men of Punjab-Sind tempts to the guess that they may have come from the Indus valley, perhaps by coastwise voyage, but there is as yet no conclusive evidence for this. At "Ur of the Chaldees," which was then at the northern edge of the Persian Gulf, the Sumerians established their first great city, and by the thirty-fifth century before our era had laid down most of the lines which later Mesopotamian civilizations were to follow.[4]

" Aryans " and " Semites." — Little is known about the physical type of either the aboriginal population or the conquering Sumerians. It has been surmised, however, that the latter were " Aryans," or " of Indo-European stock." This does not tell us much, but in any event it is clear that their language was Indo-European, and this appears to have been thoroughly assimilated

by the subject population. Further, there was indubitably an inter-mixture with other breeds that eventually made the Sumerians virtually indistinguishable from the sturdy Babylonians and Assyrians with whom the numerous bas-reliefs of later times have made us familiar. It also happened that soon after the invasion the Sumerian overlords had to struggle hard against the pastoral nomads who began to drift into their territories from the north. These Semitic-speaking shepherds (perhaps the " Asiatics " and Shepherd Kings of Egyptian history), who had led a wandering life in Arabia and the grasslands fringing the Fertile Crescent, probably were somewhat different in physical makeup from the southern Mesopotamians yielding allegiance to Sumer. Certainly there is no doubt that their language was markedly different, being of the agglutinative, guttural, Semitic type.

Ascendency of Akkad. — Slowly the erstwhile nomads took over the culture of the tillage peoples among whom they settled, interbred with them, and set up strong kingdoms of their own. By the year three thousand or thereabouts, Akkad, center of the Semitic-speaking Mesopotamians, gradually pushed outward, and on its southern border came into conflict with Sumer. Sometime in the first quarter of the third millennium a powerful ruler, Sargon I, founded a dynasty in Akkad. Legend has it that he was a gardener's son whose mother committed him to the river in a boat of reeds, and that he later served in the household of an Akkadian king. Much better attested is the fact that Sargon succeeded in carrying his rule over the greater part of Mesopotamia. Indeed, the records suggest that he reached the shores of the Mediterranean, " the Sea of the Sunset." In Sargon's old age revolts broke out, and it was left for his grandson, Naram-Sin, to restore the vanished splendors of Akkad by extending his domains even beyond the limits reached by his great predecessor. Naram-Sin utilized Sumerian scribes for the bureaucracy of his empire, with the consequence that correspondence carried on with Syria by Egyptian diplomats almost fifteen hundred years later was in cuneiform rather than hieroglyphic script. So persistent were the Sumerian patterns. . . .[5]

Priest-King and Divinity Incarnate. — Before the reign of the " Divine Naram-Sin " (*c.* 2795–2739), as he was called by his awed subjects, the rulers of the Mesopotamian cities bore the title of *ishakku* or *patesi,* which may be translated as " tenant-farmer of the city-god." [6]

This is the familiar phenomenon of the priest-king. When one of these sacerdotal rulers succeeded in establishing a dynasty in

Mesopotamia, he was also honored with the name of *lugal*, " possessor." Personal charisma in a certain sense and the charisma of office had become capable of being inherited. Great was the prestige of Naram-Sin; he was regarded not as the recipient of charisma but as its source; i.e., as himself a god. Moreover, Naram-Sin's godhead was transmitted to the offspring of his loins; earthly divinity became hereditary.

Sumerian Renascence. — But the gods themselves may weaken, and by the middle of the third millennium Sumer had resumed its old supremacy over Akkad. Men now worshiped the ruler of Ur, " the Divine Dungi, conqueror of foreign lands, establisher of the land of Sumer, who tirelessly causes anarchy to depart." [7] Last of the great kings drawing their chief support from southern Mesopotamia, Dungi further extended and consolidated the sway of Sumerian civilization. Cuneiform writing, baked clay tablets, astral lore, a relatively accurate calendar, and similar culture traits persisted in the Near East for millennia, and some of them still survive in the Western world. (For example, division of time on the basis of sixty had its origin in Sumeria.)

Babylonian Sway: Hammurabi the Law-Giver. — In the last quarter of the third millennium the Sumerian centers near the Persian Gulf were overshadowed by Babylonia, a Semitic-speaking city lying on the Euphrates farther north. This marks the beginning of the great age of Hammurabi, ruler of " the Gate of God " (*Bab-el*). In addition to the famous stele containing the code of laws which were edited and promulgated under his sanction, over fifty of Hammurabi's letters have been discovered. These show that he controlled a highly organized system of government which supervised nearly every phase of life — economic, familial, moral, legal — in his wide dominions. The Semitic-speaking Amorites (" Westerners ") to whom he owed his first push upward to Babylonian power had originally come from Syria, so that Hammurabi's sway in this and neighboring western regions probably rested on a basis firmer than that possessed by any Mesopotamian conqueror before him. Moreover, even the hard-bitten upland Assyrians and Elamites of the eastern marches bowed before his overmastering might, as did also the once invincible Sumerians. The result of these Babylonian victories was that Hammurabi and his bureaucracy successfully administered the affairs of an empire that curbed within its borders a jostling horde of peoples and their conflicting cultures.[8]

The Apparatus of Rational Domination. — Under such circumstances, his writ as traditional-charismatic sovereign, and even

as the " Divine Hammurabi," ran with full efficacy only in Babylon and its immediate environs, and even here it had to be strengthened by all the apparatus of rational domination and by the ultimate sanction thereof — physical coercion. Law in its strict sense,
bearing with it enforcement of impersonal decisions by delegated
officials of a central authority (see the section on " Embryonic
Law," Chapter One), played a large part, as it must in any country where the controls of vicinally limited sacred societies run at
cross purposes. Under such circumstances, gossip, ostracism, and
like " spontaneous " pressures diminish in efficacy, and thereby
help to engender the Guilt = Punishment equation (characterized,
as Faris says, by official efforts " to make the punishment fit the
crime "). The stele bearing the Code of Hammurabi shows him
as an earthly divinity receiving his laws from the sun-god — a
typical attempt to get supernaturalistic reinforcement for regulations that have already lost a large part of their sacred character.
To be sure, these instruments for the regulation of an extensive
territory were forged from a mass of customs and embryonic and
full-fledged laws having strongly sacred traits in the societies
where they developed. Nevertheless, the rational hammering to
which they were subjected in the effort to give them more general
forms rendered them almost unrecognizable to those who had
once seen them only as unique configurations within an " emotional halo."

    Discriminatory Laws: Patrician and Plebeian. — Hammu-
rabi's rational craftsmen did their work well, for the code is
strikingly secular; it contains no regulations touching matters
of sacred or supernaturalistic ritual and lore. Crime has been
stripped of the element of blood-feud vengeance and is dealt with
as an offense against the state, which relentlessly but impersonally
subjects it to controls ultimately reducible to the application of
the *ultima ratio.* Complete equality before the law, however, is
not in evidence. The code therefore lacks in this respect a
thoroughly rational basis — for the obvious reason, to name no
others, that any empire recently won and consolidated by conquest would necessarily be stratified.

    At the tip of the Babylonian pyramid was the king, and just be-
neath this capstone came the patrician layer, in all probability
made up of the ablest members of the groups that had successively
dominated the various regions of the empire, with the latest com-
ers in the most privileged niches. These patricians (*awelu*) possessed a great many of the perquisites of rank, including the right
to exact heavily disproportionate retaliation for personal injuries

but — *noblesse oblige!* That is to say, the aristocrat could also be more severely punished for his offenses and, guilty or not guilty, had higher fees to pay.

It seems fairly clear that by Hammurabi's time there had arisen a tendency to deprive the nobles of some of their immunities for the benefit of the king, on the one hand, and the plebeian freemen (*muskinu*), on the other. The latter, probably comprising " share-croppers " of the erstwhile " tenant-farmer of the city-god," together with artisans, small merchants, and wage-earners in general, could not so luxuriously revenge themselves for injuries to their persons as could the nobles, for they had to accept financial recompense if it was offered. On the other hand, however, they were more lightly punished, and in particular were the beneficiaries of a much lower scale of fines and fees. Favored in these respects, it may well be that the plebeians buttressed the secular absolutism that was arising at the cost of patrician feudal prerogatives.

Slaves and the Lex Talionis. — The bottom blocks in the Babylonian social pyramid were the slaves (*ardu* — " heads "), who could be owned by both plebeians and patricians. A lively trade in human chattels went on continually, for most domestic service and arduous manual labor rested on their shoulders. The lot of the slaves could easily have been worse, however, for they were permitted to accumulate property, and could even purchase other slaves or their own freedom. Furthermore, in Hammurabi's time they had the right to marry free women (although in most cases they were given slave girls as wives), and the children of such mixed unions were legally classed as freemen. Further, the offspring of slave concubines and patricians might take the rank of the father under certain circumstances. It should not be assumed, however, that the slave led an enviable existence; judicial discrimination weighed heavily upon him. To take only one of many examples: if the slave struck a freeman, Hammurabi's code required the cutting off of his right ear. Here the *lex talionis,* the Mosaic " An eye for an eye, and a tooth for a tooth," would have been relatively merciful — and, in fact, there were numerous attempts to apply it in the code wherever social stratification did not interfere.

From all this it is clear that the degree of rationalism attained in the classical penology of Beccaria, to take the obvious instance of the Guilt = Punishment equation, far transcends anything attained in Babylonian society, legalistic and secular though it was in some respects.

Women and Property. — As compared with many other early societies, women enjoyed a considerable measure of freedom, although the " double standard " was much in evidence, not merely in custom but in the law itself. It seems likely that a large part of the liberty accorded to females rested on the high regard for property rights which was so marked a feature of Babylonian social thought. Thus the wife remained in control of the dowry she brought to her union (which was dealt with as a civil contract), and could spend it as she saw fit. If divorce took place, the " discontracting parties " had to run the gantlet of an elaborate scheme for repaying or otherwise adjusting the bride price and the dowry. Furthermore, alimony, although relatively rare, was legally possible.

The laws dealing with property were extraordinarily exact and detailed, showing that Babylonian civilization, although basically agrarian, was strongly commercial in spirit. The greater number of the clay tablets that have come down to us deal with business matters, and in Hammurabi's code a wide range of property disposal was recognized: dedication, gift, barter, sale, lease, deposit, loan, and pledge. Inheritance of property evidently loomed large in the Babylonian mind, for nearly one law in ten (23 out of 250) dealt with this topic.

Evidence of extensive culture contact throughout the far-flung empire, and beyond its borders as well, is to be found in the laws regulating shipping and caravan traffic; they cover an amazing number of contingencies and bear witness to the high degree of organization that the transportation industry had attained. Even Egypt offers nothing comparable.

Crime and the Courts. — The portions of the code devoted to criminal law reveal a list of sanguinary punishments ranging all the way from impaling and burning to the putting out of eyes that pried into forbidden secrets. Because of this, much has been said about Babylonian cruelty, but it is well to remember that in the England of King James (he of the Authorized Version), over two hundred crimes were punishable by death, and that the repertoire also included drawing and quartering, branding on cheek and forehead, cropping of ears, and like pleasantries. We have already noted the fact that the *lex talionis,* although present in principle, was not consistently applied because of the stratification of Babylonian society. Deviations were not all the result of social discrimination, however, for there was some effort to take account of motive. Instance : if a defendant on trial for killing a man could prove that his act was unintentional, he was released on payment of a fine graded according to the rank of the deceased. Similarly, the owner of a goring ox was punished only if he had previously known the animal to be vicious (a provision later copied into a Hebrew code). Interesting attempts to put the " eye for an eye " principle into effect are exemplified in provision for the execution of the son of any architect who built so carelessly as to cause the death of his employer's son. There were several similar " reciprocities."

Court procedure affords what is probably an example of tendencies toward secularization. In earlier laws higher tribunals were composed of priests, but by Hammurabi's time civil officials had almost entirely taken their place; the only remaining sacerdotal function was the administering of the oath before the gods. It should be noted, however, that this was not the perfunctory matter that it comes to be in thoroughly secularized cultures: witness the fact that, in affairs of which the defendant alone had knowledge, his oath (if he dared take it) was regarded as sufficient — the solemnity of the act was so great that perjury seems not to have been thought possible. It is not advisable, then, to attribute to Babylonian juridical practice more than *tendencies* toward secularization; sacred and supernaturalistic sanctions were far from powerless. Social thought was quite as much swayed by lore as by science, if not more so.[9]

" Wisdom Writings." — There is a striking dearth of other than priestly, legal, and commercial records in all the Mesopotamian civilizations; Breasted is quite correct, in this respect, in pointing out the superiority of Egypt.[10] The poet and the sage were not held in high honor for their own sakes. An apparent exception is offered by the Gilgamesh Epic, which is of course magnificent literature (and it furnishes, among other things, the prototype of the Hebrew story of the Flood). But the use made of it was primarily liturgical, and apart from its folklore the epic does not offer much of interest to the student of social thought. Most relevant for our purposes is the " wisdom literature ": precepts, counsels, proverbs. In an early list of admonitions, perhaps going back to Sumerian times, is found the equivalent of that maxim, " Return good for evil," so frequently appearing in the social thought of the major civilizations. In the same list are injunctions to hospitality, mercy, reconciliation, and choice of a virtuous wife that reveal much practical social wisdom, but like the preliterate proverbs we quoted in Chapter One, they are all cast in concrete terms. From a much later period, the ninth century before Christ, comes a pessimistic plaint of human folly and the solace of death that reminds one of the Hebrew *Ecclesiastes* or the Egyptian *Dia-*

logue with His Soul of a Man Weary of His Life; here again, however, the heights of abstraction are not reached. A collection of proverbs that goes back to at least the time of Hammurabi contains these: " Strife you find among servants, gossip among barbers "; " The strong live by their own wages, the weak by the wages of their children "; " He is altogether righteous and good, yet he is clothed in rags." [11] Surely, surely, there were *wise* men before Agamemnon!

Babylonian Collapse. — And to continue in the Greek vein:

> The day shall surely come when sacred Troy shall fall,
> And Priam, and the people of the ash-speared Priam — all.

Or, to seek light from the Far East: " The Great Happiness does not come twice."

Which is to say, with reference to our present theme, that the enfeebled hereditary divinity transmitted by the " Divine Hammurabi " further diminished in efficacy. At the beginning of the second millennium his dynasty fell before the raids of the Hittite " Kings of the Sea Country " and the invasion of the Kassite highlanders from the plateau of Iran. The Hittites withdrew, but the Kassites remained, setting up a dynasty that endured at Babylon for some six hundred years. Their conquest marks the appearance in Mesopotamia of the horse, called by the cowering Babylonians " the ass of the mountains." Once again the drama that Oppenheimer regards as basic to the formation of the state was enacted: pastoral nomad subjugated settled agriculturist.[12]

Like previous invaders of " the Land between the Rivers," the Kassites adopted Sumerian customs, and their leader proclaimed himself " King of the Four Regions, King of Sumer and Akkad, King of Babel." The new rulers worshiped the gods they found in possession, and for a time won the good will of the conquered. Adding little to the culture they assimilated, losing one Babylonian dependency after another, and leaving very few records behind, the Kassites finally succumbed before the attacks of other eastern highlanders, the Elamites and the Assyrians.

Assyrian Rise and Fall. — The latter people had been a threat to Babylonian power ever since the fourteenth century, and the successful campaigns of Tiglath-Pileser I, about 1090–1060 B.C., carried his ferocious iron-wielding Assyrians across the domains once held by the Hittites and their neighbors the Mitanni, and brought him tribute from the Phoenician cities and other erstwhile Egyptian dependencies on the Mediterranean coast. His immediate successors, pressed hard by nomadic Aramaeans and " Chaldeans," could not hold the ground he had gained. Eventually, however, the caravan-intercepting herdsmen of the grassland fringe, destroyers of material prosperity and political organization, were subjugated. Soon thereafter — some eight-hundred-odd years before our era — the armies of Assyria once more extorted tribute from Sidon and Tyre, and a century later conquered Palestine. Undergoing many vicissitudes of good and evil fortune, the Assyrian empire finally collapsed toward the end of the seventh century B.C. After an interregnum enlivened by the forays of the Medes (an Aryan-speaking people whose capital lay in the highlands of Iran), and by a transitory Babylonian renascence that carried the Hebrews into captivity, the vastest Near Eastern empire of all was created from the ruins of its forerunners by the hardy Persian hillsmen under the leadership of Cyrus, King of Kings (*regnebat c.* 558–528 B.C.). But this brings us to the verge of Chapter Four, " The Mobile Background of the Greco-Roman World," and we must retrace our steps.

The Crudity of Assyrian Law. — The Semitic-speaking Assyrians who conquered the land beyond and about the Tigris brought with them their tribal god Asshur, and as his people made good their mastery, he became the national patron of all Assyria. Myres vividly describes him and his followers:

Asshur was a stern friend, and a ruthless enemy; no Assyrian monarch dared ascribe his achievements but to the command and the ruling of Asshur. Was Asshur angry? then the best-planned strategy would go awry. No aggression was too unprovoked, no atrocity too cruel, to be perpetrated on the enemies of " Asshur, my good Lord." No ancient nation — not even Rome — has practised *Realpolitik* . . . with the callous fanaticism, the sheer indifference to humane pretences, which mark Assyrian warfare and, still more, Assyrian diplomacy. What its expectant victims thought of it is written large in Jewish prophecy.[13]

To an even greater degree than is the case with Babylonian thought, we must rely upon Assyrian laws for our data. A code of the thirteenth or fourteenth century B.C. has been found which appears to have been in effect over a region quite as extensive as that which once yielded jurisdiction to Hammurabi. Curiously enough, the Assyrian code seems almost entirely free of the influence of the Babylonian, in spite of the great prestige of the latter and the use of a common cuneiform script; administrative and legal terms, officials, and procedure are different. Moreover, the Assyrian is much more uncouth and immature than the Babylonian, although the latter represents a period at least six centuries earlier. Again, the Assyrian is much less general; it seems to be little more

than a compilation of prevailing practices, and is hardly worthy
of being termed a code. Finally, it bears within it great inconsistencies; impulsive savageries and equally impulsive provisions for
mercy, both foreign to the calculated rational domination of Hammurabi, mark the Assyrian compilation.[14] It may be, however, that
as the Assyrians became accustomed to the administration of a
great empire they stripped their laws of the peculiarly limited and
local traits so strikingly stamped upon the fourteenth-century collection. Unfortunately, nothing has yet been unearthed which
throws any light on conditions after the ninth century B.C., when
the Assyrian empire, long a going concern, entered upon its greatest era.

Inferior Status of Woman; Ownership. — Only about half of
the fourteenth-century code, comprising some eighty-seven legible
laws, is available. Of these, about two-thirds are devoted to
women, who occupied a position much inferior to that granted
them in Babylonia. When discussing sex discrimination in Chapter
One, we quoted the Russian proverb, " A husband is father of his
wife "; its Assyrian equivalent would be, " A husband is owner of
his wife." Indeed, wives or daughters could be pawned, so to
speak, and if redemption proved impossible, the creditor could
dispose of them to others if consent was given by the debtor.
Moreover, the husband alone had the privilege of divorce and,
unlike the situation in Babylonia, stood in no danger of having to
pay his wife alimony, although he did have to compensate her
father, to whom ownership reverted, for the loss of her virginity.
Moreover, the father could reclaim, through the divorced wife,
the dowry she had originally brought with her.

The Assyrians were at one with the Babylonians in the high regard in which they held private property, although only about one-
fourth of the extant laws relate to it, and these primarily to real
estate and irrigation rights, always important in the " fluvial civilizations " of the Near East. In addition, there are eight laws
which deal with the wrongful sale of animals, children, or slaves
held in pawn; had we the other half of the code, this number might
be increased.

Equality before the Law. — Criminal law deviates strikingly
from that of Babylonia, for there is no provision for the differential punishment of the non-slave male population; the patrician
could not disproportionately retaliate for personal injuries. Considering the date of the Assyrian code, it seems evident that there
had not yet been time to adjust it to the social stratification arising
through imperial conquest; no legal distinctions were made be-

tween patrician and plebeian. The embryonic stage of criminal
law had been left behind, however, for there is little evidence of
private vengeance or of go-betweens privately hired to compose
feuds between families. The Assyrian state stood supreme and administered its punishments (far more barbaric than those of
Babylonia) through its own officials. All the criteria of positive
law were therefore present. At the same time, notice should be
taken of the fact that penalties appear often to have been for the
benefit of the plaintiff rather than for the whole body of citizens
or the state, with the exception of one sanction frequently applied;
namely, a month in the king's service.

Epitomizing, we may say that Assyrian social thought, as represented by law, was distinctly cruder than its Babylonian forerunner
— at least in the middle of the second millennium B.C. Some
instructive contrasts could be drawn with Hittite social thought
on the basis of information derived from sources of the same
kind, for the code of the cosmopolitan Hittites was notably
milder than even that of the Babylonians.[15] More relevant matters claim our attention, however, and we proceed at once to another region of the Near East exhibiting social thought of a
far more complex character than any we have yet encountered in
this chapter.

" The Gift of the Nile." — In fertility the Nile valley resembles the rich alluvial lands of Mesopotamia, but is quite unlike
them in other respects. Except at the fan-shaped Delta, with a
convex seafront of about one hundred and fifty miles and with a
depth, to the point of the triangle where the river is a single
stream, of about one hundred, the Nile valley is very narrow in
proportion to its length. The width ranges from a maximum of
fifteen miles near the northern end to a minimum of about two
near the First Cataract, six-hundred-odd miles south of the Mediterranean. The Delta has long been called Lower, and the Valley
ribbon beyond, Upper Egypt. The stretch above the First Cataract has never been considered part of Egypt *per se,* although the
valley as far as the southern confines of Nubia, over twelve hundred miles from the river's mouth, was sometimes under Egyptian
rule (more often nominal than real).[16]

The first dwellers in Egypt proper did not all belong to one
breed, but to three, which when fused brought forth types showing
pervasive similarities. Sergi (herein followed by later anthropom-
etrists) has classed them with the dark-whites of the Mediterranean fringe, at least as far as the upper classes are concerned,
although under the sun of the Nile the Egyptians burned to a red-

dish bronze. Other breeds, such as the Nubians and the Negroes of the extreme south, the Semitic-speaking nomads from the northeast, and miscellaneous Hittites, Mitanni, Greeks, and Persians, from time to time brought in new elements, among the dominant strata in particular (Ikhnaton!), but without fundamentally altering the numerical preponderance of types arising primarily from the first fusions.[17]

Totemism in Egypt? — The earliest inhabitants were nomadic hunters, who entered the Nile valley (perhaps twenty thousand years ago) as the grassland plains surrounding it slowly dried out.[18] They apparently brought with them one of the most widespread principles of social organization and thought known to man; namely, totemism. Its essence consists in the practice of claiming some non-human material entity, inorganic or organic (usually the latter), as ancestor of a kinship group, and of giving its name to the group or its members or both. Other features frequently found are abstention from the use of this eponymous ancestor as food, and incest taboo where the other members of the totem are concerned, thus leading to exogamy. In its classical form the totem is always an animal, which is never killed by its human " descendants " except in religious ritual, and these " descendants " always maintain among themselves the incest taboo, but the classical doctrine has been so uncritically applied that it has fallen into disrepute. For this reason, among others, virtually no mention was made of totemism in Chapter One. In discussing it here, we are not exposed to the assumption that we regard it as basic to or even of major significance in preliterate life; our remarks bear primarily on the Egyptian phenomena [19] as evidence of a system of implicit social thought.

The valley dwellers have left behind them many pictures which show them hunting, fighting, or working the soil under the apparent sanction of ensigns or standard-like emblems representing, among other things, falcons, cows, elephants, antelopes, and the like. This was long termed zoölatry, but recent scholarly opinion [20] assigns a possible totemic significance to these standards, calling them the " rallying marks " [21] of totemic clans (see note for terminological discussion).[22]

In many preliterate totemic groups, authoritative rule lies in the hands of the elders; in the language of Chapter One, totemic gerontocracy maintaining traditional domination is not uncommon. In Egypt, recorded religious traditions refer to a past, not far removed from the beginning of the historic period (*c.* 4000 B.C.), in which groups of men were ruled by the *saru*, i.e., by the elders. This is one more bit of evidence showing that it is possible, although not yet proved, that totemic organization held sway in prehistoric Egypt.[23]

The Nome Vanquishes the Totem. — When the clear light of history begins, however, the clan is a thing of the past; the nome has taken its place. The difference between the two may be stated thus: the clan is organized on the basis of kinship, the nome on the basis of territory (compare Greek *genos* and *deme*). The original Egyptian word is *spat,* meaning " division," and its hieroglyph represents a rectangular piece of ground divided into squares by intersecting lines. There is much other evidence to show that the sign indicated an essential feature of the nome; namely, that it was a settled group, perhaps originally a clan, that had adapted its social organization to a specific plot of the Nile bottomlands which it then methodically diked, irrigated, drained, tilled, and otherwise cared for. In other words, the needs of Nile agriculture helped to impose territorial organization on groups that may once have been united only in the totemic bond.[24]

The ensign was retained as a symbol of the nome, and each ensign gave its name to the territory it ruled; " the eponymous patrons of the nomes . . . [played] this part down to the end of Pharaonic civilization." [25] It must be noted, however, that the ensign did not always remain the same, and thereby hangs a tale.

Wars of Nome-God and Capital-God. — Every nome capital had its gods, some of whom presided in one only, while others — Horus the falcon, Hathor the cow, and Seth the antelope — ruled over several. In the first case the god of the capital city is blended or clearly connected with the ensign of the nome; that is to say, the totem of the clan remains that of the town. In this new capacity the totem usually becomes at least partially human in appearance. In the second case, where the same god is found holding sway over several nomes, the result is usually two patrons: the older one, the local totem, degraded from his rank but still kept as ensign of the nome (usually in non-human guise), and the new patron, the lord of the capital, manifesting himself either in a non-human shape *distinct* from the ensign or, more frequently, in humanized form. Moret, the leading Egyptologist of contemporary France, explains this state of affairs as follows:

. . . the god of the nome, where he is different from the god of the capital, is usually an ancestor, or a conquered patron who has yielded the effective lordship over the territory to a successor. After some social and political change, he has been supplanted, but not destroyed, by the god of the capital.[26]

In many cases this change is shown to have been brought about by combat:

. . . the invaders perpetuated the memory of their conquest by allowing the ensign of the former occupants to survive in humiliating conditions [mutilation; a falcon with its claws sunk in a vanquished antelope, etc.] . . . these allegorical figures preserve the living memory of the wars waged by rival clans or peoples for the possession of the nomes.[27]

Analysis of the list of nomes shows that over half were of the two-patron type indicating conquest, and among the victorious patrons occur frequently Horus, under his own name or in different forms, Hathor, who figures in the traditions as his wife but who governs cities in her own right as well, and their common enemy Seth, often defeated but still powerful, with many cities claiming him as god. In spite of the splitting-up of the soil and of worship which the multiplicity of nomes and their gods reveals, however, well-marked tendencies toward religious and political centralization appeared even before the founding of the early dynasties; the nomes had in some measure been forced together into a few larger aggregates, each clustered about a common chief god. It is perhaps this phenomenon which Breasted has in mind when he speaks of a First Unity [28] in the protohistoric period, perhaps as much as a thousand years before the First and Second Thinite Dynasties (3315–2895 B.C.), which are the earliest in the historical record.[29] In other words, the nomes were being welded into kingdoms before the dawn of attested Egyptian history.

The Osiris Myth and Its Social Significance. — Many of the protohistoric kings called themselves Servants of Horus, a title that is of great importance in the relation of the Pharaoh (" great house ") to the Osiris myth, as we shall later see. The god Horus was a god of light and the upper air, an inhabitant of the entire celestial kingdom, a falcon (in the earliest hieroglyphic writing the sign which determines the idea of " god " is the falcon on his perch). Now in addition to the Servants of Horus who held sway in Lower Egypt, there were also numerous kings who rendered allegiance to Seth. This god appears sometimes as an antelope, sometimes as a greyhound or anteater. These animals seem to have been originally the totems of a group of clans in Upper Egypt who succeeded in imposing their rule on many of the nomes of that region. Seth soon came to symbolize the forces opposed to the Servants of Horus, the god of light and the sky, and in this capacity personified darkness, the thunder, the storm, the deadly Khamsin wind of the desert, and the gods of the much-feared

" Asiatics." Periodically, in the setting of the sun, the waning of the moon, and eclipses, Seth tears out the eyes of Horus, and Horus retaliates by castrating Seth. If, as Moret thinks likely, these legends preserve an echo of pre-dynastic battles between the Delta nomes of Horus and the Valley nomes of Seth, it is interesting to note that the god Thoth, who intervened between the two contending parties and assuaged their wounds, held sway at Hermopolis, strategically situated at the juncture of Lower and Upper Egypt.

As a result of a series of combinations and recombinations too intricate to recount here, Horus the Elder (the form in which we have thus far encountered him) yielded place to Osiris the father-brother, Isis the mother-sister, and Horus the consanguine child. Osiris seems to have been the god of a group of Delta nomes influenced by fertility rituals. He was slain and hacked in pieces by his brother Seth (prototype of Satan), but Isis brought the fragments together and through her magic arts had herself impregnated by the dead god and gave birth to Horus, " the Avenger of his Father." [30] Henceforward Horus the Elder virtually disappears from Egyptian religion, his place and his attributes having been taken over by Horus the Child. The legend has been interpreted thus:

Osiris-Anzti, King of . . . the Delta, symbolizes one of those chiefs who concentrate in their own person the hitherto diffused authority of the clan . . .

At the same time as the clans become sedentary and the power is individualized in Osiris, the marriage custom changes. Being attached to the soil, man no longer goes out of the clan to look for a wife; exogamy is succeeded by endogamy; Osiris marries his sister Isis. Hence a sacred prestige attaches to the consanguine marriage, which will continue to be a feature of Egyptian manners. The institution of marriage, which the couple Osiris and Isis are supposed to have revealed to men, marks the evolution of a society from the uterine system, in which each woman of the clan believes herself impregnated by the totem, to the paternal system, in which the husband is the true father.

Nevertheless, the Osirian family retains traces of the earlier social system, and these traces will survive indelibly in Egyptian society. . . . Like Horus, every Egyptian child will mention that he is " born of such-and-such a mother," and will seldom give the name of his father. . . .

In sum, beneath the anthropomorphic legend of the agricultural god, we see the development from clan to family, and the movement from the power of the community to that of the individual. That is why the kingship of Osiris served as a foundation for the later institution of monarchy; that is why his reign is always recalled in the texts as the most ancient pattern of a lawful, civilizing government.[31]

Pharaoh as Osiris and Ra, Nile and Sun. — But the significance of Osiris is even greater than this, for as a fertility god he symbolizes the alluvium-bearing Nile itself, as well as the yearly resurrection of vegetation which the beneficent inundation brings. The preservation of the body of Osiris is absolutely necessary if he is to beget upon Isis his posthumous son Horus. It is this which explains the anxious care bestowed upon the bodies of the dead Pharaohs, the kings whose awe-inspiring labors, both cause and consequence of the charisma bestowed upon them, finally led to their deification. When they were crowned they in some sense became Horus, and they also participated in the fate of Osiris during life and death.

Copying his lord Osiris, Pharaoh is " he who gives water to the earth." At the moment when Seth seems about to triumph, when the Nile dwindles and the black earth turns to powder, Pharaoh casts into the river the written order for the flood to begin, and lo! the waters rise.

Great in majesty is Pharaoh; more than Osiris, more than Horus, is Pharaoh. Long before the Thinite kings, the astronomers of Heliopolis in Lower Egypt created a calendar (4241). They chose as the starting point for their year the middle of June, the time of the rising of the Nile (although the star Sothis provided a fixed point of reference). Heliopolis was simply the Greek name for the city the Egyptians called " the House of Ra," and Ra was the deified Egyptian sun itself, the sun-god. By some process not yet altogether clear, Pharaoh became the personification of Ra as well as of Osiris and Horus. On his coronation the king " rose " on his throne like the sun in heaven, and through a system of thought similar to that of ancient China, he continued to " rise " every day in order to ensure the reappearance of " the orb of beneficence." [32]

Egyptian Social Monism. — With the control of both Nile and sun centered in himself, the ruler became the very embodiment of the Egyptian course of nature, and hence he inaugurated the great seasons of agricultural labor by turning the soil with a mattock, opening the irrigation canals with a pick, and cutting the first-fruits of the harvest with a sickle. Here again the Chinese analogy comes to mind. Eventually, by the time of the Memphite dynasties at the beginning of the Old Kingdom (2895–2540), the belief in the necessity of the Pharaoh's functions issued in such strict and effective control by his officials that all private property in land disappeared; the whole of the arable area of Egypt became the monarch's domain:

In the imagination of the people the king possessed magic secrets so potent that the products of all nature " came forth at his voice " as soon as he uttered the master-word; so he was the great " provider " for his people; he " presided over the provisions for all living beings." [33]

In this way there was created for the Pharaohs a right to rule founded upon their perfect identity with the gods, the first kings of mankind, confirmed by tradition and sustained by the magic rites which gave to the king all the material and moral powers of divinity. In order that the Pharaohs might be sure of eternal life they simply had to be identified with Osiris in every possible way. Periodically rejuvenated by an Osirian ritual during life, the same ritual, applied to their dead bodies, reanimated them as Osiris had been similarly reanimated for all eternity, and simultaneously re-vivified the whole of Nature.

   The Rise of Ra and of Pharaoh's Autocracy. — Under the Memphite rulers, however, the powerful priests of Heliopolis (like Hermopolis strategically situated at the juncture of Delta and Valley) saw to it that the Pharaoh's attributes as incarnation of Ra, the sun god, were steadily augmented. From the Fifth Dynasty (2680) onward, Ra began to attain spiritual ascendency over Horus and Osiris, although an open conflict was averted by ingenious reconciliation of rôles. Thus, for example, it was by Ra's order that the murdered Osiris had been resuscitated by Isis and other gods. Again, it was through a divine tribunal sitting at Heliopolis that Osiris was " justified " (*maâu*), in spite of the accusations of Seth, and promoted to the rank of an " upper god " like Ra. Horus presented a more delicate problem, for in his earliest rôle as Horus the Elder, the divine falcon, he had been a rival of Ra, the sun. A solution was found by admitting him to the company of Ra as Horus the Child — in other words, as a secondary deity deriving his title merely from the fact that he was his father's son, and a posthumous son at that.

   As Ra, king of the world, the Pharaoh's autocratic powers reached their greatest expansion. Rising with his heavenly counterpart at dawn, he went about the royal business as one who, like Louis XIV, " *le Roi Soleil*," could calmly say, " *L'État, c'est moi.*" Essential to the task of administering his vast realm were the Pharaoh's functions of " commanding " and " judging." Commanding consisted in " uttering words " in which he " spoke justice " (*maât*). Judging was " dividing words," making a decision between one thing and another. These acts of the king, essentially similar to the Chinese magical realism in which the word created the thing signified,[34] constituted justice, truth (*maât*) — that is, public law. There were as yet no codes analogous to that of Hammurabi; law was improvised by the king's decrees, as occasion demanded, on the basis of traditional lore :

> Law was "what the King loves"; the opposite was "what the King hates"; and what he hated above all was that "his word should be transgressed." Pharaoh's subjects did not discuss the law given by the King: . . . "I am the King's true liegeman, I am the Great God's true liegeman; I love good, I hate evil; what the God loves, is acting justly." [35]

The Faith of the Pyramids. — Source of all law, owner of all land, center of all divinity, the Pharaoh realized in his single person the powers that in Europe could have been embodied only by a pope-emperor. And just as there was but one living man in whom the natural and the social orders of Egypt were centered, so there was but one dead man upon whose fate in the after-life all else depended, and he too was Pharaoh. The incredibly arduous labors entailed in the building of the Pyramids, labors that must have enlisted nearly the whole population of Egypt, Upper and Lower, had far greater significance than mere gratification of the vanity of an earthly ruler, as has been strikingly pointed out :

> It is almost impossible to conceive such a gigantic effort . . . demanded by every King in his turn. It gives one some idea of the material power and moral authority of Pharaoh; *it enables one to see the better into the mentality of the people which worked for the salvation of a single man,* the master whose protection was perhaps despotic, but pretended to the justice, foresight, and benevolence of a god; it helps one to understand the religious reverence with which a whole people bowed down before the dead body of the King, who conquered death by the grace of Osiris, and protected his kingdom after his decease. We see that the royal pyramid was an act of *faith.*[36]

Pharaoh Himself Is Judged. — And yet in spite of the faith that moved to such mighty works, we find that the era of the Great Pyramids, which began with the Fourth Dynasty (2840), did not long endure. Starting with the Fifth Dynasty (2680), the larger part of the resources of the kings went into great temples honoring Ra. Their tombs were correspondingly of smaller dimensions, but what they lacked in masonry they made up for in prayers inscribed on the granite walls of the inner chamber. The men de-

voted to the business of praying, the priests of Heliopolis and elsewhere, were beginning to exert influence that was eventually to
have dire consequences for the autocratic rule of the Pharaohs.
By the end of the Fifth Dynasty (2540) Pharaoh, in theory the
earthly god-priest from whom the lesser clergy derived all efficacy,
found himself confronted by an oligarchy of prelates who " went
over his head " in appeal to the heavenly powers. They had been
initiated by their calling into the innermost secrets of the religious
rites, and dared to subject the Pharaoh himself to the judgment
of Ra. It seems that the earlier logic (or pre-logic) that had made
possible the complete identification of Ra and Pharaoh had given
way to one in which the latter, while still divine, had to be " justified " (*maâu*) before Ra if he was to attain immortality. Moreover, the Egyptian habit of personifying the attributes of the divine ruler had generated a goddess, daughter of Ra, called *Maât,*
Justice, before whom the Pharaoh himself had to render account
of his actions. Breasted points out still another source of the conception:

> It was [the] . . . impressive vision of an enduring state and its ever-
> functioning organization which contributed substantially to the larger,
> more comprehensive meaning of the Egyptian word " Maat," till it had
> come to signify not only " justice," " truth," " righteousness," which the
> men of the Pyramid Age discerned as something practiced by the indi-
> vidual, but also as an existent social and governmental reality, a moral
> order of the world, identified with the rule of the Pharaoh. The chief
> judge in the Egyptian courts of justice wore on his breast a lapis lazuli
> image of the goddess *Maat* and to indicate the winning litigant, the judge
> was accustomed to turn this symbol towards the winner as the two liti-
> gants stood before him.[37]

Priests and Princes: Oligarchs. — Emboldened by the belief in
powers before whom even the priest-king-god would be judged,
the clerics engaged in a practice not yet extinct in even the Western
world: they vested in themselves the complete control of the
" fields of the god " which served as perpetual endowments of the
temples of Ra. Moreover, these priests were not only exempt from
taxation (or its equivalents) and supervision, but also claimed
authority at court as the result of kingly concessions rashly made
in return for prayers and other professional services.

The next stage in the pruning of the Pharaoh's prerogatives
was marked by the growing independence of the provincial nobility, the nomarchs. As Egypt advanced in population, wealth,
and complexity, it was no longer possible to follow the patrimonial
practice of drawing the rulers of the nomes and other high officials

from the family of Pharaoh alone, as had previously been the custom. Powerful officials not in the kingly line managed to entrench themselves as semi-autonomous nomarchs, as miniature Pharaohs within the confines of their own nomes. They even dared to call upon the gods of their own cities rather than Ra as sanctioners and witnesses of their practice of *maât*. Indeed, they went further than this: they claimed to share in immortality, not merely in the underground Osirian life, but in the celestial domain of Ra. " The detailed royal ritual is not yet engraved on their tombs, but at least they have won the principle; heaven is open to them after death, as to the King." [38] Inasmuch as religious and civic rights were inseparable, the priests and princes acquired claims, eventually to become hereditary, to administrative offices, with a privileged position beside the Pharaoh in this life and the next.

Disorganization and Plebeian Revolt. — This whittling-away of spiritual and temporal autocracy could not fail to have far-reaching social consequences. To engage in a single great act of faith preserving the natural and social orders is one thing. To be badgered by the rival bureaucrats of priests, princes, and Pharaohs is another. Discontent reared its seditious head among the common folk. These commoners included not only the traditionalistic husbandmen and herdsmen, but also a dangerously large class of artisans living in the towns, together with no inconsiderable number of mobile traders, sailors, and "caravaneers" who brought the precious luxuries of the outside world, and many necessities as well, into " the Gift of the Nile."

Down to the last Memphite dynasty (2540) the commoners seem to have benefited very little by the gradual developments that yielded so many advantages to the oligarchy of priests and nomarchs. At long last, however, a series of usurpations, wars between nomarchs and between nomarchs and Pharaohs, so weakened the forces of traditional, charismatic, and rational domination that the masses rose in revolt — here, there, everywhere:

. . . civil and religious rights had gone to whoever was strong enough to take them, and the individual had given rein to his appetites and kicked over every kind of discipline . . . the common people of Egypt [flung] . . . itself on the prey. Sometimes oppressed and always forgotten, it took its revenge on the recognized authorities and overwhelmed them in a wave of violence and rapine.[39]

The appalling situation is clearly foreshadowed in a number of literary documents, is strikingly described in others, in still others evokes profound reflection freed from the burden of traditional lore (an unprecedented thing in Egypt of the day), and finally, in the social thought of sage and priest, calls forth Messianic prophecies.

Machiavellian Precepts and Proverbial Kindliness. — In *The Teachings Addressed to Merikere,* an unknown ruler of a city split off from the domain of Pharaoh gave his son " the counsels of craft and patience which his difficult position inspired." [40] He mentions revolts of nomarchs, defeat of the troops of Pharaoh by the Thebans, and attacks by " Asiatic " nomads, of whom he says:

> Behold the wretched Asiatic . . . he can never abide in one place, his legs are ever in motion, and he is always fighting since the days of Horus [the Elder]. He conquers nothing, but neither is he conquered. [41]

Again the conflict of nomad and tiller, foretaste of the day when the Hyksôs, the Shepherd Kings, at last conquering something, were to rule over the Egyptians. But there is much more in the *Teachings* than Machiavellian precepts, echoes of disorder, and observations about nomads. Breasted seems entirely right in calling attention to the continuance of the pervasive influence of *maât* as exemplified by such utterances as: " More acceptable is the virtue of the upright man than the ox of him that doeth iniquity "; " Comfort the mourner, afflict not the widow, deprive not a man of the possessions of his father "; " Be not harsh, kindness is seemly "; ". . . embellish thy seat in the necropolis as one who hath done righteousness (*maât*)." [42]

Certainly this is far from systematic social thought, but proverbial wisdom it undoubtedly is, and the part such lore has demonstrably played in later formulations, Oriental and Occidental, is by no means inconsiderable. The Hebrew Book of Proverbs, for example, contains a large number of sayings gleaned from the " wisdom literature " of Egypt. This included, in addition to the *Teachings* discussed above, the *Instruction* of Kagemni, the *Precepts* of Ptah-hotep, the *Teaching* of Amen-em-apt, the *Maxims* of Ani, the *Negative Confessions,* the Ptolemaic *Precepts,* and several minor collections. Like proverbial lore elsewhere, these adages are traditionalistic, practical, concrete, and useful as means of social control. Humane considerations are by no means lacking, but the politic or the expedient is usually uppermost. [43]

Crisis, Release, Introversion, Foreboding. — Social thought of a more relevant type is splendidly illustrated in this same disorganized period — at a later stage of disorganization, perhaps —

in the *Collection of Sayings* attributed to Onkhu, a priest in the House of Ra. Onkhu offers in these utterances an instructive spectacle of the release (in William James's and Teggart's sense — see Chapter Seven, section on " The Effects of Liberation ") engendered by crisis. The revolutionary situation in which he finds himself is so astounding that he abandons the style of the wisdom writings and " seeks unknown words, expressed in new language, free of all repetitions of the usual formulas, and removed from the traditions left by our ancestors." [44] For perhaps the first time in Egyptian history, a thinker attempts to cast off the guidance of the past — which in times of social disorganization always appears as external restraint — and to find within himself, through personal meditation, the clue to the good life for man and society. Soon, however, Onkhu's reflection gives way to lamentation: " Changes are going on; . . . every year weighs heavier than the last . . . all men are criminals; on all which was respected they turn their backs." [45]

Pessimism and the Hope of Justification. — Small wonder, then, that writers more capable of sustained introversion should indite pessimistic dirges. A thousand years before Job and the Preacher men proclaimed to those who would hear the vanity of all things. In one a harp-player chants, in mood of deepest scepticism, the futility of the efforts of the Pyramid-builders:

> Behold the places thereof;
>> Their walls are dismantled, . . .
> None cometh from thence
>> That he may tell us how they fare; . . .
> Encourage thy heart to forget it,
>> Making it pleasant for thee to follow thy desire,
> While thou livest . . .
>> Lo, no man taketh his goods with him.
> Yea, none returneth again that is gone thither.[46]

How like the Rubaiyat!

> They say the Lion and the Lizard keep
>> The Courts where Jamshyd gloried and drank deep: . . .
> Ah, make the most of what we yet may spend,
>> Before we too into the Dust descend; . . .
> Not one returns to tell us of the Road,
>> Which to discover we must travel too.

Far more pessimistic than the *Song of the Harp-Player*, individuated and disillusioned though he was, is the *Dialogue with His Soul of a Man Weary of His Life*. So unrelieved is his gloom that

Breasted calls him the Misanthrope. At the beginning, the man recommends death to his soul as a blessed release from woe, but like the harp-player the soul remembers the neglected and violated tombs of the great, " whose offering-tables are as empty as those of the wretched serfs dying like flies . . . along the vast irrigation dikes." [47] There is but one solution; namely, the following of the maxim, " Eat, drink, and be merry, for tomorrow we die."

Up to this point there is little essential difference from the *Song of the Harp-Player,* but the author of the *Dialogue* goes on to a conclusion vastly more significant: life, in his own day and generation at least, offers even less than death. Lamenting his own unfortunate lot — " Lo, my name is abhorred " — he continues with a great social diatribe, worthy of an Amos, in which a recurrent note is his loathing of his demoralized fellows and the injustices they perpetrate. Returning to the contemplation of death, he idealizes it as release from suffering. He even expresses the Job-like hope that although the immortality of the Osirian rites is a delusion, a second life at least long enough to be " justified " — i.e., to be favorably judged by *Maât* before the throne of Ra — will give solace to his soul. Thus persuaded, the soul of the unhappy man at last yields, and passes on to be with " those who are yonder." [48]

Messianic Prophet: Ipuwer. — Last of all in this survey of the writers of the " times of trouble " are Ipuwer and Nefer-rohu, two writers who have been called prophets in the specific Hebraic sense of that term, perhaps because of their appearance in " times of trouble," their scathing description and probing analysis of social ills, and their penchant for describing remedies of the distinctly idealistic type. Ipuwer is an old sage of the Tenth Dynasty (*c.* 2200 B.C.) who reveals to his royal master the anarchic state of affairs of which the latter, sunk in sloth or dotage, chooses to be blissfully ignorant. First, the circumstances responsible for the turmoil: " Asiatic " invasions; plebeian (*huru* — poor) uprisings; destruction of titles to property; insecurity so great that " no one tills the ground "; high mobility — " Tents, that is what men build "; unemployment; famine and plague; falling birth-rate; reversal of traditional values — in a word, revolution.

These things, dreadful as they are, says Ipuwer, have generated conditions even more dreadful: kings are being abducted by the riotous poor; Pyramid tombs are broken open; collection of revenues is impossible; frightened officials desert their posts because of repeated assaults. The revolution has overturned everything: the nobles and former rich are in distress, and if possible flee the country; brutal, greedy, and stupid plebeians arrogate to themselves all the wealth; the newly rich manifest the utmost insolence, especially if they were menials before the revolution; noblewomen serve their former slave-girls and yield their bodies to commoners — " He who used to sleep without a woman from poverty, now finds noble ladies . . ."; the children of the high-born can no longer be distinguished from the baseborn.

Most important of all, the magical and religious secrets which were the monopoly of the kings, the princes, and the priests have been disclosed to the masses and, not content with equality on earth, they storm the gates of paradise. The example set by the rebellious oligarchy has taught the plebeians to demand for themselves a future in heaven like the kings'. Up above every man will be summoned before the tribunal of Ra, and not content, like the Misanthrope, with mere " justification " in the sight of *Maât,* will by means of virtue (or magic!) pass all barriers and become a god.

There is only one remedy, says Ipuwer, for this universal frenzy. The exalted and truly righteous must take refuge with the gods, reminding them of " the offerings, the sacrifices, which the men of the old days piously paid," and must put their trust in the goodness of Ra, the " Shepherd," who " will throw cold water on the fire." [49] The end of the text is incomplete and there is some doubt as to which passages refer to Ra and which to an ideal sovereign who will carry out Ra's will for Egypt, but in any case the utopian and Messianic note is clear, as Breasted indicates:

> The element of hope, that the advent of the good king is imminent, is unmistakable in the final words: " Where is he today? Doth he sleep perchance? Behold his might is not seen." With this last utterance one involuntarily adds, " as yet." The peculiar significance of the picture lies in the fact that, if not the social programme, at least the social ideals . . . already included the ideal ruler of spotless character and benevolent purposes. . . . This is, of course, Messianism nearly fifteen hundred years before its appearance among the Hebrews.[50]

Nefer-rohu's Prophecy, Propaganda, Prediction, Plan? — Apparently hopes of this sort were widely prevalent; some scholars maintain that Ipuwer's prophecy is part of a whole *corpus* of similar utterances, many of them of prior date. In any case we know that he soon had a successor, the Heliopolitan priest Nefer-rohu. This prophet, real or spurious, was active about the time of King Amenemhet I (1995–1965 B.C.), a great ruler in that brilliant Twelfth Dynasty which did so much to make the later portions of the period called the Middle Kingdom (2160–1660 B.C.), a time of order and prosperity. Nefer-rohu made his prophecy as impressive as possible by giving it a fictitious antiquity of a thousand years. He confidently asserted that Amenemhet, who at the beginning of his reign was simply a sovereign of Upper Egypt, would become ruler of Lower Egypt as well and put an end to the " time of troubles " — as indeed he did. Breasted raises the question as to whether the prophecy was a shrewd bit of political propaganda devised by Amenemhet to make his conquest of the Delta easier. It may have been this, or a prediction after the event, or a genuine example of social forecasting. Perhaps — who knows? — it was the latter, for Nefer-rohu frankly disclosed the fact that the new Pharaoh was not a son of the old royal line. Propaganda or prediction after the event would hardly have revealed so damaging a fact. It is possible, moreover, that Nefer-rohu was not only a successful social forecaster but also a skilled social planner (if there can be any such!); at all events, he set forth a program to be followed by his ideal ruler. This had two chief requisites: first, extermination of the invading " Asiatics " and Libyans; and second, the building of the " Wall of the Ruler " to cut off entry from the northeast, " so that the Asiatics shall not be suffered to go down into Egypt. They shall beg for water after their traditional manner, in order to give their flocks to drink." [51] Inasmuch as Amenemhet's prestige was already so great that civil strife had waned — " Those who . . . devised rebellion . . . have stilled their mouths for fear of him " — there would then be no obstacles to the restoration of order within the borders of Egypt: " Justice (*maât*) shall return to its place, and injustice shall be cast out." [52]

Oligarchy Defeated, Aides Distrusted. — Right again! Under the Theban Pharaohs, of whom Nefer-rohu's ideal ruler made real was the first, much was done to extend the sway of *maât*. Amenemhet I labored mightily toward this end, although in the very nature of the case he had to utilize as his administrators men who had grown up in the disorganized era before the restoration of unity, and who hence were not entirely trustworthy. In fact, he seems never to have had full confidence in his subjects, and his gloomy presentiments were justified, for in his old age an attempt was made to assassinate him. In his *Teachings,* addressed to his son, he gave counsel anticipatory of Machiavelli's advice in *The Prince:*

> Hearken to that which I say to thee,
>   That thou mayest be king of the land, . . .
> That thou mayest increase good.
>   Harden thyself against all subordinates.

The people give heed to him who terrorizes them . . .
When thou sleepest, guard for thyself thine own heart;
For a man has no people
In the day of evil.[53]

Nevertheless, the reforms instituted by Amenemhet I were slowly carried through by his successors, and the era known as the Rule of the Just Laws dawned. Their task made easier by the levelling effects of the revolution, the Theban Pharaohs broke the remaining power of the oligarchy of nomarchs and priests. *Immortality and " Liberty ": Social Pacifiers.* — But what of the most dangerous group of all? What of the plebeians? The problem seems to have been solved, as ever, by " a judicious mixture of force and consent." For force, a reorganized army with bronze weapons; for consent, a revival of the Osirian faith that gave to the masses assurance of personal immortality. Under the Twelfth Dynasty there was established in Upper Egypt a holy city of Osiris, and his cult seems to have become the equivalent, so far as its public significance was concerned, of that of Ra under the Memphite dynasties of the Old Kingdom. To be sure, a poor man would not be buried with all the magnificence of an earthly Pharaoh, but what did that matter?

His obscure name, traced on a wooden tablet, or an ostracon, would be followed by the qualification, " Osiris N., Justified . . . Privileged Lord . . ."; in the next world he would have the divine offerings; and he would go to heaven like a Pharaoh.[54]

When we recall the fact that religious and civil life were inseparably intertwined, it becomes apparent that the concessions above indicated necessarily brought with them " a share in government, admission to the offices, employments, and secrets of the royal administration." [55] Moreover, the peasant was emancipated from serfdom; he rose to the rank of " a free, hereditary tenant with a legal status." [56]

The Eloquent Peasant. — This is not to say that he thenceforth had no troubles, for the *Tale of the Eloquent Peasant* plainly shows the contrary. It is a vivid story of his age-long struggle, as serf or as freeman, against the grasping greed of Egyptian officialdom:

A needy peasant sets out for market with his laden donkeys. One of these nips a mouthful of grain on property in charge of an unscrupulous official, who has barred the public path in order to bring about such a happening, and who immediately seizes the pretext to rob the peasant. Hastening to plead his case before the steward under whom the unjust official serves, he manifests such a gift for bombastic rhetoric that the delighted steward brings him before the royal judges in order that Pharaoh may hear and be amused. Not knowing that under the Rule of the Just Laws which Pharaoh has created his case is already won, the peasant is put through his paces to the extent of nine successive appeals, each more magniloquent, more high-flown, than the last. He displays complete knowledge of the accepted social thought of the Middle Kingdom, and if he dares to lecture the royal judges, it is because the Pharaoh has made a point of acquainting all his subjects with the duties expected of officials. The story has a happy ending for, as Maspero puts it, " the King caused his donkeys and their load to be restored to him, and in addition, he gave six slaves, male and female, to the eloquent wind-bag who had amused His Majesty." [57]

Pharaonic Socialism. — One outstanding implication of this edifying tale, as Hertzler points out,[58] is that the actual level of administrative performance often fell considerably short of the standard upheld by the ruler. Another inference lying ready to hand is that appeal to higher officials, and even to the Pharaoh himself, may have been encouraged as part of a general drive toward centralization. Certain it is that the lower orders were on the whole loyal to the Theban monarchs (especially to vigorous rulers such as Senusert I, contemporary of Hammurabi), even though the burden laid upon them was heavy. Not only had the peasant been freed from serfdom, but the artisan also enjoyed a new liberty:

The craftsmen, hitherto attached to the workshops of the King, the temples, or the nobles, were now freed, and as it were, secularized . . .
No doubt the craftsman, like the peasant, had to make a " declaration " and to pay registration-duties, but once he had settled with the fiscal authorities he was free . . .[59]

Further, the channels of vertical social mobility were more widely open than ever before; through the office of bureaucratic scribe, in particular, the gifted son of the plebeian could rise above his father's rank. An ideology making for the circulation of the élite arose:

The scribe is released from manual tasks; it is he who commands. . . . No scribe fails to eat the victuals of the King's House . . . his father and mother thank God for it.[60]

Peasant, craftsman, and scribe — all participated in the service of the state, but the first two were guided by the third, the bureaucrat. Some compensation for their subordinate rôles they had, however, for after the state had taken its share of harvests and receipts, the rest became their property as a sort of " wage " or " gift " from the Pharaoh. Conditions such as these were favorable to the growth of a middle class (*nemhu*) acquiring wealth by labor and dependent on no master but the monarch himself. Material interests as well as participation in the Osirian ritual helped to cement allegiance.

The Pharaoh Enjoins Justice. — It was probably at about this time that the traditional address delivered by the Pharaoh to high state officials before their assumption of office took form. Under the title of the *Installation of the Vizier* it thereafter played an important part in Egyptian social thought; *maât* became more and more a *civic* virtue. Some of the most significant passages follow:

> Behold it (the vizierate) is not to show respect-of-persons to princes and councillors; it is not to make for himself slaves of any people . . .
> Behold, when a petitioner comes from Upper or Lower Egypt (even) the whole land, . . . see thou to it that everything is done in accordance with law, that everything is done according to the custom thereof, [giving] to [every man] his right . . .
> Forget not to judge justice. . . . Look upon him who is known to thee like him who is unknown to thee; and him who is near the King like him who is far from [his house].[61]

Here, surely, is rational domination in highly developed form. The famous Rule of the Just Laws is at hand — but before this beneficent rule could attain its fullest efficacy, an even greater degree of solidarity than that prevailing in the first half of the Middle Kingdom (2160–1660 B.C.) was necessary. How was it attained? Not primarily by consolidation from within — i.e., not chiefly through immanent development — but as a result of what Toynbee has called " challenge-and-response," the equivalent of Teggart's " intrusive factor " and " release." (See Chapters Seven and Twenty.)

Ethnocentrism vs. the Shepherd Kings. — It will be recalled that Babylon was raided by the Hittites about 1925 B.C., a date which coincides with the early part of the Twelfth Dynasty in Egypt. During the " time of troubles " that preceded the advent of the Middle Kingdom, " Asiatics " apparently contributed much to the general disorganization, as we have already seen. Now about 1900 B.C. one of the Theban Pharaohs, Senusert II, seems to have extended the hospitality of Egypt to other Asiatic migrants, *presumably from Palestine,* who had been expelled from their homes as a consequence of the Hittite inroads.[62] Sometime near 1760 B.C. the Kassites, riders of " the ass of the mountains," set up their rule in Babylon, and within a relatively short time thereafter the Egyptians once more had to defend themselves against " Asiatics on the march." Were they the Kassites themselves, or were they Palestinian peoples set adrift by the Kassite disturbances? We noted above that a group of Palestinians had been driven into Egypt by the Hittites two centuries before; did they make common cause with the newcomers? Whatever happened, Egypt soon lay prostrate under the Shepherd Kings, the Hyksôs, who profaned temples, looted cities, and placed upon their leader the double crown of Pharaoh. After about a century of Hyksôs misrule, the Egyptians rose in revolt and expelled the invaders. Theban rulers once more ascended the throne, and the New Kingdom, sometimes called the Empire, started on its triumphant way.[63]

Kingdom Becomes Empire. — The royal authority only gained by the conflict with the Shepherd Kings : the Rule of the Just Laws reached its climax, and the whole of Egypt formed " Pharaoh's Fields " — the country had never been more completely in the moral and material possession of the monarch than at the beginning of the New Kingdom. Moreover, the great age of Egyptian imperialism dawned; in the sixteenth and fifteenth centuries B.C., Nubia was conquered and an Egyptian army reached the banks of the Euphrates. In Mesopotamia, however, a reaction set in against the new masters, and in 1479 B.C. the great battle of Megiddo ("Armageddon") was fought. This, when followed by other campaigns, gained for Egypt the hegemony of the Near East for over a century, i.e., until 1360 B.C.[64] Egyptian diplomacy spread its network further than it ever had before, even utilizing cuneiform writing, as we have already noted, in its voluminous correspondence and records. Moreover, a policy of intermarriage with Babylonian, Mitannian, and Hittite princesses helped to reinforce the bonds of conquest and diplomacy with those of kinship.

At the end of the reign of Ikhnaton, however, the Concert of Nations directed by Egypt abruptly ceased. Syria fell into the hands of the Hittites; Palestine was abandoned to the Amorites and the *Habiru* (nomads apparently the same as those known to us as the Hebrews), and Egypt itself was in uproar.[65] What had happened?

From Ra to Amon to Aton. — This question can be answered only when the changes undergone by Egyptian religion are understood. Attention was called to the fact that after the " time of troubles " the masses were pacified by a democratization of Osirian immortality. We must now take note of the fact that this was accompanied by a complete readjustment of the Heliopolitan cult of Ra. The Theban monarchs had brought with them from Upper Egypt a local god called Amon, from whom they claimed descent. The powerful Theban priesthood succeeded in identifying Amon with Ra, and the Heliopolitan priests, their power broken by the revolution, were forced to accept the interpretation. Thenceforth Amon-Ra, with his great temples at Karnak and Luxor, became the most widely worshiped of all the incarnations or aspects of Ra. Under the sway of the almost theocratic priesthood, many sovereigns proclaimed their descent from him through the adoption of names such as Amenemhet, Amenhotep, Amenophis. Sun-god though he was, however, Amon-Ra retained a limited and even anthropomorphic character; he stood guard at the *Egyptian* frontiers, where he had built the gates restraining all strangers from entering his inviolable domain. Moreover, he was identified with the *Egyptian* Pharaoh, not with the ruler of a world empire.[66]

In the days of Amenophis III (1415–1380), the emperor under whom the Egyptian hegemony was most far-reaching, there began to develop the worship of the sun in a new form, not as the anthropomorphic Amon-Ra, but as the solar disk with outstretched wings, Aton (whose name recalls Adonai, the " I am that I am " of the Old Testament).[67] In spite of the fierce resistance offered by the Theban priests, a great religious overturn was effected in the reign of his successor, Amenophis IV: Amon was driven from his temples, his inscriptions obliterated, his priests thrust out of office, and the Pharaoh's name changed to Ikhnaton, " Glory of Aton."

The Hybrid, Heretic King and His Monotheistic Imperialism. — This ruler was one of the offspring of the mixed marriages inaugurated during the imperial epoch. In his veins flowed the blood of the Aryan-speaking princes of Mitanni, a Syrian strain derived from his mother Tii, and, of course, a Theban infusion.[68] The biological intermixture as such perhaps meant little, but it does indicate a motley cultural heritage. With such a background, plus the demands of empire, it is small wonder that Ikhnaton adopted a universal faith, a solar monotheism devoted to the beneficent life-giving father of all that exists — earth, water, plants, Egyptians, and *foreigners*. In the beautiful hymns Ikhnaton is reputed to have composed, no distinctions are drawn between strangers and Egyptians (in fact the strangers are mentioned first). All men are in the same degree Aton's sons and must regard themselves as brothers — anticipation of "God hath made of one blood all nations of men." For perhaps the first time in history, religion is conceived as a bond uniting men of differing color, language, and customs. As Breasted puts it:

It was universalism expressed in terms of imperial power which first caught the imagination of the thinking men of the Empire, and disclosed to them the universal sweep of the Sun-god's dominion as a physical fact. Monotheism was but imperialism in religion.[69]

And Moret:

. . . only the King of Egypt is left as the qualified mediator between Aton and humanity . . . through him [Ikhnaton] alone the divine benefits will be extended to the men of Nubia, Syria, and Egypt. Mystic and altruistic enthusiasm are here mingled with political astuteness and national egoism . . .

In this . . . [Ikhnaton] was distinguished from a Sargon or a Hammurabi, who did not attain the same degree of comprehension of the great problems of international policy.[70]

Climax and Collapse. — Social thought had passed from totemic loyalties, the rivalries of nomes and their conquering deities, devotion to Pharaoh as Nile or as Sun of Egypt, to exalted mystic cosmopolitanism transcending the confines of these limited sacred societies and including the whole known world in a new supernaturalistic-ethnic-political union. The detached universalism of the stranger, i.e., of the man in whom culture contact and the comparison of peoples has generated that power to abstract from the concrete and particular which is one aspect of mental mobility, manifested itself in the person of the Heretic King. In his willingness to say, in effect, *Ubi bene ibi patria,* he passed beyond the bounds of the social thought that up to his time had dominated Egypt.

But mingled with his gold was dross; fanaticism and weakness prevented him from making peace with foes at home and from conquering enemies abroad. Under his immediate successors the vast empire crumbled so badly that not even the mighty Ramesids (1300–1169 B.C.) could wholly restore its glories. His heir, Tutankhaton, "Living Image of Aton," changed his name to Tutankhamon, "Living Image of Amon," under the influence of the priests of Amon, who had regained all their former power. All? Far more than before! As a preliminary step they established

title to one-seventh of the land of Egypt, and then, by debasing
the Osirian ritual to the level of magical incantation that assured
immortality to the purchaser regardless of violations of *maât,*
dragged the masses in their train. No social thought of any novelty or consequence came from the sacerdotalists or their dupes.
Finally, the First Priest of Amon became Pharaoh, but the theo-
crat and his successors reigned over a shrunken domain. The native Egyptians ceased to be a serious fighting force; Nubians,
Negroes, and Berbers settled in the fertile territories they had so
long coveted. To be sure, the Berber Kings who reigned at Bu-
bastis in the eleventh century B.C. maintained the old claims to
Syria for a long time; the Hebrews feared Egypt only less than
they feared Assyria and Babylonia. Moreover, material prosperity did not seriously diminish, and personal piety survived the
inroads of magic. Traders from Phoenicia and later from Ionia
and mainland Greece set up their stations in the Delta and traf-
ficked busily; Greek mercenaries, drawn by what to them were
rich rewards, bolstered the supine Pharaohs against attack. When
Athens was rising to the dominion of men's minds there was still
wealth and comfort in the Nile valley, as Herodotus garrulously
related, but the spacious days of empire and even of independence
were gone. After the Persians came Alexander, and the succeeding Ptolemaic interlude was closed by the clash of Roman arms.[71]
Finis Aegyptiacus.

Israel: Blood, Its Bonds, and Mishpat. — The ancient Hebrews belonged to that large but formless and dispersed group
of Semitic-speaking nomads whom the Egyptians called " Asiatics." They inhabited the southern grassland margin of the Fertile Crescent and the pastures and oases of the Arabian Peninsula.
Probably closely related by blood to the Amorites, Aramaeans,
the " bitter and hasty people of the Chaldees," and the Hyksôs
or Shepherd Kings, their wanderings led to much intermixture
with the Hittites, Canaanites, and other Near Eastern groups.

Hebrew social organization, when the historical record opened,
was based on the patriarchal family. The " ruling father," " possessor," " lord," or *baal* presided over an array of wives, concubines, sons and their families, daughters until marriage took them
elsewhere, and slaves. As among the Assyrians, wives were considered the husband's property, and their number was usually determined by his wealth, inasmuch as outright purchase was the
rule. Patriarchal authority had wide scope; e.g., power of life
and death over children — of which an instance is afforded by
Abraham's contemplated sacrifice of Isaac. Such authority was

not unlimited, however, for certain well-recognized customs held the father in check; tradition could not be lightly flouted.

These " omnibus families," akin to the Greek *genos,* were ordinarily units of a larger whole, the clan (see note 22, this chapter, about terminology). This organization seems to have been based primarily on the need for protection against blood-feud vengeance and, of course, for exacting such vengeance from others. The largest, oldest, or strongest of the families exercised a sort of preëminence, imposing its *baal* as head of the clan. Here again, however, authority was limited by tradition; the council of elders made up of the heads of all the clan families guided the chieftain in the path of *mishpat.* This *mishpat* was simply the distillate of the accumulated rules of right conduct forming part of the clan's traditional heritage. Although it is usually translated as " justice " or " righteousness," it was in no sense abstract, and in this respect at least resembles *tao, dharma, maât,* and other symbols of the sacred phases of social life. In fact, *mishpat* may be thought of as the concrete core of traditional domination.

The fact that the clan functioned chiefly in blood-feuds naturally made its fundamental bond the claim to blood-kinship (although, after appropriate ritual observances, outsiders might be adopted into it). Hand in hand with solidarity against foes without went an *ethôs* of brotherhood within. Struggle for the common welfare was enjoined, and when successful, distinctions were granted and recognized by the clan as a whole. Moreover, there was much mutual aid in time of crisis, and although family ownership and inheritance were well developed, certain types of property, notably in grazing grounds and wells, were held by the clan in common. The practice of exogamy, together with vicinal proximity to and conflict with other nomads, sometimes massed several clans into a tribe. Tribal units were originally dominated by elders having virtually theocratic powers, but in later periods the elders often yielded to charismatic warrior-chieftains.[72]

Spirits, Mana, Gods, Church. — Animism and animatism were both in evidence among the early Hebrews. Every extraordinary object, event, or person was believed to have an indwelling spirit, known as an *el* or " power," which was also its *baal* or " possessor." [73] In other words, to be " possessed " by an *el* was literally to be owned by it in the same way as the *baal* or " ruling father " of the patriarchal family owned his dependents.

These animistic *elohim* (plural of *el*), able to leave their habitations at will, also had animatistic or manaistic traits. They were charged with a mysterious energy, called *kodesh,* making contact with them dangerous. *Kodesh* has the same ambivalent meaning as the Latin *sacer* from which " sacred " is derived: holy and taboo, or blessed and cursed. Instance the sacred ark of Yahweh:

> Uzzah put forth his hand to the ark of God, and took hold of it; for the oxen stumbled. And the anger of Yahweh was kindled against Uzzah; and God smote him there for his error; and there he died by the ark of God.[74]

Yet in spite of their perilous character, the *elohim* were regarded as friendly in the main. The localities to which they were fixed were usually " high places," sometimes guarded by a *kahin* or " diviner," prototype of the *kohen* or priest. Each clan or tribe had its own chief divinity, always considered the ancestor of the group. Worshiped at the " high place " where the divinity had manifested " extraordinariness," the ritual always had a *group-representative* character. Herein the ancient Hebrews exemplify the situation epitomized by Durkheim in the phrase, " No religion without a church."

The ritual involved animal sacrifice, and some sacred object, usually a stone, was daubed with the resulting blood, thus renewing the blood bond between the *el* and his offspring.[75] Some writers, notably Robertson Smith, see totemism in such conduct, and maintain that the pig and other tabooed animals were regarded as totemic ancestors. Recent research casts doubt on this hypothesis, but as long as it is not made all-explanatory it need not be ruled entirely out of court.

In addition to this worship of the ancestor of the clan or tribe, there was also worship of family ancestors, represented by small images in human form called *teraphim*. Traces of this are to be found in the Old Testament as late as the time of David (*regnebat c.* 1020–980 B.C.).[76] Here again the group-representative character of supernatural entities among the early Hebrews is apparent.

The Coming of the Hebrews. — Cross-currents of migration throughout the Near East, noted here and there in previous sections of this chapter, carried Semitic-speaking peoples into Palestine at least three thousand years before Christ. Assimilating Sumerian culture early, these peoples — for whom we shall frequently use the Biblical term " Canaanites " — developed a complex civilization that carried on commercial and diplomatic correspondence with Babylonia in cuneiform writing, and, as we have seen, with Egypt as well.

The general disorganization of the Egyptian empire that accompanied the quarrels between the adherents of Amon-Ra and of Aton, in the latter days of Ikhnaton's ill-fated reign, had as its immediate consequence the ruin of the Pharaohs' military power in all of Syria. This was probably hastened by the onset of the Hebrews (*c.* 1375 B.C.), some of whose ancestors had probably fought as *Habiru* mercenaries in the ranks of the Babylonians centuries before. The Hebrews at first succeeded in occupying only the hill country of Canaan, where they continued to follow the nomadic way of life and to uphold its *mishpat.*

Fairly soon, however, many of them filtered down into the Canaanite cities and villages, and followed urban occupations or practiced agriculture. This mingling of cultures was accompanied by interbreeding, and had it not been for occasional fresh invasions from the desert, the nomadic heritage would have been notably lessened and perhaps hopelessly diluted.

The " Asiatics " Assert Themselves. — The latest of these invaders arrived about the twelfth century before our era, settling in the hills of southern Canaan. The newcomers, who exercised great influence on their predecessors, had apparently been among those " Asiatics " who invaded or took refuge in Egypt. They may have entered at the time of the Hyksôs, and they told of the preeminence of one of their number, Joseph, who had been " set over all the land of Egypt " as Pharaoh's vizier. As the story had it, they later fell into disfavor, and were used as slaves in the construction of state buildings and the like. An especially rebellious Hebrew, Moses, was said to have escaped to the desert near Mount Sinai. There he apparently found refuge with clans worshiping a strange deity named Yahweh (or Jehovah). Adopted into the Yahweh worship, he returned to Egypt full of faith in the power of this god to deliver his people.

The deliverance did occur, and Yahweh was given the credit, thenceforth receiving the devotion of Moses's fellow-clansmen. Moses led them to Sinai, Yahweh's holy mountain, where they made a covenant with the other Yahweh-worshiping groups, agreeing to the common observance of certain rituals and to the first henotheism of the Hebrews; namely, the promise to serve no other than Yahweh. " Thou shalt have no other gods before me . . . for I Yahweh thy god am a *jealous* god."

Armed with this new faith, the followers of Moses slowly moved on to and invaded Canaan, settling in the south. Peace was soon made with the Hebrews who had preceded them, to whom they communicated their enthusiasm for Yahweh. Elaborate genealogies were developed that linked all the Yahweh wor-

shipers with one or another of twelve tribes having a common
ancestor, Jacob or *Isra-el* (" God rules ").

Culture Conflict in Palestine. — From the time of Sargon I
and the " Divine Naram-Sin," viz., about twenty-eight centuries
before our era, Syria had been a dependency of Sumeria and
Babylonia, as we have already noted. Not until the Hittites and
Kassites wrenched away the pillars of Babylonian imperialism,
beginning about 1700 B.C., did Palestine pass into other hands
for any great length of time. Its Canaanite inhabitants paid quite
as much attention to trade and property as did the Mesopotamians : private ownership of land, mortgages, and exaction of interest were firmly established. The resemblance did not cease here :
they worshiped the Babylonian mother-goddess Ashtart in addition to their own *elohim* and *baalim*. The consequence was the
widespread practice of fertility rituals that, like those of Babylon, included sacred prostitution.

When the first contingent of nomadic Hebrews encountered
this civilization, they at first rejected it, for the *mishpat* of the
desert granted little place to private ownership of land and none
to fertility orgies. But as they gradually trickled into the Canaanite villages and urban centers, they took over a great deal of
Canaanite culture; a process of assimilation began that not even
the onset of the Yahweh-worshiping clans from the south permanently interrupted.

There was no massing of the Hebrews as a whole against the
Canaanites; groups of clans and tribes fighting in a scattered and
desultory way seized what territory they could and left the rest
to the prior inhabitants :

And Yahweh was with Judah; and he drove out the inhabitants of the
hill-country; for he could not drive out the inhabitants of the valley,
because they had chariots of iron. . . .

Yet the children of Manasseh could not drive out the inhabitants of
those cities; but the Canaanites would dwell in that land.[77]

And the land in which the Canaanites dwelt was quite as often
as not better adapted to agriculture and trade than that occupied
by the newcomers. Sporadic conflict went on for centuries, but
finally a *modus vivendi* was achieved : cities that could not be conquered but that were nevertheless greatly inconvenienced by repeated sieges granted full political rights to the Hebrews, and the
latter reciprocated by adopting a number of Canaanite tribes *en
bloc* as " sons of Israel." The result, naturally, was amalgamation :

And the children of Israel dwelt among the Canaanites, . . . and they took their daughters to be their wives, and gave their own daughters to their sons.[78]

New Yahwehs for Old. — The racial and cultural hybrids issuing from these unions [79] were naturally more numerous in the areas where the Canaanites had been most thickly settled; i.e., in urban and agricultural regions. The upland and desert margins harbored groups relatively unmixed in blood and, although no longer wanderers, still cherishing the nomadic *mishpat.* Early in Hebrew history, then, there appeared antagonism between those near-nomadic tribesmen clinging to the old Yahweh of the desert and the settled devotees of a new Yahweh who took on many of the traits of the deities previously worshiped by the Canaanites.

Conspicuous exponents of the earlier standpoint, of the " old Yahweh," were certain groups such as the Rechabites, Kenites, and Nazarites. They went to extremes, wishing even to abolish agriculture and urban life, associating these as they did with the worship of the *baalim.* Other intransigeant groups were the roving bands of ecstatic, dervish-like *nabim,* heirs of a long desert tradition, of whom we shall have more to say when discussing the prophets.

The new Yahweh was less exclusive than the old: the name *elohim,* originally plural, came to be applied to him in the singular, and he was also thought of as the *baal* or owner of various sacred objects. The " high places " became his shrines, and he appropriated the names of the former possessors. " The cult that went on at these sanctuaries was the same that had always been maintained at them, only now it was rendered to Yahweh."[80] This included even the sacred prostitution previously mentioned; [81] as the *nabim* or " proclaimers " put it, " Israel went a-whoring after strange gods."

Judges and Kings. — When the Hebrews first settled in Canaan they had felt no need of a central government; the ancient system of patriarchy and gerontocracy seemed to suffice, except for those intertribal disputes which the " judges " were called upon to settle. These arbiters were simply outstanding local leaders, approved by the elders, who had also gained the charisma of virility and skill through success in warfare. Finally, however, they were confronted by problems beyond their powers; the Philistines, from whom the land of Palestine is named, made their disturbing entrance on the scene. Apparently an Aryan-speaking people, they may have been a contingent of the " Peo-

ples of the Sea " who harried the Egyptian coasts at the time of
the Great Migrations within the dawning Greek world (discussed at length in Chapter Four). It has even been surmised
that they were fleeing from that Cretan turmoil, marked by the
final fall of Cnossus, which occurred some twelve centuries before
Christ. Hard-fighting warriors, with body-armor and feathered
helmets, the Philistines routed the Canaanites and Hebrews west
of the Jordan and took possession of the southwestern coast.
To the challenge they offered the Hebrews responded by choosing
Saul as the first of the " kings."

Saul was really not much more than an influential tribal chieftain, for his kingdom was simply a loose federation of tribes
which chose him for their " servant." [82] Retaining a " judge "-
like simplicity in his kingdom in the hills, he sought valiantly to
uphold the nomadic ideals. All his days Saul battled with the
Philistines, but they were not finally checked until the time of
his successor, David. In the story of David's conflict with Goliath,
the giant Philistine champion, we probably have an epic pervaded by the nomadic ideal, i.e., the unarmored shepherd wielding a primitive weapon, the sling, defeats the full-panoplied
bearer of elaborate arms made by urban artisans.

From King to Despot. — But when his kingdom became
secure against attack, David slowly drifted away from the *mishpat* of the desert, and in middle age assumed certain prerogatives
of the Oriental despot. Repentance gained for him the esteem
of his fellow-tribesmen and subjects, however, so that to succeeding generations he symbolized the ideal Hebrew ruler (and
hence figured largely in the Messianic hope).

This was not the case with his son Solomon, who almost
wholly abandoned the nomadic ideals for those of the Canaanites.
Not content to support his régime through gifts, spoils, and
tribute (in accordance with the " collegial " *mishpat* of the
desert), he imposed forced labor and taxation, proceeding on
the Canaanite theory that the people and the land belong to the
king. Palaces, temples, and fortresses were built in profusion,
and in addition, foreign trade was monopolized. A by-product
of the last-named activity was a large harem of foreign wives,
acquired through the making of trade treaties. These wives
occasionally led Solomon to honor strange gods; nevertheless,
throughout most of his life he was a dutiful worshiper of
Yahweh. Not the old Yahweh of the desert *mishpat,* however;
the new Yahweh sanctioning the agricultural-urban *mishpat* of
the Promised Land gained his allegiance.

Revolt, Secession, Consolidation. — Public resentment was soon aroused. The burdens of the régime were grievous to bear, and in addition the desert *mishpat* was violated. An unsuccessful revolt served to bring into the open the two conflicting theories of the state implicit in the two rival *mishpats.* The nomadic type was similar to the governmental compact: rulers were looked upon as servants chosen by the people to guard the interests of all. Following the tribal pattern, public affairs were on a " collegial " basis: every man had a voice and stood on practically the same level as his fellows. The Canaanite theory, on the other hand, resembled Hobbesian absolutism: the state was held to be an aggregation of individuals who had irrevocably yielded their rights to an absolute ruler in return for the protection he gave from " the war of each against all."

Solomon's son Rehoboam went further in the direction of absolutism, casting aside the restraints imposed by the council of elders and following the advice given by the younger warriors and courtiers.[83] The result was another revolt, which this time was successful; northern Israel split off. Yet, in spite of opposition and cleavage, the institution of monarchy consolidated its powers. The old tribal leadership was completely replaced by courtiers, counsellors, and professional soldiers or *gibborim* who held the unruly in check. An elaborate officialdom appeared, bringing with it the beginnings of rational domination.

Class Conflict and the Nomadic Ideal. — All this signified the emergence of a privileged class which, together with the increasing burden of taxation, divided the population into two opposing groups: the creditor patricians, and the debtor peasants and laborers.

During the storms engendered by these differing centers of pressure, the upholders of the nomadic *mishpat* compiled the Covenant Code.[84] Dating from the ninth century B.C., but based on older formulations, it " was the simple statement of the old customs of right which had prevailed in Israel and were to prevail." [85] Toward dependents and inferiors this code was peculiarly favorable: the poor were to be protected against oppression, interest on loans was forbidden, and widows and orphans were to be shielded.

As in the nomadic period proper, loyalty to near relatives and to fellow-Israelites was enjoined. Such ethnocentrism usually involves a dualistic ethic, and the Covenant Code is no exception: lying, cheating, and violence were not condemned when dealing with the " they-group." [86] This aspect of Hebrew law later had interesting results, for in Christian countries the Jewish money-lender was permitted to charge a high rate of interest to outsiders, but was forbidden to do so within the " we-group ".[87] Far down the centuries the nomadic *mishpat* both stimulated the mutual aid of fellow-tribesmen and " separated the peoples."

Clairvoyants and " Proclaimers." — Those who were most active in keeping the nomadic *mishpat* before the Hebrews as that which Yahweh required were the great eighth-century prophets. We know that they did not spring forth overnight; even before the Hebrews left the desert there had existed among them confraternities of wandering ecstatics having traits strikingly similar to those of shamans and certain types of medicine-men. In Canaan they were looked upon as clairvoyants, and for a small sum they would " reveal " the whereabouts of lost or stolen goods and the like. They continued their practice of travelling in bands, and deliberately cultivated ecstatic frenzy as the technique for obtaining divine revelations.

Bound by tradition to the life of the desert, these " holy men " were always a conservative force " standing for loyalty to the ideals of the nomadism of the days gone by, hostile to the advance of civilization and culture. . . ." [88] As the monarchy developed, these seers took a more and more active part in public affairs, defending the rights of the poor, instigating revolt, and warning presumptuous rulers. As a result, they came to be looked upon as " proclaimers " of righteousness or *mishpat* rather than as clairvoyants. As Eiselen puts it, they were forthtellers rather than foretellers. There was no sharp break, however, in the prophetic tradition; for example, ecstatic traits, often accompanied by what would now be termed symptoms of mental disorder, were retained to the very end.[89] This could hardly be otherwise, for upon it depended their recognition as emissaries, bearers of the divine charisma,[90] of Yahweh.

Emissary prophets, not *exemplary* prophets! [91] This distinction is vital to an understanding of Amos, Hosea, and their like. " The Lord Yahweh hath spoken; who can but prophesy? " [92] recurs, in essence, again and again. The Hebrew prophets considered themselves as the mouthpieces of Yahweh, as emissaries with a trenchant message, not as exemplary representatives of the life of contemplation and mysticism. It is this active quality which distinguishes the Hebrew *nabi* from the Hindu ascetic, the Egyptian priest, or the Brahman exponent of the highest *dharma*. The Hebrew prophets have a long line, but we shall deal specifically with only Amos, Hosea, Micah, and Ezekiel.

Amos the Unafraid. — The first half of the eighth century
B.C. was remarkably peaceful in Palestine, for the westward
expansion of the Assyrian Empire kept many of Israel's troublesome neighbors busy in warding off attacks. Trade flourished and
wealth rolled in; the result was much pomp and circumstance
among merchants, courtiers, and ecclesiastics alike.[93] Yet the
poorer classes reaped little benefit: taxes remained high, there
was much foreclosing of mortgages, and the legal tribunals were
corrupt. The wealthy lived in great extravagance and debauch-
ery, utterly ignoring the plight of the poor.[94]

It was in the midst of this situation that the prophet Amos
appeared (*c.* 750 B.C.). In his mode of gaining a livelihood and
his dwelling-place a better representative of the nomadic *mishpat*
could scarcely be conceived, for he was a shepherd from the
rugged southern hills. Journeying to the cities to eke out his
livelihood and to sell wool, he observed with indignation the
violations of the old sacred order. The *ethôs* of mutual aid had
been completely cast aside; Hebrews were selling fellow-Hebrews
into debt, and in many other ways [95] were flouting the blood bond
and its obligations. " Let *mishpat* roll down as waters," cried
Amos, " and *mishpat* as a mighty stream." [96] Although he did
not openly incite to revolt, his repeated proclamations that a
society based on injustice could not long endure fell little short of
" seditious utterance," and the *gibborim*, the henchmen of the
king, must have eyed Amos askance.

Characteristic of the reactionary radicalism of Amos is the
fact that most of what he denounced had been warned against
frequently in principle, and often in specific precept, in the Covenant Code. But Amos never implied that he was preaching anything new; his strength lay precisely in his reawakening of tradition. He did, however, broaden the sphere of Hebrew ethics
slightly, for in proclaiming the doom of a corrupt Israel he also
proclaimed the doom of its corrupt neighboring states, not because they were " lesser breeds without the law," but because
they were unjust and licentious.

Hosea the Long-Suffering. — Ten years or so after Amos
had proclaimed his message, Hosea began his peculiar career.
The signs of social upheaval that Amos saw on the horizon had
become realities. After the death of Jeroboam II in 743 B.C.,
wars of succession stripped the patricians of their wealth and
still further ground down the poor. Marauders plundered and
Assyria threatened. The vacillating foreign policy of the Hebrew
rulers led them alternately to pay tribute to Assyria and to seek

an Egyptian alliance. Hosea denounced the injustices wreaked on the poor by princes and priests, poured scorn on the fruitless attempts to gain security by playing off one great power against the other,[97] and condemned the " murderers " who successively usurped the throne.

We should note in passing that Hosea had drifted away from the desert *mishpat* in some measure, for he gave his approval to monarchy so long as it did not involve misdoing in the sight of Yahweh. In other words, he verged on assertion of the divine right of kings, but also maintained that when a king did wrong it was *prima facie* evidence that the charisma of the Almighty had departed from him.

As far as Israel and its present iniquitous rulers were concerned, said Hosea, there could be but one issue: Israel would be " swallowed up," made to " eat unclean food in Assyria," where " the Assyrian shall be their king." [98] After this time of discipline and trial ordained by Yahweh to teach his children obedience, proclaimed the prophet, the old order would be restored.

Hosea was also greatly concerned about the unfaithfulness of Israel in cult observances. The *baalim* were being worshiped by the peasants to ensure the fertility of their fields, and sacral harlotry was consequently rampant. Hosea declared that Yahweh himself was the giver of the products of the soil, and that Israel was Yahweh's wife who had deserted him and was playing the harlot with the *baalim*. This, as we have seen, was more than mere metaphor, but in addition Hosea's own peculiar domestic destiny lent it figurative meaning. He had married a temple prostitute — commanded, as he said, by Yahweh — in order to remind everyone that Yahweh's wife, Israel, was a harlot too. Israel's infidelity was the root of all her troubles, said poor Hosea, and the Assyrian captivity which he foresaw was to be only temporary — just long enough to bring Israel to her senses and back to Yahweh her forgiving spouse, even as Gomer would some day leave.her evil ways and return to her loving husband Hosea.[99]

With the best will in the world, it is difficult to avoid seeing in Hosea's conduct some trace of that emotional instability elicited and fostered by the tradition of the ecstatic seers.[100] But unstable or not, his premonitions of Israel's doom were borne out by subsequent events. In 734 B.C. Tiglath-Pileser III of Assyria took captive some of the border tribes. Thirteen years later one of his successors conquered the northern kingdom and carried most of its population captive to Assyria. In spite of Hosea's assurances to the contrary, repentance was of no avail; they were never returned to their native land. Only Judah, the southern kingdom, remained.

Micah, Foe of the Cities. — Judah remained for a brief respite, but only on sufferance; the power of Assyria finally waned, but that of Babylonia correspondingly waxed. It was only a question of time before the highroad between Egypt and Mesopotamia would be cleared of the obstinate and stiff-necked folk who persisted in living amid the passing chariot wheels.

As soon as the brief respite began, the prophet Micah made his protest against the injustices that had arisen in Judah. Like Amos he came from a nomadic hamlet in the hills, and he too was a man of the people who spoke to them in a direct, untutored way. The similarity does not stop here, for in the vigor and bitterness of his denunciations one seems to hear another Amos. Micah, however, not only vented his fury on the urban patricians but also " proclaimed " against the oppression of the peasant classes by the landed gentry [101] (who, by the way, had become urbanized).

But with all his flaming zeal, Micah was neither monarchomach nor revolutionist; Yahweh, not man, was to remedy social evils. That is to say, he did not challenge the rule of righteous kings, for their very righteousness attested their charismatic powers. Yet after all, Micah was sufficiently subversive, for he regarded the urbanization of Israel as the major causal factor in the deterioration of Hebrew society, and his remedy was simple: to wit, destruction. Israel could never regain her nomadic integrity without the laying waste of those cities of iniquity where " the heads thereof judge for reward, and the priests thereof teach for hire, and the prophets thereof divine for money . . . therefore shall Zion for your sake be plowed as a field, and Jerusalem shall become heaps." [102] This done, it would be possible to return to the purity of simplicity, and hence to Yahweh's favor.[103]

The Significance of the Eighth-Century Prophets. — Micah, Hosea, and Amos played a very important part in the conflict of cultures in Canaan. When the brotherhood *mishpat* of the desert was being displaced by the stratified *mishpat* of the cities, they reasserted the nomadic sense of values. It was impossible completely to restore the desert standards, but they did succeed in separating the worship of Yahweh from that of the *baalim,* and thus in diminishing the Canaanite element in Judaism.

By the same token, the importance of magic in Hebrew religion was markedly reduced, for the cult of the *baalim* had been strongly magical. Weber maintains that the stress laid by the prophets on the ethical, anti-magical requirements of Yahweh had far-reaching results in the economic life of the Western world. These results flow from the fact, says Weber, that Calvinism drew heavily on the Old Testament, and thus confirmed the anti-magical, rational bent that was so conspicuous in *early* modern capitalism.[104]

However this may be, the prophetic protest remained a force to be reckoned with in Judaism. To be sure, there were reactions in favor of the Canaanite fertility rituals, and the rise of an organized priesthood checked the ecstatic influence. Nevertheless, in the Deuteronomic Code, the Holiness Code, and other priestly adaptations of the prophetic standards, Yahweh reappeared as a god of brotherhood and benevolence among the Chosen People. Concessions were made to the Canaanite point of view, inasmuch as recognition was given to the many feasts and ceremonies which had been developed since the adoption of the agricultural festivals; but for all that, the nomadic *mishpat* still loomed large.[105]

Organismic Conceptions vs. Individuation. — Parallel with the new developments we have recounted went others tending toward the breakdown of family and clan solidarity and the growth of individualism. For the early Hebrew groups, J. M. P. Smith's statement of their underlying organismic thought applies:

> The individual involves the group in the results of his crime. The group has sinned through a member; therefore the group must suffer punishment. Nor is it at all essential that that member of the group who committed the offense be punished rather than some other member or members. The social body has offended and that body must suffer — the particular member of the body that suffers is a matter of slight consequence. When one member suffers, all the members suffer with it.[106]

There were exceptions to this organismic rule even in the Covenant code, the oldest body of laws in the Old Testament, and as time went on they increased in number.[107] Nevertheless, many centuries passed before a self-conscious doctrine of individualism developed in Israel. When it appeared, it was used to justify practices differentiating the " person " from the " plurality pattern " that had long been going on. We have already noted the individuating if not individualizing effects of culture contact in Canaan; clan loyalties dissolved, and " individuals cut loose from the laws of common humanity " emerged.

Urbanization, trade, industrialization, class cleavage, and the like all furthered this tendency. Paradoxical as it may seem, the prophetic message also held within it the germ of individualism. When whole tribes went over to the Canaanite worship, only those members who in some way lacked the feeling of group solidarity could hearken to the prophet.[108] Moreover, the continued emphasis on ethical ideals could not but be destructive of morals — if we grant the validity of the familiar distinction between morals and ethics.

Far more important, in all probability, were the effects of the Babylonian Captivity. During this first exile (586–538 B.C.) the Hebrew state was virtually non-existent, and no one knew when, if ever, repatriation would take place. Many of the less traditional Hebrews found their way into the realms of Babylonian culture, and when the Captivity ended a large number chose to remain in their new home. The promises of the synagogue began to take the place of the Promised Land; religion became personal rather than national in implication.

Ezekiel, Denier of Solidarity. — It is therefore in Ezekiel, the prophet of the Exile, that we find individualism most clearly expressed. (Jeremiah's individualism, although the outgrowth of the impending doom of the Exile, was of a more personal character and hence is less relevant here.) [109] Ezekiel had undergone the Babylonian Captivity while still a youth, and was greatly distressed because of the hopelessness with which his fellow-exiles viewed their plight. Holding to the old doctrine of solidarity, for good and for evil, they held that they were suffering because of the sins of their fathers as well as their own.

The reaction of Ezekiel was to preach extreme individualism: each person sustains his own individual relation to Yahweh. One man's crimes do not bring condemnation upon the heads of other men, nor, conversely, does the righteousness of one secure immunity for others who have sinned. Going still further, he asserted that in the coming judgment the past life of the individual will not count; the only thing of importance will be his actual status when judgment is passed.[110] Ezekiel therefore not only broke away from the old conception of the solidarity of the family or clan, but also jumped to the opposite extreme of atomistic individualism:

> The fact of the essential unity and continuity of each life is ignored; life is considered from the point of view of actions, not character. The ties of heredity and environment which link a man to his fellow-men and often involve the innocent with the guilty in the temporal disaster, are not given due consideration.[111]

Individualism and Immortality. — Ezekiel's break with the past was too sudden to have much immediate influence on his more traditional contemporaries; moreover, his immediate successors, Deutero-Isaiah and Jonah, were primarily concerned about the destiny of the nation. In fact, not until the belief in immortality developed among the Hebrews did individualism really take deep root. This belief at first encountered much opposition because the worship of family ancestors, or *teraphim,* to which we have already called attention, had been repudiated by the worshipers of Yahweh even before the Canaanite admixture was partially purged away. Only with (1) increasing emphasis on the individual, (2) the rise of the idea of retribution, and (3) the dawning sense of fellowship with Yahweh did the belief in immortality win a final victory.

The first of this trio of influences is illustrated in passages promising long life (or a miraculous conquest of death) to the individual: " He hath swallowed up death forever; and the Lord Yahweh will wipe away tears from off all faces." [112]

The second, the idea of retribution, is clearly stated by Job when he maintains that he will be " justified ":

> . . . I know that my Redeemer liveth,
> And at last he will stand up upon the earth:
> And after my skin, even this body, is destroyed,
> Then without my flesh shall I see God;
> Whom I, even I, shall see, on my side,
> And mine eyes shall behold, and not as a stranger.[113]

The life after death in which Job here proclaims his faith is only a temporary one; like the Egyptian Misanthrope long before him, Job merely expresses the belief that he will have the opportunity to see his righteousness vindicated by Yahweh, and will then descend to Sheol to be among the dead, who slowly pass from their shadowy, chthonian existence and from memory.

Job also supplies some of the most striking evidences of the sense of fellowship with Yahweh, but it was not until the late Psalms that this led to a definitely enunciated belief in immortality:

> But God will redeem my soul from the power of Sheol;
> For he will receive me. . . .[114]

> Thou wilt guide me with thy counsel,
> And afterward receive me to glory.[115]

Persian Influences on Hebrew Thought. — After the conquests of Cyrus, Persian thought had much to do with the further development of the Hebrew idea of immortality, and it seems advisable to pause for a moment in order to gain some notion of the Persian beliefs.

In the teachings of Zoroaster, the Persian sage, the universe is primarily a stage for the contest between good and evil — in fact, the creation occurred only in order that this contest might take place. The struggle between the powers of light and the powers of darkness is a perpetual drama that will cease only when good, personified by the god Ormuzd, vanquishes evil, represented by Ahriman. Ormuzd has as his helper the Persian redeemer Mithras, the slayer of the sacrificial bull whose blood, streaming over the believer, makes him " whiter than the snow." Winged beings, strangely like Jewish angels in the Apocrypha, aid Ormuzd and Mithras in their task of redemption, but the diabolical Ahriman, " Prince of the Powers of the Air," also has flying hosts at his command. The children of light, who side with the beneficent Ormuzd, receive everlasting blessedness; the children of darkness, the dupes of Ahriman, are consigned to the flames of hell.

The effects of this elaborate other-worldly doctrine did not make themselves fully apparent in the canonical books of the Old Testament, but they nevertheless can be traced.[116] It was in the inter-Testamental period, however, that the angelology of the Persians saturated Jewish lore. Thence, as well as by direct transmission, it passed over into Christian doctrine, with consequences that are still strikingly evident — but more of these matters in Chapter Six, " Christian Social Thought from Beginnings to Thomas Aquinas."

Future Golden Age and Messiah. — Quite as important in Hebrew social thought as the belief in immortality was the Messianic hope. This took two forms: hope of a new age in which Israel would rule the nations, and hope for an ideal sovereign, a Messiah.

The first of these can be traced as far back as the pre-prophetic period, and by the time of Amos the people were definitely expecting a " great day of Yahweh " which would be a " day of light." The later prophets modified this: first would come a day of doom and then, after punishment and repentance, a glorious future. In this new world, Israel was to be the spiritual leader of all nations, war to cease, the soil to become unusually fertile, and animals no longer to harm mankind or each other. These external changes, however, were to be only the " outward signs of inward grace ":

> . . . they shall teach no more every man his neighbor, . . . saying know Yahweh; for they shall all know me, from the least of them unto the greatest of them, saith Yahweh.[117]

Now the coming of this glad day is not inseparably bound up, in all the prophetic writings, with the advent of the ideal king, the Messiah. Nevertheless, it centers in him in many striking passages, some of them distinctly reminiscent of Egyptian forerunners. Sometimes the Messianic hope is connected with the glory of the Davidic dynasty, but not always. In virtually every instance, however, the Messiah is given divine attributes, and his rule is said to have no limit:

> His name shall be called Wonderful, Counsellor, Mighty God, Everlasting Father, Prince of Peace. Of the increase of his government and of peace there shall be no end, upon the throne of David, and upon his kingdom, to establish it, and to uphold it with justice and with righteousness from henceforth even for ever.[118]

Still more influential than this conception of a Messiah reigning in more than earthly splendor is that of the Suffering Servant. Although it was originally meant to apply to an individual, it later signified the nation as a whole. The Suffering Servant is a vivid presentation of the thought that the redemption of man and of the nations is to be effected not by force but by vicarious suffering: " He was wounded for our transgressions, he was bruised for our iniquities; the chastisement of our peace was upon him; and with his stripes are we healed." [119]

Many interpretations of this striking passage and its associated ideas, in Deutero-Isaiah and elsewhere, have been offered. The least unsatisfactory is that repeated defeat led the Hebrews to despair of other than moral victories over their oppressors, and consequently to exalt the rôle of suffering by giving it a vicarious significance. This interpretation perhaps offers a solution, but to many minds the form taken by the Messianic hope in the Suffering Servant still remains unexplained. Its influence on the rôle of Jesus lends it major significance in Christian thought. Jewish thought, however, has also been much affected by the Suffering Servant conception.

Summary of the Chapter. — The most easterly of the Five Lands, Punjab-Sind, perhaps represents a link between ancient Far and Near East, for its civilization may have had some relation to that of Sumeria, and hence to the other Mesopotamian cultures. At the present stage of our knowledge, however, no general priority can be claimed for any.

In Sumeria a complex culture developed as early as sixty centuries ago, and it furnished patterns followed not only in Mesopotamia but also in Syria and elsewhere. The great Babylonian law-giver, Hammurabi, was one of the first great exponents of rational domination; the code he promulgated was strikingly secular. It was not wholly rational, however, for social stratification played a considerable part in determining penalties. Women had a very large measure of freedom, but the high regard in which property was held had much to do with this. Criminal law inflicted drastic penalties; there was some attempt, however, to take account of mitigating motives. Laws dealing with shipping and the caravan traffic testify to a wide range of culture contacts. Assyrian law was distinctly cruder than its Babylonian forerunner and its Hittite contemporary, in both form and content. Women were held as property, and punishments inflicted for crime often seem needlessly savage, even for that early period. Real estate laws and irrigation rights reflect the preoccupation with water supply, so characteristic of the bottomlands agriculture of much of the Near East.

Egyptian social thought of the implicit type appears in the phenomenon of clan totemism. This soon merged in territorial organization centering around the nome. Finally, with the rise of the Osiris myth, the development from clan to family and from totemism to centralized political authority received an appropriate ideology. The Pharaoh, symbol of family and sovereignty, came to be an earthly god upon whose fate in the after-life the destiny of all Egypt depended. Social monism akin to that found in China made the preservation of his body in the Pyramid tomb of supreme importance, so that in the task of preparation for death he became absolute during life.

Eventually, however, discontent appeared, and first the oligarchs and then the populace threatened Pharaoh's power. The social disorganization of the time brought forth many pessimistic forebodings strikingly similar to those found in the Bible; further, Messianic prophecies strengthen the parallel. The restoration was accompanied by a " grant " of immortality to the plebeians, as well as by diminution of the rights of the erstwhile oligarchy of princes and priests.

Under the revived monarchy the Rule of the Just Laws, clearcut manifestation of rational domination, made its appearance, and was strengthened after the interregnum of the Shepherd Kings. Egyptian imperialism began its far-reaching conquests, and finally Ikhnaton, a hybrid Pharaoh representing the inter-racialism and interculturalism of the Empire, inaugurated a universalistic religion that was a reflection of the times and his own background. This faith was that of Aton, the solar disk, shining alike upon Egyptians and strangers. The imperialistic ideology was too drastic, however, and under stress crumbled before Egyptian ethnocentrism and the armies of Egypt's enemies. A decline set in that was interrupted only by occasional strong dynasties, and although even a weakened Egypt was still strong enough to harry the Hebrews, its great days were over.

The Hebrews were originally wanderers, and only after many vicissitudes did they settle in Palestine. Culture contact with the Canaanite inhabitants brought on a long-drawn-out struggle between nomadic sacred conceptions and the more secular social thought of the urban and tillage contingent. This struggle was exemplified in the conflicting theories of the state held by the nomadic " judges " and " kings " on the one hand and the rising despots on the other. The contest between Yahweh and Baal provides another relevant illustration.

The prophets were most conspicuous in the fight for the nomadic way of life. Amos was particularly incensed by the violations of the brotherhood *ethôs* of the desert that disparities in wealth and consequent class cleavage brought with them. Hosea was much more clearly an heir of the " ecstatic tradition," and devoted a greater portion of his message to assaults on the fertility rituals of the " Canaanized " Hebrews, although he did not lose sight of social injustices. Micah held that the source of the social disorganization of the time was the cities, and proposed their destruction in order to facilitate the return to tradition.

This tradition was sapped in another way by the lapse of belief in clan and family solidarity that accompanied culture contact and urbanization. When the Hebrews were carried into captivity, many of them became so individuated that they chose to remain in Babylon, and Ezekiel, the prophet of the Exile, preached an extreme atomistic individualism. Not until the belief in immortality gained general adherence, however, did religious individualism triumph. Foreshadowed by Job, the doctrine was clearly enunciated in the later Psalms and, in the inter-Testamental period, angelology and related supernaturalistic doctrines resulting from Persian influence greatly reinforced it.

Other types of reaction to the frustrations that culminated in the Exile and the loss of autonomy were the belief in a future golden age and in the coming of an ideal ruler who would rectify all injustices and reign with wondrous beneficence. A variant of the latter belief is the conception of the Suffering Servant, in which hope for earthly blessings is apparently dependent upon the idea of vicarious sacrifice or atonement. This proved to be of literally tremendous significance in the development not only of Jewish but also of Christian social philosophy.

Recent efforts to decipher Minoan Linear Script A have led some investigators to hazard the assumption that the early migrants to Crete not only came from a region of the Near East, localized as lower Anatolia (for which there is substantial archaeological evidence), but also that they wrote in a variety of Akkadian. This would establish a very close link between the Near East and the Aegean civilization (dealt with in the early part of the next chapter) that so notably influenced Greek developments. It must here be stated, however, that there is as yet no general acceptance of the Akkadian thesis; what may eventually turn out to be genuine decipherments are at present highly selective, fragmentary, and at best merely plausible.

On the basis of what must now be conceded to be the actual decipherment by Michael Ventris, assisted by John Chadwick, of Minoan Linear Script B as proto-Greek, T. B. L. Webster has developed an elaborate thesis to the effect that the Minoan and Mycenaean civilizations were strongly affected by Near Eastern predecessors and contemporaries. This was particularly the case, contends Webster, with regard to political structure; highly centralized rule along Near Eastern lines was established in Crete, the Argolid, and contiguous regions. Also using archaeological evidence and Greek documents, Webster has done much to sustain his thesis, but it is still viewed as somewhat too sweeping to be fully credited.

In any case, ties between the Near East and the world that eventually came to be called Greek today seem to have been firmer than was supposed a generation or two ago.

Turning to another topic, also relevant for the early part of Chapter VI, "Christian Social Philosophy to Thomas Aquinas," it can be said that the discovery of the Dead Sea Scrolls has borne out those parts of the present chapter dealing with Babylonian, Persian, and similar influences on Hebrew social thought. Moreover, Becker's treatment in Chapter VI (in the sections headed "Sects among the Jews," "Jewry outside the Promised Land," and "Jesus, Founder of a Jewish sect") of Hebrew social thought during the Dead Sea Scrolls period has been shown to stand in no present need of major correction, but merely of specific reference to the Scrolls. Further, on the basis of evidence long antedating that provided by the Scrolls, he discussed the Suffering Servant doctrine in the present chapter, and in Chapter VI he presented the ascetic Essenes, since viewed as the probable scribes of the Scrolls, as having had an impact on early Christian thought. To quote (p. 218): "It is highly unlikely that Jesus could have remained uninfluenced by their teachings."

CHAPTER IV

The Mobile Background of the Greco-Roman World and Its Effects on Social Thought

MIRACLE AS MIRAGE. — When men speak of Greece, there arises, in the minds of all who have felt the magic of the writers of the famous fifth century, a picture of Athens, "the city white like lime, high-towered and many-peopled." The fascination exercised by this ideal Athens nevertheless has its dangers; under its sway some scholars have forgotten or ignored influences that would make "the Greek miracle" more understandable and, perhaps, no miracle at all. If the present chapter is to offer any satisfactory explanation of the marvelous mental mobility of the Greeks, and particularly of the Athenians, some discussion of the cultures upon which Athenian civilization was based must be included. This is particularly necessary in view of the fact that we shall be compelled to trace the possible effects of Greek mentality upon that of Rome — if we are to pyramid hypotheses we must be fairly sure of foundations.

The Helladic Peoples. — Before the invasions of the Greek peninsula by the pastoral nomads from the north, the Ionians, Achaeans, and Dorians who later became the Hellenes of Classical times, there flourished a rich bronze culture throughout the whole Aegean area, most complex in the islands, especially in Crete, the center of the Minoan culture, but also well developed on the mainland, where the Mycenaean culture predominated.

These bronze cultures, all of them bearing traces of Egyptian influence, were far superior to anything developed by the northern invaders for at least five centuries after the Great Migrations; instead of being a race of godlike geniuses who "made gentle the life of the world," modern research shows them to have been barbarous destroyers who ruined a complex civilization that they were unable to match for half a millennium, and who then succeeded only by building upon its achievements.

From remote Neolithic antiquity there were in the insular and littoral regions of the Aegean and eastern Mediterranean a dark-white, short, non-Nordic people basically akin to the dark-whites of Egypt. The race is commonly called Mediterranean. In addition, there was also a dark, short-skulled " Armenoid " or " Hittoid " people inhabiting the uplands of Asia Minor and the Grecian and Morea peninsulas.

The insular and littoral Mediterraneans remained in the Neolithic stage until well into the fourth millennium B.C., except for those on the island of Crete, who seem to have used bronze somewhat earlier. Increasingly close contact with Egypt and Phoenicia apparently stimulated the Cretans markedly, for their culture rapidly grew more complex, and at about 2200 or 2000 B.C., at the same time that the brilliant Eleventh and Twelfth Dynasties of the Middle Kingdom bloomed in Egypt, the scattered village communities of Crete came together, or were forced together, into a strong monarchical state, the capital of which was Cnossus. There the ruler built a great stone palace and received the tribute of his subordinate princes; maritime relations with Egypt became closer, and a flourishing trade sprang up. Expansion went on gradually, with minor fluctuations, until about 1700 B.C.; at this time a general disaster seems to have overtaken the island, and for a period variously estimated at from twenty-five years to a century, Minoan culture in Crete lay dormant. Suddenly, however, it burst forth in a renascence that surpassed its former greatness; Crete began the final ascent to those heights from which, Euphorion-like, it forever fell.

Before the zenith was reached, however, certain processes worked themselves out on the mainland, and their outcome played the decisive part in the Cretan collapse; the northward expansion of Minoan culture after the cataclysm above mentioned must be taken into account.

The littoral Mediterraneans and upland Hittoids of the Grecian and Morea peninsulas passed by fitful stages from polished stone to bronze, but they seem to have had no contact with the bronze Minoan culture of Crete during this transition period. A distinct advance in cultural complexity was registered when, apparently with little or no period of " incubation," Minoan culture appeared on the southern shores of Morea, i.e., the Peloponnesus, in full force about 1700 B.C. The Mycenaean culture, as distinct from the Minoan, was born, and soon developed to a point where it almost equaled the culture of the Cretan renascence; by 1500 or 1400 B.C., as a result of Minoan decadence, Mycenae was the artistic center of the Aegean world. The offshoot showed more vigor than the parent stock.

The First Stages of the Migrations: the Ionians. — The two or three centuries that elapsed between the time when the Minoan culture reached the mainland and the development of a distinct Mycenaean offshoot were not empty of other processes; the mainland itself underwent great changes during the time that acculturation by the expanding island power to the south was going on. For centuries, perhaps beginning as early as the end of the third millennium B.C., a pastoral folk from the region of the Hungarian and Wallachian plains had been pushing slowly southward, sometimes amalgamating with the prior Hittoid inhabitants of the occupied areas, sometimes displacing them by the simple process of taking the grasslands and leaving the barren hills to anyone who would stay there. There is much difference of opinion as to whether the northerners were fair-haired and blue-eyed; it is certain that the Hittoids were dark. In point of language and economy the latter afforded a marked contrast; they spoke nothing that remotely resembled anything Indo-European, and were tillage peoples; the newcomers, on the other hand, were the progenitors of Greek, an Indo-European tongue, and were pastoral or semi-pastoral nomads.

Their importance for the Cretan penetration of the interior was this: they probably had little other than stone and crude copper implements, and no really good pottery, down to as late as 1600 B.C., when the Cretans reached them with bronze weapons and fibulae and the consummate vases and beakers of the island workshops. Slowly the northerners traveled southward with their herds, a few miles farther each year; pressure from behind left them no rest. It is probable that contact with the Hittoids had brought about some social disorganization, for they offered no great resistance to the spread of Minoan culture. About 1580 B.C. these wild northern folk learned the use of bronze, and by 1450 B.C. vases of Minoan style had reached the very foothills of Olympus.[1]

Not content with having seized the northern peninsula, the nomads trickled southward into the Peloponnesus, where the indigenous population was more dense and more difficult to displace. Hence a good deal of amalgamation with the Hittoids seems to have taken place; here it was that the new people, now of mixed blood and simple semi-pastoral and tillage economy, took on a still larger number of Minoan culture traits and became known as Ionians (not to be confused with the *Asiatic* Ionians, to whom we shall most often refer). The Minoan elements remained largely external, however; the wares of Crete were eagerly desired and used, but little domestic manufacture went on — perhaps because of lack of suitable materials. Further, the Ionians were slow to take to the water, and the water was a chief conditioning factor in the Minoan culture; the Cretan was a sailor or he was nothing.

The Achaean Flood. — Beginning with about the sixteenth or fifteenth century, the scene shifts again; a fresh group of pastoral nomads, probably akin to those who became Ionians, invaded the upper peninsula and, at what seems a remarkably rapid rate, overran the Peloponnesus as well, conquering the Ionians who had come before them. The latter in some instances fled before the Achaeans, as these latest migrants were called, and a considerable number of refugees won a foothold in Attica and the Cyclades among the Mediterranean and Hittoid peoples who had not previously been appreciably disturbed by the nomad invasions. The Ionian refugee contingent was not large in proportion to the settled population, however, and a minimum of strife seems to have ensued; the groups merged so completely that the myth of common " Pelasgian " origin grew up. Further, the Ionians set up no state; there was relatively little social stratification other than that already established.

The Achaean invasion of the remainder of the peninsulas was far otherwise. Almost everywhere nomad chieftains and their followers established themselves as rulers of subject populations. The early Mycenaean culture, as yet little different from the Minoan, was adopted by the newcomers with astonishing thoroughness and rapidity; within fifty years there was even a renewal of the cultural elaboration that had been checked by their onslaught.

But what of the Cretans? Where were they during these troublous times? Just where they had always been, on the sea, profiting from both sides alike, setting up trading stations and penetrating inland when the situation demanded it, but always with a trump card in case of difficulty — their galleys. Trade with the rapidly developing Mycenaean centers on the islands and coasts continued, but they were steadily becoming self-sufficient; the real opportunities were to be found among the oncoming Achaeans before the latter had conquered the Mycenaean centers.

And among the Achaeans went the Cretans, bartering bronze and gold for hides, amber, and slaves. Soon relations were established that were as close to being friendly as the times allowed; Cretan and Achaean worked together, one on the sea, the other on the land. But even on the sea, as Glotz puts it, " the Achaeans were doing their apprenticeship. When they arrived in Greece they had not even known what the sea was." [2] . . . Finally the old relation of master and pupil was no longer adequate; even the devious ways of the sea no longer held any mystery for the landsmen. When the littoral Mycenaean culture areas fell prey to the Achaeans, the new rulers welded them into homogeneous units able to cope with the Cretan thalassocrats in war, trade, or piracy.

For a time, however, the dominance of the islanders persisted; the bearers of the Minoan culture still acted as middlemen whenever their superior naval strength permitted, and they still exacted tribute from the mainland peoples whenever they could. But a day came when the Achaean sea-lords grew tired of being exploited by the Cretan thalassocracy; they became fully competent to carry their own vases and bronzes to Egypt and the western seas. Finally, growing resentment against the exploitation practiced by the Cretan sea-kings culminated in the rising of a united Mycenaean world against the thalassocrats who had given them all the more complex elements in their culture.

Crete was not well fortified; the long years of Aegean hegemony and comparative peace had dulled the fighting spirit of the islanders, and about 1400 B.C. the glorious palace of Cnossus was given to the flames by Mycenaean conquerors. The center of the Aegean world shifted to Argolis, the point in the eastern Peloponnesus where the Mycenaean culture of the mainland reached its zenith, and a new period of expansion set in.

The Mycenaean civilization, under its Achaean masters, extended farther than the Minoan had ever done under the Cretans; remote provinces were brought into one market: isolation gave way to accessibility. In spite of expansion, the new culture did not equal the artistic standard set by its predecessor. Further, it must not be supposed that the Achaeans, in taking over Mycenaean culture, had dropped all their own characteristics. The fierce ardor of the herdsman persisted, and the extension of the new civilization was not due to purely economic influences, peaceful exchange, or colonization by mutual consent. Piracy revived; depending on the folk to be faced, ships went off laden with warriors or with merchandise. When the warriors established themselves on an island or bit of coast, they used it as a base for further journeys of adventure and plunder; the Achaeans gradually spread themselves over the whole Aegean area, and even ravaged the coasts of southeastern Asia Minor.

The Dorian Catastrophe. — There is a limit to such extension of domain; " by dispersing themselves the Achaeans had grown dangerously weak. In going off to every shore of the Mediterranean they left many gaps behind them. Gradually bands of the same race, speaking a dialect of the same language, came out of Illyria, and made their way across Pindus, ever pressing farther towards the south. The Dorians were coming into history." [3]

The invasion, like the others before it, was merely a slow infiltration at first; from about 1300 to 1200 B.C. the Achaean-Mycenaean forts were apparently able to stem the tide. Then, quite suddenly, the defenders were routed; some scholars say that this marks the appearance of the leaf-shaped iron sword that cut its triumphant way through all Europe. Certain it is that the Dorians were bearers of a Danubian iron culture that the earlier migrants had not had.

At any rate, there can be no doubt that the defenders were utterly routed; the terrible savagery of the inroad everywhere sent the stricken peoples flying, mad with terror, and in their terror they themselves became terrible to those who stood in their path. Many Achaeans sought refuge in Attica with those Ionians whom they had themselves expelled from the Peloponnesus two centuries before, and there, cowering beyond the mountain passes, they waited for the Dorian hosts to pass by. Many of the Ionians, and Achaeans as well, thinking the situation desperate, fled by sea to the islands of the east and the shores of Asia Minor, where a new culture later bloomed — the *Asiatic* Ionian, to which extensive reference will later be made. Most of the Dorians, however, seeing the fertile plains of Messenia and the southern Peloponnesus before them, passed by the little, rocky " goat-pasture " behind its ramparts of the Parnes range, and pushed on to the south — there is nothing to show that Attica was ever invaded by any considerable body of Dorians. The latter were no longer landsmen only; on their journey from the north, they like the Achaeans had taken to the sea, so that when they reached the southern end of the Peloponnesus, they hesitated not at all, but embarked in battle array for Crete. Cnossus fell for the last time, and for three thousand years only " orts of blackened bone " marked the spot where King Minos had once held sway.

At first when the Dorians sacked a city, they could in a way rebuild it or have it rebuilt; the Mycenaean culture did not collapse immediately, and the Dorians were after all nearly two centuries in reaching Crete. Toward the end, however, there came tribes who could destroy but not build nor even keep, chieftains who bore the proud title of " sacker-of-cities," who burned and shattered, and then could make no more of their conquest than to live as huddled war-parties among the ruins.[4]

The Flight from Attica. — There was of course no complete destruction of the culture of their forerunners by the Dorians, and this is even more true of the inhabitants of Attica. In that sheltered peninsula, escaping as it did from all but the backwash of the Dorian invasion, no sharp break with the Mycenaean culture ever occurred. Yet the effects of the march of the men of iron were clearly felt in Attica: it was the final struggle of the Great Migrations, when the whole Aegean area was in the wildest confusion. Ionians and Achaeans and their surviving predecessors were roving about the narrow seas desperately striving for a foothold. Relatively little conflict seems to have accompanied the settlements of refugees in Attica, but there was nevertheless some displacement of their forerunners, and these, mingled with the Achaeans who could not get a grip on the mainland, joined the surging hordes of other peoples who had been similarly expelled and were also fleeing by sea. These motley swarms fought their way across the stepping-stone islands of the Cyclades and Sporades until they clutched the irregular coastal fringe of Asia Minor and held it fast.

Thus came the fugitive settlers to what was afterward Asiatic Ionia — came in the turmoil and shouting of the " uprooting of peoples " to the first great frontier of the Greek world.

Mental Mobility and Athenian Mentality. — It is now high time that we indicate more directly the bearing of all this on the theme of the present chapter, which, it will be recalled, is entitled " The Mobile Background of the Greco-Roman World and Its Effects on Social Thought." Attention has been paid to physical and social mobility, but mental mobility is of course what we have had primarily in mind. It should by now be apparent that mental mobility cannot be briefly defined, but some idea of the meaning of the term has doubtless been given in foregoing chapters, if only by contrast with its antonym, mental immobility. Here it will be sufficient to state that it is a correlate of that form of social change in which secularization is strikingly manifest, and that it involves, among other things, mental mutability, release of inhibitions and energies, crisis (as defined by Thomas), rationalism, and attitudinal plasticity that sometimes reaches the extreme of personality disorganization.

We are here concerned with mental mobility in Hellenic history, and particularly in the history of Athens, for both the agility of intellect and the fickleness of character possessed by the Athenian citizen had no parallel in the ancient world; nothing can be found that is really comparable to the Age of Pericles until we reach the modern period with its urban, cosmopolitan culture. Pater has given us this comment:

"The citizen of Athens," observed that great Athenian statesman in whom . . . *the mobile soul of Athens* became conscious, — "The citizen of Athens seems to me to present himself in his single person to the greatest possible variety . . . of thought and action, with the utmost degree of versatility." . . . the example of *that mobility, that daring mobility, of character has seemed to many the special contribution of the Greek people to advancing humanity*. It was not however of the Greek people in general that Pericles was speaking . . . but of Athens in particular; of Athens, that perfect flower of Ionian genius. . . . Its very claim was in its grace of movement, its freedom and easy happiness, its lively interests; but its weakness is self-evident, and was what had made the political unity of the Greeks impossible. . . .
. . . Athens . . . was the willing victim of its own gifts, its own flamboyancy, well-nigh worn out now by the mutual friction of its own parts, given over completely to hazardous political experiment . . . ever ready to float away anywhither, to misunderstand, or forget, or discredit, its own past.[5]

The relation of this type of mental mobility and social instability to the population movement and culture contact made possible by navigation in the thalassic Aegean region is closely similar to conditions prevailing in the rising urban centers of Europe, especially in Italy, during the later phase of the Crusades, the Age of Discovery, and the Commercial Revolution. Indeed, there is some discernible relation to the modes of behavior found in the great cities of modern times, as has already been suggested — hence the importance, for an understanding of at least the immediate antecedents of our own era, of the " case " afforded by Hellenic Athens.

Asiatic Ionia, the Greek Frontier. — To begin with, it should be noted that Asiatic Ionia, settled by one-time " Athenians," provided the initial stimulus that finally gave rise to the Age of Pericles. These early Ionian settlements are sometimes called " colonies," but they really were not colonized at all if by that term we intend to denote the founding of a settlement by a portion of an ethnic or cultural group and the planned maintenance of reciprocal relations by the mother-city and the colonists. As we have indicated, Ionia was largely settled by fugitives during the time of the Great Migrations, when no connection with the primary culture areas could well be maintained. The thalassic area

within which such settlement took place made it possible for contact to be reëstablished at a comparatively early date, but the
essential criteria of colonization were nevertheless lacking.[6]

Instead of colonists, the Ionians might better be called frontiersmen; they became as different from the sedentary peoples they
left behind as did the " English Tartars " (Burke's name for the
wide-ranging denizens of the American frontier) from the re-
spectable citizens of Massachusetts and the other Atlantic colonies. Indeed, Turner has expressly pointed out the similarity in
process:

> The frontier does indeed furnish a new field of opportunity, a gate of
> escape from the bondage of the past; and the freshness, and confidence,
> and scorn of older society, impatience of its lessons, have accompanied
> the frontier. What . . . [the Ionian coast] was to the Greeks, breaking
> the bond of custom, offering new experience, calling out new institutions
> and activities, that, and more, the ever-retreating frontier has been to the
> United States directly, and to the nations of Europe more remotely.[7]

As a consequence of the movement to Ionia, *all* ties with the
home-lands were broken. As Gilbert Murray has so forcibly put
it, " For the fugitive settler on the shores that were afterwards
Ionia, there were no tribal gods or tribal obligations left, . . .
no old laws; . . . household and family life had disappeared
. . . and he had left the graves of his fathers, the kindly ghosts
of his own blood. . . ." [8] Under the stress of the new situation
and its concomitant crisis, old folkways were dropped, old customs
and laws abandoned,[9] as has been amply demonstrated by the
scholars who have studied the changes recorded in the Greek
Epic.[10] The frontiersmen were predominantly male; few women
and children had survived the desperate flight: consequently, culture contact on the most intimate plane, the sexual, began almost
at once. " A man was not now living with a wife of his own race,
but with a dangerous strange woman, of alien language and alien
gods." [11] The earlier pastoral culture was considerably modified;
Lydian and Carian foods and clothing were of much influence;
the family took on matriarchal traits; strange gods came to be
worshiped; mental mobility and social change manifested themselves.

The Sea and the Colonies as Secularizers. — Had it not been
for the thalassic nature of the Aegean, with its numerous " breaks
in transportation " and its consequent ease of navigation even for
crude vessels, similarity between the Ionian Greeks and those of
the home-lands would have been reduced to a very scanty measure

indeed. As it was, the Ionians (and others as well) began to levy toll on Aegean commerce, piracy and warfare involved all the peoples of the East Mediterranean littoral, commerce and trade sprang up along the short-distance sea routes, peaceful intercourse gradually became established, and culture contact began to blur the lines of difference separation had drawn. In time the term "Ionian" was once more applied to certain of the home-land Greek peoples as well as to the migrants, and the islands and shores of the Aegean became a fairly uniform culture area.

The process of "uniformation" was furthered by the practice, early adopted by the Asiatic Greeks and soon imitated by the home-land peoples, of sending out colonies that maintained commercial relations with the metropolis, or mother-city. Daughter-cities dotted Magna Graecia, the bleak Cimmerian shores of the Black Sea and the Sea of Azov, Cyrenaica, Sicily, Corsica and Sardinia, South Gaul, Epirus and Illyria, and one lone outpost was even set up at the mouth of the unfriendly Nile, the trading station of Naucratis. These were genuine colonies, founded with an eye to commerce, and it is upon these and the Phoenician ventures that Heeren probably based his generalization that commercial nations are the only genuine colonizers.[12] He confused them, however, with the fugitive early-Ionian settlements, with the Greek frontier, largely because the modern archaeological and philological evidence upon which the discrimination is based was lacking in his day. No sharp line can be drawn, but the difference is nevertheless there;[13] extreme individuation was much more marked on the frontier than in the commercial colonies, inhibition less powerful, release more complete, innovation less suspect, individualism more explicit, atomization more thorough, secularization further advanced.[14]

The colonies, however, contributed mightily to the breakdown of the sacred community and the rise of the secular society, for although the processes were slower, they were irreversible to a degree not characteristic of the frontier. Rapid disorganization is often succeeded by rapid reorganization, whereas a slower rate often issues in a type of social atomization that is much more thoroughgoing, especially if a metropolitan economy prevails. This was the case in the colonies; the wine of disorganization brought about only a mild exhilaration, a state of euphoria and expansiveness, and the sacred community changed slowly and calmly, via a cycle much like that adumbrated by Turgot, into a society which in the equilibrium it achieved was more thoroughly secular than any prior to the fifteenth century of our era.[15]

Commerce and the Secular Stranger. — Now one of the significant things about the Ionian frontier, and a point wherein it differs from almost every other example, is that the earlier period of extreme individuation and disorganization seems not to have been succeeded by strong reaction, by rigid reorganization. This is probably due to the fact that the era of colonization got under way about the time the first reactions were brewing; culture contact with home-land Greeks and barbarian peoples checked incipient reorganization to such an extent that the sacred community was never effectively reëstablished by the Greeks proper.

Several factors were responsible for this: among the most powerful seems to have been commerce. Trade with the colonies flourished; the whole Aegean area throbbed with busy traffic; the cities were filled with swarms of strangers — Greeks from other cities and not a few barbarians. Commerce and the stranger! They go hand in hand. The old hostility to newcomers, so strikingly enduring in the Spartan *xenelasia,* gave way, in the commercial Greek cultures, to the precise reverse — strangers were welcomed. The merchant, for example, was gradually admitted to the *polis;* he had not the rights of a citizen, to be sure, but he had something more — the privileges flowing from the practice of commercial hospitality.

The very fact that strangers were thus permitted to come and go argues that the isolated communities of the Aegean area had begun to become accessible; some social disorganization had already taken place. The stranger of course accelerated the process; he brought with him new folkways, new mores; his frequent shifts of domicile strengthened his own detached commercial tendencies, and this detachment communicated itself to the peoples among whom he temporarily sojourned — not being himself emotionally bound by the established ties of kinship and locality, his cool disinterestedness came to lessen the unifying warmth of the in-group. He possessed a certain objectivity, that peculiar mixture of concern in the immediate event and indifference to the final issue. He was the confidant of the disaffected and restless, for his simultaneous nearness and remoteness inspired a certain confidence. He was free from local conventions, and by neglecting to observe customary usages helped to weaken those usages.[16] Finally, he subjected everything to rational scrutiny and disregarded the specific differences of the various intimate primary groups with which he came in contact, thus practicing a certain habitual abstraction that caused him to acquire an " intellectual bias " and to communicate that bias to others. Surely there is some significance in the fact that the stranger in his first well-marked historical form appears in conjunction with commerce, using " that most interesting of all abstractions, money," [17] and with phonetic writing, then the most abstract of all methods of recording human speech. *Abstraction and mental mobility go hand in hand.*

The Vogue of Reason. — If the essential characteristic of philosophy is abstraction, i.e., detachment from the unique and concentration on the recurrent, we have a clue to the reason for the close association of commercialism and philosophy found, for example, in such men as Thales. We can see why *not only Greek philosophy but the first genuine philosophy saw the light in the frontier cities of Ionia.* In view of the assertions frequently made by enthusiastic Egyptologists such as Elliot Smith, this is an untenable statement, for according to them Greek philosophy was merely an offshoot of " the wisdom of the East." Burnet, a modern authority on Greek philosophy, has paid his respects to this latter theory thus:

. . . in some quarters Oriental cosmogonies are still paraded as the source of Greek philosophy. The question is not one of cosmogonies at all. The Greeks themselves had cosmogonies long before the days of Thales, and the Egyptians and Babylonians had cosmogonies that may be older still. . . . These things, however, have nothing directly to do with philosophy. *From the Platonic point of view, there can be no philosophy where there is no rational science.* It is true that not much is required — a few propositions of elementary geometry will do to begin with — but rational science of some sort there must be. Now rational science is the creation of the Greeks, and we know when it began. We do not count as philosophy anything anterior to that.

It is true, of course, that science originated at the time when communication with Egypt and Babylon was easiest, and just where the influence of these countries was likely to be felt, and it is a perfectly fair inference that this had something to do with its rise. On the other hand, the very fact that for two or three generations Greek science remained in some respects at a very primitive stage affords the strongest presumption that what came to Hellas from Egypt and Babylon was not really rational science. . . . Of course everything depends on what we mean by science. If we are prepared to give that name to an elaborate record of celestial phenomena made for purposes of divination, then the Babylonians had science and the Greeks borrowed it from them. Or, if we are prepared to call rough rules of thumb for measuring fields and pyramids science, then the Egyptians had science, and it came from them to Ionia. But if we mean by science what Copernicus and Galileo and Kepler, and Leibniz and Newton meant, there is not the slightest trace of that in Egypt or even in Babylon, while *the very earliest Greek ventures are unmistakably its forerunners.* Modern science begins just where Greek science left off, and its development is clearly to be traced from Thales to the present day.[18]

This same point has been stressed by Park, who says that reason and reflective thinking, strictly defined, came into vogue if not into existence in the Greek city-states.[19] Habitual abstraction (the product of the comparison of peoples), writing and prose, a money economy, and an urban culture could not arise except under peculiarly favorable conditions; the clear recognition of conceptual, as distinguished from perceptual, knowledge is no matter-of-course, everyday occurrence — man has for a long time been *homo faber, homo loquens,* and even *homo sapiens,* but he has been *homo rationalis* only since yesterday, and even now his claim to the proud title is uncertain.

In the foregoing pages the relation of secularization to the other processes working themselves out in Ionia has frequently been dwelt upon; this emphasis is not peculiar to the writer, however, for Burnet has said much the same thing:

> The spirit of Ionian civilization had been thoroughly secular, and this was, no doubt, one of the causes that favoured the rise of science. . . . No one who has once realized *the utterly secular character of Ionian civilization* will ever be tempted to look for the origins of Greek philosophy in primitive cosmogonies.[20]

" The utterly secular character of Ionian civilization! " Little did those curious travelers, those merchants enamored of the shining coins of Gyges, those traders thumbing the papyrus invoices of the Phoenicians, those tale-makers fascinated by their own eloquence, those scribes struggling manfully to write in the everyday speech — little did they know of the new habit of thought they themselves were establishing, and still less of the achievements that this habit of rationality would make possible.

The Metics, Importers of Goods and Ideas. — When all these effects of the intrusion of strangers (termed Metics by the Athenians) were noted, certain of the more bucolic Greeks raised their voices in protest; Metic commercial perfidy became a favorite target for the native-born moralist.

It was not long before the Athenian dislike of the Metics active in economic affairs also manifested itself with regard to philosophic interlopers; they were labeled *sophoi* or Sophists, i.e., " knowers," and the word acquired even in the fifth century an unfavorable sense.[21] " The fact that these distinguished men were foreigners made them unpopular at Athens. The Athenian public was full of prejudices, and that against ' the foreigner ' was particularly well developed." [22] There can be little doubt that such dislike was due to the fact that the newcomers, both Metic traders and Metic philosophers, were disturbing to the most deep-rooted of motor habits, the most settled of beliefs, the most sacred bonds of the community, and to the self-esteem of the elders who saw their own wisdom disregarded by novelty-seeking youth. As time went on, however, the Metics won their way in spite of difficulty, and their schools as well as their banks flourished. As Glotz says:

> It was impossible that a class which imported goods, and with them ideas, from all over the world . . . should never know any other means of action than money, and should confine all its ambition to gain. The liberal careers also attracted the Metics. . . . Sophists appeared from every side; Protagoras came from Abdera, Gorgias from Leontion, Prodicos from Ceos, Hippias from Elis, Polos from Acragas. They brought with them all the ideas which were being worked out in the Hellenic world, but *especially those which best suited men who were emancipated from local prejudices and eager for practical novelties.*[23]

The effects of this influx soon became manifest among the native-born. Witness the fact that Plato represents Socrates hesitating, in his early manhood, between the Ionic doctrines and the Italic doctrines (offshoots of the Ionic), also current.[24]

This conflict of philosophies is significant, for it points to the growing intellectual ascendency of Athens. Burnet probably has this in mind when he says:

> Athens is the only place where the Ionic and Italic philosophies could come into sharp conflict like this, and the middle of the fifth century is the only time at which it could happen.[25]

In other words, the sudden shift in relative position resulting from the Persian Wars had made Athens the most accessible of all Mediterranean centers, and just at the period of her highest accessibility, with its great commercial advance and differentiation, numerous Metic philosophers visited or took up permanent residence in Athens.[26] The young Socrates, to choose once more the most striking example, thus came into direct or indirect contact with most of these men,[27] and also with the mobile commercial Metics of the Piraeus, for he was born about 470 B.C., " and his early manhood was spent in the full glory of the Periclean age," [28] the age of philosophy and prosperity.

Socrates the Rationalist. — Thus it was that *Socrates was influenced by practically every theory extant in the Greek world in the middle of the fifth century, and by the division of labor* (differentiation) *inherent in the metropolitan economy as well.*[29] His powerful mind assimilated the varied fare offered it, and the result was the most thoroughgoing rationalism the world had yet seen; he was the first champion of the supremacy of the intellect as a court from which there is no appeal; he was the first to insist, without modification or compromise, that a man must order his own life by the guidance of his own intellect, without regard for mandates of external authority or for impulses of emotion. Here we have " the intellectual bias " of the Ionian thinkers applied by the great Athenian to human conduct as well as to the affairs of the gods or the occasional divagations of the heavenly bodies. What Thales was in the world of Nature, Socrates was in the world of Man.

His relentless rationalism spared nothing, and he therefore was a rebel against authority as such; he did not hesitate to tell his companions that an old man had no rational title to respect unless he was also wise, or that an uneducated or stupid parent had no claim to the obedience of his children on rational grounds. " Knowledge and veracity, the absolute sovereignty of the understanding, regardless of all prejudices connected with family or city — this was the ideal of Socrates, consistently and uncompromisingly followed." [30] Unreasoning, spontaneous loyalty to the *polis* — the only sort effective in that day — had disappeared so far as Socrates and his fellow rationalists were concerned, in spite of the *Crito* and other protestations to the contrary, *just as such loyalty had disappeared in the secular society of Ionia almost a century before.* The elemental, non-rational bonds of the Athenian sacred community, already badly frayed by the economic individualism correlated with the accelerated development of metropolitan economy, began to snap one by one when the accelerated development of rationalistic and individualistic attitudes, as personified in Socrates and his followers, threw upon them what may well have been the final rending load. The character-attitudes of the Athenian youth, conditioned by patterns for a fixed world and already weakened by the flux of the metropolitan economy,[31] could not resist the final shattering impact of the new formulas. The great disorganizing power of these formulas derived from the fact that they provided rationalizations sanctioning many kinds of individuated behavior toward which suppressed tendencies had been generated by the unrest of the time, but which had been at least partially restrained by the disapproval of the Athenian elders who had inculcated the traditional character-attitudes. When such traditional character-attitudes disintegrate there is nothing to take their place, for deep-seated urges soon overwhelm the feeble barriers of reason, and there appear " individuals cut loose from the laws of common humanity." Of course, someone may say that the laws of common humanity are not worth following, and that, for example, the disintegration of the Athenian political structure was a small price to pay for those marvelous achievements of the Great Age of Pericles which only the release accompanying individuation made possible. That may indeed be true, but in any event it does not concern us here; what does concern us is the undeniable fact that the trial and condemnation of Socrates came about because he had a large share in the political breakdown of the *polis* of his birth. " The execution of Socrates was the protest of the spirit of the old order against the growth of individualism." [32]

Moral Flexibility and Political Decadence. — But the old order, in spite of executions, could not long survive the disintegrating influences set loose by the Persian Wars, and defeat by the Spartans in the Peloponnesian War marked the virtual collapse of Greek city life as it had been known to the men of Marathon.[33] The oligarchy of the Thirty for a time promised a restoration of the old state of affairs — one of the first things they did was to pass a law prohibiting instruction in public speaking[34] — but nothing could stem the rising tide of individuation, and the oligarchs were soon ousted by the mobile men of the Piraeus. Thereafter individuation ran riot;[35] in the single field of military service, for example, we find Athenian officers acting independently of their country, in the pay of foreign powers, whenever it chanced to suit their own individual advantage — Conon, Xenophon, Iphicrates, Chabrias, and others.[36] The soldiers and sailors became as thoroughly insubordinate as had the Ionians before Lâde three-quarters of a century earlier;[37] the campaign in Sicily proved them thoroughly untrustworthy. The leading men of Athens became notoriously open to bribery in all sorts of public matters,[38] and the surest way to preferment was a ready purse. Even at an earlier period, when the individuating influences of the Persian Wars had not yet exerted their full effect, some flagrant cases of selling information to the enemy occurred, as the examples of the great leaders Themistocles and Miltiades show.[39] The citizenry manifested the utmost fickleness, now exalting a favorite, now casting him down — no consistency, no stability.[40] Even a large proportion of the " old true-blue Athenians," as they have already been called, were utterly disorganized; the walls of the *polis* had given way, and nothing remained

to save them from themselves unless . . . unless . . . a new
plan of social organization, along rational lines, could be devised
to take the place of the old.

   Plato, Foe of Mobility. — So thought at least one of these dis-
mayed conservatives — Plato. A scion of one of the old families,
a contemner of the Metics and their innovations, Plato had been
drawn to Socrates by the latter's ethical bent as well as by his
condemnation of " the sweaty, greasy democracy of the Piraeus,"
and not by his individualistic tendencies, for Plato was vehement
in condemning that individualism which it had been the life-work
of Socrates to foster ! [41] Instead, " Plato laid down the principles
of aristocratic idealism imbued with religion," [42] and he sought
his model for the rational State that was to save the Athenians
from themselves in Sparta, archfoe of democracy, determined
enemy of innovation, and most unintellectual of all Greek states.
Curious, and yet comprehensible; the Spartan organization was
admired by Plato because the old order, the sacred community,
survived there — the citizen absolutely submissive to the authority of the state, and not looking beyond it. Hence he saw in Sparta
the image of what a state should be — because it was relatively
free from that individualism which characterized his master
Socrates and which he himself (in so far as his rationalistic speculations in political philosophy inclined others to individualism)
was actively engaged in promoting ! Yet we should not be too
critical of Plato; he did truly observe the phenomena of individuation, the rise of mental mobility, and for that we could pardon
even grosser inconsistencies.

   Pater has eloquently described the utterly disorganized political situation with which Plato was confronted; the flux into which
the Athenian character had passed as it became more and more
mobile; the contrast to such mobility afforded by that Dorian
tradition of immobility, of Spartan stability, upon which he ultimately based his political faith; and the incongruous rational
structure he reared upon so irrational a foundation:

   . . . in the Athens of Plato's day, as he saw with acute prevision . . .
centrifugal forces had come to be ruinously in excess of the centripetal.
Its rapid, empiric, constitutional changes, its restless development of
political experiment, the subdivisions of party there, the dominance of
faction, as we see it, steadily increasing, breeding on itself, in the pages
of Thucydides, justify Plato's long-drawn paradox that it is easier to
wrestle against many than against one. *The soul, moreover, the inward
polity of the individual, was the theatre of a similar dissolution* [43] . . .
the Heraclitean flux, so deep down in nature itself — the flood, the fire —

seemed to have laid hold on man, on the social and moral world, dissolving or disintegrating opinion, first principles, faith, establishing amorphism, so to call it, there also. All along, indeed, the genius, the good gifts of Greece to the world had had much to do with the mobility of its temperament. Only . . . the defect naturally incident to that fine quality had come to have unchecked sway.

Mobility! We do not think that a necessarily undesirable condition of life, of mind, of the physical world about us. 'Tis the dead things, we may remind ourselves, that after all are most entirely at rest, and might reasonably hold that motion . . . covers all that is best worth being. And as for philosophy — mobility, versatility, the habit of thought that can most adequately follow the subtle movement of things, that, surely, were the secret of wisdom, of the true knowledge of them. It means susceptibility, sympathetic intelligence, capacity, in short. . . . Yet to Plato motion becomes the token of unreality in things, of falsity in our thoughts about them. *It is just this principle of mobility . . . that . . . he desires to withstand.* Everywhere he displays himself as an advocate of the immutable.[44] . . . the key to Plato's view of the Sophists . . . is that *they do but fan and add fuel to the fire in which Greece, as they wander like ardent missionaries about it, is flaming itself away.* . . . they were really developing further and reinforcing the ruinous fluidity of the Greek, and especially of the Athenian people.[45] . . . Those evils of Athens . . . came from an exaggerated assertion of the fluxional, flamboyant, centrifugal Ionian element in the Hellenic character. . . . They could be cured only by a counter-assertion of the centripetal Dorian ideal, as actually seen best at Lacedaemon; by way of simplification, of a rigorous *limitation* of all things, of art and life, of the souls, aye, and of the very bodies of men, as being the integral factors of all beside. It is in those simpler, corrected outlines of a reformed Athens that Plato finds the " eternal form " of the State, of a city as such, like a well-knit athlete, or one of those perfectly disciplined Spartan dancers. His actual purpose therefore is at once reforming and conservative.[46] . . . " The Republic " . . . is the protest of Plato . . . against the principle of flamboyancy or fluidity in things, and in men's thoughts about them. Political " ideals " may provide not only types for new states, but also in humbler function, a due corrective of the errors, thus renewing the life, of old ones. But like other medicines the corrective or critical ideal may come too late, too near the natural end of things. The theoretic attempt made by Plato to arrest the process of disintegration in the life of Athens . . . by forcing it back upon a simpler and more strictly Hellenic type, ended . . . in theory.[47]

The Athenian Collapse. — " Ended . . . in theory." Yes, just that. From the beginning of the fourth century, the disintegration of Athenian political life proceeded unchecked, as was inevitable from the very nature of the processes involved, and one

disaster followed another: first the protracted misery of the
internecine feuds that made of the Pan-Hellenism of Isocrates
a hollow mockery, then the irruption of the hard-bitten Mace-
donians under Philip and Alexander, and finally the degradation
of the whole of Greece to the rank of a mere Roman province
called Achaea. To be sure, even when Athens presented " a mourn-
ful picture of weakness and anarchy " her economic life flowed on
almost unchecked; [48] the metropolitan economy, international in
its very nature, was but little affected by the decline of the city-
state — by the passing of that *polis* which had once held men's
loyalties above all else. Not only this: Athens fulfilled in her
political impotence the proud boast of Pericles; she became the
teacher of Greece, and of the whole known world — in her
Lyceum the keen-eyed realistic stranger, Aristotle the Ionian
Stagirite,[49] who knew and thought again all that the Greeks of all
time had ever known and thought, began a conquest of posterity
that for two thousand years and more was to make the very name
of Greece a proud proclamation of the victory of " mobility,
versatility, the habit of thought that can most adequately follow
the subtle movement of things." All this and more might be said
of the glory of the city in her decline,[50] and yet Athens, the Athens
of Marathon, Plataea, and Salamis, the Athens of the Periclean
Age, the Athens that the poets and philosophers of the famous
fifth century had conjured up out of the formless void, was gone
from the face of the earth forever.

Summary of Hellenic Analysis. — The end of the tale has
come, but a summary of the processes involved may prove a useful supplement: (1) The settlement of Ionia under frontier conditions, and the later expansion of Greece, generated in metropolitan Ionia, a full century before similar phenomena appeared
in Greece proper, tendencies toward rationalism, secularization,
social atomization, and extreme individuation that were largely
responsible both for the achievements and the failures of the
thereby " mentally mobilized " Ionians. (2) As a result of a
series of minor changes which were primarily due to Ionian influence and which, although fairly rapid in themselves, together
comprised a type of change that may be called slow alteration,
the Athenian state reached a stage of political development before the Persian Wars that made it a potential commercial rival
of Miletus. (3) This potentiality was translated into a greater
actuality when, as the result of an intrusive factor in the form of
the Persian Wars, the vicinal position of Athens suddenly shifted
to the center of the Mediterranean world. (4) This rapid muta-

tion enormously increased the vicinal accessibility of Athens and in turn produced the accelerated development of metropolitan and international economy and of rationalistic and individualistic tendencies. (5) The accelerated development of Athenian metropolitan economy greatly increased the division of labor, the prevalence of pecuniary valuation, and the number of mentally mobile Asiatic-Ionian Metics resident in Athens, all of which had a marked mobilizing influence on the mentality of the stable citizens to whom the political strength of Athens had largely been due. (6) The accelerated development of Athenian metropolitan economy also brought with it an influx of Ionian Metics from the most highly secularized, rationalistic, mentally mobile classes, and these Metics spread their individualistic doctrines among the Athenians, thus providing rationalizations of the prevalent unrest generated by the sudden impact of pecuniary valuation and new "vanity-values," which rationalizations in turn increased the unrest. (7) The Metic philosophers also influenced a group of Athenian intellectuals — historians, dramatists, and philosophers — of whom Socrates was the most striking example. (8) These intellectuals added their influence to that of the Ionian newcomers in rapidly disseminating doctrines that still further increased the mental mobility prevalent among Athenians of the latter half of the fifth century. (9) One aspect of this mental mobility, individuation, finally reached such a degree that the attitudes necessary for the maintenance of a stable political structure disintegrated, and although the metropolitan economy continued to flourish, the Athenian state collapsed. (10) Plato and other individuated but theoretically conservative Athenians hoped to reconstruct it on a rational basis, but in the very nature of the case their efforts met with no success, and the *polis* as an effective form of political organization remained forever a thing of the past.

The Mental Mobility of the Hellenistic World. — A new chapter for Hellenism begins with the great conquests of Alexander. The Alexandrian empire promptly fell to pieces upon the death of its founder, but its significance for the diffusion of Hellenism was not thereby entirely destroyed. On the paths of his marches Alexander founded seventy cities, all of them named after himself. According to a leading authority, these cities were " founded as special centers of culture or points of defence, and organized as such with a certain local independence. These cities . . . were the real backbone of Hellenism in the world. . . . Many were upon great trade lines, like the Alexandria which still exists." [51] Others were garrison towns in distant provinces or outposts guarding the frontiers against the barbarians. It was Alexander's purpose " to discountenance sporadic country life in villages and encourage town communities. The towns accordingly received considerable privileges. . . . The Greek language and political habits were thus the one bond of union among them, and the extraordinary colonizing genius of the Greeks once more proved itself." [52]

In this fashion, then, was Hellenism diffused throughout Macedonia, Syria, Egypt and a great number of smaller states. The various Hellenistic cities were closely connected by a thriving maritime commerce. In particular, one might mention the growing preëminence of Rhodes and of Alexandria. In both cases commercial success was closely followed by intellectual achievements. Rhodes became a center of philosophy and oratory, and Alexandria, with its great libraries, museums, and corps of savants, took undisputed leadership in erudition and science. The mental mobility implicit in the Hellenic tradition, however, gave to the various Hellenistic kingdoms a lack of stability and an incapacity to unite that resulted in constantly unsettled political conditions, with never-ending intrigues and more or less overt conflicts. As always, they were unable to combine effectively, even in the face of common danger. At a certain point, it became quite obvious that the growing military power of Rome contained a serious threat to the future independence of the Hellenistic states, but even when Pyrrhus of Epirus made a bold and serious attempt to check Roman expansion, his Hellenistic allies refused to come to his assistance. Later the Roman conquest of Achaea was materially aided by its internal dissension.

In the later days of Hellenism, mental mobility as a personality trait was the most conspicuous characteristic of the Hellenistic population. This comes out very clearly in the unfavorable opinion of the Greeks of the Hellenistic period held by many Romans who nevertheless professed themselves great admirers of Greek culture and civilization. In his defense of Flaccus, Cicero made the following observations: " If ever there was a Roman of Greek predilections it was I. . . . But moral strictness and truth in giving evidence that nation has never practised; they have no idea of the importance, weight and authority of this matter." [53] In a letter to his brother on the duties of a provincial governor, Cicero warns him against intimacies with Greeks, asserting that only a few of them are still worthy of ancient Hellas, and that most are fickle and deceitful. In another place, he says of the Greeks that

he is " sick of their want of character (*levitas*), their obsequious-
ness, their devotion, not to principle, but to the profit of the
hour." [54] This, coming not from a Cato but from a man who himself earned a not-unfounded reputation as a trimmer, is a severe
indictment. It appears to have reflected the common opinion in
Italy. Thus Strabo describes the Alexandrians as excessively fickle,
volatile, and given to the pursuit of pleasure. From all this it
seems evident that mental mobility, secularization, and liberation
from old restraints had proceeded to such a point as to be seriously
destructive both of individual character and of social cohesion.

The Rise of Rome. — In the fourth century B.C., when an extraordinary mental mobility was producing in the Greek city-states
a remarkable efflorescence of culture on the one hand and a dissolution of political cohesion on the other, there was in the process
of formation a new and much more powerful empire which was
destined to be the cultural heir of Greek civilization. The story
of the gradual ascendancy of Latium and of Rome over the other
Italian states and subsequently over the whole civilized world is
a long and complicated one. Fortunately we need deal here with
only those aspects of this development which are particularly
relevant in determining the general mental climate out of which
the social thought of Roman writers arose.

The three chief powers in Italy up to 500 B.C. were the Etruscans, the Samnites, and the Latins. The political independence of
Latium was originally preserved by several factors : first, the
struggle between Greeks and Etruscans which made Latium a
buffer between two spheres of influence; second, a rather difficult
terrain, consisting in large part of marshy plains, and hills on
which agriculture was at first difficult; and third, access to the sea.
This last factor was of enormous significance in the rise of Latium,
as it made it culturally accessible to the currents of civilization
flowing in from Greece, Etruria, and Carthage. The constant
danger of attack from several sources, however, welded the inhabitants into a well-knit sacred community, intensified by a love
of the soil which had been turned to agriculture with such great
difficulty.

Growing Power and Greek Gifts. — Rome quite early became
the leading city in Latium, a fact signalized by an important commercial treaty with Carthage. For a period she had an Etruscan
dynasty, upon the expulsion of which there was set up a sort of
republic of the patrician families. With the growth of economic
opportunity and commercial accessibility the proportion of plebeians greatly increased. In the first place, " the commercial im-

portance of Rome attracted settlers from other parts of Italy,
especially Latium, just as the class of *metoeci* [Metics] was
created by a similar development at Athens." [55] The importation
of artisans for industry, and the annexation by conquest or agreement of adjacent Latin territories, with the accompanying destruction of local aristocracies and the liberation of their
" clients," also worked in the same direction. In all these respects,
then, we see a gradual weakening of the immobilizing ties of the
sacred community.

The sacking of Rome by the Gauls about 390 B.C. revealed the
insufficiency of a purely patrician army and led to the widening
of the basis of citizenship. By granting civic privileges and military duties to the plebeians, Rome immensely augmented her military power and also made possible considerable increases in social
mobility. The increasing accessibility of Rome is well reflected in
the development of Roman religion. While on the one hand the
ancient nobility of Etruscan origin imposed an Etruscan style of
religious architecture and of worship, the deities which were
worshiped in these shrines were not of Etrurian but of Greek
origin. " The plebeian immigrants from the Hellenized cities of
Latium develop trade and industry and bring with them a number
of cults, some of them Greek but adopted by the Latins, and others
Latin but modified by the Greeks." It is significant that " all the
new gods have to do with trade and industry." [56]

A long series of wars was necessary for Rome to defeat the
Etruscans and the Samnites and to become master of Italy; another to destroy her chief rival Carthage; and another to bring
to heel the independent Hellenistic states. These series of wars
had enormous financial and social repercussions on Roman life.
Most important was the enormous increase of wealth, consisting of indemnities exacted, land annexed, slaves captured, and
booty carried off. Capitalists of the senatorial class bought up
vast tracts of newly-acquired land from the state with money
legally or illegally gained in military operations, and farmed
them on a scientific basis with slave labor. A new class of wealthy
citizens sprang up composed of army contractors and commissars.
Groups of business men formed companies which leased from
the state the right to exploit various recently-acquired natural
resources. While on the one hand there thus grew up an enormously wealthy landlord and business class, on the other the small
freeholders in Italy were steadily diminishing in numbers and importance and a large rural and urban proletariat was in the process of formation.

The wars against Macedonia, the conquest of Syracuse, and the wars against Mithridates were of special significance in Roman intellectual and cultural development. Rome had always respected the intellectual and artistic eminence of Greece, and the close contact incidental to the political conquest and governance of the Greek states did much to intensify this attitude. Rome wished to be regarded not only as the political conqueror of Greece but as its spiritual successor, and hence as a real part of Greek civilization. Important in this connection was the presence in Italy of the thousand Achaean hostages who formed a highly selected group of the most enlightened and educated men from the cities of the Achaean League. These men, who were not allowed to return to Greece, were often welcomed by the more progressive Romans, and they did much to spread the cosmopolitan, secular culture of Hellenism. The most eminent of the Achaean hostages was Polybius of Megalopolis, who was an intimate of Scipio, the conqueror of Numantia and Carthage. To Polybius we owe our first scientific history of Rome, and his sociological theories were largely influenced by his reflections on that history.

The conservative and bucolic forces led by Cato were intransigently opposed to this extension of Greek influences. They keenly felt the danger to their sacred community of the rationalistic cosmopolitanism of the Hellenes. They were, however, fighting a losing fight. In every department of life the Greek influence was manifest, and especially in art, literature, and religion. Roman architecture and statuary took on more and more Greek forms; the national literature of Rome was largely translated from the Greek, and this familiarized the Roman populace with the Greek gods and heroes, who were promptly incorporated into the Roman religion, usually, but not always, under Latin names.

Republic Gives Way to Empire. — The growing concentration of wealth and power in the hands of the Roman senators produced revolutionary agitation for a transference of power from the senate to the popular assemblies, for the division and redistribution of the large estates, and for an extension of the franchise. This agitation gave rise to the bloody civil wars in the course of which the original issues were largely forgotten. With the pursuit of a frankly imperialistic policy, and the acquisition of enormous new provinces, Rome became *de facto* an empire, and the old republican constitution was no longer workable. What emerged clearly as a result of the civil wars was that henceforth the army would play a leading rôle in internal politics. Its support had become absolutely necessary for political rule within the state. Moreover, events had clearly established that the army could not be used to carry out any large and disinterested political programs; it was interested only in immediate material gain. From this, two conclusions for the development of Roman political life naturally followed. First, the inevitable trend was towards a personal military dictatorship. Caesar was the first clearly to perceive this fact. Second, a policy of more or less continuous imperialistic expansion and conquest was inevitable, for only by new plunder and grants of land could the army be kept satisfied.

Thus it happened that the first century B.C. was an epoch of transition from the old idea of a community of free city-states (on the Greek model) to the Oriental conception of a world-state ruled by one man. The social wars merely accelerated the tendencies towards the concentration of wealth and power which had previously existed. Though the great estates changed hands with every change in the political situation, they continued to grow larger and to become more and more the property of a few wealthy capitalists. Great fortunes became common; the number of millionaires greatly increased. Vertical social mobility was intense: by clever financial and political manipulation, freedmen and the children of slaves amassed considerable fortunes. Rome became the business center of the world: enormous transactions in the Roman wheat supply, the Italian exports of olive oil and wine, in tax farming, and the like, were daily carried out. Numerous Roman citizens spent their lives abroad in various business pursuits. (In one of the Eastern wars Mithridates slew some eighty thousand of these Roman traders!) The flow of capital from the provinces raised the wealth of Italy to tremendous heights, and led to a great expansion of industry. The provinces, however, were being rapidly bled white.

Particularly was this so in the East, where repeated requisitions and conquests and the unscrupulous tactics of tax-farmers and Roman bankers had plunged the formerly prosperous cities into an ever-increasing misery of debt. In part this accounts for the fact that Hellenistic thought became increasingly pessimistic about the things of this world and increasingly disinclined toward either profound philosophical speculation or careful scientific observation. Philosophy more and more turns to ethics, and particularly to an ethics of renunciation. The three leading philosophic schools, Stoic, Epicurean, and Cynic, all teach a " detachment from life," a mode of self-concentration which makes one indifferent to the vicissitudes of fortune.

After the horrors of the protracted civil wars, the peace initiated by the Empire of Augustus was gladly welcomed both by Rome and by the provinces. It is true that the Empire meant the end of political freedom and responsibility for Roman citizens, but this was a sacrifice which was willingly made on the altar of peace and stability, and Augustus was shrewd enough to retain certain of the older republican forms, and to maintain the special privileges of Italy, and particularly of the Roman senatorial class, in the Empire.

The Roman Peace and Urbanization. — The first two centuries of the Empire under Augustus and his successors formed an epoch of unrivalled internal peace and prosperity. The ideal of permanent peace seemed now for the first time realized, and its benefits were extended to what was in effect the whole civilized world. A second great achievement of the Empire was the extension and promulgation of that Greek culture which Rome had received from Hellenistic sources. This culture was transmitted to many areas — Spain, Britain, Gaul, parts of Germany, the north coast of Africa, central Asia Minor, the Caucasus and Transcaucasia, Syria, Palestine, Arabia, and so on. This culture was transmitted, not by coercion or political pressure, but by the prestige of Rome and the compelling attractiveness of its example. The cosmopolitan and urban character of this culture is well indicated by Rostovtzeff:

> The Roman Empire never was or tried to be a world-wide state of a national type — a state in which one nation subdues and forcibly assimilates other nations to itself: it became by its constitution more and more cosmopolitan. What gave it strength and substantiality and enabled it . . . to hold together . . . was its culture which all shared and all prized. . . . But for some trifling local variations this culture was the same everywhere. Like our modern culture it belonged to dwellers in towns and was closely connected with the Greek conception of the city. . . . There was no impassable gulf between town and country; and the town more and more attracted the rural population and inoculated them with a taste for town habits. Thus one of the chief tasks of the empire in its civilizing mission was to spread the urban method of life in places that knew nothing of it until they were conquered by Rome.[57] . . . The empire was a world-wide state, consisting of a number of urban districts, each of which had for its center a well-organized town or city. In these towns, and especially in the capital, lived that part of the population which directed the social and economic life of the empire.[58]

The urbanization and Romanization of the extensive Roman provinces would not have been possible if it had not been for an imposing series of military frontiers which not only preserved peace and order and defended Roman civilization, but even served in a special way to promote it. The inhabitants of the strips of frontier territory lived a peculiar sort of life. Half a million men, recruited in Italy or the provinces for twenty- or twenty-five-year periods, lived in permanent fortified camps strung along the frontiers. Around these barracks there grew up settlements, called *canabae*, of innkeepers, winesellers, dealers in war booty, and women (who were often married to the soldiers). After retirement, the soldiers quite commonly elected to stay in the district in which they had served their terms, and became farmers or tradesmen. In this fashion the *canabae* grew into villages and towns, and thus originated many important European cities, e.g., Cologne, Mainz, Strasbourg, Vienna, Budapest. These towns became important frontier markets, extensively visited in times of peace by the neighboring barbarians, and by traders from many remote districts. Here the visitors often spent extended periods in contact with Greco-Roman culture, and after leaving contributed in turn to its further diffusion.

Commerce, the City, and the Roman Road. — In the fields of transportation and communication the achievements of the Empire were impressive. An enormous area, including all the peoples fringing the Mediterranean, was closely linked into a single unit by a remarkable system of land and water routes. A series of magnificently-built roads converging on Rome spread out to the Atlantic, to the North Sea, to the Dardanelles and the Black Sea. Other systems covered Asia Minor, Syria, North Africa, and Britain. It is safe to say that almost every town of the least importance was linked up with main highways and readily accessible. Along these highways official couriers traveled by special post at an average of fifty miles a day. We are told that " Constantinople could be reached from Rome in twenty-four days and Alexandria in fifty-four. . . . *Such speeds would have been considered good in England of the seventeenth century. . . .* The roads were one of the most potent means whereby the Roman government created a citizenship transcending barriers of language, nationality, and color." [59] Sea transportation, while not so sure and steady as land transport, was much cheaper and was extensively used. The Mediterranean was in fact " a Roman lake." Every part of it was connected by shipping with every other part. Similarly, the great rivers of western Europe, the Nile, and the Black Sea were extensively navigated. After Pompey's war with the pirates, piracy seems to have given comparatively little trouble and the dangers to navigation were much more from nature than from man.

Along with the improvement of communication and transport there was under the early Empire a vast increase in commerce. Trade was maintained even with such distant markets as those of China, India, central and southern Africa, Arabia, central Asia, Russia, Germany, and Scandinavia. But more important was trade *within* the Empire, between Italy and the provinces, and among the provinces. This was stimulated by the purely nominal customs dues which interposed no effective barriers to free trade. " By securing safe communications, the government enabled every class and every race to exercise that form of activity which it found most congenial." [60] With the increase of commerce, the class of traders grew larger, and within it the Syrians, Arameans, and Jews played an increasingly important rôle. Their frank commercialism and detachment from local prejudices, their position as secular strangers, undoubtedly served to break down yet further whatever traditionalism and insularity still lingered on.

The new wealth created by this commerce and expanding industry was reflected, above all, in an increasingly comfortable and even luxurious urban life. Rome, with a population of more than a million, " became by degrees the most magnificent [city] in the world, and the pleasantest to live in." [61] The public buildings were remarkably large and beautiful, and were elegantly appointed. There were innumerable temples, forums, triumphal arches, commemorative columns, and statues, in addition to numerous libraries, museums, public baths, parks, shops, markets, and immense theaters and circuses. For the workers, employment was readily available, and the lowest classes were maintained by the state. Public amusements were a regular feature, as were occasional free distributions of money or food to the people by the state. While no other city could match Rome in these respects, almost every town, even the smaller and newer provincial ones, took Rome as a model. According to Rostovtzeff :

One may say without exaggeration that never in the history of mankind (except during the nineteenth and twentieth centuries in Europe and America) has a larger number of people enjoyed so much comfort; and that never, not even in the nineteenth century, did men live in such a surrounding of beautiful buildings and monuments as in the first two centuries of the Roman Empire.[62]

Resignation, Hedonism, and Rationalism. — We have now sketched the general social conditions of the Empire, and it remains only to describe the kind of mental climate which it in large degree helped to form. We have previously noted how the des-

perate situation of Greece had helped to make popular the Stoic
and Epicurean philosophies. It was these philosophies for Everyman, particularly Stoicism, and not the refined speculation of
Plato and Aristotle, which the Romans of the Augustan age acquired as part of the Hellenic tradition. In part, this was because
of the period in which the main Roman contact with Greek culture occurred, and in part it was because of the relative intellectual simplicity of these doctrines; their concreteness and their
applicability to practical problems were more in accord with the
peculiar characteristics of Roman mentality. Stoic doctrine was
clear, logical, and easily learned. In its later phase it treated the
form of government as unimportant, and advised the individual
to turn away from public affairs in order to concentrate on moral
improvement, self-discipline, and the cultivation of a sense of
duty. To Romans of the Augustan age, living under a dictatorship, it is easy to see how apposite and convenient this advice must
have seemed.

The relatively sudden extension of Greco-Roman culture over
the whole civilized world and the greatly intensified social interaction produced by the unification of so wide an area produced
important tendencies towards rationalism. The successive breaking down of narrow provincialisms, the widened mental horizons,
provided particularly fertile ground for the Stoic conception of
natural, universal law common to all mankind. This law was
viewed as the expression of divine reason which, single in spite of
its various manifestations, underlies and permeates all existence.
The doctrine of Stoicism won many converts among the highest
social classes in the Empire. The Emperor Marcus Aurelius is
perhaps the best example. Yet this doctrine, in spite of its undoubted dignity and moral elevation, carried but little conviction
to the mass of the population. It was too austere and rigorous,
and did not seek to provide much comfort for the dangers and
hardships of mortal existence.[63] In particular, it offered no consolation for death and no theory of personal immortality. But the
severe bloodshed and constant dangers of destruction during the
social wars had made some such anodyne a necessity for the bulk
of the population. It is therefore not surprising that Neo-Pythag-
oreanism, with its strong interest in a future life, should have
gained more and more of a foothold. The same may be said of
the Eleusinian mysteries.

Much attention has been paid throughout this chapter to the
individuating and secularizing effect of mental mobility in the
evolution of Greco-Roman society. An individualistic hedonism

and a scientific or materialistic rationalism are the natural outcome of this configuration of mental processes. Epicureanism provided the most cogent and dignified defense of this type of philosophic position in the ancient world. In spite of extraordinary
defamations by its opponents, Epicureanism secured numerous
converts, but many of them were far from the actual spirit of
Epicurus's teachings, and used his formulas to justify a life of immediate sensual enjoyment.

   Revulsion against Rationalism: the Syncretic Cults. — Thus
by the third century A.D. the rationalistic elements of Greek
philosophy were fast being displaced by various mystic, magical,
or religious ideologies. A notable increase in religious feeling was
occurring in the lower classes, and the upper classes were being
more and more influenced along religious lines by their social inferiors. Numerous proselytizing sects and cults were taking shape
in the East and beginning to move westward. " These religions
. . . were favored by the conditions of life due to the existence
of a world-wide state. Together with traders and artisans from
the East, these beliefs made their way into almost every commercial center, especially seaport towns, and there formed closed
religious societies. The empire put no obstacles in their way." [64]
The close interaction of these various creeds with each other and
with the older local cults of Latin or Greek origin led to " syncretism," the attempt to reconcile and blend these creeds with one
another, to view them as mere variants of a single idea. Mystical
and religious ideas were fused with the older philosophy by
Plotinus and his disciples. The official state religion had by now
entirely lost its vitality and its hold over the minds of men, and
the final battle for supremacy occurred between the mystical Neo-
Platonism of Plotinus on the one hand and Christianity on the
other. It was the latter which most nearly fulfilled the spiritual
requirements of the times and which conquered. For the triumph
of Christianity, in spite of its long persecution, there are undoubtedly many reasons, not the least of which was a shift of
interest from this life to the life to come. But it is surely not presumptuous also to see in the triumph of early Christianity a decisive reaction against the extremes of mental mobility, of scepticism, rationalism, individualism, and secularization which for
a time the Roman Empire had achieved for many of its educated
classes. For the early Christian, mental immobility was assured
by the acceptance of dogma on faith, secularism was abandoned
for a purely religious view of the world and man's rôle in it, and
individualism was overcome through membership in a body which

possessed the most intense group sentiment and which often required of the individual the ultimate sacrifice, martyrdom. And beyond doubt, " the blood of the saints was the seed of the Church."

Greco-Roman Thought about Mobility and Kindred Topics. — With this background in mind, it is now possible to deal directly with the various statements (few formulations reach the level where they can be dignified by the term " theories ") made by Greek and Roman writers on such topics as migration, culture contact, mental mobility, and cultural and social change. In view of space limitations, if for no other reason, we cannot offer an exhaustive survey. Moreover, we do not make the claim that the authors quoted are the " original sources " of the ideas they advance; in many instances they have had a host of predecessors whom we do not mention. Further, the authors we have chosen have in most cases a great deal more to say on the themes of this chapter and other topics of sociological interest than can be noted here; we merely offer samples. Once more, the treatment of the material is not systematic, for systematization would be virtually impossible without a highly artificial separation of phrases from contexts and much duplication. A simple chronological arrangement seems best. Some order is brought into the medley by the procedure of rephrasing the more important generalizations in modern terminology, but danger lies in this method unless the original is readily available for comparison, and we have therefore provided numerous quotations.

The writers laid under contribution are Herodotus, Thucydides, Plato, Aristotle, Strabo, Cicero, Caesar, and Seneca. These men were not scientists in the modern sense; we expect from them suggestion but not hypothesis. Suggestion, however, may be worth while — *vixere fortes ante Agamemnona!*

Before culling these suggestions, however, another word of warning is in order. The writers chosen frequently refer to migration, culture contact, mental mobility, and cultural and social change as if they were rare and exceptional. As it is, however, we know that at first man was a slow wanderer or drifter, following food,[65] that culture contact is by no means a rare occurrence, but on the contrary is the very warp of human history,[66] that the diffusion of culture has frequently been the result of minor, normal migrations,[67] and that social change is continuously going on.[68] In other words, social change may be a process of slow alteration as well as of rapid mutation; but the writings of the men we are considering usually deal with the surprising and the exceptional.

Aside from this there seem to be few serious difficulties, except that the various phenomena we are considering must usually be inferred from accounts of culture contact cast in moralistic or ethnocentric terms.

Herodotus and His Anecdotes. — "The Father of History," for example, says little or nothing about the trading journeys of his fellow-countrymen to Naucratis, the little Greek colony near the Canopic mouth of the Nile, but notes the haughty attitude of the Egyptians toward their young and pushing "inferiors," the Hellenes:

> They have an aversion to using Hellene customs: in a word, they are the most conservative of all nations. This is a point in which all the Egyptians are punctilious.[69]

Again, he says relatively little about the wide-ranging pastoral nomadism of the Scythians, but notes their aversion to adopting the mores of the secular stranger, the Greek merchant:

> They [the Scythians] avoid as much as possible the importation of foreign customs, and have a particular aversion for those of Hellas . . .[70]

He either knows or cares little about the perpetual invasions and conquests of the Sart regions of Persia by the Massagetae (variously known as Turanians, Daha, and Sacae), but he offers an anecdote about "Persians" which clearly points to the nomadic abstemiousness and stern discipline seized upon by later writers as the fundamental reason for their formidable fighting power:

> . . . a certain Artembares . . . made the following suggestion to the Persians, which they disclosed to Cyrus: — "Since Zeus gives supremacy to the Persians, and to you, O Cyrus, command of warriors, after the downfall of Astyages, take heart. We have a circumscribed country, one that is rough; but if we leave it, we shall find a better one . . ."

> When Cyrus heard this, he disapproved of the idea and said: "Do so, but prepare yourselves to be ruled, not to rule. For from luxurious lands come men who love luxury. The same land cannot be prolific in wonderful fruit and in mighty warriors."[71]

Further, he implicitly points to the contrast between the "iron horse-archers" the Persian ruling class once were, and the softened potentates they later became when the mores of the agriculturists of Iran had broken the nomad morale; the old Greek, for all his garrulousness, is a worthy forerunner of Ibn Khaldūn:

The Persians adopt foreign manners with wonderful facility. They thought the Median dress was fairer than their own, and adopted it. In battle they wear Egyptian breastplates. Directly they hear of any new luxury they procure it, and have introduced from Hellas a system of pederasty. They are polygamous, and also keep concubines.[72]

Here are a series of observations pointing plainly to migration, culture contact, and mental mobility; they could be supplemented by many more, for Herodotus was not an inveterate gossip and the father of *Kulturgeschichte* for nothing.

Thucydides, Student of Migration and Its Concomitants. — Even the historian of the Peloponnesian War, usually the model of the " history is past politics " school, could not refrain from a few simple, common-sense observations concerning non-political processes; indeed, migration receives at the hands of Thucydides one of the earliest explicit treatments:

. . . Hellas appears to have had no stable sedentary population until a comparatively recent date, and to have been subject in earlier times to migrations, in which populations were easily dislodged from their homes under pressure from some more numerous body of intruders. There was no trade and no security of intercourse by sea or by land. Each community lived at a subsistence level by its own local production, without accumulating capital or investing it in the land, since none could foresee when the next invader would deprive them of their homes, which they had not yet learnt to fortify. They also took it for granted that their bare daily bread would be as easy to gain in one place as in another. For those reasons they migrated readily, and therefore did not develop great manpower or great armaments. The richest territories . . . were particularly exposed to changes of population. The fertility of the soil produced accumulations of power, which resulted in ruinous civil disorders, and at the same time these countries were more eagerly coveted by foreigners. On the contrary, Attica, which enjoyed the longest unbroken immunity from civil disorders owing to the thinness of its soil, never lost its original population; and one of the strongest proofs of my contention that the comparative development of other countries was retarded by migrations is to be found in the fact that the most important victims of war and civil disorders in the rest of the Hellenic world found an asylum, as refugees, at Athens, became naturalised there from remote antiquity, and so still further increased the population, with the result that they subsequently overflowed from Attica and planted colonies in Ionia.[73]

Thucydides has here made several statements about the history of Attica that modern researches do not completely bear out, as we have seen, but his implicit generalizations, right or wrong, are worth noting: (1) a stable, sedentary population is necessary for the accumulation of large amounts of capital; (2) the habit of moving from place to place may be acquired as a result of historical processes; (3) the richest territories are those most subject to changes of population, a generalization pointed out by House; [74] (4) civil disorders, i.e., the class struggle, develop concomitantly with the increase of capital; (5) refugees frequently bring great advantages to the countries that receive them; (6) population may increase by slow accretion from without; and the like.

In another passage Thucydides hints at the condition upon which Goethe's Mephistopheles thus commented, " War, commerce, and piracy are an indivisible trinity ":

. . . in ancient times both the Hellenes and those Barbarians whose homes were on the coast of the mainland or in the islands, when they began to find their way to one another by sea, had recourse to piracy.[75]

Thucydides also points out the reason for the inland location of the older Greek cities, giving a historical basis for a peculiarity upon which, as we shall see, both Aristotle and Plato speculated:

. . . when navigation had become general and wealth was beginning to accumulate, cities were built upon the sea-shore and fortified; peninsulas too were occupied and walled-off with a view to commerce and defence against the neighboring tribes. But the older towns both in the islands and on the continent, in order to protect themselves against the piracy which so long prevailed, were built inland . . .[76]

He was also aware of the importance of vicinal location for the development of trade: Corinth was situated at " a break in transportation ":

Corinth, being seated on an isthmus, was naturally from the first a centre of commerce; for the Hellenes within and without the Peloponnese in the old days, when they communicated chiefly by land, had to pass through her territory in order to reach one another. Her wealth too was a source of power, as the ancient poets testify, who speak of " Corinth the rich." When navigation grew more common, the Corinthians, having already acquired a fleet, were able to put down piracy; they offered a market both by sea and land, and with the increase of riches the power of their city increased yet more.[77]

Plato, Urban Sociologist. — It remained for Plato, however, to make the first cardinal generalizations in urban sociology; he had observed the lax morality of Corinth and Athens, and he was anxious to build up a new *polis* with the simplicity, stability, and sincerity which he believed existed in Sparta:

ATH. And is there any neighboring state?

CLE. None whatever, and that is the reason for selecting the place.

ATH. Then there is some hope that your citizens may be virtuous; had you been on the sea, and well provided with harbors, and an importing rather than a producing country, some mighty savior would have been needed, and lawgivers more than mortal, if you were to have a chance of preserving your state from degeneracy and discordance of manners. But there is comfort in the eighty stadia; although the sea is too near, especially if, as you say, the harbors are so good. Still we must be satisfied. The sea is pleasant enough as a daily companion, but has also a bitter and brackish quality; filling the streets with merchants and shopkeepers, and begetting in the souls of men uncertain and unfaithful ways — making the state unfriendly and unfaithful both to her own citizens, and also to other nations.[78]

In a passage in *The Laws* he also makes several observations concerning colonies and the causes of social change which have been commented upon by Giddings as follows: " In no later writing that I know do we find in so few words so many cardinal generalizations as these lines contain upon the nature and behavior of human society." [79] Here is the passage:

Cities find colonization in some respects easier when the colonists are of one race, which like a swarm of bees goes from a single country, friends from friends, owing to some pressure of population, or other similar necessity; or because a portion of a state is driven by factions to emigrate. And there have been whole cities which have taken flight, when utterly conquered by a superior power in war. This, however, which is in one way an advantage to the colonist or legislator, in another point of view creates a difficulty. There is an element of friendship in the community of race, and language, and laws, and in common sacrifices, and all that; but inasmuch as such colonies kick against any laws which are other than they had at home, although they have been undone by the badness of them, yet because of the force of habit they would fain preserve the very customs which were their ruin; and the leader of the colony, who is their legislator, finds them troublesome and rebellious. On the other hand, the conflux of several populations might be more disposed to listen to new laws; but then, to make them combine and pull together, as they say of horses, is a most difficult task, and the work of years. . . . I was going to say that man never legislates, but that destinies and accidents happening in all sorts of ways, legislate in all sorts of ways. Either the violence of war has overthrown governments, and changed laws, or the hard necessity of poverty. And the power of disease has often caused innovations in the state, when there have been pestilence, and bad seasons continuing during many years.[80]

Some of Plato's generalizations may be formulated in modern terminology thus: (1) strangers are not controlled by the mores of their temporary stopping-place, hence their presence tends to bring about social disorganization; (2) isolation is favorable to social stability; (3) it is relatively easy to control homogeneous colonies if the institutions of the homeland are preserved, however imperfect these institutions were and are; (4) heterogeneous colonies will submit to innovations more readily than will homogeneous, but it is some time before such innovations pass beyond the formal stage; (5) catastrophes may be immediately antecedent to social change; (6) social disorganization and social change are correlated.

Aristotle and Anonymity. — The great Stagirite does little more than sum up the arguments of Plato and others about the best location for a city, but he does it admirably. The element of migration is much more explicit in his comment than in the Platonic original:

> Whether a communication with the sea is beneficial to a well-ordered state or not is a question which has often been asked. It is argued that the introduction of strangers brought up under other laws, and the increase of population, will be adverse to good order (for a maritime people will always have a crowd of merchants coming and going), and that intercourse by sea is inimical to good government.[81]

Perhaps the earliest recognition of the rôle of the city in promoting anonymity and thereby facilitating mental mobility is contained in the following passage, also by Aristotle:

> . . . where the number of the citizens is too many . . . it is more easy for strangers and sojourners to assume the rights of citizens, as they will easily escape detection in so great a multitude.[82]

Strabo the Wide-Ranging. — In spite of the flashes of insight scattered throughout their works, most Greek writers following Plato and Aristotle — Polybius, Eratosthenes, and others — have little to give us that is relevant to the present theme. Not until we come to Strabo, who finished the final revision of *The Geography* between the years 17 and 23 A.D., do we find an *embarras de richesses.* Our only difficulty is in selecting the passages most significant for our purposes from the great number that are relevant. It is perhaps best to begin with a disavowal of geographic determinism by Strabo the geographer:

> Arts, forms of government, and modes of life, arising from certain (internal) springs, flourish under whatever climate they may be situated; climate, however, has its influence, and therefore while some peculiarities are due to the nature of the country, others are the result

of institutions and education. It is not owing to the nature of the country, but rather to their education, that the Athenians cultivate eloquence, while the Lacedaemonians do not, nor yet the Thebans, who are nearer still.[83]

This disavowal does not commit him to a barren cultural determinism, however; he is always willing and eager to reckon with those factors of the geographic environment which promote communication, migration, and so on. Further, he sees that certain types of migration result in culture contact and mental mobility, as the following excerpts show (note the re-statement of Thucydides's theory about Corinth and the " break in transportation ") :

Corinth is said to be opulent from its mart. It is situated upon the isthmus. It commands two harbours, one near Asia, the other near Italy, and facilitates, by reason of so short a distance between them, an exchange of commodities on each side.

As the Sicilian strait, so formerly these seas were of difficult navigation, and particularly the sea above Maleae, on account of the prevalence of contrary winds, whence the common proverb,
     " When you double Maleae forget your home."
It was a desirable thing for the merchants coming from Asia, and from Italy, to discharge their lading at Corinth without being obliged to double Cape Maleae. For goods exported from Peloponnesus, or imported by land, a toll was paid to those who had the keys of the country. This continued afterwards for ever. In after-times they enjoyed even additional advantages, for the Isthmian games, which were celebrated there, brought thither great multitudes of people. . . .

The temple of Venus at Corinth was so rich, that it had more than a thousand women consecrated to the service of the goddess, courtesans, whom both men and women had dedicated as offerings to the goddess. The city was frequented and enriched by the multitudes who resorted thither on account of these women. Masters of ships freely squandered all their money, and hence the proverb,
     " It is not in every man's power to go to Corinth." [84]

Comana is populous, and is a considerable mart, frequented by persons coming from Armenia. . . . The inhabitants are voluptuous in their mode of life. All their property is planted with vines, and there is a multitude of women, who make a gain of their persons. . . . The city is almost a little Corinth.[85]

He contrasts the type of social structure found in these focal points of population movement, where mental mobility is high, with the simpler type of sacred community found among the pastoral nomads, and points out how contact with Greek and Roman mores, brought about by the rise of navigation, tended to bring with it disorganization of the nomad society:

And when we consider the amount of fraud connected with trading speculations even amongst ourselves, what ground have we to wonder that Homer should have designated as the justest and most noble those [Scythians] who had but few commercial and monetary transactions, and with the exception of their swords and drinking cups, possessed all things in common, and especially their wives and children, who were cared for by the whole community according to the system of Plato. . . . And this is still the opinion entertained of them by the Greeks; for we esteem them the most sincere, the least deceitful of any people, and much more frugal and self-relying than ourselves. And yet the matter of life customary among us has spread almost everywhere, and brought about a change for the worse, effeminacy, luxury, and over-refinement, inducing extortion in ten thousand different ways; and doubtless much of this corruption has penetrated even into the countries of the nomads, as well as those of the other barbarians; for having once learnt how to navigate the sea, they have become depraved, committing piracy and murdering strangers; and holding intercourse with many different nations, they have imitated both their extravagance and their dishonest traffic, which may indeed appear to promote civility of manners, but do doubtless corrupt the morals and lead to dissimulation, in place of the genuine sincerity we have before noticed.[86]

Strabo has undoubtedly exercised a great deal of influence upon those social theorists who trace the rise of the class state to the conquest of tillage peoples by pastoral peoples. As we shall see when we speak of Gumplowicz, Oppenheimer, Ratzel, Cowan, and others, Strabo has given in the following statements an anticipation of many points of importance in their theories:

All, or the greatest part of them [the Scythians], are nomads. . . .
Between these people, Hyrcania, and Parthia as far as Aria lies a vast and arid desert, which they crossed by long journeys, and overran Hyrcania, the Nesaean country, and the plains of Parthia. These people agreed to pay a tribute on condition of having permission to overrun the country at stated times, and to carry away the plunder. But when these incursions became more frequent than the agreement allowed, war ensued, afterwards peace was made, and then again war was renewed. Such is the kind of life which the other nomads also lead, continually attacking their neighbours, and then making peace with them.[87]

The nomads are more disposed to war than to robbery. The occasion of their contests was to enforce the payment of tribute. They permit those to have land who are willing to cultivate it. In return for the use of the land, they are satisfied with receiving a settled and moderate tribute, not such as will furnish superfluities, but the daily necessaries of life. If this tribute is not paid, the nomads declare war. Hence the poet calls these people both just, and miserable, for if the tribute is regularly paid, they do not have recourse to war. Payment is not made by those who have confidence in their ability to repel attacks with ease, and to prevent the incursion of their enemies.[88]

This might almost pass for an abstract of Oppenheimer's *The State*!

Again, Strabo has pointed out one of the effects of isolation, viz., the development of the psychical basis for such "anti-stranger" manifestations as the Spartan *xenelasia*, although he draws his example from another source:

> The rough and savage manner of these people [the mountaineers of Spain] is not alone owing to their wars, but likewise to their isolated position, it being a long distance to reach them, whether by sea or land. Thus the difficulty of communication has deprived them both of generosity of manners and of courtesy. At the present time, however, they suffer less from this, both on account of their being at peace and the intermixture of Romans. Wherever these [influences] are not so much experienced people are harsher and more savage.[89]

Cicero and Maritime Mobility. — Among the Roman writers Cicero is especially important for our purpose. His observations upon the mental mobility of maritime cities are more detailed than those of either Plato or Strabo:

> Maritime cities are . . . exposed to corrupt influences, and revolutions of manners. Their civilization is more or less adulterated by new languages and customs, and they import not only foreign merchandise, but also foreign fashions, which allow no fixation or consolidation in the institutions of such cities. Those who inhabit these maritime towns do not remain in their native place, but are urged afar from their homes by winged hope and speculation. And even when they do not desert their country in person, their minds are always expatiating and voyaging round the world.

> There was no cause which more deeply undermined Corinth and Carthage, and at last overthrew them both, than this wandering and dispersion of their citizens, whom the passion of commerce and navigation had induced to abandon their agricultural and military interests.

> The proximity of the sea likewise administers to maritime cities a multitude of pernicious incentives to luxury, which are acquired by victory or imported by commerce; and the very agreeableness of their position nourishes the expensive and deceitful gratifications of the passions. And what I have spoken of Corinth may be applied, for aught I know, without incorrectness to the whole of Greece. For almost the entire Peloponnesus, the Enianes, the Dorians and the Dolopes, are the only

inland peoples. Why should I speak of the Grecian islands, which girded by the waves, seem as if they were all afloat, together with the institutions and manners of their cities? And these things I have before noticed do not respect ancient Greece only; for all its colonies likewise are washed by the sea, which have expatriated from Greece into Asia, Thracia, Italy, Sicily, and Africa, with the single exception of Magnesia. Thus it seems, as if fragments of the Grecian coasts had been appended to the shores of the barbarians. For among the barbarians themselves none were heretofore maritime, or inclined to navigation, if we except the Carthaginians and Etruscans; one for the sake of commerce, the other of pillage. Here then is one evident reason of the calamities and revolutions of Greece, because she became infected, as I before observed, with the vices which belong to maritime cities. But yet, notwithstanding these vices, they have one great advantage; it is, that all the commodities of foreign nations are thus concentrated in the cities of the sea, and that the inhabitants are enabled in return to export and send abroad the produce of their native lands to any nation they please, which offers them a market for their goods.[90]

Here are several generalizations which, to be sure, may not be valid, but which are none the less important: (1) the mental mobility associated with the type of migration peculiar to trading centers gives rise to social disorganization; (2) mobility in the broadest sense is a *mental* phenomenon, and may arise in a particular individual when no significant change in his geographical location has occurred; (3) culture contact is facilitated by geographical conditions making " transthalassic " movement easy; (4) the extension of the market is accompanied by the decline of agricultural and military interests; (5) the political disunion of Greece was an outgrowth of the social disorganization concomitant with a high rate of migratoriness and mental mobility; and the like.

Caesar the Observer. — Cicero's contemporary, Julius Caesar, certainly had excellent opportunities to observe the effects of migration and culture contact, and in his *Gallic Wars* shows that such opportunities were not altogether lost. Speaking of the various tribes against which campaigns have been conducted, he says:

Of all these, the Belgai are the bravest, because they are the furthest from the civilization and refinement of [our] Province, and merchants least frequently resort to them, and import those things which tend to effeminate the mind. . . .[91]

Upon their territories bordered the Nervii, concerning whose character and customs when Caesar inquired he received the following information: — That there was no access for merchants to them; that they suffered no wine and other things tending to luxury to be imported; because they thought that by their use the mind is enervated and the courage impaired: that they were a savage people and of great bravery.[92] . . .

It is not without significance that both the Belgai and Nervii, although partly sedentary, practiced pastoral nomadism; Caesar's observations sound strangely like the comments of Herodotus upon the Scythians and those of Strabo upon the " nomads."

Again, Caesar points out how the combined influences of accessibility and a culture making navigation possible produce similarity in the cultures of certain coastal areas:

The island [Britain] is triangular in its form, and one of its sides is opposite to Gaul. One angle of this side . . . is in Kent, whither almost all ships from Gaul are directed. . . .

The most civilized of all these nations are they who inhabit Kent, which is entirely a maritime district, nor do they differ much from the Gallic customs.[93]

Seneca the Moralist. — It is from the rhetorician and practical ethicist Seneca that the most valuable passage, for present purposes, is gleaned. He comments on the movement of large numbers of the population to the city of Rome, and analyzes the motives which seem to account for such movement:

Look, I pray you, on these vast crowds, for whom all the countless roofs of Rome can scarcely find shelter: the greater part of those crowds have lost their native land: they have flocked hither from their country towns and colonies, and in fine from all parts of the world. Some have been brought by ambition, some by the exigencies of public office, some by being entrusted with embassies, some by luxury which seeks a convenient spot, rich in vices, for its exercise, some by their wish for a liberal education, others by a wish to see the public shows. Some have been led hither by friendship, some by industry, which finds here a wide field for the display of its powers. Some have brought their beauty for sale, some their eloquence: people of every kind assemble themselves together in Rome, which sets a high price both upon virtues and vices.[94]

Paraphrasing, his conclusions are as follows: (1) the large city offers opportunities for differentiation along highly specialized lines; (2) both the elementary segmental cravings and the most highly sublimated desires may best be gratified in the large city; (3) movement to the city is largely determined by a prior process of individuation; (4) the highly specialized person finds the best market for his abilities in the city; and the like.

Summary of the Chapter. — The mental mobility fostered by the peculiar situation of the Asiatic Ionians was transmitted to the Greeks, and particularly to the Athenians, so effectively that the efflorescence of intellect and the decadence of political cohesion that marked the teacher also manifested itself in the pupil. When Rome became heir of the culture of Hellenism, a similar process of transmission of mental mobility became apparent. But after all Rome was exposed to a world vastly greater; Greek influences alone do not account for the mobile types of thought and conduct that appeared in the later days of the Empire. Urbanization and individuation, exceeding even the Hellenistic example, were initiated and diffused by the revolution in communication made possible through Roman colonization, citizenship, highways, and pacification of the seas.

Turning to the reflection in social thought of the situations thus engendered, we noted that, although Herodotus (484–425 B.C.) said little that was explicit about migration and culture contact, his writings abound in descriptions of the *effects* of these phenomena, and that with Thucydides (471–400 B.C.) the treatment becomes more definite and direct. When Plato (427–347 B.C.) wrote his various treatises, mobility, isolation, social change, and disorganization were placed in the foreground of the discussion. Aristotle (384–322 B.C.) added little to Plato's arguments, but, perhaps as a result of the influence of Hippocrates (460–359 B.C.), he dealt with migration even more explicitly, and was one of the first to consider the rôle of the city in promoting anonymity. Strabo (63 B.C.–21 A.D.) disavowed geographic determinism, and pointed to a valid contrast between the types of social structure found in focal points of mobility and in isolated societies — a contrast borne out by modern investigations. Cicero (106–43 B.C.) in detail, and Caesar (100–44 B.C.) in passing, were concerned with the mobility and accessibility of coastal areas. Just as Strabo had used Corinth, Seneca (4 B.C.–65 A.D.) used Rome as a source of information regarding the effects of urbanization, and showed rare insight in his analysis of the processes involved.

The decipherment, in 1952, of Minoan Linear Script B (see p. 134) has changed many of the details relating to the antecedents of Greek social thought as recorded in the earliest parts of this chapter. However, the main outlines are still reasonably accurate, in large measure because Becker, basing his treatment on his unpublished doctoral dissertation, "Ionia and Athens: Studies in Secularization" (U. of Chicago, 1930), refused to accept the Evans thesis (taken over *in toto* by Toynbee) that Mycenae was a mere Minoan colony. For the Minoans, some of the necessary revisions in Becker's treatment are to be found in his article, "Church and State in the Cosmos of Crete," *International Review of Social History* (Amsterdam), vol. i, Part II (Fall, 1956), pp. 253-95.

CHAPTER V

Classical Theories of the Origin of Society and the State

DISTINCTIONS WITH DIFFERENCES. — In attempting a résumé of the theories of the origin of society and the state prevalent in the Greek and Roman cultures commonly called "Classical," a few observations concerning terminology should be made. Although today the concepts society, state, and government are distinct categories to the informed student of the social sciences, such was not the case until the later Middle Ages or early modern times, and even in many modern writers, notably the legalistic type of political scientist, a certain vagueness seems to persist. Even though there were preliminary attempts at distinguishing between these concepts in both classical and medieval times, as in Aristotle's discussion of the nature of a constitution and Marsiglio of Padua's notion of the delegation of lawmaking power, still it was not until the publication in 1576 of Jean Bodin's *Six Books Concerning the Republic* that a clear distinction was made between these three terms.[1] By the state we mean, to quote from one of the better manuals, " a sovereign community, politically organized for the promotion of common ends and the satisfaction of common needs ";[2] while the government represents " the collective name for the agency, magistracy, or organization, through which the will of the state is formulated, expressed, and realized."[3] The term " society " is a still broader concept. Willoughby has well distinguished between the nature of society and of the state: " We thus distinguish between the conception of an aggregate of men as politically organized — as constituting a body politic — and the same community of men as forming merely a group of individuals with mutual economic and social interests. The body politic is this social body plus the political organization. An aggregate of men living together and united by mutual interests and relationships we term a society."[4]

Not only the lack of differentiation between these concepts in ancient times makes the study of the Classical theories of the origin of the state confusing to the modern reader, but an equal misunderstanding may arise if one does not remember that the view of a state in the works of Greek, Roman, and early medieval writers was that of the city-state of Classical times. Not until the time of St. Thomas Aquinas, and more particularly that of Machiavelli, do we find theorists getting much beyond that conception, and even they rather modified than abandoned the Classical notions.[5] Bodin, again, seems to have been the first one resolutely to turn his back upon the notion of limitation of numbers in a state and to take the ground that sovereign organization is the fundamental characteristic of that institution.[6] Naturally, then, the early conception of the nature of the state as a limited city-state would modify to some extent any theories regarding its origin.

Theories of Socio-Political Origins from Homer to Socrates. — As is well known, some of the earliest records of Greek literature are to be found in the Homeric poems. In them we find no particular theories regarding the state, but rather a description of the political conditions in the early stages of Greek society, conditions which have been well summarized in the works of Seymour and of Keller.[7] Modern comparative ethnology has shown that in many important respects these conditions were not widely different from the state of semi-tribal, semi-feudal political conditions wherever they occur. Aristotle seems to have believed that in those days the kings were permitted to reign by the sufferance of the people and were chosen by them. Janet criticizes this conception and shows that, like all similar tribal kings, their power was thought to be derived from a divine source; they were traditional-charismatic leaders.[8] Says Janet:

> Aristotle describes the monarchy of the heroic times as a monarchy which rested upon the consent of the people and was hereditary according to law. It is impossible, however, to discover in Homer any traces of this popular origin of monarchy. Rather it was held that the monarchy had a divine origin. It was said that the power of the kings was derived from Jupiter. Their power, like the power of the patriarch, was absolute and did not tolerate any opposition.[9]

The functions of these Homeric kings included those of the priest, judge, and military leader. Their rule was of a patriarchal nature:

> The monarchy was still of a patriarchal type; the kings were called " the shepherds of their peoples "; the welfare and safety of the people were their chief solicitude.[10]

In addition to the kings, there were assemblies consisting of the elders, and sometimes of the whole people, to whom the kings submitted their proposals. The assemblies did not deliberate but gave their advice by acclamation.

Passing down some five centuries from the time of the circumstances described in the Homeric literature one finds a most striking passage in Aeschylus (525–456 B.C.), where he anticipates Lucretius by more than five centuries in a very acute description of the general course of the development of civilization.[11] Elsewhere in Aeschylus, however, we find little that relates to the present theme, and we therefore turn to the historian and traveler, Herodotus (484–425 B.C.). In Book III, 80–82 of his *History,* he introduces a dialogue as to the respective merits of the three main forms of government: monarchy, oligarchy, and democracy. While the argument is put in the mouths of Persians, there can be little doubt that the ideas were Greek. Janet is of the opinion that this is the first historic instance of a discussion of this question, which has exercised the ingenuity of political thinkers from the days of Herodotus to the present, and concerning which no general agreement has ever been reached:

> Such were the diverse opinions which were opposed to each other in this memorable debate. Here was brought for the first time the problem of the political destinies of peoples, a discussion which, in all probability, will never terminate.[12]

Socrates. — We do not have enough records of the sayings of Socrates to judge with any accuracy whether or not he may rightfully be accredited with having formulated a theory of the state. It seems reasonable to suppose that he followed the Sophists in introducing the conception of the law of nature as contrasted to human law, and thus opened up a line of thought which in its later manifestations became a fertile basis for theories of political and social origins.[13] Whether or not Socrates saw any such possibilities in his doctrine we do not know. What is universally agreed concerning the contribution of Socrates to political science is that he brought in a beginning of a rational method in insisting upon precise and exact definitions of the terminology used. Says Janet:

> It was he who brought philosophy into ethics or into politics, which meant the same thing to the ancients; and it was also he who gave to ethics the method and the authority of science.[14]

At the same time, it is quite agreed that he developed no systematic theories in any line of thought; in fact, he was opposed to any system, and had his greatest delight in making evident the ridiculous elements in the systems of his day. Janet has summed up this point well:

There was nothing scientific about the political discussions of Socrates. With him politics were above all practical and moral. He dealt with the duties of public life as with the duties of private life, without bringing up any abstract theory.[15]

Plato. — When we come to Socrates's most famous disciple and apologist, Plato (427–347 B.C.), we first come upon ample evidence of a comprehensive theory. Plato's first work on society and the state in order of composition, and the most famous of all his treatises, is the *Republic.* This is not, however, in any way a scientific treatise. Least of all is it historic. Rather is it a picture of an ideal commonwealth, devised to illustrate Plato's conception of justice; so ideal in fact, that even Plato seems to have doubts regarding the possibility of its practical operation.[16] Opinions regarding its value to social science have varied. Pollock says: "The Platonic Republic, I think, must be considered as a brilliant exercise of the philosophic imagination, not as a contribution to political science." [17] Nettleship is perhaps a little more appreciative when he says:

The whole Republic is . . . an attempt to interpret human nature psychologically. The postulate upon which its method rests is that all the institutions of society, class organization, law, religion, art, and so on, are ultimate products of the human soul, an inner principle of life which works itself out in these outward shapes.[18]

In the *Republic,* Plato explains the origin of society (or in his terms, the state) as having its basis in the differentiated wants of mankind and the resulting division of labor. It by no means purports to be a historical account. "We may call it a logical picture of the origin of society, in this sense, that it illustrates what the existence and maintenance of society demands, and how these demands can best be satisfied, taking these demands in a logical order." [19] A state, according to Plato, is an integration of those having needs and those fulfilling them, every person belonging to both of these classes. The three primary needs of man being food, dwellings, and clothing, the fundamental requirement in the differentiation of the inhabitants of the first society was that one should be a husbandman, another a builder, another a weaver, and still another a shoemaker. Therefore, he says, every notion of a society in its period of inception must include four or five men. Not only was this division of labor essential to the existence of a society, but it was also of great value in bringing about the production of goods superior to those which could have been produced by a single man if compelled to care for all of his wants — that is, division of labor produced the specialist. On further reflection, Plato saw the necessity of adding other classes in the composition of his commonwealth. That the husbandman, builder, weaver, and shoemaker might have tools, there had to be carpenters and smiths. Then, to furnish oxen for the husbandmen and leather for the shoemaker, as well as cloth for the weaver, it was necessary to add shepherds and herdsmen. Further, as it was impossible to locate a city in a habitat which would be self-sufficing, there had to be a merchant class which would go and bring from neighboring cities such things as the state did not possess. And, that they might not return empty-handed, the amount of home production must be increased beyond the amount of home consumption, in order to enable the merchants to take something to offer in return for what they desired. This increased home consumption would of necessity entail a greater number of husbandmen and artisans, and as in many cases the merchants would be compelled to cross the sea, sailors would be essential to the success of their trip. On further reflection, however, Plato considered that it would be impossible for trading to go on in a city without a market-place: hence, there should be brought into being retail merchants who could care for the local trade. Finally, the class of hirelings and slaves was needed to make the state natural and perfect.

It is unnecessary to point out that his whole social scheme had for its basic principle exchange based upon a division of labor. Following this description of the origin of the state Plato goes on to give a picture of primitive life as he conceived of it.[20] This description of almost idyllic felicity bears a striking resemblance to Rousseau's picture of the life of man in a state of nature as painted in his *Discourse on the Origin of Inequality Among Men.* It should be borne in mind, however, that the resemblance between the two descriptions lies entirely in the conception of the primitive freedom from restraint and the resulting happiness, and not in external similarity, for Plato pictures a much more advanced stage of culture than does Rousseau.

But after all, this picture of primitive life hardly satisfied Plato's conception of the ideal state. The life in which the mere bodily wants were satisfied was inadequate — such a state was a mere " city of pigs." To secure perfection there must be a certain degree of luxury. Luxury, in turn, would call into being new classes whose services would be needed in providing for the new wants, and hence there would appear courtesans, sculptors, painters, embroiderers, musicians, poets, dancers, modistes, barbers, cooks, confectioners, nurses, tutors, and physicians. This great augmentation of the wants of the people would necessitate the extension of the borders of the state. Such territorial aggression, however, would in turn bring on war with the neighboring peoples. Since war, like everything else, could not be carried on successfully without individuals specially adapted to such a profession and devoting their time exclusively to it, a new class of soldiers or guardians had to be provided.[21]

Such is the origin of society or the state, for, as is evident to any student of social science, Plato has made no differentiation between the two, and, if one were to judge by strict canons, what he describes is not a state at all, but is merely an organized society.[22] His picture also reflects, as we have seen, the Greek conception of the limited nature of the ideal state as regards population and geographic extent. It comes in for all the criticism which may usually be directed against the products of uncontrolled speculation, but even this imaginative description is not as inaccurate as might be supposed, if viewed in harmony with Plato's method of approach. Nettleship has stated this in an admirable way:

We have now to notice a second feature in Plato's method; the state is to be looked at in its origin and growth. The phrase, "origin of society," suggests to us at first the most elementary state of society historically discoverable; but we must put that idea aside, for that is not what interests Plato here. He is not concerned with an historical enquiry, such as how Athens came to be what she was, but with this question: Given the fact of society as it is, what are the conditions which its existence implies, what is it in human nature which makes society exist? . . . We should have a modern parallel to this method if a sociologist, taking England, as it is, were to set out from the idea that, since life would not go on at all if its necessaries were not provided, the life of England rests ultimately on its industrial organization, and were to proceed to ask whether there was any principle of good or bad, right or wrong, discoverable in this industrial organization.[23]

This exposition of Nettleship's is most illuminating, and should prevent any unfair criticism of Plato arising from a misunderstanding of his viewpoint. Nevertheless, it is perhaps permissible to point out some of the main criticisms which might be brought against such a picture of the origin of society. In the first place, Plato's theory, like the social contract fallacy, implies knowledge prior to experience, an error which Hume exposed with great lucidity. It assumes that without any previous experience people would perceive the utility of coöperation and the division of labor, and as a result initiate social relations. Not only is this theory philosophically erroneous, but it is contrary to history and ethnography. Although in a crude sense there was undoubtedly a division of labor among animals [24] which was carried over into human society with ever-increasing scope and intensity, still the division of labor by highly specialized vocations is a relatively late arrangement in human society.

The fundamental fact to be noted is that the basis of society in its origin was the native tendency of the human being toward association, and not reflection and a perception of utility. Furthermore, although geographic, economic, and political factors have had a tremendous influence in shaping and hastening socialization and social evolution, none of them furnishes the fundamental cause of association, whereas man's biological makeup does.[25] Nevertheless, Plato offers a brilliant and incisive analysis of social organization, if not of social origins, and one which has been advanced in more or less recent times.[26] Certainly increased wants and the resultant increase of commerce and industry have been among the most potent factors in the progress of civilization, and it would be no more than tearing down a man of straw to criticize Plato for a lack of knowledge of modern anthropological method.

Barker, in his brilliant study of the political thought of Plato and Aristotle, criticizes the above explanation of the origin of society from the standpoint of psychology. He points out that Plato formulates his classes in society on the basis of the threefold division of the mind according to his system of psychology. The appetitive function of the mind was represented by the economic classes; the spirited by the military; and the rational by the governing. Barker points out that this radical separation of the classes of society is based upon a faulty conception of psychology which makes an unnatural division of the mind.[27] Though this may be true, it was an error which persisted until late in the nineteenth century.

In Book III of the *Laws,* as might be expected from the difference in the nature of the two works,[28] Plato gives a radically different explanation of the origin of society and the state. Instead of the transcendental *a priori* creation there is found a sober attempt to trace the origin of society.

In the first place, he calls attention to the necessity of getting a proper perspective as to the amount of time required for the evolution of society. With an insight strikingly modern, Plato lays it down as his opinion that the time essential for the development of complex social organization must have been vast and incalculable — infinite ages, in fact. To him the history of the past was one which recorded the successive rise and decline of civilizations — in other words, he was definitely a cyclical thinker. He follows this orientation with respect to time by an account of a great deluge, like that related in Genesis, which destroyed a majority of mankind. Only a few hill shepherds survived, and they were ignorant of the mechanical arts and political rules which had been a part of the accumulated knowledge of those who had perished.[29] It will be noticed that he does not here attempt to account for the origin of man, whose existence for ages prior to the deluge he takes for granted. In the sixth book of the *Laws*, however, he sets forth his views on the subject: " Every man should understand that the human race either had no beginning at all, and will never have an end, but will always be and has been, or that it began an immense while ago." [30]

From this scanty beginning in a few shepherds and their flocks, society developed through an immense period of time. In the *Laws* he gives another idyllic sketch of the early life of mankind which resembles Rousseau's picture of what he believed to be the most perfect period of human existence, namely, that of patriarchal society just prior to the emergence of civil society. The desolation of the primitive people created a feeling of affection and good-will towards one another; and, while they had enough to satisfy their wants, still there was not enough of surplus to cause enmity. It was, in short, a ruder but more virtuous association than was to be found in any subsequent age. They had no written laws, nor indeed any written language, thus coming within our preliterate category. The only authority was that of the head of the family, the patriarch.

The next step in the growth of society came when the shepherds left the mountains, congregated in the foot-hills, and commenced agriculture. Each group brought with it its peculiar laws and customs. The beginning of legislation took place when these groups selected arbiters who reviewed the various family laws, selected the best, and presented them to the chiefs for the government of the tribes. Society thus passed from the patriarchal family stage into the tribal condition, and concomitantly therewith rational domination began to emerge. The next advance came about when the tribes vacated the foot-hills and settled in the villages in the plains, where tribal kingship originated. The fourth and final step in the evolution of the state came when several villages united into a confederation.[31] The account of this fourth stage, or the formation of the Dorian Confederation, is one of the most interesting in the whole history of the theories of political origins, for it seems to be one of the first explicit Western statements of the theory of the governmental compact.[32] Plato thus describes the process:

> The case was as follows: Three royal heroes made oath to three cities which were under a kingly government, that both rulers and subjects should govern and be governed according to the laws which were common to all of them: the rulers promised that as time and the race went forward they would not make their rule more arbitrary; and the subjects said that, if the rulers observed these conditions, they would never subvert or permit others to subvert those kingdoms; the kings were to assist kings and peoples when injured, and the peoples were to assist peoples and kings in like manner.[33]

In some respects this account of social and political development offered in the *Laws* is almost modern. The emphasis on the great amount of time essential to the course of social evolution, the progress from the patriarchal family to tribal society, the subsequent origin of the kingship, and the integration of the tribes into a confederacy, if not in accord with the theories of the most critical of modern ethnologists, is quite in agreement with the classical or comparative school as represented by men like Spencer and Morgan. The account of the development of industry from the first pastoral stage, through the beginning of agriculture, to the rise of the mechanical arts and commercial activity, is ingenious and approximately in agreement with semi-modern writers (Bücher, *et alia*) expounding a " stage-theory " of economic history, although Plato leaves out the preliminary steps of direct appropriation, the hunting period, and the domestication of animals. The patriarchal origin of society has now been quite generally abandoned as a theory, though it received its most forceful exposition and support from so recent and able a writer as Maine, and as Zimmerman has shown, is by no means wholly untenable.[34] Ethnologists are rather generally agreed, moreover, that the patriarchal family was an actual institution at a later period which, indeed, did roughly correspond to the nomadic pastoral " stage." [35] Although Plato did not clearly envisage the most primitive form of industrial life and social organization, as might be expected, still he stated a correct correlation between a later type of industrial and social development. Although the idea of the patriarchal origin of human society has been severely criticized, still there is not only a tendency to reject such extreme substitutes for this theory as the theories of promiscuity and communism advanced by men like Lubbock, Bachofen, Morgan, and Briffault, but also to doubt whether or not the maternal type of descent actually preceded the paternal in all cases, or even in the majority.[36] Further, although Plato manipulates the steps in social evolution somewhat to suit his particular purpose in describing the local conditions with which he was acquainted, on the whole it may be said that his account of social and political origins in the *Laws* is more accurate and complete than most others down to the time of Bodin, if not to the time of Hume and Ferguson. It was certainly more complete than that of Aristotle, which, indeed, is so closely similar that it may well have been a condensed adaptation from Plato.

Viewed subjectively, the basis of social relations is justice, according to Plato, and justice, in its most general sense, consists in the social division of labor.[37] This principle of the division of labor, as mentioned above, extends not only to individuals but also to classes. By thus making justice depend upon the proper division of labor, Plato harmonized his subjective view of the basis of society and the state with the notion of social origins present in the *Republic*.

Plato's conception of the ideal state, with its communism among the ruling and military classes, is a utopian conception, based, as many utopias are, on the contention that man can control his own social relations and that social organization is an art rather than a continuous growth.[38] The temptation to gain an easy victory by criticizing it is great, but Plato himself had serious doubts about the practicability of his scheme, and in the *Laws* he devised his second-best state, or the best state possible in the existing condition of society. Here private property and family life were to be permitted, but Plato shows his limited Greek horizon and his Pythagorean number-mysticism when he insists that there shall always be 5,040 members of this state ($5,040 = 1 \times 2 \times 3 \times 4 \times 5 \times 6 \times 7$, and 7 has occult powers) ; the rulers were to have the duty of regulating population so as to perpetuate such a condition.[39]

Summary of Plato's Theories. — In his search after an adequate definition of justice, Plato was led into making an analysis of society and of the state. He outlined an organic theory of society and found not only the economic but also the ethical basis of society to be embodied in the functional division of labor. In this respect he contributed what is probably the most penetrating analysis of the economic foundations of society to be found in the works of any writer of antiquity.

He recognized the existence and the importance of the factor of mentality, sometimes called "the organization of the social mind," although he considered it as merely the sum of the individual minds in the social group. Adopting the premises that man can control his own social relations and that concerted volition would be the necessary result of similar external surroundings and stimuli, he constructed one of the most complete of the utopian plans for an ideal society of which history bears any record. (It is interesting to note that, aside from its communistic aspects, this utopia of Plato provided for the first comprehensive scheme of eugenics in the history of Western social or biological philosophy.)

Especially interesting are Plato's speculations in historical sociology. With almost the perspective of a nineteenth-century evolutionist, but with much less dogmatism, he discerned something of the true nature of social development and the time requisite for its consummation, and presented theories of his own on the subject which were fairly penetrating for one possessed of scanty data.

Aristotle. — The next person to claim our attention is Aristotle (384–322 B.C.), the pupil and opponent of Plato and the tutor of Alexander the Great. Aristotle is one of the most interesting figures of all history, not only for his individual knowledge and achievements, but for the great influence which, owing to more or less accidental circumstances, he exerted on posterity. There can be no doubt that no other philosopher of antiquity has had an influence on succeeding generations which even remotely compares with that exerted by Aristotle. His writings are among the few which have ever enjoyed the honor of competing with the Bible for a period of at least three hundred years. Says Robinson, speaking of the influence of Aristotle during the period of the domination of scholastic philosophy:

He was called "The Philosopher," and so fully were the scholars convinced that it had pleased God to allow Aristotle to say the last word upon each and every branch of knowledge, that they humbly accepted him along with the Bible, the church fathers, and the Canon and Roman law, as one of the unquestioned authorities which together formed a complete guide for humanity in conduct and in every branch of science.[40]

The most distinct contrast between Plato and Aristotle lay in the matter of method. Plato was primarily imaginative and "deductive "; Aristotle was first of all observational and "inductive." [41] Others may have described this difference as accurately, but few have done it as vividly as Pollock, who says:

> Plato's splendor of imagination and charm of language have indeed deserted us; but we get an exact observation of men and things and a sound practical judgment which set us on firm ground and assure us of solid progress. A balloon is a very fine thing if you are not anxious to go anywhere in particular; a road is common, and the traveling on it may be tedious but you come to the journey's end. Plato is a man up in a balloon who hovers over a new land, and now and then catches a commanding view of its contours through the mist. Aristotle is the working colonist who goes there and makes the roads. The more one considers his work, the more one appreciates his good sense, his tact in dealing with a question in the best way possible under the given circumstances, and his candor towards the reader. [42]

While Pollock's generalizations are undoubtedly true when the social theories of Plato and Aristotle are taken as a whole, in regard to the particular subject under discussion, namely, the origin of society and the state, Plato's account in the *Laws* is more complete and accurate than that presented by Aristotle.

Although Aristotle is regarded as the father of the theory of evolution, he gives no description of the origin of man beyond the following: " But the primeval inhabitants of the world, whether they were born of the earth or were the survivors of some destruction, may be supposed to have been no better than ordinary foolish people among ourselves; such is certainly the tradition concerning earth-born men." [43]

When, however, he considers the origin of the state or society (for he fails almost entirely to differentiate between the two concepts in his discussions of genesis, although he afterward does so to some extent in his analysis of the constitution of the state), he has a definite theory to offer. Instead of opening his famous *Politics* by a digression on abstract questions and then proceeding to illustrate them by conditions speculatively conceived, Aristotle immediately plunges into an analytical discussion of the origin and utility of the state. In the first place, he says that for the perpetuation of the race there must be a union of the sexes; this is the primary requirement for the existence of the state. Next comes the necessary relation of master and slave (necessary that both may be preserved), and out of these two fundamental relations of man and wife, master and slave, arises the family, which he defines as " the association established by nature for the supply of man's everyday wants." [44]

Aristotle's conception of the nature of these family relations is worthy of notice. His view of the relations of the sexes is widely at variance with that of Plato as expressed in the *Republic*. Instead of the community of women, the equality of the sexes, and the participation of women in the same occupations as men, Aristotle championed a strict monogamic family in which the father was to be the unquestioned ruler and adultery was to be punished by a loss of the privileges of citizenship.[45] Moreover, women must not share in the same pursuits as men; the place of women is in the household, managing domestic affairs.[46] Aristotle was also a firm believer in the natural right of slavery. Those gifted with knowledge and foresight are by nature designed to rule, and those possessed primarily of bodily strength, with little intellect, are destined for service.[47] This does not seem to be mere speculation, for there is every evidence that he was firmly convinced by the empirical data then available of the practical truth of such an assertion. He says:

But is there any one thus intended by nature to be a slave, and for whom such a position is expedient and right, or rather is not all slavery a violation of nature? There is no difficulty in answering this question, on grounds both of reason and of fact. For that some should rule and others be ruled is a thing not only necessary, but expedient; from the hour of their birth some are marked out for subjection, others for rule.[48]

Although some over-sentimental readers may be shocked at this frankness, there can be no doubt that Aristotle was much nearer the truth than certain democratic writers of later days, particularly those of the eighteenth century and after, who discoursed about the natural biological equality of all men.[49]

Beyond the family arises the village as the next form of association. It is produced when several families unite for a more complete type of association than that which aims merely at the supplying of everyday needs. The village, as he conceives it, is, in its most natural form, purely a genetic aggregation — a " colony " from the family.

The state, or the third and highest form of society, comes into being when several villages are united into a single community which is self-sufficing. Having its origin in mere provision of the actual physical necessities of life, the state has persisted because it affords opportunity for the complete development of man's social nature. Why? Aristotle answers, in the most important dictum of Classical times as far as sociology is concerned, because *man is by nature a social being,*[50] and the state is not an artificial

creation, but simply the natural outgrowth of man's social tendencies and needs. Although all animals are social, man is particularly so by virtue of his unique gift of the power of speech —
a point which modern sociologists, following Mead, have only
begun to exploit to the full.[51] Therefore, since society is essential
to man's perfect development, society is logically prior in importance to the individual, and prior in time to the *developed*
personality. Consequently, anyone who is either able or willing
to live entirely apart from society must be abnormal, " either a
beast or a god." [52]

In the last part of his treatment of the origin of the state
Aristotle seems to hint that he regarded the state as the political
organization of society, and distinguished between the two concepts. He says :

A social instinct is implanted in all men by nature, and yet he who
first founded the state was the greatest of benefactors. For man when
perfected is the best of animals, but, when separated from law and justice, he is the worst of all; since armed injustice is the most dangerous,
and he is equipped at birth with the arms of intelligence, and with moral
qualities which he may use for the worst ends. Wherefore, if he have not
virtue, he is the most unholy and savage of animals, and is the most full
of lusts and gluttony. But justice is the bond of men in states, and the
administration of justice, which is the determination of what is just, is the
principle of order in political society.[53]

This passage might be amenable to interpretation as a belief
in the pre-political stage of society and the necessity of the formation of political society to curb the natural evils of man — a
conception exceedingly popular at a later period, but taken in
connection with the general tenor of his political doctrines there
seems to be little doubt that Aristotle believed the state to be an
organic growth. Pollock is of this opinion when he points out
that if later political theorists had given proper attention to
Aristotle's dictum of the inherent sociability of man, they would
have been saved from that fatal fallacy of the theory of a pre-
social state of nature and the ensuing social contract.[54]

From the historical point of view Aristotle's account of social
genesis is neither as complete nor as accurate as that given by
Plato in the *Laws,* and he also fails to analyze the social division
of labor with the same acumen that Plato showed in his *Republic.* The shortcomings of Aristotle's account of social and
political genesis have been summarized by Jowett:

The accustomed method of dividing the whole into its parts is logical
rather than historical: that is to say, they are the parts into which it can

be dissected, not the elements out of which it has grown. It is not the historical method which resolves institutions and facts into their antecedent elements. Aristotle does not investigate the origins of states, but only divides a genus into species or a larger part into the lesser parts or unities out of which it is made up, or shows how an existing state may be preserved or destroyed. We must not expect him to give an analysis of primitive society, such as would be found in a modern writer on anthropology. His observation and experience were almost confined to Hellas. The earliest forms of property and society were unknown to him. He does not appear to have heard of marriage by capture, and does not distinguish between endogamy and exogamy. The " horror naturalis " which forbids marriage within near degrees of relationship, was to him an established fact. He seems to have supposed that there had existed from the first some rude form of the family, like that of the Homeric Cyclops, in which the individual savage gave the law to his own household. But he does not examine how this lowest form of human society passed into the village and the village into the state. Nor does he seriously attempt to gather the ancient customs of Hellas from the usages of contemporary barbarians, although he occasionally lights upon this path of enquiry which had already been indicated by both Thucydides and Plato.[55] Nor does it occur to him that the ties of family or caste may be so strong that the growth of the state is stunted by them; nor, on the other hand, that the life of cities may be so intense as to make any larger political unity impossible.[56]

The truth of this last part of the criticism is well attested by the very experience of the Greeks themselves in their many and unsuccessful attempts to form a political unity out of the various city-states.

Again, Aristotle was mistaken if he meant to imply that society is temporally prior to the individual (many writers assert that he meant only *logical* priority). Neither is prior to the other, rather both are complementary and each essential to the perfection of the other.[57] Says Giddings:

The individual, therefore, is not prior to society, or society to the individual. Community is not precedent to competition, or competition to community. From the first competition and community, society and the individual have always been acting and reacting upon each other.[58]

And as a recent manual trenchantly puts it : " The sharp separation of person and plurality pattern is impossible." [59]

In Book IV of the *Politics*, Aristotle undeniably gives a clear statement of the organismic theory of society, which was common throughout later history and was especially elaborated during the later part of the nineteenth century by Spencer, Schäffle, Lilienfeld, and Worms.[60] Although he does not develop the theory or carry out the analogy in detail, still there can be no doubt that he understood the principle involved. In the artisans, husband-men, and laborers he locates the sustaining system; in the traders the distributive system; and in the warriors, legislators, rulers, and judges he discovers the regulative system. To be sure, he does not trace the order of their development and differentiation, and he fails to see that their combination in one class is the first stage, and that progress comes through differentiation of structure and function, but in a general way he gives an elementary outline of the theory.[61]

In Books VIII and IX of the *Nicomachean Ethics,* Aristotle finds the subjective basis of the state and society to be friendship. This is merely an elaboration of the doctrine laid down in the beginning of the *Politics* that man is by nature a social being. Because of his inherent sociability he desires friends and cannot exist happily, if at all, without them. Society or association is the motive of friendship. Friendship is the concrete form in which man's social nature manifests itself.[62]

Aristotle, like Plato, gave license to his imagination in the construction of an ideal commonwealth, but discussion of his utopia does not properly come within the scope of this chapter. All that is necessary to point out is that, like the conception of Plato, it was to be a small city-state where all the citizens might know each other, and, in spite of Aristotle's criticism of com-munism, there were traces of it in his ideal state, as, for example, in the common meals.[63] This picture of a utopian state, with its limited Greek horizon and with stability as its ideal, has little more than a curious interest for the modern political student. As Bury remarks:

> The Republic of Aristotle's wish is not quickened like Plato's by strikingly original ideas; it is a commonplace Greek aristocracy, with its claws cut, carefully trimmed and pruned, refined by a punctilious education, without any expansive vitality, and like Sparta leaving no room for the free development of the individual citizens. If the cities of Hellas had been moulded and fashioned on the model of the city of Aristotle, they could hardly have done what they did for European civilization.[64]

Summary of Aristotle's Theories. — Aristotle has been the most influential of all writers on social philosophy, both on ac-count of the depth of his insight into social processes, and be-cause of the strong effect he exerted on medieval thought. He made many advances over Plato in his investigation of the basis and justification of political and social relationships. In the first place, Aristotle introduced the systematic-empirical method of studying social phenomena, while Plato had relied almost entirely upon the speculative line of approach. But probably more important than this was his direct and clean-cut assertion that man is by nature a social being. This dictum, had it been heeded by later writers, would have precluded any possibility of the erroneous doctrine that society was founded in and through an original social contract based upon the doctrine of conscious self-interest. As a deduction of his postulate of man's inherent sociability, he pointed out the necessity of social relations for the complete development of the human personality, and made plain the abnormality of the wholly non-social being.

Aristotle presented an explanation of social evolution in terms of utility, an expansion of the social nature, and the scope of the desire for, and need of, society. In this respect he made a considerable advance over Plato, who had advocated the utilitarian and economic explanation, almost to the exclusion of the hereditary basis. Although Aristotle's interpretation was more inclusive and well balanced, he fell far short of the analytic thoroughness of Plato, particularly in his analysis of the economic foundations of society.

In his criticism of Plato's communistic scheme he advanced arguments against that particular form of communism which for completeness and scientific accuracy leave little to be said on the subject. But his own project for an ideal commonwealth was not much more satisfactory than that of Plato, for both were permeated with the Greek ideals of exclusiveness, provincialism, and localism, as well as with the notions that social stability is the end most to be sought in the institutions of society, and that society is prior to the individual in importance.

The subjective basis of society Aristotle believed to be embodied in friendship, in the analysis of which he approached Giddings's theory of the " consciousness of kind."

Finally, Aristotle gave a more complete statement of the organismic analogy than did Plato — in fact, the latter really confined himself to assertion of organic unity. (For a discussion of the difference between " organismic " and " organic," see pp. 688–692.)

Background of Post-Aristotelian Greek Theories. — Post-Aristotelian philosophy was distributed among some six different schools: the Academy, the members of which followed Plato; the

Peripatetics, or followers of Aristotle, who devoted themselves particularly to natural science; the Cynics; the Cyrenaics; the Stoics, and, finally, the Epicureans.[65] It is with the last two only that we need be greatly concerned in this brief history of social thought — and, indeed, they absorbed most of the doctrines of the Cynics and Cyrenaics, respectively. While all these schools were represented by leaders who were prolific writers, practically all the works of the Greek Stoics and Epicureans have been lost, and our main source for their ideas is the miserable, gossipy collection of fragments compiled by Diogenes Laertius early in the third century of the Christian Era to amuse an "intellectual" damsel with whom he was quite friendly. The works of their Roman followers have been better preserved, and we shall take them up later in the discussions of Lucretius and Seneca.

The distinctive sociological characteristics of the Stoic and Epicurean social philosophy are not difficult to account for on the basis of the conditions of the time, as we saw in the preceding chapter. The swallowing up of the Greek city-states in the imperial system of Alexander and the disorder which followed the disintegration of his empire naturally led, on the one hand, to the cosmopolitan serenity and the resignation of the Stoics, and, on the other, to the individualistic and materialistic doctrines of the Epicureans, who valued society and the state solely for their aid in securing a superior degree of convenience and safety.

The Stoics. — The school of philosophy founded by Zeno (c. 350–c. 260 B.C.) in the latter half of the fourth century B.C. — a school which lasted until the close of the period of the domination of the Western Roman Empire — interpreted society in terms of rational thought, and held with Aristotle that all men must be social, both for the development of their own personalities and for the proper discharge of their duties toward their fellow-beings. The Stoic conception of society was far broader than that of the other schools of philosophy, to whom the world was either Greek or barbarian; their cosmopolitan conception of a world-society and citizenship did much to develop the idea of the essential brotherhood of mankind. Especially important in their ethical doctrines was their emphasis upon the law of nature as the proper guide for moral conduct.

The Stoic views of society had a marked relation to their views of God, man, and the world. The Stoics were avowed theists and looked upon the universe, man, and society as products of divine handiwork. God had created the material universe and man; human institutions were but the feeble imitation of divine wisdom, secured by man's imperfect assimilation of divine guidance. This divine wisdom emanated from God in the form of the *Logos* and might be absorbed to some degree by the rational nature of man. Such views naturally led to an attitude of human resignation, for what happened was God's will. It also produced a fundamentally religious and pietistic outlook upon social processes and problems.

The Stoic doctrines among the Romans reached their highest development in Epictetus (about 90 A.D.) and in the emperor Marcus Aurelius (121–180 A.D.). In fact, the loss of the Greek originals has made these two writers the main sources for the Stoic theories sketched above.

Summary of Stoic Doctrines. — The Stoic contribution to theories of social and political origins may be summed up as follows: [66] (1) The first systematic development of the theory of " natural law " as the dominant force in the universe, exerting controlling influence on social relations as well as on physical occurrences. (2) The conception of society as based on an " ethical imperative " — a rational perception of men's relation to their fellow-beings which demands their participation in society for a two-fold reason: the perfect development of their own personalities, and the discharge of their duties toward the remainder of society. " They [the Stoics] maintained that the state was an organization of human community life, which originates by reason of a social instinct implanted in man by nature." [67] (3) A conception of a sort of citizenship in the world: this phase of Stoic speculation broke through the Greek city-state horizon of Plato and Aristotle and might have led to the development of international law had there been any independent states left (Rome had absorbed them all). [68] Stein goes so far as to say that the Stoic writings of Cicero and Seneca furnished the main sources for the later development of international law by Hugo Grotius. [69]

The Epicureans. — Quite different from these doctrines were those of the school of philosophy founded by Epicurus (342–270 B.C.). Epicurus desired to interpret the origin of all things in a purely natural and materialistic manner which would preclude any necessity for supernatural intervention. [70] Hence the Epicurean attitude towards society was in fundamentals exactly the reverse of the Stoic position; the former might in fact be called evolutionary materialists. They combined the atomic theory of Democritus with Heraclitus's doctrine of flux or eternal change, and the resultant doctrine constituted the classic evolutionary philosophy of pagan times. They did not deny the existence of the gods, but they did hold that the gods had nothing whatever to do with the material world, man, or society, which had evolved in a wholly naturalistic fashion. Hence religion, based on the fear of the gods and efforts to placate them, was deemed the chief bane of humanity. The Epicureans, then, repudiated the whole theistic view of things and frankly accepted a materialistic philosophy (which does not mean, as so many have imagined, a gross hedonism or any justification of vulgar corporeal indulgence). They believed happiness to be the highest aim of man, but their view of happiness was that of the founder of their school, a civilized and cultured person.

Making use of his rationalistic method of procedure, Epicurus accounted for the evolution of man from a wild savage to civilization through the process of invention prompted by necessity.[71] Applying this philosophy to the origin of society and the state, he offered one of the first explicit theoretical accounts of the appearance of society and the state through a mutually binding contract entered into by the component population.[72] The Old Testament references to Yahweh's covenant with Israel deal primarily with the unity of the religious congregation, and Plato's reference to the contract was simply a description of a governmental compact. Diogenes Laertius has preserved for us some alleged sayings of Epicurus on this subject which give a fairly clear idea of his views:

Natural justice is a covenant of what is suitable, leading men to avoid injuring one another and being injured.

Those animals which are unable to enter into an agreement of this nature, or to guard against doing or sustaining mutual injury, have no such thing as justice or injustice, and the case is the same with those nations, the members of which are either unwilling or unable to enter into a covenant to respect their mutual interests.

Justice has no independent existence; it results from mutual contracts, and establishes itself wherever there is a mutual engagement to guard against doing or sustaining mutual injury.[73]

Granting the Sophists as possible exceptions, it may be said that the Epicureans hereby made the first striking statement of the individualistic attitude to appear in social philosophy. In marked contrast to Plato and Aristotle, Epicurus taught that the interests and happiness of the individual are prior to the interests of society, and that society and the state exist simply for the protection of the individual.[74] Giddings has concisely summed up this whole matter:

With cosmopolitanism, however, came individualism, and with it the final word of Greek philosophy upon social relations. Epicureanism, with its emphasis upon individual initiative and individual happiness, contended that the society is best which imposes minimum restraints upon the individual will. From this doctrine as a premise, the conclusion was inevitably reached that social and legal relations rest wholly upon individual self-interest, and the desire of each to secure himself against injury. The true origin of society was therefore to be sought in contract or consent. So the teaching of Plato and Aristotle was turned about. The assumption that society creates and moulds the individual became the dogma that individuals, for individualistic ends, create society.[75]

The criticism which we have already directed against the quasi-Aristotelian doctrine that " the whole is prior to the part " also applies to the Epicurean dogma that " the part is prior to the whole." The false antithesis, " individual vs. society," need not appall us, because in social life there are neither fixed " individuals " nor a " society " remaining always the same. When we observe particular " societies " closely enough, we recognize that they arise from the continual intersecting of human wills and their attendant desires; the latter in turn are not dependent upon the innate biological equipment of their possessors alone, but also upon countless social relations. To quote Todd on this point: " Is the individual made for society or society made for the individual? Neither. Which was prior? Again, neither. They are complementary and indispensable to each other." [76]

Summary of Epicurean Doctrines. — The Epicureans presented a conception of society diametrically opposed to that held by the Stoics, for the former maintained that society had its only basis in conscious self-interest which led to the inception of social relations in order to escape the evils and inconveniences of a nonsocial and isolated condition. Such a theory, as has been noted, was based on that fallacious conception of society which opened the way for the later development of the doctrine of the presocial state of nature and the foundation of social relations in a contract. With the possible exception of the Sophists and Plato, Epicurus was the first to premise an initial agreement, though it was more after the nature of the governmental compact than the social contract. Thus, as compared with the cosmopolitan and idealistic Stoics, the Epicureans were marked individualists and evolutionary materialists.

Polybius. — The last of the important Greek writers in the field of social theory was the historian Polybius, the first real formulator of historical methodology.[77] He wrote his *History* while a hostage in Rome from 167–151 B.C. In the sixth book he makes a digression to explain the causes of the excellence of the Roman system of government, and as an introduction to this he gives an account of the origin of society and of government which forms his chief contribution to social thought.

Beginning, like Plato, with the premise of a deluge that destroyed the majority of mankind, he traces the genesis of social relations and political organization. The survivors of the deluge multiplied by natural means, and through instinct and a sense of weakness sought the society of others of their kind. As among animals, the strongest took the lead. Banding together like animals they followed the strongest and bravest, who set up a despotism based upon physical force. Morality then developed slowly from the punishment of ungrateful individuals by the group. If an ingrate attempted to injure his benefactor the others would imagine themselves in the place of the injured man, would sympathize with him, and wreak vengeance upon the injurer. From a sense of sympathy there thus grew up a conception of duty and justice. The leader of the people, if he ruled according to the principles of justice, would impress the citizens with the fact that he gave every man his just reward, and they would perceive the utility of such political organization and pledge their loyalty to the ruler. Reason thus took the place of instinct and brute force as the basis of government.[78]

Polybius next proceeds to classify governments in a manner very similar to that adopted by Plato and Aristotle, and traces the usual cycle in which these forms supposedly recur. Kingship, the first type, degenerated into tyranny when the kingship became hereditary in a family and there was no longer any need to rely on the equitable administration of justice for security in holding the office. Then the ruler exploited the kingdom to support himself in luxury and gave no heed to the rights of his subjects. This caused plots against the ruler, and the people, following the lead of the highest-minded citizens, overthrew the dynasty. The people, grateful to these leaders for their deliverance, installed them as rulers. This third form of government constituted an aristocracy. The rule was equitable as long as the original aristocrats lived, but their sons, not sharing their fathers' experience of oppression, gave themselves up to unrighteous living and unlawful rule. The resulting government constituted the fourth type, oligarchy. The people, then, remembering the experience of their fathers with unjust rule and their own with the oppression of several rulers, dared to set up neither a kingdom nor an aristocracy, and so administered the government themselves. This fifth type was a democracy. This also went well in the first generation, when the memory of oppression was fresh, but the second generation followed their own selfish interests and democracy degenerated into anarchy, the sixth and last type. This period of mob rule ended only when it had evolved another king, and thus the cycle of transformations started again.[79]

The only way in which this undesirable cycle could be ended was by simultaneously combining the best elements of a kingdom, an aristocracy, and a democracy in one government. This plan, said Polybius, had been devised by Lycurgus at Sparta and had grown up gradually in Rome. At Rome the consuls represented the kingship, the senate the aristocracy, and the people the democracy.[80] This, as Dunning remarks, was the first formal statement of the system of checks and balances in constitutional government;[81] one which was revived by Machiavelli, and was succeeded by the more famous scheme of Montesquieu.

Summary of Doctrines of Polybius. — The contributions of Polybius to social theory, which are quite as important as his contributions to history, may be summed up as follows:

(1) A plausible account of social genesis, probably the best offered until the researches of recent ethnologists. The theory of the association of primitive men because of a vague perception of likeness and a sense of weakness in isolation, although unprovable, was and is a much more tenable hypothesis than the rationalistic contract theories later in vogue. The origin of government in force, subsequently strengthened and rendered more permanent by reflection leading to a conviction of the utility of such relations, is in accordance with the views of some scholars even at the present day. It was this same line of argument which David Hume used nearly two thousand years later in his attack on the doctrine of the origin of society and government through a social contract.[82]

(2) An account of the origin of morality and justice through the group sanction or disapproval of certain practices believed to be beneficial or detrimental to the supposed welfare of the group. This is also in accord with an influential section of modern opinion and has been made the central thesis of two well-known works — the *Physics and Politics* of Walter Bagehot, and the *Folkways* of W. G. Sumner.

(3) The first clear statement of the theory of reflective sympathy as the subjective basis of social relations — a theory which was later developed by Spinoza, Hume, and Adam Smith, and

which was the basis of Giddings's earliest theory of society. Recent research has cast some doubt upon the validity of the theory as it is ordinarily applied,[83] but it was for a long time surprisingly fruitful.

(4) The first comprehensive statement of the theory of the necessity of checks and balances in preserving a stable form of government.[84]

(5) Finally, Polybius presented one of the clearest statements of the prevalent classical conception of the cyclical nature of the historical process [85] — a view taken up by Ibn Khaldūn and Machiavelli, and recently revived by LeBon, Gumplowicz, Spengler, Pareto, Sorokin, and others.

Lucretius. — Polybius was the last of the Greek social philosophers, and even he was almost a Roman. Although from what evidence we have it seems that the Romans contributed little to social thought in the form of original theories, nevertheless it is among the Roman followers of the later Greek schools of philosophy, like the Stoics and Epicureans, that we have to look for our most complete statements of the Greek theories, modified no doubt by Roman culture, but the best information of the kind that remains. Unfortunately the minds of the Romans were of a legal and practical character, little given to constructive speculative philosophy. Says Pollock: " The Romans were great as rulers and administrators, and they created systematic law. But in philosophy they were simply the pupils and imitators of the Greeks, and showed themselves as little capable of invention in politics as in any other branch." [86]

Nevertheless, several of the Roman writers " adapted Greek principles with considerable ingenuity " and inasmuch as the books of the original Greek writers have disappeared, we must pay some attention to their imitative successors.[87]

The chief representative in Rome of the Epicurean school was the philosophic poet Lucretius (*c.* 99–55 B.C.), probably the greatest mind that Roman blood and culture produced. So little remains of the writing of Epicurus that certainty as to the degree of originality possessed by Lucretius cannot be reached. It is apparent, however, that Lucretius adopted the general philosophical view of Epicurus and admitted his discipleship with pride.[88] If, as Pollock states, statesmen should go back to Aristotle (which is, to say the least, doubtful), certain it is that much more warrant exists for the contention that ethnologists and sociologists should return to Lucretius — if not to ascertain scientific truth on every occasion, nevertheless to find a remarkably close approximation to what recent researches have revealed on the subject of the early history of man.[89]

Lucretius considered that the idea of the existence of the world " from all eternity " was an untenable position; he believed that it must have had a relatively recent origin. All animals, including man, he held had sprung from the earth; they were generated by the moisture of the soil and the heat of the sun. He clearly discerned the meaning of the struggle for existence, declaring that some species had been preserved rather than others because of their superior craft, courage, or activity.[90] Early mankind was tall of stature, strong, hardy, and little affected by the elements. Men obtained their food at first by gathering berries and acorns, and dwelt in caves and thick forests.[91] Mere sexual instinct, devoid of sentiment, caused the propagation of the species. Soon they armed themselves with clubs and stones, captured wild beasts for food, and used skins for clothing.[92] In time, man came to have a hut for a place of abode and took a wife to dwell with him in a relatively permanent matrimonial arrangement. Family life softened the rude nature of primitive man, and neighbors, feeling their mutual needs and interests, made agreements to refrain from injuring each other. Justice had its origin in sympathy or pity for the weak. This social concord Lucretius did not think universal, but held that it must have prevailed among the greater part of mankind, or else the species could not have maintained its existence. The leaders in this primitive society, who were first chosen for their beauty and strength, soon began to build cities, to fortify them, and to distribute cattle and fields among their retainers. Soon wealth became more important than either strength or beauty in determining leadership. The wealth of the early kings, however, aroused the envy of the rest, the less fortunate " rose up against them " in an orgy of slaughter, and government forthwith degenerated into anarchy. But the wiser men led the rest of the people into making a compact for mutual protection and the ensuring of order, and the people, tired of violence, readily acquiesced in this plan. The state and stable government were thus established by means of a mutual compact.[93] Lucretius's description of the origin of government and of the means of its overthrow is worth quoting, for it is one of the few statements of this theory which have come down to us in any degree of completeness:

At length the leaders began to build cities, and to found fortresses, as a protection and refuge for themselves. They also divided the cattle and fields, and allotted them according to the beauty, strength, and understanding of each individual; for beauty was then much esteemed, and strength had great influence. Afterwards wealth was introduced, and gold brought to light, which easily robbed the strong and beautiful of their honor; for men, however strong, or endowed with however beautiful a person, generally follow the party of the richer. . . .[94]

Kings therefore [Lucretius previously explains how the wealth of the kings attracted envy and brought about their downfall] being deposed and slain, the ancient majesty of their thrones, and their proud scepters lay overthrown in the dust; and the illustrious ornament of the royal head, stained with blood beneath the feet of the rabble, mourned the loss of its supreme honor; for that which has been too much feared before, is eagerly trodden down.[95]

Power, accordingly, returned to the lowest dregs and rabble of mankind, while each sought dominion and eminence for himself. But at length the wiser part taught them to establish a government, and made laws for them, that they might consent to observe order; for mankind, weary of passing their life in a state of violence, were worn out with contentions; on which account they fell submissively under the power of laws and strict ordinances. For because every one in his resentment, prepared to take revenge for himself more severely than is now allowed by equitable laws, men for this reason became disgusted with living in strife.[96]

Summary of the Doctrines of Lucretius. — Correlating the current accounts of the customs of " primitive " peoples and the previous theories of poets and sages, Lucretius produced a theory of social development which, in all its aspects, was infinitely superior to anything presented by any other writer down to the critical period of eighteenth-century philosophy: (1) the struggle for existence; (2) the survival of the fitter; (3) the mode of life among primitive peoples; (4) the origin of language, fire, industry, religion, domestic relations, and the arts of pleasure; (5) the sequence of culture epochs; (6) and the development of commercial relations. These points are all set forth with a clearness, accuracy, and modernity which precludes the possibility of the reading into his writings of later ideas which did not occur to him. Shotwell has thus estimated the nature and significance of Lucretius's achievement: " It is a poem for the twentieth century, in this sense perhaps the most marvellous performance in all antique literature. Any survey of antique processes of mind as they bear upon the development of the historical outlook would be sadly incomplete without an examination of *De Rerum Natura.*"

Cicero. — Powerful thinker that Lucretius was, however, he never greatly influenced his immediate posterity; Horace was the only Roman writer much affected by his principles. The Epicurean theories were too subtle to attract the attention of the forthright Roman citizen, and they were of course quite repugnant to the Christian writers because of their denunciation of *religio* as the chief cause of human misery.[97] Hence, it is to Cicero, a would-be eclectic with strong Stoic leanings, and Seneca, a professed Stoic, that we must turn to gather the general views on political theory held at Rome between 100 B.C. and 100 A.D. Carlyle says on this point:

> Cicero has left us in the fragments of the " De Republica " and in his treatise " De Legibus " a very interesting and significant account of the political theory fashionable in the first century before our era; while Seneca's writings serve to illustrate some general tendencies of political thought one hundred years later. With the assistance of these writers we can in some measure reconstruct the general outlines of the political conceptions which influenced the Lawyers and the Fathers. We can at least learn from them the commonplaces of political philosophy in their days, the notions current among the educated men of the period.[98]

Although opinions as to the degree of originality possessed by Cicero may differ, most writers agree that it was not great, and many deny him any at all. Pollock says that " Nobody that I know of has yet succeeded in discovering a new idea in the whole of Cicero's philosophical writings, and the portions of his work on the ' Commonwealth ' which have come down to us are no exception to this." [99] Dunning is a little more charitable to Cicero, and says: " That the thought of Cicero follows very closely to the suggestions of Polybius cannot be denied, but to conclude that the Roman made no contribution to political science beyond that of the Greek is a step hardly warranted by the facts." [100] But whether or not Cicero was at all original, he is valuable as a sort of general repository of earlier Greek philosophy. Carlyle has well stated his significance in social theory: " Cicero is a political writer of great interest, not because he possesses any great originality of mind, or any great power of political analysis, but rather because in the eclectic fashion of an amateur philosopher, he sums up the commonplaces of the political theories of his time. When we read him we feel that we learn not so much what Cicero thought as what was generally current in his time." [101]

When we attempt to organize Cicero's political theories, however, we find that his very eclecticism, no matter how valuable it may be in preserving the generalities of social theory current in his day, is nevertheless a source of considerable confusion because of the conflict of opinions and his own non-committal attitude when presenting several different views.[102] " It must be remembered that Cicero's eclecticism is in part the expression of a certain incoherence in his philosophical conceptions, and that it is not a matter for any great surprise that we should find him holding together opinions hardly capable of reconciliation." [103]

Cicero was familiar with two conceptions of the origin of the state: (1) the Epicurean doctrine of the non-sociability of "natural man" and the growth of society and the state out of the utility of mutual defense; and (2) the Aristotelian and Stoic conception that man is naturally inclined to the society of other men. [104] It seems reasonable to suppose, on the basis of the general nature of his writings, that Cicero supported the Stoic position. He refers disparagingly to the Epicurean doctrine in his *De officiis* (where he follows Panaetius): "Neither is that maxim true which is affirmed by some, that human societies and communities were instituted from the necessity of our condition, because we cannot without the help of others supply what our nature requires." [105] In opposition to this, Cicero holds that society is a natural institution; man being made for society, and that the greatest society — the state — has grown gradually from the elementary form of association, the family. Participation in a state is the natural method of human life, and the state cannot be considered as any chance association of men with diverse objects and methods. [106] It must be an association founded upon justice and law, and must have for its purpose the furthering of the well-being of all the citizens. Though the form of government may vary, the state must always be founded upon the basis of justice and the common well-being. Government, whether in the hands of one, a few, or all, is legitimate if the original bond of justice and common welfare is preserved. An unjust government is not to be designated as merely corrupt; in reality, such conduct dissolves the very state itself. [107] This is the main substance of Cicero's thought on the origin and nature of society, the state, and government. We may now examine some specific points in greater detail.

Cicero gives two distinct, but on the whole harmonious, accounts of social origins; one in Book I, Chapters XXV–XXVI of his *De republica,* and the other in Book I, Chapter XVII of his *De officiis.* In his *De republica* he follows Aristotle in the belief in the inherent sociability of man, and discovers the origin of human society in the "gregarious instinct" of mankind rather than in a perception of the mutual utility of associated activity. In support of this theory he points to the fact that men are so constituted that they spontaneously seek society, even when possessed of an abundance of material wealth and in no need of mutual assistance.

This social instinct also leads men to form a type of governmental organization in order that social unity may be preserved. The location of the headquarters of the social group will be determined by natural conditions; a strong central position, fortified by nature, would of course be the ideal situation.[108] Cicero states his case thus:

A commonwealth is a constitution of the whole people. But the people is not every association of men, however congregated, but the association of the entire number, bound together by the compact of justice and the communication of utility. The first cause of this association is not so much the weakness of man, as a certain spirit of congregation which naturally belongs to him. For the human race is not a race of isolated individuals, wandering and solitary; but is so constituted that even in the affluence of all things, and without any need of reciprocal assistance, it spontaneously seeks society.

It is necessary to presuppose the original seeds of a commonwealth, as it were, since we cannot discover any primary establishment of the other virtues, or even of a commonwealth itself. These unions, then, formed by the principle which I have mentioned, established their headquarters originally in some central positions, for the convenience of the whole population; and having fortified them by artificial and natural means, they have called this collection of houses a town or city, distinguished by temples and public squares. Every people, therefore, which consisted of such an association of the entire multitude as I have described — every city which consists of an assemblage of the people — and every commonwealth which embraces every member of these associations — must be regulated by a certain authority in order to be permanent. This intelligent authority should always refer itself to that grand first principle which established the commonwealth. It must be deposited in the hands of one supreme person, or entrusted to the administration of certain delegated rulers, or undertaken by the whole multitude.[109]

Following Polybius, Cicero indicated his preference for the mixed form of government, but showed that he considered monarchy the best alternative.[110]

In his *De officiis*, Cicero gives both an objective description of the genetic growth of society and a subjective interpretation of society in terms of friendship and like-mindedness. He shows his belief that the commonwealth grows out of the family through the gradual expansion of the latter. He praises the society of "those of the same manners," emphasizes the value of like-mindedness in society, points out that friendship is a most important constitutive force in society, and shows that maximum friendship is possible only among the like-minded. In all this emphasis on like-mindedness, Cicero reminds one of Giddings's insistence upon the necessity of the "consciousness of kind" in any stable society. Cicero phrases these doctrines as follows:

For as it is a common natural principle among all animated beings that they have a desire to propagate their own species, the first principle of society consists in the marriage tie, the next in children, the next in a family within one roof, where everything is in common. This society gives rise to the city, which is, as it were, the nursery of the commonwealth. Next follow the connections of brotherhood, next that of cousins; and when they grow too numerous to be contained under one roof, they are transplanted to different dwellings, as it were to so many colonies. Then follow marriages and alliances, whence spring more numerous relationships. The descendants by this propagation form the origin of commonwealths; but the ties and connections of blood bind mankind by affection. For there is something very powerful in having the monuments of our ancestors the same, in practising the same religious rites, and in having the same places of interment. But among all the degrees of society none is more excellent, none more stable, than when worthy men, through a similarity of manners, are intimately connected together; for as I have often said, even when we discern the "honestum" in one another it touches us, and makes us friends to the man in whom it resides.

Now though every virtue of every kind attracts and charms us to the love of those who possess it, yet that love is strongest that is effected by justice and generosity. For nothing is more lovely, nothing more binding, than a similarity of good dispositions; because among those whose pursuits and pleasures are the same, every man is pleased as much with another as he is with himself, and that is effected which Pythagoras chiefly contemplates in friendship, "that many may be one." A strong community is likewise effected by good offices mutually conferred and received; and, provided these be reciprocal and agreeable, those amongst whom they happen are bound together in close association. . . . And those friendships are most agreeable that are cemented by a similarity of manners.[111]

Thus, as Carlyle puts it, to Cicero the "commonwealth is an organic development out of the natural association of the family, and at the same time it is the expression of the consent of the common will, for every citizen has his share in its control."[112]

In his conception of the growth of the commonwealth, Cicero's views resemble Burke's thesis that the state is an organic growth rather than a mechanical product.[113] He describes the gradual development of the Roman constitution in much the same terms as Burke pictured the growth of the English system in his polemic against the French Revolution:[114]

But our Roman Constitution, on the contrary, did not spring from the genius of one individual, but from that of many, and it was established not in the life-time of one man, but in the course of several ages and centuries. For, added he [Scipio], there never yet existed any genius so vast and comprehensive as to allow nothing at any time to escape his attention, and all the geniuses in the world united in a single mind, could never within the limits of a single life, exert a foresight sufficiently extensive to embrace and harmonize all, without the aid of experience and practice.[115]

Finally, in his analysis of slavery, Cicero seems to give some ground for the opinion that he foreshadowed the ideas of Seneca and the Church Fathers or Patristic writers; namely, that human institutions grew out of the necessity of checking the evils of human nature — *ergo,* that the state must be an organization which grew up in consequence of the depravity of human nature and as a remedy for it. This opinion, however, is erroneous, for though Cicero may have maintained that slavery grew out of innate disparities and moral perversity, he certainly did not hold the view that the state was a product of human depravity, but on the contrary regarded it as the noblest work of man.[116]

Summary of the Teachings of Cicero. — Cicero followed Plato in attempting to describe an ideal commonwealth, but he did not feel the need of constructing a plan for a utopian society, since he considered that the Roman commonwealth possessed all the essential characteristics of a perfect state. He accepted Aristotle's dictum of the natural sociability of man rather than the Epicurean doctrine that society results from a sense of weakness in isolation or a perception of the utility of association, but he did emphasize the advantages of associated life while denying that they furnish the basic cause of society. He also agreed with Aristotle as to the value of friendship and like-mindedness as the psychical basis of association. From the Stoics he derived his doctrine of the brotherhood of man, and from Polybius he appropriated the theories regarding the classification and cycles of government and the value of checks and balances. In short, it was his summing up of the various contemporary theories into a readily accessible body of social thought that constituted Cicero's main achievement.

Seneca. — We now come to a consideration of Seneca (3 B.C.– 65 A.D.), who gives us a picture of the social theories, as they appeared to a Stoic philosopher and statesman, prevailing about a century after Cicero's eloquent tongue was forever stilled. Seneca was no more a profound philosopher than was Cicero and, like the latter, he tended to be a rhetorician, but he was more consistent than Cicero, being a professed adherent of a single philosophical school — that of the Stoics. Although Cicero probably could more accurately be classed as a Stoic than anything else, still his streak of scepticism and eclecticism gave him an irresponsible freedom and inconsistency, utterly foreign to the writing of the more systematic Seneca.[117]

The great difference between Seneca and Cicero is the former's refurbishing of the fateful idea of a primitive state of society, a golden age, which was followed by the era when the conventional institutions of society were called into being as a remedy for the evils which had brought the golden age into anarchic collapse. " The most important difference between Seneca and Cicero is to be found in his developed theory of the primitive state of innocence, the state before the conventional institutions of society existed, and the consequent theory that these institutions are only the results of, and the remedies for, the vices of human nature." [118] This was a very significant doctrine, for it was eagerly taken up by the Fathers and had considerable vogue all through the early Middle Ages.

Seneca rarely refers to a law of nature, but he frequently refers to nature itself as that perpetual and unchanging test of merit to which men must conform if they are to realize the true end and enjoyment of life. " In the main, he seems to conceive of it (nature) as the permanent principle and end of life, not as identical with its primitive forms. We shall have to consider the question presently in relation to his conception of the primitive character of society, and we shall see then that while he may occasionally, at least, use the word ' nature ' as representing the primitive, yet his general tendency is to look upon the completest perfection of human nature in a developed society as being the true ' nature ' in man." [119]

In Epistle 2 of Book XIV of his *Epistulae morales,* Seneca sets forth his theory of the primitive condition of society in the golden age of pristine innocence. In this period of primordial felicity, mankind lived without coercive authority, gladly obeying the wise, and consorting without distinctions of property or caste. His explanation of the course of events which brought about the transition from this primitive stage to modern society is strikingly like that given by Rousseau in his *Discourse on the Origin of Inequality among Men.* The main cause for the breakdown of the primitive arrangements was the origin of private property; the people became dissatisfied with common ownership, and the resulting lust after wealth and authority rendered necessary the institution of political power to curb the cravings of man.[120] Carlyle has epitomized this famous letter as follows:

Before the existing age there was an age when men lived under other conditions; in other circumstances; an age which was called the golden. In this primitive age men lived in happiness and in the enjoyment of each other's society. They were uncorrupt in nature, innocent, though not wise. They were lofty of soul, newly sprung from the gods, but they were not perfect or completely developed in mind and soul. They were innocent, but their innocence was rather the result of ignorance than of virtue; they had the material out of which virtue could grow rather than virtue itself, for this properly belongs only to the soul trained, and taught, and practised: men are born to virtue, but not in possession of it. . . . In this primitive state men lived together in peace and happiness, having all things in common; there was no private property. We may infer that there could have been no slavery, and there was no coercive government. Order there was of the best kind, for men followed nature without fail, and the best and wisest men were their rulers. They guided and directed men for their good, and were gladly obeyed as they commanded wisely and justly. The heaviest punishment they could threaten was expulsion from their territories. . . . As time passed, the primitive innocence disappeared; men became avaricious, and, dissatisfied with the common enjoyment of the good things of the world, desired to hold them in their private possession. Avarice rent the first happy society asunder. It resulted that even those who were made wealthy became poor; for desiring to possess things for their own, they ceased to possess all things. The rulers grew dissatisfied with their paternal rule; the lust of authority seized them, and the kingship of the wise gave place to tyranny, so that men had to create laws which should control the rulers.[121]

Several points in Seneca's disquisitions on the origin of social and political institutions are worthy of notice. In general, the whole doctrine of a primitive golden age bears a striking resemblance to the Christian doctrine of that blessed state before the dreary time when " in Adam's fall we sinned all." Nevertheless, Seneca paints a less roseate picture of the primeval Eden than did many later defenders of the excellence of the state of nature. He held, in fact, that this primitive period was essentially an undeveloped epoch rather than an ideal one; a number of his successors regarded the primitive condition as the natural in the full laudatory sense of the word. But Seneca championed the view that social institutions are devices for controlling human wickedness resulting from the corruption of man, rather than as means for securing greater happiness and social efficiency. " Seneca thus looked upon the institutions of society as being the results of vice, of the corruption of human nature: they are the conventional institutions made necessary by the actual defects of human nature rather than the actual conditions of ideal progress." [122]

In his *De clementia,* I, Seneca shows a decided bent toward the theory of the divine source of government and the divine authority of the ruler — doctrines very common in the Patristic period.[123]

Seneca is particularly important in the history of social theories because he was the source for a large proportion of the social doctrine of the Church Fathers. They felt free to draw upon him, for his writings on religion bore a close resemblance to Patristic conceptions. (This led to a wide-spread myth that he was a friend of St. Paul.) Seneca's doctrine of the corruption of human nature, combined with the doctrine of the primitive state of innocence, was admirably adapted to transformation into the Christian doctrine of the bliss of Eden and the subsequent Fall. Says Carlyle:

> We have already seen in Cicero some traces of this theory of the corruption or faultiness of human nature; in Seneca it is more clearly and explicitly drawn out. And if we now put this together with his theory of primitive life, we see that Seneca's view is, in all important points, the same as that of the Christian Fathers, that man was once innocent and happy, but has grown corrupt. And further, we find that what Cicero only suggests as the cause of the subjection of man to man, Seneca holds of the great institutions of society, property and coercive government; namely, that they are the consequences of and the remedies for vice.[124]

As already noted, Seneca's conception of the primitive golden age was transformed by the Fathers into the conception of the condition of mankind before the Fall. " The Fathers conceive of the state of man before the Fall much as Seneca conceives of the Golden Age, and they account for the disappearance of the primitive conditions of that age by the theory of the Fall. By the Fall man passed out of the state of nature into the state in which the conventional institutions of society are necessary." [125] This influence of Seneca did not extend merely to the earlier Fathers, but, as Carlyle points out, was still strong at the time of Gregory the Great. " It is probable that Gregory the Great is here following St. Augustine, but the general source of the authority can hardly be mistaken; it is the same Stoic doctrine of a primitive state in which the conventional institutions of society did not exist, of which we have already spoken so often. The primitive state of

man was to these Fathers, as it had been to the Stoics like Posido-
nius and Seneca, a condition without coercive government: in the
state of nature men did not need this." [126] Like Seneca, the Fathers
did not conceive of coercive government as existing in the state of
nature. It was occasioned by sin, but it was not illegitimate; rather
it was a divinely appointed remedy for sin.

Seneca's influence, moreover, did not cease with the Patristic
period; Stein has pointed out how the Stoic doctrines, with their
ideas of the brotherhood of man, were able to furnish the basis
for the system of natural law philosophy and international law
which grew up in early modern Europe. "Seneca's writings,
Cicero's *De finibus,* and especially the latter's *De officiis* (well
known to be only a free translation of a work of Panaetius), furnished the sources from which Grotius formulated his doctrine of
natural right." [127]

Summary of Seneca's Theories. — Seneca's chief contribution
to social philosophy was his revival of the ancient Greek conception of the primitive stage of society as a golden age, alleged
to have been followed by the period of the origin of the conventional institutions of society (as a remedy for the evils which crept
in and brought the golden age to an end). In this age of "golden
innocence" mankind lived without coercive authority, gladly
obeying the wise, and without any distinctions of property or
caste. The main cause for the breakdown of this arrangement was
the origin of private property. The people became dissatisfied
with common ownership, and the resulting lust after wealth and
authority rendered necessary the institution of political authority
to curb these growing evil propensities. The chief importance of
this doctrine is not its enunciation by Seneca, but its adoption by
the Christian Fathers. They identified it with the state of man before the Fall, and thus reinforced the already extremely retrospective character of Christian social philosophy. Finally, Seneca
played an important part in the growth of the notion of "natural
right."

Plotinus. — Another philosophic development among the Romans which had important consequences in the history of social
theory was Neo-Platonism, a school of thought which found its
main representative in Plotinus (204–270 A.D.). With its renunciation of the world of sense, its tendencies toward unlimited
credulity, and its hostility to rationalism or scepticism, it furnished the general intellectual setting which was adopted by
Patristic and medieval theology. It thus militated strongly against
any movement toward a scientific conception of social processes

and institutions. Neo-Platonism, the conception of a former golden age, and the eschatological view of society, which was drawn as much from Persian religions and the pagan mysteries as from Christian texts, all combined to make up the other-worldly and anti-rational intellectual environment in which Christian theology and social philosophy flourished.

The Roman Lawyers. — In their efforts at formulating a distinction between the *jus naturale* (natural law) and the *jus gentium* (conventional law), the Roman Lawyers or legists of the imperial period seem to have indicated a belief in the existence of a primitive state of nature like that pictured by Seneca. The *jus naturale* was apparently based upon usages common to the primitive stage, and the *jus gentium* on the practices which had developed after the growth of the conventional institutions of organized society.

The method followed by Justinian in drawing up the Roman law enables us to examine the conceptions held at different times. In the *Digest* are to be found the doctrines of the great lawyers of the second century and the early part of the third century; in the *Code* may be found the imperial constitutions from the second to the sixth centuries, which illustrate the development of the principles of Roman law; while in the *Institutes* is to be found the law as finally formulated in the sixth century. The theories of the *Digest* and *Code* may first be considered.

In stating the distinction between the *jus naturale* and the *jus gentium,* the jurists of the *Digest* (e.g., Ulpian, Florentinus, and Tryphoninus) seem to imply, as already noted, the existence of the primitive state of nature postulated by Seneca. Says Carlyle:

> The impression which these passages leave upon us is this: that the writers have present to their minds some primitive circumstances, some primeval or natural institutions of the human race as distinguished from even the oldest and most universal conventional institutions of human society. . . . We venture to think that here we trace the influence of that mode of thought about the primitive conditions of human life which we have seen in Seneca, and which we may gather was representative of the general character of at least some Stoic theories.

> We may think therefore that the distinction made by Ulpian between the jus naturale and the jus gentium is really connected, though Ulpian may not have been fully conscious of the fact, with a tendency to conceive of some state of nature as lying behind the actual conditions of human life. . . . At least whatever doubt we may continue to feel as to the true significance of Ulpian's distinction and definition, there can be little doubt that the tendency of legal theory was towards the distinction between the primitive and conventional of which we have spoken.[128]

From the nature of the writings of the lawyers we should expect no long philosophical or historical account of how society and the state came to be, but they do present a very definite theory as to the source of political authority, and it is interesting to note that along with the conception of a primitive state of nature, they also held the theory of the foundation of government upon the consent of the people, or in other words upon a governmental compact between ruler and ruled. They thus combined in an undeveloped form these two elements in the theory of origin of the government which were so common in late medieval and early modern times. Carlyle, after a close examination of all the writers of the *Digest*, comes to the conclusion that from the beginning of the second century to the sixth there was no conception of the basis of the authority of the emperor known to Roman law except that of the consent of the people. Though the emperor might be absolute and might gain his power by means most remote from the consent of the people, nevertheless the theory remained that his power was founded upon popular consent. Some of the best parts of Carlyle's treatment of this subject may be quoted:

The Roman lawyers of the second century and onwards deal briefly indeed, but very distinctly, with the question of the ultimate source of authority in the State, and we think that, so far, they do very clearly carry on the tradition represented by Cicero. They do not conceive of the Roman citizen as having any direct share in the actual administration of the Commonwealth, but in their view the Roman citizens are the sole ultimate source of authority, whether legislative or administrative. . . . The medieval theory of the social contract, which, so far as we know, was first put forward definitely in the end of the eleventh century, may have relations with such ancient forms of the theory as are perhaps suggested by Cicero and had been developed by Plato, and perhaps by authors whose works have now disappeared. We shall see that the medieval theory is related primarily to the traditional ideas of the Teutonic races on government, and to the course of the history of the Teutonic empire and kingdoms. But at the same time, the theory of the Roman Lawyers with respect to the people as the sole ultimate source of authority in the State seems to us to be clearly an undeveloped form of the theory of contract. We might call it the theory of consent, which is not the same thing as the contract in any of its forms, but is the germ out of which the theory of the contract might very well grow. . . .

. . . Few phrases are more remarkable than this almost paradoxical description of an unlimited personal authority founded upon a purely democratic basis. *The Emperor's will is law, but only because the people chose to have it so.* Ulpian's words sum up in a single phrase the universal theory of the lawyers; so far as we have seen, there is no other view known to the Roman jurisprudence. From Julianus, in the early part of the second century, to Justinian himself in the sixth, the Emperor is the source of law, but only because the people by their own legislative act have made him so.[129]

From the second century, then, to the sixth, we have seen that the Roman law knows one, and only one, ultimate source of political power, and that is the authority of the people. It may of course be said that this is the merest abstract theory, that during this time the imperial power was obtained by every method, but never by that of popular appointment; that the legislative authority of the people was only a name and a pretence, and it must be noticed that Justinian seems even to speak of the Emperor as the sole " legislator " as though, in fact, the legislative authority of the Roman " populus " had wholly ceased. But still the ultimate authority of the people subsisted, and so came down till it touched the new Teutonic theory of law and political authority, a theory which again knew nothing of any legislative authority in the State apart from the whole body of the State.

We think that the legal theory that all political power is derived from the people, is at least one of the sources from which the theory of the social contract sprang. It is far from being the same theory, but it seems to us to represent an elementary form of the same conception.[130]

In Justinian we also find a trace of that theory of the divine source of political authority which was to play so prominent a part in the theories of the Christian Fathers, but in Justinian it seems to have meant nothing more than a recognition of the agency of God in political affairs as well as in all the other matters of the world. On this point Carlyle remarks:

It is true that in Justinian we also find some trace of a conception out of which there grew another theory of the authority of the ruler. The first words of the rescript we have just quoted are, " *Deo auctore nostrum gubernantes imperium, quod nobis a caelesti majestate traditum est.*" In another rescript also prefixed to the Digest, we read, " *quia ideo imperialem fortunam rebus humanis deus praeposuit, ut possit omnia quae noviter contingunt et emendare et componere et modis et regulis competentibus tradere.*" In another place still he speaks of God subjecting all laws to the Emperor, whom he has given to man as a living law. These phrases may be compared with those of Seneca and Pliny . . . and with the patristic conception of the relation between God and the ruler, which we shall presently have to examine; but in themselves the words of Justinian can hardly be pressed to mean more than that the providence of God rules even over the matters of the State.[131]

In the *Institutes* of Justinian the theories of the *Digest* regarding the source of political authority are adopted practically without change, though there seems to be a little clearer distinction drawn between the *jus naturale* based upon the primitive state of nature and the *jus gentium* based upon the institutions of conventional society. In the *Institutes,* however, there is no clear conception of a pre-political condition of mankind,[132] and for that reason we shall not deal here with the doctrines there presented.

It should be plain that all the criticisms leveled against the doctrines of the " natural state of man " in the foregoing pages also apply to the Roman dogma of *jus naturale,* for this was implicitly based on a theory quite as objectionable as the most naïve speculations of Seneca. Because we thus cavalierly dismiss the theorizing of the Roman lawyers on this point, however, it should not be inferred that the modern social theorist has nothing to learn from them. On the contrary: the social theorist, and particularly the sociologist, should pay close attention to the brilliant and precise formulations of basic legal relations (which are also social relations) laid down centuries ago by the Roman jurisconsults. They gave excellent definitions of such important relations as *majestas, dominus, subjecti,* and the like; if the sociologist is careful to distinguish between the strictly legal and the strictly sociological aspects of these relations, a great deal can be learned that will aid in the sociological analysis of fundamental interhuman relations such as supraordination and subordination, domination and submission, and a host of others.[133]

Summary of the Doctrines of the Legists. — In concluding this hasty survey of Classical theories of the origins of society, the state, and government, we must take note of the important conception developed by the Roman lawyers regarding the origin and nature of political authority. It is the opinion of recent and reliable authorities that from the second to the sixth centuries A.D. there was but one legal theory of this authority, and that was that it had its foundation in the consent of the people. However remote from popular consent might be the method by which the emperor at any time rose to power, the theory remained the same. That this conception had a very great influence upon the later developments of the theory of a social and especially of a governmental contract, and of popular sovereignty, is beyond doubt. Another important allied doctrine was that of the absolute nature of secular authority.

The social thought of Plato and of Aristotle, as presented in the present chapter, stands in need of more intensive treatment from the standpoint of sociology of knowledge. For Plato, see Francois Ollier, *Le Mirage Spartiate* (Paris: E. de Boccard, 1933).

CHAPTER VI

Christian Social Philosophy to Thomas Aquinas

WHEN JEW MET GREEK AND ROMAN MET BOTH. — Christianity as a social and religious phenomenon arose out of a definite historical configuration; it did not spring suddenly from a vacuum, but was a natural product of hopes and fears prevalent in the Jewish and Greco-Roman world of the period.

After their return from the Babylonian captivity the Jews reverted in part to their older ideals of a sacred society, but with the coming of the armies of Alexander they began more and more to absorb the secularizing culture of Hellenism. Greek colonies and cities were established in Palestine, and eventually all things Greek became fashionable. Under the tolerant rule of the Ptolemies many Jews became " sophisticated " (in the original sense); they looked upon the religion of Yahweh as barren and provincial.[1] The more severe rule of the Seleucids (following 198 B.C.) saw further Hellenization; even the position of high priest fell into the hands of a member of the pro-Greek party, Jason. He built a gymnasium and introduced Greek games, with their athletic nudity so alien to Jewish mores; even the priests neglected their sacred duties as a consequence. These and other inroads caused the faithful to fear that Yahweh would be completely forgotten.

The secularizing effect of culture contact was unwittingly checked, however, when Antiochus Epiphanes came to the throne of Syria in 175 B.C. Not satisfied with the extent of voluntary progress in Hellenization, he sought to accelerate the process by force. The temple was plundered and an altar to Zeus set up on the site of the altar to Yahweh; by royal decree all Jewish religious rites were forbidden. This attempt at sudden overturn evoked the usual reponse: a renascence movement got under way. Under Maccabean leadership the faithful Jews revolted, and in 165 B.C. won their religious freedom; a few years later political liberty followed. Thereafter the Jews split into two parties: the Hellenists, who eventually became the Sadducees, and the Judaists or Chasidim, who stood for loyalty to Yahweh and finally became the Pharisees. The renascence movement soon encountered difficulties; the current of Greek influence gained headway, and shortly before the coming of the Roman legions in 63 B.C., coins with Greek inscriptions were issued.

When the *Pax Romana* spread over Palestine, Jewish political independence of course passed away. Soon the Maccabean dynasty was displaced by Herod the Great, a Roman appointee whose "reign" (40–4 B.C.) reached to the threshold of our era. Edomite by birth, Jew by adoption, at heart a thorough Hellenist, he did everything in his power to spread Greek culture, even going so far as to subsidize the Olympic games, then on the point of death from financial anemia. Diplomatically enough, he also sought to retain the favor of the Judaists by lavishly rebuilding their temple, but they readily discerned where his real affections lay, and greeted the news of his death with cheers.

From that time (4 B.C.) until the beginning of the great Diaspora in 70 A.D. the Judaists who adhered most closely to the ideal of an ethnocentric sacred society were constantly in revolt against Roman rule. Thousands of Jewish patriots were crucified, and many charismatic leaders came forward to fill the rôle of national savior or Messiah. It was about the middle of this period that the obscure events (not regarded by the Romans as sufficiently important to be recorded) associated with the beginning of Christianity took place.

Sects among the Jews. — Christianity was in its early stages a Jewish sect, and in order to understand it properly some knowledge of its contemporary competitors is necessary. These were represented by the Sadducees, the Essenes, the Pharisees, and the Zealots.

The Sadducees, as already noted, were the heirs of the more ardent Hellenists, especially among the upper classes. Few in number, they had little popular following, but their influence went far among the rich and the higher ecclesiastics. Theologically conservative, accepting neither the doctrine of resurrection that had accompanied the drift away from simple tribal *mishpat* nor the complex oral interpretation of the sacred writings developed by the Pharisees, they held themselves bound only by the obvious letter of the law. Traditional ritual duties fulfilled, they then felt free to follow Greek fashions in thought and conduct. These denatured Jews of course did not favor the renascence movement; they were strong in the court party, paid much attention to politics, and favored friendly relations with foreigners, particularly if the latter had favors to dispense.[2] The Messianic hope had no appeal for them; a continuance of the *status quo* was all they asked. Partially secularized, urban and urbane, pro-Greek, upper-class: the Sadducees.

Another type of Hellenistic influence, entirely different in character, gave rise to the sect of the Essenes. Although commonly classed as an extreme branch of the Pharisees, they might with almost equal right be called a Jewish branch of the Pythagoreans and Stoics (a view defended by Josephus). Certainly Pythagorean parallels are easy to find: aspiration for bodily purity, high regard for celibacy, white garments, refusal to take oaths, rejection of animal sacrifices (which brought the Essenes into conflict with Jewish orthodoxy), prayer at sunrise, dualistic view of soul and body, pre-existence and immortality of the soul, and the like. About all they lacked was Pythagorean vegetarianism and belief in transmigration of souls. Although authorities differ, it is also claimed that, like the Pythagoreans, the Essenes lived in monastic communities, possessing goods and taking meals in common. They would neither engage in trade nor hold slaves — the latter especially noteworthy in an age of widespread servitude — and were distinctly pacifistic until the time of the final clash with Rome. It is highly unlikely that Jesus could have remained uninfluenced by their teachings.

But be this as it may, there can be no doubt that he had little use for the doctrines of the sect with the largest popular following; viz., the Pharisees. These were the successors of the Judaistic Chasidim or " pious ones " of the Maccabean period, and lived in fervent hope that Yahweh would soon send his Messiah to save their oppressed nation. Strictly legalistic in their reverent acceptance of both the sacred writings and the accumulated oral interpretations thereof, the Pharisees were religiously active, but politically passive; the only way to hasten the coming of Israel's savior was for loyal Jews to observe the ritual law in all its severity. No province of life was left unregulated by these representatives of traditional domination, and it soon became impossible for simple village folk, far from the centers of the cultus and cramped by poverty, to be good Pharisees. The latter spoke scornfully of " the people of the land " (*amme-ha-aretz*), and these in turn eagerly welcomed charismatic *nabim* who, like Jesus, denounced Pharisaic preoccupation with minute ritual requirements and the accompanying Pharisaic neglect of nomadic *mishpat*.

It was among these villagers, as well as in the ranks of the urban poor, that the Zealots found most of their recruits. Like the Essenes, they have been called (somewhat inaccurately, it is true) an extreme branch of the Pharisees, but there the connection ends. Instead of being political quietists, the Zealots were fiery nationalists who gladly resorted to violence for the attainment of their goals. Claiming to serve God only and recognizing no earthly master, they struggled against everyone, whether Jew or Gentile, identified with the " let-alone " rich and the Hellenized or Roman ruling classes. Their allegiance went to any promising malcontent who seemed likely to be the Messiah, so long, but only so long, as he evinced his mission by active preparation for, or better still, actual leadership in overt revolt. Strongest in Galilee, they made up part of the following of Jesus during the time when he was thought to be the Messiah who would become literal " king of the Jews " through armed uprising.

If the Sadducees may be likened to Anglican prelates amenable to " popish influences " in the time of the Stuarts, the Essenes may perhaps be compared to the Quakers, the Pharisees to rigid but non-political Calvinists, and the Zealots to the rash and violent Levellers. Like all analogies, this is shaky on more than one leg, but its chief defect is this : no provision can be made for the Jews of the dispersion.

Jewry outside the Promised Land. — But after all, these dispersion Jews did not really constitute a sect, however different from the Jews of the homeland they may have become. Beginning with the end of the eighth century B.C., when the northern kingdom fell and thousands of Israelites were carried away by the Assyrian conqueror, the dispersion continued with the collapse of the southern kingdom and the subsequent Babylonian captivity, until Jews were to be found almost everywhere. This all took place *before* the great Diaspora that followed the destruction of the Temple by the Romans ; we might justifiably speak of the early and late dispersions, or the dispersion and the Diaspora, if we wished to be extremely precise.

Although the dispersion Jews held in the main to the fundamental tenets of traditional Judaism, they were much more influenced by and tolerant of the Hellenistic movement than were the Jews of Palestine. Strongly steeped in Greek philosophy, they owed to it, among other things, the practice of allegorizing the sacred writings when confronted by some absurdity more obvious than ordinary — incipient rationalism engendered by culture contact. Among Greco-Jewish writers none can compare in importance with Philo, inhabitant of Alexandria, the great center of the dispersion. He sought to harmonize Hebrew and Greek thought, with the consequence, as might be expected, that his works were not considered orthodox by the Jewish priesthood. They later proved popular, however, with the Church Fathers. One of the most important products of the Jews of Alexandria was the Septuagint, the Greek translation of the Hebrew Scriptures, rendered necessary by the fact that many of the dispersion Jews could neither read nor speak the homeland tongue.

Unlike the Palestinian Jews, those of the dispersion carried on a vigorous proselytizing campaign. Jewish monotheism and ethical ideals won numerous thoroughgoing converts, and in addition many Gentiles who were not quite thoroughgoing enough to undergo the Jewish rite of circumcision became regular attendants at the synagogues. (Such Gentiles, by the way, probably provided Paul with a substantial proportion of his recruits.) In addition to serving as centers for the dissemination of missionary propaganda, the synagogues of the dispersion played an important part in de-localizing the Jewish religion by rendering it less dependent upon the Jerusalem temple worship and its ritual. They were also a factor in making Judaism more and more a religion of sacred books, thus helping to make the Jews spiritually at home everywhere — and nowhere.

Throughout all the period of oppression, revolt, and dispersion there was one ray of hope for the faithful Jew within or without the Promised Land, and that was the confidence that in due time God would send his Messiah to redeem his chosen people and save them from their oppressors. Conceptions as to who this Messiah was to be varied widely. Some expected national salvation at the hands of a king of the royal line of David. For other thinkers and dreamers the hoped-for Messiah was a semidivine personage already waiting in heaven for the proper time to reveal himself and rescue God's people. Since Israel's present evil plight was due to sin, they thought, the only hope was to practice repentance and righteousness, until such time as sufficient evidence of devotion had been given, whereupon God would send the Messiah. By waging war with divine aid upon the enemies of the chosen people, this leader would bring the whole earth under the benevolent but firm Jewish heel. All the nations would then be judged, and the righteous, including both the living and the resurrected dead, would be gathered to serve Israel's God in the new world — the Messianic age, or the kingdom of Heaven. When the idea of retribution developed, it was thought that both the righteous and the wicked would be resurrected, the former to be rewarded, and the latter to be punished.[3]

Jesus, Founder of a Jewish Sect. — Although Christianity as it emerged into the Roman world combined ideas derived from several different sources, it received its initial impetus from Jesus of Nazareth, a Jewish carpenter and teacher of Galilee, who was born during the closing days of the reign of Herod the Great. His whole life was spent during a period when rebellious outbursts on the part of the Judaist parties were especially frequent; longing for national liberty was intense. Born of humble parents, he very probably received what education he had from teachers at the local synagogue. His home, we may assume, was like that of many other pious Jewish families of his day; certainly his knowledge of the sacred writings seems to testify to childhood familiarity. The family probably considered themselves members of the Pharisaic sect, but it is likely that they could not be as punctilious in the observance of the fine points of the law as could many Pharisees, and doubtless were scornfully dubbed by some " the people of the land." [4] Apart from sectarian wrangles, however, they could hardly have been other than loyal Jews, visiting the temple at Jerusalem each year at the time of feasts, mourning the sad state of their nation, and hoping for redemption at the hands of God's Messiah. Jesus's native village was less than an hour's walk from Sepphoris, the largest city in Galilee. When he was only a boy this city was burned and two thousand Jews were executed by the Romans because of the revolt of Judas the Galilean; Jesus must have heard many tales of these nationalistic martyrs.

Of Jesus's life before the age of thirty we have no authentic account, although there is some speculation, based on inferential evidence only, that he may have lived for a time with one of the Essene groups. He first appears in the records, however, as a disciple of John the Baptist, a stern preacher of repentance as a preparation for the coming Messianic age: "Repent ye, for the kingdom of God is at hand." Clad like a nomad of the desert fringe, eating the same scanty fare, this *nabi* seems almost another Amos, "herdsman of Tekoa." Jesus was baptized by John, and at once began to preach a similar message. One great difference in method soon became apparent, however: Jesus did not remain isolated in the desert places as did John, but traveled about among the people announcing that the Messianic age was imminent and that all who would have a part in it should prepare themselves by adopting a new way of life. This did not call for extreme asceticism, however, nor did he himself follow the striking practices of his forerunner. Perhaps Jesus's experiences in

Sepphoris, the large city near his home, had made him too urban to be much attracted by John's stark mode of life.

It was an easy matter in those days to gather a following, especially if the salvation of Israel was the burden of the message, and before long Jesus had a group of disciples. Most of them, it seems, were attracted by his striking personality and their hopes that he would prove to be a successful revolutionary leader, rather than by any abstract principles he expounded. At least one and probably two of the disciples belonged to the revolutionary Zealot party, but in spite of the hopes of these and other followers, it is not likely that Jesus thought that he himself was to be the Messiah whose imminent coming he was announcing.[5] He was therefore an emissary prophet, although his later followers looked upon him as exemplary. Traveling and preaching in various parts of Palestine for well over two years, he eventually aroused the suspicion of the local officials in Galilee, the hearty hatred of the Pharisaic and Sadducean parties in Jerusalem, and finally the wrath of the higher Roman authorities. Opposition finally crystallized around three main points:

(1) As one of "the people of the land" Jesus thought the Pharisees were too much concerned about ritual minutiae while they "left undone the weightier matters of the law, justice, and mercy, and faith"[6] — essentially the charge leveled by Amos. For Jesus, the righteousness demanded by the law as required for the new Messianic age was one of broad principles rather than legal technicalities. The Pharisees held, however, that the faithful observance of the details of the law was necessary for the safety of the Jewish people before God. Encouraging the populace to neglect ritual duties was therefore highly reprehensible.

(2) As a proclaimer of the kingdom of God, the coming age in which God would have complete control, Jesus also had much to say about the formation of a community based on that hope. He did not speculate about the nature of the kingdom: it was simply to include all ethical and religious ideals, was to come "soon," and was to be followed by the end of the world and the judgment. All Jesus's emphasis was upon the ethical and religious preparation of the community which was "looking for the kingdom," and the two commandments which summed up the entire law, he said, were these: "Thou shalt love the Lord thy God with all thy heart, and with all thy soul, and with all thy mind," and "Thou shalt love thy neighbor as thyself."[7] Not only should friends be loved, but also enemies. Moreover, the evil-doer should not be resisted; if struck on one cheek, offer the other. In this

doctrine of non-resistance Jesus may have been influenced by Pythagorean teachings as mediated by the Essenes; it is likely that he also owed much to the ideal of the Suffering Servant presented by Isaiah (see Chapter Three).

Although Jesus conceived these ideals as belonging primarily to the Messianic era, he believed that it could be entered into even before its coming by beginning to follow its way of life.[8] When this teaching is related to the political situation of the time one can readily see that it would inevitably arouse opposition. Not to resist the oppressive Roman was to the Pharisee and especially to the Zealot unthinkable, and to love the tyrant would be treason, for it would mean the surrender of the nationalistic hope of the Jews. Jesus even went so far as to sanction payment of the hated Roman tax: " Render unto Caesar the things that are Caesar's, and unto God the things that are God's." [9] Little wonder it was that Judas, who seems to have been a Zealot, betrayed Jesus to the Roman authorities when it finally became apparent that he would not fight for Israel nor for himself as Israel's Messiah.

(3) Furthermore, the Roman governors of the time were suspicious of anyone with too large a following. Although Jesus's followers were chiefly simple peasant folk like himself, when they showered him with kingly honors on the occasion of his last visit to Jerusalem he was seized as a dangerous revolutionary. Urged on by the Pharisees, the Sadducees, and the Zealots (who wanted their leader Barabbas released), the Romans gave him a summary trial and executed him by crucifixion, as they had thousands of other real or supposed malcontents.

The Social Teachings of Jesus. — Jesus's ethical ideal had a two-fold basis: (1) the religious idea of the presence of God; and (2) the conception of the infinite and eternal value of the soul. The first outstanding sociological characteristic of this ideal is an unlimited, unqualified individualism, which has its basis in the religious idea. As a child of God, chosen to be in fellowship with him, the individual may regard himself as infinitely precious. Such an individualism is radical, transcending all natural barriers and differences. Furthermore, he who has consecrated himself to God is united with other individuals who have done the same; they have all yielded themselves to the same divine will. This gives rise to an intense sense of fellowship and brotherhood which recognizes the worth of every human being. Hence arises the second sociological characteristic of Jesus's ideal; namely, an absolute universalism.[10]

Although Jesus's message was not a program of social reform, but primarily a summons to prepare for the coming of the kingdom of God, it is possible to determine his attitude on various social matters. In his teaching no particular attention is given the state, and Jewish nationalism and all its expectations are entirely ignored. For Jesus, the kingdom of God was to be the rule of God and not of the Jewish people; he made it plain that the Roman Empire existed, and had a perfect right to exist, because God permitted it.[11] His outlook on economic questions was also very simple, as Troeltsch indicates: " God allows everyone to earn his living by means of work; if distress should arise, then love can help; wealth, however, must be feared on account of its danger to the soul. . . . Further, all questions of property are considered solely from the standpoint of the consumer, whose practice must remain modest if it is to remain healthy, and who fills up all the bare spaces created by poverty with the exercise of a thoughtful generosity." [12] Although his message shows particular sympathy for the poor, it is not restricted to them. There is no trace of a struggle against oppression, except in his struggle against false religious leaders.

On the question of the family, Jesus's teaching is more detailed. " Indeed, the idea of the family," says Troeltsch, " may be regarded as one of the most fundamental features of His feeling for human life. The value which each individual possesses within the monogamous family (the sense of being a person) and the intimacy of the family bond are in fact also inwardly connected with the religious individualism and universalism of His teaching. Hence His insistence on the indissolubility of the marriage bond, and on the limitation of sex intercourse to married people, even for men." [13]

Jesus seems to have had no thought of definitely organizing a community or church to practice and spread his doctrines. His message was rather the summons to prepare for the coming of the kingdom of God. This preparation, for the present at least, was to take place within the framework of the present world order, in a purely religious fellowship of love, with an earnest endeavor to conquer self and cultivate virtue. Even the kingdom of God, when it came, was not to be *primarily* a new social order, for although it would create a new order, it would be one not concerned with state, society, or family.[14] In short, the eschatological, other-worldly note was dominant in his teaching.

Culture Contact and Syncretism in the Early Empire. — The Mediterranean world of the first century was politically a unit, and for the upper classes there was also far-reaching intellectual homogeneity. Greek ways of thinking were accepted everywhere, and educated people in all parts were acquainted with Greek literature, dramā, and philosophy. Although Latin was spoken in the West, the Greek tongue was spoken everywhere; in fact, it had become a *lingua franca* making for free interchange of thought in all parts of the empire. And this interchange went on apace, for the peace which came with the empire rendered travel secure. Pirates had been driven from the sea, and the excellent military roads penetrating to the farthest extremes of the *Pax Romana* made land travel relatively swift and safe.

But with unity and mobility came a certain disorganization. The religious life of the empire was in a state of unrest. The sacred bulwarks represented by the old Roman religion had long since fallen into decay, and as secularization advanced many turned to philosophy to find an answer to the riddle of existence. Some espoused Stoicism, others took up Epicureanism, others found refuge in the philosophies of Plato or Aristotle. All these, however, had become primarily religious in tone; they were far from being wholly secular — indeed, they never had been. Stoicism, with its doctrine of the divine immanence and of the natural equality and brotherhood of all mankind, was accepted by most of the upper classes as their religion.

Yet a large number seemed not to be satisfied with the practice of virtue and the guidance of reason. Philosophy, even when strongly imbued with sacred notions, did not fully assuage the religious unrest. Many men, therefore, and especially those of the lower classes, turned to find help outside themselves in a mystic union with God. Even the Stoic felt this need: " No man is good without God," wrote Seneca. And again: " Can anyone rise superior to fortune save with God's help? " [15] To meet this demand there were at hand numerous " mystery " sects, some native to the Greek world, others hailing from the Orient. Among the former were the mysteries of Dionysus, and of Demeter at Eleusis, and among the latter those of Isis, of Mithras, and of Cybele, the Great Mother of the Gods. In many respects the two kinds were parallel, although the Oriental ones were exotic growths in the Greco-Roman world which they had penetrated, and were in addition actively proselytizing.

All the mysteries had certain characteristics in common. Among them were these: (1) an elaborate symbolism which provoked in the initiate the sense of regeneration, redemption, and the forgiveness of sins through a reconciliation with God by the means provided by the cult; (2) an esoteric knowledge of God, derived from revelation, giving the initiate a new outlook on life and a sense of " cosmic security "; (3) a sacramental drama reënacting the sufferings, death, and resurrection of the special deity of the cult; (4) identification with this deity through participation in the sacramental drama, in which the worshiper attained a new life by partaking of the savior-deity's death, and sharing in his revived and eternal life; (5) the promise of a glorious immortality which could not be impaired by bodily death; and (6) a personal religion open to everyone without regard to rank or accident of birth. The sacramental drama was usually accompanied by an intense funereal sadness at the death of the hero; a phase of painful suspense; then, when the tension was at the very breaking point, overwhelming and unrestrained joy at the savior-hero's resurrection. In many cases there was considerable emphasis upon the efficacy of the symbolic eating of the flesh and drinking of the blood of the slain god. In the Taurobolium of Mithraism, for example, the initiate actually sat under a grating on which the bull was slaughtered, and was bathed both within and without by the redeeming blood. " There is a fountain filled with blood, drawn from Immanuel's veins " — " Wash me in the blood of the Lamb." . . .

Paul, Universalizer of Jesus's Sect. — The execution of Jesus naturally dashed the hopes of his enthusiastic followers. Their aspirations soon came to life again, however, when the account of Jesus's resurrection from the dead gained currency. He who they had hoped would be a political Messiah during his lifetime they now believed was destined to play the part of the heavenly Messiah who would soon return from his place at God's right hand to effect the salvation of the Jewish nation. With great enthusiasm these first Christians sought to convert their fellow-Jews to a belief in Jesus's Messiahship. On becoming members of the Christian sect, these converts submitted to an initiatory rite of baptism, as had the followers of John and Jesus. They also joined with the rest of the Christian fellowship at stated intervals in a sacramental eating of their *heros* (this practice is now claimed by some Protestants to have been " a simple repast in memory of Jesus's last meal with his disciples "). It was as a Jewish sect with " mystery " traces, therefore, that Christianity began. At the hands of Paul, however, one of the Hellenistic Jews of the dispersion, it was to become much more.

Paul was a Jewish citizen of Tarsus in Asia Minor, a city near the great Hellenistic center of Antioch. Brought up as a strict

Pharisee, he was sent as a young man to study in Jerusalem at the feet of Gamaliel, one of the famous doctors of the law. It was while Paul was still in Jerusalem that the Christian sect arose, and as a strict Pharisee and monotheistic Hebrew he joined actively in persecuting the Christians for their blasphemy in giving divine honors to a man. But before long Paul was himself converted to Christianity as a result of a vision, sometimes said to have been epileptic in character, through which he was convinced that the resurrected Jesus had appeared to him. The next ten or fifteen years of Paul's life are rather obscure. After three years in Arabia and a brief visit to Jerusalem he then went to Antioch in Syria. Here he appears to have begun his active preaching and to have formed his purpose to be an apostle to the Gentiles, preaching first in Antioch, and later in the nearby regions of Asia Minor.

It was during this period that the question arose as to whether the Gentile converts would have to undergo the Jewish rite of circumcision. Most of the Jewish Christians thought they should, but Paul, confronted by the task of converting the Hellenistic inhabitants of Antioch and vicinity, held they should not, that personal acceptance of Jesus as the Messiah (the Christ, in Greek) was sufficient. This question was settled at the famous Council of Jerusalem, at which it was decided that the Gentile Christians need not be circumcised provided they contributed to the expenses of the mother church. Paul's position was a very important one for the future of the new religion, as it made it possible, in principle at least, for Christianity to transcend all cultural and racial limitations.

Finding the Antioch church becoming less and less sympathetic with his point of view, Paul wandered farther afield. During the next decade his labors centered in Greece, Macedonia, and the nearby portions of Asia Minor, with the Greek cities of Corinth and Ephesus as his headquarters. Here he founded several congregations over which he exercised pastoral care, often by correspondence — hence the famous Epistles.

In Greece there came about an important change in Paul's message. Before this time he had presented Jesus as the resurrected Messiah who would soon come again to establish the kingdom of God. These were distinctly Jewish concepts, and Paul was at first baffled because he seemed unable to make them appeal to the Greek mind. As he studied the Greeks, however, he became convinced that Christianity could meet their needs even better than their native mysteries, and he also found in the vocabulary and ideology of the Greek mystery sects a convenient vehicle for presenting his gospel (good news) about Jesus. It had the advantage of being familiar to his Greek hearers, and still would not be untrue to his own basic conceptions — for after all, even a Pharisee, when reared in a Hellenistic milieu, could hardly avoid taking over some of the ideas then so common. Paul found that his new technique worked; this the Greeks could understand, and this he himself could preach with conviction. Henceforth the resurrected Jesus became the dying and risen hero-savior by whose death eternal life was won for those who believed in him. The initiatory rite of baptism became not only a pledge of repentance and a means of ritual purification — features present as early as John the Baptist — but also symbolized or effected a mystical union with the savior and birth into a new life. The communal meal, at first not clearly sacramental in form, though definitely so in essence, became by *explicit* doctrine the actual consumption of the body and blood of Christ, i.e., communion. The baptized believer was " a new creation in Christ Jesus," and the indwelling divinity was a continuous presence that supplied guidance for both the individual and the religious community. In all probability, however, Paul did not consciously copy any of the mystery religions. It was simply that their concepts were common coin in the Greek world of that age, and that Paul therefore found them adequate to express his own message concerning Jesus.

In thus making Christianity " the mystery of Christ," Paul did not give up his Jewish heritage, for he perpetuated the authority of the Hebrew sacred writings, proclaimed in characteristic Jewish fashion the imminent coming of the Messiah, and preserved a good part of the spirit and teachings of Jesus. As a result of this Jewish heritage, the ethical standards of Christianity were considerably different from those of some of the Greek mysteries; sexual orgies, for example, were frowned upon. Again, as a prophet Paul belonged to the distinctively Hebrew " emissary " tradition, although he did not have the well-marked ecstatic, almost shamanistic traits of some of them. He felt himself forced to do as he did; his message was " laid upon him " almost as if it were a compulsion neurosis. " Woe is me," he said, " if I preach not the gospel." [16]

To what class of society Paul belonged we cannot say. We know that he possessed Roman citizenship, which he prized highly. This would seem to align him with the upper economic levels, for most of the opposition to Rome was among the poor. But, in addition to this and to his professional training in the

Jewish law under Gamaliel, he also knew and practiced the trade of tent-making, by which means he supported himself while engaged in itinerant preaching. Was he a member of the upper classes, or was he an artisan? We cannot say definitely. Nor can we say with assurance why it was that Paul's preaching bore most fruit among the lower classes. Was it because he himself was a member of the lower classes, and feeling most at home with them made his appeal to them? Was it owing to the egalitarianism of the early Christian communities, where distinctions of class were disregarded and even a slave could hold important positions? Or was it a result of the fact that Paul's technique of presenting Christianity as a Greek mystery appealed particularly to this stratum of the populace? These may all have been important factors, but in any case there can be no doubt that Christianity was at first a religion of the under-dog, although perhaps it is too much to say, with Nietzsche, that it was " a faith for women and slaves."

Paul's career was brought to an end when he was arrested in a Jewish riot in Jerusalem. After several years in prison he was finally taken to Rome for trial, where he probably suffered martyrdom in one of the outbursts of hostility against the Christians.

The Pauline Conception of Equality. — The ethic of Paul remained essentially similar to that of Jesus, but certain further developments should be noted.[17] For example, the ideas of individuality and universalism became intensified and appreciably narrowed. The infinite worth of the individual was now related to Christ, in whom the believer lives and moves. The fellowship in brotherly love became the general union of all believers through life in the actual mystical life-substance of Christ, in virtue of which they became members of the body of Christ. Further, the universalism was expressed in the missionary effort to convert the whole world to Christ.

In connection with the idea of individualism there arose a peculiar problem with relation to the ideas of equality and inequality; namely, how far does equality extend? *The idea of equality which is implied in individualism was for Paul limited to the religious sphere.* All individuals are equal in their common sinfulness and need: " All have sinned, and fall short of the glory of God."[18] Further, all are equal in that wherever individuals surrender to salvation through grace, that grace is given in equal measure to each.[19] This was expressed in the common participation of all in the common worship, where, as we have seen, even slaves could lead. But the question arose in the mind of Paul as to whether all men have the same right to be redeemed out of this equality of unworthiness and need into the equality of the possession of grace. Further, are all alike destined to share in the second kind of equality? If this second kind is not achieved, is it due to the will of man or of God? Paul says it is due to the inscrutable will of God — an answer, be it noted, that could have been returned by a Greek tragedian or one of the later Hebrew prophets. God has willed that some should be saved sooner, some later; although Paul thought that in the end all would be saved.

But as already noted, he was very cautious about carrying over the religious equality into secular relationships. When he considered the inequalities of human life in ordinary affairs, the inequalities due to ability and to the social and political situation, he had no idea of removing them. The existing differentiations of national and social life were foreign to the religious interest, and were simply accepted as divine ordinances. This idea Paul worked out in his metaphor of the organism in which each of the members, both the exalted and the baser, has its place of service in the life of the whole. Thus every kind of work and capacity, even the least, is honored; all worthy action is the service of God. Both those who exercise authority and those who obey do so " as unto God "; therefore, inequalities should be willingly accepted.

One reason for this attitude on the part of Paul was his eschatological conviction of the imminence of the end of the world and of Christ's return, so that the acceptance of the present inequalities could be taken as only temporary. His chief reason, however, was that inasmuch as the whole world and its order are guided by God, inasmuch as the existing order and social institutions are predestined and allowed by God's will, Christians must therefore submit and adapt themselves to them. This emphasis on the will of God brought in the idea of predestination, which cut the nerve of the idea of absolute equality, and in addition eventually provided justification for Calvinism.

State, Family, Property: Conservatism and Radicalism, Mixed. — Paul accepted the state of his time, the Roman Empire, as an institution permitted by God, and even prized it as an institution which cared for justice, order, and external morality. " Let every soul be in subjection to the higher powers: for there is no power but of God; and the powers that be are ordained of God." [20] In this Paul drew heavily on the Stoic doctrine of the moral law, the *jus naturale,* written on the heart and embodied even in the heathen state and legal system. But together with the order of the state there was also recognized the whole order of society, with its unequal distribution of property and divisions of class and rank. Christians, when differences arose, were not to resort to the state authorities, but to arbitrators from among their own group. They were to avoid trades and forms of social intercourse connected with heathen worship. On the whole, the Christians were to respect the existing régime and to make use of it, at the same time retaining a spirit of inner detachment and independence.

Paul's attitude toward the family was essentially conservative. Although for reasons unknown to us he eschewed marriage and looked upon the sex life with suspicion, such matters, naturally enough, played a very important part in his thought. Marriage was his figure for the relation of Christ to his church. He accepted the existing patriarchalism as the natural order; the husband was to be recognized and obeyed as the head of the family, and the wife and children were to be subject to him. Nevertheless, this was considerably tempered by the ideas of individualism and equality: the husband was to treat the members of his family with the love and respect due to fellow-Christians, and this extended even to the relation of master and slave. In the religious and moral realm, as we have seen, freeman and slave, wife, husband, and child were all equal.

The whole problem of economics and property was regarded essentially from the standpoint of the consumer. The Christians of this time had a distinct leaning toward small groups closely bound together by personal relationships, in which the Christian ethic of love could more easily be carried out. Paul's churches were essentially communities of this sort, remote from the great legal organization of the giant state. Accepting the conditions and distinctions of Roman society as Paul did, emphasis was laid on philanthropy; individuals were aided and social conditions allowed to remain as they were. This ideal could, of course, be carried out successfully only in an economic situation where general conditions were comparatively tolerable.

Pauline Christianity therefore contained both conservative and revolutionary elements, with the conservative predominating. The conservatism, however, was not founded upon love and esteem for existing institutions, but rather upon a mixture of contempt, submission, and recognition. Acceptance of existing social conditions was looked upon as submission to God and his will.

This attitude produced the conservative principles of patience and suffering within " the world," the ordinances of which are permitted by God, the possibilities of which Christians use for their own ends, and the continuance of which they endure because inwardly they are unaffected by them.

Yet there were also within Paul's thought radical and revolutionary aspects directed toward the development of religious personality and the fellowship of such personalities among themselves. " In fact," says Troeltsch, " a religious doctrine like that of Christian monotheism, which takes religion out of the sphere of existing conditions and the existing order and turns it purely into an ethical religion of redemption, will possess and reveal the radicalism of an ethical and universal ideal in face of all existing conditions." [21] It is this element in Christianity which was the source of many later attempts at radical social change. Even though the radicalism lies below the surface, it exercises a profound transforming influence and ventures on the most searching interference with the social order. It does this sometimes by indifference to the existing conditions, as when Christianity later helped to destroy the Roman state by alienating people from its ideals; and sometimes by submitting existing conditions to the corrosive test of its own ideals and values. Although Paul's Christianity was predominantly conservative socially, his monotheism and universalism and his belief in redemption and its ethico-personal inwardness contained an essential radicalism. Yet because the radical individualism and universalism of Christianity proceed only from the religious idea and are related to supernaturalistic values, a social conservatism is always possible.

Emperor and Galilean: the Struggle with Rome. — When Christianity first arose, its devotees were looked upon as a sect of the Jews, and since the Jewish religion was one of the legal religions of the empire, the Roman authorities were in the beginning quite tolerant.

Soon, however, the practices of the Christians made them very unpopular. For example, the convert to the new faith left off his worship at the pagan temples, and as a consequence the trades connected with the temple worship declined. Further, the seclusiveness and secrecy of the early Christians caused them to be suspected of all kinds of gross conduct, such as sodomy, incest, cannibalism, and black magic. Even when these offenses did not figure in the charge, the populace deeply resented the sly way in which proselytizing Christians would slip into houses and " pervert " their inmates, causing at the very least divisions within families. Hence the first persecutions were not the result of official proscriptions of the new religion, but rather were popular outbursts against a sect that was becoming more and more heartily despised. During the reign of Nero, advantage was taken of the general attitude toward the Christians by placing the blame for the burning of Rome upon them in order to divert suspicion from the emperor. Thousands were thrown to the lions, torn asunder by dogs, or burned alive. In a short time, however, the charge of arson was changed to that of " hatred of mankind." Thereafter, whenever popular feeling ran high, out burst the shout, " Christians to the lions."

Once the difference between the Christians and the Jews was recognized by the officials, the Christians became in many ways obnoxious to the law. In the first place, they necessarily constituted unlawful or at least extra-legal societies, and of these the authorities were always suspicious. Next, their societies practiced a new and unlawful worship, for the Christ was neither a national god nor one officially recognized; their secrecy also laid them open to suspicion of magic, which was forbidden by law. Most important of all, however, was the fact that the Christians maintained a unity independent of and contrary to the imperial unity, and moreover, possessed a wide-reaching organization. This was entirely contrary to the fundamental principle of Roman domination; namely, to rule by dividing. All subjects were to look to Rome alone, but the Christians looked to a non-Roman unity, and regarded themselves as Christians first and Roman subjects afterward. When Rome refused to accept this secondary allegiance, they ceased to consider themselves Roman subjects. This, however, was but one instance of the spirit of insubordination and obstinacy which many ancient writers attributed to the Christians. Under the emperor Domitian it led to charges of treason being placed against them because of their refusal to worship Caesar, an elementary duty of the Roman citizen. Christianity was proscribed, not as a religion, but as interfering with the organization of society which the empire inculcated and protected.

Nevertheless, there was no *general* official persecution of Christianity during the first two centuries of the present era. Whatever action was taken was by local administrators, and " was in accordance with the general powers and instructions to all the governors of provinces, to maintain peace and order, and to seek out and punish all persons whose action disturbed, or was likely to disturb public order." [22] But though no official persecution of the Christians *per se* occurred, their continued unpopularity caused them to live in constant fear of crowd upheavals, and of the consequent administrative action. It was not until A.D. 250, however, that the Roman state deliberately set about to obliterate Christianity. Under Decius the Christians were accused of refusing to worship the ancient deities (looked upon as being the traditional protectors of the state); they were therefore charged with atheism and treason, and many were put to death. Diocletian later (303 to 313 A.D.) persecuted them on the same charges. Only under Constantine, when the Christian God was proclaimed the protector of the state and Christianity was made the official state religion, did the persecutions dwindle to insignificance; later flareups, such as those under Julian the Apostate, were of limited scope and duration, however important they seemed to be at the time.

The Fathers as Belated Stoics. — The Christian Fathers as a source of religious dogma and authority during the Middle Ages have a degree of importance in the history of theories of social relations and groups scarcely second to that of the Scriptures, for during the Middle Ages their writings enjoyed almost equal authority. Although these writings are spread over at least six centuries (from the time of the apostles to the era of Charlemagne), there is sufficient coherence in their doctrines to allow the Patristic period to be discussed as a whole. Carlyle says on this point: " We think that it is true to say that in the main the Fathers represent a homogeneous system of thought." [23]

The basic social theories of the Fathers agree in many points with those of Aristotle and the Stoics. This is true, for example, of their belief that mankind is by nature social and that the existence of society cannot be attributed to an original contract or compact. " For God, since he is kind, wished us to be a social animal," wrote Lactantius, about A.D. 300.[24] Furthermore, he declared that the existence of man in society cannot be attributed to an agreement based on perceived utility. Man did not enter into society because he wished assurance of safety or the advantages of a division of labor, but because it was a mandate of his nature.

As to man's original nature the Fathers agreed with the Stoics. Seneca had held that in the beginning there had been a golden age in which man was essentially good, happy, and in no need of coercive institutions. From this state, according to Seneca, man had fallen, and as a result the present institutions of society arose. The Fathers took over this doctrine bodily, identifying

Seneca's golden age with the state of Adam and Eve before their sin and expulsion from Paradise.

The Fathers likewise followed the Stoics in holding that the law of nature, the *jus naturale,* ruled before the Fall. This law was considered as divinely ordained and revealed through reason to all men. In this primitive state the natural law provided for the equality of all men, but the Fall introduced a new element into the situation; namely, sin. And with the appearance of sin there had to be a revision of the original natural law in order to deal with it. Hence arose a relative natural law which ordained the present inequalities and coercive institutions, both as punishments for sin and as remedial measures to mitigate its evil effects. All the social institutions which from the point of view of the Fathers were necessary evils were held by them to be the results of original sin; these included, among other things, the patriarchal dominion of the male, private property, slavery, and finally, the state.

Hierarchy, Property, and Economic Life in Patristic Thought. — The whole social structure of the world as they knew it was accepted by the Fathers: professional and labor organization, distribution of wealth and property, and social stratification. Following Pauline precepts, these social distinctions were ignored in principle within the church's own circle and allowed to remain in every other sphere. On the part of the Fathers, moreover, there was no thought of social reform. Before Constantine it was sufficient to renounce the forbidden professions and occupations connected with heathen worship; the rest of the social order was taken for granted. After Constantine, however, all occupations came to be looked upon by the Fathers as forming an integral part of the social order; by participating in them, therefore, Christians were upholding the divine order of the state. And since the taint of idol-worship had been removed, Christians were now free to take part in the army and in official and economic life in general. Furthermore, there was no idea of a " calling " to a specific occupation, as in Calvinism and the doctrine of Aquinas, for the Fathers considered the original state of man to have been an equality from which differences in estate came through sin. The division of labor was thought of as a divine arrangement adapted to the needs of a fallen humanity. The various occupations were therefore regarded with indifference, and the fact that any man found himself in one rather than another was charged up to chance.

In early Patristic doctrine it was held that all possessions were originally destined for all, but that sin and its ensuing greed brought about maldistribution. That is to say, the institution of private property arose because of sin, which thereafter made primitive communism impossible. Property, however, was looked upon as having a twofold danger: the spiritual danger of pride, and the physical danger that the poor might lack absolute necessities. The problem thus raised was dealt with in two ways: (1) in the monasteries private property was abolished, and an attempt was made to restore primitive communism; (2) outside the monasteries private property was permitted, but was to be held in trust for charity, and shared with those less fortunate. But although the Fathers were well aware of the suffering caused by the prevailing social system, and were not willing to adapt themselves to it without some protest, they did not dream of social reform, much less of making any radical change. The immediate aim of charity was not the healing of social wrongs or the getting rid of property, but rather the revealing and awakening of a new spirit of love. The aim was this new spirit, not a new social order. To the wealthy who might be tempted to the sin of pride in giving, however, the Fathers pointed out that almsgiving was an act of justice, not of mercy, inasmuch as man has a natural right to that which he needs. Furthermore, those who had possessions necessary to their function in society were to maintain toward them a spirit of detachment, of freedom from all pleasure in property as such. But it should be noted that the conception of functional necessities, when linked with the acceptance, however reluctant, of the existing òrder, resulted both in theory and practice in virtual sanction for everything currently associated with particular niches in the social hierarchy. A king, for example, could plead that a richly jeweled scepter was necessary to his function as a king — QED. The upholders of the *status quo* therefore had very little to fear from even the most searching application of Patristic theory concerning wealth. Herein the Fathers resembled the *dharma*-teaching Brahmans.

Work, too, was looked upon by the Fathers as a consequence of the Fall and therefore as a punishment for sin. It was encouraged, however, because hard work was the means by which private property was acquired and almsgiving made possible; further, it was looked upon as having certain remedial aspects as well. Useful as a discipline of the body, prized as an education in sobriety and industry, work became an obligation; Paul's injunction, " If a man will not work neither shall he eat," was taken seriously and strictly enforced whenever possible. As a result the Patristic doctrine increased the sense of the duty of labor, but of course did not reach the level of intensity achieved by Calvin's teachings.

There was no developed thought on economic questions — that did not come until the time of the Schoolmen. Trade was accepted, and yet it was suspected, both because it presupposed pleasure in possessions and gain, and because it ran counter to the principle of love " to enrich oneself at the expense of others." It was therefore considered as belonging on a lower level than agriculture, craftsmanship, and manual labor. When fixing his prices, all that the tradesman might ask was the cost of production plus the additional amount necessary for a moderate profit — a position later to be developed into the famous Scholastic doctrine of the just price. The taking of interest was completely forbidden, but practice, as usual, lagged behind precept. At the same time, a sufficient number of Christians were deterred from systematic usury to make the field a fertile one for the Jews, as Jews had no chance to be saved anyway.

The Family, Women, and Slaves according to the Fathers. — A very important place was given to the family in Patristic thought. The monogamic family was considered the basis of society and the state, and high and strict ideals were set before its members, for not only did the Fathers uphold monogamy, but also chastity before marriage (for both husband and wife) and conjugal fidelity. They also taught that parents should exercise an ethical and religious discipline in the care of children, and should reject all regulation of the birth rate by infanticide, exposure, abortion, contraception, or any other means. Further, they refused to sanction divorce, deriving their argument from the New Testament: " What therefore God hath joined together, let not man put asunder." [25]

But in spite of the high esteem in which the Fathers held the family as a social institution, it was regarded, with its patriarchal domination by the male and its " conjugal rights," as a consequence of the Fall. The family was but another instance of that coercion which had replaced the freedom of the primitive state. The overlordship of man had been established when Adam and Eve were driven out of Paradise. All this tended to take from woman, and especially from the married woman, much of the freedom she had enjoyed, with regard to property in particular, in the late pagan régime of Rome. The common attitude of the early Fathers was that woman is not and cannot be man's equal in the affairs of this world, and by Tertullian's time she was explicitly exhorted to remain in her home and perform her housewifely duties. Her status of course became considerably less free, and she was considered the handmaiden of her husband, who had almost complete power over her, legally and otherwise.

The reasons for this Patristic estimate of woman, so strikingly similar to Paul's, were threefold. In the contemporary Roman world, nearly every form of amusement tended to rouse violent sexual passions; the age was one of almost unrestrained license. The attitude of the Fathers therefore seems to have been in one of its aspects a reaction against the mores of the period. Another reason is to be found in the growth of asceticism and monasticism, with its emphasis on celibacy and virginity. Marriage came to be thought of merely as a substitute for a worse evil, that of fornication. Jerome, in speaking to a young girl who had made a vow of virginity, showed that he considered virginity more desirable than marriage: " Do not court the company of married ladies. . . . Learn in this a holy pride: know that you are better than they." [26] Finally, the authority of Paul was granted great weight, and as we have seen, he had no high regard for woman or the married state.

In the teachings of the Fathers as a whole, then, the sex ethic was split into two parts not readily reconciled. On the one hand, there was the ascetic ideal, intended to be carried out by the monastic groups, with its emphasis on celibacy and the purity of the unmarried state. On the other, marriage was looked upon as a divine institution, consecrated and completely justified. This cleavage probably arose as the hope of Jesus's second coming slowly lost its immediacy. Ascetic celibacy for all could be upheld as long as there·was a vital belief in the imminent end of the world, but as years passed and eschatological fervor waned, concessions to the lusts of the flesh and the need of maintaining the race were made. The family had to be brought within the scope of religious control, however, and therefore it was sanctioned, but without abandoning the earlier ideal. Hence the necessity of keeping the two divergent conceptions in watertight compartments.

Slavery was also considered as one of the inevitable results of the Fall. According to the Fathers it was not God's purpose to have one man possess lordship over another, since before the Fall all men were free and equal. But sin made slavery necessary and natural in the sense of the relative natural law; it became a legitimate institution. Slaves were consequently admonished to obey even cruel masters. Instance the fact that Ambrose, apparently echoing Paul's injunctions to Onesimus, said in speaking of a slave: " For he is born one of them; he should endure it patiently; obeying not only good masters, but harsh ones as well." [27]

But again as in Paul's doctrine, slavery was looked upon as affecting only the body. In religious matters master and slave were on an equal footing, though necessarily unequal under human law while sojourners in this earthly city. " The slave may be superior in character to his master," wrote Ambrose; " no condition of life is incapable of virtue; the flesh can be enslaved, the mind free." [28]

Thus the Fathers changed nothing whatever in the laws dealing with slavery; the institution was accepted as appointed by God, and this was also the attitude with regard to the laws of the state which kept the slave in bonds. To repeat: the aim was a new spirit, not a new social order.

Patristic Theory Concerning Church and State. — For the Fathers the outstanding instance of those coercive institutions necessitated by the Fall was furnished by the state. Like work or slavery, it is both a punishment for sin, compelling men to submit to its laws, and at the same time remedial in that it introduces an element of order into a world which would otherwise be subject to the disorder of sin. Irenaeus, in his work *Against Heresies,* stated this theory clearly:

> For since man, by departing from God, reached such a pitch of fury as even to look upon his brother as his enemy, and engaged without fear in every kind of restless conduct, and murder, and avarice, God imposed upon mankind the fear of man, as they did not acknowledge the fear of God, in order that, being subjected to the authority of man, and kept under restraint by their laws, they might attain to some degree of justice, and exercise mutual forbearance through dread of the sword suspended full in their view. . . . Earthly rule, therefore, has been appointed by God for the benefit of nations, and not by the devil.[29]

This statement of Irenaeus is interesting also in that it assumes that the end of government is justice, another point wherein most of the Fathers agreed with the Stoics. Many of them also insisted, as the Stoics had not, that unjust rulers would sooner or later feel the wrath of God as punishment for their iniquity.

Patristic writers were unanimous in regarding the state as existing by divine authority. This doctrine they supported chiefly by texts from the Gospels and from Paul's writings. Jesus's statement, " Render therefore unto Caesar the things that are Caesar's; and unto God the things that are God's," was frequently cited; as were also Paul's words: " Let every soul be in subjection to the higher powers; for there is no power but of God; and the powers that be are ordained of God." Even in times of persecution this doctrine of the goodness of secular authority as such was upheld; persecutions were attributed to evil rulers rather than to the state itself. Even after the time of Constantine, however, the Fathers never permitted the evil and the sinful aspect of the state to be wholly overlooked.

The right of rule was held to depend not upon any personal characteristics of the ruler, nor upon any grant of authority by the people, but upon the immediate grant of God — a sort of " charisma of office." In this the Fathers disagreed with the Stoics, who held that imperial authority was derived from the people and had as its end the care of the common weal. The Fathers accepted the doctrine of the divine right of kings, holding that the imperial authority, even under pagan rule, came from God himself. The emperor ruled either " by the grace of " or " by the wrath of " God, according as the people deserved to have a good or a bad emperor. As to whether obedience was to be rendered the person or the sacred office of the emperor, most of the Fathers held that it was to be paid the latter.

The emperor administered laws according to the standard of the relative natural law, and all Roman law was supposed to correspond to this standard. This inaugurated a method of testing and limiting laws which was followed by all the Fathers, so that Origen could say: " One may only obey the laws of the State when they agree with the Divine Law; when, however, the written law of the State commands something other than the Divine and Natural Law, then we must ignore the commands of the State and obey the command of God alone." [30]

The conception of the divine nature of secular authority was later a sad stumbling block to the church when it came into conflict with the secular government. Two divine institutions might readily exist side by side, without involving any question as to superiority, as long as there was perfect harmony; when conflict came, however, it was difficult to decide which was to take precedence. The majority of the early Fathers maintained that the church was absolutely supreme in matters of faith and morals, whereas the state was supreme in the secular sphere. Ambrose went even further, affirming the right of the church to own and control property as a divine possession which could not be taken by the state; this was the beginning of the extension of church authority over temporal affairs. However, only one of the early

Fathers, Chrysostom, makes an unqualified statement of the
superiority of the church to the state:

> The prince holds in his hands material weapons, while the priest has
> only spiritual ones. The king wages war against barbarians, the priest
> against demons. . . . We read in the Old Testament that the priests
> anointed the kings, and today the prince still bends his head beneath the
> hands of the priest. . . . Thus we understand that the priest is superior
> to the king, for he who receives the benediction is evidently inferior to
> him who gives it.[31]

A Tale of Two Cities: Augustine. — By far the most outstanding of the Fathers was Augustine (354–430 A.D.), Bishop of
Hippo in North Africa. He represents in the main the type of
social thought we have just been discussing, but several ideas
that demand special attention are contained in his masterpiece,
The City of God, written to refute the charge that Christianity
was responsible for the sack of Rome by Alaric in A.D. 410. In this
great work, incorporating most of his social teachings, Augustine
presented his doctrine of the two cities: " the city of men " and
" the city of God."

He agreed with the other Fathers as to the natural origin of
human society, the nature of man before the Fall, and the rise
of coercive institutions in society, including slavery, as a result of
the Fall. Holding definitely predestinarian views (perhaps related
to the Manichaeism in which he so long believed), he quite consistently maintained that slavery was part of God's plan for certain persons, and joined to this the Aristotelian argument as to
the natural inequality of mankind. Private property, in his view,
is the creation of the state, and exists only in virtue of its protection. The right of property is also limited, he thought, by the
use to which it is put; a man who does not use his property rightly
has no valid claim to it.

Augustine also differed from the other Fathers and from Cicero
(one of the Roman thinkers heavily drawn upon) as to the place
assigned to law and justice in the state. Cicero had defined the
state as a multitude of men united in their agreement upon law
and in the common enjoyment of that which is useful to them.
Augustine rightly interpreted this as meaning that there could be
no Christian state without justice, because where there is no justice there can be no law, and then, for reasons best known to himself, went on to deny that there could be any justice in a pagan
state such as Rome. Cicero's definition he applied exclusively to
the divine state, in which there is fixed law and definite forms of

justice, and proceeded to give a definition of the state which would apply to Rome as he conceived it (leaving out all reference to law and justice), as " a multitude joined together in the common enjoyment of the things which it loves." [32] Whether Augustine realized the eventual significance of this change may well be doubted, but it is clear that it makes the *just* state entirely dependent on the church, and unjust states are given no Christian sanction whatever, but are condemned as pagan. The way was thereby opened for the anathematization of any ruler declared to be either pagan or unjust, or both. The journey of Henry IV to Canossa began in the time of Augustine . . .

The origin of the state Augustine ascribed to man's defective nature under the régime of sin since the Fall. He did not regard the institution of government, however, as itself sinful, but rather as in accord with the divine purpose of creating some system of order and discipline whereby men's vices might be restrained if not eradicated. The state is therefore a remedial institution. The ruler is the representative of God on earth, and as such is entitled to the obedience of his subjects. It is not only his right but his duty to use the coercive and protective power given him.

It should by now be apparent that Augustine did not think out very clearly the relation which should exist between the state and the church. Carlyle says on this point:

> There is no doubt that he conceived of the Temporal Power as being inferior in dignity and greatness to the Spiritual Power, but I do not think that he had very clearly before him what we call the questions of the relation of Church and State. . . . I do not think that it is safe to found upon the writings of St. Augustine the conclusion that he would have looked upon the Church as being in its proper nature in any relation of authority or supremacy over the State. [33]

Nevertheless, in his description of the city of God we get a picture of a theocratic state in which the state is identical with the church, except in officers. In this commonwealth only the faithful can be citizens. And from the church the state receives its power and attains its highest end, the unity and government of Christians. Quoting Robinson:

> The State . . . merges . . . in the Church, and the civil power becomes the weapon of the Church, the legislator and the magistrate are but sons of the Church, bound to carry out the Church's aims. . . . The Empire becomes the instrument and vassal of the Church. [34]

Thinking of the earthly state as Augustine did, it was quite natural that he should look upon it as being vastly inferior to that eternal state of the spirit and of the hereafter. The fundamental distinction, however, between " the city of men " and " the city of God " was apparently not that between church and state, but rather between two societies, the one composed of the wicked and the other of the godly. On earth these societies are mixed, and it is only as a symbol that the church stands for the city of God. The city of God is that mystical society of all those who, both now and in the hereafter, have accepted orthodox Christianity. Because of his doctrine of predestination, Augustine held that not all members of the church belong to the city of God, but he was equally positive that no one outside the church could belong.

Augustine's great work dominated Christian thought for centuries. It " set over against the declining world of ancient Rome the eternal commonwealth of God's elect, and sketched in fervid rhetoric the ideals and interests of that church here on earth which strives toward the kingdom of heaven." [35]

Defenders of Theocracy; Organismic Notions. — Although Augustine and some of the other Fathers may be said to have laid the basis for justifications of theocracy, there were few attempts to utilize their labors until well into the eleventh century. This was probably owing to the general dearth of theoretical interests that became evident when, as Seeck puts it, the ancient world went into a decline.[36] The exploits of pagan or half-Christianized chieftains occupied nearly all of the attention of the dwindling intellectual class; there was no time for critical reflection. At the most men framed far-fetched philosophies of history on the foundation of fantastic interpretations, allegorical and otherwise, of the Christian epic. The Muse Clio was compelled to accept such sorry consorts as Rhabanus Maurus (776–856 A.D.), his pupil and disciple Walafrid Strabo (c. 809–849 A.D.), and John Scotus Erigena (d. 877). Heinrich von Sybel has commented on the work of these and other imitators of Orosius and Cassiodorus, two mediocre Fathers, as follows:

> This period possessed no idea of historical judgment, no sense of historical reality, no trace of critical reflection. The principle of authority, ruling without limitation in the religious domain, defended all tradition, as well as traditional dogma. Men were everywhere more inclined to believe than to examine, everywhere imagination had the upper hand of reason.[37]

While Sybel's severe judgment is perhaps justified in the cases mentioned, one should not forget the terrific handicaps under which men labored in the Dark Ages and the early Middle Ages.

Moreover, the annalists and chroniclers were by no means contemptible as recorders of facts, however incompetent they may have been in generalizing from them. Again, efforts at systematic interpretation of historical trends were not infrequent. It must be granted, however, that the prevailing Christian ideology acted as a distorting influence and in addition diverted attention from " worldly things." The great Crusader Villehardouin and the isolated Frankish historian Nithard showed strong secular interests, but they were exceptions; it must be conceded that in general the Christian philosophy of history left little room for the kind of causal interpretation of history that is today in favor. The will of God was everywhere invoked as a direct explanation. At the very best, we are merely given fairly accurate accounts of scattered events.

Augustine's *City of God,* then, long remained without a successor; it was not destined to stimulate social thought, but rather to constitute one more of the reasons for intellectual stagnation. The stimulus came when, with the growth of feudalism, the revival of Roman law, the growth of canon law, and the consolidation of ecclesiastical power, the relations of church and state became a problem that confronted men at every turn of their every-day affairs. Roman law brought to the fore the theories of popular sovereignty and secular absolutism, and the canon law strengthened the theocratic tradition deriving from the Fathers.

The struggle of the church with the state became acute when Pope Gregory VII released the subjects of Henry IV, the rebellious secular head of the Holy Roman Empire, from their oaths of allegiance. As will be recalled, Henry capitulated and made the journey to Canossa, where under peculiarly humiliating circumstances he was forced to admit the supremacy of the papacy. One of the most forceful statements upholding Gregory's right to compel secular rulers to bow the knee was furnished by the fiery priest Manegold of Lautenbach (d. after 1085), who clearly enunciated the principle of a governmental compact as the basis of political authority. Although his statement was but an epitome of the general theory of the period, he must be given credit for explicitly and definitely formulating it for the first time, apparently, in the history of Western Europe. Tyranny was defined as the breaking of the original compact by which the ruler was placed in power, and such breach was held to constitute a valid basis for rebellion.[38]

The theocratic doctrine of the state received its fullest exposition, however, in the *Polycraticus* of John of Salisbury (1120–

1182), an English cleric who had studied under Abélard. The authority of the prince, he declared, is distinctly inferior to that of the priest; in fact, the prince is the servant of the priesthood. This theory he stated in his doctrine of the two swords, the one held by the church, the other by the state. " He declares that it was from the church that the prince received the material sword as the minister of the priesthood, in order to be able to discharge that part of the priest's office which the spiritual power could not worthily exercise." [39]

Further, John put forward an influential conception of the fundamental difference between the legitimate prince and the tyrant. The supreme mark of distinction between the two lies, he said, in the fact that the prince obeys the law and rules his people according to it, whereas the tyrant nullifies the law and reduces the people to slavery. The prince is necessarily subject to the divine law and equity, and must rely on the clergy in order to make his enactments consonant with it. If he fails either in this or in his obligation to procure the welfare of all his subjects, declared John, he must be deposed, and in the effort even tyrannicide is permissible, for if tyrants are not struck down by the hand of man, they will surely be smitten by the hand of God.

John was also an exponent of the organismic theory of society, which he developed in detail. The state, he declared, is a divinely animated body conducted on the basis of the highest equity and controlled by reason. The soul of the body is the clergy, the head the prince, the heart the senate, and to the stomach and other internal organs correspond various public officials. The eyes, ears, and tongue are the governors of provinces; the hands are the military forces and subordinate authorities; and the feet are the agricultural classes and the artisans. In this picturesque fashion he puts forward the theory that a " well-ordered constitution consists in the due allotment of functions to the members of the commonwealth and in the right condition, strength, and composition of each and every functionary body." [40]

The Angelic Doctor and the Four-Fold Law. — Neither Manegold of Lautenbach nor John of Salisbury possessed much influence on their contemporaries, however; in fact, they have never at any time been outstanding in Christian social thought. Let us turn to a figure that overtops even Augustine in the long tradition of the church, the *doctor angelicus,* St. Thomas of Aquino (*c.* 1225–1274), commonly called Aquinas in order to distinguish him from the numerous other saints bearing the same given name. This thinker, probably the greatest of the Middle Ages, undertook the gigantic task of reconciling all accumulated knowledge with Christian theology and, as might be expected, found it necessary in doing so to construct a complete philosophy of life and society. His sources included the theories of Aristotle, the Stoics, Cicero, Augustine and the other Fathers, Neo-Platonism, and the theology of the church. Of his many writings, his *Summa theologiae, De regimine principum,* and his commentary on Aristotle's *Politics* are the most important in the development of his social and political philosophy.

A Neapolitan noble by birth, he joined the Dominican order in 1243 against the wishes of his family. Recognizing his uncommon ability, his spiritual advisers sent him to Cologne and Paris to study under Albertus Magnus, the greatest Schoolman of his age. Here he acquired the degrees of Bachelor, Master, and Doctor of theology, afterward teaching at Cologne, Paris, Rome, and Naples. In these crowded years of teaching and writing (he died before reaching his fiftieth year), Aquinas was constantly consulted on important civil and ecclesiastical questions, and for good measure was active in preaching. In the Roman Catholic church his influence has never ceased, and his works were chosen by Pope Leo XIII in 1879 as the basis of present theological instruction.

His social theories can best be approached through his doctrine of four-fold law: (1) *eternal law,* God's own will and purpose for the universe; (2) *natural law,* the progressive expression of this eternal law in reason; (3) *human law,* the application of natural law to human needs and the basis of the human social order, deriving its authority through conformity with natural law; and (4) *divine law,* supplementing human reason and human law in regard to man's eternal destiny, salvation, as revealed in the sacred Scriptures.[41]

Aquinas agreed with Aristotle and Cicero that man is naturally social and that the origin of society was due to human spontaneity and community of interests. Man is formed for society and is truly human only in association. Society, then, rests on a basis of natural law. Further agreement is manifest in his contention that natural law is essentially an expression of human reason. He adds, herein following Aristotle closely, that reason possesses an impulse toward its goal, so that he who follows natural law is led onward toward man's true end.

Inequality, Coercion, and the Principle of Plenitude. — Aquinas's conception of natural law, however, differs rather widely from that of the Stoics and the early Fathers. Whereas the

latter thought of it as standing for the essential equality of all
men, the *doctor angelicus* thought of it as standing for an essential human inequality. Instead of regarding the primitive state
of man as one in which communism would have developed, he
thought of it as one in which man's natural inequalities would
have expressed themselves, so that all the plurality patterns of
society, such as the family, state, and the like, would have developed, but on a voluntary, not a coercive basis. Hence it was
only coercion, not the institutionalized groups themselves, which
the Fall introduced.

Furthermore, instead of identifying the absolute natural law
with divine law, Aquinas was very careful to make a distinction
between the two. For him the natural law belongs only to the
realm of nature, whereas divine law belongs to supernature. The
former is known only through reason, the latter only through
God's miraculous grace. Reason and nature are sufficient to enable man to achieve a certain measure of happiness and virtue,
but are not sufficient to enable him to attain the vision of God,
which is man's true end. This consummation is achieved by going
beyond nature, in accordance with divine law, by means of God's
miraculous free gift of grace. Reason and natural law are therefore subordinate and preparatory to grace, which before the Fall
imparted to man both a moral and a mystical perfection. The
Fall is no longer thought of as the loss of the " absolute law of
nature " but as the loss of grace. As a result the natural law of
reason also became dimmed, and assumed a new form involving
coercion as both penalty and remedy for sin. Another consequence
of the Fall is to be found in the unjust and irrational inequalities
of position and destiny found in society.

This opposition of nature and grace the prince of the scholastics overcomes, however, by a system of degrees, which in the
development of reason leads upward from nature to grace. Here
the Aristotelian idea of development, or rather that of hierarchical classification of ends, is applied. The distinction between the
absolute and the relative natural law is no longer important, for
they are both only different degrees in the realization of natural
law. The Christian ethic therefore became relative, with the
radical and revolutionary ideals at the top as " counsels of perfection," and the relative standards below. While the church
signified the permanent presence of the absolute, only the relative need be realized by persons. What men failed to realize in
this life could be made up later in purgatory. Furthermore, man's
progress upward from one stage to the next depends upon nothing

in his own nature, but rather is achieved only by means of a
divine miracle at each step. God is thought of as the end and final
cause of the whole process, " drawing all men unto Himself " —
a truly Aristotelian conception.

This hierarchical pattern, held Aquinas, is one which characterizes the whole universe, which is indeed one and yet contains
within itself all the degrees of imperfection and perfection —
" the principle of plenitude." Not only does the individual pass
through many phases, but society also ascends from one plane to
another through its graded social organization, from the lowest
slave up to the king. " The ordered variety of the ecclesiastical
hierarchy is meant to repeat upon a higher plane, in the realm
of Grace, the harmonious variety of the natural order and of the
order of the State." [42] In a certain sense, then, " whatever is, is
right," for anything less than plenitude would be less than perfection, and God is perfect.

Aquinas a Patriarchal and Organic Thinker. — This theory
of society is characterized by Troeltsch as patriarchal and organic. As organic it emphasizes the unity of human society in
relation to its absolute goal, at the same time holding up the
idea that each individual member is supremely important and has
a definite place within the ordered whole. It also involves the
division of service and labor in the achievement of the common
goal. Membership necessarily brings with it the obligation to
assist every other member to enter into his spiritual inheritance.
This aspect of Aquinas's theory, says Troeltsch, is a direct development of the complete religious individualism of Jesus. From
the radical and critical principle thus provided, it follows that
unjust institutions, which are not consonant with the law of God,
may and must be altered; that godless rulers must be deposed or
warned; and that rebellion may on occasion be justified.

The patriarchal aspect of Aquinas's theory is its conservative,
stabilizing side. Society is full of inequalities of every kind, and
its members are enjoined to a voluntary acceptance of and submission to them. By the ruling classes they are to be utilized as
an opportunity for the exercise of charity and devotion toward
their less fortunate brethren; and by others as occasions for dis-
playing the virtues of trust, patience, and humility to those above
them. All social relationships are modeled on the family, with
its patriarchal domination of the husband over the wife and children, and the corresponding willing subordination of those pa-
triarchally ruled. This aspect, Troeltsch says, is Aquinas's version
of Jesus's universalism of love. But as we have seen, patriarchal-

ism explicitly recognized the existing social hierarchy and emphasized the duty of every man to remain within his own class and to be content with his present position — here granting authority to Pauline teaching.

Both the patriarchal and organic points of view find a common ground in the conception of "calling," which now arose as a rational constituent part of the social system. The division of labor was for Aquinas, as we have seen, the result of the inequality of human capacities. Therefore the organization of society according to class and profession is not something produced by sin, but something willed by God in accordance with his purpose of grace. No man may try to rise beyond the limits of his class, nor forsake the calling inherited from his father.

It follows that Aquinas had no idea whatever of social reform. Whereas the early church accepted the social order as something fixed and incapable of being reformed, tolerating it simply as the sinful corruption of the order of natural law, the medieval church, as represented by this scion of nobility, accepted the social order, with all its glaring inequalities and its sadly relative approximations to the ideals of the church, as *the natural, necessary, logical world-order*. To seek to reform the social order would be to meddle with something God had planned in accordance with the principle of plenitude.

The Subjection of Woman, Slavery, and Private Property Justified. — In connection with the rational character of natural law and the hierarchical nature of the world and of society, Aquinas taught a developmental theory of the rise and progress of social structures and institutions. The family is the original and fundamental form of social life, and is the first result of that natural reason which formed men into communities. The purpose of the family consists primarily in the birth and education of offspring, and this purpose leads to monogamy, to the holding of private property as the wealth of the family, and to the right of inheritance. The sensual sexual side of marriage is ignored, since the aim of marriage is limited solely to the rational reproduction of human beings. The family relationship is held, as we have seen, to be a specially hallowed example of what.all human relationships ought to be. In regard to the position of woman, Aquinas followed Aristotle in considering her completely subordinate to man:

The woman is subject to the man, on account of the weakness of her nature, both of mind and of body. . . . Man is the beginning of woman

and her end, just as God is the beginning and end of every creature . . .
Woman is in subjection according to the law of nature, but a slave is
not.[43]

Aquinas accepted slavery as a conventional institution, not as
a natural one. While it did not belong to man's original state,
it may be justified now on the ground of utility. Slavery is supported by two arguments, the one Aristotelian and the other
Augustinian. Following Aristotle and the principle of plenitude,
the erstwhile Neapolitan noble held that among the souls of men
there are different grades of perfection, giving rise to the obvious
inequalities among individuals. It is natural, therefore, that the
superior should control and direct the inferior, and that the
feeble and foolish should be controlled by the strong and wise.
Following Augustine, he justified slavery as being one of the
results of the Fall, for it was then that humanity was first placed
in circumstances which gave rise to the condition of master and
slave. Slavery is a punishment for sin. The rights of the master,
however, are not unlimited. Slaves are to be subject to their
masters in servile work and in obedience to the orders that fall
within the limits of the master's power, but beyond these limits
the slave is by nature free. In marriage, for example, the slave is
free from the control of his master, and should not be sold
separately from his family. Aquinas distinguished between certain acts done by the slave in obedience to his master and others
in which the slave possesses full human rights, and hoped that
the hardships of slavery could be mitigated if slaves were coun-
selled to accept their position as a spiritual discipline in preparation for a higher freedom in the hereafter.[44]

In his doctrine of private property Aquinas differed little from
the Fathers. He maintained that it is lawful and not contrary to
nature, but that nevertheless private rights cannot be permitted
to interfere with the common right of mankind to the necessaries
of life. Almsgiving, he argued, is an act of love and mercy, but
is also an obligation, for temporal possessions, while they may
be private as regards ownership, are not so as regards use —
in so far as they are superfluities, they belong to others who may
have need of them. When poverty or distress require it, property
belongs to the community as a whole. If a man finds a fellow-man
in dire need, and does not himself possess what is needed to aid
him, he may without moral fault take the rich man's property
and give it to the needy.[45] (This sounds almost like the principle
characterized by Sumner as " A and B put their heads together
to decide what C shall be compelled to do for D.")

*Economic Traditionalism and the Fear of Urban Seculariza-
tion.* — The whole economic organization of society, in the view
of Aquinas, is based on the necessity of labor and on the division
of labor which that involves. This leads, in accordance with
natural law, to the organization of " estates " engaged in the
same kind of work. These functional-hierarchical groupings are
to be preserved in order to protect the food supply. Individuals are to be restricted to their own " estate " grouping
(" class " is not an accurate designation here — see note 34,
Chapter One) and to their own work in order not to disturb
the social organization. This is the traditionalist spirit, says
Troeltsch, as opposed to the rationalism of capitalism. And he
says:

It is expressed in the differentiation according to rank, of the way of
life, and in the injunction to the political authorities, through a policy of
protection of food supply and of the regulation of prices to maintain for
each individual the income according to his rank. It is the standpoint of
the conservation of food supplies which is closely connected with the
maintenance of permanent professional groups [*Stände* or " estates "]
in which the same trade or calling is handed on, without variation, from
father to son, through many generations.[46]

A positive value is assigned to work. It is not only the means
of existence, but is also the means of gaining sufficient property
to enable the performance of the duty of maintaining a family
according to the standards of one's estate. (Here we notice that
the purely consumer's standpoint of the early church has been
discarded.) But work also has an ascetic value, destroying carnal
ideas and preventing the distraction caused by sensual pleasures.
Moreover, when viewed as a result of the Fall it leads also to
humility. Labor is thus both a penalty and a means of salvation.
    Wisely enough, so far as the interests of the medieval ecclesia
were concerned, Aquinas condemned trade and commerce, on
the whole, except as a means of securing the commodities which
the community lacks. His ideal community was a town, strongly
agrarian, which by a system of orderly exchange of goods with
the surrounding country under its rule would constitute an economic unit as nearly self-sufficient as possible. Commerce is justified, therefore, only to supply the community's needs; it should
not be engaged in for gain.
    One reason for Aquinas's condemnation of trade was the
fraud committed in the markets by the traders, especially in
the practice of haggling over prices. Such a practice, said the
greatest of the Schoolmen, is likely to lead to cheating. There is,

he insisted, a just and natural price for everything, and this all barter and trade should observe. Here we have the full-fledged doctrine of just price; it was destined to play a great part in the world, and is even now far from extinct.

A second and probably more important reason for Aquinas's condemnation of trade and commerce was his desire to preserve unchanged the sacred communities of the faithful; a native of an Italian city-state, he was able to observe on every hand the secularizing effects of the culture contact engendered by the Crusades and the ensuing lust for Levantine goods and the sequins of the followers of Mohammed. In addition, his familiarity with Aristotle's comments on Plato furnished him with a number of ready-made generalizations, which with little change he made his own in *De regimine principum:* (1) commerce brings strangers into the *polis,* and the resulting culture contact fosters mental mobility, which in turn leads to social disorganization; (2) " a nation of shopkeepers " soon becomes unwilling and unable to go to war, and therefore exports should consist only of unavoidable surpluses, while imports should be pared to the bone of bare necessity; (3) the city-state should not be on the coast, for maritime cities are notorious for their lax morals, the result of cosmopolitanism and a high rate of transiency; [47] (4) it should, however, be near enough to the sea to get necessary supplies from abroad, so that on the whole the golden mean of an intermediate position should be chosen. [48]

The State Not a Necessary Evil. — According to Aquinas the state is one of the developments of natural law, for as reason worked itself out in human society, the state sprang up naturally out of the family and family relations, which gradually extended to include the community and finally the whole race. Aquinas, therefore, did not consider the state as a necessary evil, as had the early Fathers. Instead, it is the natural and necessary foundation for the preservation and development of human well-being. Although God is the source of all authority to govern, he has placed the political sovereignty in the hands of the people, who are God's instrument in calling the state into existence. The people, therefore, may set up the kind of state they wish, entrusting their sovereignty, according to human law, to a king, to an aristocracy, or to a republican form of government. Although the state is a natural institution, the particular form which it assumes rests upon a compact between rulers and ruled. The princes therefore derive their power from the people, and bear a responsibility to rule justly and in such a way as to promote the highest virtue.

All this, by the way, would have had a familiar ring in the ears of a follower of Mencius, a thousand years earlier.

The particular form of organization for the state which Aquinas preferred was a compromise, approaching the form later known as the limited monarchy. Under this form of constitution the power would be given to one ruler who had under him others also possessing powers of government. Such a mixed constitution, said Aquinas, is the best: for it is partly kingdom in that there is one ruler, partly aristocracy in that many have authority, and partly democracy in that the people choose their rulers. The state is organized, therefore, on the same pattern as the universe, a structure in which the individuality of the particular members is carefully preserved, and yet in which the members are arranged in an ordered series of classes and ranks. It is also noteworthy that he does not have in mind one state, but many — again the principle of plenitude, direct reflection of the Europe of his day.

Considering the conditions under which Aquinas grew up in Naples, it can occasion small wonder that he recognized the fact that occasionally a wicked ruler broke the compact to rule his people for their good and became an exploiting tyrant, governing only for his own interests. When this occurs, declared the courageous churchman, the people possess not only the right but the duty of revolution, and in an elective monarchy the tyrant may be deposed. He rejected tyrannicide, however, as likely to lead to anarchy.

Nature and Grace, State and Church. — Following Aristotle, Aquinas attributed to the state a twofold function: one temporal, consisting in the preservation of the physical welfare of its citizens and the maintenance of order and peace; and one spiritual, plainly evident as the ethical task of promoting the moral well-being of men and assisting them to lead a virtuous life. The state consequently seeks to preserve and develop man's natural abilities. As a member of the natural order, man might thus conceivably attain to the full stature of his *natural* virtue in the conditions of human society. But man is more than natural; he is also spiritual, and has a supernatural end which consists in his union with God in " the beatific vision." This is not to be achieved by the exercise of purely natural capacities, but only through a life of grace and virtue. Man therefore belongs to two orders, that of nature and that of grace. As a member of the order of nature he looks to the rule and authority of the temporal sovereign; as a member of the order of grace he looks to the church. Man's supreme end is the beatific enjoyment of God, and any lesser ends are to be looked upon merely as means to the higher life of grace. The state therefore is not an end in itself, but is only instrumental as leading up to grace.

"The natural end of a people formed into a society," wrote Aquinas, "is to live virtuously; for the end of any society is the same as that of the individuals composing it. But since the virtuous man is also determined to a further end, the purpose of society is not merely that man should live virtuously, but that by virtue he should come to the enjoyment of God." This latter, however, cannot be brought about by any human direction, but only by the aid of the divine kingdom; and "The administration of this kingdom has been committed, not to the kings of this world, but to priests, in order that the spiritual should be distinct from the temporal." [49]

This naturally leads up to the relation of church and state. Since the ruler who directs men to their ultimate end should hold sway over those who have the care only of intermediate ends, "it is evident that the king should be subject to and obey that authority which is placed in the hands of the priest." [50] But this "authority in the hands of the priest" is also temporal. "For the relation of the good life of nature to the supernatural life of blessedness as a means to an end is one which necessitates the supervision of the means by that ruler whose principle concern is with the end." [51] Consequently, he argued, the pope is to be obeyed above every other ruler in temporal as well as spiritual affairs.

This dualism of two orders of rule Aquinas therefore transcended by making the spiritual supreme, but he did it in a way much more subtle than that blared forth in Manegold of Lautenbach's or John of Salisbury's tracts. State and church are not mutually exclusive, he said; they are complementary. The Christian man, as a citizen of both, is really in organic affiliation with only one great social organization. The two parts can be distinguished as state and church, but they are welded into indissoluble unity by the ultimate end of every earthly act, man's destined union with God in "the beatific vision." Aquinas stood for an ecclesiastical unity of civilization under the sway of the pope, highest link in the earthly chain reaching upward to God.

Summary of the Chapter. — Christianity began as a Jewish sect, but was strongly influenced by ideas current in the Hellenistic world. Its initial impetus was derived from Jesus of Nazareth, who preached an unlimited, unqualified individualism and an absolute universalism of love. He seems to have presented no program of social reform, but to have devoted his efforts to inducing people so to live that they could enter into the kingdom of God even before its imminent coming. This kingdom, when it came, was not to be primarily a new social order, for although a new order would be created, it would not be one concerned with family, society, or state. Otherworldliness was a prominent feature of Jesus's teaching, and this eschatological emphasis has been predominant in Christianity ever since.

The extensive culture contacts of the Greco-Roman world in the first century of our era brought the followers of Jesus close to the various mystery cults in which the element of salvation through identification with the god or hero was stressed. Paul, a Hellenistic Jew of the dispersion, brought this into relation with the individualism and universalism of Jesus, and thereby succeeded in making a highly successful appeal to the Gentile world. In particular, the lower classes were strongly attracted. It should be noted, however, that in Pauline doctrine the individualism and universalism of Jesus were intensified and narrowed. The infinite worth of the individual was related to Christ, and the universalism was expressed in missionary effort. Sharp distinction was made between religious and secular equality; Paul had no idea of championing the latter. Moreover, he affirmed the *status quo*. Pauline Christianity is therefore a mixture of conservative and radical traits, with the conservative predominating.

Persecution of the early Christians was not at first a governmental policy, but simply an outburst of popular antipathy. Later, when the illegal activities of the Christians made them obnoxious to the authorities, systematic persecution was launched upon. It must be borne clearly in mind, however, that Christianity was not proscribed as a supernaturalistic doctrine, but as a set of sacred practices drastically interfering with the organization of society which the Roman Empire inculcated and protected. Finally, when Rome could not wipe out the ever-growing church, it joined hands with it.

The Fathers of the church agreed in many respects with Aristotle and the Stoics in their fundamental social theories. They held, for example, that mankind is by nature social, that there had been a golden age free from coercive institutions, and that absolute natural law ruled before the Fall. Relative natural law prevailed thereafter, and under it, as the result of sin, such institutions as the patriarchal dominion of the male, private property, and the state were instituted. A functional conception of property that did not seriously challenge the existing order was

256   EARLY AND MEDIEVAL CHRISTIANITY

a feature of Patristic doctrine, as were also the notions of work
as both punishment and remedy for sin, and of trade as morally
inferior. Marriage was looked upon as a divine institution, but
virginity was upheld as an ideal. Slavery was held to be one of
the inevitable results of the Fall, as in Paul's doctrine, and in
further agreement with him, master and slave were dealt with
on an equal footing religiously. There was no developed theory
of the relation of church and state, but secular authority was held
to be divinely granted. Among the early Fathers only Chrysostom
made an unqualified statement of the superiority of the church to
the state.

Augustine agreed with the other Fathers in most of his social
theories, but differed in some respects. One of these was his acceptance of the Aristotelian doctrine of the natural inequality of
mankind; the other Fathers had held that men are by nature
equal. Another was his limitation of the conception of the just
state to that sanctioned as such by the church, and by implication
the granting of the right of revolution to the subjects of unjust
states.

More direct justifications of theocracy were provided in the
eleventh century by Manegold of Lautenbach and John of Salisbury, two forthright defenders of the papacy against the empire.
A far more influential apology, however, came from the pen of
Thomas Aquinas, who in addition offered several other important modifications of and innovations upon the prevailing social
theories. Most important among such alterations was the
apparent transcending of the dualism of church and state
by making them both subservient to the ultimate end of
man, union with God in "the beatific vision."

Recent research, beyond that noted on p. 134 with reference to the Dead
Sea Scrolls, in archaeology, the Biblical and related documents, theology
(in the broad sense), and so on, makes it debatable: (1) whether Jesus
viewed himself as an emissary prophet — he may have come to accept assign-
ment to the role of Messiah; (2) whether individualized interpretations,
with regard to any and all of the leading figures discussed, having psychiatric
implications, are fully tenable in view of the broadly general character of
many of the patterns of group conduct involved; (3) and whether anything
beyond an invidious *ad hominem* point is cored, in spite of sociology of
knowledge possibilities, by referring to Aquinas as a "Neapolitan noble
by birth."

CHAPTER VII

The Meeting of East and West and the Advance of Secularism

H OW CULTURE CONTACT CAME ABOUT. — Europeans usually have little appreciation of the effect the Moslem East has had upon the Western world. Even professional historians often fail to give due weight to such instances of close culture contact and cross-fertilization of cultures as are afforded, for example, by the Moorish invasions of the Spanish peninsula, the Crusades, and the ensuing trade with the Levant.

On the other hand, they often attach too much importance to the revival of the theories of Aristotle. The really significant thing about this revival is not the theoretical modifications as such which it produced, but the witness it bears to the contact of the Mohammedan and Christian cultures, and especially to contacts within the far-flung Mohammedan culture area. Some of Aristotle's most important writings first reached Europe of the Middle Ages through the translations of the Spanish and Provençal Jews (the Ibn Tibbon family of translators, among others), who themselves had received the Greek fire from the Moors of Spain. The Moors, being good Moslems, made the *haj* or pilgrimage to Mecca at least once in their lives, and sometimes oftener, as we may see from the example of the greatest Moslem traveler, Ibn Battūta of Tangier.[1] First and last this astonishing man journeyed some seventy-five thousand miles (four trips to Mecca and return making up a good part of the sum, although he also traveled to China and elsewhere). By means of these frequent pilgrimages culture contact with the Arabian East was maintained, and the Arabian East was the center of secular learning and enlightenment when Europe was deep in the sacred Dark Ages.[2] The Greek writings were not merely utilized to buttress a sacred book, as was often the case in Europe; they exercised a formative influence on secular affairs. Commentaries on Plato, Aristotle, and Strabo were written by Moslems before the eleventh century that Europe did not equal until the seventeenth.[3]

Certain it is, at any rate, that the cross-fertilization of non-material cultures represented by the use of translations of Aristotle in the great European university centers produced nothing startlingly new in the thirteenth century, either in the writings of Aquinas or in those of his contemporaries. To be sure, the cogitations of the Schoolmen were of considerably higher grade than the disquisitions of Maurus and Erigena, and this superiority may in part be due to Aristotle's writings, but after all they had little interest in the affairs of this world, in such " secular commonplaces " as the foundation and disruption of states and the fate of peoples. Mass movements like the earlier Crusades and the slow nibbling of the Commercial Revolution did far more toward the overthrow of the sacred society of isolated Europe and the establishment of an incipient secular society than did all the syllogisms of the Stagirite.

In other words, culture contact with the East was most effective in the realm of material culture. The Crusades and trade with the Levant were the great mediating agencies in this field, and were of course almost inextricably intertwined. For example, the Venetians and others transported Crusaders to Asia Minor and brought back Levantine goods; warfare and commerce ran their courses side by side. In spite of this fact, however, it seems likely that the adventurous folly of the Crusades was the prior agency in effectively acquainting the Western world with the rich store of goods the East had to offer, with the seductive mores of the infidel, and with the various Christian and near-Christian heresies flourishing in Asia Minor. Witness the well-known fact that the Templars were infected with Gnostic and similar doctrines picked up during their long residence abroad, which heresies, along with other things, they diligently spread throughout Christendom on their return. The Commercial Revolution, on the other hand, did not really begin to get under way until the early fourteenth century, although it must be admitted that when it did the trickle of culture contact started by the Crusades broadened into a flood, and Europe's wall of isolation crumbled.

Then came release, for out through the breaches burst the heaven-storming Titans of the " conspirital societies " of Italy, individuals cut loose from the laws of common humanity, to be sure — but what individuals! One can understand, if not sympathize with, Nietzsche's raptures; men of mighty energy, astounding versatility, and appalling wickedness appear on the scene, men *released* from the bonds of " the Thirteenth, Greatest of Centuries." Culture contact had done its work.

Unrest and Culture Contact. — Culture contact, however, cannot be taken for granted; it does not " just happen "; it must be accounted for in the specific configuration in which it occurs. In some instances mere geographical proximity is a sufficient explanation; in others, more far-reaching considerations are involved. The latter is the case in regard to the extensive culture contacts of the period under discussion; geographical proximity affords no explanation whatever, and the phenomenon of *unrest* must be brought into the foreground.

Now, how is unrest generated, and how did it produce culture contact in the period considered?

To begin with, unrest is present in some degree in any culture. Someone has said that " walking is but a process of falling forward that is continually interrupted "; Thomas and Znaniecki's well-known generalization might be cast in a similar form: " Social stability is but a process of continually reorganizing a continually disorganizing plurality pattern." [4] Even when an ideology, with its concomitant mores and institutions, has slowly brought order out of chaos and become dominant, as did the Christian Epic among many of the European peoples during the eighth, ninth, and tenth centuries, subversive forces are forever at work. If the dominance of the ideology is to be maintained, either such forces must be eliminated or the tension and unrest resulting from their intrusion must be drained off by providing outlets.

These outlets may merely dissipate the tension and thereby temporarily lessen the unrest; such dissipation frequently finds a vent in " the crowd that dances," to use Park's graphic phrase. On the other hand, channels for tension-energy are often found in " the crowd that acts " (also a phrase of Park's coining). In the first type, tension seems to find an outlet in behavior predominantly involving the autonomic or sympathetic nervous system; in the second, the central nervous system appears to be more directly involved. The Dancing Mania of the Middle Ages, the Great Revival of 1800, and the Flagellant epidemic are examples of the first; the First and Second Crusades, the Klondike rush, and the storming of the Bastille afford instances of the second.[5] To use terms that must not be taken too seriously, the one is introverted behavior, the other is extraverted; in either type of activity, tension-energy is translated into physical movement and unrest is lessened.

In order to understand the application of the above statements to the period being discussed, it is necessary to refer to an earlier era. At the end of the Dark Ages, Europe was as nearly static (in the sense of lack of cultural innovation) as it has ever been before or since. Isolation prevailed, as the accounts of voyages and attitudes toward other peoples show; by the ninth and tenth centuries religious sanctions had already attached themselves to and fixated much social behavior. A sort of isolated sacred society arose Phœnix-like from the holocaust of Latinized and Germanic cultures; Western Christendom emerged from the welter of the Migrations with a relatively high degree of basic cultural unity. In other words, the period of social disorganization, release, and individuation that marked the Merovingian and early Carolingian régimes in central Europe was followed by a period of social reorganization and inhibition that even the collapse of the empire of Charlemagne did not seriously interrupt.

Many factors were operative in bringing about this reorganization, but lack of space forbids their discussion; the threat of the Day of Doom is among the most conspicuous. Although but partial, although by no means as thoroughgoing as the eventual consolidation of Christendom in the thirteenth century, the degree of reorganization effected by these factors even in the earlier period was considerable. In fact, so many accustomed outlets were dammed up with such relative suddenness that tension and its associated unrest began *again* to become rife. The hard-won dynamic equilibrium effected by reorganization was soon threatened by an increase in processes of disorganization; the hold of the sacred community upon its newer, less Latinized members weakened considerably in the early part of the eleventh century.

To make matters worse, the eleventh century was visited by a series of terrible famines — 1005, 1016, 1094. Of all the factors that are associated with tension and unrest, hunger seems to be the most important, as Dashiell's experiments on various types of animal " drives " or urges seem to indicate; hungry animals manifest about sixty per cent more restless activity than those activated by any other need.[6] During the first two of the famine periods listed above, aimless wandering became so prevalent that it took on the aspect of genuine collective behavior; tension and unrest carried thousands of hapless souls up hill and down dale, looking for they knew not what, just as they did in the England of More's time. The partially reorganized social order was seriously threatened by this activity, at once symptom and cause of disorganization,[7] and every effort was made to stop wandering,[8] but even the death penalty seems to have been of little avail. " The milling of the human herd," to use Park's phrase, went on with the inevitability of the natural process it was. Its earlier extreme forms soon abated, to be sure, but all through the eleventh century we find traces of its persistent disorganizing and preparatory influence.[9]

Further, all Europe was in a state of turmoil because of political and ecclesiastical grievances. As Prutz has said:

Everywhere in the Occident, turn where one might, discontent and demand for amelioration or at least change, of existing conditions prevailed; everywhere the urge to escape from the unendurable present by means of one bold stroke made itself felt.[10]

Once more, pestilence contributed its share to the prevailing unrest. Hecker has pointed out the relation between the Black Death and the Dancing Mania of the fourteenth century; it is not without significance that in 1094, the year before " *Dieu le vult!* " greeted Urban's announcement of the First Crusade, a plague of unknown variety raged from Flanders to Bohemia. The stricken populace perished in droves, and in the following year the disorganized survivors flung themselves into the swollen flood of the Peasants' Crusade. In other words, the " milling " became a " stampede " that partially passed over into a collective act with an over-determined symbol — the Holy Land.

The First and Second Crusades were of course not solely due to the particular influences named; several other " moments," to speak with the Germans, played their part. Nevertheless, the surprising extent to which the lower classes participated in the movement would be incomprehensible without taking into account the unrest generated by famine, discontent, and pestilence; the Holy Land became in a sense a place where all the ills of this world would be alleviated, an earthly Paradise, a symbol of escape. Further, plenary indulgence was promised to all who participated in the conquest of the heathen in possession of the sacred places of Christendom. The Crusades were thus a means of release for those restless persons, particularly in the ruling strata, who found even the partially reorganized world of the eleventh century too straitly confining. What wonder that everyone in Europe who was *loose,* morally and socially, plunged into the orgy of slaughter and pillage that broke out long before the real enemy was reached?

Mixture of Mores and Growth of Trade. — The First Crusade resulted in the setting up of several Frankish states in Syria that endured for the better part of a century. As is usually the case, peaceful relations with the erstwhile foe were established, and a flourishing trade in the goods they had to offer sprang up along the borders of the Kingdom of Jerusalem and the principalities of Edessa, Antioch, and Tripoli.

The mixture of folkways and mores so often a source of social disorganization soon manifested itself as a result of this culture contact. Ernest Barker has thus described the process:

> The barons alternated between the extravagances of Western chivalry and the attractions of Eastern luxury: they returned from the field to divans with frescoed walls and floors of mosaic, Persian rugs and embroidered silk hangings. Their houses, at any rate those in the towns, had thus the characteristics of Moorish villas; and in them they lived a Moorish life. Their sideboards were covered with the copper and silver work of Eastern smiths and the confectioneries of Damascus. They dressed in flowing robes of silk, and their women wore oriental gauzes covered with sequins. Into these divans where figures of this kind moved to the music of Saracen instruments, there entered an inevitable voluptuousness and corruption of manners.[11]

This softening of a group of hardy conquerors as a result of culture contact soon had its inevitable consequences; the Frankish domains were recaptured by the Saracens, and an era of more or less continuous crusading ensued — indeed, conflict had never entirely ceased at any time from 1095 on.

In spite or because of this conflict, however, trade and peaceful intercourse continued; the expelled Franks who were forced to return to their native lands, and even those who returned from the early successes of the First Crusade, brought back with them needs and cravings that only goods from the Levant could fill. Their example and the real utility of some of their imported culture traits awakened a general demand for Levantine wares in Europe, and the Venetians, Genoese, and other Mediterranean traders reaped a rich harvest. The beliefs and theories of the hated infidel, his non-material culture, eventually made a considerable impress on the West, particularly in chemistry and mathematics, *but the field in which culture contact was soonest effective was the material.* Soon we find the Italian trading peoples becoming marginal; they learned to tolerate the Moslem and then to imitate him; the fighting Crusaders found them but half-hearted allies during the latter part of the twelfth century and thereafter. They did not want to spoil their sources of supply; having worked out a *modus vivendi* with the foes of Christendom, they were not anxious to have it disrupted by fanatical Christians. A little conflict when trading interests were threatened was all well and good, but conflict for the general weal of the sacred society of the West — no!

The Shift from Sacred to Secular. — This sacred society, with the marginal exceptions noted above, had achieved a notable degree of integration by the thirteenth century. The release afforded by the Crusades had drained off some of the restless elements, and the in-group feeling aroused by the struggle with the infidel had welded much of Christendom into a body presenting a united front to the common foe in spite of internal dissension. The power of the church steadily increased, the era of cathedral-building set in, and the Franciscan reforms quieted unrest for a time. Nevertheless, the very processes which made the unity of the thirteenth century possible contained the seeds of disorganization, for as we have seen, the Crusades brought about culture contact with the East, and thus made the point of climax the point of incipient disorganization as well.[12] Slowly the stream of Levantine goods and customs broadened into a torrent, the Commercial Revolution began, and the Italian city-states danced like their own stout carracks on the very crest of the advancing waves of secularism that have since flooded the modern world. An accessible, secular society, made accessible by the Crusades [13] and secular by commerce,[14] began to take form and shape. The Middle Ages passed their zenith; the Age of Faith was about to be transmuted into the Age of Commerce and Discovery. Once again traditional ties were broken; once again men became " individuals cut loose from the laws of common humanity "; once again release supplanted inhibition. " The century of transition " [15] ran its fateful course.

The optimistic eighteenth-century philosophers wrote their fulsome screeds on progress and human perfectibility during the period when man's mental horizon had just been immeasurably extended by the amazing scientific, philosophical, and literary activity of the preceding century, the century of Bacon, Harvey, Kepler, Galileo, Descartes, Huyghens, Boyle, Newton, Locke, Spinoza, and Leibniz. It is therefore highly probable that they had their own era of the Enlightenment in mind when they spoke of the energizing effect of release from traditional bonds; nevertheless, they might well have been speaking of the early " conspirital societies " of Italy most deeply affected by the meeting of East and West, for at no time set down in the historical record have the processes of release, individuation, and secularization been more manifest than in the fourteenth century, the age of Can Grande della Scala, Dante, Boniface VIII, Pierre DuBois, and Marsiglio of Padua.

The Effects of Liberation. — Release from the bonds of the *milieu natale,* as Durkheim puts it, or from the kinship group, or from the isolated sacred society, does indeed sometimes strip men of large sections of their human nature, if by that term we mean the cultural conditioning that has overlaid and transformed the crude undifferentiated urges of the biological organism. Further, the resulting partial individuation (the process can never be complete) does often seem to be correlated with vice and crime of the most revolting sorts; " Progress is a terrible thing " —

> He calls it Reason, uses it but
> More bestial to be than any brute. . . .
> He sees no filth but he must poke his nose in't.

But Goethe also pointed out (with recent effect upon Toynbee, among others) that the human being frequently is in need of an external stimulus, an intrusive factor, if he is to realize his fullest capacities:

> Man's efforts lightly flag, and seek too low a level.
> Soon doth he pine for all-untrammeled sloth.
> Wherefore a mate I give him, nothing loth,
> Who spurs, and shapes, and must create though Devil.

In other words, individuation frequently releases energies that otherwise would never come to their own; as Whitehead says, " the great ages have been the unstable ages." [16] Men break with the code of their time, but they accomplish great things. The same point has been noted by Teggart:

As a result of the breakdown of customary modes of action and of thought, the individual experiences a " release " from the restraints to which he has been subject. . . . we hold ideas simply because nothing has occurred to disturb them; the fact is that . . . unless we encounter flaw or jar or change, nothing in us responds. [James asks] . . . to what . . . do men owe their escape? and to what are improvements due, when they occur? In general terms, he says, the answer is plain: " Excitements, ideas, and efforts are what carry us over the dam." Ideas in particular he regards as notable stimuli for unlocking what would otherwise be unused reservoirs of individual initiative and energy. This effectiveness he ascribes to the fact, first, that ideas contradict other ideas and thus arouse critical activity, and second, that the new ideas which emerge as a result of this conflict unify us on a new plane and bring us to a significant enlargement of individual power.[17]

It is quite probable, in the light of the above, that the surprising achievements of the late medieval (or early modern) period were

due, first, to the breakdown of the isolated sacred society effected
by the meeting of East and West in the Crusades and the ensuing
trade with the Levant, with its resulting individuation; and second, to the conflict of ideas engendered by the flood of new material and non-material culture traits later brought in by the Age of
Discovery, the Commercial Revolution, and the Revival of Learning.[18] (The rise of the bourgeois class of course played a large
part, but in a sense this was merely one aspect of the Commercial
Revolution.)

By and large, the period we have just discussed represents in
striking form the phenomena correlated with unrest, culture contact, release, and mental mobility; no other era in European history affords quite so detailed and vivid a picture of what eventually
happens when a highly organized but relatively isolated culture
is suddenly brought into new relationships with other cultures.[19]
Only a few of the salient features have been sketched; and those,
needless to say, somewhat superficially. The growth of urban centers, the decay of the feudal system, the ever-increasing extent of
the market, the rise of a thoroughgoing money economy, the
breakdown of the doctrine of just price, the appearance of the
wandering scholars, the secularization of learning, the paganism
of the Humanists, the expansion of Europe — all these things
should be considered if a complete analysis were to be given, and
we shall later focus upon some of them. For present purposes,
however, consideration of the culture contacts occasioned by migrations issuing from unrest and culminating in the Crusades and
their associated trade with the Levant is sufficient. Some insight
into the social dynamics of " the Fourteenth, Century of Transition," has perhaps resulted — that, at any rate, was and is the
desideratum.

Mohammedan Expansion. — Two of the most important
things to bear in mind concerning the foregoing analysis are the
fact that it could be duplicated, *mutatis mutandis,* within the
Moslem world, and the further fact that all the processes of social
disorganization manifested in Italy (to take the most obvious
European example) were in full swing at least two centuries
earlier among the devotees of Allah and his prophet. The sudden
surge of the Arabian nomads and the cohorts they swept in their
train carried them across North Africa, into Spain, beyond the
Pyrenees, across Mesopotamia into Persia and North India, and
far down the African coast — all within one hundred years after
the death of Mohammed. By the ninth and tenth centuries sectarian strife had assumed serious proportions, and the rivalries

of worldly princes were at least equally devastating. Expansion brought disorganization of the sacred society; change was steadily in the direction of secularization. The upshot was that a Moslem social thinker came into possession of abundant experience of the ways in which civilizations are transformed, and was able to analyze the dynamics of the history of his own people in so thoroughly general a way that his theoretical results are transferable, in part at least, to the dynamics of other cultures.

Ibn Khaldūn. — The first writer after Polybius, then, to apply the equivalents of modern ideas in historical sociology was not a European. All the rich lore of the Moslem travelers, the ripe culture of the Greeks, the instructive spectacle of socially disorganized Mohammedan and Christian cultures, and his own experience as a diplomatist and statesman were the heritage of that greatest of early modern geographers, historians, and sociologists, the Berber of Tunis, Ibn Khaldūn (1332–1406). His importance far overshadows that of such predecessors as Ibn Idrisi, for he achieved the feat, unique for his time, of regarding history as a natural process; Polybius at last finds a successor. Anticipating Vico and Turgot, he stressed the continuity of historical development and at the same time the importance of " intrusive factors " (due, among other things, to the migrations of the desert dwellers, the Beduin and Berber nomads). In marked contrast to the static or eschatological conceptions of Christian historiography contemporary with him, he advanced the thesis that history is but a composite of processes of social change, and insisted that psychical and situational factors act in such close concert that they may frequently be considered as but two aspects of the same series of happenings.

Ibn Khaldūn has been much praised, but no translation of his great *Prolegomena to History* is available in English. Flint paid a good deal of attention to him in *The History of the Philosophy of History,* and in this secondary way only has he become known to English-reading social scientists. The only complete translation in any Occidental language, in fact, is that of DeSlane, *Les prolégomènes d'Ibn Khaldoun,* which appeared in 1863.[20] The first notice taken of the great Moslem by the scholarly world of the West appears to have been a translation of excerpts from his writings by Silvestre de Sacy in 1806, and the first time that great importance was accredited him seems to have been in an article (in French) by Joseph von Hammer-Purgstall in 1821,[21] which included a translation of chapter or section headings. This was followed in 1835 by the first article in English, by Jakob

Grefve,[22] which also was accompanied by a translated list of chapter titles.

His direct influence on sociologists probably dates from 1899, when Gumplowicz published his *Sociologische Essays*, for in this book was a chapter on Ibn Khaldūn, " An Arabian Sociologist of the Fourteenth Century." [23] Owing to the stress laid upon the conflict theory of social development by Gumplowicz [24] and Ratzenhofer,[25] and by Ward, with his social karyokinesis,[26] the really significant aspects of the Berber's doctrine, so far as migration, culture contact, and mental mobility are concerned, were almost totally obscured. The present-day champion of the conflict theory, Oppenheimer, has only praise for Ibn Khaldūn, but the German writer notes only those parts of the Moslem's work which fit into his agrarian reform program, as may plainly be seen from the 1926 edition of *Der Staat*.[27]

The conflict theory is of great importance, but the significance of Ibn Khaldūn's social thought is by no means limited to this narrower context within sociological theory. In the *Prolegomena* is to be found a wealth of material, brilliantly analyzed, concerning immanent social factors in nomadic and sedentary life, corresponding closely to sacred and secular structures, and concerning the dynamic relationship holding between these two forms within a larger social area. These less known aspects of his work have been selected here on the basis of general relevance to the themes of this chapter (in Chapter Nineteen we deal with the conflict theory phases at some length).

" *Things Born of Civilization.*" — The work with which we are concerned was written as a prolegomenon to history, or is what we might term " critical historiography." In the Moslem world there had grown up the well-established " sciences which have tradition as their object." [28] The method consisted in a complicated system of checking and cataloguing the *isnads,* or bearers of tradition, so as to know just who they were, from what sources their traditions came, and what degree of confidence could be assigned to them. The most important of these disciplines had grown up about the Sunna and the Sunnite traditions. Ibn Khaldūn's genius grew out of his recognition that this method, itself traditionalized, had several inherent tendencies to error, which he classified as seven, but which for our purposes may be reduced to three. In the first place, error may often result from the partiality or partisanship of the authors, and in the second place from over-credulity on the part of historians concerning the quality and adequacy of their sources. It will be seen that even here, in "partiality" or "partisanship," a social factor was recognized, but had Ibn Khaldūn confined himself to these two sources of error, his work would have been but an extension and refinement of existing Moslem historiographic methodology.

But then came the "insight leap," made possible by his rich background experience with both sacred and secular structures which his unusual mind was able to conceptualize in brilliant fashion. The third and by far the most important source of error, said Ibn Khaldūn, is an "ignorance of the nature of things which are born of civilization." [29] To avoid such errors one must know the causes and conditions of social events, and must have a perspective of social change. It is especially this latter point which he emphasized: society is in a continual process of transition, now rapid and overtly manifested, now latent. All historical facts are related to an epoch, to a people, and to a particular kind of social grouping, and have meaning only within this relativity.

This led to his definition of the "true object of history," a definition which sums up the object-matter dealt with throughout the *Prolegomena:*

[History endeavors] . . . to give us an understanding of man's social state, or civilization, and to teach us of the phenomena which are naturally connected with it, viz: savage life; the refinement of the mores (*mœurs*); the nature of family and tribal solidarity; the various types of superiority which one people gains over another, and which lead to the birth of empires and dynasties; distinctions of rank; the occupations to which men give themselves, such as the lucrative professions, occupations related to (the necessities of) life, to the sciences and to the arts; and all the changes which the nature of things may bring about in the character of the society.[30]

But in general it may be said that history *per se,* in its purely exterior form, was thought of by Ibn Khaldūn as a descriptive retracing of events, as a branch of knowledge which passes from people to people. This may be evidenced by some of his other writings, notably the *History of the Berbers.* The *Prolegomena,* however, he thought of as embodying a science *sui generis,* having a special object of study — namely, human society — and utilizing special techniques of its own. It should focus on this object in an attempt to determine the inherent, and to distinguish this from the accidental. Any attempt to label Ibn Khaldūn as a "sociologist" would be anachronistically futile. Rather one should attempt to follow his thought in its various contexts in an effort to arrive at a general appreciation of his work as a whole, an appreciation which, because of great similarity in point of view and object-matter, may make contributions to, though not growing up within, the framework and content of sociology.

It has been noted that his methodology was oriented toward the problems of historical documentary criticism. This led to his larger formulation of the laws of society and social change, which should act as points of critical reference in determining the validity of documentary or traditional evidence. The logico-observational character of his work is striking throughout. Though living in a society having strong secular tendencies, his was not a period of a purely "sensate" or empiricist mentality. Both experimental and supernatural elements were conceived as realities, and could be harmonized by reason, much as with Plato, Aristotle, Thomas Aquinas, and many others. This may be a strength or a weakness, as one wishes to view the matter. But this has no very immediate bearing on the validity of his work as a system for the analysis of "things born of civilization." The supernaturalistic elements refer almost entirely to ultimate realities and ultimate causes. Only on rare occasions did he bring them in as "explanations" of his more immediate problems. Though it may do some violence to his deeper thinking, most of his references to Allah may be thought of purely as ritual "asides."

The range of his empirical data was based largely on his very wide personal experience, plus a thorough knowledge of the Arabian writings and documentary sources of the time. It is given in illustrative form, but always with reference to careful analysis rather than mere description. To some he may seem to be seriously handicapped in range of materials. But, much as with Durkheim, Weber (to a large extent), and others, Ibn Khaldūn's reputation rests upon his peculiar treatment of this material, rather than upon exhaustiveness. The data with which he grappled may be conceived of as a series of crucial experiments testing the salient points of his theories. His was a case of the human mind trying to *comprehend* rather than catalogue the specifically social factors in man's living and doing.

Basic to the entire *Prolegomena,* and often referred to throughout, are the distinctions which may be made between man and all other living beings.[31] Man has science and the arts; he alone has need of regulatory authority;[32] he has industry and work, "economic" ways of procuring the necessities of life; he has "sociability," both as a psychological tendency or sentiment and as a result of the exigencies of his needs and wants;[33] and man lives in social estate, an *état social* having two fundamental dialectical forms, nomadic life and sedentary life. There is system or " meaningful configuration " throughout the universe, and this applies to things pertaining to society. Presumed randomness, " chance," he reduced to " hidden causes," which led him always to search beneath the surface of the apparent.

Such a position naturally leads to a historical determinism. Machiavelli, with all his determinism and its related pessimism, pleaded for national unity in Italy. Ibn Khaldūn was never the pleader, the spokesman of reform; he accepted the decadent dynasticism of his time as the inevitable result of manifold social processes. But his determinism is wisely relativistic. He was concerned with the typical forms of historical sequence. His law of similarity, that " the past and future resemble each other as two drops of water," [34] refers to the general form, contours, and limits of social phenomena. Within these limits the polar law of dissimilarity operates; there is a *suite de vicissitudes,* trendless flux, and variation from society to society.

Human Geography. — Ibn Khaldūn devoted an early section of the *Prolegomena* to those factors and forces which are not " born of civilization," but which exert at least some influence on the forms and sequences which constitute any society.[35] This section is quite obviously limited by the geographical knowledge available to him, but his point of view was, again, sane and well balanced. The influence of these factors he considered to be indirect. Climate and geography fit into his general schema of analysis as a background of conditional limits. Demographic factors, gross bodily traits, the most general psychical differences, and finally the type of civilization that is possible depend upon climate in the sense of whether or not they will be in close conformity with a mean type, or norm of civilization, or whether, at least in some respects, they will have radically deviating tendencies. Climate also acts as a principle of absolute limits; beyond certain extremes there can be no civilization at all. Between these two poles lies the point of optimum favorability for civilization. Within any one climate there is a wide range for the variation of social factors. Within the temperate climates are found geographical differences more or less favorable to desert nomadic, pastoral nomadic, agricultural, or sedentary life. These factors have some bearing on the general social forms, and also may affect social action through the food factor, the kind of diet helping to produce physical and moral sturdiness or flabbiness. This section may be taken as a short overture to his central theme, the deep-rooted, abiding contrasts between nomadic and sedentary life.

Esprit de Corps *and Nomadic Life.* — Nomadic life and sedentary life, conceived of as social processes, constitute two major polar types, and are basic to Ibn Khaldūn's whole frame of reference. But within the general " rural " population he distinguished three types of social life, a distinction which must be borne in mind if the well-rounded character of his work is to be properly appreciated.[36] First, there is the more purely agricultural type which lives in villages and hamlets. It is also to be found in territories lying about cities, and is an important demographic factor in replenishing a naturally diminishing city population.[37] Like all of these rural peoples, the agriculturalists lead a very plain and simple life, restricting themselves practically to the bare necessities of existence. Then there are those who occupy themselves with the raising of sheep and cattle. They have greater territorial mobility than do the agriculturalists, but do not penetrate into the desert to any great extent; they might be called pastoral nomads. Finally there are the breeders of camels, who have the greatest mobility of all, and who are found in the desert much more frequently than are the pastoral nomads. It is especially with this group of desert nomads that Ibn Khaldūn dealt in his analysis of nomadic life, and he used it as a type case of *esprit de corps* (*'Asabijja*). Within this group he felt that the Arabs were the most typical because they were occupied exclusively with the raising of camels.

One of the most important questions in an attempt to break down the vague substantive " society " into its fundamental factors concerns the nature of the social bond, the *lien social.* In what way is a measure of stability in society achieved? One of the best ways of solving such a problem is to attempt to discover where evidence of social integration may most clearly be found, where other social factors seem to be at a minimum, and where the bonds of social solidarity are typified. Ibn Khaldūn adopted just this method. As the best conceptualization of the social bond, from a working hypothesis point of view, he used the term *'Asabijja,* which has been translated *esprit de corps,* and which, as we shall see, corresponds quite closely to the concept of sacredness as a factor in social organization or in social action. *Esprit de corps* he found in purest, most typical form in nomadic life.

In the Arabian tribes of desert nomads the two factors which he regarded as most important in the rise of society, viz., the need for subsistence and the need for defense, are clearly seen. Simplicity of life, roughness of customs and habits, lack of all superfluous " veneer," bravery, and high tribal solidarity for purposes of defense and mobility — all this is in harmony with the requisites of a desert life and the raising of camels. Here one might think that rather than Ibn Khaldūn's *Prolegomena* it is Demolins's *Comment la route crée le type social* that is being considered. But Ibn Khaldūn placed much more emphasis on the social organization and structure to be found in such circumstances, on the factor of social cohesion itself, and on the functional relation of this factor to other social factors; and he placed much less emphasis on the " causal " efficacy of the geographical factors themselves. Herein he resembles Heeren.

A number of social conditions are critical in the development and maintenance of *esprit de corps*. The fact that these tribes are independent of outside controls, and particularly of outside protection, that there is concentrated on them alone the responsibility for their existence, is extremely important. They must be constantly on the alert, ready to act quickly, and to act in a concerted, unified manner. He claimed that the control of a higher authority weakened the energy of peoples; these nomads are free from such control. It is here that we should find, to paraphrase Durkheim, " the elementary forms of the solidary life." Add to this the necessary stress on sacredness developed in such a situation and we might say, " and of the stable life."

As a typical concomitant of *esprit de corps* is to be found the " bond of blood " or parentage. This is neither a mysterious *deus ex machina* brought in to give a sudden " explanation " of his most critical problem, nor is it considered to be an invariable or immutable factor. It is defined essentially as an ensemble of attitudes, sentiments, and former modes of habitual action with reference to other members of the tribe. With these desert nomads the dominance, forcefulness, and maintenance of the blood ties is furthered by " purity of blood." They are isolated from contacts with peoples having different customs and character (which is what Ibn Khaldūn really meant by " race "). He brought out even more clearly what is meant, and also what is not meant, by the " bond of blood " in a section about patronymics. A man may be taken into a tribe, and if he adopts the tribal name, symbol of " heeding " or " having a care for " the sacred customs, he can be accepted on equal footing. Everything possible is done to sever all ties with and to annul all influences of the tribe of his birth. In short, the only heuristic value added by the term " bond of blood " in Ibn Khaldūn's work is to point to the particular kinship form which these desert nomadic tribes take and within which *esprit de corps* manifests itself.

Although cohesion and solidarity may be found in almost ideal-typical form in the nomadic tribe, it is by no means a homogeneous group of individuals functioning as an undifferentiated unity. Within the tribe, smaller groups such as the immediate family and the extended kinship group are recognized. Starting from this fact, his interest in the problem of power manifests itself. The right of commanding the tribe is not held in each of its branches but belongs to a single family. But he made the very significant claim that the fact of living in society and *esprit de corps* are the elements of which the body politic is composed. Far from being a political explanation of society, his work might much better be considered a distinctly social or even sociological explanation of political power and various political forms.[38] Actually, however, his theory is one-sided in neither respect; as is typical of his thought, he emphasized the mutual interdependence of *esprit de corps* and the problem of power relationships.

Islam Critically Examined. — As has been noted, Ibn Khaldūn's method, on the empirical side, is illustrative, but illustrative in such a way as to constitute test cases — almost " critical experiments " (which we discuss in Chapter Twenty as " culture case study "). Significantly enough, he applied this type of analysis to his own religion. It was customary, even prerequisite, that the *imam* (religious leader of Islam) should be of the tribe of Koreish. He considered it not enough to state, as was usually done, that one of the " motives " of such a rule was the attraction of divine favor because the prophet himself was of the tribe of Koreish. There must be some more definitely social reason, a common system of ends rather than one highly rationalized motive. The Koreish tribe, he claimed, was the noblest, the oldest, the strongest — and had the greatest *esprit de corps;* by reason of this fact, it alone could integrate the several *esprits de corps* of the Hedjaz tribes about a common end. But he also recognized that the tribe of Koreish had gone through exactly the same stages (see below) as any dominant tribe must. It had enjoyed its era of luxury and ease, and its *esprit de corps* had consequently been weakened. Any attempt to preserve membership in the tribe of Koreish as a prerequisite for religious leadership was therefore nothing but an almost meaningless vestige of an earlier social situation. That the prerequisite *was* preserved, he saw very clearly, was another sign of the decadent state of Islam as a whole.

Some serious objections, partly growing out of present-day historical knowledge, and partly out of more recent developments in sociological theory, could be raised concerning his interpretation of the rise of Islam. The Koreish tribe, at the time of Mohammed, did dominate Mecca, but it was by no means typical of desert nomadic tribes. Mecca was a trade center, and the Koreish tribe held control as a sort of commercial syndicate, operating in oligarchical fashion. Such a society would tend to be more secular than sacred (or *esprit de corps*) in nature.

On the theoretical side, these conditions are more in harmony with the fact of the appearance of Islam. In spite of the appeal of the charismatic leader, a prophetic movement rarely arises in a familistic structure, or isolated sacred society, unless that society has in some way become accessible and thereby has begun to disintegrate or to fail in its power to absorb all the elements within its normal range of influence. Mohammed, the bearer of the charisma (he was an epileptic), in his reaction against the materialism of the Koreishites met with strong opposition in Mecca. He had to flee with a small group of followers (further proof of lack of Koreish integration) to Medina, where, after an actual battle, an organization strong enough to influence his own tribesmen was finally achieved.

Some of Ibn Khaldūn's historical data were inadequate, and, from the point of view of contemporary sociological theory, did not deal adequately with the question of prophetism. There are other geneses of *esprit de corps* (which he would admit, taking desert nomadic life as an ideal type), such as the one growing up about Mohammed as its charismatic leader. But once this movement was started the name and prestige of the tribe of Koreish were coveted. The analytical factors which Ibn Khaldūn used were by no means lacking: leadership, *esprit de corps,* and the inevitable cycle of affluence and decay.

Urbanization and Sedentary Secularism. — Ibn Khaldūn never reached a high degree of consciously refined abstraction. But in attempting to explain social phenomena he was led to classify them into types, built on the basis of culture case study, which could be used as elements or factors in societal situations, rather than as mere descriptions of concrete social realities. We have already seen this in his use of *esprit de corps.* As a polar type set in contrast with nomadic life, with its strong *esprit de corps,* he placed the sedentary life of cities, characterized by a very marked weakening of the *esprit de corps.* These two types constitute the most critical elements in his frame of reference. Between these two poles the cyclical processes of his social dynamics run their course.

Sedentary life is essentially a way of living, a mode of social life, and is used as a social *factor,* just as is the *esprit de corps* concept. It may also be thought of as a process, very similar to what we term the process of secularization. Sedentary life is found in its most typical form in cities, particularly in the capital of an empire.

Lying back of social life is a hierarchy of needs or wants which range from the absolutely essential to sheer luxury. Within the hierarchy there is a fairly clear-cut dichotomy between want-satisfaction among the desert nomads and among the city dwellers. The large city population cannot all be primarily concerned with the provision of physical necessities. Sedentary life is characterized by a luxury of styles and ostentations. On the dynamic side, once this process starts it continues to develop in importance; it becomes an irreversible trend toward more and more luxury, ease, and " refinement " of tastes. " One form of luxury calls forth another ";[39] sedentary life eventually engenders a great wave of sensate culture (to use Sorokin's terminology).

Sedentary life of course has its more specifically " moral " or institutional side. *Esprit de corps* and social control in general are noticeably weakened. Among many other things, Ibn Khaldūn mentioned dishonest, vulgar, and obscene speech as being characteristic of this tendency. There is a gradually augmenting abandonment of many regulatory norms of behavior. Tranquillity and repose, brought about under the protection of a specialized military organization, break down the morale and bravery of a city population; a " let the government do it " and " don't care " attitude takes deep root. Processes of association, and even the factor of *esprit de corps,* are not, however, totally lacking in cities.[40] Institutionally, a city will be conquered or destroyed before complete " normlessness " (Durkheim's *anomie*) takes place. Ibn Khaldūn saw that *esprit de corps* in city life takes the form of a sort of secular " associationalism," strikingly exemplified in the growth of political factions and cliques that may give rise to a conspiratal society like that of Machiavelli. Blood ties and kinship bonds naturally tend to be minimized.

We have emphasized these factors because they constitute the most critical reference points in Ibn Khaldūn's theory, viewed as a *system* of social analysis. There are many more special problems which he treated quite brilliantly. The germs of an economic theory are to be found in the *Prolegomena.*[41] The problem of the formation of cities, as such, is treated at great length.[42] The analysis of religion as a social factor, the beginnings of a sociology of religion, is brought in on several occasions. Rural-urban migration and other demographic problems are often considered.

An especially important phase of his work, constituting a large part of the *Prolegomena,* is one in which the main thread of social dynamics or cyclical social processes becomes the growth and decay cycles of dynastic imperial government. (One should not forget, however, that the secularizing sedentary life, as a process containing within itself the seeds of its own destruction, is basic to the socio-political series of changes with which he deals; individuation, as a social factor, is more important in his analysis than the problem of political relations as such.)

Political Life-Cycles. — In the genesis and evolution of political controls, *esprit de corps* is all-important. Within the desert nomadic tribes, as has been pointed out, the germs of sovereignty are to be found in the chief as traditional leader. At this level it rests on a sacred basis, the source of authority being moral. A directional trend is implicit in such a situation which *may* lead to true sovereignty.[43] The chief's power may become augmented, there may be a wider use of force and constraint, or even the establishment of rational domination. In coming in contact with other tribes and other *esprits de corps,* either a balance of power will be established or weaker tribes will be absorbed by the more powerful. In this latter case the newly developed " super-tribe " will extend its conquest and domination until eventually it will be in a position to attack the reigning dynasty. Then it will either conquer the empire or be absorbed within it, depending largely on the condition of the latter, i.e., on the phase in the cycle of decadence. This is the general schema of the evolution of political power, and *esprit de corps* is its most critical element. It is arrived at from data concerning dynastic life-cycles in Moslem history, but it may also be viewed as a valuable sociological monograph concerning the rôle of social integration, or *esprit de corps,* in the development and maintenance of the state (as we shall later see when discussing conflict theories of political origins).

Esprit de corps is closely related to and tends to be concomitant with blood ties. This Ibn Khaldūn related to the dynastic form of empires. A family group within the larger tribal organization may take on a special importance, and in the foundation of an empire a particular family, the family of a chief, becomes a focus of social control. Such families have *per se* the same cyclical tendency of development and decay as do empires. The family must have a strong supporting party back of it; this is oftentimes " collegial " in character. Once the empire is established, sheer traditionalism, habit, and moral obligation — that is, attenuated sacred attitudes — may come to take the place of the intensely sacred force of *esprit de corps,* and even of the actual support of the " collegial " party which was influential in establishing the empire. Often freedmen and clients of the family come to take the place of such a party during the established phase; a patrimonial grouping upholds the state. At the same time, sedentary life, secularization, individuation run their course toward inevitable decay.

At one point in his analysis of social dynamics Ibn Khaldūn developed a theory of the circulation of the élite which is almost identical with Pareto's famous treatment of the same subject.[44] In the sedentary life there is a premium on ruse rather than on force. Those skilled in ruse, the " foxes " in Paretian terms, have their day. The " lions," strong in *esprit de corps* (persistence of aggregates), are pushed down in the social scale; but they are not afraid to use force and may eventually cause a complete realignment of social classes and controlling elements.

It should be noted, however, that Ibn Khaldūn fully realized the limits of applicability of this cyclical process. It is not rigid; *la suite de vicissitudes,* trendless flux, played too important a part for that. There may be vicinally isolated areas where nomadic life is so deeply entrenched (notably the Berber tribes in the Maghreb) that the process does not get a chance to start. Even in the life-cycle of empires as such there is room for variation; in some areas there is a relative continuity of sedentary life from one empire to another. Ibn Khaldūn also recognized ethnic continuities larger than the tribal. His work as a whole has the merit of containing many ramifications and operating with complexly interconnected factors, but always in a perspective of relatedness and never of sheer random variation.

The Significance of Ibn Khaldūn. — Starting from an attempt to make of society a special object of study, Ibn Khaldūn was led to analyze it, to break it down into scientifically utilizable categories, and to develop generalizations from his materials that have a permanent interest and permanent value for that movement of thought known as sociology, in spite of the fact that it was originally designed as a framework for critical historiography and in a time and place where sociology as such was wholly foreign. We have called attention to but a few of the parallels and anticipations to be found in the *Prolegomena;* other writers have noted a great many more.[45] For example, mention is often made of the fact that Ibn Khaldūn followed Aristotle in his theory that man is by nature social, as well as the fact that there is some trace of Plato in the great Berber's corollary: namely, that man is social because his wants are so varied and extensive that they can be supplied only by coöperative effort. There are also strong traces of other Classical social thinkers in the doctrine that the conflict of desires produces quarrels and leads to the necessity of setting up government in order to assure order and stability. Further, the material presented in the foregoing sections shows that he insisted upon the necessity of homogeneity for the existence of a stable state with almost the emphasis of a Giddings — and small wonder, when one considers the similarity between *'Asabijja* (translated as *esprit de corps*) and " consciousness of kind." Again, Ibn Khaldūn's analysis of the influence of physical environment upon social organization was more thorough than that of any other study of the subject until the time of Bodin, if not until that of Montesquieu.[46] All in all, Ibn Khaldūn rather than Vico has the best claim to the honor of having founded the philosophy of history in its present form, and his grasp of the factors involved in the historical process was firmer and more modern than that of the Italian of three centuries later.

More important than any of these specific theories, however, were the point of view and method characteristic of this Moslem thinker. *He possessed an almost completely secular attitude toward the state,* and in this respect can be compared only to the similarly secularized and diplomatically experienced Machiavelli of almost a century later. Rosenthal puts it thus:

When the two men are placed side by side and their thinking with regard to the state centered upon, one finds that they had in common a separation of the state from religious influence, from the supremacy of the church, and an untheological, fully secular method of observing political affairs. Both thought in a thoroughly realistic way, did not permit themselves to be guided by ethical and metaphysical considerations, and unemotionally observed the state as it really is.

The significance of this for the history of the human mind is great. As early as the fourteenth century the culture of Islam produced a representative of the best in historical realism in this social scientist who anticipated important modern theories concerning the nature of the state and the forces that influence it.[47]

In closing our discussion of Ibn Khaldūn, we cannot do better than quote Schmidt's estimate of this thinker who was centuries in advance of his time and yet was a product of that time:

After all, Ibn Khaldūn as a man is most clearly and significantly revealed in the great work he left behind. Here he lives more truly than in the turbulent activities of his diplomatic career. His nature is reflected in his observations on human society, his rigorous demand that it be studied comprehensively and with scientific accuracy, and his faithfulness, so far as time and circumstances permitted, in meeting this requirement. He is a solitary figure, towering above his age, yet to be explained in the way he himself regarded as proper in the interpretation of every historic phenomenon. The law of growth and decay of social groups which he himself discerned cast him into oblivion; the same law has led to his discovery and the recognition of his genius. It has been asked whether a man can be a leader if he has no following, forms no school, and exercises no strong influence in his own time or on the generations immediately succeeding him. He who finds a new path is a pathfinder, even if the trail has to be found again by others; and he who walks far in advance of his contemporaries is a leader, even though centuries may pass before he is recognized as such and intelligently followed. Not only those who, consciously or unconsciously, bring about changes in the world that are at once noticeable, but also those who, sooner or later, affect its thinking, are constructive forces in human society.[48]

Turmoil in Christendom; Its Effects in France. — The social disorganization of the Moslem world to which Ibn Khaldūn's writings bear such eloquent testimony was paralleled by the break-up in the unity of Christendom that set in shortly after the early Crusades, and that got fully under way at the beginning of the fourteenth century. In the Europe of that day every man's hand seemed against every man's, and of unity there was none:

War seems the universal occupation — war *in excelsis* of course between those two mighty opposites of medievalism, those majestic figures now almost lost to view in the gathering mists of time — the Pope and the Emperor — but war also between Emperor and vassal, between Emperor and commune, between town and town — war between Guelph and Ghibelline, between black Guelph and white Guelph, between street and street, almost between house and house — everywhere turbulence, confusion, anarchy![49]

This condition of social disintegration was most evident in Italy, for there the aftermath of the Crusades wreaked most havoc, and there the trade with the Levant continued to lap away the foundations of order, but even when we turn away from Italy, " garden of the Holy Roman Empire," and gaze at its neighbor, France, we still see the secularizing effect of the meeting of East and West, although we see it in a widely different form.

Culture contact produced disorganizing but nevertheless different results in France because ever since the twelfth century France had been a rising power at the very time when the empire, shattered by the fatal struggle with the papacy, was a falling power. The greatness of France was foreshadowed in the early Crusades, for it played such a leading part in them that they were called *Gesta Dei per Francos* and all Christians were given the generic name of Franks by the Moslems of the East. It will be recalled that it was along the borders of the Frankish states in the Holy Land that trade with the erstwhile foe became flourishing, and that when these little states were overthrown and their alien inhabitants forced to flee to their native land, Saracen culture traits in great number were brought into France. Perhaps one may venture the guess that the great renascence of the twelfth and thirteenth centuries that gave France the leadership in monasticism, scholasticism, literature, architecture, and civilization generally was not wholly unrelated to culture contact with the East. Finally, it was in France that the great movement toward the national state had its beginning; the French monarchy successfully combated the disruptive forces of a feudalism that in its death-throes was still powerful enough to rend Italy asunder. It is with this rise of secular absolutism that we shall now concern ourselves.

Pierre DuBois, Exponent of Nationalistic Secular Absolutism. — Although in theory there was a duality of powers as between the church and the state in the Middle Ages, we have already seen that men like John of Salisbury and Thomas Aquinas definitely inclined to the view of the superiority of the clerical or spiritual power. Moreover, the great popes of the age, like Innocent III, were able to make good such pretensions. The papal claims did not abate with the close of the thirteenth century, but actually increased with the pronouncements of Boniface VIII at the opening of the fourteenth — " I am Caesar, I am Emperor." [50] Yet Boniface could not realize his claims in practice, and a doctrinal attack was launched against the church by Pierre DuBois and Marsiglio of Padua which paralleled the political defiance of the church by Edward I and Philip the Fair and the physical assault upon Boniface by Nogaret. Indeed, Pierre DuBois so far departed from the medieval system as to attack not only the clerical position but also the conception of the medieval empire and the feudal system. He was by implication as much a critic of Dante as of John of Salisbury. He was one of the first exponents of secular absolutism and of the omnipotence of the state, and he not only foreshadowed the national monarchy of France but offered a plan for its realization. [51]

Pierre DuBois was a French lawyer at the court of Philip the Fair. He was born in Normandy about 1255 and died about 1321.

Although he wrote a large number of pamphlets, only two of his works are relevant here: his *De abbreviatone*, written about 1300, and his more famous *De recuperatione terre sancte*, composed between 1305 and 1307. The latter treatise on "The Recovery of the Holy Land," although offered as a plan for the defeat of the infidel in the East, was really most important as a vehicle for his views of the relations between church and state and for his conception of the ideal French national monarchy and the reforms necessary to achieve it. Nevertheless, it once more bears witness to the effect of the meeting of East and West; as Figgis puts it, "The whole spirit of the book is secular and modern." [52]

A leading reason for the failure of the Christians to capture and retain the Holy Land was their general social and political disorganization, attributed by the secular absolutists to interference by the pope in temporal matters. In the following paragraph DuBois set forth his belief in the disastrous nature of papal intrusion:

Because of his sanctity the Pope should aspire only to the glory of pardoning, praying, giving judgment in the name of the Church, preserving peace among Catholic princes, so as to bring souls safe to God; but he shows himself to be the author, promoter, and exerciser of many wars and homicides, and sets an evil example. It depends on him to conserve his ordinary resources without being turned from the care of souls; it is in his hands to rid himself of worldly occasions and to avoid the cause of so many evils. If he will not accept so great an advantage, will he not incur the reproaches of all men for his cupidity, pride and bold presumption? [53]

DuBois proposed to remedy the situation by handing over the temporal authority of the pope to the king of France. In return for this concession, the king was to support the pope through a generous annual pension. Unity in Christendom was to be still further advanced by bringing all of it under the domination of the French king through force, persuasion, and alliances. One of the most effective ways in which the unity of Europe under France might be forwarded would be to make France itself as efficient and attractive as possible. This would both attract outsiders to union and also prepare France for its greater responsibilities. It is in his outline of the reforms most desirable in France that DuBois presents the proposals which make him the most original social theorist of the declining medieval period.

In preparing the way for his suggested reforms he foreshadows

Montaigne and Montesquieu by his critical, secular attitude toward the past. He condemns that slavish adherence to the past which binds us to its faults and leads us to continue outworn customs and institutions. Institutions are not intended to last forever or to be the objects of unthinking worship. They are valuable only in so far as they are adapted to a given period and set of conditions.

DuBois's scheme of reform rested, as we have seen, upon the dual conception of the supremacy of France in Europe and the absolute domination of the king in France. As a student of Roman law he was a believer in secular absolutism. Hence the first essential reform in France was for the king to crush feudalism and secure unity and order. In this connection he makes many suggestions concerning military methods and reforms which will make the royal armies more effective. Even more important was the prophetic nature of such a program in relation to the approaching appearance of the national state system in its first form of dynastic absolutism. When peace and unity had been established on the ruins of feudalism, the king should undertake a number of essential reforms in order to put France in the best possible internal condition and to make it well fitted to gather Europe under its domain. In outlining such a program of national reconstruction he reminds one of Fichte's famous " Addresses to the German Nation " given at the beginning of the nineteenth century.

DuBois's Program for Social Reconstruction. — Next to the abolition of feudalism, the most important innovation suggested was the reconstruction of the church. We have already noted his proposal that the pope should surrender all temporal power to the French king and accept a pension in its place. The archbishops and bishops likewise were to be required to hand over their goods to lay authorities and to be content with pensions. The monks also were to turn over their property in trust to laymen and live on an annual stipend paid from the income. The nunneries were to be curtailed in size and in part converted into schools for girls. Celibacy was no longer to be required of the clergy, though those who felt certain of their capacity to practice it might be encouraged to do so. In this way the power of the French king would be enormously strengthened by removing the rivalry of the church and by giving him greatly extended resources.[54]

DuBois's suggestions as to educational reform were novel and interesting. He laid great stress upon the value of education for both war and peace. He proposed to wipe out most of the existing system of education. In its place he would substitute a rational hierarchy of educational institutions: elementary schools would provide instruction in the Bible, grammar, history, and science; more advanced institutions would carry the student into a study of languages, logic, and the rudiments of theology; and professional schools would be provided for those desiring to prepare themselves in law, medicine, and theology. In the whole educational system greater efficiency was to be secured through the preparation of concise and abridged textbooks which would eliminate confusion and the useless freight of argumentation and authority embodied in the typical medieval manuals.

Special stress was laid upon adequate instruction in languages, particularly in the Oriental languages. Even if the Moslems were conquered it would still be necessary to convert them, and such conversion would be fatally handicapped unless the Christians could speak the Oriental languages and thus be able to argue with and convince their Mohammedan subjects. In this connection DuBois offered his original scheme for the education of women. Many have too hastily taken this as evidence that DuBois was a fourteenth-century feminist, but such was not the case. Women were not to be educated because it was an inherent right of their sex; rather they were to be educated because they could be useful in overcoming the infidel.[55] They were to be given special instruction in Oriental languages and then shipped off to the East to marry Mohammedan husbands. Their linguistic facility would then allow them to convert their husbands to Christianity, proselyte effectively, and honeycomb the East with traitors to the Mohammedan cause, which would make the victory of the Christians much more certain and rapid. Further, the presence of these women in the East after the conquest would increase the rapidity with which the Moslems could be converted to the true faith.

DuBois also suggested many reforms in legal procedure. He would wipe out the abuses connected with ecclesiastical courts and special privileges of the clergy. Moreover, he held that the civil law badly required a thorough overhauling and recodification in a single clear and logical system. Further, courtroom procedure was to be simplified, made more economical, and designed to produce justice. He would no longer have witnesses examined in court, but would have them submit their testimony in the form of sworn depositions. Nor would he permit rhetorical speeches by counsel in court; each side was to be compelled to submit its case to the court in the form of a written brief accompanied by all essential depositions. In other words, the legal " tricks of the trade " were to be eliminated and justice made sure, swift, and economical.

International Conciliation. — Finally, DuBois made an attractive proposal for securing international peace prior to the time when the union of Europe might be secured under the dominion of France. Such unity was essential if the Crusade was to succeed, and he therefore proposed a general council of Christendom, to be called by the pope. Here all disputes among the Christian nations were to be settled and the energy of the faithful thus conserved for the assault upon the infidel. His interesting provisions for boycott and arbitration, to be applied primarily to recalcitrant Italian cities, are set forth in the following passages:

If any shall presume, contrary to this good ordinance, to make war against their Catholic brothers they shall forthwith incur the loss of their goods, and so also shall all those who aid them by fighting, victuals, arms, or other necessities of life or of warfare, of any description; and after the end of the war the survivors, of whatever age, condition, and sex, shall be forever removed from their possessions, and they and their heirs shall be sent to populate the Holy Land. . . . Thus therefore those who begin a war, and those who wilfully lend them help and counsel, communicate with them, or supply them with any manner of victuals, water, fire, or other necessities of life, shall be punished by the lord Pope, and they shall not be excommunicated nor anathematized, in order to avoid the danger to their souls and an increase in the numbers of the damned; for it is far better to punish them temporarily than eternally. . . .

But since these cities [the Italian republics] and many princes, recognizing no superiors in their lands, who may do them justice according to the laws and customs of the localities, will strive to enter into disputes, before whom are they to proceed and to take litigation? It may be replied that the [general] council may ordain the election of three religious or lay arbitrators, prudent, experienced, and faithful men, who shall be sworn to choose three prelates as judges, and three other persons from each side, men of substance, and such as are obviously incapable of being corrupted by love, hate, fear, greed, or anything else. These shall come together in a suitable place, and having been strictly sworn, and presented before their coming with the articles of the petition and the defence, fully set forth, shall receive witnesses and instruments, and, first rejecting all that is superfluous and beside the point, shall diligently examine them. They shall listen to the examination of each witness by at least two men, sworn and faithful and true; the depositions shall be written down and very diligently examined, and most carefully kept by the judges, to prevent fraud and falsehood. . . . In giving judgment, if it be expedient, let them have assessors who are to their knowledge faithful and skilled in divine and canon and civil law. If either party be discontented with their sentence the same judges shall send the process and judgment to the apostolic seat, for it to be amended

or altered by the Supreme Pontiff for the time being, as shall seem good
to him, or if not, to be confirmed for a perpetual memorial and registered
in the chronicles of the Holy Roman Church.[56]

Summary of DuBois's Proposals. — We find in the writings of
Pierre DuBois an attack upon some of the most characteristic of
medieval institutions: the temporal power of the pope, the secular
holdings and authority of the Church and its magnates, the "two
powers" system, and the feudal pattern of politics and society.
He likewise foreshadowed or advocated many later developments
in France, Europe, and the world: the subordination of the papacy, the Gallican Church, the secularization of church property,
the destruction of feudalism, the establishment of the national
monarchy, secular absolutism, the Code Napoléon, and the League
of Nations. We may well conclude with Power that "however
wild may be some of his practical proposals, however much he
owes to his contemporaries, and however he may be still clogged
by the conceptions of the Middle Ages, Pierre DuBois was an
original thinker and a herald of the modern world."

Dante's Plea for the Vanishing "Two Powers" System. —
But even though "a herald of the modern world" appeared at the
very beginning of the century of transition, we must not assume
that from 1300 on there were no voices pleading for the restoration of the past. Many men looked backward for their vision of
the perfect society, and among them was the illustrious Italian
poet, philosopher, scholar, and statesman, Dante Alighieri
(1265–1321).

Certainly he had every reason to wish for a sweeping change in
the conditions under which he lived. The factional struggles arising from the release and individuation rampant in the Italian city-
states ran their course in Florence, Dante's native spot, and
shortly after the dawn of the fourteenth century he fell foul of
both the party of the pope and that of the French king. He was
banished, and for nineteen weary years wandered from city to
city, from country to country. In his bitterness he characterized
himself in these stinging words: *Florentinus natione non moribus*
("Florentine by birth but not by character").

The key to Dante's character, and to his social theory as well,
is to be found in the fact that "world peace was the target at
which all his shafts were sped." It is interesting to note that the
two other members of the trio who lent luster to the first quarter
of the fourteenth century, Pierre DuBois and Marsiglio of Padua,
also longed for an end of the strife that surrounded them. How-

ever much they may have differed in other respects, they were all greatly concerned with the problem of preserving peace in Christian Europe. With Dante, indeed, it was the dominating practical passion of his life, for it was not only the root of his political activity, the basis of his *De monarchia* and omnipresent in other prose works, but was also a leading thread in the *Commedia*. Indeed, not a few scholars look upon the Divine Comedy as fundamentally a Ghibelline political pamphlet designed to advance the prospects of Can Grande della Scala in the unification of Italy. Although this may be true, it would be unfair to Dante if we were ever to lose sight of the fact that his aim was always peace, never mere partisan advantage. It is because in his day he saw no other approach to the desired consummation that he so ardently advocated world-empire and a world-emperor. " To him the empire meant peace, that peace on earth which is the image of the heavenly peace that passes all understanding." And, as Smith goes on to say :

> But he is not content simply to assume that peace is a desirable possession for all humanity. He will show why it is. He will prove it by his strong logic. He will found it on the testimony of Holy Writ and the teachings of only less holy philosophy. Syllogism by syllogism he will establish it and make both it and the means to attain it clear and convincing for all but those whose hearts are blinded by prejudice and greed.[57]

Dante followed Aristotle in holding that man is by nature a social animal, requiring government for the regulation of group life.[58] Of all types of government, imperial sway is preferable : " There must, therefore, be one to guide and govern, and the proper title for this office is monarch or Emperor. And so it is plain that monarchy or the Empire is necessary for the welfare of the world." [59] In order to ensure unity and world-peace this monarchy must be a world-monarchy : " This [unity] cannot be unless there is one prince over all, whose will shall be the mistress and regulating influence of all the others." [60]

This peace and world-monarchy had hitherto been realized but once — namely, in the Roman Empire — and Dante adds to the logical argument for a world-monarchy certain historical considerations by bringing evidence to support his argument that God favored the Roman Empire. He had no critical historical spirit at all, and accepted the myths in the *Æneid* and Livy as verified or verifiable historical facts. For example, Rome was founded by pious and godly men. Again, Rome succeeded so remarkably in reducing the Mediterranean world to subjection that the most reasonable hypothesis is that God sponsored this expansion and the resulting world-peace. Once more, the Holy Roman Empire was the direct successor of the Roman Empire, and hence might claim to have carried over the divine favor accorded to the latter.

The final problem is whether the secular power comes directly from God or is conferred upon the secular rulers by the pope, the "vicar of God." On this question Dante has no doubts. Secular power is derived directly from the Almighty, wholly independent of the parallel derivation of spiritual power from the same omnipotent source:

> Two ends, therefore, have been laid down by the ineffable providence of God for man to aim at: the blessedness of this life, which consists in the exercise of his natural powers, and which is prefigured in the earthly Paradise; and next, the blessedness of the life eternal, which consists in the fruition of the sight of God's countenance, and to which man by his own natural powers cannot rise, if he be not aided by the divine light; and this blessedness is understood by the heavenly Paradise. . . .

> Therefore man had need of two guides for his life, as he had a two-fold end in life; whereof one is the Supreme Pontiff, to lead mankind to eternal life, according to the things revealed to us; and the other is the Emperor, to guide mankind to happiness in this world, in accordance with the teaching of philosophy. . . .

> It is therefore clear that the authority of temporal Monarchy comes down, with no intermediate will, from the fountain of universal authority; and this fountain, one in its unity, flows through many channels out of the abundance of the goodness of God.[61]

Indeed, the electors in the medieval scheme did not really exercise their own discretion in electing an emperor, but merely announced God's choice. Therefore, the universal empire is vindicated by the requirements of mankind, the course of history, and the divine source of the secular authority. World-peace will be ensured by the universal church and the universal empire, equally derived from God and independent within the range of legitimate authority assigned to each.

It will be observed that Dante, better than any other writer (not excepting Aquinas), realized in his program the theoretical duality and balance of powers implicit in medieval doctrine. At the same time, the oft-quoted statement of Bryce that the *De monarchia* was an epitaph rather than a prophecy was comprehensively true. Both church and empire were really going into eclipse. Nationalism had already begun to supplant medieval feudal imperialism, and the Protestant revolt was soon destined to rend Christendom asunder. Even before this took place the infidel poured over Eastern Europe and was only turned back with the greatest difficulty from the gates of Vienna itself. Dante's great plea for peace went for naught.

Marsiglio of Padua, Utilitarian and Spokesman for Imperial Secular Absolutism. — The moribund Holy Roman Empire did not have to rely wholly on Dante's impassioned defense; it was upheld with equal force and originality by Marsiglio of Padua (1270–1342), who brought out his *Defensor pacis* in collaboration with John of Jandun in 1324, approximately twelve years after Dante's attempt to resuscitate the Empire in *De monarchia* and twenty after DuBois's challenge to both empire and papacy in *De recuperatione terre sancte.*

Marsiglio's work contains a much more systematic consideration of the origin of society and the state than does Dante's or DuBois's, though it is no less devastating in its criticism of the church. In describing the origins of society Marsiglio adopted a strictly utilitarian approach to the subject, reminiscent of the Epicureans and prophetic of Machiavelli, Hobbes, and Bentham. Society, says Marsiglio, starts with the family, but this is inadequate to meet the needs of a well-rounded life. Families therefore unite to supply those mutual necessities which cannot be realized in isolation. Coöperative effort, then, is the initial impulse to and the chief bond of society. But man is not only naturally coöperative; he is also combative because of the inevitable conflict of interests between individuals. Justice and morality arise as soon as man perceives that there are certain types of action which are to be commended, as improving coöperative capacity, and others which must be restrained in order to make coöperation possible. The resulting rules of conduct, which stimulate coöperation and restrain conflict, make up the body of what is known as natural law.

Natural law is adequate in content to constitute the basis of social control, but to be effective it must be enforced: the state and government are therefore essential to any well-ordered existence. Throughout this whole process of social and political genesis man is guided by his reason, which is keenly aware of utility; hence Marsiglio's theory of society is not merely rationalistic, but utilitarian. That such a doctrine of social origins diverges tremendously from that set forth by the Fathers and Aquinas is apparent. Allen thus comments on the significance of this highly secular line of approach:

It strikes at the root of medieval orthodoxy. It is the view of Machiavelli: it is, even, an approximation to the view of Hobbes. It gets rid at once of the transcendental element in ethics. It is quite strictly utilitarian. On this view right and wrong have no reference whatever to a final end of man in another life; no necessary relation at all to any cosmic purpose.[62]

Although the state has as its original and immediate purpose the repression of anti-social action, its complete and ultimate function is to realize what Marsiglio designates as *tranquillitas*. By this Marsiglio means the perfection of social coöperation — complete harmony and coördination of abstract crowds, groups, and abstract collectivities [63] — a conception not unlike that set forth by Mackenzie and Hobhouse in our own day in their philosophical revaluation of the organic analogy. Marsiglio would have this state of *tranquillitas* realized in the same way that Plato aspired to bring about social justice; namely, through the social division of labor. Marsiglio specifies the following classes as necessary in society if perfect social differentiation and coöperative effort are to be achieved: judges, soldiers, farmers, money-dealers, architects, tailors, artisans, merchants, and priests. It is a chief task of government to see to it that all of these classes exist, that the personnel is adequate to the needs of the society, and that each citizen is assigned his proper position in this functional scheme. Marsiglio argues his case thus:

The state, according to Aristotle, is a perfect community, comprising every element of sufficiency in itself, and instituted for the sake not merely of living, but of living well. The latter part of this definition indicates the ultimate purpose of the state; for they who live politically not only *live* — beasts and wild animals do that; but they live *well*, even though they may be wanting in the liberalizing products of civilization and enlightenment. As the object of the state is that men may live and live well, we must first treat of living, and of its modes; for the state is necessary for everything undertaken by the community of men comprising the state.

. . . concerning living and living well, in the mundane sense of the good life, and concerning the things which are essential to that life, renowned philosophers have given an almost complete demonstration. They have reached the conclusion that for fulfilling that life a civil community is necessary; for perfect life cannot be attained otherwise. . . . Since man is born unprotected from his environment, and is thus liable to suffering and destruction, he needs arts of diverse sorts whereby he may ward off obnoxious things. And since such arts cannot be employed save by a number of men, nor preserved save through their communication from age to age, it is necessary for men to congregate in order to acquire what is useful and escape what is injurious.

Among men thus congregated contention arises naturally, which, if not regulated by the rules of justice, leads to division and strife, and finally to the dissolution of the community. It is, therefore, necessary to introduce into the community the rule of justice and to set up a guardian, or protector. Since it is the function of the guardian to restrain dangerous transgressors and others who are agitators or who seek to harass the community from within or without, the state must have within itself the means of repression. . . .

We may then summarize what we have said. Men are associated together for the sake of living sufficiently — that is, to obtain the things which are necessary to themselves and to transmit such things from generation to generation. This congregation in its perfected form, containing the limit of sufficiency in itself, is called the state. The various things needed by those desiring to live well cannot be procured by men of a single rank or office. It is necessary that there be diverse ranks or offices among the members of the community, each rank or office contributing something which man needs for the sufficiency of life. These various orders or offices constitute the multiplicity and diversity of the parts of the state.[64]

Anticipations of Later Theories. — Next to this utilitarian theory of society, the most noteworthy contributions of Marsiglio to social science were his doctrines of the nature of law, majority rule, representative government, and secular absolutism. The science of jurisprudence is the science of creating and improving the group life of man and his coöperative activities. Law, in practice, is the body of rules which advance this objective. These precepts of social expediency which constitute law can be discovered by any reasonable person, though of course the learned and expert are more competent for the exercise of this function. Yet, to be effective, law must not only be discerned; it must be promulgated and enforced. Marsiglio's conception of law has been stated thus:

Law is essentially a judgment as to what is just and advantageous to the community. It is an imperative expression of the common need, formulated by reason, promulgated by the recognized authority, sanctioned by force.[65]

Such conceptions led Marsiglio to inquire into the ultimate authority behind law, and this he found to reside in the whole body of the citizens or in the elected representatives of a majority of these citizens. Marsiglio preferred an elective monarch and an

elective legislature, though the *Defensor pacis* cannot well be regarded as a brief for parliamentarism. Marsiglio thus sets forth
his defense of majority rule:

It is only to the whole body, or the majority, of the citizens that the
authority of making or instituting law pertains. Only out of the delibera-
tion and will of the whole multitude is the best law produced. . . . For
a majority can more readily than any less number discern the defect in
a law proposed for enactment; for the whole community is greater in
importance and worth than any part; and general utility is more apt
to be found in a law issuing from the community, since no one knowingly injures himself. . . .

The authority for making laws pertains either to the whole body of
citizens, or to a single one or to the few. It cannot pertain to one man,
for he, looking rather to his own than to the common interest, can,
through ignorance or malice, produce a bad law, whence a tyranny
will arise. For the same reason it cannot pertain to the few; they likewise in making law plan for a particular interest and not for the common
good; we see this in oligarchies. For the opposite reasons, lawmaking
pertains to the whole body of citizens or to a majority. For all citizens
must be duly regulated by law, and no man knowingly does injury or
injustice to himself; therefore, all, or at least most, desire a law adapted
to the common good of the citizens.[66]

Even in his day Marsiglio apparently had to meet the argument
of the differential psychologist that the majority are mostly of
inferior intelligence, and he disposes of this contention, to his own
satisfaction, as follows:

The power of making the laws should belong to the whole body of
citizens, for there is no law-giver among men superior to the people themselves. The argument that there are an infinite number of fools in the
world may be met by pointing out that " foolish " is a relative term, and
that the people know their own needs best and will not legislate against
their own interests.[67]

Marsiglio recognized that actual governmental power must be
delegated. He himself preferred a monarchy to a democracy or
an aristocracy, held that the monarch should be elected, and advanced the contractual conception that the king should be deposed
if he violated the terms of his agreement with the people:

The actual administration must be in the hands of a single person or
group of persons. Perhaps a king is the best head for the state, but the
monarch should be elected and not hold his office hereditarily, and should
be deposed if he exceed his powers.[68]

As a good student of Roman law, Marsiglio was a thorough believer in secular absolutism. He based his belief not only upon his utilitarian analysis of social genesis and his conception of popular sovereignty, but also upon a complete rejection of the pretensions of the church to temporal power and to immunity from the civil power of the state. The greater portion of Part II of the *Defensor pacis* is devoted to an attempt to prove four major contentions: (1) the church as such has no justifiable claim to any kind of coercive jurisdiction; (2) the clergy as such have no claim to immunity from secular jurisdiction; (3) neither pope nor clergy have any right to govern or even to speak for the church; and (4) the clergy have no justifiable title to property.[69]

In formulating the ground for his attack upon the church, Marsiglio resembles Pierre DuBois in assigning the chief responsibility for the wars and disorders of Christendom to the papal and clerical lust for temporal power and prestige:

In our preceding pages we have found that civil discord and dissension in the various kingdoms and communities is due, above all, to a cause which, unless it be obviated, will continue to be a source of future calamity, — namely, the claims, aspirations, and enterprises of the Roman bishop and of his band of ecclesiastics, bent upon gaining secular power and superfluous worldly possessions. The bishop of Rome is wont to support his claim to supreme authority over others by the assertion that the plenitude of power was delegated to him by Christ through the person of St. Peter. . . . But in reality no princely authority, nor any coercive jurisdiction in this world — to say nothing of *supreme* authority — belongs to him or any other bishop, priest or clerk, whether jointly or severally.[70]

In attempting to undermine the papal claims, Marsiglio used historical as well as logical and legal arguments. He assailed the very cornerstone of Catholic historical claims: namely, the doctrine of Petrine supremacy and the original papacy of Peter. He claimed that Paul rather than Peter was the first bishop of Rome, and that if Peter ever came to Rome it was after the visit of Paul.[71]

Not only did Marsiglio deny to the pope any spiritual power; he likewise denied that either the pope alone or the pope and the lesser clergy combined possessed the supreme spiritual power. The ultimate spiritual power was to be found in the whole body of believers, who could function practically only when assembled in a general church council. Marsiglio thus foreshadowed the Conciliar Movement of the next two centuries, though he did not advocate the immediate assembling of a church council to deal with the ecclesiastical problems of his day. The clergy, he contended, could neither remit sins nor hold the keys of heaven and hell. Their sole legitimate function was to give instruction in the methods of salvation and to administer the sacraments. There was therefore no real need for any ecclesiastical hierarchy, the priests being able to exercise all the necessary duties of the clergy.

It would scarcely be necessary to emphasize by way of summary the diverse and decisive ways in which Marsiglio departed from the accepted medieval scheme of things. It is not too much to say that the *Defensor pacis* contained within itself, whether its authors understood it or not, the germs of most of the subsequent innovations and interests in social and political philosophy down to the close of the eighteenth century. In one way only, was it anachronistic: namely, that, unlike Pierre DuBois's " Recovery of the Holy Land," it set forth the outworn claims of the medieval empire instead of forecasting the national state.[72]

The Conciliar Movement and the Reversal of Authority. — An important break with the medieval system of affairs was associated with the Conciliar Movement of the first half of the fifteenth century (1409–1439). It grew out of the rival candidatures of the popes Urban VI and Clement VII and the resulting Great Schism. It was necessary to settle the problem of the supreme ecclesiastical power in order to approve the right pope and bring harmony to an organization whose whole message and work rested upon the premise of unity of doctrine and organization. As a result, some four general church councils were summoned: Pisa (1409); Constance (1414–1418); Basel (1431–1443); and Ferrara-Florence (1438–1439).

The Conciliar Movement in its essence represented the extension of Roman law to the church. Pierre DuBois and Marsiglio of Padua had applied Roman law to the secular government, and Marsiglio had arrived at the conception of popular sovereignty and representative government. Although himself chiefly concerned with secular affairs and the subordination of church to state, even Marsiglio had contended that the ultimate power of the Catholic Church resided in a church council representative of the whole body of believers. Gerson, Nicholas of Cues, and the jurists of the age carried the Roman law, and especially the Roman law of the corporation, over into the realm of church government, with results quite subversive of the medieval view of the church and of the derivation of spiritual power. The accepted conception of the Middle Ages was that the pope was the vicegerent of God on earth and that divine power was conferred upon the pope by God, streaming down from the pope through the hierarchy of the church to the humble believers in the ranks of private Christians.

The Conciliar Movement reversed this doctrine. Applying the Roman law to the church, the theorists of the Conciliar period held that the supreme power in the church resided in the whole body of believers. The rank and file of the faithful Christians could not, of course, function directly in mass-meeting. It was essential that they be represented, in the same way that they found it necessary to function through their representatives as citizens of the secular state. For all practical purposes, therefore, the supreme spiritual power was located in a general church council. The pope was regarded as an administrative convenience who might call and preside over councils and conduct the affairs of the church during the interims between councils. The pope was not needed, however, to call a council; it might be assembled without his authority. When the Roman law of the corporation was applied to him the pope was defined as the presiding officer of the corporation of believers. In other words, the Conciliar Movement made the pope the vicar of the church rather than the vicar of God; it applied to the church the doctrines of popular sovereignty and representative government and undermined the mediæval view of the nature, power, and functions of the pope.

Nicholas of Cues, Organismic Theorist. — For the purposes of the history of social theory, it is important to note that this development of representative government greatly aided the progress of a similar trend in secular society — a trend furthered if not initiated by the writings of Marsiglio and others. Indeed, the greatest writer of the Conciliar period, Nicholas of Cues (1401–1464), himself extended his views to the realm of secular society and civil government. His basic conception of society was that it is an organism in which every element has its definite function to perform in working for the harmony of the whole. In this connection Nicholas worked out the most extensive elaboration of the organismic analogy which was produced until the appearance of certain nineteenth-century theories of society and the state. Like Paul von Lilienfeld far later, Nicholas made use of the conception of social and political pathology. Reviving the Platonic analogy, he designated the ruler as the physician-in-chief of the sick state, who has the duty of prescribing for its ills according to the best advice of political philosophers past and present.[73] Nicholas contended that popular consent is the sole basis of political obligation; it is both a divine principle and a natural right. All men are by nature free; hence government must spring from the consent of the governed. Men are by nature equally endowed with power; therefore, if any are superior to others, their position of ascendency depends upon the consent of the rest. He reconciled the doctrine of popular sovereignty with the medieval dogma of the divine derivation of secular power by claiming that God works in and through persons. Yet one should remember that Nicholas did not have in mind the contemporary conceptions of representative government or the individualized doctrine of consent developed by the Levellers and other theorists of the Commonwealth period. He meant by representative government and popular consent simply representation by the medieval " estates " which stood for definite economic, class, and ideological interests.

We may therefore say that in the fifteenth century there existed in embryonic form all the major doctrines of the contract school of the seventeenth and eighteenth centuries: sovereignty, natural law and natural rights, the state of nature, the social contract, and the popular basis of civil authority. Indeed, Æneas Sylvius Piccolomini (1405–1464), later Pope Pius II, in his *De ortu et auctoritate imperii Romani,* seems to have distinguished definitely between the social and the governmental contract, and to have anticipated Richard Hooker by more than a century. Most of these doctrines show strong traces of such Classical influences as Aristotle's conception of the " virtue of the many," the Roman theory of secular absolutism and popular sovereignty, and the Roman law of the corporation.

Summary of the Chapter. — We have ranged far afield, and it is time that we see where this chapter has taken us. To begin with, we noted that the concerted effort put forth by Christendom in the Crusades was both symbol and symptom — symbolic of the unity attained, and symptomatic of the unrest destined to culminate in disunity. The culture contact that was both concomitant and aftermath of the Crusades was considered, and the associated trade with the Levant and its part in the early Commercial Revolution given due weight. The processes of liberation (or release) and individuation were then analyzed, together with their manifestations in both Christendom and the Moslem world. Ibn Khaldūn, a great Moslem who reflected on the social disorganization rife all around him, was then given extended attention and his high rank among social theorists stressed. Next we considered a strongly secularized thinker, Pierre DuBois, whose project for a campaign against the Moslems was at bottom both evidence of collapse of the unity that would make such a Crusade successful and presage of the national state. Along with the disorganizing effects of culture contact from without went the revival of Roman law and its cultivation at royal and imperial courts, with the consequence that the conception of secular absolutism, so deadly to the medieval idea of the " two powers " still cherished by Dante, was introduced and increasingly accepted. Further, all the forces operative tended to favor national unity as against feudal decentralization. The rising tide of the Commercial Revolution brought in on a moderate scale the dynamic influence of capital, and this steadily submerged more and more of the stability, routine, and provincialism of the medieval agrarian economy. The new stock of capital gradually enabled the secular absolutists to command a paid bureaucracy and army and thus to reduce to subjection the recalcitrant feudal lords. As we saw, Marsiglio of Padua was a spokesman for *imperial* secular absolutism, and although his forthright attack on the papacy brought in a note distinctly off the medieval key, he was in a certain sense anachronistic in his defense of the empire, for everything pointed to the future ascendency of the national state. Eventually a still more modern trend was initiated by the Conciliar Movement, for in its extension of the conceptions of Roman law to the church, theories of popular sovereignty and representative government directly antagonistic to medieval notions of the powers of the pope were introduced. Consequently, by the middle of the fifteenth century all the major doctrines of the contract school of two centuries later were already in operation. The outcome of all these disintegrating processes was that the foundations of the Middle Ages were thoroughly undermined; secularization advanced to new fields.

Two or three decades ago, many historians deprecated the use of such terms as the Dark Ages. Here and there today, however, it is conceded that large parts of Europe *were* relatively isolated in vicinal, social, and mental senses, during the period in question — *relatively*. Another term, the Crusades, is open to much graver objection. There were indeed great differences between the First Crusade and the Sixth, for example, and these should at least have been mentioned in even the limited space available. Moreover, the interpretations of the First Crusade primarily with reference to collective behavior can justifiably be criticized; for many of today's sociologists, collective behavior itself seems in some contexts to be a rather dubious category. It verges on over-simplified physiological psychology.

Turning to other matters, let it be noted that there is now a very good English translation by Rosenthal of Ibn Khaldūn's *Prolegomena*. On the basis of the divergences between this and the French translation, and the cross-checking of these with Schimmel's German translation, Becker would today be inclined to regard Ibn Khaldūn as a reactionary radical hoping for the favor of Allah by a return to "the purity of simplicity." In other words, he would not be treated as so fundamentally secular a thinker, although there would be no attempt to deny the many secular components of his analysis.

CHAPTER VIII

The Expansion of Europe, Humanism, and the Protestant Revolt

STRICTLY INACCURATE. — In this chapter we shall be compelled to include a number of highly diverse trends in the development of social thought. Moreover, a good deal of the discussion will be negative in tone; i.e., the effort will be made to show that certain factors to which great influence is conventionally ascribed did *not* have the effect on social change in general and social philosophy in particular attributed to them.

The reader is asked to bear in mind most of the sketch of the historical background given at the beginning of Chapter Seven, for the tendencies therein noted continued to exert an all-pervasive effect on European developments in the period now to be examined. In addition, account should be taken of the fact that in October, 1492, Columbus landed on San Salvador in the Bahamas, and that in May six years later Vasco da Gama reached Calicut on the coast of India. The expansion of Europe, which had previously inched along a tortuous path, suddenly strode with seven-league boots. Trade with the Levant continued to be of some importance, but from 1500 on the awareness of a great new world beyond the Pillars of Hercules steadily increased. Isolation again gave ground to accessibility, and a Dryden triumphantly proclaimed in the *Annus Mirabilis:*

> Instructed ships shall sail to rich commerce,
>   By which remotest regions are allied;
> Which makes one city of the universe,
>   Where some may gain and all may be supplied.

But let us now turn to the first of our negative analyses.

The Insignificance of Humanism in Social Change. — A generation ago it was fashionable to assign great importance in the development of modern civilization to the period conventionally called the Renaissance. In the works of the aesthete Symonds, for example, one finds the general thesis that the Middle Ages were centuries of general and relatively uniform stagnation, the paralyzing shell or envelope of which was burst by the potent forces arising from the new appreciation of Classical literature and the remarkable developments of chromatic and plastic art during the two centuries following 1450. The most diverse results have been assigned to such factors, not even excepting the rise of modern science, the mastery of oceanic navigation, and the birth of the national state system.

Now the results of a generation of historical scholarship have been such as totally to dissipate this illusion. In the first place, we have learned much more about the real nature of the Middle Ages. It has been shown that they cannot be dealt with as a unified period, for there was an enormous gulf between the culture of Merovingian France and the Italy of Dante. They were not an era of uniform cultural stagnation; from the twelfth century onward there was a steady, if gradual, intellectual and scientific improvement, and the Renaissance, *as such,* did little to stimulate these tendencies in any unique manner. In the second place, it has been shown that it is manifestly inaccurate and misleading to throw together all the multifarious and diverse cultural developments of the period from 1450 to 1700 and assign them to the Renaissance. If this term is to have any specific meaning whatever, it must be held to refer to Humanism and the developments in art. The latter, for various reasons, may justifiably be left out of this discussion.[1]

As to Humanism, it can scarcely be proved that the laudable increase of interest in, and approval of, the literatures of Greece and Rome produced any remarkable intellectual revolution, least of all any marked impulse to renewed scientific curiosity. The only direct contribution which Humanism made to the new science lay in the recovery and reading of some of the writings of the Greek scientists who had far more modern and acceptable ideas on scientific matters than those of most medieval figures, but instances of this sort were very few and relatively unimportant. Although it must be confessed that their knowledge proved of little value to science, it is true that the most encyclopedic of all the Greek scientists, Aristotle, had been known to the Schoolmen in translations from the Arabic at the end of the eleventh century, and in excellent translations and editions of the Greek originals from the close of the thirteenth century onward.[2] *The Humanists were much more attracted by rhetorical and mystical pagan works than by the scientific treatises of antiquity.* Cicero and Neo-Platonic writers loomed far wider on the horizon than Aristarchus, Archimedes, or Hipparchus. As Robinson has judiciously said:

. . . Plato was as incapable in the fifteenth century of producing an intellectual revolution as Aristotle had been in the thirteenth. With the exception of Valla, whose critical powers were perhaps slightly stimulated by acquaintance with the classics, it must be confessed that there was little in the so-called " new learning " to generate anything approaching an era of criticism. It is difficult, to be sure, to imagine a Machiavelli or an Erasmus in the thirteenth century, but it is likewise difficult to determine the numerous and subtle changes which made them possible at the opening of the sixteenth; and it is reckless to assume that the Humanists were chiefly responsible for these changes.[3]

The most significant and potent impulse given by Humanism to intellectual and scientific advance was an indirect one, consisting in a revival of interest in the things of this world. The intellectual classes among the pagans, by contrast with the Christians, had been singularly little interested in the supernatural world or the destiny of the soul. They were primarily concerned about the most satisfactory type of life here on earth. Philosophy was designed to teach how to live successfully rather than how to die with assurance of ultimate safety. This dominant *secular* interest had been lost for approximately a millennium on account of the Christian absorption in the problems and technique of the salvation of immortal souls; had not Augustine himself warned against becoming too much engrossed in earthly interests lest assurance of successful entry into the New Jerusalem be jeopardized? As men like Petrarch and his followers and successors came to read more of pagan literature and to approve it heartily, they were inevitably infected with the virus of the secular orientation of the Greek and Roman past, and there arose the amusing situation of actually pious Humanists enthusiastically recommending what was frankly branded by Augustine as an integral portion of the City of the Devil.[4] Erasmus admitted that the appellations St. Socrates and St. Cicero were neither inappropriate nor sacrilegious. He thus openly expressed his preference for pagan writers when compared with even the most illustrious Schoolmen:

Whosoever is pious and conduces to good manners ought not to be called profane. The first place must indeed be given to the authority of the Scriptures; but, nevertheless, I sometimes find things said or written by the ancients, nay, even by the heathens, nay, by the poets themselves, so chastely, so holily, and so divinely, that I can not persuade myself but that, when they wrote them, they were divinely inspired, and perhaps the spirit of Christ diffuses itself farther than we imagine; and that there are more saints than we have in our catalogue. To confess freely among friends, I can't read Cicero on " Old Age," on " Friendship," his " Offices," or his " Tusculan Questions " without kissing the book, without veneration towards that divine soul. And, on the contrary, when I read some of our modern authors, treating of politics, economics and ethics, good God! how cold they are in comparison with these! Nay, how do they seem to be insensible of what they write themselves. So that I had rather lose Scotus and twenty more such as he (fancy twenty subtle doctors!) than one Cicero or Plutarch. Not that I am wholly against them either; but because, by the reading of the one, I find myself better, whereas I rise from the other, I know not how coldly affected to virtue, but most violently inclined to cavil and contention.[5]

That the generation of an interest in the secular world was an impulse in the direction of scientific curiosity, as compared with the supernaturalism of Patristic and Scholastic Christianity, cannot be denied; yet it was but a feeble and indirect urge which was probably far more than offset by the antiscientific tendencies of the Humanistic movement in education. It was the mystical and aesthetic, rather than the scientific and rationalistic, attitude which was promoted by the spirit of Humanism, and at its very best it could do no more than to produce the learning of a Scaliger or Casaubon. And, finally, what slight indirect impulse Humanism may have given to secular studies and science was obstructed or frustrated by the revival of supernaturalism and bigotry in the period of the Reformation and Counter-Reformation. By the time scholarship had recovered from this blow, the " merchant adventurers," explorers, and scientists had created a new world of fact and ideas quite foreign to Erasmus, Luther, Baronius, and Loyola alike.[6]

The invention of printing, which came as a result of the labors of Coster and Gutenberg in the period of Humanism, was a very important contribution to the ultimate development of a technique which is so much a thing of coöperative effort and effective communication as modern science, but here again the service was indirect and incidental rather than causal. There was no immediate flood of radical or scientific literature. The majority of the books printed during the first century or so after Gutenberg were not scientific and critical, but pious, religious, and theological — usually a reproduction of those which had appeared as a result of the patient and persistent efforts of medieval copyists in the monastic *scriptorium* in the centuries before the invention of printing. It was not until the sixteenth and seventeenth centuries that books reflecting the beginnings of the new thought and science were printed in any considerable number. Neither did printing make it easier to produce heterodox literature: the European governments made unlicensed printing a serious offense — in some states a capital crime! — and established a thorough censorship of the licensed presses. The precarious nature of the printing profession in regard to the issuance of novel scientific or philosophical works is well illustrated by Osiander's famous preface to Copernicus's work, in which Osiander, to protect his press, implied that probably Copernicus was only joking.

All in all, then, we may say that the Revival of Learning, particularly in its Humanistic aspect, had little effect on the deeper currents of social development.

The Continuing Chaos in Italy. — It is perhaps a bit unfair to the rediscoverers of Plato and Cicero, however, to expect that their exhortations to civic virtue could have any effect on the seething whirlpool manifest in those parts of Europe most disorganized by that too-rapid advance of secularization of which the earlier phases were analyzed in the previous chapter. England, Germany, France, and Spain had regained some measure of stability under the aegis of the national state, but Italy was still paying the penalty of precipitate innovation. As Hearnshaw says:

> Intellectually and æsthetically in the van of all European peoples, morally and politically she lagged far in the rear. Her people, widely divergent in race and culture, were utterly degenerate and corrupt; she had lost all military capacity; her princes were craven and criminal; her Church was secularised and incredibly depraved; she was torn by violent schisms and incessant intrigues. No bond of any sort of unity held together her struggling atoms. . . . Hence the study of Italian politics in the fifteenth and sixteenth centuries is like an attempt to solve a complicated puzzle. One dominant fact, however, emerges from the study. It is that in the game of politics as played in Italy at that time no rules of honor or morality whatsoever were observed. Treasons, betrayals, poisonings, assassinations, perjuries, hypocrisies, sacrileges, infidelities — all kinds of base and hateful villainies — were employed without scruple or remorse.[7]

It was in the light of such facts as these that Giddings constructed his ideal-typical " conspirital society," of which he says: " [This type] . . . arises in populations that, like the Italian cities at their worst estate, have suffered disintegration of a preexisting social order. Unscrupulous adventurers come forward and create relations of personal allegiance by means of bribery, patronage, and preferment. Intrigue and conspiracy are the social bonds. The social type is Conspirital."[8]

From the point of view of the sociology of knowledge (*Wissenssoziologie*) it is highly significant that Dunning could say that no writer was ever more of a child of his environment than was the greatest social philosopher of this period in European history, Nicolo Machiavelli (1469–1527).[9] Why? Because Machiavelli's analysis was frankly based upon the premise that intriguing self-interest and insatiable desires constitute the mainsprings of all human activity.

Nicolo Machiavelli and His Point of View. — The man whose sobriquet came to be synonymous, in the mind of Butler, with that applied to a certain cloven-footed gentleman ("Old Nick" — the Devil), not only had a low estimate of the human nature he observed around him, but also made one of the most acute analyses of that contemporary human nature to be found in literature. With a point of view essentially similar to that of Ibn Khaldūn, he went beyond Plato and Aristotle by separating ethics from politics. It is this which has caused him to be regarded as a counsellor of evil and unscrupulous doctrines, but it seems that such a charge is hard to substantiate. All that he did was to cut beneath the surface of his contemporaries' "speech-reactions" and get at their basic behavior; he simply endeavored, in a cold and dispassionate manner, to discover and reveal those methods whereby the Italian despots were able to succeed. If there was anything in his writings apart from the sincere and scientific desire to record matters as he observed them, it may well have been irony rather than iniquity.[10]

In spite of certain innovations, however, Machiavelli's analysis of society was not systematic or well balanced; hence it was long regarded as a mere rule-of-thumb discussion of political motives and a guide for the self-seeking despot or imperialistic republic. Machiavelli's works are much more abstract and general than they seem at first glance, but it is true that the theory they contain is implicit rather than explicit; hence the slight esteem in which they were long held was a pardonable error. As far as Machiavelli had any formal theory, he copied directly from Polybius; and this too detracted from his rank as a social thinker.

His method was professedly historical, but he reversed the usual mode of procedure; i.e., he speculated upon the activities of his contemporaries and, having reached an empirical generalization, he resorted to history to find some example to support his conclusion.[11] This is not the historical method at all, strictly speaking, but the discredited illustrative method; yet we should not be too hard on Machiavelli — many modern social theorists follow a practice in all respects similar, and quite as erroneous.

It might be well to point out here that though the *Prince* is frequently regarded as the most important or even the only book by Machiavelli on political and social philosophy, such a view is wide of the facts. His *Discourses on the First Ten Books of Livy* in reality contain his most profound observations in these fields. The *Prince* is a handbook for the successful tyrant or autocrat; the *Discourses* treat of those fundamental social and political facts essential to the wise management of a prosperous and expanding republic.

Machiavelli's Doctrines of Motivation and Social Control.— Inasmuch as the place of Machiavelli in social theory is largely due to his analysis of the social and political motives prevalent in the Italy of his day, we may now consider at length what he has to say upon these subjects. The pivotal point in his social philosophy is the doctrine of the insatiability of human desires and the correlated assumption that this characteristic furnishes a sufficient motive for all social activity:

It was a saying of ancient writers, that men afflict themselves in evil, and become weary of the good, and that both these dispositions produce the same effects. For when men are no longer obliged to fight from necessity, they fight from ambition, which passion is so powerful in the hearts of men that it never leaves them, no matter to what height they may rise. The reason of this is that nature has created men so that they desire everything, but are unable to attain it; desire being thus always greater than the faculty of acquiring, discontent with what they have and dissatisfaction with themselves result from it. This causes the change in their fortunes; for as some men desire to have more, whilst others fear to lose what they have, enmities and war are the consequences. . . .

Moreover, as human desires are insatiable (because their nature is to have and to do everything whilst fortune limits their possessions and capacity of enjoyment), this gives rise to a constant discontent in the human mind and a weariness of the things they possess; and it is this which makes them decry the present, praise the past, and desire the future.[12]

In his analysis of " human nature " and the means which a ruler should adopt to control men, Machiavelli is no less disillusioned than Hobbes, and his statements, right or wrong, are more impressive because they are more frank, blunt, and straightforward in tone. For example, in speaking of whether it is better for a prince to be loved or feared by his subjects, he says:

This, then, gives rise to the question " whether it is better to be beloved than feared, or to be feared than beloved." It will naturally be answered that it would be desirable to be both the one and the other; but as it is difficult to be both at the same time, it is much more safe to be feared than to be loved, when you have to choose between the two. For it may be said of men in general that they are ungrateful and fickle, dissemblers, avoiders of danger, and greedy of gain. So long as you shower benefits upon them, they are all yours; they offer you their blood, their substance, their lives, and their children, provided the necessity for it is far off; but when it is near at hand, then they revolt. And the prince who relies upon their words, without having otherwise provided for his security, is ruined; for friendships that are won by rewards, and not by greatness and nobility of soul, although deserved, yet are not real, and cannot be depended upon in time of adversity.

Besides, men have less hesitation in offending one who makes himself beloved than one who makes himself feared; for love holds by a bond of obligation which, as mankind is bad, is broken on every occasion whenever it is for the interest of the obliged party to break it. But fear holds by the apprehension of punishment, which never leaves men. A prince, however, should make himself feared in such a manner that, if he has not won the affections of his people, he shall at least not incur their hatred. . . .

A prince then should know how to employ the nature of man, and that of beasts as well. . . . It being necessary then for a prince to know well how to employ the nature of the beasts, he should be able to assume both that of the fox and that of the lion; for whilst the latter cannot escape the traps laid for him, the former cannot defend himself against the wolves. A prince should be a fox, to know the traps and snares; and a lion, to be able to frighten the wolves; for those who simply hold to the nature of the wolves do not understand their business.

A sagacious prince then cannot and should not fulfil his pledges when their observance is contrary to his interest, and when the causes that induced him to pledge his faith no longer exist. If men were all good, then indeed this precept would be bad; but as men are naturally bad, and will not observe their faith towards you, you must, in the same way, not observe yours to them; and no prince ever yet lacked legitimate reasons with which to color his want of good faith. . . .

But it is necessary that the prince should know how to color this nature well, and how to be a great hypocrite and dissembler. For men are so simple, and yield so much to immediate necessity, that the deceiver will never lack dupes. . . .

For instance, a prince should seem to be merciful, faithful, humane, religious, and upright, and should even be so in reality; but he should have his mind so trained that, when occasion requires it, he may know how to change to the opposite. And it must be understood that a prince, and especially one who has but recently acquired his state, cannot perform all those things which cause men to be esteemed as good; he being often obliged, for the sake of maintaining his state, to act contrary to humanity, charity, and religion. And therefore it is necessary that he should have a versatile mind, capable of changing readily, according as the winds and changes of fortune bid him; and, as has been said above, not to swerve from the good if possible, but to know how to resort to evil if necessity demands it.[13]

This attitude can be fully understood only in the light of Machiavelli's conspirital environment and the fact that he regarded everything as subordinate to the welfare and continued existence of the state. He makes this clear in Book III of the *Discourses:* " For where the very safety of the country depends upon the resolution to be taken, no considerations of justice or injustice, humanity or cruelty, nor of glory or of shame, should be allowed to prevail. But putting all other considerations aside, the only question should be, What course will save the life and liberty of the country?"[14] As Meinecke's *Die Idee der Staatsraison in der neueren Geschichte* clearly shows, this amoral conception of " reasons of state" has played a fateful rôle in modern history.

Machiavelli was shrewd enough to discern that no universal rule could be laid down which would hold good for the government of all classes of people. Discussing the question as to whether gentle or rigorous methods are to be preferred in governing, he contends that " in attempting to reconcile these two opposite opinions, we must consider whether the people to be governed are your equals or your subjects. If they are your equals, then you cannot entirely depend upon rigorous measures, nor upon that severity which Tacitus recommends. . . . But he who has to command subjects, such as Tacitus speaks of, should employ severity rather than gentleness, lest these subjects should become insolent, and trample his authority under foot, because of too great indulgence. This severity, however, should be employed with moderation, so as to avoid making yourself odious, for no prince is ever benefited by making himself hated."[15]

Men are easily corrupted, regardless of how virtuous and well-educated they may originally have been,[16] says Machiavelli, and there is a persistence in these passions and desires which makes it possible to forecast the future by a study of the past:

Whoever considers the past and the present will readily observe that all cities and all peoples are and ever have been animated by the same desires and the same passions; so that it is easy, by diligent study of the past, to foresee what is likely to happen in the future in any republic, and to apply those remedies that were used by the ancients, or, not finding any that were employed by them, to devise new ones from the similarity of the events. . . .[17]

Wise men say, and not without reason, that whoever wishes to foresee the future must consult the past; for human events ever resemble those of preceding times. This arises from the fact that they are produced by men who have been, and ever will be, animated by the same passions, and they must have the same results. It is true that men are more or less virtuous in one country or another, according to the nature of the education by which their nature and habits of life have been formed. It also facilitates a judgment of the future by the past, to observe nations preserve for a long time the same character; ever exhibiting the same disposition to avarice, or bad faith, or to some other special vice or virtue.[18]

Machiavelli was an analyst of social behavior keen enough to comprehend the tenacity with which a people cling to their customary practices, and he emphasized the fact that in making any change or reform, at least the semblance of the old institutions must be retained. To quote:

He who desires or attempts to reform the government of a state, and wishes to have it accepted and capable of maintaining itself to the satisfaction of everybody, must at least retain the semblance of the old forms; so that it may seem to the people that there has been no change in the institutions, even though in fact they are entirely different from the old ones. For the great majority of mankind are satisfied with appearances, as though they were realities, and are often even more influenced by the things that seem than by those that are.[19]

This shows that he was fully aware of the difficulty of breaking up "the cake of custom," as Bagehot would call it, but because of his low estimate of the intelligence of the masses, he believed that they could be easily duped by clever social perversion (in Wiese's special sense).

One of the most striking contrasts between Machiavelli and the Classical writers was his insistence upon the necessity of extending the dominion of a state if it was to remain successful. The contrast between this conception and those of the Platonic city with its 5040 members and the Aristotelian *polis* where all the citizens are acquainted is immediately apparent. To be sure, Machiavelli held that theoretically the best political existence would be in a state without internal dissensions or desires for external aggrandizement, but that this could not be realized in practice:

But as all human things are kept in a perpetual movement, and can never remain stable, states naturally either rise or decline, and necessity compels them to many acts to which reason will not influence them; so that, having organized a republic competent to maintain herself without expanding, still, if forced by necessity to extend her territory, in such a case we shall see her foundations give way and herself quickly brought to ruin. And thus, on the other hand, if Heaven favors her so as never to be involved in war, the continued tranquillity would enervate her, or provoke internal dissensions, which together, or either of them separately, will be apt to prove her ruin. Seeing then the impossibility of establishing in this respect a perfect equilibrium, and that a precise middle course cannot be maintained, it is proper in the organization of a republic to select the most honorable course, and to constitute her so that, even if necessity should oblige her to expand, she may yet be able to preserve her acquisitions.[20]

Machiavelli here seems to have anticipated the idea advanced by Herbert Spencer that perfect social equilibrium is unattainable in the static form and that only a moving equilibrium is possible.[21] In this he was far in advance of the Greeks, who sought to secure a perfect social equilibrium in their ideal, restricted, non-expansive city-state. Machiavelli went further, however, than the desire for mere territorial expansion; he also insisted that a country must provide for an increase of population if it desires to achieve greatness: " Those who desire a city to achieve great empire must endeavor by all possible means to make her populous; for without an abundance of inhabitants it is impossible ever to make a city powerful. This may be done in two ways; either by attracting population by the advantages offered, or by compulsion. The first is to make it easy and secure for strangers to come and establish themselves there, and the second is to destroy the neighboring cities, and to compel their inhabitants to come and dwell in yours." [22] This second plan might be carried out in three ways: (1) by a confederation of republics with no single sovereign power; (2) by the Roman method of associating with a republic other states, but at the same time reserving the sovereign power to itself; and (3) by making the conquered peoples subjects and not associates. Of these methods he considered the second the best.[23]

He thoroughly understood the value of a common religion in keeping a people united, and advised the rulers to encourage everything which tended to increase religious fervor. That is to say, he did not value religion for its intrinsic spiritual benefit, but solely in a purely utilitarian sense as an aid in maintaining political unity and allegiance:

Princes and republics who wish to maintain themselves free from corruption must above all things preserve the purity of all religious observances, and treat them with proper reverence; for there is no greater indication of the ruin of a country than to see religion contemned. . . , everything that tends to favor religion (even though it were believed to be false) should be received and availed of to strengthen it; and this should be done the more, the wiser the rulers are, and the better they understand the natural course of things. Such was, in fact, the practice observed by sagacious men; which has given rise to the belief in the miracles that are celebrated in religions, however false they may be. For the sagacious rulers have given these miracles increased importance, no matter whence or how they originated; and their authority afterwards gave them credence with the people. . . .[24]

Psycho-Sociological Theories in the Discourses. — Machiavelli also makes some generalizations concerning the action of crowds which are of interest to sociologists and psycho-sociologists. Contrasting the conduct of a number of people in differing situations he says: " United in one body they are brave and insolent, but when afterwards each begins to think of his own danger, they become cowardly and feeble." [25]

In regard to the judgment of deliberative assemblies, he arrived at about the same conclusions as Spencer, Lecky, LeBon, and Sighele:

Those who have been present at any deliberative assemblies of men will have observed how erroneous their opinions often are; and in fact, unless they are directed by superior men, they are apt to be contrary to all reason. But as superior men in corrupt republics (especially in periods of peace and quiet) are generally hated, either from jealousy or the ambition of others, it follows that the preference is given to what common error approves, or to what is suggested by men who are more desirous of pleasing the masses than of promoting the general good.[26]

The truth of Machiavelli's contention concerning the low intelligence of a popular assembly and the ease with which a demagogue can gain ascendency over it is unhappily afforded much too ample confirmation by history.

Of the social effect of prestige he was informed to a certain degree, for he says: " Nothing is so apt to restrain an excited multitude as the reverence inspired by some grave and dignified man of authority who opposes them. . . . I conclude, then, that there is no better or safer way of appeasing an excited mob than the presence of some man of imposing appearance and highly respected." [27]

The influence of imitation is also noted in the following passage: " Timasitheus inspired the multitude with a sentiment of religion, and they always imitate their rulers. And Lorenzo de'Medici confirms this idea by saying: ' The example of the prince is followed by the masses, who keep their eyes always turned upon their chief.' " [28]

Summary of Machiavelli's Theories. — This completes the review of some of Machiavelli's leading contributions to social theory. They are extremely fragmentary and almost inextricably interwoven with political considerations, but may be summed up under the following heads:

(1) He made a beginning toward bringing back politics to the scientific standpoint from which it had been treated by Aristotle, and to a certain extent applied historical data to its elucidation. This was a considerable departure from the speculative deductions which had been made by the writers of the medieval period. He began the task which Bodin was to carry forward.[29]

(2) As did Ibn Khaldūn, he effected a complete separation of politics from ethics.

(3) His analysis of motives showed, to his own satisfaction at least, that the ultimate ground for all political and social activity among men proceeds from a narrow self-interest, and that men are satisfied with material prosperity and a sense of protection and mutual advantages.

(4) In his analysis of mankind he arrived at the conclusion that men are possessed of insatiable desires and of boundless ambition and selfishness.

(5) Proceeding from these two conclusions, he laid down certain timely rules of conduct for the prince, to the end that he might avail himself of this analysis of human motives and thereby circumvent the wiles, deceits, and treachery of the masses through excelling them in all these respects when the occasion demanded.

(6) He abandoned the Classical ideal of the small city-state and passed beyond Aquinas in advocating territorial expansion and the formation of ever larger political entities.

(7) He developed no rounded system of explicit social theory, but contented himself with compiling treatises which were admirably suited to his times and impregnated with implicit generalizations valid in certain other periods.

The Rediscovery of Plato and the Neophobia of the Utopian Writers. — For those who were less absorbed by the immediately practical than Machiavelli, another type of outlet for discontent with the world as it then was came into view when the writings of the ancients were rediscovered by the Humanists. Plato in particular proved attractive to a certain type of mind. The Arabs had cared little for his poetic method, his flight from a world of flux and change, and Ibn Khaldūn had almost ignored him, but he was enthusiastically welcomed in Europe when Greek scholars brought his writings West and the new printing press scattered them abroad. Ideal commonwealths, pictures of a world where the lion and the lamb lie down together, were fabricated after the pattern of the *Republic,* and provided discontented intellectuals with slings and arrows for a literary attack on the *status quo.* Some historians have contended that the attack was measurably successful, but they have fallen prey to the *post hoc ergo propter hoc* fallacy; it was but the surface foam on a current of influences that would have brought about social change if no utopias had ever been written, or if Plato and his commentators had flickered out in the vast pyre of the Alexandrian library.

In virtually every instance the desire of the utopian writers was for the return of a golden age, for refuge from a reality too stern to be confronted with equanimity. In Mumford's phrase, they wrote "utopias of escape." The writers of the so-called Renaissance, who continued to serve as models, were inclined to apotheosize the Classical notions concerning the desirability of fixity (Machiavelli provides one of the few exceptions), and the putative Reformers, who were nearing the zenith of their influence, were quite sure that they wanted a static, changeless social order — after they had once established *their* sacred society of the faithful and subservient. The disorganizing effect of culture contact, of "commixture of manners," engaged the almost exclusive attention of these epigoni of the Greeks. Isolation, quiescence, stability, and mental immobility were the ideal characteristics of any society.

As a consequence, a good deal of attention is paid in most of the utopias to the problem of preserving these havens for the blessed free from the devastating effects of change. More's *Utopia,* for example, written in the years 1515 and 1516, shortly after the publication of Amerigo Vespucci's account of his voyages, tells of the cutting of a " deep channel " between the whilom country of Abraxa and the rest of the continent, so that Abraxa became an isolated island; its name then was changed to Utopia. This channel was dug at the command of the good king Utopus, who, having molded his subjects to his will, wished them forever to remain in his image, as it were. Strangers who brought useful arts were welcomed, but were carefully " cared for " in order that they might not infect the natives with the itch for innovation. Further, means were taken to control the movements of the natives themselves, evidently in order to prevent any release of tendencies that might be thwarted and seeking an outlet, as the following lines plainly show:

If any man has a mind to visit his friends that live in some other town, or desires to travel and see the rest of the country, he obtains leave very easily from the . . . local authorities when there is no particular occasion for him at home: *such as travel, carry with them a passport from the Prince, which both certifies the license that is granted for travelling and limits the time of their return.* . . . If they stay in any place longer than a night, everyone follows his proper occupation . . . but if any man goes out of the city to which he belongs without leave, and is found rambling without a passport, *he is severely treated, he is punished as a fugitive, and sent home disgracefully; and if he falls again into the like fault, is condemned to slavery.* If any man has a mind to travel only over the precinct of his own city, he may freely do it, *with his father's permission and his wife's consent;* but when he comes into any of the country houses, . . . he must labor with them and conform to their rules: and if he does this, he may freely go over the whole precinct; being thus as useful to the city to which he belongs as if he were still within it. Thus you see that there are no idle persons among them, nor pretences of excusing any from labor. *There are no taverns, no alehouses nor stews among them; nor any other occasions of corrupting each other, of getting into corners, or forming themselves into parties.* . . .[30]

Apparently More has some insight into the processes of social change, for he permits movement only when *no release* from the most rigid social control is involved (the statutes of laborers prevailing in his day probably indicated the direction of his analysis). No individuation, no release of biological tendencies or temperamental attitudes, no opportunities for crowd-forming, no milling about, no interstimulation and orgiastic behavior — not if More can help it! (Other phases of his thought will be dealt with later.)

Francis Bacon's *New Atlantis* was published more than a century later than *Utopia* — in 1629, three years after Bacon's death, to be exact — and although incomplete, still lets us see that Bacon's interest was not political, as was More's, but scientific. He longed for an ideal country where experimental science, zealously pursued, would at last give men dominion over things, " for nature is governed only by obeying her." In his thought-kingdom, science is made the civilizer that binds man to man. Nevertheless, he was solicitous lest the ways of a harsh world corrupt his ideal, and took measures to prevent change and at the same time introduce new " light " from abroad! In speaking of the foundation of the Atlantidean régime by the good King Salomana, he says:

This King . . . therefore, taking into consideration how sufficient and substantive this land was, to maintain itself without any aid at all of the foreigner . . . and recalling into his memory the happy and flourishing state wherein this land then was, so as it might be a thousand ways altered to the worse, but scarce any one way to the better; though nothing wanted to his noble and heroical intentions, but only (as far as human foresight might reach) to give perpetuity to that which was in his time so happily established, therefore among his other fundamental laws . . . he did ordain the interdicts and prohibitions which we have touching the entrance of strangers . . . doubting novelty and commixture of manners . . . this restraint of ours hath only one exception, which is admirable; preserving the good which cometh by communicating with strangers, and avoiding the hurt. . . .

When the king had forbidden to all his people navigation into any part that was not under his crown, he nevertheless made this ordinance; that every twelve years there should be sent forth out of this kingdom two ships, appointed to several voyages; that in either of these ships there should be a mission of three of the fellows or brethren of Salo-man's House [an institute for research], whose errand was only to give us knowledge of the affairs and state of those countries to which they were designed; and especially of the sciences, arts, manufactures and inventions of all the world; and withal to bring unto us books, instruments and patterns in every kind . . . thus you see we maintain a trade, not for gold, silver, or jewels, nor for silks, nor for spices, nor any other commodity of matter; but only for God's first creature, which was light; to have light . . . of the growth of all parts of the world.[31]

Evidently Bacon wanted to eat his cake and have it too — wanted to have the technical, scientific, and other benefits of culture contact without the changes in mores and institutions such contact engenders. Wary of " commixture of manners," he yet fancied that the material culture of a people could change and still leave the cherished precepts and laws of good King Salomana with as much effectiveness as ever. Had he read Cicero as carefully as he had read Plato and Aristotle, he would have perceived that even when people " do not desert their native country in person, their minds are always expatiating and voyaging around the world." Mental mobility apparently may be the result of indirect culture contact, and does not necessarily involve migration on the part of the person acquiring such mobility; there may be " vicarious migration."

Bacon was also responsible for the reissue of the proverb *Magna civitas magna solitudo,* " a great city, a great desert "; his comment, too, is enlightening — " because in a great town friends are scattered, so that there is not that fellowship, for the most part, which is in less neighborhoods." [32] In other words, he said that (1) social isolation may be concomitant with the extreme vicinal accessibility of the city; and that (2) the more intimate relationships of the sacred society or primary group are likely to be wanting in urban centers.

Thomas Campanella was Bacon's contemporary, a man only seven years younger; he was an Italian Dominican who suffered in the cause of the new science. Caught between the fire of the Spanish Inquisition and the rising tide of the Protestant revolt, he was seven times tortured for his heresies. His utopia, *The City of the Sun*, was written during his twenty-seven years in prison before his final escape to the France of Richelieu, where his writings were declared orthodox by the Sorbonne. One might expect something very startling to come out of such catastrophic vicissitudes, but truth to tell, there is very little in *The City of the Sun* that is comparable even to the backward-looking radicalism of More or the scientific heterodoxy of Bacon. For our purposes he merely serves as the ever-present exception that proves the rule; he was comparatively tolerant of strangers, apparently not seeing in them the source of Bacon's dreaded " corruption of manners ":

To strangers they are kind and polite; they keep them for three days at the public expense; after they have first washed their feet, they show them their city and its customs, and they honor them with a seat at the Council and public tables, and there are men whose duty it is to take care of and guard the guests. But if strangers should wish to become citizens of their State, they try them first a month on a farm, and for another month in the city, then they decide concerning them, and admit them with certain ceremonies and oaths.[33]

Some misgivings concerning culture contact Campanella apparently had, but they were not very grave. In fact, he shows little insight into the processes of social change; he puts no such limitations on travel as does More, for instance. Apparently the institutions of his city are so superior that other nations will adopt them in preference to their own:

They navigate for the sake of becoming acquainted with nations and different countries and things. . . . They assert that the whole earth will in time come to live in accordance with their customs. . . .[34]

Perhaps the only significant thing in this quotation is his recognition of the fact that the dominance of one culture pattern is theoretically possible, and that communication or purposeful diffusion may play a large part in spreading such a pattern. By and large, however, Campanella's utopia is of antiquarian interest only; it throws little light on the course of social thought.

Fear of the new is somewhat more evident in the work of James Harrington, the author of the detailed and prolix utopia, *Oceana* (name indicative of the expansion of Europe!), published in 1656 during the time of the Commonwealth. When the Restoration put an end to the Cromwellian régime, Harrington was thrown in jail, where he suffered from scurvy and at last became insane. When he had been made a complete wreck in body and mind, his gracious Majesty restored Harrington to his family. In spite of his enfeebled health, Harrington had the urge to write as strongly as ever, and he composed a long treatise to the effect that " they were themselves mad who thought him so." But mad or not, only one short passage from the *Oceana* seems relevant here :

> Lacedæmon, being governed by a King and a small Senate, could maintain itself a long time in that condition, because the inhabitants, being few, having put a bar upon the reception of strangers, and living in a strict observance of the laws of Lycurgus . . . might well continue long in tranquillity. For . . . not receiving strangers into their commonwealth, they did not corrupt it.[35]

Here is apparent not merely the influence of Plato but of the sacred society from which Plato himself derived his ideal — Sparta, " archfoe of democracy, determined enemy of innovation, and most unintellectual of all Greek societies."

Enough has been said by now to show that the Humanistic influence on the utopian writers was not productive of a zealous desire to escape from the vestiges of medievalism everywhere evident in the sixteenth century, but rather to realize a completely strait-jacketed social order, a society more static than the much-abused Middle Ages ever saw. We may best characterize the utopians, therefore, as reactionary radicals.

Thomas More and the Details of His Utopia. — This reactionary radicalism is especially evident in the work of Sir Thomas More (1478–1535), the leading North European social philosopher of the period of Machiavelli. He was a devout Catholic to the end of his days; several times was on the verge of becoming a " religious," once in the rôle of a Carthusian monk; and was a Humanist to whom even the learned Erasmus paid deference. There can be little doubt that along with the influence of his beloved Plato went a strong infusion of Apostolic, Patristic, and Scholastic social theory. More is noted for his incisive indictment of the social evils of his time, and more particularly for the ideal commonwealth (modeled, as we have noted, along the lines of Plato's *Republic*) which he outlined as a remedy for these evils. More's *Utopia* left very little if any more freedom to the individual than did Plato's scheme, in spite of the fact that he regarded his plan as immediately practicable, whereas Plato admitted that only " when kings are philosophers, or philosophers are kings " would his ideal be possible of realization.

The *Utopia* was a reaction against the miseries attendant upon the early Commercial Revolution in England. The practice of raising wool for the export trade with Flanders carried with it a tremendous number of enclosures and their accompanying evictions. Vagabondage and pauperism were the fate of the yeomen dispossessed of their holdings during the fifteenth and sixteenth centuries. Confusing effect with cause, laws were passed to stop wandering in the hope of thereby quelling social unrest (More was equally shortsighted, as the passages already quoted show), but in spite of all the penalties, thousands of " sturdy beggars " footed it up hill and down dale, aimlessly searching for something they could not name. In addition to his attack upon enclosures and sheep-raising, More also criticized other phases of the Commercial Revolution, such as the growth of monopoly and private property in the means of production. He also attacked the cruel criminal law and drastic punishments then in vogue in England and throughout Europe, the extravagance of supporting a standing army in idleness, and numerous other evils of his time. As a fair example of More's gift for invective may be quoted his diatribe against the enclosures :

But yet this [the keeping of an idle standing army] is not only the necessary cause of stealing. There is another, which, as I suppose, is proper and peculiar to you Englishmen alone. What is that, quoth the Cardinal? forsooth my lord (quoth I) your sheep that were wont to be so meek and tame, and so small eaters, now, as I hear say, be become so great devourers and so wild, that they eat up, and swallow down the very men themselves. They consume, destroy, and devour whole fields, houses, and cities. For look in what parts of the realm doth grow the finest and therefore dearest wool, there noblemen and gentlemen, yea and certain abbots, holy men no doubt, not contenting themselves with the yearly revenues and profits, that were wont to grow to their forefathers and predecessors of their lands, nor being content that they live in rest and pleasure nothing profiting, yea much annoying the weal public, leave no ground for tillage, they inclose it all into pastures; they throw down houses; they pluck down towns, and leave nothing standing, but only the church to be made a sheep-house. And as though you lost no small quantity of ground by forests, chases, lawns, and parks, these good holy men turn all dwelling-places and all glebeland into desolation and wilderness. Therefore that one covetous and insatiable cormorant and very plague of his native country may compass about and inclose many thousand acres of ground together within one pale or hedge, the husbandmen be thrust out of their own, or else either by cunning or fraud, or by violent oppression they be put besides it, or by wrongs and injuries they be so wearied, that they be compelled to sell all: by one means therefore or by other, either by hook or crook they must needs depart away, poor, silly, wretched souls, men, women, husbands, wives, fatherless children, widows, woeful mothers, with their young babes, and their whole household small in substance and much in number, as husbandry requireth many hands. Away they trudge, I say, out of their known and accustomed houses, finding no place to rest in. All their household stuff, which is very little worth, though it might well abide the sale: yet being suddenly thrust out, they be constrained to sell it for a thing of nought. And when they have wandered abroad till that be spent, what can they then else do but steal, and then justly pardy be hanged, or else go about a begging. And yet then also they be cast in prison as vagabonds, because they go about and work not: whom no man will set a work, though they never so willingly proffer themselves thereto. For one shepherd or herdsman is enough to eat up that ground with cattle, to the occupying whereof about husbandry many hands were requisite.[36]

In the constructive part of his program for social rehabilitation was a plan for a socialistic community where all the shortcomings which he found in his own day and generation were to be eliminated. More has therefore been called the father of modern socialism by some writers, but this is wholly inaccurate. In the first place, he was not even the father of so-called utopian socialism: Hebrew prophets, Chinese sages, Plato, and many of the exponents of a golden-age social philosophy have equal claim to the title. All that More contributed was a striking modernization of the perennial hope and a name that caught the popular fancy. In the second place, " utopian " socialism is undoubtedly poles removed from the " scientific " variety, whatever one may think of either. No one was more zealous in pointing out the deficiencies of the former than was the man whose name is most often linked with the latter, Karl Marx — unless it was his *alter ego* Engels, with his devastating book, *Socialism, Utopian and Scientific.*

The salient features of the second book of the *Utopia,* wherein More builds up his constructive theory, may be epitomized as follows:

(1) The abolition of private property.

(2) The division of labor according to common-sense methods and general adaptability.

(3) The retention of family life as the unit of social organization — herein differing markedly from Plato.

(4) The abolition of money as the " root of all evil."

(5) The reduction of the working day to six hours, with due

provision for recreation, education, and protection against the entry of what More regarded as vice.

(6) Freedom of religious belief.

(7) A government monarchical in form, but providing for the election of the monarch by the people through an indirect process.

How different these proposals were from the conditions then in vogue is apparent to all familiar with the history of the period. More made the following defense of the abolition of private property:

> Now I have declared and described unto you, as truly as I could the form and order of that commonwealth, which verily in my judgment is not only the best, but also that which alone of good right may claim and take upon it the name of a commonwealth or public weal. For in other places they speak still of the commonwealth, but every man procureth his own private gain. Here where nothing is private, the common affairs may be earnestly looked upon. And truly on both parts they have good cause so to do as they do. For in other countries who knoweth not that he shall starve for hunger, unless he make some several provision for himself, though the commonwealth flourish never so much in riches? And therefore he is compelled even of very necessity to have regard to himself, rather than to the people, that is to say, to other. Contrawise there, where all things be common to every man, it is not to be doubted that any man shall lack anything necessary for his private uses, so that the common storehouses and barns be sufficiently stored. For here nothing is distributed after a niggardly sort, neither there is any poor man or beggar. And though no man have anything, yet every man is rich. For what can be more rich, than to live joyfully and merrily, without all grief and pensiveness; not caring for his own living, nor vexed or troubled with his wife's importunate complaints, nor dreading poverty to his son, nor sorrowing for his daughter's dowry? . . . Here now would I see, if any man dare be so bold as to compare with this equity, the justice of other nations; among whom, I forsake God, if I can find any sign or token of equity and justice.[37]

In the matter of the division of labor he is not as solicitous or thoroughgoing as Plato, for the latter viewed the question from the political as well as the industrial standpoint. Of this principle More says:

> Husbandry is a science common to them all in general, both men and women, wherein they be all expert and cunning. In this they be all instructed even from their youth: partly in their schools with traditions and precepts, and partly in the country nigh the city, brought up as it were in playing, not only beholding the use of it, but by occasion of exercising their bodies practising it also. Besides husbandry, which (as I

said) is common to them all, every one of them learneth one or other several and particular science, as his own proper craft. That is most commonly either clothworking in wool or flax, or masonry, or the smith's craft, or the carpenter's science. For there is none other occupation that any number to speak of doth use here. . . . But of the other aforesaid crafts every man learneth one. And not only the men, but also the women. But the women, as the weaker sort, be put to the easier crafts: as to work wool and flax. The more laboursome sciences be committed to the men. For the most part every man is brought up in his father's craft. For most commonly they be naturally thereto bent and inclined. But if a man's mind stand to any other, he is by adoption put into a family of that occupation, which he doth most fantasy. Whom not only his father, but also the magistrates do diligently look to, that he be put to a discreet and an honest householder. Yea, and if any person, when he has learned one craft, be desirous to learn also another, he is likewise suffered and permitted.

When he hath learned both, he occupieth whether he will: unless the city have more need of the one, than of the other. The chief and almost the only office of the syphogrants [magistrates elected by every thirty families] is, to see and take heed that no man sit idle: but that every one apply his own craft with earnest diligence.[38]

More made the following naïve provision for family life, the regulation of numbers, emigration, and colonization in his Utopian kingdom:

But now I will declare how the citizens use themselves one towards another: what familiar occupying and entertainment there is among the people, and what fashion they use in the distribution of every thing. First the city consisteth of families, the families most commonly be made of kindreds. For the women, when they be married at a lawful age, they go into their husbands' houses. But the male children with all the whole male offspring continue still in their own family and be governed by the eldest and ancientest father, unless he dote for age: for then the next to him in age is placed in his room. But to the intent the prescript number of the citizens should neither decrease, nor above measure increase, it is ordained that no family which in every city be six thousand in the whole, besides them of the country, shall at once have fewer children of the age of fourteen years or thereabout than ten or more than sixteen, for of children under this age no number can be prescribed or appointed. This measure or number is easily observed and kept, by putting them that in fuller families be above the number into families of smaller increase. But if chance be that in the whole city the store increase above the just number, therewith they fill up the lack of other cities. But if so be that the multitude throughout the whole island pass and exceed the due number, then they choose out of every city certain citizens, and build up a town under their own laws in the next land where the inhabitants have much waste and unoccupied ground, receiving also of the same country people to them, if they will join and dwell with them.[39]

Even the upholders of traditional domination in preliterate societies, the elders, have more social *savoir faire* than this! They know that " of children under this age " — fourteen — a " number " *can* be " prescribed and appointed "; population increase is not left to chance. Further, More seems never to have had the least inkling of the fact that " waste and unoccupied ground " would not always be available if population increased at the rate he calmly contemplated. To be sure, he did propose that the Utopians systematically colonize vacant territory, but the essential difficulty still remains.

Many other more or less ingenious or ingenuous devices were outlined by More, but they must be passed over for lack of space. The quotations given are sufficient to indicate the general tenor of the work for which he is famous. Although he was doubtless inspired by the loftiest and most unselfish motives, his scheme comes in for much of the justified criticism that Aristotle directed against Plato's proposals, to take no more recent attack into account. More was an honest man, and he knowingly paid for his integrity with his life when he clashed with Henry VIII, first over the latter's assumption of the headship of the English church, and second over his royal master's divorce of Catherine and marriage to Anne Boleyn. If sterling character, coupled with wit and a Latin style second only to that of Erasmus among his contemporaries, could gain for More high rank as a great social thinker, his place would be assured. Inasmuch as these things, excellent as they are, do not enter into the estimate, we must say, on the basis of the *Utopia,* that he was not a theorist of the first rank — whereas the morally suspect Machiavelli, for example, was. Let us conclude by quoting Mims's strikingly apt characterization: More was " an essentially reactionary idealist who, beneath his enthusiasm for the new currents of Humanism, strove to perpetuate the paternalistic spirit of the rapidly disintegrating medieval world " (see note 41).

The Negative Intellectual Effect of the Protestant Revolution and the Catholic Reaction. — Even less than the Renaissance did the movements conventionally known as the Reformation and Counter-Reformation *directly* promote a scientific and critical point of view or encourage interest in mundane and secular affairs. It has been assumed by many that the Renaissance produced the Reformation, but it seems that this is true only in the sense of a somewhat ironical remark once made by Robinson to the effect that the mythical Renaissance may have caused the mythical Reformation. Between Humanism and Protestantism there was little real intellectual affinity or genetic relationship, however much there may have been of personal identity and interrelationship between Humanists and Reformers. If any of the Protestant Reformers derived inspiration from the Humanists, it was from the piety and Christianity of the scholars and not from their Humanism. If Luther was impelled to ecclesiastical and doctrinal reform by his study of Erasmus's writings, it was due to the ideas of Erasmus the Christian and not to those of Erasmus the Humanist. The exuberance of Erasmus over the writings and doctrines of St. Cicero could never have been the starting point for the theological views and intellectual attitudes of a Luther, a Calvin, a Baxter, or a Knox. Cicero's motto, " We who search for hypotheses are prepared both to refute without prejudice and to be contradicted without resentment," could hardly have been the fountain-spring whence Calvin derived the canons of hospitality applied in his treatment of Servetus.[40]

The important point is that, strictly speaking, Humanism, on the one hand, and Lutheranism and Calvinism, on the other, were fundamentally divergent and opposed. Humanism was a moderate and rather unconscious revolt against the otherworldliness of Patristic and Scholastic Christianity; the Protestant revolt brought with it an all-pervading revival of even the grosser forms of supernaturalism, diabolism, miracle-mongering, witchcraft, and a host of other phases of this general culture-complex. In short, Humanism and the Reformation were highly divergent in general cultural orientation and intellectual outlook, and we may agree with Erasmus that if Luther hatched the egg which he (Erasmus) had laid, it was quite a different bird from that which Erasmus had intended. Smith's criticism of Pearson's lack of superior and definitive erudition on such matters as the Renaissance and Reformation is undoubtedly justifiable, but it seems that Pearson stumbled on materials which led him to formulate exactly the correct interpretation of the divergent viewpoints of Erasmus and Luther in the famous chapters of his *Ethic of Free Thought*.[41]

Some Protestants have taken great pride in the elimination of many alleged idolatrous practices of the Catholics which was effected by the Reformation, but their exultation rests upon dubious foundations. By so doing they enormously weakened the emotional power of the church and took from it one of its most potent forces, the aesthetic appeal to eye and ear. The rich emotion-bearing ritual and liturgy of the Catholic Church is far better adapted to attracting and holding the mass of faithful believers than the metaphysical dogmatism of Calvin or the savage vocal emotionalism of our evangelical Protestant sects of the cruder sort. And no candid critical observer is likely to regard the miracle of the mass and its attendant ritual, or the images of Jesus, the Virgin, and the Saints, as more or less pagan and idolatrous than baptism or various phases of Protestant soteriology and theology. The necessary and desirable qualifications upon exuberance over the higher intellectual tone of Protestantism have been formulated thus:

The defection of the Protestants from the Roman Catholic Church is not connected with any decisive intellectual revision. Such ardent emphasis has been constantly placed upon the differences between Protestantism and Catholicism by representatives of both parties that the close intellectual resemblance of the two systems, indeed their identity in nine parts out of ten, has tended to escape us. The early Protestants, of course, accepted, as did the Catholics, the whole patristic outlook on the world; their historical perspective was similar, their notions of the origin of man, of the Bible, with its types, prophecies and miracles, of heaven and hell, of demons and angels, are all identical. To the early Protestants, as to Catholics, he who would be saved must accept the doctrine of the triune God and must be ever on his guard against the whisperings of reason and the innovations suggested by scientific advance. Luther and Melanchthon denounced Copernicus in the name of the Bible. Melanchthon re-edited, with enthusiastic approval, Ptolemy's astrology. Luther made repeated and bitter attacks upon reason, in whose eyes he freely confessed the presuppositions of Christianity to be absurd. Calvin gloried in man's initial and inherent moral impotency; and the doctrine of predestination seemed calculated to paralyze all human effort.

The Protestants did not know any more about nature than their Catholic enemies; they were just as completely victimized by the demonology of witchcraft. The Protestant revolt was not begotten of added scientific knowledge, nor did it owe its success to any considerable confidence in criticism. As Gibbon pointed out, the loss of one conspicuous mystery, that of transubstantiation — " was amply compensated by the stupendous doctrines of original sin, redemption, faith, grace, and predestination " which the Protestants strained from the epistles of St. Paul. Early Protestantism is, from an intellectual standpoint, essentially a phase of medieval religious history.[42]

Without attempting in any way to pass judgment upon the theological merits of the positions taken by Protestant Reformers, it may be pointed out that the majority of historians have now accepted the view that the great significance of the Reformation lay in the political and economic movements associated with it, rather

than in the purely religious and theological problems and issues
involved. In line with the suggestions made long ago by Sleidanus
and Harrington, contemporary writers — among them Max
Weber, Troeltsch, and Tawney — have shown that the most vital
phases of the Reformation period were the rise of independent
sovereign states and of those ideals and practices of the modern
bourgeois business-man which God was supposed to have initiated
and to have given his unqualified approval.[43]

Intellectually speaking, the Reformation was most decidedly
backward-looking. Theologically it assumed to go back to the
Apostolic age. Luther denounced the universities, designated reason as the devil's most seductive harlot, reveled in devil- and miracle-mongering, *and was the first important European to condemn
the Copernican theory*. The philosophical anthropology of Calvin, with its morbid basis in the concept of human treason before
God, and his predestinarian theology are alike intellectually depressing and abhorrent. And no person could be less sympathetic
with science and critical philosophy than a fanatic like Knox.
Moreover, the Protestant emphasis on the infallible nature of the
Bible was in some ways more dangerous and obstructive to scientific advance than the Catholic dogma of an infallible church
which might periodically alter its tenets *sub rosa* or *Rota*.[44]

About the only contribution to the rise of the secular spirit
which can be assigned to Protestantism is the indirect aid which it
gave to rebels against ecclesiastical tyranny over the freedom of
expression. This was foreseen and deplored by Bossuet. As he
clearly pointed out, once the unity of Christendom had been
broken by the Protestants, there was no reason why the process
should not go on indefinitely and lead to the multiplication of innumerable Protestant sects, thus making it impossible to enforce
any unity of doctrine. It was in this matter of rendering ecclesiastical interference with thought less easy and effective, through
promoting the disunity of Christian belief and organization, that
Protestantism aided, if at all, in advancing the secular *Weltanschauung*. In a minor sense Calvinism, with its emphasis on the
God-given calling of money-making, may be said to have promoted
those phases of applied science that have been closely related to
modern industry and the practical applications of the " theory of
business enterprise." [45]

The reaction of the Protestant revolt on Catholicism was in-
tellectually more disastrous than its effect upon the followers of
Luther and Calvin. The cultural degradation which came with the
Catholic defense-reaction in the Counter-Reformation can best be

gauged by the contrast between a typical pre-Reformation Catholic like Erasmus and the most characteristic figure in Counter-Reformation Catholicism, Ignatius Loyola. Although no movement founded by an Erasmus could have produced a Voltaire, as the most cursory comparison of the *Adages* with the *Philosophical Dictionary* will readily demonstrate, neither would it have naturally led to the creation of the Jesuit order. The church had been growing more tolerant and more appreciative of secular learning, but it was put on the defensive by the Protestant assaults and soon felt it necessary to recover, revivify, and vigorously defend dogmas which had been allowed partially to lapse.[46] Protestantism and Counter-Reformation Catholicism collaborated in enacting one of the most degrading and depressing scenes in the history of Western civilization — the witchcraft mania of the sixteenth and seventeenth centuries.[47]

Indirect Protestant Influence on Social Thought. — In its *indirect* effects upon social theory and practice the Protestant revolt made for three things in particular: nationalism, capitalism, and Puritanism. The princes of northern Europe were eager to escape from the control and financial exactions imposed by that greatest of international states, the Roman Catholic Church. Seeing in Luther's theological revolt a convenient moral cloak for their secular ambitions, these rulers, following the lead of Frederick the Wise of Saxony, supported Protestantism with enthusiasm. The great rallying-point was the *cuius regio euius religio* clause of the Peace of Augsburg (1555), but the princes were more interested in the *regio* than in the *religio,* and the " religious " wars did not cease until independent national sovereignty was recognized in western Europe at the close of the Thirty Years' War in the terms of the Treaty of Westphalia. We may therefore say that Protestantism coöperated with the capitalistic revolution in supplanting feudalism by national centralization, and thus indirectly fostered changes in social thought.

Protestantism made an attractive appeal to another group in western Europe; namely, the rising middle class which had been created by medieval industry and commerce, particularly by the trade with the Levant during and after the Crusades. With the expansion of Europe overseas the bourgeoisie were still further strengthened, and at the same time they found the medieval Catholic restrictions on business enterprise ever more irksome. They welcomed Protestantism as a movement of revolt from restrictive Catholic ideals and precepts in the economic field. Luther gave little encouragement to rising capitalism, but Calvin was reasonably sympathetic, and especially praised the virtues of thrift and pecuniary accumulation. Soon Protestant divines were preaching from the parable of the three stewards and from the perverted text, " Seek ye not your own but your neighbor's wealth." Money-making was soon represented as the most God-given of secular achievements; the medieval limitations on the profit economy were rapidly abrogated. The ethic of Protestantism was quickly and thoroughly adapted to the spirit of capitalism and business enterprise.

Calvinism and Capitalism. — One of the most enlightening contributions of sociology to the analysis of religious structures is the revelation, as set forth by Max Weber and others, of the link between capitalism and Calvinism. Despite the overstatements made by some of Weber's uncritical followers, there is little doubt that a close relation has existed in modern times between these two movements, and that they have profoundly influenced each other. For present purposes it may be stated that the Calvinistic religious bodies were representative of the middle class, and that the rise and development of these bodies was conditioned by the economic interests of the bourgeoisie, who in turn owed their position as a trading and capitalist class to the faith established by Calvin at Geneva.

The spatial distribution of this form of Protestantism coincided at an early date with the vicinal location of the rising commercial classes : Swiss cities on the trade routes between northern and southern Europe; the commercial cities of France; the provinces bordering on the Rhine, that aorta of the early Commercial Revolution; the Netherlands, with their highly developed banking and commerce and their extensive shipping activity; England, in which Calvinistic Puritanism and the new capitalism arrived together a hundred years later than on the Continent; and finally, America, the scene where both Calvinism and commercialism have achieved their most complete triumphs. Venice and Florence, it should be noted, were also sympathetic to the faith, but certain factors which cannot be discussed within present space limitations prevented any thorough and permanent acceptance. There is one notable exception to the spatial coincidence of commercialism and Calvinism — Scotland; that country lacked a bourgeois class and, just as in Germany, the nobility provided the fighting front of the Protestant revolt. In the course of time, however, the association of commercialism and Calvinism also became established among the Scots, to a degree that was not paralleled in some of the countries where the correlation was earliest manifest.

The mentality of the bourgeoisie contains certain constant features which are reflected in Calvinistic religious organization and doctrine. Among these the most important are the high development of self-consciousness and the prevalence of an activist attitude toward life. To these primary factors others of secondary importance may be added: the general high level of culture and education, the financial security and physical comfort in evidence, the sense of class superiority which is fostered, and the direct effect of business and trade upon its code of ethics. All in all, it may be said that the net result of these factors is the tendency of the Calvinistic bourgeois to think in terms of persons more than of forces, and in terms of personal merit and demerit more than of fortune and fate.

Protestantism and Puritanism. — The third in the trinity of major tendencies forwarded by the Protestant defection from Rome was Puritanism, or " intra-worldly asceticism." This rested upon four major foundations. In the first place, the Protestants alleged that the Roman Church had been becoming too worldly in the centuries before Luther; hence they tended to stress purity and withdrawal from fleshly activities. They were scarcely consistent, however, as may be seen in Luther's attitude toward the marriage of the clergy and toward sexual relations, and in the enthusiasm of the Protestant business classes for economic aggrandizement. In the second place, the Protestants laid more stress upon the word of Scripture than did the Catholics; they really revived the Old Testament. This was full of restrictive regulations; e.g., the Sabbatarian laws. The Protestants thus tended to give a new vitality and currency to ancient prescriptions which limited personal freedom with great severity. Finally, the commercial classes among the Protestants, preëminently the Calvinistic Puritans, were engaged at the time in various practices which were economically and ethically of somewhat dubious character, though by no means as severely judged then as now. We refer to such enterprises as the slave trade, the rum trade, smuggling, semilegalized piracy, and the like. In order to allay their consciences the Puritans gave special attention to worship throughout the week as well as on the Sabbath, and to restrictions making for " purity " (especially chastity) in personal life. They frowned severely upon earthly indulgences and upon the ways of the flesh. Protestantism therefore tended to inculcate a rather negative type of morality, and also served to make it more a matter of sexual chastity than of social justice and altruism. This view of ethics has been peculiarly appropriate to capitalism and has been zealously promulgated by the custodians of the contemporary economic order.

Let us now examine the relation of Puritanism (especially of the Calvinistic type) and bourgeois capitalism a little more closely.

The dropping of the *concilia evangelica* by Protestant groups meant for them the disappearance of the dualistic extra-worldly asceticism of Catholicism. The stern religious characters who had previously gone into monasteries now had to practice their religion in the light of the world. For such an intra-worldly asceticism an adequate ethic was gradually created through the dogmatic pronouncements of Protestant divines. Celibacy was not required, marriage being viewed simply as an institution for the rational bringing up of children; sexual intercourse was supposed to be confined to purposes of reproduction. Poverty was not required, as in some of the Catholic orders, but the pursuit and administration of wealth were brought under the doctrine of stewardship; the wealthy man could not wander astray into reckless enjoyment, but had to conduct his life along rational and ascetic lines in accordance with the divine plan. Thus Sebastian Franck was correct in summing up the spirit of Calvinism in the words, " You think you have escaped from the monastery, but everyone must now be a monk throughout his life."

The wide significance of this transformation of the ethical ideal can be followed down to the present in the countries where Protestant intra-worldly asceticism has reached its highest development. It was until very recent times plainly evident in those portions of the United States most influenced by Calvinism. Although the church and the state are separate, nevertheless no person in a position requiring public confidence — lawyer, banker, or physician — could lightly ignore religious affiliations; when he took residence in a new community he was always asked to what religious body he belonged, and his prospects were good or bad according to the answer he returned. The motto " Honesty is the best policy " is eminently Calvinistic, an expression of intra-worldly asceticism, not a mere slogan of cynical opportunism. It is based on the belief that God will take care of his own, the belief in predestination, election, and reprobation. Moreover, it must be said that the belief received ample pragmatic verification; as one English Calvinist put it: " The Godless cannot trust each other across the road; they turn to us when they want to do business; piety is the surest road to wealth." For a modern statement of this same Calvinistic confidence, the reader need turn only to the utterances of Roger W. Babson. Such men are not at all hypocritical or giving vent to " cant "; they are merely expressing certain logical consequences of Calvinism.

The acquisition of wealth, made easier if not possible by intra-worldly asceticism, led to a dilemma in all respects similar to that into which the medieval monasteries fell: the efficiency possible in a sternly ascetic community led to wealth, wealth to luxury, luxury to fall from grace, and this again to the necessity of conviction of sin and renewed asceticism. Calvinism sought to avoid this difficulty by the theory of stewardship; man was only an administrator of what God had given him. All fleshly joys — gluttony, intemperance, concupiscence — were roundly condemned, but were not to be evaded by flying from the world into monastic seclusion. On the contrary, the person who would be sure of his state of grace was required to prove it to himself and others by a specific type of conduct unmistakably different from the way of life followed by the " natural man." This desire for proof of salvation gave the person an incentive methodically to supervise a state of grace in his own conduct, and thus to penetrate it with asceticism. Such ascetic conduct meant a rational planning of the whole of one's life in accordance with the assumed will of God; moreover, it could be required of everyone who laid claim to salvation. The religious life of the saints, as distinguished from the natural life, was no longer to be extra-worldly, to be cut off from the currents of daily existence by the walls of the monastic community, but was to be intra-worldly — in the world and yet not of it. This rationalization of conduct in the press and bustle of worldly affairs for the sake of the world beyond was the consequence of the concept of " calling " inherent in ascetic Calvinism. Weber has discussed this as follows:

> Christian asceticism, at first fleeing from the world into solitude, had already ruled the world which it had renounced from the monastery and through the Church. But it had, on the whole, left the naturally spontaneous character of daily life in the world untouched. Now it strode into the market-place of life, slammed the door of the monastery behind it, and undertook to penetrate just that daily routine of life with its methodicalness, to fashion it into a life *in* the world, but neither *of* nor *for* this world.

The rationalistic type of conduct inaugurated by the Calvinistic concept of " calling " quickly gave to the entrepreneur following this belief a fabulously clear conscience and — what was perhaps of greater importance — assured him of faithful and industrious workers if they too were Calvinists. The reward of the ascetic devotion practiced by the Calvinistic employee was the evidence of eternal salvation. This was to such persons complete compensation for their ruthless self-exploitation in the interests of their similarly ascetic exploiter, for the evidence of salvation, in an age when religious discipline took control of the whole of life to an extent inconceivable to us now, represented a reality quite different from any it has today. In the Calvinistic church admission to the Lord's Supper was granted only to the ethically fit, and their ethical fitness was in turn identified with business honor — while no one inquired into the actual content of the "bloodless bundle of logical categories" formally held as the faith requisite to salvation. So powerful and so subtly although unconsciously refined an organization for the production of capitalistically-minded individuals has never existed in any other church or religion. Calvinistic Puritanism and modern capitalism for a long time went hand in hand.[48]

Protestant Support for Secular Absolutism. — In relation to the state, Protestantism tended to stress the absolute power and divine right of the secular ruler. This proceeded from two sources. In the first place, the divine right of the king was advanced in Protestant lands as a substitute for and check upon the divine right of the pope. In the second place, Protestantism owed its success to the support of friendly secular rulers, and therefore was not loth to second their claims to temporal absolutism. This led them to adopt the Pauline doctrine of passive obedience. Luther, while not much given to theorizing about politics and not much interested in the state as such, was nevertheless positive enough in his support of passive obedience, as Allen shows:

. . . no true Christian can set himself so to oppose his ruler, be he good or evil, but will rather suffer all manner of injustice. The Scriptures speak quite plainly. God has commanded obedience to magistrates in all things lawful by the law of God and has forbidden active resistance in any case and for any cause. The inferior magistrate must obey his superior; the duty of the common man is simply to obey the magistrate. "God Almighty has made our princes mad"; but he has ordered us to obey them; and whoso resisteth shall receive damnation. It is not a question of how magistrates came to be where they are. Luther insists simply that God has commanded obedience to such magistrates as there are. Simply because this is so and for no other reason whatever, we must regard our magistrates, good or bad, as set over us by God. "I will side always," he declared in 1520, "with him, however unjust, who endures rebellion and against him who rebels, however justly." To plead rights in the face of God's plain command is impious as well as illogical.[49]

Calvin accepted the doctrine of passive obedience as thoroughly as Luther and stated it at far greater length. On this point he was completely logical and consistent. The king was to be obeyed in all commands which did not expressly violate the revealed will of God. No matter what the degree of secular injustice and oppression, the subject should obey his ruler and trust to God to punish oppressive and wicked princes. The following sentences from Calvin's *Institutes of the Christian Religion* amply illustrate Calvin's extreme concessions to the principle of passive obedience:

The first duty of subjects towards their rulers, is to entertain the most honorable views of their office, recognizing it as a delegated jurisdiction from God, and on that account receiving and reverencing them as the ministers and ambassadors of God. . . .

From this, a second consequence is, that we must with ready minds prove our obedience to them, whether in complying with edicts, or in paying tribute, or in undertaking public offices and burdens which relate to the common defence, or in executing any other orders. " Let every soul," says Paul, " be subject unto the highest powers." " Whosoever, therefore, resisteth the power, resisteth the ordinance of God " (Rom. xiii, 1, 2). . . .

But if we have respect to the word of God, it will lead us farther, and make us subject not only to the authority of those princes who honestly and faithfully perform their duty toward us, but all princes, by whatever means they have so become, although there is nothing they less perform than the duty of princes.

. . . whatever may be thought of the acts of the men themselves, the Lord by their means equally executed his own work when he broke the bloody sceptres of insolent kings, and overthrew their intolerable dominations. Let princes hear and be afraid; but let us at the same time guard most carefully against spurning or violating the venerable and majestic authority of rulers, an authority which God has sanctioned by the surest edicts, although those invested with it should be most unworthy of it, and, as far as in them lies, pollute it by their iniquity.[50]

Melanchthon and Natural Law. — Philip Melanchthon, the third of the trio of leading early Protestant Reformers, also accepted the conception of royal absolutism and passive obedience in most of his formal writings on the subject, but also he brought into his social and political philosophy a doctrine which, with later modifications and elaborations, was designed to constitute the foremost justification of resistance to tyrannical government: namely, the theory of natural law and natural right. Melanchthon's view of natural law was, to be sure, much more theological and less cosmological and historical than the early view of the Stoics or the later conceptions of the contract school, but it contained within itself the germs of what became in the hands of John Locke the cornerstone of the doctrine of rightful rebellion. To quote Dunning's summary:

Melanchthon's system is based on the concept of natural right (*ius naturae*) or, what is the same thing from a different point of view, natural law (*lex naturae*). This law consists in the perception which God has implanted in the human mind of the practical principles concerning, first, the existence of God himself and the obedience due to him; and second, the civil institutions which promote his glory. The precepts of natural law are summarized in the Decalogue, of which the first table (i.e. the first four commandments) determines man's duty toward God, and the second table (the last six commandments) his duty toward his fellow-man. Whatever institutions may be logically based on the Decalogue, therefore, are in accordance with natural right; but this direct revelation of God's will is not the only source from which the law of nature may be derived. The nature or end of man furnishes immediately and without demonstration certain universal principles (*sententiae communes*) — such, for example, as that man is adapted to social life — from which it is possible to derive by reasoning the practical rules of right living. Whatever may be logically deduced from these principles of human nature, therefore, must be considered as included under natural law as well as under the law of God. It is the business of philosophy — as distinct from theology — to detect and explain these fundamental principles that are written in nature, and by reason to determine in accordance with them the arrangements that are essential to physical existence.[51]

We may now pass on to a detailed consideration of the doctrine of the divine right of kings — a doctrine which in its early modern form grew primarily out of the practical necessities imposed by the secession of the Protestant princes from the jurisdiction of the Holy See.

The Divine Right of Kings. — The doctrine that kings rule by divine right is an old one, far antedating its popularity in the sixteenth and seventeenth centuries. Early preliterate peoples believed in the charismatic basis of the political power of the chieftains, and often construed charisma as religious mana.[52] In the ancient Orient the kings were viewed as at least in part divine.[53] The Hebrews represented the kings as having been indirectly chosen and approved by God through the process of having the kings announced and anointed by the prophets.[54] The Apostles frankly avowed that the civil magistrates ruled by divine will and that government was a God-given institution.[55] Dante proclaimed the doctrine of divine right as the basis for the civil aspect of the "two powers" system.[56] Pierre DuBois, Marsiglio of Padua, and William of Ockham defended the absolute and divine right of the monarch in opposition to papal pretensions to supremacy.[57]

The Protestant Revolution, however, made necessary a revival and a notable elaboration of this doctrine. It is of course true that in countries other than Protestant the growing sentiment of nationalism stimulated the new interest in the divine right of the secular rulers, but in Protestant lands, particularly in England, it was essential to erect an adequate set of pretensions on the part of the kings and princes which would serve to offset the claims of the papacy to absolute power and divine support. As Figgis has said, the purpose of the newly-elaborated Protestant doctrine of the divine right of kings was to furnish " a contradiction and a counter-theory to that of papal supremacy." His more extended statement follows:

Clearly the Pope's claim to a universal monarchy by Divine Right, and to implicit obedience on pain of damnation, must be met in similar fashion, whether in the sixteenth or the fourteenth century. The English State must assert a claim to Divine appointment. Obedience must be demanded as due by God's ordinance, and all resistance must be treated as sin. . . .

. . . in the writings of French controversialists there was developed a theory, which with slight modifications is identical with the English theory of the Divine Right of Kings. The essential notion is that the King owes his position directly to Divine appointment and is therefore accountable to God alone, and not to the Pope.

To sum up: out of the sentiment common to all Christians that subjection to lawful authority is in general a religious duty, since authority is part of the natural and Divine order, the Papacy developed a claim to complete supremacy, as the only Divinely ordained government. This claim was met by a counter-claim to Divine Right on behalf of the Imperial dignity. In the sixteenth century the doctrine was elaborated with greater rigidity, — the principle of absolute non-resistance seemed necessary to protect secular government from clerical interference. In the seventeenth century the political side of the doctrine came out most strongly, and it is seen to be the form in which alone could become popular the theory of sovereignty. It further accomplished a work in softening or preventing political changes. Its work done, it began to become obsolete at the Revolution, and tended to pass into a mere sentiment.

In its earlier phases, the divine right of kings was defended chiefly on the ground of passages from Holy Writ which represented government as an indispensable institution that God had divinely revealed, sanctioned, and established. In the seventeenth century Robert Filmer and others introduced in behalf of divine right what was known as the patriarchal doctrine. It was based upon the identification of the kingdom with the family, and of royal with paternal power. The king was held to be identical with the head of the family, and his power as natural and as indispensable as that of the patriarchal father. A genealogical argument was also attached to this point of view: it was argued that God had originally conferred all secular power upon Adam, and that the kings represented the existing repository of this power originally bestowed upon Adam and handed down through the line of subsequent patriarchs and kings. This put the divine right position on a more defensible basis, for it was relatively easy to refute a Scriptural passage or to cite a contradictory text. As Figgis has expressed it: "The patriarchal conception of society is far from being the essence of the theory of the Divine Right of Kings; it is merely the best argument by which it is supported."

Nevertheless, the patriarchal view in one way served to weaken the argument of those in favor of divine right, in that it put the defense of the doctrine on the ground of nature. This offered opponents the opportunity to attack it on the basis of the natural rights theory at a time when the theological conception of politics was dissolving before the naturalistic approach. It is not surprising, therefore, that the two most effective attacks upon the divine right theory in the seventeenth century were made by those two great exponents of natural right, Algernon Sydney and John Locke. Moreover, their books were directed specifically against Filmer. Hence, although Filmer's patriarchal argument powerfully extended and buttressed the divine right position for the time being, "his method paved the way for its overthrow." (Among the other leading writers supporting the doctrine of divine right we should certainly mention Tyndale, James I, Berkeley, and Bilson in England; and Barclay and Blackwood, two Scottish writers domiciled in France.)

The essentials of the fully developed doctrine of the divine right of kings have thus been stated:

(1) *Monarchy is a divinely ordained institution.*

(2) *Hereditary right is indefeasible.* The succession to monarchy is regulated by the law of primogeniture. The right acquired by birth cannot be forfeited through any acts of usurpation, of however long continuance, by any incapacity in the heir, or by any act of deposition. So

long as the heir lives, he is king by hereditary right, even though the usurping dynasty has reigned for a thousand years.

(3) *Kings are accountable to God alone.* Monarchy is pure, the sovereignty being entirely vested in the king, whose power is incapable of legal limitation. All law is a mere concession of his will, and all constitutional forms and assemblies exist entirely at his pleasure. He cannot limit or divide or alienate the sovereignty, so as in any way to prejudice the right of his successor to its complete exercise. A mixed or limited monarchy is a contradiction in terms.

(4) *Non-resistance and passive obedience are enjoined by God.* Under any circumstances resistance to a king is a sin, and ensures damnation. Whenever the king issues a command directly contrary to God's law, God is to be obeyed rather than man, but the example of the primitive Christians is to be followed and all penalties attached to the breach of the law are to be patiently endured.

The following passages set forth the English variety of the doctrine in the language of the time:

We will still believe and maintain that our Kings derive not their title from the people but from God; that to Him only they are accountable; that it belongs not to subjects, either to create or censure, but to honour and obey their sovereign, who comes to be so by a fundamental hereditary right of succession, which no religion, no law, no fault or forfeiture can alter or diminish. . . . Obedience we must pay, either Active or Passive; the Active in the case of all lawful commands; that is whenever the Magistrate commands something which is not contrary to some command of God, we are then bound to act according to that command of the Magistrate, to do the things he requires. But when he enjoins anything contrary to what God hath commanded, we are not then to pay him this Active Obedience; we may, nay we must refuse thus to act (yet here we must be very well assured that the thing is so contrary, and not pretend conscience for a cloak of stubbornness), we are in that case *to obey God rather than man.* But even this is a season for the passive obedience; we must patiently suffer what he inflicts on us for such a refusal, and not, to secure ourselves, rise up against him. . . .

If Adam himself were still living and now ready to die it is certain there is one man, and but one in the world who is next heir, although the knowledge who should be that one man be quite lost.

The theory was commonly supported by a number of Biblical illustrations and texts, of which some of the most important may be mentioned: Samuel's description of a king when the Jewish nation demanded one; David's refusal to touch "the Lord's anointed"; the text "By me kings reign and princes decree justice"; the passage describing the vision of Nebuchadnezzar, asserting that "the Most High ruleth in the kingdom of men, and giveth it to whomsoever he will, and setteth up over it the basest of men"; the command to "render unto Caesar the things that are Caesar's"; Christ's words to Pilate, "thou couldest have no power at all against me except it were given thee from above"; the behavior of the early Christians; and above all the direct enjoining by both Peter and Paul of obedience to constituted authority: "The powers that be are ordained of God. Whosoever therefore resisteth the power, resisteth the ordinance of God. And they that resist shall receive to themselves damnation"; "Ye must needs be subject, not only for wrath, but for conscience' sake"; "Submit yourselves to every ordinance of man for the Lord's sake." [58]

As Protestantism developed in England the divine right theory was needed to defend the kings not only against papal pretensions, but also against the decentralizing influence of Presbyterianism and Congregationalism. In due time, however, secular absolutism became thoroughly established beyond any danger of successful challenge, and the political menace of Presbyterianism gradually passed. The work of the divine right theory was then finished, and it tended to lose ground and disappear. Its passing was not so much due to the fact that it was more absurd than the contending doctrine of natural right as it was to the fact that its historic mission had been accomplished. As Figgis puts it:

Not until the danger was past of a relapse into Popery or Presbyterianism, can the notion of Divine Right be said to have accomplished its work. The case of France is precisely similar. On the one hand, the Papacy claimed to excommunicate and depose the King, and to keep the rightful heir out of his inheritance. On the other hand, the Huguenots made themselves the mouthpiece of a recrudescent feudalism. . . . In the result both in France and England, the central power succeeded in establishing its supremacy, even to the point of persecuting the teachers of all doctrines which it regarded as harmful.

The Divine Right of Kings ceased to have practical importance, not because its doctrines were untrue, but because its teaching had become unnecessary. The transition stage had passed. The independence of the state had been attained. Politics, having made good their claim to be a part of the natural order, no longer had need of a theological justification. [59]

Early Anti-Tyrannical Writings. — The arguments for divine right and passive obedience naturally called forth or were anticipated by a series of writings which took the opposite point of view; namely, that resistance to authority under certain conditions is justified. If one excepts the medieval writers inspired by John of Salisbury, it may be said that the most famous school of thought defending this thesis was that of the so-called social contract theorists from Hooker to Rousseau. This, however, was chiefly a seventeenth- and eighteenth-century development. Previous to this, in the late sixteenth and early seventeenth centuries, came the anti-monarchical writers, of whom the most representative for our purposes are Duplessis-Mornay, author of *A Defense of Liberty Against Tyrants* (1579); George Buchanan, author of *On the Sovereign Power among the Scots* (1579); and Juan de Mariana, author of *On Kingship and the Education of a King* (1605).

The authorship of the *Vindiciae contra tyrannos* (*A Defense,* etc.) has long been a subject of dispute, but in a recent authoritative memoir on the topic Laski inclines toward the belief that the claim of Duplessis-Mornay is better founded than that of Languet. Duplessis-Mornay was a gifted diplomatist and scholar, and was for some time the right-hand man of Henry of Navarre, the Huguenot ruler who clinched his military ascendency over France by turning Catholic and thus gaining popular support. Duplessis-Mornay, a loyal Huguenot, became disgruntled at this turn of events and withdrew from political life, but retained such influence with his fellow-religionists that he was styled "the Huguenot pope." The Huguenots were at bottom upholders of the provincial feudatories as against the ever-waxing national state, and Duplessis-Mornay's book may be regarded as an attack upon French secular absolutism as personified in Louis XIII. It is interesting to note that this plea for tyrannicide was written about seven years after Louis had agreed to the massacre of fifty thousand Huguenots—the famous St. Bartholomew's Day of 1572. Apparently a case of "fight the devil with fire"!

In many ways the book foreshadows the chief problems raised by the social contract and revolutionary writers of the next two centuries. The author accepts the traditional view of the natural sociability of man; i.e., that man lived originally in groups completely free from external social control; it was a golden age not unlike that pictured by Seneca. "Men," says Duplessis-Mornay, "[are] by nature free, impatient of servitude, born rather to command than to obey." Political society arose as a consequence of the appearance of private property and the conflicts thereby produced. An organization was found necessary to administer justice at home and wage war abroad. As the original has it:

When the words " mine " and " thine " had entered into the world and conflicts arose among citizens concerning ownership of things, and between neighboring peoples over boundaries, it became customary to have recourse to some one who would justly and effectively see that the poor suffered no violence from the rich, or the whole people from their neighbors. When such contests and wars became more violent a permanent choice was made of some one for whose valor and diligence all had high regard. Thus kings were first established to administer justice at home and lead the army abroad. . . . Kings were ordained by God and established by the people for the benefit of the citizens. This benefit consists principally in two things — in the maintenance of justice among individuals and of security against enemies.[60]

The author of the *Vindiciae* thoroughly subscribed to the doctrine of popular sovereignty: the people, having been originally free and independent, possessed all political power; they did not surrender this when the state was established, but merely delegated the authority to their representatives and rulers. Hence, in a political sense the people are greater than the king; and likewise, the representatives of the people are superior to the king. Again we quote directly:

Since kings are established by the people, it seems to follow certainly that the whole body of the people are superior to the king. . . . Moreover, it is clear that kings were instituted for the benefit of the people. . . . There are many peoples who live without a king; a king without a people, however, you cannot imagine. . . . Since, therefore, the king exists through, and for the sake of, the people, and without the people cannot stand, who will wonder at our conclusion that the people are greater than the king? Now what we have said concerning the whole body of the people we wish also to be said concerning those who in every kingdom or city lawfully represent the body of the people.[61]

Royal government was in the beginning established by a twofold contract. The first was one between God and the people and king, in which people and king agreed to obey God, and the king promised to rule for the glory of God. The second contract was one between the king and the people, in which the king agreed to rule justly and the people undertook to obey him under these conditions: " In the first covenant or contract there is an obligation to piety, in the second, to justice. In the former, the king promises dutifully to obey God, in the latter, that he will rule the people justly; in the one that he will provide for the glory of God, in the other, that he will secure the welfare of the people." [62]

To come now to the question of the right of resistance to royal authority, the author raises the issue in the form of four questions: " (1) Whether subjects are bound and ought to obey princes, if they command that which is against the law of God? (2) Whether it be lawful to resist a prince who doth infringe the law of God, or ruin His Church: by whom, how, and how far it is lawful? (3) Whether it be lawful to resist a prince who doth oppress or ruin a public state, and how far such resistance may be extended: by whom, how, and by what right or law it is permitted? (4) Whether neighbor princes may, or are bound by law to aid the subjects of other princes, persecuted for true religion, or oppressed by manifest tyranny? "

The author answers the first question decisively in the negative. The commands of God come before those of any secular and mundane ruler. The second question he promptly answers in the affirmative. By violating the law of God the king breaks the first part of the dual contract upon which political authority rests; therefore, the people are justified in resisting the monarch. But this resistance cannot well be executed by the people as a whole. They should act through their recognized representatives, the magistrates of the kingdom. The author contends that it is likewise lawful for the people, through their representatives, to resist a prince who violates the second part of the twofold contract — namely, his promise to rule justly:

Everywhere there is between prince and people a mutual and reciprocal obligation: he promises that he will be a good prince; the people promise that if he is such they will obey him. The people are thus obligated to the prince conditionally, he to them absolutely. If the condition be not fulfilled, the people are released, the contract abrogated, the obligation *ipso jure* void. The king is faithless if he governs unjustly; the people, if they neglect to obey him while he rules justly. The people are entirely innocent of the crime of perfidy if they publicly renounce an unjust ruler or endeavor to overpower by force of arms one who without lawful right attempts to hold the kingdom.[63]

Finally, the author gives a positive answer to the fourth question. A prince is bound to aid the subjects of another prince who are being persecuted for adhering to the true religion, as this is dictated by the principle of the unity of the church. A prince should also intervene to protect the subjects of another prince against civil tyranny, on the ground of the unity of humanity. In Duplessis-Mornay the Huguenots possessed an advocate of great plausibility and rationalizing power.

The learned Scottish Humanist, George Buchanan, developed an equally vigorous plea for resistance to tyranny. His book, *De jure regni apud Scotos,* was written between 1567 and 1570, and circulated in manuscript, so that it antedates the *Vindiciae.* He held that society is based upon the social instinct of man, aided by the recognition of self-interest (inasmuch as men realize the benefits to be gained from association). Of the two the social instinct, implanted in man by nature and God, is the more important. Government was called forth by the effort to escape from the lawless and primitive state of nature. Buchanan also adhered to the view of popular sovereignty and the derivation of political authority from the people. Royal authority was based upon the consent of the people, and was established through a compact whereby the king agreed to rule justly and the people agreed to obey him under these conditions. The whole purpose of government was to bring about civil justice: the institution of kingship was devised solely to secure justice, and the original governmental compact had justice as its cornerstone. A king is by definition a prince who rules justly. All other princes are tyrants: these may either be usurpers, who have not been approved by the people, or they may be those who were legally instituted but who rule unjustly. Buchanan denounced the tyrant with great vigor, and approved enthusiastically of the right of resistance to the unjust king; he was much less logical and specific than the author of the *Vindiciae,* however, in indicating just how and by whom this resistance should be set up. Nevertheless, his actual method of treating the more or less medieval ideas that provided his starting-point make him one of the most modern writers between Machiavelli and Hobbes.

The right of resistance to an unjust monarch was defended from the Catholic point of view by the learned Spanish Jesuit, Juan de Mariana, in his *De rege et regis institutione.* Government, he held, was instituted as a means of escape from the state of nature, which, although not intolerable, was inconvenient. He dwelt at length on the condition of man in the state of nature, and reached conclusions somewhat intermediate between those of Locke and Rousseau. To quote Dunning's epitome:

In developing his conception of kingship, Mariana starts from the natural state of men, which he describes with some fulness on the general lines of Polybius's idea. In the beginning men lived like wild animals, following instinct in the procurement of food and the propagation of their kind, bound by no law and subject to no authority. The life had its advantages: nature furnished food and drink and shelter, through fruits and streams and caves; cheating, lying, avarice and ambition were unknown, and the cares of private property had not made their appearance. But, on the other hand, man's wants were greater and more varied than those of other animals, and at the same time he was less adapted than they to the protection of himself and his young from the dangers that incessantly arose from both animate and inanimate forces around him. It was to overcome these disadvantages that men grouped themselves together and submitted to the leadership of some one who displayed especial capacity in promoting their welfare. This was the origin of civil society, with all its blessings to the race. The timidity and weakness of men were the divinely implanted qualities through which the rights of humanity were to be developed.[64]

As might be expected, Mariana supported the doctrine of popular sovereignty, and contended that political authority was conferred by the people upon their rulers. As to type of government, he preferred a monarchy properly restrained by law. Although he defended the conceptions of popular sovereignty and of delegated political power, he did not elaborate the idea of a governmental contract. If a king ruled in his own interest rather than in the interest of the majority of the people, he ceased to be a king and became a tyrant. Resistance to the tyrant was upheld by Mariana. The citizen should first allow the assembly to warn the tyrant and give him an opportunity to reform, and if this accomplished nothing, the individual citizen might then slay the tyrant by any means except poisoning.

(The anti-monarchical doctrine was also espoused by Johannes Althusius, the leading Germanic political philosopher of the period, but his views may be more legitimately included in a later chapter.)

Summary of the Chapter. — We began by calling attention to the fact that the historical background of the chapter on "The Meeting of East and West and the Advance of Secularism" is in large part assumed for this one as well, and that in addition the effects of the expansion of Europe during the early Age of Discovery must be included in the present picture. The development in letters known as Humanism was then assessed, and the verdict rendered that it was of little direct importance in the social thought of the period, an opinion contrary to the one commonly entertained by those who attribute great significance to the Renaissance. It was then shown that the continuing chaos in Italy probably had more to do with Machiavelli's social insight than did whatever Humanism he may have imbibed, and his theories, remarkably penetrating where "conspiral societies" are concerned, were outlined. The failure of Humanism to engender anything basically in harmony with the trends of the period was next illustrated by the utopian writers and their essentially static proposals; More in particular was chosen to exemplify this in detail. Whatever was really novel in the work of the utopian thinkers came from other sources, notably the discovery of new lands and peoples and the resulting comparisons. We then pointed out that the Reformation really reformed nothing, that it was of no higher intellectual altitude than the Catholicism it abjured, and that the leaders of the movement were quite reactionary in their estimate of the new science. Important indirect effects of the Protestant revolt there were, however, and of these we chose to pay most attention to the relation of Calvinistic thought and capitalistic ideologies and ways of life. The part played by Protestantism in the nationalistic tendencies of the time was also noted, and the further development of the doctrine of the divine right of kings in Protestant nations was briefly sketched. Last of all, we saw how the secular absolutism of the period called forth a number of anti-tyrannical writings from both Protestant and Catholic sources. The attempts to justify resistance to royal authority represented by such doctrines are exceedingly important in the history of social thought and in *Wissenssoziologie,* for they are the precursors of the revolutionary wing of the social contract school in the succeeding century.

Recent research on the dates of Machiavelli's writings should today be taken into the reckoning by anyone who, from a sociology of knowledge standpoint, concerns himself with the "irony *versus* iniquity" problem with regard to Machiavelli.

The perennial Calvinism-capitalism problem should also be viewed afresh in the light of recent research on Christian sectarians who, although expressly rejecting doctrines of predestination and warmly accepting free-will teachings (such as those of Arminius), nevertheless played significant parts in capitalistic development. Further, note should be made of "middleman trading peoples" (also called "marginal" in a special sense) many of whom, although neither Calvinistic nor even Christian, have been and are capitalistic. Becker, in his *Man in Reciprocity* (New York: Praeger, 1956) has devoted a chapter (xv) to them.

Ambiguity in the use of secularization and related terms has crept into earlier chapters, but is especially apparent here. After all, secular absolutism is at the very least, in Becker's recent usage (see p. 42), of loyalistically sacred character. Given the usage current among most historians, the ambiguity cannot readily be eliminated, but it can be noted and the reader put on the alert.

CHAPTER IX

A Smaller and a Larger World:
Natural Science and the Comparative View

EXALTATION AND ABASEMENT. — The sixteenth and seventeenth centuries brought forth many exceedingly interesting developments in European thought; yet, if one were forced to use but two categories in classifying them, a great number might be included under " Discoveries Increasing the Scope and Relative Complexity of the Known World," and " Discoveries Diminishing the Relative Size, Importance, and Cosmic Significance of the Earth and Its Inhabitants." The first classification would include among other things the revelations of the biologists, the explorers, and the early ethnographers; the second, the astronomical discoveries associated with the names of Galileo and Newton. The work of the first group suddenly extended, to limits undreamed of a century previous, the boundaries of the known world, impressing the leaders of thought with its almost infinite complexity; the labors of the second displaced the earth from the position it had once proudly occupied in the very center of the cosmos and showed it to be a mere speck of dust in a universe immeasurably vast. The world became larger, and the earth became smaller.

Again the Expansion of Europe. — We have already pointed out at some length certain effects of the oversea explorations, but the significance of this increase in accessibility, this further breakdown of isolation, is so great that recapitulation is warranted. Historians and sociologists have long recognized that the contact of cultures is far and away the most potent force in breaking down cultural fixity and mental immobility — in other words, the most dynamic factor in history. This vitally important force had earlier manifested itself during the Crusades with certain results already noted, and had not failed to maintain itself as an important factor in European history from that time onward, but the era of its greatest potency followed the successful voyages of Columbus and Vasco da Gama. The elucidation of this set of historic influences, which has been the work of historians from Raynal to Shepherd, has probably been the most important contribution which historians have made to the subject of the setting of the work done by the early modern scientists.

First and foremost among the impulses coming from European expansion should be put the general disintegration of the medieval and feudal order and the substitution of a generally novel social and political system — in short, the actual transformation of the whole face of European civilization through the stimulation of the spirit of adventure, scientific curiosity, new knowledge, the rise of world commerce and large-scale oversea colonization, modern capitalism and capitalistic institutions, the increase of urban life, the rise of the middle class, and the gradual extinction of the feudal system by the national state. In coöperation with the Protestant *Ethik* it altered the attitude of religion toward economic practices by eliminating the social point of view and stressing the divine sanction for the ultra-individualism of modern capitalism, with its emphasis upon pecuniary profit (resulting from " stewardship ") as pleasing in the sight of God. It was this great series of interrelated transformations that laid the basis for the Industrial Revolution and that exploitation of modern science and technology which so largely produced what we call contemporary civilization.[1]

Scientific Advances. — In its specific contributions to science the expansion of Europe was by no means unimportant or negligible. Most directly influenced was the science of navigation, with its accessory sciences of mathematics, engineering, and optics. The explorations and discoveries not only enormously increased concrete geographic information of every type, but stimulated scientific cartography upon the basis of determinable latitude and longitude. Astronomy was enriched by the discovery and observation of constellations in the southern hemisphere, and by the scrutiny of hitherto known heavenly bodies from new positions on the earth's surface. Additions were made to chemical knowledge by the discovery in oversea areas of rocks and minerals of new and significant types. Botany, the *materia medica,* and zoölogy were remarkably aided and advanced by the great variety and number of newly discovered forms of plant and animal life. And a strong if not adequate stimulus was given to the movement which ultimately founded the science of anthropology through the contact with a large number of new racial and subracial types in widely differing degrees of cultural development.

With the equally marked influence of the results of the expansion of Europe on art, letters, and currents of philosophic thought this is not the place to deal. It is worth pointing out, however, that it did much to stimulate that appreciation of diversity and relativity which loomed so large in the thought of Montaigne or Bodin as compared with that of Aquinas. It is evident that this movement, as a whole, produced a new and larger world in two important senses: in the first place, by discovering the western and southern hemispheres, and, in the second place, by changing the cultural complexion of the world that had been known before 1500. It is doubly significant for the scientist, in that it not only stimulated many phases of modern science, but also did much to create that contemporary intellectual, economic, and social world in which present-day science can function.[2]

The Comparative Viewpoint. — The most important aspect of the reaction of the expansion of Europe on social science lay in the development of what may be called the comparative point of view. The Christian attitude had rested upon the assumption of the unity and uniformity of right and custom. There was one revealed religion, one correct method of life, one acceptable attitude toward private property, one proper view with respect to the family, and so on. The discoveries associated with European expansion produced a vast body of novel information bearing upon the life and customs of mankind throughout the world, both in advanced stages of civilization and in savagery and barbarism. This new body of facts served to make it evident that, "taking the round world over," there was an endless number of different ways of dealing with human problems and gratifying human desires in the fields of government, property, sex, religion, and aesthetics, and that no matter how bizarre the practice, the practitioners regarded their way of doing things as perfect and divinely revealed.

This awareness of the diversity of human customs and rationalizations naturally aroused much curiosity and speculation on the part of those given to serious thinking about human affairs. It inevitably produced an increasingly secular spirit and served to break down the traditional sacred conceptions of man and his institutions. In short, it was in this age that the comparative viewpoint gained power, and it soon led to the production of such illuminating works as Voltaire's *Essai sur les mœurs* and Montesquieu's *De l'esprit des lois.* Such fields of human intellectual endeavor as comparative religion, comparative philology, comparative jurisprudence, and comparative ethics were cultivated, in some instances for the first time.

Other Effects of a Larger World. — The oversea expansion also produced many other results affecting social and political philosophy. The discovery of preliterate men, or so-called " primitives," seemed to offer confirmation of the medieval assumptions of a state of nature anterior to established society and of a " natural man." This served to strengthen interest in the state of nature, natural rights, and the social contract theory which flourished in the seventeenth and eighteenth centuries. Again, the beginnings of ethnography, associated with the study of the manners and customs of peoples overseas, led to the collection of a large body of new information concerning the behavior of man and the varieties of mankind inhabiting the planet. This was of no little significance in relation to the development of the social sciences; i.e., of the sciences of man in his social relations. Finally, the investigation of human habitats and customs overseas and in remote parts of the Old World helped to create that interest in the subject of the interrelation between man and his physical environment which ultimately led to the rise of anthropogeography at the opening of the nineteenth century.

Montaigne and the Secular Weltanschauung. — One of the most complete repudiations of the typically medieval views of man and society is to be found in the charming essays of Michel Eyquem, generally known as Montaigne (1533–1592). He is of but slight importance in the history of social theory so far as the conventional issues of the social philosophy of the age (such as the basis of kingship, the state of nature, passive obedience, or constitutional problems in state and church) are concerned, but he nevertheless looms large because of his general viewpoint, which was markedly different from that of the orthodox Christian, whether Catholic or Protestant. He was the first great apostle of urbanity and detachment after Pyrrho, Lucian, and other leading pagan exponents of scepticism and moral relativity.

Montaigne's education and training in part explain his remarkable divergence from the orthodox patterns of thought. His religious background was highly diversified; this made it difficult for him to take seriously the pretensions of any one sect to a monopoly of divine revelation. Moreover, the range of his studies contributed greatly to his intellectual detachment and calm moderation. The typical Christian devoted himself to Holy Writ and theology, which when taken seriously rather than

"broadmindedly" are of necessity intolerant in nature and implication, and he knew little of the diverse customs of the world
outside of his limited circle of local observations. Montaigne, on
the other hand, found his favorite authors among the great pagan
expositors of secular analysis: Plutarch, Cicero, and the Epicureans. The moral relativism thereby engendered could scarcely
be accepted by those who believed that there was but one road to
salvation and that to undermine crucial Christian doctrine involved putting not merely one's own soul but those of thousands
of others in jeopardy. Further, Montaigne was born in the early
stages of the era of oversea discoveries. He was from the beginning interested in the diversity of customs and beliefs entertained
and followed by mankind in various parts of the earth. Such interests and knowledge made it difficult for him to take with due
seriousness the Christian contention that there was but a single
safe and proper way to conduct one's life.

In his attitude toward the purpose of philosophy, conceived
in its broadest possible form as the sum total of human learning
and reflection, Montaigne completely repudiated the orthodox
Christian position, which was that the chief purpose of human
intellectual effort was to secure salvation in the world to come —
in other words, that philosophy had as its chief function the
preparation of man for a safe death, and that theology was the
" queen of the sciences." Montaigne contended, on the contrary,
that the main purpose of human learning was to teach man how
to live more adequately and happily here on this earth — the essence of the secular attitude. To him the highest types of intellectual interest and discipline were what we should today call
psycho-sociology, ethnography, and aesthetics. He therefore
reversed the whole objective of life and study as it had been accepted by all of the great branches of Christendom. It was a direct
anticipation of Francis Bacon's highly secular suggestion that the
Kingdom of Man be substituted for the Kingdom of God as the
chief center of human interest and intellectual endeavor.

The starting-point of Montaigne's philosophy was poles removed from the Christian theological schema founded upon original sin, the Fall, and man's consequent total depravity. Moreover, Montaigne had little use for the accompanying attitude
of theological certainty; he was keenly — perhaps too keenly —
aware of the paucity of the information which any one individual
could obtain and assimilate ("Que sais-je?"), and was equally
convinced of the intellectual limitations of mankind as a whole.
Consequently he held that it is necessary ever to bear in mind

the relative insignificance of our information and to subject ourselves frequently to the most searching intellectual self-examination in order to impress upon us how little we really know. This was a marked contrast to the intellectual confidence of the theologian, Protestant or Catholic, who, armed with the Scriptures and the masters of theology, *knew* that he possessed the sum total of saving knowledge.

Next, whereas the Christians had emphasized the unity of all true wisdom and the uniformity of conduct essential to salvation, Montaigne was wont to stress the opposite; namely, that diversity and pluralism seemed to be the rule of nature and hence of God. He arrived at this view as a result of his almost morbid introspection of his own moods as they varied from day to day and from year to year, and also as an outgrowth of his observation of the enormous variety of human customs and beliefs reported by ancient observers and contemporary explorers. Willis has effectively expressed these foundations of Montaigne's defense of cosmic and social diversity:

> The diversity of human nature, the inconstancy of our actions, the uncertainty of our judgment, the curious, inexplicable, essentially unreasonable foundations of our opinions, these are Montaigne's favourite themes. . . . "Whosoever looketh into this narrowly hardly ever finds himself twice in the same state — If I speak diversely of myself, it is because I see myself diversely. All contrarieties are found in me at some moment and in some fashion. Bashful, insolent; chaste, lustful; talkative, taciturn; laborious, delicate; witty, dull; melancholy, gay; lying, truthful; learned, ignorant; both liberal and avaricious and prodigal./All these things I perceive in myself in some degree according as I turn myself about." . . .

> His cogitations led him over a wide field, the field of his reading (wide for those days, his library consisted of a thousand books and he was an indefatigable though impatient reader), of his experience and observation as a courtier, politician, lawyer, and country gentleman, of the illimitable and, as he grew older and more and more absorbed in his *Essays,* the increasingly fascinating field of his self. The then recent discovery of the New World, upsetting all traditional views of the size and geography of the universe — those marvellous, rich cities in the Indies, were no more alluring to the curiosity and imaginations of the Old World than were the unexplored regions of the soul to Montaigne. . . .

> Like a Mohammedan fearful of destroying any scrap of paper lest perchance the name of Allah should be written on it, Montaigne dared not ignore a jot of evidence concerning the waywardness of man. All that he could read and collect of human customs, habits, and opinions

he reported: he travelled, not, as many people do, " to find Gascons in Sicily," but to seek " Greeks and Persians " there. He was insatiable in pursuit of the diversity of other men's lives; he was fascinated by the unending list of human vagaries and foibles.[3]

It was also inevitable that in his discussion of morality Montaigne should depart widely from the orthodox Christian position; he may rightly be regarded as the most important of the semi-modern progenitors of the contemporary relativistic approach to ethical issues. Because of his secularism, Montaigne was able to attack the problem of ethics in a detached fashion — or perhaps this detachment constitutes his secularism. However that may be, there can be little doubt that his theory of ethics was empirical rather than revealed. To quote Willis again:

True morality was that way to which reason, acting upon our experience of life, and our knowledge of ourselves, pointed. He believed that the origin of all moral codes, though the codes had since become stereotyped and insensitive to realities, lay in reason, and that mankind's notions of good and evil were not, as Socrates thought, deposited in our minds by a God who created us, but were reasonably derived from men's contact with life and with themselves. This explained why the customs and moralities of different peoples and races were so different.[4]

Starting in this way, Montaigne gravely challenged many of the leading tenets of the Christian ethic. He repudiated entirely the Christian tendency to separate the body from the mind or soul, to regard the soul and its pleasures as good and the body and its enjoyments as base, and to represent bodily pleasures as separate from, but disastrous to, the operations of the mind. He held that both body and soul were equally an endowment of nature and God, that bodily pleasures were as natural and defensible as the experiences of the soul, and that in reasonable indulgence in corporeal delights the mind might actually be freshened and stimulated. He thus issued a fundamental challenge to the theological dichotomy of the world of the spirit and the realm of the flesh — the dualism of body and mind — and insisted upon viewing the human organism as a unity:

The body hath a great part in our being. . . . Those who would sunder our two principal parts and disunite the one from the other are to blame. We ought to recouple and rejoin them. We must bid the soul not to withdraw and entertain herself apart, not to despise and abandon the body (which she cannot well do except by some counterfeit apish trick), but to combine with it, to embrace, cherish, assist, and control it, to counsel and correct it and bring it back when it goes astray; in short, espouse and act towards it as a husband. . . . It is . . . , as it were, divine for a man to know how to enjoy his existence loyally. We seek for other conditions because we understand not the use of our own and we go outside of ourselves because we know not what is happening there. Thus it is in vain that we mount upon stilts, for, be we upon them, yet we must go with our own legs. . . .[5]

From such considerations it is apparent that Montaigne in no sense shared the orthodox Christian view that morality was almost entirely a matter of sexual purity or chastity; he held that sex relations in themselves were not evil, and that they need only be controlled by a sense of moderation and honor. But, more fundamentally, morality was for Montaigne something far broader than proper sexual conduct; he held that it was chiefly a matter of decency and justice. An aggressive war, the torturing of witches, or the oppression of the weak he viewed as more reprehensible than sexual offenses. Although he did not go as far in this regard as the Third Earl of Shaftesbury, the great Deist (to be discussed later), Montaigne exhibited some tendency to formulate an aesthetic approach to morality, identifying it as he did with good taste.

The conception of God entertained by men has tended to conform to their general world outlook and personal philosophy, and so Montaigne conceived of God as a sort of magnified Montaigne — detached, tolerant, and complacent in the face of the diverse follies of fallible mortals.

Quite apart from his theories, Montaigne is also interesting as a personality: he is an excellent example of the heightened self-consciousness, egocentricity, scepticism, moral relativism, and general mental mobility that develop in some individuals exposed to the full impact of increased accessibility. He was a product of the contact of cultures, a man so keenly aware of the diversity of human thought and custom that he lived the detached life of a stranger among his compatriots and contemporaries. Walled in by his thousand books, they yet provided the medium whereby his mind " went voyaging and expatiating about the world." He was truly urbane, for in all essentials this country gentleman lived an urban life; his mental mobility was directly connected with his secular, cosmopolitan outlook — an outlook that would have been impossible in the isolated, sacred European society of three centuries before. The world, for better or for worse, had grown larger.

Jean Bodin, Systematic Exponent of Comparative and Historical Method. — In previous chapters we saw that the Moslem world had also grown larger, several centuries in advance of the

European, and that while the disorganization attendant upon
expansion was producing thinkers like Ibn Khaldūn, Christendom, previously isolated, was barely beginning to reach out into
the new secular world that intrusive factors had begun to bring
into being. As soon as secularization was well under way, the
same strife and turmoil that induced Ibn Khaldūn to reflect upon
the cyclical rise and fall of dynasties made itself felt in Europe;
the belief that "progress is a terrible thing" received fresh confirmation. It may be, however, that if not the physical at least the
intellectual strife of the period was, as Lichtenberger points out,
"productive of great thinkers not only in theology but in those
scientific and practical interests which increasingly were dominating men's minds. Here was laid the basis for the doctrines of the
physiocrats and the mercantilists so important in economic theory of a later period and the origin of the doctrine of sovereignty
which from this time on engaged the thinking of political philosophers." [6] "Challenge-and-response," to employ Toynbee's theory of social and cultural dynamics, was evoking its usual results.

At any rate, it is certain that many brilliant social theorists
flourished during the era in question, and among them was the
author of the *Six Books concerning a Republic,* Jean Bodin
(1530–1596). We mentioned Ibn Khaldūn at the outset of this
discussion of Bodin because of the resemblance some of the latter's doctrines bear to those of the great Moslem. There is a bare
possibility that culture contact may have been at work here as
elsewhere. This possibility arises because of the fact that although
Bodin's father was French, his mother, according to a report current among his contemporaries, was a Spanish Jewess whose family had sought refuge in France as a result of the persecutions
under Ferdinand and Isabella. [7] The activities of the Provençal
Sephardim in translating the Classical writers have already been
noted; it may well have been that they also brought to the town
of Angers, where Bodin was born, some knowledge of the Moslem writers as well. Certainly the similarity between several doctrines held by Ibn Khaldūn and Bodin is striking enough to warrant further investigation by some curious student of the history
of social thought.

The theory of the origin of empire in the conquest of tillage
peoples by herdsmen formed a large part of the Berber's contribution, as we have seen; the Frenchman does not mention the
nomad-agriculturist conflict, but he clearly expounds the conflict
theory of the rise of the state:

. . . before there was either city or citizen, or any form of a Commonweale amongst men, every master of a family was a master in his own house, having the power of life and death over his wife and children, but after that force, violence, ambition, covetousness and desire of revenge had armed one against another, the issues of wars and combats giving victory unto the one side, made the other to become unto them slaves; . . . Then that full and entire liberty by nature given to every man, to live as himself best please, was altogether taken from the vanquished. So the words of Lord and Servant, Prince and Subject before unknown unto the world, were first brought into use. Yea, Reason and the very light of nature leadeth us to believe very force and violence to have given course and beginning unto Commonweale . . . herein it appeareth Demosthenes, Aristotle and Cicero have mistaken themselves, in following the error of Herodotus, who saith that the first Kings were chosen for their justice and virtue; and have hereof feigned unto us, I wot not, what heroic and golden worlds; an opinion by me by most certain arguments and testimonies elsewhere refelled.[8]

Further, the cyclical theory set forth by Ibn Khaldūn seems to find an echo in the teaching of Bodin, for in his philosophy of social change the latter presents a doctrine in striking contrast to the static theories of earlier European writers; indeed, it has quite a modern ring — "alteration" and "conversion" sound strangely like "evolution by slow adaptation" and "evolution by rapid mutation." The setting in which these terms occur is about as follows:

Bodin points out that however desirable theoretically may be stability and perfection in government, it is practically unattainable. No state, however well established and flourishing, can long remain in a stable condition "by reason of the changes of worldly things, which are so mutable and uncertain." These changes may take place in either or both of two ways, "alteration" (slow adaptation) or "conversion" (rapid mutation), for Bodin says:

Now I call that a Conversion of a Commonweale, when as the State thereof is altogether changed; as when a Popular estate is changed into a Monarchy; or an Aristocracy into a Democracy; or contrarywise; for as the change of customs, laws, religion or place, it is but a certain kind of Alteration, the State and sovereignty continuing still; which may also to the contrary itself be changed, without any change of religion, or laws, or any other things also, besides them which belong unto sovereignty.[9]

Again, his comments on the influence of "the soil" on personality recall Ibn Khaldūn's remarks on the abstemiousness of the desert shepherds:

. . . men of a fat and fertile soil are most commonly effeminate and cowards: whereas contrarywise a barren country makes men temperate by necessity, and by consequence, careful, vigilant and industrious.

The fact that the trading town is frequently a " free city " over which the territorial state has little control is implicitly pointed out by Bodin:

. . . the barrenness of the soil doth not only make men more temperate, apt to labor, and of a more subtile spirit; but also it makes towns more populous: for an enemy affects not a barren country, and the inhabitants living in safety do multiply and are forced to traffic or to labor.

Further, Ibn Khaldūn's statements about city dwellers are partially paralleled by Bodin, although the latter may of course have been influenced in this by the Classical writers or Aquinas:

As for the inhabitants upon the sea coast, and of great towns of traffic, all writers have observed, that they are more subtle, politic, and cunning than those that lie far from the sea and from traffic.

Last of all is a remark that shows how the Age of Discovery and Colonization had already begun to start men thinking about social change and the effects of the expansion of Europe:

The transportation of Colonies works a great difference in men. . . .[10]

Paraphrasing those of Bodin's generalizations that show marked similarity to some of Ibn Khaldūn's (which may be unsound but are none the less of great historical interest), we may say: (1) the state in its historical form is often due to conquest; (2) class distinctions are frequently to be traced to a conqueror-conquered relationship; (3) the family or kinship bond is prior to any form of political supraordination or subordination; (4) the most stable social structure is but a moving equilibrium maintained by processes of social disorganization and reorganization; (5) social change may take the form of slow adaptation or rapid mutation; (6) various segments of a culture may change without any appreciable corresponding change in other segments; (7) agriculturists are frequently characterized by a lack of fighting vigor; (8) the discipline imposed by scanty natural resources is sometimes advantageous; (9) trading cities are often so located as to be relatively safe from attack; (10) city dwellers are more mentally mobile than isolated peoples; (11) colonization is an important source of personality change. But even though the similarity of theory apparent here may indicate a real connection, we should be unfair to Bodin if we were to imply that he had nothing of his own to give. Many writers in the field have held that the French publicist was the most systematic writer on social and political theory between his own day and that of Aristotle. This may be an exaggeration, but certainly he was one of the first writers in western Europe to take social philosophy out of the realm of pure deduction and to place it upon the basis of such historical knowledge and ethnographic data as were available in the latter part of the sixteenth century — data derived from areas far removed from those drawn on by his Mohammedan forerunner. Instead of relying wholly on deductions from assumed principles, as did most Western writers of his day, Bodin also had recourse to historical facts, as he understood them, as well as to the descriptions of popular usages and customs reported by ancient observers and by explorers contemporary with him (though the amount of material to be derived from the latter source was limited when he wrote). His work in this regard was highly rudimentary, and for this and other reasons his modernity should not be unduly stressed; nevertheless, it may be said that he started the historical and comparative methods in social philosophy on the way to their eighteenth-century culmination in the work of Montesquieu. Let us again examine some of his doctrines, without reference to the possibility of Ibn Khaldūn's influence.

Bodin held that the unit of society was the family:

The beginnings of all civil societies are derived from a family, which is (as we say) itself a natural society, and by the father of nature itself first founded in the beginning together with mankind. But when reason, by God himself ingrafted in us, had made man desirous of the company and society of man, and to participate together both in speech and conversation; the same so wrought, as that proceeding farther from the love of them that were domestic and their own, it extended farther, to take pleasure in the propagation and increase of families. So also families by little and little departing from their first beginning, learned by civil society to imitate the natural society of a family.[11]

Larger associations were composed by family increase, the break-up of these large family groups, and their later union through the influence of sympathy and the desire for coöperative endeavor. Although Bodin held that the "state is an association of families and their common possessions, governed by a supreme power and by reason,"[12] at other times he took the position that society, as well as the state, is composed of a large number of groups, such as guilds, corporations, colleges, companies, congregations, and communes, which exercise definite functions in society and are subordinated to the supreme political power of the state. In this way he foreshadowed the group conception of society and the state later set forth in great detail by Gierke and his followers, such as Maitland, Figgis, Cole, Laski, Duguit, and other pluralists.

Bodin thus traced the genesis of society from an original family which expanded, dispersed, and was in time reunited through the operation of the "social instinct" and the perception of the utility of coöperative activity. Developed society was essentially a union of lesser constituent groups organized for the purpose of carrying on trade, worship, and similar activities. *But although society itself might have had this peaceful origin, the state and sovereign power developed out of force, through the conquest of one group by another.* In his view of the original state of man Bodin took the position that it was one of disorder, force, and violence. He rejected, and refuted with vigor, the conception of "heroic and golden ages" as descriptive of man before the rise of political society. He thus parted company with Seneca and others among the pagan philosophers. It was in the establishment of civil society that man discovered his way out of this inconvenient, if not intolerable, state of nature.[13] In this manner Bodin furnished suggestions for two later groups of theorists whose interpretation of political origins were radically opposed to each other. From his views of early man, the state-of-nature writers derived no little stimulus to formulate the doctrine of a social contract as the method of securing peace and order. His own contention that the state arose in force was in harmony with the writings of Hume, Ferguson, and others who vigorously opposed the contract school.

Perhaps the most original aspect of Bodin's writings related to his view of sovereign power as the test of the state. He defined sovereignty as "supreme power over citizens and subjects, unrestrained by laws."[14] Sovereignty originally resides in the people, but they may confer it upon either a single or a plural ruler, provided they do so for life and do not limit the bestowal as to any specific purpose or period of time. In what way did Bodin's conception of sovereignty denote an advance beyond the views of earlier writers? He did not outstrip William of Ockham or Marsiglio of Padua in insisting on the unlimited nature of secular authority, but he did transcend them in separating the conception of secular absolutism from a particular ruler or rulers and in defining it as an abstract principle. As Allen puts it: "It may be said that what Bodin did was to detach the notion of sovereignty from circumstance and see it as a legal theory logically necessary in all associations for other than specifically limited purposes. In doing this, in detaching the idea of sovereignty from all association with Emperor, Pope, or king, and attempting to define its nature apart from all circumstance, he was doing, perhaps, what had never quite been done before." Here we see the growth in the power of abstraction that always seems to accompany the widening of the limits of the known world; the isolated sacred society and its limited mental range gives ground to the accessible secular society and its accompanying increase in rationalistic thought.

Another innovation lay in his insistence that the possession of sovereign power was the supreme test of the existence and independence of the state. To quote from Allen once more: " It may, indeed, be said that Bodin was the first to declare that the distinguishing mark of the state was its recognition of legal sovereignty." [15] In this way Bodin fits into the line of descent in the development of the doctrine of political sovereignty which runs from the Roman Lawyers through Marsiglio, William of Ockham, Bodin, Hobbes, Blackstone, Bentham, Austin, Hegel, Droysen, Treitschke, and Burgess. As long as the doctrine of absolute secular sovereignty was accepted as a basic political and legal truth of the highest validity and relevance, Bodin's place in the history of political theory loomed large on this account alone. If, on the other hand, the challenge to monistic and absolute sovereignty proclaimed by the contemporary pluralists is sound, then Bodin helped to formulate and transmit a fallacy as untenable as the social contract doctrine and infinitely more mischievous.

Bodin as a Human Geographer. — A phase of the social theory of Bodin for which he is traditionally most distinguished is his view of the relation between geographical factors, such as climate and topography, and the social behavior of man. He is often placed in the genealogy of anthropogeography and regarded as the father of those developments which are associated with such names as those of Montesquieu, Herder, Ritter, Ratzel, Reclus, Vidal de La Blache, Brunhes, Newbigin, Semple, Hessinger, *et al.* There is some warrant for this, as the excerpts from Bodin's writings, given when we were discussing possible influence by Ibn Khaldūn, go to show. Nevertheless it would be more accurate to place him as the last of the ancients, including Hippocrates, Cicero, Vitruvius, and Aquinas. His anthropogeographical conceptions, with the exception of the few we have already noted, were not founded upon close observation of geographical conditions or the behavior of man, but upon Aristotle's theory of the four elements, Hippocrates's doctrine of the four humors, and astrology. His work was that of synthesizing the old lore rather than of launching out in the direction followed by later students of the relationship between man and his physical environment.

Bodin's doctrines concerning geographical factors in history were elaborated as a guide to statesmanship. He held that the wise ruler must know the characteristics of his subjects before attempting to legislate for them. This would not only improve his rule but also do much to avert the possibility of dissatisfaction and revolution. The theoretical foundation of Bodin's conception rested first upon the Hippocratic doctrine of the " humors " which make up the human body: black bile, yellow bile, blood, and phlegm. The particular mixture of these, in the case of the individual, determined his physical health and his so-called " temperament " as bilious, sanguine, choleric, or phlegmatic. (Where is the great novelty of Kretschmer's mode of analysis?) Next came his blocking off of the planet into climatic zones. He divided the world into three climatic zones on both sides of the equator, each thirty degrees in width. Those occupying the area from the equator to thirty degrees north he described as the peoples of the south. Those living from thirty degrees north to sixty degrees north he designated as the peoples of the intermediate area — the middle climates. Those living north of the sixtieth parallel he called the peoples of the north. (He ignored, however, all those dwelling south of the equator.) Finally, he stated his views as to the astral influences affecting these peoples, from which one might learn many of their characteristics. The peoples of the south are under the domination of Saturn, Venus, and the sign of Scorpio. They are therefore given to physical lust on the one hand, and to intellectual contemplation on the other. Sexual activity is particularly marked among the peoples of the south: in Germany the men and women bathe together without any disturbance, whereas in Spain it is not thought wise to let them sit together even during mass. The peoples of the middle climates are presided over by Jupiter and Mercury; hence they are distinguished for power and agility. Those in the northern areas are under the sway of the Moon and Mars, which makes them strong and brave but leaves them stupid. The southern peoples have a melancholic temperament; and those of the northern zone a phlegmatic temperament; and those of the middle zone have a sanguine temperament in the northern portion and a choleric in the southern. Thus equipped,

Bodin felt able to generalize as to the complex of traits which characterized the peoples in each of these major climatic zones.

Bodin finds the greatest contrasts between the peoples of the southern and the northern zones:

We have said (speaking in general) that the people of the South are of a contrary humor and disposition to them of the North; these are great and strong, they are little and weak; they of the North are hot and moist, the others cold and dry; the one hath a big voice and green eyes, the other hath a weak voice and black eyes; the one hath a flaxen hair and a fair skin, the other hath both hair and skin black; the one feareth cold, and the other heat; the one is joyful and pleasant, the other sad; the one is fearful and peaceable, the other is hardy and mutinous; the one is sociable, the other solitary; the one is given to drink, the other sober; the one is rude and gruff-witted, the other advised and ceremonious; the one is prodigal and greedy, the other is courteous and holds fast; the one is a soldier, the other a philosopher; the one fit for arms and labor, the other for knowledge and rest.[16]

Like the pagan writers, Bodin concluded that the peoples of the middle area were quite obviously superior to those of the north and the south — it is to be observed that the " middle climates " now referred to France rather than to Greece and Italy! As he quaintly observes:

And the wisdom of God hath so well distributed his graces, as he hath never joined force with excellence of wit, neither in men nor beasts; for there is nothing more cruel than injustice armed with power. The people therefore of the middle regions have more force than they of the South, and less policy: and more wit than they of the North, and less force; and are more fit to command and govern Commonwealths, and more just in their actions. And if we look well into the histories of all nations, we shall find, that even as great armies and mighty powers have come out of the North; even so the hidden knowledge of philosophy, the mathematics, and other contemplative sciences, are come out of the South; and the political sciences, laws, and the study thereof, the grace of well-speaking and discoursing, have had their beginning in the middle regions, and all the great empires have been there established.

Bodin also pointed out that there is a sort of cultural division of labor among mankind based, as he believed, upon the differential effect of climate:

The people of the South are made and appointed for the search of hidden sciences, that they may instruct other nations. Those of the North for labor and manual arts; and those of the middle betwixt the two extremes, to negotiate, traffic, judge, plead, command, establish Commonwealths, and to make laws and ordinances for other nations.[17]

On the basis of theoretical assumptions even more absurd than those which buttressed his doctrine of the characteristics of the inhabitants of the three climatic zones, Bodin contended that the peoples of the west resemble those of the north, and the peoples of the east those of the south. Likewise, those living at high altitudes are similar to inhabitants of northern climates, while those living at low levels resemble the peoples of southern zones. Nevertheless, Bodin did not believe in complete, rigid geographical determinism; he held that education, laws, and institutions might exert a powerful modifying influence upon those characteristics of peoples which grew out of their geographical situation.

In Bodin's general contention that the statesman should acquaint himself with the characteristics of his subjects and that these traits are *influenced* to a considerable degree by geographical factors there was much truth. Likewise, many of the qualities which he assigned to the inhabitants of various zones were in part correct; their characterization was the product of the observations of travelers since the time of Herodotus. But with the best will in the world, there is little or nothing that can be said in defense of the mass of vagaries by means of which he attempted to explain the genesis and development of these traits. Montesquieu is said to have formulated his laws of climatic influences upon the basis of experimentation with a sheep's tongue; ludicrous as this procedure may have been, it was a vast advance in attitude and methodology as compared with Bodin's exploitation of astrology and Hippocratic physiology.

In his other important work in this field, the *Methodus ad facilem historiarum cognitionem,* Bodin brought out the first specific and detailed treatise on historical method and one of the most explicit of the early philosophies of history. The emphasis was distinctly more on the interpretation of history than upon the criticism and use of sources; there was throughout the same stressing of geographic factors in history which we have already discovered in the *Six Books concerning a Republic.* The *Method for Understanding History* was much more a forerunner of the opening chapters of Buckle's *History of Civilization in England* than of the contemporary manuals on historical method by Bernheim, Langlois and Seignobos, Keyser, and others.

Summary of Bodin's Contributions to Social Philosophy. — It is not difficult to discern the similarity between his conception of the origin of the state and that held by Ibn Khaldūn, Hume, and Ferguson, later developed by Gumplowicz and other writers of the conflict school. His definition of sovereignty as the " supreme power in a state unrestrained by law " is a starting-point of modern political science. In his doctrine of the single-family origin of society he followed Aristotle and anticipated Blackstone and Maine. His theory of the group basis of civil society gave several authors the suggestions which they pushed to the extreme characteristic of the writings of Gierke and his many followers. In coördinating ethics and politics, he paved the way for Grotius, and his suggestions as to the influence of sympathy in society were in line with the later developments of this doctrine by Spinoza, Berkeley, Hume, Ferguson, Adam Smith, and Sutherland. By premising a lawless state of primitive freedom, he gave an impetus to that old tradition which received its fullest elaboration a century later in the writings of the contract school, with its assumption of an unregulated state of nature. In his work on historical interpretation he presented one of the first attempts at a philosophy of history, a line of investigation earlier attempted by Ibn Khaldūn and later exploited by Vico, Voltaire, Turgot, Herder, Condorcet, Comte, and Buckle. Finally, his analysis of the influence of physical environment upon social behavior was the most elaborate and systematic that had appeared up to this time, though not as original as is usually affirmed.

The Scientific Revolt and Its Results in Astronomy. — But in spite of Bodin's receptivity where other social philosophies and the data of oversea exploration were concerned, he was curiously impervious to ideas deriving from the scientific inquiries carried out in his time. This is the more remarkable for the reason that the natural science with which he might have become acquainted, had he been sufficiently alert, was not a sudden outburst but a gradual growth from the time of Gerbert onward. There was no one specific cause: the new knowledge from the East, the new intellectual life promoted by the rise of the towns and their universities, the gradual pushing back of the boundaries of the unknown places of the earth — all these reagents and many more combined to bring about a cumulative ferment that finally issued in the series of scientific achievements for which the sixteenth and seventeenth centuries are famous. Why Bodin was unaffected by these innovations we do not know, but unaffected he apparently was.

Like so many other periods of innovation, the era was marked by a spirit so belligerently secular that we may justifiably use the term " revolt " in characterizing it. The scientific movement was much more than a revolt, to be sure, but we should egregiously misunderstand it if we were to lose sight of the fact that it was in strong rebellion against the speculative method and supernatural goal of scholasticism. There was abroad in Europe a passionate conviction that a new body of saving knowledge, wholly secular in character, was to be found through the observation of nature, and that in this procedure the scholastic technique, for all its undoubted logical sophistication, was impotent because, as Bacon expressed it, " Nature is more subtle than any argument."

Perhaps one major reason why the first results of early modern science were so impressive was the fact that effort was directed toward the solution of a majestic and imposing problem; namely, the nature and laws of movement of the heavenly bodies. Few would claim that Kepler and Galileo were greater scientists than Huyghens and Leeuwenhoek, but the field of their labors was one designed to give their results a more compelling interest. It should be remembered, of course, that the cosmology of the early sixteenth century, although cherished by the Schoolmen and immortalized by Dante, was not a Christian but a pagan product. One is moved to an ironical smile when he contemplates the intimidation of Copernicus, the persecution of Galileo, and the martyrdom of Bruno at the hands of Christians for uprooting a wholly pagan cosmology and theory of celestial mechanics. The Scriptural cosmology was one which represented the earth as a minute slab of earth and water supported on the void and lighted with heavenly bodies of varied candle power which studded the canopy of the heavens at no great distance from the earth.

Copernicus did little to modify the Hellenic celestial mechanics accepted by Christendom beyond exchanging the positions of the sun and the earth in the vast and complicated arrangement of fixed crystalline spheres, thus transforming it from a geocentric to a heliocentric system — *die kopernikanische Wendung*. Giordano Bruno, however, perceived clearly the implications of the shift from a geocentric to a heliocentric universe, and set them forth with impressive clarity and comprehensiveness. Among his theories damaging to the cosmology of the Christian Epic were such things as : the lack of finite limitations on or a fixed center for the universe; the fallacy of the doctrine of rigid crystalline spheres, with the substitute conception of the free motion of the heavenly bodies in space; the relativity of space, time, and motion; the ever-changing positions and relations of the heavenly bodies; the similarity or identity of the constituent materials in the heavenly and earthly bodies; and above all, the particularly disconcerting notion of the plurality of worlds. When to these challenging innovations in cosmic philosophy was added a tendency toward the popularization of such doctrines, it is not hard to understand why a Catholic Church of the Counter-Reformation type should interfere and arrange the speedy incineration of Bruno. Most of his views were at the time pure guesswork, but many have been confirmed by subsequent developments in celestial mechanics, astrophysics, and chemistry.

The succession of figures who laid the definitive basis for the celestial mechanics which held the field largely unchallenged until the era of Einstein consists of Tycho Brahe, Kepler, Galileo, and Newton. Tycho Brahe, quite in the spirit of old Hipparchus, carried on a careful study of the heavens and gathered concrete data of great value for later theorists. The first of these was his assistant, Johannes Kepler, who showed that the planets moved in elliptical rather than circular paths, that they traveled most rapidly when nearest the sun, and that there was a constant relation between the cubes of their distance from the sun and the squares of their times of revolution. Galileo founded dynamic mechanics by his famous law of falling bodies, arrived at as a result of a classic example of experimental science — an achievement so significant that Bergson is said to have remarked that modern science came down from heaven along Galileo's inclined plane. Isaac Newton combined Kepler's third law with Galileo's law of falling bodies in his famous law of inverse squares or universal gravitation, which was not only the crowning achievement of seventeenth-century science but also the inspiration for much of the Deistic philosophy and theology of the eighteenth century. The old heavens, not merely of Genesis and the astrologers but of Aristotle and Ptolemy, were wiped away, and a new cosmos of infinite expanse and complexity was substituted.

Astrophysics and Deism. — These scientific advances served to modify the conception of God and the universe entertained by many among the educated classes. The laws of motion worked out for the celestial bodies helped to break down the notion of an arbitrary God which had prevailed during the Middle Ages. He had been supposed to function chiefly in connection with some unusual occurrence such as a volcanic eruption, a comet, an earthquake, or an inundation, whereas he now came to be regarded as a law-giving and law-abiding being — the distinctive doctrine of the Deists. Likewise, the heliocentric universe and the new knowledge of its extent served to magnify the notion of God, for if one were to retain the theistic interpretation of nature at all, this newly discovered universe necessarily required a much more powerful and magnificent deity than the primitive tribal god of the ancient Hebrews, mundane, geocentric, and grossly anthropomorphic in many of his characteristics. The transformed views of God and the universe of necessity sooner or later brought changes in religious beliefs and practices, thus modifying many social institutions which had rested upon the foundations of earlier supernaturalistic conceptions.

"*Natural Religion.*" — A group of English Rationalists were the first to endeavor to state systematically the significance of the new knowledge deriving from the advance of science and the discoveries overseas for the reconstruction of the prevailing view of the world, God, man, and society. Lord Herbert of Cherbury (1583–1648) and Charles Blount (d. 1693) attempted to formulate the principles of a new or Deistic religion based upon reason and alleged to have been found in all essential phases among all peoples at all times. This "natural religion" rested upon five fundamental tenets: (1) the existence of God; (2) the worship of God; (3) the view that the promotion of better living was the chief end of worship; (4) the contention that better living must be preceded by the repentance of sins; and (5) the belief in a world to come, in which man would be dealt with in accordance with his daily life here on earth. This religion was justified on the basis of the assertion that it was reasonable and universal, whereas Christianity had been defended upon the contention that it was " a stumbling-block to the wise," and unique.

Alexander Pope in his *Universal Prayer* (1737) and other writers of like spirit later endeavored to develop and express a theory of the physical universe and of God compatible with the new astronomy and natural science. The petty God of the ancient Hebrews who " walked in his garden in the cool of the day " was manifestly not adequate to serve as the ruler of the new universe which had been revealed by the astronomers from Copernicus to Newton. It was therefore necessary greatly to magnify God in order to create a supernatural being suitable to the requirements of the Newtonian cosmic perspective. Further, the Christian notion of God had been one of divine arbitrariness. God, to the Christian, was functioning wholeheartedly only when he was apparently leading nature to deviate from its normal course by means of such manifestations as earthquakes, volcanic eruptions, tidal waves, comets, and the like. Pope and his associates were impressed with the new "laws" and processes "revealed" by natural science, and came to regard God as a law-making and law-abiding God. He was held to be especially manifest in the unending repetitions and orderly behavior of nature. Natural law was identified with divine law, God being regarded as the source of all natural manifestations.

Shaftesbury's "Gentleman-God." — The Third Earl of Shaftesbury (1671–1713) made another contribution to the reconstruction of the conception of God. The Hebrew and Christian God had frequently been regarded and described by the ultra-orthodox as an arbitrary, jealous, inconsistent, cruel, and revengeful being — a God who was, as Mark Twain remarked, guilty himself of all the sins and crimes for which he severely punished mankind. The gentle and aesthetic Shaftesbury was repelled by all this. Montaigne had earlier protested against the orthodox " slanders " on God, and held that God probably had more majestic and godlike responsibilities and interests than counting the hairs on the head of each individual daily or taking a census of the sparrows at nightfall. In other words, the divine activities were held by Montaigne to be on a divine level and of a divine character. Shaftesbury went further : he maintained that although the attributes of God far transcended the human imagination, men should at least go so far as to credit God with the urbanity and decency possessed by a cultivated English gentleman of the year 1700. It is for this reason that Shaftesbury is often mentioned as the first man to assert that God might be a gentleman. The result, then, of Deism and rationalism was greatly to magnify and dignify the prevailing conception of God; nevertheless, many of the orthodox of that age regarded these beliefs as equivalent to atheism. Most of the adherents of the new doctrines, however, including even Voltaire, believed thoroughly in the new Deistic God, and actually were thoroughgoing theists who were merely critical of " revealed religion."

The Attack on Revelation. — A number of very interesting and vital contributions to the interpretation of religion and the estimate of Christianity were offered by the group just discussed and certain other thinkers. David Hume, for example, suggested that religion be studied in a realistic fashion by psychological methods, as one would any other phase of human behavior. Hobbes, Spinoza, and Astruc laid the foundations for Biblical criticism by questioning the Mosaic authorship of the Pentateuch and encouraging what later came to be the well-founded scholarly interpretation of the sources, authors, and dates of the books of the Bible. In this way the orthodox doctrine of revelation was directly discredited at its very source while the undermining process was going on indirectly through the accumulation of scientific knowledge that challenged the scientific views embodied in the Bible. Matthew Tindal, Thomas Chubb, and Henry St. John Bolingbroke drew a sharp contrast between " true " and " historic " Christianity. True Christianity was made up of the teachings of Jesus, whereas historic Christianity was the Christian religion as it existed in the worship of the Catholics and Protestants of the seventeenth and eighteenth centuries, bearing, so these writers contended, only the most remote resemblance to the teachings of Jesus. These Deists accepted true Christianity as a valid religion because of its embodiment of the five basic tests mentioned above, but rejected historic Christianity without the slightest hesitation. Conyers Middleton, in his *Letter from Rome* (1729), for the first time adequately pointed out the large number of pagan elements which had entered into the syncrasy known as historical Christianity, and also called attention to the unreliability of the Christian Fathers as historians and chroniclers of the rise of the Faith. He showed that theirs was a credulous age, given to forgery, allegory, and miracle-mongering, however high the motives of the faithful. The great historian Gibbon explained the triumph of Christianity in the early centuries of our era as the result of secular causes rather than of divine intervention and support. Woolston, Middleton, and Hume attacked the conception of the miraculous and offered withering criticisms of the Christian belief in miracles. Hume's arguments have probably never been equaled in logical coherence and factual accuracy by any similar critic — indeed, many scholars regard them as the first sweeping refutation of the theory of miracle-working and its services to the faithful. Hume laid particular stress on the difficulty of proving the occurrence of a miracle and on the impossibility of using a miracle as proof of the validity of Christianity. He contended (1) that no occurrence could be a miracle unless it could be proved to be contrary to all known or probable scientific facts and processes; (2) that testimony concerning a miracle could not be accepted unless the veracity of the human witnesses was so impeccable that nature was more likely to vary from its normal course than such witnesses were to lie or be mistaken; and (3) that even though a real miracle was established, it could not be proved to be a miracle wrought by God, as it was freely admitted by the orthodox theologians that the Devil could work miracles at will to deceive faithful Christians.

Obviously there were important social implications of the views of these heterodox thinkers. Shaftesbury, for instance, suggested that the aesthetic basis of morality was sounder than the theological, rejecting the current notion that what was moral was what led one safely to salvation, and contending that the test of the moral was the contribution of any act to the increase of the true and the beautiful in human life. One modern writer describes him as a Greek among the Puritans; this is a vivid characterization, but its current connotations may give an erroneous impression of Shaftesbury — after all, he was a deeply religious thinker. Pope and others attacked the conventional Christian tendency to degrade man as man, to regard him, in his secular sense, as a vile entity unworthy of interest or study. The Deists, however, rejected this " vermicular attitude," upheld man as the supreme achievement of God's creative ingenuity, and contended that to depreciate man was an indirect insult to God.

By thus rehabilitating man in his secular setting the Deists made possible the rise of those sciences which are devoted to a study of the nature of man and his social relations. Hitherto only theology had been regarded as of any real significance, because it was man's soul which was important and theology was the technique for assuring its redemption. With the growth of the secular interest there inevitably came a great increase in the desire to improve social conditions by eliminating abuses and oppression and by increasing human happiness. In other words, secularism immediately suggested reforms in institutions, something in which a logical orthodox Christian could scarcely find any absorbing interest, inasmuch as he was supposed to be chiefly concerned with salvation, and many of his spiritual mentors expected secular civilization and material things to pass away fairly soon in any event. This interest in reform was best expressed by Helvétius, Condorcet, and Bentham, whom we shall consider in the chapter on progress. The rationalistic philosophy, in all its aspects, was best summarized in the various writings of Tom Paine — not an original writer, but an organizer and expositor of a high order, and a courageous crusader for truth and justice as he conceived them.

Although this rationalistic movement began in England, it soon gained headway on the Continent. Voltaire visited England in his earlier years and became the greatest of all exponents of the philosophy of freedom and enlightenment because of his versatility, his courage and zeal, and his international reputation. Diderot and the Encyclopedists, following Bayle, systematized, classified, and rendered available to the reading public the essentials of the new learning and philosophy.

Celestial Mechanics and the Notion of a "Natural Order." —
It has long been recognized by historians of social thought that
the phenomenal rise of science from 1500 to 1700 also had a remarkable influence upon the development of social, political, and
economic philosophy during the course of these and the succeeding centuries. For example, students of human relations were
profoundly impressed by the fact that Newton, in his law of inverse squares or universal gravitation, had discovered what was
believed to be a very simple explanation of the nature and movements of the physical universe. It was held that equally simple
explanations could be found for social phenomena. As Sorokin
puts it:

> The extraordinary progress of physics, mechanics, and mathematics
> during this century called forth an extraordinary effort to interpret
> social phenomena, in the same way that mechanics had so successfully
> interpreted physical phenomena.[18]

For example, the English Deists and the French *philosophes*
contended that natural laws governed society as well as the physical universe, and they created the concept of a "natural order"
to which, as the divine and physical norm, social institutions should
conform. In the field of political theory there were revived and
further developed the notions of the state of nature, natural law,
the origin of society in a social contract, and the right of revolution. In economics this notion of "naturalism" was used to defend the economic aspirations of the rising commercial or middle
class. In early modern times the absolutist state and the new
commercial activities led to widespread state interference with
certain money-getting activities. In due time, however, there arose
a group of thinkers (to be considered in detail later) who held
that inasmuch as God ruled the world of human activities as directly and thoroughly as he did the world of nature, man should
not try to interfere in this process through human legislation.[19]
If he did, he not only interfered with the divine regulation of
affairs but might even be regarded as offering an affront to God
himself; man should therefore repeal his obnoxious and obstructive legislation and let God dominate. The Almighty could best be
assured of a free hand through the existence of a régime of unlimited competition and complete *laissez faire*. In this way the
astronomical and other scientific advances of the sixteenth and
seventeenth centuries lay at the foundation of the movement for
free trade led by the Physiocrats and the classical economists, and

also furnished the basis for the opposition to factory legislation championed by the latter.[20]

In the field of social philosophy at large, the chief results were attempts to draw analogies between physical forces and laws on the one hand, and social factors and processes on the other. Ultimately this type of thought led to such developments as Comte's social physics, Herbert Spencer's purely physical interpretation of social life in Part II of his *First Principles*,[21] and Giddings's attempt to correlate physical and psychical factors in Book IV of his *Principles of Sociology*.

Berkeley's Excursion into Social Physics. — It was to this field of social philosophy that Bishop George Berkeley (1685–1753) devoted his attention. (Although he might well be dealt with in one of the chapters dealing primarily with eighteenth-century matters, his obvious relation to the themes of this chapter justifies his inclusion.) He was evidently profoundly impressed by Newton's law of inverse squares, and felt that he could apply it to social and moral phenomena. His essay embodying this attempt is entitled *Moral Attraction* (1713); it draws an analogy between the operation of physical forces in the universe and the psychical attraction between individuals in society. Although his attempt to correlate physical and social forces, or in other words to give a mechanistic explanation of society, is very crude and elementary, still there can be no doubt that he did make the effort, and that he thereby foreshadowed the work of Carey, Barcelo, Haret, Winiarski, and many others.

Berkeley shows that there is an attraction between all the bodies in the solar system, and likewise that in the minds of men there is a principle of attraction which operates in a similar manner, drawing people into the various forms of sociation. The nearer that physical bodies are placed to each other, the stronger will be their mutual attraction; so also among men those most closely related or resembling each other are most strongly attracted to each other. But at the same time those physical bodies most remote from one another have an attraction for each other, though it may be imperceptible, and if the stronger attraction of the bodies in close proximity were removed, then these remote bodies would be drawn together. In the same way, if two men who are different meet in a place inhabited by individuals differing from both more than they do from each other, then these two individuals will feel a mutual attraction. (As will be noted, this bears a certain resemblance to Giddings's theory of the " consciousness of kind," but Berkeley did not offer it as an explanation of association, but rather as a result of the " social instinct," which he was content to explain by the theological assumption that it was due to divine action.)

On the other hand, there are centrifugal forces in the universe which prevent all the bodies in the solar system from uniting in one mass; similarly, in society, individual passions and desires tend to obstruct the perfect action of the "social instinct" — sociation includes dissociation as well as association.

The attractive force in the solar system, he holds, cannot be explained in any other way than by the immediate action of God, and neither can the principle of human associativeness. It does not originate, he says, from education, law, or fashion, but is an original gift of the creator. As the attractive principle of the universe is the key to natural phenomena, so is the " social instinct " the source and explanation of all the various actions of man in society which may be called moral or social.

Although Berkeley stops short of trying to find a psychological explanation for the "social instinct," the method which he introduces — namely, analogy between physical and mental forces, and influence of the "social instinct" upon social activities — makes this essay one of the most interesting contributions to social philosophy up to his time. As early as 1713 there was a writer who had formulated at least the rudiments of Giddings's contention that " sociology insists that one fundamental logic underlies the objective or physical, and the subjective or volitional explanations of social phenomena." Berkeley also foreshadowed that emphasis on sympathy as a factor in society which later in the century was to be elaborated by Hume and Adam Smith. The following is the relevant part of the text of his important essay:

From the contemplation of the order, motion, and cohesion of natural bodies, philosophers are now agreed that there is a mutual attraction between the most distant parts at least of this solar system. . . . And as the larger systems of the universe are held together by this cause, so likewise the particular globes derive their cohesion and consistence from it.

Now if we carry our thoughts from the corporeal to the moral world, we may observe in the Spirits or Minds of men a like principle of attraction, whereby they are drawn together in communities, clubs, families, friendships, and all the various species of society. As in bodies, where the quantity is the same, the attraction is strongest between those which are placed nearest to each other, so it is likewise in the minds of man, *caeteris paribus,* between those who are most nearly related. Bodies that are placed at the distance of many millions of miles may nevertheless attract and constantly operate on each other, although this action does not show itself by a union or approach of those distant bodies, so long as they are withheld by the contrary forces of other bodies. . . . The like holds with regard to the human soul, whose affection towards the individuals of the same species who are distantly related to it is rendered inconspicuous by its more powerful attraction towards those who have a nearer relation to it. But as those are removed the tendency which before lay concealed doth gradually disclose itself. . . . These are natural reflections, and such as may convince us that we are linked by an imperceptible chain to every individual of the human race.

The several great bodies which compose the solar system are kept from joining together at the common center of gravity by the rectilinear motions the Author of nature has impressed on each of them. . . . After the same manner, in the parallel case of society, private passions and motions of the soul do often obstruct the operation of that benevolent uniting instinct implanted in human nature; which, notwithstanding, doth still exert, and will not fail to show itself when those obstructions are taken away. . . .

And as the attractive power in bodies is the most universal principle which produceth innumerable effects, and is a key to explain the various phenomena of nature; so the corresponding social appetite in human souls is the great spring and source of moral actions. This it is that inclines each individual to an intercourse with his species, and models everyone to that behavior which best suits the common well-being. Hence that sympathy in our nature whereby we feel the pains and joys of our fellow creatures. . . . In a word, hence arises that diffusive sense of Humanity so unaccountable to the selfish man who is untouched with it, and is, indeed, a sort of a monster or anomalous production.[22]

Summary of the Chapter. — At the beginning of the chapter we pointed out that man's abode became both larger and smaller in the period discussed: larger because of the oversea ventures and the gradual appreciation of the fact that new continents and not merely " new islands of the Indies " had been discovered; smaller because science showed the earth to be " a tiny mote floating in the dust of a cosmic back alley." The effects of the expansion of Europe during the later phases of the Age of Discovery were then analyzed, and Montaigne was chosen as an example of the secularizing effect of the comparison of cultures. His scepticism was dealt with at length, his rôle as progenitor of Deism noted, and his urbanity and mental mobility briefly mentioned. We then called attention to another writer of the sixteenth century, Jean Bodin, and dwelt upon the similarity of certain of his doctrines to those of Ibn Khaldūn. Bodin's place as an early combat theorist, exponent of the monistic doctrine of sovereignty, psycho-sociologist of the " sympathy school," precursor of social contract political philosophy, anthropogeographer, and philosopher of history was then discussed, and his failure to make use of the new natural science dawning in his day was commented upon. Next, the scientific revolt and its results in astronomy were passed in review, and the effects upon Deism, rationalism, and " natural order " theories were given due weight and the attack on revealed religion was noted. After this, the influence of astrophysics and celestial mechanics upon attempts to draw analogies between physical and social processes was discussed, and Berkeley's excursion into social physics adduced as an example of such analogies.

The ethically relativistic point of view, exemplified by Montaigne and others.discussed in the present chapter, has of course had expounders (who were not in all cases advocates) at least as far back as Herodotus. The evidence regarding diversity in ethical precept and practice has long been known; the peoples taken into account have varied, but their deviations have often resulted in relativistic conclusions, on the part of many of their varied observers, that in essence are strikingly similar. At the same time, many other observers, quite as well informed, have refused to draw such conclusions! They may be termed, if not ethical absolutists, at least antirelativists. Debate, often acrimonious, between the representatives of the opposing camps, as well as among those who cannot readily be classified with the extremists, has gone on for a long time, and shows few signs of waning.

Sociologists are often placed entirely within the relativistic group, both by themselves and others. The author responsible for the present edition, however, feels that even among sociologists there have been too many eminent writers not fundamentally identified with relativism, whether extreme or moderate, to warrant any such all-inclusive placement. Further, he feels that even though sociology is in his view the basic social science (see Preface to the First Edition), this does not entitle the sociologist to make final pronouncement on issues that properly concern all "men of knowledge" (to use Znaniecki's apt designation). We may grant, with Dickens, that Uriah Heep was much too 'umble, but we must also grant that Alfred Jingle was much too bumptious.

Turning to less general matters, it may be well to note that the chapter might well have included some reference to Masonry as, in its inception at least, of Deistic character. For the sociologist, such voluntary associations bearing well-marked ideologies are or should be of great interest. Further, the ways in which Freemasons have come to define their roles in this or that social context have much significance for sociology of knowledge.

The present interest in deductive models of social systems, with its parallel interest in mathematical formulations amenable to computer techniques, might lead to interest in earlier models such as Berkeley's, although perhaps the latter, and others like it, may be thought to fall in the category "curiosity."

CHAPTER X

New Nation, New Citizen:
The Vogue of Contract Doctrines

SECULARIZERS: MONARCH AND NATION. — We have dealt at length with a number of influences that helped to usher in the early modern period, and among these was the growth of secular absolutism. It is now necessary to consider this in greater detail and in relation to certain other factors, notably the increasing power of the national state, if we are properly to understand the social theories then prevalent. It was necessary to justify the existence of secular absolutism, to defend the national state against ecclesiastical claims, to vindicate absolute monarchy, and later, as the bourgeoisie rose to power, to justify popular sovereignty, representative government, and the right of revolution. Although it is exceedingly difficult to account for the emergence of the social contract theory on the basis of the above-listed necessities alone, there can be little doubt that its ready acceptance was primarily due to the general social situation.[1] But we anticipate; let us first see what the historical background was like.

The Commercial Revolution and the National State. — In discussing the disorganizing effects of culture contact during the late medieval period and in analyzing certain phases of the Humanist movement and the Protestant Revolt, we noted the fact that both Renaissance and Reformation, as ordinarily understood, were but phases or results of that great transformation which marks the origin of the modern world and the national-state system — the Commercial Revolution. By this is meant not only the discoveries, the revival of trade, and the "intervention of capital," but also the reactions of these innovations upon the whole basis of European civilization. The permanent intellectual progress which followed the so-called revival of the fifteenth century was not so much the result of the resurrection of an antique culture as it was the product of the new mental mobility which came from the contact of cultures and the intellectual curiosity stimulated by the discoveries.

The chief impulse that the Commercial Revolution brought to the growth of national states came from the rise of the middle class and their alliance with the monarchs in the attempts to destroy the anarchy and decentralization of the feudal system. Hitherto the kings had been compelled to depend upon the feudal lords for the administration of law, the provision of royal funds, and the military protection of the realm. It could scarcely be supposed that the feudal lords would render effective aid to any policy designed to limit their powers or terminate the political order to which they owed their existence. There was, therefore, no possibility of bringing about that important step in the political development of the Western world, the destruction of medieval feudalism, until a new class had arisen with sufficient strength to furnish the kings with the loyal aid necessary to cope with the recalcitrant upholders of the old order, and until a source of royal income had been provided which would enable the kings to hire loyal officials and armies without relying for their financial support upon feudal taxes. Both of these all-important prerequisites for the growth of administrative centralization, political concentration, and the rise of the dynastic national state were supplied by the Commercial Revolution. A loyal officialdom, opposed to the feudal aristocracy, appeared in the new *noblesse de la robe* — the middle-class merchants and lawyers who filled the royal offices. Through the "intervention of capital," through the flood of wealth streaming into the royal treasuries from the national share in the profits of the new commercial and industrial enterprises, the kings were provided with the indispensable financial power to hire their own administrators and to support a national army independent of the feudal lords.

The Wars of Political Centralization. — The emergence of the national dynastic state in modern times was first manifested in the case of England. Occasioning factors were the appearance, in 1485, of a shrewd and vigorous monarch in the person of Henry VII, and the circumstance that in England alone had the feudal nobility been gracious and self-effacing enough to prepare for their destruction by a war of mutual extermination — the War of the Roses (1455–1485). Henry VII filled the royal coffers by taxing the feudal nobles through the use of " Morton's Fork " and other ingenious devices, haled recalcitrant and rebellious feudal lords before the Court of the Star Chamber, and encouraged the new commerce by treaties such as the *Intercursus Magnus* and by subsidizing explorers such as the Cabots. His son, Henry VIII, broke with Rome and gave a quasi-religious basis to the growing English nationalism. Elizabeth profited by the labors of her father and grandfather, and her reign witnessed the first great cultural expressions of English nationalism, as well as the emergence of England as a leading naval and colonizing nation. By the close of the Tudor period (1603), England had become a highly centralized dynastic national state. Feudalism in its political aspects had passed, and the middle class had so developed its political strength that a half-century later it was able to demonstrate its superiority over the crown.

After a brief but brilliant development of Portuguese nationalism (1498–1580), Spain was next in the order of national development. Charles V had been an imperialist rather than a nationalist, and had hoped to revive the medieval Empire, but his son and heir in Spain, Philip II (1555–1598), was a true Spanish nationalist. He attempted to bring unity not only to Spain but also to the Spanish possessions in the Netherlands. His over-ardent nationalism, however, brought disruption rather than centralization, and in 1567 the Dutch, led by William the Silent, broke into active revolt. The new Dutch national state declared its independence in 1581, and secured the European confirmation of its action at Westphalia in 1648.

A century after England had emerged from civil war with a strong national monarch at the head of the state, Henry IV, the founder of the French Bourbon dynasty, came forth victorious over his opponents in the civil war and was crowned king in 1589. Capturing not only Paris but France " by a mass," he began with his great minister, Sully, the building of the dynastic national state in France. His work was cut short by his death at the hand of the assassin, Ravaillac; but his work and plan were carried on with vigor and determination by the great ecclesiastics and statesmen, Richelieu and Mazarin, until by the time of the suppression of the Fronde, in 1652, the feudal system as a dominating political power in France had passed away. The fruit of the work of Henry, Sully, Richelieu, and Mazarin was appropriated by Louis XIV, in whose reign France not only reached the height of its dynastic centralization, but attained to the cultural primacy of Europe. The Thirty Years' War (1618–1648) in Germany brought with it a multitude of nationalistic movements and demonstrated the fundamentally political nature of the Protestant Revolt. The stirrings of national ambitions in Bohemia (1618–1620) and in Denmark (1625–1629) were speedily repressed, but Sweden forged to the front as a great national state (1630–1632) and maintained its position until it was lost through the overweening ambition of the warrior king, Charles XII (1697–1718).

The Treaty of Westphalia first gave general European recognition to the growing national-state system and to the existence of independent national sovereignty. It brought diversity rather than unity to Germany, however, and necessitated the postponement of German unification until the latter part of the nineteenth century, when this anachronistic and belated process disturbed the peace of the world. But if a unified national German state was not the product of this general period of the development of dynastic national states, there appeared the dynasty and the state which were ultimately to bring centralization and unity to Germany — Prussia under the Hohenzollerns. After having developed from robber barons into wealthy city magnates of Nuremberg in southern Germany, the Hohenzollerns appeared upon the North European stage through the purchase of the mark of Brandenburg from the bankrupt Emperor Sigismund by Frederick Hohenzollern in 1415. Through fortunate marriage arrangements the dynasty secured the possession of Prussia in 1618. The basis of the Prussian bureaucracy and military system was laid by Frederick William, the Great Elector (1640–1688), and the process was carried to completion by Frederick William I (1713–1740). Starting with these contributions of his ancestors, Frederick the Great (1740–1785) was able by diplomatic skill and military genius to raise Prussia to the rank of a first-rate European power and to create that German political dualism which erected a final barrier to German national unification until Austria had been humiliated and finally ousted in 1866.

In the latter part of the seventeenth century Poland acquired a degree of power which enabled it to save Christendom from the Turk in 1683, but unfavorable geographical situation, ethnic, religious, and social diversity, and unrestrained feudal anarchy prevented Poland from securing permanent national unity and condemned it to a steady decline into a century and a half of dismemberment and servitude. Even semi-Asiatic Russia did not remain immune in this general European process of national differentiation and centralization. Under its barbarous and brutal but able ruler, Peter the Great (1696–1725), political power was centralized, a national royal army was established, European manners and customs were introduced, and Russian foreign policy was given a westward orientation. By 1721 the Baltic provinces had been taken from Sweden and the all-important "window to the West" secured. Although neither Prussia nor Russia was seriously affected by the direct impact of the Commercial Revolution, the growth of nationalism in these states during the seventeenth and eighteenth centuries was indirectly almost wholly a result of the political reactions of this great economic movement. In both states nationalistic policies were adopted in obvious imitation of the administrative and military methods of the monarchs of the new national states. The Great Elector aped the policies, methods, and measures of Richelieu, Mazarin, and Louis XIV; and Frederick I took as his model William III of England. Peter the Great learned from England and Holland the secrets of the new industry and commerce, while from Louis XIV he obtained his pattern for political centralization and military reorganization. By the middle of the eighteenth century, then, national states had been created in most of Europe. Only in Germany, Italy, and the Balkans was this process postponed until the next century.

The Rise of Mercantilism. — The growth of nationalism during the period of the Commercial Revolution was forwarded by forces other than political centralization. The nationalistic commercial policy known as Mercantilism, which developed more or less universally after 1500 as the general body of economic and commercial doctrines which governed European trade and industry until the middle of the nineteenth century, operated strongly in the way of increasing national consciousness, self-interest, and jealousy, and was a potent stimulant to international friction. Commerce during this period became little other than collective or national piracy, in which the " rights " of other nations were ignored or denied, but there can be little doubt that national consolidation was thereby greatly furthered.

The Upsurge of National Literatures. — In addition to this powerful economic impulse to nationalistic and militaristic policies, a strong intellectual influence arose in the remarkable development of vernacular literature, in spite of the spell of the Classical revival known as Humanism. Italy produced Machiavelli, Guicciardini, Ariosto, and Tasso; France, Rabelais, Montaigne, Corneille, Molière, and Racine; Spain, Cervantes, Lope de Vega, and Calderon; Portugal, Camoëns, Miranda, and Ferreira; England, More, Spenser, Shakespeare, Jonson, Marlowe, Bacon, and Milton; and Germany, Sachs, Ayrer, Opitz, and Fleming. Even Holy Writ was no longer a unifying force in literature, but in the translations of Luther and the King James Version became a powerful vehicle in the development, popularization, and improvement of the vernacular language and a subtle and effective force making for nationalistic divisions. The vernacular literature not only gave literary expression to the growing differentiation of national cultures, but constituted a national possession of first-rate importance which served as a patriotic inspiration for the generations to come.

Before the end of the eighteenth century, then, Europe had ceased to be either feudal or imperial and had come to be primarily national in political organization, economic policy, and intellectual tastes and expression. What was further needed to perfect the nationalistic system was the thrill furnished by the French Revolution and its results, and the provision of a real nervous system for the new nationalism in the improved or revolutionized methods of communication and transportation which came in as a phase of the Industrial Revolution.

The Increasing Power of the Middle Class. — In England during the period marked by the growth of nationalism the new middle class effected the greatest transformation of the social and political order which was accomplished before the nineteenth century. By the beginning of the seventeenth century the power of the feudal nobility had generally vanished, serfdom had disappeared, and the restrictive guild system of industrial organization had been practically eliminated. Before the close of the century, through successive concessions from the king and through the revolutions of 1649 and 1688–89, the bourgeoisie had dethroned two autocratic monarchs, had eliminated royal arbitrariness in politics and law, had brought about the predominance of Parliament in the government, and had enacted into a constitutional document those guarantees which have since come to be recognized, whatever one may think of democracy, as the most fundamental bulwarks of the democratic system. Although oppressive religious disabilities, exclusive property qualifications for participation in political life, and the perpetuation of many of the social phases of medieval feudal aristocracy all operated to prevent England from being classed as a democratic nation in 1700, the fact that the middle class had created a constitutional system and had secured complete ascendency in Parliament — the popular branch of the government — constituted an epoch-making step toward the ultimate realization of democracy.

In France, even more than in Tudor England, the Commercial Revolution at first made rather for the development of royal absolutism than for the growth of constitutional or representative government. The Estates-General, summoned in 1614 for the last time in nearly two centuries, quite failed as compared with the achievements of the English Parliament; and hope of a gradual growth of legislative supremacy in France, such as had taken place in England, perished. The political power of the feudal nobility was crushed by Richelieu's centralizing policies and by the suppression of the Fronde in 1652, but they retained their social and economic privileges until the "August days" of 1789. The French Revolution of 1789 to 1795 was the product of the faulty tactics of the *ancien régime,* of the revolutionary political theory of the English Whigs, of the intellectual impulse from the French *philosophes,* and of the American example of a successful experiment with revolution and the beginnings of democracy. The "third estate" had been too weak in 1614 successfully to oppose the combined strength of the monarch and the first two estates; but its strength had so increased by 1789, as a result of the effects of the Commercial Revolution, that it was able to coerce the monarch, the weakened nobility, and the clergy, and it proceeded to dispense with not only the vestiges of feudalism but also the guidance of the church and the control of the monarch. The calling of the Estates-General in 1789 is worthy of passing mention here, because the first instance in history of the exercise of universal manhood suffrage occurred quite incidentally in the election of the deputies of the third estate. The most significant changes associated with the French Revolution were the abolition of those economic and social aspects of feudalism which still persisted, and the establishment of a constitutional monarchy in 1791 and of a republic in 1792. Though many of these reforms proved transitory, their effect was never entirely lost; and they constituted the stimulus and precedent for the more gradual development of French democracy in the nineteenth century.

In all other important European states, with the exception of the abortive reforms of Joseph II of Austria and the benevolent despotism of Frederick the Great, the old régime with all its medieval institutions and practices remained practically undisturbed until the nineteenth century. It was not until after the disintegrating influence of the French Revolution was spread throughout Europe by Napoleon, and particularly until the Industrial Revolution had still further increased the numerical strength of the bourgeoisie, that this class was able to carry its liberalizing activities with some degree of success into central, southern, and eastern Europe.

The establishment of an aristocratic republic in America in the closing years of the eighteenth century marked an important transition in the development of political structures. Although

American society and politics abounded, at the beginning, in un-democratic features, the new state had been founded through revolution from established authority. Moreover, it was one of the first examples in history of an extensive federal republic and of a government organized on the basis of a written constitution formulated by a national constituent convention. It therefore stimulated the growth of constitutionalism and republicanism elsewhere, most notably in France; and it laid the foundations for what became in the nineteenth century the most ambitious experiment that had yet been conducted in the democratic control of political institutions. In America, as in England and France, the revolutionary movement was organized by the bourgeoisie made up of planters, merchants, and the professional classes.

The Political Doctrines of the Bourgeois Revolutions. — In the period between 1500 and 1800 many notable advances were made toward anti-feudal forms of social theory that in some instances, at least, made for representative government, or even for egalitarian democracy. The most significant and influential of these, as already noted, was the doctrine of a social contract as the explanation of the origin and justification of social institutions and political organization.

This doctrine, as distinguished from the earlier theory of a governmental compact, apparently was first enunciated by Æneas Sylvius in the middle of the fifteenth century, as has already been pointed out, but it did not become an important dogma in social and political theory until it was expressed by the English churchman, Hooker, and the German jurist, Althusius, at the opening of the seventeenth century. It received systematic exposition in a number of classical works, particularly those of Hobbes, Pufendorf, Spinoza, Sydney, Locke, Rousseau, Kant, and Fichte (to be dealt with in following sections). It was not necessarily a democratic doctrine, and it was used by some of its adherents, most notably by Hobbes, to defend royal absolutism. In the hands of Locke and Rousseau, however, it worked strongly for the destruction of the divine right theory, and it also provided a theoretical justification for altering the existing political order when it had become subversive of the terms of the supposed original contract. In other words, it provided a doctrinal foundation for political revolutions, and it was used to inspire and justify the great revolutions of the seventeenth and eighteenth centuries in England, France, and America.

In spite of our ability to trace this chain of influences, it must be said that the emergence of the social contract doctrine is very difficult to account for on the sole basis of the existing social situation. Carlyle has made clear the general diffusion of the doctrine of a governmental compact during the medieval period,[2] and we have just noted the part played by Æneas Sylvius. Giddings has insisted that the social contract theory naturally emerges in a society where political relations have long been based on parliamentary procedure and a tradition of legality, and where there is a considerable degree of homogeneity in the population.[3] The fact that the first definite instances of the enunciation of the theory may be assigned to churchmen who had been under the sway of the long-established legal systems of the Roman faith and the Church of England lends plausibility to at least a part of Giddings's theory. Again, Ritchie has pointed out the prevalence of actual contractual associations in the seventeenth century, such as the Mayflower Compact, the Solemn League and Covenant, and the " associations " of the Commonwealth period, and has further indicated the value of the contract doctrine to those writers who were seriously endeavoring to establish and justify political liberty.[4]

Finally, it should again be noted that the social contract theory bore a definite relation to the economic and political conditions of the period. As earlier sections have done something to show, the growth of commerce and capital emphasized the importance of contracts in the sphere of economic activities, and also made possible the existence of strong national states. The origin and justification of these powerful political organizations offered an impressive problem to social philosophers, and the doctrine of social contract was the first important " solution " of this problem. Further, the increased numbers, power, and ambition of the new middle class brought them into conflict with the absolute monarchs, for the latter tried to tax the trade of the merchants for all that the traffic would bear. To justify the bourgeois resistance, the theory of natural rights, the social contract, and the right of revolution were most convenient and appropriate.

It should always be borne in mind that the majority of the exponents of the contract theory did not advance it as a literal historical explanation of the origin of the state, but rather as an analytical interpretation of its existence. Many eager critics have made undeserved capital out of their misunderstanding of this important aspect of the contract theory. This of course is not to defend the analytical interpretation; as we shall later see, Hume showed that the analytical foundations of the doctrine were fully as weak as its pseudo-historical basis.[5]

The revolutionary versions of the social contract theory powerfully stimulated the development of the doctrine of popular sovereignty. Another important contribution was the doctrine that " life, liberty, and property " are the natural and inherent rights of all men. This theory, first stated by Fortescue at the close of the fifteenth century, was again enunciated by the Levellers, an English sect recruited from the poorer classes in the middle of the seventeenth century, and was given a permanent position in political theory through the influence of John Locke. It was widely at variance with the contemporary social and economic *status quo,* and it was highly influential in combating the conditions sanctioned in and through the *status quo,* especially when demands for " natural and inherent rights " became part of the programs of the radical parties in the various countries. In addition to their early formulation of the doctrine of natural rights, the Levellers made another significant contribution to the general body of democratic political theory: namely, the doctrine that every citizen should be accorded the right of participating in political activity through the exercise of the suffrage. Another important doctrine making for effective parliamentarism was that which was most vigorously expounded by Locke: viz., the legal supremacy of the legislative or popular branch of the government. Finally, the utopian schemes of such writers as More, Bacon, Campanella, and the prerevolutionary socialists in France made provision for the introduction of some degree of social democracy.

It is most significant, however, that during this entire period there was no systematic analysis of the meaning and implications of democracy, nor, with the doubtful exception of Mably in France, Paine in England, and Jefferson in America, was there any important defense of democracy as the ideal form of government. Most of the radicals regarded a constitutional monarchy or, at the most, an aristocratic republic as the ideal form of government. Montesquieu and Rousseau, for example, both held that a democracy would only be tolerable in a very small state and could never be successful in an extensive country. In short, all the theories of the period which have been briefly summarized above were mere fragmentary contributions, most of them shot through with value-judgments, rather than comprehensive and critical discussions of the nature and validity of democracy itself.

The historical background should now be fairly clear; we may properly turn our attention to the many differing versions of the social contract theory and their varying theoretical and practical consequences.

Hooker: Explicit Contractualist. — The work of Richard Hooker (1552–1600), was almost as suggestive as that of Bodin.[6] Although his treatise, *The Laws of an Ecclesiastical Polity* (1594–1600), dealt primarily with the defense of the Anglican Church, he devoted a portion of the first book to a discussion of society and government in general.

Hooker emphasized the fact that government originated in the consent of the governed and must be administered according to law. He thus agreed with the previous doctrines of a governmental compact and popular sovereignty.[7] This doctrine of a compact as the origin of government was an old one. It had appeared in the writings of the Confucian followers of Mencius, the Brahmans of the *shastras,* the Sophists, Epicurus, Lucretius, the Roman Lawyers, Manegold of Lautenbach, Aquinas, Marsiglio, William of Ockham, Nicholas of Cues, and the monarchomachs of the sixteenth century, such as Hotman, Languet, Duplessis-Mornay, Knox, and Buchanan. Nevertheless, no previous writer — with the exception of Æneas Sylvius (who did not, however, explicitly state and systematically develop his theory) — had advanced the doctrine of a social contract; namely, that society arose by the deliberate agreement of men to escape from the evils of a pre-social condition.[8] Hooker, however, definitely set forth this doctrine of a social contract, and it seems certain that he may be accorded the rather questionable honor of having first stated the theory as such.[9] Hooker did not, however, go as far as Hobbes; he did not claim that man in the state of nature was unsocial, but on the contrary agreed with Aristotle on this point. At the same time, Hooker asserted that sociability must be supplemented by a covenant which embodies the rules according to which association is to be guided and restrained. Owing to the chronological importance of Hooker's formulation of the social contract, it seems advisable to quote the precise passages from his work, italicizing those that seem most important:

We see then how Nature itself teacheth laws and statutes to live by. The laws [of nature] which have been hitherto mentioned do bind men absolutely even as they are men, although they have never any settled fellowship, never any solemn agreement amongst themselves what to do or not to do. But forasmuch as we are not by ourselves sufficient to furnish ourselves with competent store of things needful for such a life as our nature doth desire, a life fit for the dignity of man, therefore to supply those defects and imperfections which are in us living singly and solely by ourselves, *we are naturally induced to seek communion and fellowship with others.* This was the cause of men's uniting themselves at the first in politic societies, which societies could not be without government, nor government without a distinct kind of law from that which hath been already declared [natural law]. *Two foundations there are which bear up public societies — the one, a natural inclination, whereby all men desire sociable life and fellowship; the other, an order expressly or secretly agreed upon touching the manner of their union in living together.* The latter is that which we call the law of a common weal, the very soul of a politic body, the parts whereof are by law animated, held together, and set on work in such actions as the common good requireth. . . .

We all make complaint of the iniquity of our times; not unjustly, for the days are evil. But compare them with those times wherein there were no civil societies; with those times wherein there was as yet no manner of public regiment established, with those times wherein there were not above eight righteous persons living upon the face of the earth; and we have surely good cause to think that God hath blessed us exceedingly, and hath made us behold most happy days. *To take away all such mutual grievances, injuries, and wrongs, there was no way but only by growing unto composition and agreement amongst themselves; by ordaining some kind of government public, and by yielding themselves subject thereunto;* that unto whom they granted authority to rule and govern, by them the peace, tranquillity, and happy estate of the rest might be procured. . . .

So that in a word all public regiment, of what kind soever, seemeth evidently to have risen from deliberate advice, consultation, and composition between men, judging it convenient and behoveful; there being no impossibility in Nature considered by itself, but that men might have lived without any public regiment.[10]

Many other interesting suggestions were advanced by Hooker. Especially important was his primary reliance upon reason rather than authority, which marked a departure from certain phases of scholasticism.[11]

Suarez and Mariana. — Another churchman of this period, the Spanish Jesuit, Francis Suarez (1548–1617), in his *Tractatus de legibus ac Deo legislatore* (1612), expanded the doctrines of Aquinas by devoting especial attention to the function of law as a regulating principle in human association. To Suarez man was almost a " legal animal," so minutely did he analyze his dependence upon law.[12] In this respect he made his chief advances beyond Aristotle and Aquinas (for he accepted their dictum that man is by nature social); he linked up the view of the natural sociability of man with the social contract doctrine. He held that while men were naturally impelled to live in groups, no orderly or organized social life was possible without that act of collective will which came to be known as the social contract. Lilley says on this point:

> For him organized society, the distinctly political community, is a necessary expression and result of man's social nature. Without the voluntary act which constitutes society men are merely a multitude of unrelated or accidentally associated wills. From that state of primitive confusion they extricated themselves by the act of reason which recognized a common good to be sought and the act of will which constituted themselves into a society capable of achieving it. Thus the political society, the mystical body pledged to the pursuit of the common good, came into existence through the deliberate act of its members voluntarily sacrificing their individual liberty to this end. It is already the Social Contract theory of Rousseau.[13]

Another important element in the work of Suarez was his harmonizing of the doctrine of popular sovereignty with the theory that monarchy is the best type of government. While the supreme power resides in the people, they may alienate it from themselves and confer it upon the ruler by an act of popular will. Once this power is delegated, it is irrevocable except in the case of tyranny on the part of the monarch. Suarez admitted the legitimacy of tyrannicide in the latter case.[14]

Suarez's contemporary and fellow-Jesuit, the Spanish writer Juan de Mariana (1536–1624), offered an interesting interpretation of the early history of human society in his *De rege et regis institutione* (1605). In the beginning men had lived like animals, without authority and guided only by instinct, but free from the greed and artificial immoralities of civilization. Man, however, had greater wants than other animals; his offspring was less rapid in developing to maturity, and he was less protected by his native equipment from natural dangers and external enemies. To live in safety from attack men therefore had to group themselves together and submit to the authority of some capable leader who was able to direct the resulting political society along lines conducive to the general welfare.[15] Although a believer in the natural sociability of man, Mariana may therefore be said to have implied the social contract in his theory of civic origins. His somewhat sentimental picture of the state of nature probably approached nearer to that advanced by Rousseau in parts of his famous second *Discourse* than the views of any other writer of the period, and his theory of the influence of the prolongation of infancy was directly in line with that elaborated in the late nineteenth century by John Fiske.[16]

Althusius, Supposed Federalist. — We include the eminent German social theorist, Johannes Althusius (1557–1638), in this chapter focusing on contract doctrines for the somewhat paradoxical purpose of showing that he does not belong here.

Althusius has long been regarded as the outstanding exponent of the theory of the contractual foundation of the state on a federal basis. This interpretation has in part come about through the use of the first edition of his work rather than the second and third (where his sociological theories were more fully expressed), and in part as a result of viewing his doctrines through legalistic rather than sociological lenses. The main expositors of the traditional view have been the German jurist, Otto von Gierke, and his English disciples, Maitland and Figgis. The following quotation from Figgis admirably summarizes the *erroneous* interpretation of Althusius:

> To Althusius, however, the contract is social, it is the mutual agreement of all to live in an ordered society . . . the rights of sovereignty belong not to the ruler, whether one, many, or few, but to the members of the association. The sovereignty of the people becomes the foundation of the State. . . . This federalistic idea is to be found in Althusius and through him connects itself with the medieval theory of community life. There is not much difference between the idea of the *communitas communitatum* which the Middle Ages meant by the commons, and Althusius' notion of the State as above all else a *consociato consociationum*. . . . The novelty in him is his view of the State as entirely built up on the principle of associations. . . . Althusius starts, not, like some writers on politics, from the top, but from the bottom; the unit of civil life is for him not the individual but the family, and he rises by a series of concentric circles from the family to the town, to the province, and the State. His State is a true *Genossenschaft,* a fellowship of all the heads of families, and he takes care to prevent the absorption of local and provincial powers into the central administration. It is not merely that he allows rights to families and provinces; but he regards these rights as anterior to the State, as the foundation of it, and as subsisting always within it.[17]

Friedrich, editor of the best text of Althusius and author of the latest authoritative commentary thereon, seems completely to have overthrown the above interpretation. It now appears that Althusius's doctrines must be approached through the field of sociology, or at least of social biology, rather than through that of the medieval and early modern law of the corporation and the medieval theory of voluntary functional association.

Althusius's definition of politics shows at the outset that his approach was sociological: " Politics is the science of linking human beings to each other for a social life. . . . Therefore, it is called the science of those matters which pertain to the living together." As Friedrich points out:

> If one approaches Althusius through Gierke, he gets the impression that Althusius is developing a system of public law. But Althusius was interpreting the State as the community organized for coöperation toward the attainment of common purposes. The natural conditions of such communal life are the subject-matter of politics, its legal consequences belong to jurisprudence.[18]

To this process of living together in a political community Althusius gave the name of *symbiosis,* being apparently the first modern writer to use the term in such a manner. To the members of the body politic he applies the concept, *symbiotici,* meaning literally, those who live together. The origins of society and the state, then, are not to be found in a contract of any kind. They are natural socio-biological phenomena. This sets Althusius apart from the current legalistic theorizing of his day. As Friedrich observes: " In thus emphasizing a biological basis of political life which precedes all thinking and willing, Althusius seems rather far removed from the trends of political speculation which became dominant after the middle of the seventeenth century."

This socio-biological doctrine of Althusius may have been a result of the fact that his German compatriots at the time were taking the lead in reviving the Greek biology and launching a new era in biological observation. Otto Brunfels, Jerome Bock, and Leonard Fuchs had just founded modern botany in Germany. Valerius Cordus, also in Germany, had laid the basis for biological classification, and Conrad Gesner in Zürich had revived Aristotelian biology on a vast scale, embellishing it by an original investigation of the behavior and traits of animals. Another influence was the supposed exemplification of biological symbiosis in the German town life of the period, with its highly developed communal character.

The notion of a biological basis of social and political life provided Althusius with his theory of the origins of political power. The latter arises, in last analysis, out of the fundamental conditions of life " in a community living together by nature (*consociatio symbiotica*)." This upsets the conventional interpretation of Althusius's conception of the nature of political association; namely, as a voluntary affair manifesting itself in a complex set of contractual relations. As Friedrich does well to emphasize:

When Althusius talks about the state, the body politic, as a 'consociatio symbiotica,' he thinks of it as a vital phenomenon, as a natural phenomenon which leaves no choice to the individual. The notion that the people could choose in this matter is simply inconceivable from Althusius' point of view. . . . The truth is that the difference between public and private functions tends to disappear, just as it does in modern socialism, if all groups including the state are looked upon as natural phenomena to be explained sociologically and not legally.

It was this fact which made possible the extreme secular absolutism in the political theory of Althusius, and explains why he could go much further along this road than even Bodin. " One must not forget," writes Friedrich, " that Althusius could with greater confidence attribute such a position to the state, because in the last analysis the state embraced everything and everybody. . . . Althusius' state devours the entire community, becomes òne with it."

What becomes of the prevailing theory which portrays Althusius as the great federalist, as the expositor of the view that the state is a conscious federal unity based on the voluntary contractual relations of lesser constituent groups, themselves contractual in character? From what has gone before, we can readily see that it completely evaporates. This is especially true when we follow the exposition in the second and third editions of his book. Any contractual basis for a symbiotic group, whether the family, the guild, or the state, is entirely fanciful. Private agreements have no place in Althusius's theory of association, for in it the state " devours the community." If there is any contractual relationship, it is purely an implicit and tacit affair, as when the citizen of a state today yields allegiance to a constitution adopted long ago.

Along with the idea of a contract goes the notion of the federal character of the state. This too fades out before Althusius's emphasis on the unitary nature of political society: " The word federalism is misleading, I believe, because Althusius never wearies of emphasizing the unitary, collectivistic nature of any symbiotic group." Instead of a federalistic state of a voluntaristic character, Althusius envisaged a unitary state on a completely deterministic basis. *His state was the prototype of the Fascist and Communist states of today:*

It is perhaps worth noting that to-dąy the two most intense embodiments of the idea of state absolutism, namely Italy and Russia, have both developed systems which exactly correspond to what Althusius sets forth. In Italy the system is a hierarchy of corporations, whereas in

Russia it is a hierarchy of Soviets or councils. But how far are we in fact from a similar situation, with our organized interest groups? [19]

Grotius and International Law. — The famous Dutch scholar and statesman, Hugo Grotius (1583–1645), may for all practical purposes be regarded as the founder of international law, though Pierre DuBois, Gentilis, and Hooker had earlier made valuable suggestions. He is most noted for his systematic work in this field, which was chiefly embodied in the famous *De jure belli et pacis.* In his " Prolegomena " to this work he advanced important doctrines regarding the origin and foundation of social institutions. Although he interpreted society, in its most general sense, as the natural expression of human nature, with its " appetite for society," he was convinced, on the other hand, that the state had its origin in a contract.[20] In his work on international law Grotius endeavored to promote likemindedness in regard to the essentials of international policy.[21] Although Grotius's work in international law was an innovation, his confusing and inconsistent theory of sovereignty and denial of popular sovereignty are considered retrogressive.[22]

In the general period of Grotius and Hobbes there appeared a number of interesting developments centering mainly around the names of certain utopian writers — Campanella, Bacon, Harrington, and other less fanciful ideologists such as Filmer and Milton — and about the political documents of the Commonwealth.

Three Utopians. — *The City of the Sun,* written by the Italian friar, Thomas Campanella (1568–1639), presented an imaginary utopian society, which, aside from the communistic tendencies which it advocated, is mainly interesting in the present context, for its attempt at a psycho-sociological interpretation of society and the state. In a manner strikingly similar to that later developed by Comte, he maintained that society was based upon the principles of power, love, and intelligence, and that it could operate successfully only when these had received proper distribution and recognition in the organs of social control and political administration.[23]

Bacon (1561–1626) is noteworthy as the philosophic herald of the approaching age of experimental science. He railed against the domination of custom and tradition in political and social usages, as well as in the field of scientific enterprise. He was equally inconsistent, however, in both fields. Not only did he reject the scientific discoveries of Copernicus, Kepler, and Galileo because they did not accord with the canons of Pure Induction, but in addition he perpetrated works on social and political philosophy that were hopelessly antiquated and obscurantic, the only partial exception being his unfinished utopia, *The New Atlantis*,[24] already dealt with in an earlier chapter.

Bacon's chief innovation lay in his repudiation of medieval methods and interests. He not only denounced the medieval absorption with deductive dialectic as a method of acquiring knowledge, on the ground that " nature is more subtle than any argument," but also suggested that we should surrender the primary medieval interest in the Kingdom of God and transfer our attention to the Kingdom of Man — namely, to human society and its problems. He held that the chief task set for man was to make the earth a better place for human habitation, and contended that this could be done more effectively through natural and applied science than through theology. In other words, he dethroned theology as " queen of the sciences," and suggested that earthly rather than heavenly salvation should be the chief objective of mankind.

Harrington (1611–1677), in his *Oceana,* presented a constitution for the Commonwealth government under the disguise of a utopia. Harrington is perhaps most worthy of note for having developed a definite theory of social causation (cf. Chapter VIII, pp. 313–314). He combined an economic and a psychological interpretation of society. In his economic approach to the problem he insisted that the type of government is determined by the distribution of property: in other words, that the political system depends upon the economic and that government follows property. He also contended that there was a natural intellectual aristocracy in society which should have a dominant place in legislation and social control. Harrington argued that the ideal commonwealth was one in which property was sufficiently distributed so that a narrow minority could not control and oppress the whole commonwealth, and in which the system of elections would bring into play the political ingenuity of the intellectual aristocracy. As he stated his ideal: " A legislator who can unite in one government the goods of the mind with the goods of fortune comes nearest to the work of God, whose government consists of heaven and earth." [25]

Minor Pros and Cons. — The *Patriarcha* of Filmer (d. 1653) was an attack on the doctrine of the contractual origin of government that is of significance here primarily because it called forth Locke's elaborate refutation (to be discussed later). Although Filmer appealed to reason rather than to authority and made a good case against the contract doctrine, his own substitute — namely, patriarchal authority bestowed upon Adam by God — was even less valid than the contract doctrine.[26] By putting the argument on grounds of nature rather than theology, however, Filmer marks the transition from the theological to the natural rights and utilitarian conception.

The chief contributions of the Commonwealth period to social and political philosophy were the individualizing of the conception of a social contract by the assumption that every citizen must be a party to the contract; the appeal to the law of nature to establish the rights of man; and the formulation of the doctrine of popular sovereignty and the right of revolution.[27] John Milton (1608–1674), among others, worked over these doctrines, and derived a philosophical statement of them which he promulgated with sufficient coherence to secure their recognition.[28]

Hobbes, the Ruthless Logician. — In spite of the previous developments of the social contract doctrine, it remained for the English philosopher, Thomas Hobbes (1588–1679), to give that conception its first classic statement. Going far beyond any of the previous writers in the detailed and " remorseless logic " with which he analyzed the situation, he premised a pre-social state of nature which was a " war of all men against all men." [29] He flatly denied the dictum of Aristotle that man is by nature social, stoutly maintained that all society is for gain or glory, and vehemently asserted that any permanent social group must originate in the mutual fear which all men have toward each other.[30] He was as unsparing as Machiavelli in his analysis of human nature, and agreed with the latter's conclusion that all human activity springs from man's insatiable desires. To escape the miseries of the turbulent and unregulated state of nature, said Hobbes, all men agreed to unite into a civil society for their mutual protection, and in so doing they made an irrevocable transfer of their individual powers to the general governing agent or sovereign.[31] He did not, however, hold that either the state of nature or the contract was necessarily true in a historical sense. His analysis was psychological, and he has been correctly called the " father of social psychology." [32] It was the irrevocable nature of the contract and the conception of unlimited sovereign power which distinguished the doctrines of Hobbes from those of the majority of the other members of the contract school. Besides this voluntary contract, Hobbes contended that there might be another type, based upon force, where a conqueror compelled submission on the pain of death.[33] In this latter version Hobbes is in line with the vital principle of the conflict school represented by Gumplowicz. Hobbes's conception of the nature and attributes of sovereignty was a valuable contribution, but he confused the state and the government and erroneously ascribed sovereign power to the latter.[34]

Pufendorf's Attempted Reconciliation. — The German statesman and philosopher, Samuel Pufendorf (1632–1694), attempted a reconciliation of the doctrines of Grotius and Hobbes in his *De jure naturae et gentium* (translated as " The Law of Nature and of Nations "). His ethics were primarily those of Grotius, while his political doctrines were mainly Hobbesian.[35] He held that the social instinct in man would account for the existence of the family and lesser social groups, but that a contract was necessary to bring the state and government into being. Although Pufendorf began his analysis of the state of nature with the assumption that it was a state of peace, he ended with practically the same conclusion as that postulated by Hobbes in his *bellum omnium contra omnes*. Pufendorf's conception of the contract was twofold. First, there was a social contract which embodied the agreement to unite ; then a vote was taken to determine the form of government desired ; and finally the arrangement was ended by a governmental contract between the governors and the governed regarding the principles and limits of administration. Pufendorf thus united more clearly than Hooker the concepts of a social and a governmental contract.[36] His conception of sovereignty was as confusing as that of Grotius, for although he defined it as a supreme power in the state, he held that it must be limited to what a sane man would term " just action." [37]

Spinoza, Libertarian Contractualist. — The Jewish philosopher, Baruch Spinoza (1632–1677), was in his political theory a member of the contract school. He agreed with Hobbes's doctrine of a pre-social state of nature which was one of war and universal enmity.[38] Society, he maintained, had a purely utilitarian basis in the advantages of mutual aid and the division of labor.[39] To render this advantageous association secure, however, it was necessary that its utilitarian basis be supplemented by a contract, thus giving it a legal foundation and guaranteeing to each person in the society the individual rights which he possessed prior to the contract. He claimed that the contract was rendered valid only by the superior advantages which it offered, and that the sovereign was such only as long as he could maintain his authority. This justification of rebellion Spinoza considered to be the only safe guarantee of just rule and individual liberty.[40] Spinoza was mainly interested in using the contract as a buttress for liberty, whereas Hobbes had been chiefly concerned in utilizing it to justify absolutism.[41]

In his *Ethics* Spinoza gave a clear statement of the theory of reflexive sympathy, earlier hinted at by Aristotle and Polybius, and later revived and developed by Hutcheson, Hume, and Adam Smith, and which occupied a prominent position in Giddings's system of sociology. (We shall later see what Scheler's analysis leaves of this theory in the chapter on " Sociology in the Germanic Languages.")

Sidney and Locke, Opponents of the Patriarcha. — The *Patriarcha* of Filmer called forth two better known works in refutation of its thesis. The first was Algernon Sidney's (1622–1683) *Discourses Concerning Government.* He criticized Filmer's work in detail, proclaimed the origin of government in the consent of the governed, and declared himself for the indefeasible sovereignty of the people.[42] Of all English writers in the seventeenth century, Sidney was perhaps the most effective assailant of absolute monarchy. He favored a mixed government combining elements of monarchy, aristocracy, and democracy.

The other refutation of the *Patriarcha* constituted the first of John Locke's (1632–1704) *Two Treatises of Government,* but the second treatise was far more epoch-making in its doctrines, for Locke here set forth his important conception of the social contract and his justification of revolution. In his views on the state of nature, Locke differed radically from Hobbes, Spinoza, and even Pufendorf, in that he denied that it was by any means a condition of war or disorder. The chief and immediate cause of man's leaving the state of nature was the increase of property and the desire to use and preserve it in safety. (This emphasis upon the safety of property might perhaps have been expected from an apologist of bourgeois revolution.)

Locke made the most direct claim of any writer of the school for the historicity of the social contract as the agent for initiating civil society; indeed, he maintained that it must be assumed to lie at the basis of all civil societies in existence.[43] He differentiated clearly between the society formed by the contract and the government to which it delegated the functions of political control.[44]

Rousseau, Last of the Classical Contract School. — The erratic and romantic Rousseau (1712–1778) was the author of several essays that in one way or another bore on the social contract theory, and in addition wrote the first book that carried " The Social Contract " as its main title.

It is virtually impossible to get any consistent theory out of a comparison of Rousseau's various writings, but if we give as much weight to the rhapsodical passages as to the soberer qualifications (which have all the look of afterthoughts), it is possible to say that for him the happiest age of the human race lay in the past, in the *jeunesse* of mankind, in the period of the Patriarchs,[45] and that the social contract became necessary only because with advancing culture *un noir penchant à se nuire mutuellement* manifested itself. Man turned his hand against brother man.[46]

In his later writings, however, Rousseau abandoned his praise of mankind's youth and went almost as far as Hobbes in proclaiming the radically evil strain in human nature. Although he perhaps did not preach the doctrine of " the war of each against all " with the same vehemence as Hobbes, there can be no doubt that he went at least as far as Locke in saying that the uncertainties and inconveniences of the pre-political state rendered the institution of civil society imperative. The only way in which civil society could be instituted, and united power and general protection secured, was through the medium of a social contract.[47] This contract gave rise to the state or civil community, and *not* to the government.[48] Rousseau thus distinguished between state and government and made sovereign power the prerogative of the state. Governmental power he regarded as delegated only. His definition of sovereignty as the absolute power in the state, growing out of an expression of the general will, was probably his chief innovation in political philosophy.[49]

Although the importance of his conception of popular sovereignty is generally conceded, historians now tend to ascribe less weight than they formerly did to Rousseau's dogmas as direct causal influences in the French Revolution. Moreover, few men have been further removed from the temperament of the practical revolutionist than the hypersensitive, unstable Rousseau.[50]

Now that we have surveyed a broad range of social contract doctrines, let us examine in detail one especially influential version and an equally significant criticism of it. In other words, let us present the views of Locke and Hume.

This choice of participants in the debate is amply justified, for John Locke was himself the apologist of the English revolutions of 1649 and 1688–89, and he indirectly furnished, through Jefferson, Rousseau, and others, a great deal of ammunition for the philosophical defense of the American and French revolutions of 1776 and 1789. Locke's *Second Treatise of Government* is the most representative work of the social contract school. Equally distinguished among the critics of social contract doctrine was David Hume (1711–1776); his attack upon this widely accepted theory of social and political origins was admittedly the most comprehensive and deadly set forth in the period under consideration.

John Locke Defends the Social Contract. — Locke, like Hobbes, Pufendorf, and Spinoza, starts with the premise of a state of nature (which premise will be examined at length in the succeeding chapter), but in his conceptions of the conditions found therein, he stands nearer to Pufendorf than to either of the others. Indeed, he seems to go back to the theory of Grotius and Hooker, the latter of whom he quotes with considerable frequency. Dunning has put it well when he says that Locke's conception of the state of nature is that of a pre-political state and not that of a pre-social state.[51] Locke held that while this natural state was one of liberty it was not one of war, for by the state of war is implied that state which ensues when a person uses force without right against another. This may occur in civil society as well as in the state of nature. He thus describes the latter:

To understand political power aright and derive it from its original, we must consider what state all men are naturally in, and that is a state of perfect freedom to order their actions, and dispose of their possessions and persons as they see fit, within the bounds of the law of nature, without asking leave or depending upon the will of any other man.

A state also of equality, wherein all the power and jurisdiction is reciprocal, no one having more than another, there being nothing more evident than that creatures of the same species and rank, promiscuously born to all the same advantages of nature, and the use of the same facilities should also be equal one amongst another, without subordination or subjection, unless the lord and master of them all should, by any manifest declaration of his will, set one above another, and confer on him, by an evident and clear appointment, an undoubted right to dominion and sovereignty.[52]

Following Aristotle directly, or indirectly through Hooker, Locke holds that man has been endowed with a nature which compels him to seek society and enjoy and perpetuate it. The first society was between man and wife, the second between parents and children, and the third between master and servants. He points out, however, that such societies, or any other societies of men, are not political societies unless there are: (1) a union into one body; (2) a common law; and (3) an authority to decide controversies and punish offenders.[53] These are the three canons of distinction between civil societies and all other societies. Quite at variance with Hobbes, Locke maintains that an absolute monarchy is not a form of civil society at all, for under such circumstances the monarch has both the executive and legislative powers in his hands, and there is no impartial judge or any other way of appeal open to his subjects.

Men being by nature " free, equal, and independent," they cannot be subjected to political control without their consent. He concluded, therefore, that civil societies must have had their beginning in the consent of the people. This was undoubtedly the case even in the primitive patriarchal monarchies, said Locke, for there are innumerable examples which show that men have always been in the habit of withdrawing from the rule under which they were born and setting up new governments for themselves. Moreover, for a man to submit to the laws of a state and dwell within its borders does not make him a member of it, any more than it makes a man a member of a family to partake of its hospitality and dwell with it. This is shown to be true by the example of foreigners living in a country other than their own, who must submit to its laws, but who are not thereby made members of that state. Nothing can make a man a member of a civil society or state except "his actual entering into it by positive engagement and express promise and compact." Locke sets forth his belief in the social contract in the following words :

Men being, as has been said, by nature all free, equal, and independent, no one can be put out of this estate and subjected to the political power of another without his own consent, which is done by agreeing with other men, to join and unite into a community for their comfortable, safe, and peaceable living, one amongst another, in a safe enjoyment of their properties, and a greater security against any that are not of it. This any number of men may do, because it injures not the freedom of the rest; they are left as they were, in the liberty of the state of Nature when any number of men have so consented to make one community or government, they are thereby presently incorporated, and make one body politic, wherein the majority have a right to act and conclude for the rest. . . .

And thus, that which begins and actually constitutes any political society is nothing but the consent of any number of freemen capable of a majority, to unite and incorporate into such a society. And this is that and that only which did or could give beginning to any lawful government in the world.[54]

The Economic Basis of the State. — Men having been by nature free, there must have been some very good reason for their having submitted to political control. This reason was primarily the preservation of their property, the enjoyment and possession of which was very uncertain in the state of nature. Property itself had a very interesting history. In the most primitive times, before there was a medium of exchange universally agreed upon, there was no incentive for production beyond a man's needs, for the surplus would only spoil. With the invention of money, however, there came a commodity which would persist indefinitely and which might be exchanged for perishable products. Men were thus urged to produce beyond their necessities, and disproportionate degrees of wealth came into being. As Rousseau traced civil society to the private ownership of land, so Locke made it rest upon the invention of money. Locke thus expounds his theory of the economic basis of the state:

If man in the state of Nature be so free as has been said, if he be absolute lord of his own person and possessions, equal to the greatest and subject to nobody, why will he part with his freedom, this empire, and subject himself to the dominion and control of any other power? To which it is obvious to answer, that though in this state of Nature he hath such a right, yet the enjoyment of it is very uncertain and constantly exposed to the invasion of others; for all being kings as much as he, every man his equal, and the greater part no strict observers of equity and justice, the enjoyment of the property he has in this state is very unsafe, very insecure. This makes him willing to quit this condition which, however free, is full of fears and continual dangers; and it is not without reason that he seeks out and is willing to join in society with others who are already united, or have a mind to unite for the mutual preservation of their lives, liberties, and estates, which I call by the general name — property. . . .

The great and chief end, therefore, of men uniting into commonwealths, and putting themselves under government, is the preservation of their property; to which in the state of nature there are many things wanting.[55]

The Limits of Legislative Power. — Upon entering civil society man gave up the two distinct powers which he possessed in the state of nature: namely, the right to do anything for his preservation which he could in accordance with the law of nature, and the privilege of punishing anyone who disobeyed it. He agreed to conform to civil law and to assist the state in the punishment of those who disobeyed its decrees. In all civil societies the will of the majority must rule; otherwise there can be no more stability in civil society than in the state of nature. The first great act of political society must be to establish the supreme authority — the legislative. But the utmost extent of this supreme authority in the state is confined to acts conducive to the public good:

> Though the legislative, whether placed in one or more, whether it be always in being or only by intervals, though it be the supreme power in every commonwealth; yet, first, it is not, nor can possibly be, absolutely arbitrary over the lives and fortunes of the people. . . . Their power in the utmost bounds of it is limited to the public good of the society. Secondly, the legislative or supreme authority cannot assume to itself a power to rule by extemporary arbitrary decrees, but is bound to dispense justice and decide the rights of the subject by promulgated standing laws, and known authorized judges. . . . Thirdly, the supreme power cannot take from any man any part of his property without his consent. . . . Fourthly, the legislative cannot transfer the power of making laws to any other hands, for it being but a delegated power from the people, they who have it cannot pass it over to others.[56]

The Right of Revolution. — Distinguishing between the state and the government, as Hobbes had not done, Locke showed how the government might be dissolved without destroying the state. The social contract produced the state; the governmental contract established the government, defining the rights of the governed and the power of the rulers. Revolution disrupts the government, not the state:

> He that will, with any clearness, speak of the dissolution of the government, ought in the first place to distinguish between the dissolution of the society and the dissolution of the government. That which makes the community, and brings men out of the loose state of Nature into one politic society, is the agreement which every one has with the rest to incorporate and act as one body, and so be one distinct commonwealth. The usual, and almost only way wherein this union is dissolved, is the inroad of foreign force making a conquest upon them.[57]

There are two great causes which justify rebellion or the dissolution of governments: (1) the altering of the legislative, and (2) acts by the legislative or executive, or both, contrary to the terms of the original compact. As to who shall judge of this violation of the compact, Locke answers unhesitatingly that it must be the people. The legislative and executive are both the deputies and trustees of the people, and surely no one is to judge of the acts of an agent with greater right or justice than the principal. Here is seen the doctrine which was the fundamental basis for the moral and legal justification of the English and American revolutions. Locke's own words on these subjects are as follows:

Besides this overturning from without, governments are dissolved from within:

First. When the legislative is altered, civil society being a state of peace amongst those who are of it, from whom the state of war is excluded by the umpirage which they have provided in their legislative for the ending of all differences that may arise amongst any of them; it is in their legislative that the members of a commonwealth are united or combined together into one coherent living body. . . .

There is, therefore, secondly, another way whereby governments are dissolved, and that is, when the legislative, or the prince, either of them act contrary to their trust.

Here it is likely the common question will be made, Who shall be the judge whether the prince or legislative act contrary to their trust? This, perhaps, ill-affected and factious men may spread among the people, when the prince only makes use of his due prerogative. To this I reply, The people shall be judge; for who shall be judge whether his trustee or deputy acts according to the trust reposed in him, but he who deputies him and must by having deputed him, have still a power to discard him when he fails in his trust? If this be reasonable in particular cases of private men, why should it be otherwise in that of the greatest moment, where the welfare of millions is concerned and also where the evil, if not prevented, is greater, and the redress very difficult, dear, and dangerous.[58]

Locke held that there was not only a moral and legal *right*, but also a moral and social *obligation* to launch a revolution if the ruler or rulers violated the terms of the governmental contract. Government was designed to perpetuate and protect the natural rights of man: specifically, life, liberty, and property. When these rights were destroyed and the contract was violated, the fundamental purpose of the establishment of political society was thereby nullified. Hence, in order to preserve the very basis of organized society and render secure the goal of the original social contract, the people should rise up and oust the faithless rulers and install others, who would agree to observe the terms of the contract which embodied and protected the natural rights of mankind.

David Hume Attacks the Social Contract. — At first sight it may seem rather difficult to classify what Hume considers the ultimate social fact. Ostensibly he considers that the sex instinct is the primary cause of society. At the same time, however, he assigns great influence to sympathy, tracing it back into the animal kingdom. Finally, he describes as the chief advantage of society that mutual aid which comes only through association. By a careful study of all these statements, a consistent theory may be derived. To begin with, the sex instinct causes male and female to associate spontaneously; from this conjunction arises the family, which is held together at first by that sympathy which always springs up among relatives, and in time by the influence of custom and habit which makes them sensible of the advantages of society. The family group expands, and sympathy and the advantages of mutual aid hold it together. Man's selfishness, however, makes these forces inadequate to the requirements; *to give security to property, government had to be instituted.* This must have had its beginning in a primitive arrangement, which, however, was no formal agreement or promise, but simply a slowly growing sense of common interest. Hume therefore attributes the origin of civil society to a sort of implicit convention that might perhaps be called a tacit contract to preserve property.

This seems rather inconsistent with Hume's reputation as the greatest of the early critics of the social contract. Upon examination, however, it may be seen that Hume's conception of the original " contract " is radically different from that held by the classical contract school. While the contract must be accepted as the *implied* basis of the original combinations of mankind, still it was not at first a formal or complete agreement, but was rather a gradual growth. Any conception of a formal agreement was far beyond the notions of the primitive. A chieftain would gain the consent of the group to lead them in war. Later, as a result of the advantages of concerted group action under common leadership, the group gradually perceived the utility of submitting to control, and submission tended to become more frequent. In time it became habitual. This was all that the original contract could have been as a historical fact.

Force, Not Contract, the Basic Factor. — Hume considered as the height of nonsense the belief that the contract was the literal foundation of the governments of his day. All the governments then existing or of which there was any record had been founded upon *force,* exerted through usurpation or conquest. Echoes of Hindu *danda* and anticipations of *Der Staat ist Macht!* Neither was a contract the basis for the change of governments; here as well force had been the dominating factor. Nor was the original formal contract a philosophical verity any more than it was a historical actuality. Hume made it clear that philosophically and psychologically the doctrine of a social contract as the origin of a civil society was as untenable as the historical argument for its existence. He showed that it implied knowledge prior to experience

— that people could know the advantages of government before government had come into existence. This assertion, Hume contended, was palpably unsupportable either logically or psychologically. The only basis for the origin of civil government is force, and the only cause of allegiance as a moral obligation lies in the reflection that without government society could not exist.

The Idyllic State of Nature a Fiction. — Further, and perhaps most important of all as distinguishing Hume from the contract school, he rejected absolutely the doctrine of a pre-social state of nature, calling it a mere fiction like the golden age of the poets. Man, said he, must be adjudged social from the beginning. Moreover, *men* had invented the supposed laws of nature from a sense of utility and the force of necessity. In his treatment of the "Origin of Justice and Property," Hume is perhaps more exact and modern in his reasoning than in any other part of his social philosophy. Although we hereby anticipate the next chapter, let us present his rejection of the whole notion of the state of nature:

This state of nature, therefore, is to be regarded as a mere fiction, not unlike that of the golden age, which poets have invented; only with this difference, that the former is described as full of war, violence, and injustice; whereas the latter is painted out to us as the most charming and most peaceable condition that can possibly be imagined. . . . The storms and tempests were not alone removed from nature, but those more furious tempests were unknown to human breasts, which now cause such uproar, and engender such confusion. Avarice, ambition, cruelty, selfishness were never heard of: cordial affection, compassion, and sympathy, were the only movements with which the human mind was yet acquainted. Even the distinction of mine and thine was banished from the happy race of mortals and carried with them the very notions of property and obligation, justice and injustice. This, no doubt, is to be regarded as an idle fiction. . . .

We may conclude that it is utterly impossible for men to remain any considerable time in that savage state which precedes society; but that his very first state and situation may justly be esteemed social. This, however, hinders not but that philosophers may, if they please, extend their reasoning to the supposed state of nature; provided they allow it to be a mere philosophical fiction, which never had, and never could have had any reality.[59]

Obedience as a Social Cement. — Man, he says, being born in a family, cannot avoid maintaining society, for he is impelled thereto by necessity, inclination, and habit. At the same time, it is essential that he establish political society so that life may be safe, peaceable, and *profitable.* Therefore, he maintains, the whole fabric of government may be considered as having but one purpose — the administration of justice. All the other departments of government, and even the clergy (so far as their earthly work is concerned), have their only function in assisting and promoting the administration of justice. Though justice is so essential to the preservation of society, and men realize this fact, still, owing to the weakness of human nature which prefers the minor enjoyments of the present to the abstract good of the future, the perception of the advantage of justice is not sufficient. As a consequence, it is essential that government be instituted and the principle of obedience, which is essential to support that of justice, be enforced. While many may hold that obedience will be no better enforced than justice, Hume contends that there are several things which go to prove the opposite. In the first place, the love of dominion, much stronger in the human mind than the love of duty, impels men to seek the dangers and cares of government. The man who first gains the authority to govern must be possessed of certain personal characteristics, such as bravery, integrity, or prudence, which will attract respect and admiration. In time a certain degree of respect will be attached to birth and rank. The prince endeavors to curb all disturbances and summons to his aid all his retainers. As government progresses, the ruler obtains means to reward these services, and in time establishes a military force to aid him in compelling obedience. Finally, habit operates to make obedience a matter of course, accepted implicitly without questioning its basis.

Nevertheless — and here is what separates him from the contract school — Hume states plainly that although these principles may seem certain and inevitable, and in accordance with human nature, it is at the same time foolish to think that human beings could discover them at once or foresee their operation. Government had an accidental and imperfect beginning; leadership was probably brought about by warfare. Here superior qualities would be more readily recognized, and the unity and discipline of the group would be better perfected. The frequent occurrence of war among primitive peoples acquainted them with the principle of submission, as already stated, and if the leader was as just as he was brave, he might even retain in time of peace the power of arbiter, as he had that of leader in time of war. Gradually, by a judicious mixture of "force and consent" he would be able to establish his authority. The benefits of government would be felt, and would be highly valued by the peaceable members of society. If the son enjoyed the same qualities as the father, the government would be strengthened by the resulting continuity and its attendant efficiency. Government even at its best, however, must have been feeble until the ruler possessed the means of rewarding his assistants and of punishing those who disobeyed his commands. Before that, government must have been extended slowly, and obedience exacted only in particular cases according to the exigencies of the moment. In due time government was no longer a matter of choice, but was rigorously enforced by the ruler and his associates, and, says Hume:

Habit soon consolidates what other principles of human nature had imperfectly founded; and men, once accustomed to obedience, never think of departing from that path, in which they and their ancestors have constantly trod, and to which they are confined by so many urgent and visible motives.[60]

In spite of this, submission is never perfect; there is always a struggle going on in a government between authority and liberty. Although there must be a greater or less sacrifice of liberty in every government, still authority should never be absolute or uncontrollable. The best government is of the type in which the power is divided among several parts. Their united strength is greater than that of any absolute monarch, and yet the administration is conducted in accordance with equal laws, known to both governed and governing. Liberty may be regarded as the goal of perfection in civil society, but in a struggle between liberty and authority the latter may "challenge the preference," since it is essential to the very existence of society.

Government Never Rests upon the Consent of the Governed. — Hume's essay on "The Original Contract" is one of the ablest attacks upon the contract theory which has ever been written, being more incisive than that of Burke, and more judicious and fair than that of Bentham.[61] In the first place, said Hume, no political party could at that time maintain its existence without some set of philosophical principles. Consequently, the Tories traced government back to the Deity, and thus tried to represent resistance as not only treason but sacrilege. The Whigs, on the other hand, claimed that government was founded upon an original contract which justified resistance in case justice was not administered. These principles were both true, said Hume, when taken in their correct meaning, which was quite other than that advanced by the contending parties. In the case of the so-called divine-right doctrine, no one who believed in a divine-right Providence would deny that the Deity must have intended government for mankind, for government is essential to the existence of society. Similarly with the contract theory: men are nearly equal in all their native characteristics; hence, if we go back to the very beginnings of government, it cannot be denied that it must have started in an implicit contract. Of course, there remains no record of this original contract, except as it may be traced in man's nature. In any case, to consider this consent as conscious, formal, all-inclusive, perfect, and guaranteeing general submission is the height of folly. Any such idea was clearly beyond the comprehension of the " savage mind." Hume then goes on to explain the general development of the idea of consent by advancing an argument of the same kind as that set forth in his essay on the origin of government — namely, by showing that its growth was gradual and made up of many instances of successive manifestations of force:

No compact or agreement, it is evident, was expressly formed for general submission; an idea far beyond the comprehension of savages; each exertion of authority in the chieftain must have been particular, and called forth by the present exigencies of the case. The sensible utility, resulting from his interposition made these exertions become daily more frequent; and their frequency gradually produced an habitual, and, if you please to call it so, a *voluntary,* and therefore precarious, acquiescence in the people.[62]

The philosophical apologists of the contract theory, said he, were not content to insist that government had its first origin in the voluntary consent of the people, but went so far as to maintain that even at the present it rested on no other foundation. If these philosophers would but look about them for examples, he said, they would find nothing to substantiate their views. On the contrary, all the governments which were then in existence, or of which there remained any record, had all been founded by either conquest or usurpation, without any pretense at allowing the people to give their consent:

Almost all the governments, which exist at present, or of which there remains any record in history, have been founded originally, either on usurpation or conquest, or both, without any pretense of a fair consent, or voluntary subjection of the people. . . .

I maintain that human affairs will never admit of this consent; seldom of the appearance of it. But that conquest or usurpation, that is, in plain terms, *force,* by dissolving the ancient governments, is the origin of almost all the new ones, which were ever established in the world. And that in the few cases where consent may seem to have taken place, it was commonly so irregular, so confined, or so much intermixed with fraud or violence, that it cannot have had any great authority.[63]

One of the favorite arguments of the contract philosophers, said Hume, had been that at the time of changing a government, if at no other, the principle of consent was operative. Nevertheless, asserted Hume, force had been the occasion of the foundation of almost all the new governments which had been instituted in history. A very few might seem to be based upon consent, but such a basis was more apparent than real, since the consent was mixed with fraud and violence. The argument derived from the instance of the establishment of the government of William and Mary in England, after the revolution of 1688, he held to be entirely fallacious. The majority of the seven hundred members of Parliament were the ones who gave their consent, not the majority of the ten million inhabitants of England. The fact that the majority of the latter would have consented if given the opportunity did not change the argument. In fact, said he, were one to choose a time when the consent of the people was least considered by those in control, it would be at the very period of the change of governments.

At the same time, Hume did not deprecate the principle of consent in the development of government; he said that it was " surely the best and most sacred of any." [64] All that he contended was that it was a principle which had probably never been applied to its full extent, and very rarely in any degree; consequently, other methods of founding governments would have to be sought and admitted. Finally, even if it were granted that the first government of " savages " was founded on the principle of contract, yet this would furnish no argument for present obedience to government; the contract, obliterated by a thousand changes, could no longer be supposed to carry with it any authority.

The Social Contract Refuted Philosophically. — Moreover, if the philosophers were not content with this historical refutation, Hume maintained that he could offer a philosophical one equally destructive to the contract theory. All moral duties, he says, are divided into two classes: those which are instinctive and do not depend upon reflection, and those which are performed entirely from a sense of obligation arising out of reflection upon the necessity of the performance for the good of society. Examples of these are justice, fidelity, allegiance. Man's natural instincts would lead him away from these principles were he not restrained by reflection and experience of the evils which result from their violation. Now, he asks, what is to be gained by making allegiance depend upon promise, which is in turn based upon fidelity? Neither allegiance nor fidelity will be observed without due reflection on the advantages arising from doing so. Then, since allegiance is just as advantageous a principle as fidelity, the reflection on the gains to be received by observing it would be sufficient to ensure its operation if it would be observed under any circumstances. Therefore, nothing is to be gained by making allegiance depend upon the obligation to keep one's word. The only reason, he says, why allegiance should be rendered is that " society could not otherwise subsist." [65] " The general obligation which binds us to government, is the interest and necessities of society; and this obligation is very strong."

The Psychical Sources of Society. — As one of the chief forerunners of the Utilitarians, Hume was as emphatic as any of the contract school in maintaining that the chief value of society lay in that mutual aid, division of labor, and greater production and security of goods which could only be the result of fixed social relations. On the other hand, as has been shown above, he avoided their cardinal error of supposing that the perception of these advantages by mankind furnished the explanation of political origins. Hume's piercing intellect was able to discern the fallacy which lay at the bottom of the contract theory: namely, that men could know and understand the advantages of social and civic relations which they had never before experienced. He therefore set forth a psychological hypothesis as to the ultimate foundation of society: the operation of the sex urge, widened through the influence of sympathy.

The Social Roots of Justice. — The rudiments of justice, according to Hume, appear in the family and are continually extended and deepened as society expands. There could be no original conception of justice, and it was later based upon a convention. This statement also savors of the contract dogma, but as Hume goes on to explain, this convention was not an express promise or agreement, nor was it instituted at once. Rather, it was simply an expression of common interest on the part of the members of society, who, by experience, became conscious of the value of security in the possession of property and in the enforcement of rights and obligations, and equally sensitive of the disadvantages which arise from the violation of these rules. Obedience was established with regard to one thing at a time, the field of justice growing hand in hand with the progress of society. Hume thus separates himself from the contract school and puts himself among those exponents of sociological jurisprudence who look upon justice as an ever-growing and changing principle that must harmonize with the needs of society at any given time. In explaining why virtue has been connected with justice and vice with injustice, Hume says that although self-interest was the cause of the original establishment of justice, sympathy with the interest of the public has been the cause of the moral approval which has come to accompany justice. Men experience the value of the observation of justice and sense the evils of injustice, and in addition they suffer indirectly through the operation of sympathy, which causes them to put themselves, by the exercise of the imagination, in the place of their injured neighbor. This approbation of justice is handed down by education, since parents perceive that the man most highly endowed with " probity and honour " is the most useful citizen, both to himself and to others.

Summary of the Chapter. — The Commercial Revolution released the throne from dependence on the feudal lords, thus fostering the growth of the national state. This process was first successfully completed in Tudor England; Spain and Holland followed in rapid succession. The situation in France was more complicated and the process more labored; the feudal system as a dominating political power survived a century and a half longer there than in England. Two more centuries passed before the national unification of Germany and Italy. A tremendous outburst of vernacular literature accompanied this national consolidation; the French Revolution and the revolutions in transportation and communication supplied the final touches to the new system. The rise of nationalism was inextricably interwoven with the rise of the middle class and the growth of constitutionalism and republicanism.

The doctrine of the social contract (not to be confused with earlier theories of the governmental compact) supplied theoretical justification for the great revolutions of the seventeenth and eighteenth centuries in England, France, and America, lending impetus at the same time to the doctrine of popular sovereignty. The only important champions of democracy *per se,* however, were Mably, Paine, and Jefferson. Hooker was the first to declare that society arose by the deliberate agreement of men to escape from the evils of a pre-social (but not unsocial) condition. Suarez, proceeding from the belief of Aristotle and Aquinas that man is by nature social, was nevertheless impressed by his dependence on law. Thus the doctrines of natural sociability and the social contract were combined. Mariana also linked these two ideas in his theory of civic origins. Althusius viewed the sovereignty of the people (embodied in lesser constituent groups) as the foundation of the state, and the social contract as the mutual agreement of all to live in an ordered society. Grotius considered society the inevitable expression of human nature, but believed the state to have had its origin in a contract. His chief contribution was in the field of international law. Among the utopians, Campanella set forth a psychological interpretation of society and the state; Bacon is noteworthy for his emphasis on secular problems; Harrington presented a constitution for the Commonwealth.

Hobbes's famous conception of human nature and early society was not dependent upon the contract in a historical sense. Pufendorf attempted to reconcile the doctrines of Grotius and Hobbes and united, more clearly than Hooker, the concepts of a social and a governmental contract. Spinoza followed Hobbes in his doctrine of a pre-social state of nature; he considered the contract as a safeguard of liberty, whereas Hobbes had used it to justify absolutism. Rousseau's major innovation was his definition of sovereignty as the absolute power in the state, growing out of an expression of the general will.

Locke advanced the theory that men submitted to political control in order to preserve their property. In his claim for the *historicity* of the social contract he differed widely from earlier speculation. In his hands, too, the doctrine became a weapon for revolution; violation by the rulers of the terms of the governmental compact entailed not only the legal right but also the moral and social obligation of the people to revolt.

In his rôle as greatest of the early critics of the social contract, Hume rejected the idea of a pre-social state of nature and denied the verity of the contract on historical, philosophical, and psychological grounds. He declared the beginnings of civil government to have been accidental and imperfect, and the basis of origin to have been force.

This chapter is an illustration of the statement made in the 1938 Preface that "the history of social thought is almost inextricably bound up with the history of political thought as traditionally received." It also illustrates the statements that "there has been a general failure, down to relatively recent times, to distinguish clearly between the state and society," and consequently that "much of the relevant speculation about social processes, structures, and the social aspects of personality — i.e., speculation about social or interhuman conduct as such — has been the work of men who believed that they were dealing exclusively with the state."

From the standpoint of sociology of knowledge, it is interesting that Hume, a Scot among Scots in spite of his contacts with the intellectual world, laid such heavy stress on the role of force. Even during his time (1711-76), ruthless violence played a key role in social control on his native heath. *Perfervidum ingenium Scotorum* was still an apt characterization.

CHAPTER XI

Migration, Culture Contact, Mental Mobility: Early Modern Theories of Social Change

COMMIXTURE OF MANNERS. — In this chapter and in several to follow we shall pay little attention to the historical background, as our method of treatment will be primarily topical. Concentration on those doctrines most clearly related to general historical trends has led to the neglect of others almost equally important, and we must therefore retrace our steps.

In the chapter on " The Mobile Background of the Greco-Roman World and Its Effects on Social Thought " something was done, it is hoped, to make clear the fact that the Greeks grappled with the problems engendered by the mingling of peoples, and that the Romans took up the theme. Here and there in succeeding chapters attention was again called to it, and the net effect should be that the reader is thoroughly aware that certain generalizations concerning migration, culture contact, and mental mobility have been commonplaces for millennia.

In almost every instance, however, the " corrupting " effect of culture contact, of " commixture of manners," engaged the exclusive attention of the Greeks and their epigoni. Isolation, quiescence, stability, rigidity, and mental immobility were the ideal characteristics of any community — even the utopias, as we have seen, were no exception.

Mandeville and the Sociology of City Life. — In England, however, at least one writer seems to have been able to view the collapse of the sacred community in a detached manner: Bernard de Mandeville, in his famous *Fable of the Bees, or Private Vices Publick Benefits,* pointed out that, whether desirable or not, " commixture of manners " was going on in large cities like London, and that certain inevitable consequences, by no means undesirable from Mandeville's point of view, were flowing therefrom. It is impossible even to hint at all the penetrating insights to be found in this cynical and witty work by a Dutch physician

living the life of a "secular stranger" in a great cosmopolitan
city; here only one quotation bearing on the relation of status-
striving to urban life can be given:

. . . the World has long since decided the Matter; handsome Apparel
is a main Point, fine Feathers make fine Birds, and People, *where they
are not known*, are generally honour'd according to their Clothes and
other Accoutrements they have about them; from the richness of them
we judge of their Wealth, and by their ordering of them we guess at
their Understanding. It is this which encourages every Body, who is
conscious of his little Merit, if he is any ways able, to wear Clothes above
his Rank, *especially in large and populous Cities, where obscure Men
may hourly meet with fifty Strangers to one Acquaintance*, and consequently have the Pleasure of being esteem'd by a vast Majority, not as
what they are, but they appear to be: which is a greater Temptation
than most People want to be in vain.[1]

Reformulated, this runs as follows: (1) contacts in the large
city are superficial, and "front" is necessary for the maintenance
of social status; (2) "front" may become an end in itself, dis-
sociated from the earlier life-organization, thus contributing to
mental mobility.

Mandeville's writings were perhaps a bit too consciously bizarre, however, to exert lasting influence, although during his
lifetime he had a great vogue. Not until David Hume, the Scottish
philosophe already referred to, appeared with his serene yet ex-
plosive writings was there apparent any serious break with the
ideal of the sacred community, for the Humanist writers, who
continued to set the pattern, were after all inclined to cherish the
Classical belief in the advantages of immobility, and the Reformers, whose influence was still almost at its peak, were quite sure
that they wanted a thoroughly rigid type of social structure — if
only they could lay the foundation of the structure.

Hume, Cultural Determinist. — The Scotsman, a true child of
the Enlightenment, begins with the note of inquiry, not of assertion. His fundamental question is: Why does one nation differ
from another? — in manners, in scientific and artistic attainments,
and in national character. His method of answering the query is
to exhaust every "moral" (psycho-sociological, sociological)
explanation before turning to the climatic and biological explanations then so popular. Indeed, he accounts for differences in terms
of the former so much to his own satisfaction that he never has recourse to the latter, although he expresses some doubt about the
Negroes.[2]

The rôle of the cultural heritage and of social control in producing *similarity* of behavior within a given culture area would naturally engage the attention of anyone considering the dissimilarity of two or more areas, and Hume says on this head:

Whatever it be that forms the manners of one generation, the next must imbibe a deeper tincture of the same dye; men being more susceptible of all impressions during infancy, and retaining these impressions as long as they remain in the world. . . .

. . . where a very extensive government has been established for many centuries, it spreads a national character over the whole empire. . . . Thus the Chinese have the greatest uniformity of character imaginable. . . .

Where any set of men, scattered over distant nations, maintain a close society or communication together they acquire a similitude of manners, and have but little in common with the nations amongst whom they live. Thus the Jews in Europe, and the Armenians in the East, have a peculiar character. . . .[3]

Hume observed, however, that all things human change, even homogeneous communities, and sought to determine the reasons for this:

Where several neighboring nations have a very close communication together, either by policy, commerce, or travelling, they acquire a similitude of manners, proportioned to the communication.[4]

The beneficial effects of such communication are especially noticeable in the emulation of a " number of neighboring and independent states, connected together by commerce and policy," because this emulation leads to the " importation " of the " sciences and liberal arts." Hume gives this example:

Greece was a cluster of little principalities, which soon became republics; and being united both by their near neighborhood, and by the ties of the same language and interest, they entered into the closest intercourse of commerce and learning. . . . Each city produced its several artists and philosophers, who refused to yield the preference to those of the neighboring republics; their contention and debates sharpened the wits of men; a variety of objects was presented to the judgment, while each challenged the preference to the rest; and the sciences, not being dwarfed by the restraints of authority, were enabled to make such considerable shoots as are even at this time the objects of our admiration.[5]

In other words, the contact of two or more *dissimilar* cultures results in the breakdown of the social control which arises when a culture area is relatively isolated, and such breakdown results in a release of energy and competitive effort. Nothing whatever is said about the " corrupting " effects of culture contact, although one would suppose that Hume, a student of the Classics, would have had ample opportunity to absorb this point of view. Perhaps he was so close to Scottish Calvinism that in overcompensation he adopted a rigid optimism quite as far removed from a realistic approach as its opposite.

Montesquieu the Urbane. — There is little or no trace of reaction against the zeal of the Reformers or the Pythagorean and Spartan asceticism of Plato to be found in Montesquieu, however — Montesquieu, that genial Gascon wine-grower, admirer of the utterly irrational British Constitution, who was nevertheless author of the first of the *philosophe* flank attacks upon the established order, the famous *Persian Letters,* and of that direct assault upon the bastions of church and state, *The Spirit of Laws.* The latter, one of the greatest books of its century, appeared in 1748. Its implications for the French Revolution do not concern us here; it need only be noted that Montesquieu seems fully aware of the effects of isolation and of the part played by migration, especially of the trading journey variety, in breaking down local mores and promoting social disorganization, while at the same time producing the phenomena of " polish," urban agglomeration, and stimulation of consumption :

The greatest part of the people on the coast of Africa are savages and barbarians. The principal reason, I believe, of this is because the small countries capable of being inhabited are separated from each other by large and almost uninhabitable tracts of land. They are without industry or arts.[6]

The history of commerce is that of the communication of people. Their numerous defeats, and the flux and reflux of populations and devastations, here form the most extraordinary events.[7]

Commerce is a cure for the most destructive prejudices; for it is almost a general rule, that wherever we find agreeable manners, there commerce flourishes; and that wherever there is commerce, there we meet with agreeable manners.

Let us not be astonished, then, if our manners are now less savage than formerly. Commerce has everywhere diffused a knowledge of the manners of all nations: these are compared one with another, and from this comparison arise the greatest advantages.

Commercial laws, it may be said, improve manners for the same reason that they destroy them. They corrupt the purest morals. This was the subject of Plato's complaints; and we every day see that they polish and refine the most barbarous.[8]

In proportion to the populousness of towns, the inhabitants are filled with notions of vanity and actuated by an ambition of distinguishing themselves by trifles. If they are very numerous, and most of them strangers to one another, their vanity redoubles, because there are greater hopes of success. As luxury inspires these hopes, each man assumes the marks of a superior condition. But by endeavoring thus at distinction, every one becomes equal, and distinction ceases; as all are desirous of respect, nobody is regarded.

Hence arises a general inconvenience. Those who excel in a profession set what value they please on their labor; this example is followed by people of inferior abilities, and then there is an end of all proportion between our wants and the means of satisfying them. When I am forced to go to law I must be able to fee counsel; when I am sick, I must have it in my power to fee a physician.

It is of the opinion of several, that the assemblage of so great a multitude of people in capital cities is an obstruction to commerce, because the inhabitants are no longer at a proper distance from each other. But I cannot think so; for men have more desires, more wants, more fancies, when they live together.[9]

Little sympathy with Plato here, to be sure, but neither do we find Hume's optimism. Culture contact *does* play a large part in the genesis of civilization, but it also breaks down the mores: it secularizes the sacred, and this inheres in the very nature of the civilizing process.

A great deal more material highly relevant to the themes of this chapter can be found in *The Spirit of Laws,* but the aphoristic style of the work makes quotation extremely difficult. It is perhaps advisable to rest content with the few quotations already made, merely recasting and making explicit these ten significant points: (1) some preliterate peoples are at a low level of cultural development chiefly because of isolation, and not because of racial or climatic factors primarily; (2) in earlier periods, commerce and communication are two aspects of the same phenomenon; (3) the history of commerce is bound up with that of conflict and of territorial mobility in general; (4) politeness and " manners," in their secondary-group connotations, are most highly developed in cultures where commerce is well developed; (5) culture contact is likely to give rise to belief in the relative nature of customs; (6) " manners " and " morals " may be mutually antagonistic, and frequently are so; (7) population density is correlated with the struggle for status; (8) the anonymity of the city makes " front " inevitable; (9) frequency of stimulation causes human beings to respond more readily to fresh stimuli (one phase of mental mobility); (10) population density is favorable to the growth of a monetary system of exchange.

Turgot and the Combat Cycle. — Shortly after the publication of Montesquieu's great work a young candidate for the priesthood, called Turgot by posterity, was admitted to the House of the Sorbonne; his ability gained for him the post of prior, in which capacity he had to pronounce lengthy Latin discourses at the solemn Sorbonic convocations. In several of these discourses, and in the rough drafts of several more, are to be found a series of sociological generalizations that make possible such assertions as "Seldom has there been born into the world a greater potential sociologist than Turgot." [10] His later career as a statesman and financier (he did not take holy orders), as well as a great Physiocratic economist, was marked by a series of important writings, but only the earlier discourses relate to the present theme.

Turgot's method of exhausting "moral" explanation before having recourse to climatic and biological explanation [11] is substantially similar to Hume's; the fundamental sameness of human nature is a methodological postulate: "the same senses, the same organs, the spectacle of the same Universe have everywhere given men the same ideas, just as the same needs and the same propensities have everywhere taught them the same arts." But in spite of this fundamental sameness, the human being as found in his social organizations is nevertheless different:

. . . all the delicate shadings of barbarism and culture existent throughout the earth . . . show us . . . at a single glance the monuments, the vestiges of every advance of the mind of man, the image of all the states through which he has passed, and the history of all the ages.[12]

He then raises the question: What has been the *modus operandi* of the social changes that have undoubtedly taken place? In order to answer this, another question must first be dealt with: How is stability, fixity, persistence of the same institutions to be accounted for?

Isolation, lack of culture contact, is one explanation, especially on the lower stages of culture.

. . . the nations, separated by vast spaces and still more by the diversity of languages, unknown to one another, were almost all plunged in the same barbarism in which we still see the Americas . . . they halt in mediocrity. . . .[13]

As culture develops, educational and religious institutions play a large part in fixating patterns, in rendering them rigid and inflexible:

The lustre of the new creates in men a respect for the nascent philosophy that tends to make perpetual the first opinions. . . . In Egypt and long after in India . . . superstition . . . made the dogmas of the old philosophy a sort of patrimony of the priestly families, who by consecrating them fettered them and made them one with the dogmas of a false religion . . . in China, the very care the emperors took to regulate research and learning and to confuse together the sciences and the political constitution of the State held them forever back in mediocrity. . . .[14]

Social change is brought about by the influence of migration and culture contact, especially through the medium of commerce, and so it comes that every nation represents a transitional stage between its neighbors — *"chaque nation est la nuance entre les nations ses voisines."* [15] Turgot of course does not mean to say that migration and correlated phenomena are the only factors in social change, inasmuch as the culture of any group undergoes some modification even if no appreciable contact with others takes place. Nevertheless, he expresses the view that "the human race would have forever remained in mediocrity" had it not been for the disruptive and releasing effect of migrations and conquests:

Interest, ambition, and vainglory at every instant change the face of the world and inundate the earth with blood. In the midst of their ravages, manners grow refined, the mind of man becomes enlightened, nations leave their isolation to draw nearer one another; commerce and politics unite at last all parts of the globe. . . .

Conquests and revolutions commingle in a thousand ways peoples, tongues, and manners. . . . Ambition, by creating great states from the crumbled remains of a host of little ones, itself puts limits to its own ravages. War now brings desolation but to the frontiers of empires; city and country begin to breathe in the midst of peace; the bonds of society hold in unity a greater number of men; the spread of enlightenment becomes more rapid and more widely extended; and arts, sciences, and manners progress at a more rapid pace. . . .

In the unequal progress of nations, the more cultured peoples mingled with the barbarians, now conquering, now conquered, who surrounded them; whether the latter received from the former their arts and their laws along with their servitude. or whether as conquerors they yielded to the natural empire of reason and refinement over force, the frontiers of barbarism were ever pushed back. . . .

Kings without authority, nobles unbridled, peoples enslaved, countrysides covered with fortresses and ravaged without end, war kindled between city and city, village and village. . . .

And yet, from the midst of this barbarism, will one day spring again the sciences and the arts *rejuvenated*.[16]

. . . if war and usurpation had been forever banished, men would have remained divided into a horde of nations speaking mutually unintelligible languages. — Man would consequently have been narrow in his ideas, incapable of progress in all branches of mental activity . . . in everything born of the contact of genius brought together from different parts of the world, and the human race would have forever remained in mediocrity. Reason and justice, if listened to, would have made everything fixed, as it has nearly done in China. But that which is imperfect should never be entirely fixed. Passions tumultuous and dangerous become sources of action, however, and consequently of progress; everything that frees men from their station, that brings varied scenes before their eyes, expands their ideas, enlightens them, animates them and finally leads them to the good and the true.

It is the tender passions which are always necessary, and which become more and more developed as humanity becomes more perfect; but also necessary are the violent and terrible passions like hatred and vengeance, which are more developed in barbaric periods, and which are equally natural. . . . Vehement fermentation is necessary for the manufacture of good wines.[17]

Significantly enough, he also points out that periods of slow and rapid social change succeed each other: " the total mass of human kind, through alternations of calm and agitation, of evil days and good, ever advances . . . toward a higher degree of perfection." [18] This is no chance utterance, either; he reformulated the statement in his *Discourse on Universal History*, written in 1751: ". . . *par des alternatives d'agitation et de calme, de biens et de maux, la masse totale du genre humain a marché sans cesse vers sa perfection.*" With minor modifications, this is a repetition of the passage in the *Second Discourse* of 1750. Thus we may say that Turgot was a true believer in the Heraclitean flux and the dictum that " Conflict is the father of all things " — and not only this: a *combat cycle* is indicated. Ibn Khaldūn has a successor!

In order to make still more clear the fundamental similarity between the doctrines of Turgot and his Moslem forerunner, we need only quote the following passage (freely translated):

The domains of rulers holding in subjection sedentary, tillage peoples finally reach a point in their development when, as a consequence of unequal rates of progress, they are surrounded by barbarous tribes. When the former were at the height of their power, they extended the domain through conquest, through colonizing the conquered areas, and through gradually civilizing them. When such states become feeble, however, the barbarians attack in their turn with advantage; the desire to dominate a rich country goads the ambition of the chiefs and the avarice of their ferocious peoples.

These torrents, these migrations of barbarous peoples who succeed each other without leaving a trace have sometimes overrun in their course peoples with a more complex culture, and in this manner alone has a record of the event reached the modern world. Then the barbarous people adopt the culture of the vanquished, because of the influence which enlightenment and reason always exert on violence, whenever conquest has not been followed by extermination. — The barbarians, once civilized, civilize their homeland culture area. The two peoples become one — a more extensive domain under one ruler.[19]

The barbarians thus become civilized, more rich, more tranquil, more accustomed to a life of ease, or to say the least, a sedentary life, and therefore they soon lose the vigor which made them conquerors unless a saving discipline puts a stop to the inroads of luxurious sloth.[20] — If not, the conquerors yield to new barbarians, the domain becomes still more extensive, the new conquerors have their age of vigor and of decadence in turn, but even their fall helps to perfect the arts and ameliorate the laws. — Thus the Chaldeans, the Assyrians, the Medes and Persians succeeded each other, and the domain of the Persians was the greatest of all.[21]

Last of all, we cannot omit Turgot's most surprising contribution: he clearly outlined the process of dominance and world-organization in its political aspects almost two centuries before the general concept was restated by the human ecologists. Had research followed Turgot's speculations, we might now be much further ahead in our sociological thinking. As it was, however, the flash of insight proved to be only a flash, and seems to have attracted no attention. The passage in which the contribution is found is part of the fragmentary outline on political geography already noted (freely translated):

General reflections on the way in which the various nations at first isolated, have cast their eyes about them, as it were, and have gradually come to know each other more and more. Progress in the extent of geographic knowledge in relation to the successive stages of human development. Concerning the principal relationships capable of uniting the peoples: neighborhood, commerce. The desire to conquer, reciprocal fears, common interests. How every people that has surpassed its fellows in development has become a sort of dominant center about which is formed a political world composed of nations . . . whose interests it can combine with its own. How several of these groups organized about such points of dominance have been formed . . . independently of and unknown to each other. How these groups have ceaselessly extended their limits until they impinge upon and become entangled with each other; eventually one single political process will bring all parts of the world into relation, and there will result but one political world, coextensive with the physical world.[22]

One is again reminded of Dryden's forecast in the *Annus Mira-bilis*, almost three-quarters of a century in advance of Turgot. It must be admitted, however, that the Frenchman leaves the Englishman in the shade so far as fullness and suggestiveness of prophecy are concerned; all that the latter can offer is mnemonic advantage. To quote the passage once more:

> Instructed ships shall sail to rich commerce,
> By which remotest regions are allied;
> Which makes one city of the universe,
> Where some may gain and all may be supplied.

Now to formulate a few of Turgot's generalizations in modern terminology by way of summary: (1) differences between cultural groups are to be accounted for without resort to non-sociological factors if possible; (2) isolation and rigid social control account for the fixity of many cultures; (3) the " cake of custom " resulting from isolation must be broken if any great social changes are to take place; (4) mass migrations attended by conquest are the means by which social control is most effectively broken in earlier cultures; (5) the release of energy in the individual following the breakdown of social control is the immediate antecedent of social change and of " progress " (increased cultural complexity); (6) the process by which personal and social change takes place is cyclical, and follows the pattern of equilibrium (fixity) → intrusive factor → tension and unrest → crisis → conflict (disorganization) → release → individuation → accommodation (reorganization) → new equilibrium; (7) the combat cycle will be repeated until the stage of world-organization under a single dominant center is eventually reached.

After Turgot it is really quite difficult to find a great deal that deals in a new way with the problem of migration attended by warfare; most of the later combat theories seem but echoes of the great Frenchman's discourses. In spite of this, however, later theorists often succeed in throwing light into obscure corners, in illuminating new aspects, although the main outline remains much the same. And of course Turgot by no means exhausted the theme of peaceful migration, although he did pay some attention to communication in general and commerce in particular. Hence the consideration of speculations and theories (we cannot yet speak of hypotheses) attempting to knit together unrelated facts must go on.

Herder, Precursor of Anthropogeography. — Let us journey into " the Gothick North," where we shall find, at Weimar,

Johann Gottfried von Herder. The writings of this man have for a long time been regarded solely from the point of view of the literary historian; his influence on the Romantic writers, especially the young Goethe, was great, and this fact has determined much of the comment upon him. The value of his thought in and of itself has been neglected; yet his greatest contribution, *Ideen zur Philosophie der Geschichte der Menschheit* (Thoughts Concerning the Philosophy of Man's History), was a remarkable work not only for its own period, but even for the succeeding century. In his tantalizingly tentative way of thinking he comes near to ideas propounded by Spencer and Darwin, and the account of the first dawnings of culture and of the ruder Oriental civilizations is marked by genuine insight, although his account of the development of Greco-Roman culture is less skillful. Further, most of the stock in trade of the Ratzelian school of human geographers is foreshadowed with considerable distinctness in the following passage:

One height produced nations of hunters, thus cherishing and rendering necessary a savage state: another, more extended and mild, afforded a field to the shepherd, and associated with him inoffensive animals: a third made agriculture easy and necessary: while a fourth led to fishing, to navigation, and at length to trade. The structure of our earth, in its natural variety and diversity, rendered all these distinguishing periods and states of man unavoidable. Thus in many parts of the earth manners and customs have remained unchanged some thousands of years: in others they have altered, commonly from external causes, yet always according to the land from whence the alterations came, and to that in which it happened, and on which it operated.[23]

In justice to Herder, however, it should be pointed out that geographic *determinism,* as distinct from geographic *conditioning,* is expressly avoided in the foregoing excerpt by the words: "in others they have altered, commonly from external causes." These external causes have frequently been associated with mass migrations, as he thus points out:

There is scarce an island, scarce a country, where the plains are not occupied by a foreign people of more recent date, while the more ancient and uncultivated nation has concealed itself among the hills. From these hills, on which they have retained their ruder way of life, they have often, in later times, effected revolutions, involving the inhabitants of the plains to a greater or lesser extent. India, Persia, China, and even the western countries of Asia, nay Europe itself, protected as it has been by its arts and the division of its lands, have more than once felt the scourge of overwhelming armies descending from the mountains: and what has happened on the great stage of the World has been no less frequent in smaller circles. The mahrattas in the south of Asia, the wild mountaineers in many different islands, and here and there in Europe the remains of the ancient brave inhabitants of the hilly countries, have made various incursions on the plains, and, when they could not be conquerors, have become robbers. . . .[24]

From other contexts it is quite plain that Herder means by "hills" both the regions called "mesas" (i.e., grassland plateaus) by Wissler and others, and hills and mountains in the more limited senses of the terms. Thus pastoral nomads would be included with the mountaineers who, "when they could not be conquerors, have become robbers." The migrations of the Huns and similar peoples are thus explicitly treated:

Whither have not these birds of prey extended their flight? More than once have their conquering pinions sped over one quarter of the Globe. Accordingly the mungals have established themselves in various countries of Asia, and improved their form by the features of other nations.[25]

The theories of Gumplowicz, Ratzenhofer, and especially of Oppenheimer, with reference to the migration and combat origins of the "historic" state, Herder succinctly adumbrates as follows:

What has given Germany, what has given polished Europe its governments? War. Hordes of barbarians overran this quarter of the Globe: their leaders and nobles divided the land and the inhabitants among them. Hence sprung principalities and fiefs: hence the villanage of the subjugated people: the conquerors were in possession; and all the alterations, that have taken place in this possession in the course of time, have been determined by revolutions, by war, by mutual agreement between the powerful, and in every case therefore by the law of the stronger.[26]

Again, the cycle theory of combat, already mentioned with reference to Ibn Khaldūn and Turgot, finds a faint echo in Herder:

Warlike mountaineers . . . have overrun the peaceful plains; climate, necessity, want, had rendered them strong and courageous; accordingly they spread themselves over the Earth as its lords, till they were subdued by luxury in milder climates, and then fell under the yoke of others. . . .[27]

The importance of water-borne migration and culture contact, so much stressed by Ratzel, Semple, Mahan, Vallaux, and others, Herder also recognizes:

The Mediterranean alone has so much influenced the character of all Europe, that we may almost call it the medium and propagator of all the cultivation of antiquity and the middle age. . . .[28]

Restating his contributions, we may say that Herder made the following generalizations relevant to the themes of this chapter: (1) culture patterns, although not exclusively determined by geographic factors, frequently are markedly influenced by them, particularly in the economic aspects of such patterns; (2) changes in folkways, mores, and institutions are frequently the result of intrusive or external factors such as catastrophes, mass migrations, and so forth; (3) semi-arid tundra and lower mesa areas are frequently the seat of pastoral nomadism; (4) settled agriculturists are frequently robbed, overrun, or conquered by pastoral peoples from less fertile areas; (5) the historic state frequently has its origins in the conquest of settled agriculturists by nomads of both the primary and secondary varieties; (6) the "softening" of hardy conquerors after becoming sedentary leads to their eventual overthrow and the starting of a new conquest cycle; (7) communication such as that made possible by easily navigable bodies of water facilitates culture contact and increase in cultural complexity ("progress").

Heeren, Synthesizer and Economic Determinist. — Herder's work, as already noted, had little direct influence upon historical and sociological thought; what little indirect influence he exerted was mediated through Heeren — a younger contemporary, one of that brilliant group of Göttingen professors of the period — who was deeply influenced by his emphasis upon commerce, communication, migration, and conflict. Indeed, Herder's *magnum opus* is recalled in the title Heeren gave his chief work — *Ideen über die Politik, den Verkehr und den Handel der vornehmsten Völker der alten Welt* (Thoughts Concerning the Politics, Intercourse, and Commerce of the Leading Nations of Antiquity). Montesquieu also exerted considerable influence on Heeren,[29] but Herder seems to have been predominant — not that Heeren did not expand and qualify Herder's insights. His knowledge of Adam Smith and Montesquieu greatly aided him in doing this, but after all he did not add anything essential to the pregnant ideas of his model.

He has performed one signal service, however, in pointing out the striking uniformity and simplicity of the mass migration-combat cycle, as it occurred in Persia and nearby areas of central Asia, as over against the relatively complex and obscure manifestations of the same cycle in Europe and elsewhere. He has also given some unusually clear and compact restatements of generalizations about Asiatic nomads (generalizations probably deriving from Ibn Khaldūn, Turgot, and Herder). Although he is a cistern, not a fountain, he has in such restatements probably furnished men like Ritter, Guyot, Kohl, Cotta, Reclus, Peschel, and other anthropogeographers with an appreciable part of their basic equipment. A relevant example of his capacity for effective restatement and condensation follows:

Multiplied and extensive as have been the revolutions of Central Asia, there reigns throughout the history of that continent a uniformity which is strongly contrasted with what we observe in Europe. Kingdoms and monarchies have arisen and decayed, and yet the same character has been constantly transmitted from the former to the succeeding dynasty. . . . The mighty empires which arose in Asia were not founded in the same manner with the kingdoms of Europe. They were generally erected by mighty conquering nations, and these, for the most part, nomad nations . . . they were formed to become nations of conquerors. Their mode of life fits them to endure the hardships of war; their limited wants enable them to dispense with much of the baggage which encumbers the marches of our regular armies; their countless herds afford an inexhaustible stock of horses for their cavalry, in which their principal strength has always consisted; for even in peace they are so continually moving about, that they are scarcely ever out of the saddle. These predatory habits are a sort of preparation for actual warfare, and inspire them, if not with the firm hardihood and cool courage of Europeans, yet with an audacity and impetuosity in attack, which spring from the habit of encountering danger, and the lust of spoil. The same fierce passions have called forth the locust-swarms of Mongols and Arabians from their steppes and deserts, and attracted from their mountains the Parthians and Persians, to sweep over and desolate the fruitful regions of Southern Asia. Having subdued the civilized nations established there, they extended their dominion as far as their predatory hordes could range, and became the founders of potent empires, exchanging without reluctance their sterile native country for more fortunate situations. An acquaintance, however, with the refinements and luxuries of the conquered kingdoms, and the influence of a milder climate, soon effected a remarkable change in the habits of these conquerors, and they adopted the manners of those whom they had vanquished, with the less difficulty, because a wandering herdsman is attached to no native spot, and knows no home. The consequence was a species of refinement, not of moral taste, but of mere sensual luxury; and the degree to which this was carried was proportionate to the fierceness of the desires by which it was prompted, and the suddenness of the transition from a savage state to one of ease and indulgence. In this manner the conquerors subdued themselves, and resigned their dominion, sooner or later, according to circumstances; while fresh tribes of conquerors, uncorrupted by success, sallied from their ancient haunts, or from other districts, to erect a new dynasty on the ruins of the former, and subsequently to undergo the same vicissitudes of degeneracy and subjugation.

Such may be pronounced a summary of the whole of Asiatic history, with the single exception of the Macedonian conquest; the only time when the Europeans have been masters of the interior of Asia. In this manner, of old, the monarchies of the Assyrians, the Chaldeans, the Persians, and the Parthians were founded, and fell; such, in the middle ages, was the history of the Arabian conquest; and such, up to the present day, has been that of the Tartarian and Mongol empires, which still subsist, though in ruins.[30]

In addition to this pithy summary, Heeren has given us a valuable passage on the influence of colonization[31] that distinctly foreshadows the work of Abbot, Seeley, Shepherd, Turner, Loria, Mathews, Gillespie, Leroy-Beaulieu, Muir, Hardy, Payne, and others:

One of the most interesting spectacles which history affords us, is the spread of nations by peaceable colonization. Despotic empires, which are only enlarged by conquest, exhibit to us no picture of this kind; the forcible transplanting of nations, a custom common to them, could never become the foundation of flourishing colonies, attended, as they at all times are, by oppression, and often by the dispersion of the captives carried away. If we look into these colonies, they will generally be found of a military cast, and intended rather, as in the Macedonian, Roman, and Russian monarchies, to guard the provinces of the empire than for the cultivation of the land. Commercial nations, on the contrary, especially when under the auspices of civil liberty, extend their navigation to distant regions; — Phoenicians and Greeks, not less than the British and Dutch, soon discover the necessity for foreign settlements; and notwithstanding all the abuses to which they are liable, abuses which the historian cannot mistake, it is still undeniable that not only their own civilization, but, in a great measure, the civilization of the whole human race, depend very much upon these peaceful means of advancement. The continual intercourse with their colonies enlivens and extends the knowledge of the mother states; and besides this, it infallibly promotes the development of political ideas, and what is founded upon it, the perfecting of civil government. The portion of the people separated from the parent country undergo some change in every new settlement, as the difference in the nature of the country and favourable or unfavourable circumstances necessarily give a new direction to the mind. In such cases, where society in a manner sets out anew, many improvements are easily and necessarily made, which could scarcely be adopted where every thing is become fixed and settled; and though it generally happens that colonies copy, in the first place, the government of the mother state, yet the difference of their foreign relations, and the enlarged sphere of action which their necessities open to them, soon lead them to different views. It is from the bosom of colonies that civil liberty nearly in all ages has set forth: Greece had no Solon till the colonies of Asia Minor had attained their highest degree of splendour; and while the parent country could only boast of a single legislator, whose object was to form citizens, and not merely warriors, nearly every colony of Greece and Sicily possessed its Zaleucus or Charondas. In this way, indeed, every commercial state may be said to live again in the colonies it has founded. And thus, amid the rise and fall of empires, the advances of man in civilization, in all its multitudinous forms, is perpetuated and secured.[32]

As a result of Heeren's influence more attention began to be paid to the geographical aspects of history; indeed, his influence upon Karl Ritter probably gives him a right to the title of " grandfather of human geography." Not only this: some scholars also claim that he was the father of the materialistic interpretation of history; Marx and Engels would therefore be somewhat belated offspring. Be this as it may, he exerted great influence on modern trends in sociological theory, although he himself owed most of his contribution to others. His rôle as summarizer was his most important part; whether he really was the father or originator of the trends traceable to him may well be doubted. But after all, originality is a rather scarce article, and Heeren, though he may have lacked it, was not exposed to the fate of so many of the putative " original "; he at least was not a self-made fool who worshiped his creator — *ein Narr auf eigne Hand.*

His period of greatest effectiveness was during the first half of the nineteenth century, a time when all the older disciplines were beginning to differentiate; the era of specialization was under way. The range covered by Heeren himself was much more restricted than that nibbled over by many of his contemporaries; his work was an ill omen for the type of scholar who took the whole world and its ways as an academic parish. Differentiation went on so rapidly that by the middle of the century we are confronted with a mighty host of human geographers, economic historians, anthropologists, ethnologists, and other social scientists, all representing offshoots of older, less specialized disciplines, and nearly all with something to say about migration and mental mobility — but here we prematurely approach the field of contemporary social theory.

Summary of the Chapter. — Although the Greeks, and following them the Romans, considered the results of culture contact entirely negative, and naïvely thought it possible to turn back the hands of the clock, Mandeville viewed the processes involved as both complex and inevitable. Hume was apparently the first to recognize the positive effects; he mentions release of energy and the benefits of competitive effort. With Montesquieu we get a more balanced consideration; he takes account both of the upheaval of mores and of cultural stimulation. Turgot's most significant contributions to the matter at hand include a theory of cyclical combat (reminiscent of Ibn Khaldūn), and an analysis of the process of dominance and world-organization which was surprisingly in advance of the thought of his time. Herder is of interest for his anticipation of the ideas both of the early evolutionists and of the human geographers. His influence on social thought was exerted largely through Heeren, who made practically no original contribution but who was invaluable as a summarizer, at the same time making explicit a great deal of what had been merely implicit in the thinking of his predecessors. He seems to have been the first to contrast the simplicity of the mass migration-combat cycle in Persia and parts of Asia with the more complex workings of the cycle in Europe and elsewhere. He also pointed out the contrast between expansion through conquest and through peaceful colonization.

In the present chapter, terms such as culture, culture contact, and the like are handled rather loosely, but this is today the case in most social-psychological, cultural-anthropological, social-anthropological, and sociological writing, to say nothing of that done by terminological borrowers. Some sociologists (i.e., Parsons) tried to deal with culture more precisely, and their practice is beginning to be more widely followed. See Talcott Parsons, *The Social System* (Glencoe, Ill.: Free Press, 1951), using index.

Of some importance for the history of social-scientific terminology, and perhaps for sociology of knowledge as well, is the emergence of culture in its present technical but nevertheless general sense of "the works of man" (Herskovits). It has long been thought that E. B. Tylor, in the 1870s, was first responsible for such emergence, but in German-speaking regions Klemm and Waitz were his forerunners by several decades, and Samuel Pufendorf by several centuries. Here see John P. Gillin, ed., *For a Science of Social Man* (New York: Macmillan, 1954), pp. 115-28, especially footnote 12, p. 115. In this reference it is not mentioned, however, that Pufendorf, although writing in Latin of doubtful quality, does specifically refer to culture as *industria humana,* thus directly anticipating the Herskovits phrase.

For a related treatment of some of the topics of this chapter, with bibliography, see Becker's article, "Forms of Population Movement: Prolegomena to a Study of Mental Mobility," Part I, *Social Forces*, vol. xv, 2 (Dec., 1930), pp. 147-60; Part II, *Ibid.*, 3 (March, 1931), pp. 351-61.

Supplementary Bibliography for Volume One

It is of the utmost importance that the reader bear in mind the fact that this bibliography, as the items in the Prefaces, the Notes, the Third Edition Comments (in small type at the end of each chapter), the Value-System Commentary, and the Appendix on Sociological Trends, *is not indexed*. In other words, the Name Index and the Subject Index deal only with the names and subjects appearing in the First Edition (1938) text *as such,* and this text, with the exception of minor corrections, is presented unaltered.

Reviewers the world over evidenced remarkable kindliness in dealing with the 1938 version, in spite of the extremely wide coverage that the nature of the treatise made necessary. Only with such encouragement would the present writer have ventured to present the original text again in 1952; thereafter the earlier goodwill was once more manifested. Now, in 1960, the risk is once more taken, with the hope that tolerance, at least, will be encountered.

Given the tremendous amount of contemporary scholarly activity, full up-to-dateness could not conceivably be achieved within any reasonable space limits, even if the present writer felt competent to achieve it. The list here provided is intended merely to offer a means whereby the reader can delve deeper in the direction of his interests, guided by searching investigators, than this treatise alone would ever have made possible.

Stress is on the fairly recent, but a few references of earlier date are given when it seems obvious that they should have been included in the first place. Now and again, items listed elsewhere in this treatise are included here if the present writer's orientation is indicated or has been markedly influenced by them; some of his own books and articles, understandably enough, fall in this category! Apart from such considerations as these, preference has often gone to works that contain bibliographies, in footnotes or otherwise. Further, articles and books that survey the various works of given authors, grouped in "schools" and the like (albeit singly now and again), rather than the writings of the authors themselves, figure prominently—need for brevity forced this in *most* cases. In addition, there has been an effort to list convenient "paperbacks"; in some cases passages or entire books that would otherwise be hard to come by, will thus become available. Had it seemed advisable to list well-known standard writings, such as those of Plato, Hegel, Max Weber, and others, the bibliography would have been in some respects more useful (*many* "paperbacks" are in print), and certainly more lengthy—but a line somewhere was unavoidable.

Abbreviations of journals, etc., follow the keys at the beginning of the Notes; what is not to be found in the keys is not abbreviated. The abbreviation bib. or bibs. is used for bibliographies, n. for notes, fn. for footnotes, sel. for selected, II or III for "also very useful for Volume II" (or III), PB for paperback, ext. for extensive, and so on.

Albright, W. F.,   *From the Stone Age to Christianity,* 2nd ed. (Baltimore: Johns Hopkins, 1957). Authorit. Bib. Anchor PB.

Barker, Ernest,   *Social and Political Thought in Byzantium: from Justinian I to the Last Palaeologus* (Oxford: Clarendon, 1957).

Bastide, Roger,   *Sociologie et Psychanalyse* (Paris: Presses Universitaires de France, 1950). Refers, among oth. things, to treat. of Freud's *Totem and Taboo.*

Becker, Howard,   "Vicinal Isolation and Mental Immobility," *SF,* vol. xi, 3 (Mar., 1933), pp. 326-334. III.

————————, (with D. K. Bruner), "Some Aspects of Taboo and Totemism," *Journal of Social Psychology,* vol. iii, 3 (Aug., 1932), pp. 337-353. Att. on Freud assump. and sugg. of alt.

————————, (with D. K. Bruner), "Tabu and Totemismus: Versuch einer neuen Hypothese ihrer Ursprünge und ihrer Entwicklung," *Kölner Vierteljahrshefte für Soziologie,* vol. xii, 1 (1933), pp. 52-69.

———————— and Barnes, H. E., *Historia del Pensamiento Social,* Span. trans. of *STFLTS* (Mexico: Fondo de Cultura Economica, 1945). Portug. trans. also avail. Ital. and Polish trans. of 3rd ed. soon avail. II and III.

————————, "Processes of Secularisation: An Ideal-typical Analysis with Special Reference to Personality Change as Affected by Population Movement, Part I," *Sociological Review* (British), (Apr.-July, 1932), pp. 135-154. Part II, *ibid.* (Oct., 1932), pp. 266-286.

————————, "Säkularisationsprozesse, I. Teil," *Kölner Vierteljahrshefte für Soziologie* (Jan., 1932), pp. 283-294. II. Teil, *ibid.* (June, 1932), pp. 450-463. Trans. of above.

————————, "Social Thought of Preliterate Peoples," Part I (in Japanese) *Studies of Social Science,* publication of Hosei University, Tokyo, vol. i, 2 (Oct., 1933), pp. 126-147. Part II, *ibid.,* i, 3 (Nov., 1933), pp. 64-78.

————————, *Man in Reciprocity* (New York: Frederick A. Praeger, Inc., 1956). Ext. bib. II and III.

————————, "Church and State in the Cosmos of Crete," *International Review of Social History* (Amsterdam) vol. i, 2 (Oct., 1945), pp. 253-295. Deals with Minoan soc. and cult. Pre-Ventris-Chadwick deciph., but not inval. thereby.

————————, "A Sacred-Secular Evaluation Continuum of Social Change," *Proceedings of the Third International Congress of Sociology* (Amsterdam: Aug., 1956), vol. vi, pp. 19-41. II and III.

——————————————, "Culture Case Study and Greek History: Comparison Viewed Sociologically," *ASR*, vol. xxiii, 5 (Oct., 1958), pp. 489-504. Explic. stat. of meth. sometimes misunder. Many refs. to earlier treat. III.

Bierstedt, Robert, ed., *The Making of Society: An Outline of Sociology,* rev. ed. (New York: Random House, 1959). From Plato to pres.

Boehmer, Heinrich, *Martin Luther: Road to Reformation,* trans. by John W. Doberstein and Theodore G. Tappert. (Philadelphia: Muhlenberg Press, 1946). Meridian PB. Bib.

Bogardus, E. S., *The Development of Social Thought,* 3rd ed. (New York: Longmans Green, 1955). Over-br. and not suff. incl. II and III.

Borkenau, Franz, *Der Übergang vom feudalen zum bürgerlichen Weltbild* (Paris: Alcan, 1934). Marxist orient.; somewh. doctrinaire. Much mat. not ord. encount. II.

Breasted, J. H., *Development of Religion and Thought in Ancient Egypt* (New York: Scribner's, 1912). Torch PB. Old but still author.

Burckhardt, Jacob, *Age of Constantine the Great* (New York: Pantheon, 1949). Anchor PB. Old but stim.

——————————————, *The Civilization of the Renaissance in Italy* Introd. by Benjamin Nelson and Charles Trinkaus. Vols. i and ii (New York: Harper, 1958). Torch PB. Old but still useful. II.

Burnet, John, *Early Greek Philosophy* (London: A. and C. Black, 1892). Meridian PB. Pro-Greek but stim.

Burnham, James, *The Machiavellians* (New York: Day, 1943). Well writt., but doctrinaire and occ. superfic. II and III.

Carpenter, Rhys, *Folk Tale, Fiction, and Saga in the Homeric Epics* (Berkeley: Univ. of Calif. Press, 1946). Univ. of Calif. PB. Anti-"unitarian."

Chambliss, Rollin, *Social Thought: From Hammurabi to Comte* (New York: Dryden, 1954). II and III.

Chrimes, K. M. T., *Ancient Sparta: A Re-Examination of the Evidence* (New York: Philosophical Library, 1952). Ventur. but inform. and stim.

Clark, George, *War and Society in the Seventeenth Century* (Cambridge: The Univ. Press, 1958). II.

Clough, S. B., *The Rise and Fall of Civilization: An Inquiry into the Relationship Between Economic Development and Civilization* (New York: McGraw-Hill, 1951).

Colvin, Milton,   "Alfred Weber—the Sociologist as a Humanist," *AJS,* vol. lxv, 2 (Sept., 1959), pp. 166-168.

Cos, O. C.,   *Caste, Class, and Race: a Study in Social Dynamics* (New York: Doubleday, 1948). Parts on Hindu caste system. In some resp. anti-Max Weber. Bib. II and III.

Creel, H. G.,   *Confucius: the Man Behind the Myth* (New York: Day, 1949). Torch PB. "Confucius and the Chinese Way." Stim. and accur. III.

———————————, *Chinese Thought from Confucius to Mao Tse-Tung* (New York: New American Library, 1960). Mentor PB.

Davis, S.,   *Race-Relations in Ancient Egypt: Greek, Egyptian, Hebrew, Roman* (New York: Philosophical Library, 1952).

Deissmann, G. A.,   *Paul: A Study in Social and Religious History,* trans. by William E. Wilson (New York: Harper, 1957). Torch PB. Imp.

Dodds, E. R.,   *The Greeks and the Irrational* (Berkeley: Univ. of Calif. Press, 1951). Beacon PB. Very stim.; good ns. III.

Dussort, Henri,   "La prehistoire de la sociology à la lumiere de son present," *Cahiers Internationaux de Sociologie,* 23 (Jul.-Dec., 1957), pp. 133-141.

Fairbank, J. K., ed.,   *Chinese Thought and Institutions* (Chicago: Univ. of Chicago Press, 1957). Bib. III.

Ferm, Vergilius, ed.,   *Encyclopedia of Religion* (New York: Philosophical Library, 1945). Living Age PB. Useful compend. for prelim. surv.

Finley, M. I.,   *The World of Odysseus* (New York: Viking Press, 1951). Meridian PB.

———————————, "The Ancient Greeks and Their Nation: The Sociological Problem," *British Journal of Sociology,* vol. v, 3 (Sept., 1954), pp. 253-263.

Frankfort, Henri,   *The Birth of Civilization in the Near East* (London: Williams and Norgate, 1951). Anchor PB. Claims great deal, but stim.

Freemantle, Anne, ed.,   *The Age of Belief: the Medieval Philosophers* (Boston: Houghton Mifflin, 1955). Mentor PB. Useful.

Fustel de Coulanges, Numa Denis,   *The Ancient City* (Boston: Lee and Shepard, 1874). Anchor PB. Marred by intermix. of Greek and Rom. evid., but imp. as show. sacr. compon. in urb. estab. II and III.

Gardiner, Patrick, ed.,   *Theories of History: Readings from Classical and Contemporary Sources* (Glencoe, Ill.: Free Press, 1959).

Gerth, H. H.,

Die Sozialgeschichtliche Lage der bürger-Intelligenz um die Wende des 18. Jahrhunderts (Berlin: VDI Verlag, 1935). Sel. Bib. II.

Gewirth, Alan,

Marsilius of Padua, Defender of Peace (New York: Columbia Univ. Press, 1951). Bib.

Granet, Marcel,

Chinese Civilization (London: Kegan Paul, 1930). Meridian PB. Exc. treat., altho. at times dogmat.

Grant, Frederick C., ed.,

Hellenistic Religions: The Age of Syncretism (New York: Liberal Arts Press, 1953). Liberal Arts PB. Useful compend.

Groethuisen, Bernard,

"Les Origines sociales de l'incredulité Bourgeoise en France," *Studies in Philosophy and Social Science*, vol. viii, 1939. (New York: Institute of Social Research, 1940). II.

Hampshire, Stuart, ed.,

The Age of Reason: the 17th Century Philosophers (Boston: Houghton Mifflin, 1956). Mentor PB. Useful. II.

Harrison, Jane,

Prolegomena to the Study of Greek Religion, 3rd ed., (Cambridge: Cambridge Univ. Press, 1922). Meridian PB. Durkheim interpret.; doctrinaire. III.

Hertzler, J. O.,

"Toward a Sociology of Language," *SF*, vol. xxxii (Dec., 1953), pp. 109-119.

Hitti, Philip K.,

The Arabs: a Short History (Princeton: Princeton Univ. Press, 1949). Gateway PB.

————————, *History of Syria, including Lebanon and Palestine* (New York: Macmillan, 1951). Bib.

Hughes, E. C.,

"The Early and Contemporary Study of Religion," *AJS*, vol. lx, 6 (May, 1955), pp. 1-4.

Huizinga, Johan,

Erasmus and the Age of Reformation (New York: Harper, 1957). Torch PB. Stim.

————————, *The Waning of the Middle Ages* (London: Arnold, 1924). Anchor PB.

Jaeger, Werner,

Paideia: The Ideals of Greek Culture, 3 vols. (New York: Oxford Univ. Press, 1939-1944; 2nd ed., vol. i, 1945). Det. bibs. in n. Arist. value-judg., but thor.

James, E. O.,

The Ancient Gods, vol. i (London: Weidenfeld and Nicolson, 1960). Imp.

————————, *Prehistoric Religions: a Study in Prehistoric Archaeology* (New York: Frederick A. Praeger, 1957).

Jeffery, Arthur, ed.,

Islam: Muhammad and His Religion (New York: Liberal Arts Press, 1958). Liberal Arts PB. Useful compend.

Kilzer, Ernest, "Some Antecedents of Sociology," *American Catholic Sociological Society Review,* vol. xiii (1952), pp. 233-239.

———————, *Western Social Thought* (Milwaukee: Bruce, and Ross, E. J.,   1954). Sketchy.

Kramer, S. N., *From the Tablets of Sumer* (London: Thames and Hudson, 1956). Anchor PB.

Kroeber, A. L., *Configurations of Culture Growth* (Berkeley and Los Angeles: Univ. of Calif. Press, 1944). Elab. bib. II and III.

———————, *Style and Civilizations* (Ithaca: Cornell Univ. Press, 1957). II and III.

Larson, M. A., *The Religion of the Occident* (London: Peter Orven, 1960). Imp. for Jesus as Essene.

Leff, Gordon, *Medieval Thought: St. Augustine to Ockham* (Harmondsworth, Middlesex: Penguin Books, 1958). Pelican PB.

Lewy, Immanuel, *The Growth of the Pentateuch* (New York: Bookman Associates, 1955).

Linton, Ralph, *The Tree of Culture* (New York: Knopf, 1955). Vintage PB. Superfic. in spots, but compreh. and stim. II and III.

Lowie, R. H., *Primitive Religion* (New York: Boni and Liveright, 1924). Universal Library PB. Part. imp. for anti-Durkheim anal. Major work. III.

Margolis, Max, and Marx, Alexander, *History of the Jewish People* (Philadelphia: Jewish Publication Society, 1927). Meridian PB.

Mauss, Marcel, *The Gift: Forms and Functions of Exchange in Archaic Societies,* trans. by Ian Cussison, with an introd. by E. E. Evans-Pritchard. (Glencoe, Ill.: Free Press, 1954).

McKeown, J. E., "Sociological Misinterpretations of Plato's Republic," *American Catholic Sociological Society Review,* vol. xvi, 3 (Oct., 1955), pp. 182-197.

Mendieta y Nunez, Lucio, "Batista Vico, Precursor de la Sociologia," *Revista Mexicana de Sociologia,* vol. xv, 1 (Jan.-Feb., 1953), pp. 27-35.

Moscati, Sabatino, *Ancient Semitic Civilizations* (New York: Elek, 1957). Capricorn PB. Unus. emph.

———————, *The Semites in Ancient History* (Cardiff: Univ. of Wales Press, 1960). Brief; good.

Mousheng, Lin, *Man and Ideas: an Informal History of Chinese Political Thought* (New York: Day, 1942). Pop.; stim.

Needham, Joseph, and Wang Ling, *Science and Civilization in China, Vol. II: History of Scientific Thought* (Cambridge: Univ. Press, 1956). II and III.

Néf, J. U.,   *Cultural Foundations of Industrial Civilization* (New York: Cambridge Univ. Press, 1958). I and III.

Onians, R. B.,   *The Origin of European Thought* (Cambridge: Univ. Press, 1954).

Radin, Paul,   *Primitive Man as Philosopher* (New York: Appleton, 1927). Dover PB. Highly imp. II and III.

————————————, *Primitive Religion* (New York: Viking Press, 1937). Dover PB. Profound; exc. III.

Rand, E. K.,   *Founders of the Middle Ages* (Cambridge: Harvard Univ. Press, 1928). Dover PB. Stand. work.

Rouse, W. H. D.,   *Gods, Heroes and Men of Ancient Greece* (London: Nelson, 1939). Mentor PB. Anal. of complex. sit.

Santillana, Giorgie de, ed.,   *The Age of Adventure: the Renaissance Philosophers* (Boston: Houghton Mifflin, 1957). Mentor PB. Useful compend.

Schimmel, Annemarie, trans., *Ibn Khaldūn: Ausgewählte Abschnitte aus der Muqaddima (Civitus Gentium* series ed. by Max Graf zu Solms). Tübingen: J. C. B. Mohr [Paul Siebeck], 1951). Helpf. for comp. with Fr. and Eng. trans.

Schuhl, Pierre-Maxime,   *Essai sur le formation de la pensée grecque* (Paris: Alcan, 1934). Exc. classif. and gen. bibs.

Silver, Abba Hillel,   *A History of Messianic Speculation in Israel: From the First through the Seventeenth Centuries* (New York: Macmillan, 1927). Beacon PB. Very good for "Messianic hope."

Singer, Dorothea Waley,   *Girodano Bruno: His Life and Thought; With Annotated Translation of His Work On the Infinite Universe and Worlds* (New York: Henry Schuman, 1950).

Sombart, Werner,   Introd. by Bert F. Hoselitz, *The Jews and Modern Capitalism,* trans. by M. Epstein (Glencoe, Ill.: Free Press, 1951).

Taylor, H. O.,   *The Emergence of Christian Culture in the West: The Classical Heritage of the Middle Ages,* 4th ed. (New York: Ungar, 1957). Torch PB.

Tillyard, E. M. W.,   *The Elizabethan World Picture* (London: Chatto and Windus, 1943). Modern Library PB. Literary; useful.

Usher, A. P.,   *A History of Mechanical Inventions,* rev. ed. (Cambridge: Harvard Univ. Press, 1954). Exc. study, showing weakn. of soc. of know. *re* cert. inv.

Wach, Joachim,   *The Comparative Study of Religions,* ed. with an introd. by Joseph M. Kitagawa. (New York: Columbia Univ. Press, 1958).

Waddell, Helen,   *The Wandering Scholars,* 7th ed. (London: Constable, 1949). Anchor PB.

Weber, Alfred,   "Prinzipielles zur Kultursoziologie," *ASUP,* vol. xlvii (1920-1921). Trans. as *Fundamentals of Culture-Sociology* by G. H. Weltner and C. F. Hirschmann (New York: WPA Project, mimeographed, 1939). II and III.

Weber, Max,   "Confuzianismus and Taoismus" in his *Religionssoziologie,* vol. i, trans. by H. H. Gerth as *The Religion of China* (Glencoe, Ill.: Free Press, 1951). II.

White, Helen,   *Social Criticism in Popular Religious Literature in Sixteenth-Century England* (New York: Macmillan, 1944). Bib. in fn.

Willey, Basil,   *The Seventeenth-Century Background* (New York: Columbia Univ. Press, 1934). Anchor PB.

Wilson, J. A.,   *The Burden of Egypt: an Interpretation of Ancient Egyptian Culture* (Chicago: Univ. of Chicago Press, 1951).

Wittfogel, K. A.,   *Oriental Despotism: a Comparative Study of Total Power* (New Haven: Yale Univ. Press, 1957). Slanted but usef. III.

Wright, A. F., ed.,   *Studies in Chinese Thought* (Chicago: Univ. of Chicago Press, 1953).

Wulf, Maurice de,   *An Introduction to Scholastic Philosophy* (Scholasticism, Old and New). Trans. by P. Coffey (Dublin: Gill, 1907). Dover PB. Stand. work.

——————————————, *Philosophy and Civilization in the Middle Ages* (Princeton: Princeton Univ. Press, 1922). Dover PB. Good interp.

NOTES

The reader should be made aware of the fact that, as mentioned elsewhere, *names and topics occurring in these Notes are not indexed*. Valuable bibliographic resources will be overlooked if those wishing to make use of such resources do not pore through the Notes. The same is true of the comments at the ends of all chapters; references appearing therein are not indexed.

Other bibliographical resources are provided in the Supplementary Bibliography for Volumes I, II, III. These bibliographies contain references to other bibliographies. As DeMorgan said:

Great big fleas have little fleas upon their backs to bite 'em,
  And little fleas have lesser fleas, and so *ad infinitum*.
And the great fleas themselves, in turn, have greater fleas to go on;
  While these again have greater still, and greater still, and so on.

Levity aside, now, it may be well to direct attention to the present state of the history of social thought and, for that matter, of sociological theories. Less and less reading in these fields, to say nothing of research, is today being done by professional sociologists, and this might be viewed as justifiable if it were not for the fact that picayune notions are perpetually being swallowed as the latest novelties by the gullible. Perhaps no one need worry about the gullible; the poor, in our present economy of abundance, may not be always with us (although the writer here coughs discreetly), but the gullible certainly will. Nevertheless, there are good grounds for worry; the gullible sometimes control the sinews of research, with the result that the veriest quacks and/or ignoramuses inflict on us their pompously formulated trivialities. "Paper is patient; anything can be impressed on it"—but should not *we* begin to be impatient with the fools, charlatans, semi-literates, and "scientistic" dogmatists?

Apart from this, it seems clear that those who have recently become interested in sociology of knowledge might gain a good deal for us all by dealing with the history of social thought and of sociological theories from that standpoint. If sociology is ever to transcend its ethnic, religious, class, national, chronological, technological, and other limitations, there must be relentless probing into basic assumptions with a view to discovering what can be relied on as suitable foundations for research leading to conclusions that hold despite those ethnic...to the *n*th limitations. Circularity of this kind is the only way out of circularity of that kind; only sociology of knowledge can lay bare our basic assumptions thoroughly enough for the logic of science to be effectively applied to them. And what better materials for sociology of knowledge investigation can be found than man's ideas about life with his fellows, from the years when the sages whose very names have long since been forgotten dispensed their lore to the days when the columnists who have themselves forgotten what they said last year peddle their wares?

I pause for a reply, and not only from the columnists. "My fires are banked, but still they burn..."

Notes and Suggestions for Further Reading

LIST OF ABBREVIATIONS

A   *The Annals of the American Academy of Political and Social Science*
AA   *American Anthropologist*
AAS   *Archiv für angewandte Soziologie*
ADS   *Archives de sociologie*
AESS   *Archives of the Economic and Social Sciences* (modern Greek)
AFLB   *Annales de la faculté des lettres de Bordeaux*
AGA   *Allgemein statistisches Archiv*
AGPS   *Archiv für Geschichte der Philosophie und Soziologie*
AHR   *American Historical Review*
AIIS   *Annales de l'institut international de sociologie*
AJS   *The American Journal of Sociology*
APM   *Archives of Philosophy and Methodology* (modern Greek)
ARGB   *Archiv für Rassen- und Gesellschaftsbiologie*
ARW   *Archiv für Rechts- und Wirtschaftsphilosophie*
AS   *L'Année sociologique*
ASGS   *Archiv für soziale Gesetzgebung und Statistik*
ASPS   *Archiv für systematische Philosophie und Soziologie*
ASR   *American Sociological Review*
ASSSR   *Archives of Social Science and Social Reform* (Roumanian)
ASUP   *Archiv für Sozialwissenschaft und Sozialpolitik*
BMCPEE   *Bulletin mensuel du centre polytechnicien d'études économiques*
BNJ   *Byzantinisch-neugriechische Jahrbücher*
BSFP   *Bulletin de la société française de philosophie*
BSSR   *Bulletin of the Society for Social Research*

BWC   Harry Elmer Barnes, *History of Western Civilization*
CAH   *Cambridge Ancient History*
CH   *Current History*
CM   *Communist Monthly*
ConR   *Contemporary Review*
CR   *Cambridge Review*
CSPSR   *The Chinese Social and Political Science Review*
E   *Economica*
EA   *Encyclopedia Americana*
EB   *Encyclopædia Britannica*
EI   *Enciclopedia Italiana*
ER   *Educational Review*
ES   *Encyclopedia Sinica*
ESS   *Encyclopedia of the Social Sciences*
GE   *Grande Encyclopédie*
GGE   *Great Greek Encyclopedia* (modern Greek)
HERE   Hastings's *Encyclopedia of Religion and Ethics*
HO   *Historical Outlook*
HWBS   *Handwörterbuch der Soziologie*
IJE   *International Journal of Ethics*
JA   *Journal asiatique*
JAFL   *Journal of American Folk-Lore*
JAS   *Journal of Applied Sociology*
JASA   *Journal of the American Statistical Association*
JASP   *Journal of Abnormal and Social Psychology*
JCCL   *Journal of Criminology and Criminal Law*
JCP   *Journal of Comparative Psychology*
JDP   *Journal de psychologie*
JFS   *Jahrbuch für Soziologie*
JNCBRAS   *Journal of the North China British Royal Asiatic Society*
JP   *Journal of Philosophy*

JPE *Journal of Political Economy*
JPNP *Journal de psychologie normale et pathologique*
JPPSM *Journal of Philosophy, Psychology, and Scientific Methods*
JRAI *Journal of the Royal Anthropological Institute*
JRAS *Journal of the Royal Asiatic Society*
JRD *Journal of Race Development*
JSM *Japanese Sociological Monthly*
JSP *Journal of Social Philosophy*
JSPS *Journal of Social Psychology*
KVS *Kölner Vierteljahrshefte für Soziologie*
M *The Monist*
MEM *Mensch en Maatschappij*
MF *Mercure de France*
MP *Modern Philology*
MSOS *Mitteilungen des Seminars für orientalische Sprachen*
PA *Pacific Affairs*
PASS *Publication or Proceedings of the American Sociological Society*
PR *Philosophical Review*
PSM *Popular Science Monthly*
PSQ *Political Science Quarterly*
RASI *Reports of the Archaeological Survey of India*
RAST *Royal Asiatic Society Transactions*
RB *Revue bleue*
RDI *Rivista d'Italia*
RDIS *Revue de l'institut de sociologie*
RDP *Revue de Paris*
REO *Revue de l'Europe orientale*
RHES *Revue d'histoire économique et sociale*
RIS *Revue internationale de sociologie*

RMM *Revue de metaphysique et de morale*
RP *Revue philosophique*
RPP *Revue de philosophie positive*
RS *Rivista di sociologia*
RSe *Revue socialiste*
RSH *Revue de synthèse historique*
RSICP *Report at Sixth International Congress of Philosophy*
RUBB *Revue universitaire belge: Bruxelles*
RUS *Rural Sociology*
S *Sociologus*
SBKAWPH *Sitzungsberichte der kaiserlichen Akademie der Wissenschaften, philosoph.-histor. Klasse*
SF *Social Forces*
SJ *Schmollers Jahrbuch*
SLR *Slavische Rundschau*
SM *Scientific Monthly*
SPSSQ *Southwestern Political and Social Science Quarterly*
SR *Sociological Review*
SRE *Social Research*
SS *Social Science*
SSR *Sociology and Social Research*
SSSQ *Southwestern Social Science Quarterly*
UTQ *University of Toronto Quarterly*
VFWP *Vierteljahrsschrift für wissenschaftliche Philosophie*
VWPS *Vierteljahrsschrift für wissenschaftliche Philosophie und Soziologie*
ZP *Zeitschrift für Politik*
ZSF *Zeitschrift für Sozialforschung*
ZVS *Zeitschrift für Völkerpsychologie und Soziologie*

Each author is responsible for the notes bearing on the chapters or sections marked with his symbol in the Table of Contents, with two exceptions: (1) all references in Barnes's notes to books and articles dated 1927 or later have been inserted by Becker; and (2) all the notes have been edited by Becker.

Books and articles likely to be of interest and value beyond their specific reference function are marked with an asterisk.

NOTES

CHAPTER I

1. *G. L. Gomme, *The Village Community* (1890), "The Heisgier Community," pp. 143–46. The writings of Maine, Seebohm, Maitland, and others should be consulted for similar data. A useful compilation and commentary is Sorokin and Zimmerman's *Systematic Source Book in Rural Sociology* (3 vols., 1930–32).

It will be noted that we do not make the distinction, occasionally found, between preliterates of " higher " and " lower " cultures. Although valid, it is irrelevant for our purposes.

2. Elsdon Best, *The Maori* (1924); Raymond Firth, *Primitive Economics of the New Zealand Maori* (1929); S. P. Smith, *Hawaiki* (4th ed., 1921).

3. Consult any of the numerous folklore journals. Accounts of American preliterate communities are contained in *John C. Campbell's *The Southern Highlander and His Homeland* (1921). Excellent bibliography. Marjorie Kinnan Rawlings's novels dealing with the " Florida scrub folk " are stimulating and apparently accurate, and Boswell's *Tour of the Hebrides* is of course splendid.

4. A recently discovered American example is described by Mandel Sherman and Thomas R. Henry, *Hollow Folk* (1933). This study is not as good as it might be, however, for the writers fail to confront the problem of hereditary mental deficiency in a courageous way. Further, the questions posed by these psychologists are sociologically inadequate. The writer of the present chapter has for some time been interested in the mental immobility of the German peasant. See his " Sargasso Iceberg: A Study in Cultural Lag and Institutional Disintegration," *AJS*, vol. xxxiv (Nov., 1928), pp. 492–506. One of the best recent studies of folk mentality is Conrad Arensberg's *The Irish Peasant* (1937).

5. A splendid discussion of the nature of the " folk " as contrasted with the city *populus* or *demos* is to be found in *Robert Redfield's *Tepoztlan: A Mexican Village* (1930), pp. 1–10, 205–23. For a survey of the range of folk thought, see Stith Thompson, *Motif Index of Folk Literature* (1932).

6. If this book had been written a decade or two ago, " preliterate " would not have appeared in a chapter heading or anywhere else, for earlier social scientists habitually spoke of American Indians, South Sea Islanders, Australian blackfellows, Eskimos, and all other peoples with civilizations very much simpler than our own as " primitives." Indeed, they frequently referred to them as " savages," " nature peoples," " wild men," and what not. By using such terms they misled popular opinion and fell into grave errors themselves, for the peoples who have not yet begun to write are no more primitive, in the exact sense, than we are; and as for their savagery and wildness — well, we who have passed through the World War know that these characteristics are also to be found among Europeans and Americans. (The proponents of the " new history " [James Harvey Robinson and others] used the term " pre-literary " as early as 1908; see *The New History*, chap. ii. [This volume, although published in 1912, contains articles of earlier date.] It was always used, however, in or in close connection with the phrase " pre-literary history " to denote the field to which they felt the historian should extend his researches instead of limiting them, as did the " old history," to the period since written records have been available. This usage soon became common; for example, we find Harry Elmer Barnes referring as a matter of course to " pre-literary history " in several articles, among them " The Past and Future of History," *HO*, vol. xii [Feb., 1921], p. 48. After all, however, this meaning of the term covers only a small part of " preliterate," and it seems that credit must be given to Ellsworth Faris for introducing and

securing acceptance for the latter. See his " Pre-Literate Peoples: Proposing a New Term," *AJS*, vol. xxx [May, 1925], pp. 710–12. It should be noted, however, that Robert E. Lowie, in his *Primitive Religion* [1924], Preface, *passim*, used " illiterate " in much the same sense as Faris later [1925] used " preliterate." The usual connotations of " illiterate," however, make " preliterate " or Radin's " non-literate " distinctly preferable.) Further, earlier writers would not have spoken of the social thought of preliterates except for the purpose of contrasting it with the vastly superior thought of modern man; their favorite antithesis was primitive **versus modern. (Even at present a few writers deriving from the nineteenth** century espouse this point of view; e.g., George F. Murdock, book review, *AA*, vol. xxxiv [Oct.-Dec., 1932], p. 704: " The Arunta and the Tlingit and the Hindu [*sic*] are as important to sociology as are the experimental rat and the fruitfly to genetics." A similar belief was held by W. G. Sumner, and is vigorously defended by his follower, A. G. Keller, both in *The Science of Society* [1927] and its epitome, *Man's Rough Road* [1932].)

Such naïve social evolutionists were and are grossly in error. To begin with, the initial mistake of identifying preliterate with primitive led them to the further misconception that all preliterates possess a rudimentary intellect (" primitive " in the sense of crude), inherently incapable of complex and sustained mental processes. This view of the matter was almost certainly correct when held with regard to Neanderthal man or earlier proto-human types, but it is highly doubtful when transferred to *Homo sapiens*, who made his appearance anywhere from twenty-five to fifty thousand years ago. The native mental endowment of man in the later Paleolithic was perhaps as good as that of twentieth-century man if mere cranial capacity is an adequate index; improvements in human thought since the old stone age are probably due primarily to the increased range of culture contacts, advances in the technique of thinking, and rapid multiplication of the sum total of human knowledge. Natural selection undoubtedly has had some effect, but the time since the emergence of *Homo sapiens* has been so relatively short, and the capacities selected have been so diverse (often bearing no direct relation to the ability to engage in abstract thought, for example), that this funda-mental process of organic evolution has probably had only a secondary effect on the mental powers of post-Paleolithic man in the aggregate.

As between preliterate and modern, of course, the situation is not quite the same. There are some preliterates who, like the Bushmen, possibly may not be of the same stock as *Homo sapiens*, and to whom the considerations just advanced therefore do not apply. Recent studies by Porteus comparing the Bushmen with the Australoids, for example, show the former to be of inferior mental status. See his *Primitive Intelligence and Environment* (1937). There are others who have been exposed to selective processes of so peculiar a nature that the question as to whether their mental powers have been altered or impaired must certainly be left open until all the evidence is in. But when every objection is taken into account, it is still possible to say that for the purpose of analyzing their social thought it is quite permissible to assume, as a working hypothesis, that preliterates deriving their blood from *Homo sapiens* generally have innate mental characteristics approxi-mately similar (not necessarily " equal ") to those of at least the rank and file of their " literate " modern contemporaries. The difference between the actual ex-pressions of those mental characteristics *with which we are concerned in this chapter* resides chiefly in the great discrepancy between the cultures of which they are the heirs. (*S. D. Porteus, *The Psychology of a Primitive People* [1931], holds that Australian aborigines, among others, are definitely inferior to Europeans, whereas *Franz Boas, *The Mind of Primitive Man* [1910], maintains that there is no discoverable difference in innate capacity, a position akin to that taken by W. I. Thomas, *Primitive Behavior* [1937], pp. 770–800, " The Relative Mental Endowment of Races." A stimulating survey of pros and cons is given by *Alexander Goldenweiser, *Early Civilization* [1922], pp. 327–415 [see also his *Anthropology* (1937), pp. 407–26]; and by *F. H. Hankins, *An Introduction to the Study of Society* [1927], pp. 525–30. Probably the best discussion of the topic in any language is Richard Thurnwald's " Psychologie des primitiven Menschen," in Gustav Kafka, ed., *Handbuch der vergleichenden Psychologie* [1922]. This article is accompanied by a splendid bibliography on preliterate mentality, pp. 307–20.)

Even such carefully qualified assertions as those we have just made probably have a dogmatic ring to those who believe that the " savage " is always and everywhere intellectually inferior, by sheer force of heredity, to his " civilized " cousin " higher in the evolutionary scale." Nevertheless, there is good warrant for making them. For example, in the construction of tools, houses, boats, fishing tackle, and in the thousand and one other tasks of everyday life that make the manipulation of material objects a necessity, the preliterate sets to work just as one of us acquainted with the logic of materials would, and often shows a much higher degree of insight and intelligence than some of us might. (Hankins, *op. cit.*, pp. 394–95; Goldenweiser, *op. cit.*, pp. 405–07.) When the sequence of cause and effect is fairly obvious, the preliterate offers explanations much like those of modern man. Moreover, those who declare that there is a profound, biologically caused cleavage of kind between the thinking of modern and preliterate man have failed to note that the antithesis they set up is not between the preliterate and the ordinary member of a modern social group, but between the preliterate and the scientific expert at work in his own field. Illogical behavior, such as acting on mutually contradicting beliefs, ignoring secondary causes, and attributing surprising or sudden events to mysterious agencies, can be observed in modern life almost any day. The error here is not that preliterate peoples are wrongly observed, but that modern man is scarcely observed at all.

7. A critique of the usual method of finding " survivals " is given by Clark Wissler, *An Introduction to Social Anthropology* (1929), pp. 218–21.

8. This lack may not be altogether a disadvantage. Cf. *Paul Radin, *Primitive Man as Philosopher* (1927), pp. 61–62.

9. Paul Radin, *Method and Theory of Ethnology* (1933), pp. 262–63.

10. *Wiese-Becker, *Systematic Sociology* (1932), pp. 222–26.

11. Thurnwald, *op. cit.*, pp. 148, 151, *et passim*.

12. Ellen Churchill Semple, *Influences of Geographic Environment* (1911), p. 132.

13. Walter Bagehot, *Physics and Politics* (1899), p. 52.

14. Ratzel, *Politische Geographie*, p. 398.

15. Ogburn, *Social Change* (1923), p. 191.   16. Bagehot, *op. cit.*, p. 131.

17. P. Vidal de La Blache, *Human Geography*, pp. 325–26. This belief has found root in American thought; e.g., ". . . psychic inertia is a general trait of human, nay of animal, psychology " (Alexander Goldenweiser, " Culture and Environment," *AJS*, vol. xxi, p. 632).

18. Ogburn, *op. cit.*, p. 191.   19. *Ibid.*, p. 173.   20. *Ibid.*, p. 194.

21. The common assumption is that " racial " factors " cause " cultural inertia and that the present rapidity of cultural change in the Western world is due to inherent " Nordic " qualities. This fallacy has been commented upon as follows: " The growth of a culture that has reached the point of extremely rapid change will, within a definite period of time, say, five hundred years, be immensely greater than the growth, within the same time, of a culture that has not reached

the stage of such rapid change. If such a comparison be thought of as a race between two cultures, the one will in the same period of time greatly outdistance the other, which will seem to be left hopelessly behind. The original disparity between two such cultures may have been due to relative degrees of *isolation* or other cultural factors " (Ogburn, *op. cit.*, pp. 138–39).

22. *Ibid.*, p. 177.

23. Franz Boas, *Anthropology and Modern Life* (1st ed., 1927), p. 140.

24. P. Vidal de La Blache, *op. cit.*, p. 72.

25. *Howard Becker, " Vicinal Isolation and Mental Immobility," *SF*, vol. xi (Mar., 1933), pp. 326–34.

26. Franz Boas, *Primitive Art* (1927), p. 150.

27. The notion of " sacred society " has been advanced in the United States by Robert E. Park, who in turn probably derived the concept from Ferdinand Tönnies, *Gemeinschaft und Gesellschaft* (1887). There are of course many similar concepts current among social scientists; see the list given in Wiese-Becker, *op. cit.*, p. 225.

It should be noted that the connotations of " sacred," as used here, are not quite the same as those clustering about the term in the writings of Durkheim, Marett, and others, for these authors tend to identify the supernatural with the sacred, whereas we make a distinction between them. See also Radin, *op. cit.*, pp. 48–51.

The idea of " holiness " is transitional (logically, not developmentally) between the sacred and the supernatural. See Rudolf Otto, *Das Heilige*, translated by John W. Harvey as *The Idea of the Holy* (Oxford, reprint, 1936).

There are of course degrees of sacredness; little or no " emotional halo " is to be found surrounding some traditions, whereas others have a great deal. The sacred therefore should not be identified with the *merely* traditional! In the text we sometimes seem to disregard our own warning, but we always have in mind those phases of tradition that have binding force when, for example, we discuss traditional domination.

28. C. A. Dawson, " The Unity of the Social Group," *JAS*, vol. xi (July-Aug., 1927), pp. 569–71.

29. A. J. Todd, *The Primitive Family as an Educational Agency* (1913); Radin, *op. cit.*, p. 52; *N. Miller, *The Child in Primitive Society* (1928), chap. iv. An interesting analysis of preliterate social organization is to be found in Moret and Davy, *From Tribe to Empire* (1926); it is marred, however, by Davy's dogmatism. A fine monograph is W. L. Warner's *A Black Civilization* (1937), especially chap. iii.

30. Old as it is, E. A. Ross's *Social Control* (1901), based on articles even older (1896–98), is still worth reading on this topic.

31. Goldenweiser, *Anthropology* (1937), pp. 408–09.

32. Spencer and Gillen, *Native Tribes of Central Australia* (1901), pp. 10–15.

33. Max Weber, *Wirtschaft und Gesellschaft* (1920), p. 130.

34. " Estatism " is a translation of *Ständetum*, and " estatal " of *ständisch*. *Stand* or estate is difficult to define in its peculiar German connotation, but some light may be gained through phrases such as " The Third Estate," and through phrases making use of an alternative form, " station," such as " the rights and duties of my station," " station in life," and the like. " Stations are primarily vocational plurality patterns functioning within the total organization of economic activity. Such vocational groupings diminish or avoid the energy-consuming antagonism or aloofness of those who carry on the same function within a given folk and state " (Wiese-Becker, *op. cit.*, p. 581). *Lehrstand*, the teaching vocation, *Wehrstand*, the military vocation, and *Nährstand*, the vocation or vocations that provide the necessities of life, is a familiar German trilogy that may give added meaning to " estatism." See Morris Ginsberg's *Sociology* (1935) for a discussion of estate.

35. Max Weber, *op. cit.*, pp. 138–39. **36.** Thurnwald, *op. cit.*, p. 171. **37.** *Franz Boas, *Anthropology and Modern Life* (1st ed., 1927), p. 140. **38.** Margaret Mead, " The Rôle of the Individual in Samoan Culture," in Kroeber and Waterman, *Source Book in Anthropology* (rev. ed., 1931), p. 561.

39. A number of the earlier writers — Tylor, Lang, and others — made much use of proverbs in analyzing various aspects of preliterate culture, although they did not apply labels such as " consciousness of kind," etc. Moreover, books by A. C. Hollis, *The Masai* (1905) and *The Nandi: Their Language and Folklore* (1909), were largely based on African proverbs. Among the first sociologists to use proverbs in analyzing the social thought of preliterates was W. I. Thomas, *Sex and Society* (1907), pp. 258–80. He was followed by E. S. Bogardus, *History of Social Thought* (1922), who has erroneously been given credit for originating the method by *J. O. Hertzler, " The Social Wisdom of Preliterates with Special Reference to Their Proverbs," *SF*, vol. xi (Mar., 1933), pp. 313–26. Hertzler's article is a useful although naïve treatment of the subject. An excellent recent discussion (of which the following quotation is a sample) of African folk proverbs is given by Westermann: " The intelligence, and at the same time the moral principles, of the African find a significant expression in his folk-lore, that is in proverbs, riddles, and stories. They are not all on an equal level, especially the stories. These depend, in the form in which we hear them, largely on the personality of the narrator, and he may be intelligent, witty or dull. Of the proverbs it may be said without reservation that they are equal in value to those of European peoples. They give proof of an astonishing power of observation of men and animals, deep and mature experience of life with sane judgment, and frequently also of humour and sarcasm. They are always apt and pointed in expression and extraordinarily picturesque. The inventors of proverbs are mostly men, while many of the fairytales owe their origin and diffusion to women and mothers. How the Africans value the two categories is shown in a Twi proverb: ' A clever child is told proverbs and not stories.' Proverbs sharpen the wit, and are a mental exercise, while stories are a mere pastime. The Negro . . . is superior to the European, at least to the northern European, in the power of self-expression. In addresses at public meetings we often have an opportunity of admiring the clearness of his exposition, the sharp details in his arguments, his apt illustrations by the use of proverbs. We can only regret that so much cleverness and skill are not devoted to worthier objects than perhaps to a case dealing with the chasing away of a goat or with verbal insults. . . . Each of the proverbs is a little masterpiece; they express in concentrated and yet easily intelligible form one single thought " (Dietrich Westermann, *The African Today* [1934], p. 17).

See also the discussion in W. I. Thomas, *Primitive Behavior* (1937), pp. 785–87, and the bibliography on " Mentality, Personality, Language," pp. 801–04.

A list of books dealing primarily with peasant proverbs seems worth giving here:

Erskine Beveridge, ed., *Fergusson's Scottish Proverbs* (1924).
Wilhelm Borchardt, *Die sprichwörtliche Redensart im deutschen Volksmunde* (2nd ed., 1894).
Robert Christy, *Proverbs, Maxims and Phrases of All Ages* (1893).
J. Eiselein, *Sprichwörter des deutschen Volkes* (1840).
Julio Cejador y Frauca, *Refranero castellano* (3 vols., 1928–29).
Giuseppe Giusti, *Raccolta di proverbia toscani* (1898).
James Howell, *Proverbs and Old Sayed Saws and Adages* (1659).

V. C. Lean, *Lean's Collectanea* (4 vols., 1902–04).

D. E. Marvin, *The Antiquity of Proverbs* (1922).

*R. C. Trench, *Proverbs and Their Lessons* (1905). Best general work in English. Has excellent bibliography.

Pico Luri di Vassano, *Modi di dire proverbiali e motti popolari italiani spiegati a commentati* (1875).

40. Wiese-Becker, *op. cit.*, p. 516.

41. Thurnwald, *op. cit.*, pp. 269–301.

42. Park and Burgess, eds., *The City* (1925), p. 18.   43. Radin, *op. cit.*, *passim*.

44. *W. G. Sumner, *Folkways* (1907), pp. 13–15.   45. Thurnwald, *op. cit.*, p. 178; Charles Hose, *Natural Man* (1926); C. G. and B. Seligman, *The Veddas* (1911).

46. *Ellsworth Faris, "The Origin of Punishment," *IIE*, vol. xvi (Oct., 1914), pp. 54–67. This essay is also to be found in *The Nature of Human Nature* (1937).

47. Thurnwald, *op. cit.*, p. 209.

48. F. Müller-Lyer, *The History of Social Development* (1921), p. 269.

49. Edward Westermarck, *Origin and Development of the Moral Ideas* (1908), vol. ii, pp. 171 ff.   50. *Ibid.*

51. *Hutton Webster, *Primitive Secret Societies* (2nd ed., 1932), *passim*.

52. Arnold Van Gennep, *Les Rites de passage* (1909).

53. *R. H. Lowie, *Primitive Society* (1st ed., 1920), pp. 186–203.

54. *Bronislaw Malinowski, *The Father in Primitive Psychology* (1927); *The Sexual Life of Savages* (1929). (Thurnwald is somewhat sceptical of the thoroughness of Malinowski's investigations into preliterate contraceptive techniques; so also is W. I. Thomas, *Primitive Behavior* [1937], pp. 788–92.)

55. J. J. Bachofen, *Das Mutterrecht* (1861). Most of the evidence for the supposed existence of *universal* matriarchy prior to patriarchal family structure is assembled in Robert Briffault, *The Mothers* (1927). In spite of valid evidence and interpretation here and there, the book as a whole must nevertheless be regarded as dogmatically written to prove a thesis.

56. *Herbert Aptekar, *Anjea: Infanticide, Abortion, Contraception in Savage Society* (1931).

57. A. M. Carr-Saunders, *The Population Problem* (1922), pp. 217–20 *et passim*.

58. Wiese-Becker, *op. cit.*, pp. 307–08. The phrase " charismatic leadership " comes from Max Weber's writings, particularly his *Wirtschaft und Gesellschaft*, *passim*.   59. *Ibid.*, p. 307.

60. R. R. Marett, " Mana," *EB*, 14th ed.; A. M. Hocart, " Deification," *ESS*. *Kingship* (1927).

With relation to the paragraph ending on page 23, line 17, Goldenweiser comments: " This formulation is inexact. Such magical processes as incantations and mimetic rites are certainly impersonal. The personal-impersonal contrast obtains rather between mana and spirit. It must also be remembered that mana often operates through personal channels." Much depends here on the interpretation of the terms " personal " and " impersonal," as well as on the weight attached to " relatively." Nevertheless, Goldenweiser's remarks are relevant.

61. *Clifford Kirkpatrick, *Religion in Human Affairs* (1929), p. 228.

62. R. R. Marett, " Mana," *HERE*, vol. vii, p. 378; Goldenweiser, *Anthropology* (1937), pp. 221–25.

63. C. H. McIlwain, " Divine Right of Kings," *ESS*, vol. v, p. 176.

64. Weber, *op. cit.*, p. 141. All these forms are of course *ideal-typical*; see note 94.

65. *Ibid.*, p. 142. It must be noted that *charisma and mana are not the same*; the mana belief is simply a specific form of the much more general notion of charisma. For a psychiatric theory of a certain aspect of " negative mana " or taboo, see Howard Becker and D. K. Bruner, " Some Aspects of Taboo and Totemism," *JSP*, vol. iii (1932), pp. 337–52.

66. Clark Wissler, *Introduction to Social Anthropology* (1929), p. 259.

67. *Ibid.* **68.** Wiese-Becker, *op. cit.*, p. 226. **69.** Weber, *op. cit.*, p. 124.

70. W. H. R. Rivers, *Social Organization* (1924), p. 169.

71. *Bronislaw Malinowski, *Crime and Custom in Savage Society* (1926), p. 30.

72. *Ibid.*, p. 52.

73. Radin, *op. cit.*, p. 77. Goldenweiser, however, has pointed out that our discussion is couched in somewhat too negative terms. He is probably right; see his " Loose Ends of Theory on the Individual, Pattern, and Involution in Primitive Society," *Essays in Anthropology in Honor of Alfred Louis Kroeber* (1936), pp. 99–104. See also Goldenweiser's *Anthropology* (1937) on " pattern " and " individualism " (use index).

74. *Ibid.*, pp. 48–51.

75. Thurnwald, *op. cit.*, p. 207.

76. L. T. Hobhouse, *Morals in Evolution* (1915), p. 73; Paul Vinogradoff, *Outlines of Historical Jurisprudence*, vol. i, " Tribal Law " (1920). To be taken with a grain of salt: E. S. Hartland, *Primitive Law* (1924).

77. Even Barton, who uses the term " law " to describe the Ifugao system, makes it quite clear in his summary that his usage is inaccurate, as the following excerpt shows:

" General principles of the Ifugao legal system. — Its personal character. Society does not punish injuries to itself except as the censure of public opinion is a punishment. . . .

" Collective procedure. — Legal procedure is by and between families, therefore a family should be ' strong to demand and strong to resist demands.' A member of an Ifugao family assists in the punishment of offenses against any other member of his family, and resists the punishment of members of his family by other families. . . .

" The go-between. — No transaction of any sort between persons *of different families* is consummated without the intervention of a middle man, or go-between " (R. F. Barton, " Ifugao Law," in Kroeber and Waterman, *op. cit.*, pp. 348–49).

From this it is patent that the element of *enforcement* by a central authority whose acts are felt to be impersonal is lacking; the go-between is simply an arbitrator serving families, and his decision cannot be enforced if a family concludes that one of its members has been wronged by that decision. It is a pity that so keen an analyst as W. I. Thomas has failed to see this point, as is evidenced by his *Primitive Behavior* (1937), pp. 515–609, " Primitive Law."

78. The student might profitably consult *Franz Oppenheimer, *The State* (1912); this is an English translation of an exceedingly influential German work of which the second edition, greatly expanded, appeared in 1926 under the title *Der Staat*. Oppenheimer defends the so-called conflict theory of the origin of law. Other references are Faris (see note 46); R. E. Lowie, *The Origin of the State* (1924); W. C. MacLeod, *The Origin and History of Politics* (1931), especially chap. ii. For additional references see our sections on conflict theories of the origin of the state in Chapter Nineteen.

79. R. H. Lowie, *op. cit.*, pp. 205–55; *Richard Thurnwald, *Economics in Primitive Communities* (1932). Thurnwald's book is probably the best general survey of the subject that has yet appeared; it also contains an excellent bibliography.

80. A. L. Kroeber, *Anthropology* (1923), p. 388.

81. After a critical reading of the page proofs of the foregoing paragraphs, Alexander Goldenweiser commented: " It is not quite fortunate to speak of ' crude personal forms ' (p. 31, line 15) of non-material property among primitives in view of the fact that this form of property concept is much more congenial to the primitive way of thinking than it is to ours." We agree. The student should consult a number of works on this subject in order to clothe the skeleton of this section with flesh and blood. A few of the many excellent treatises available are:

Raymond Firth, *Primitive Economics of the New Zealand Maori* (1929).

*Elizabeth E. Hoyt, *Primitive Trade: Its Psychology and Economics* (1926).

*Bronislaw Malinowski, *Argonauts of the Western Pacific* (1922).

For further references see the Thurnwald bibliography (note 79).

82. One of the worst offenders in this regard is J. G. Frazer; his famous *Golden Bough* has spread as much error as enlightenment. Another source of overemphasis, to say the least, was E. B. Tylor's *Primitive Culture* (1st ed., 1871). His treatment of animism caught the fancy of his successors more than all the rest of his discussions lumped together.

83. *Goldenweiser, *Early Civilization* (1922), pp. 184–234, revised version in his *Anthropology* (1937), pp. 208–88. These are excellent general surveys, but there are a number of others that might profitably be consulted:

Fritz Graebner, *Das Weltbild der Primitiven* (1924).

F. H. Hankins, *op. cit.*, chap. xii, " Myth, Magic, Religion and Science," pp. 523–99. Bibliography.

*Clifford Kirkpatrick, *op. cit.*, chaps. i–ix. Excellent bibliography.

R. H. Lowie, *Primitive Religion* (1924).

*Bronislaw Malinowski, " Magic, Science and Religion," in Joseph Needham, ed., *Science, Religion and Reality* (1925).

R. R. Marett, *The Threshold of Religion* (2nd ed., 1914); *Faith, Hope and Charity in Primitive Religion* (1932); *Head, Heart and Hands in Human Evolution* (1935).

84. The classic study of animism is Tylor's *Primitive Culture*. The fourth edition (1903) was the last one revised by Tylor himself.

85. Mana was first made known to the learned world by R. H. Codrington, *The Melanesians* (1896).

86. J. T. Shotwell, *The Religious Revolution of Today* (2nd ed., 1924), p. 101.

87. Émile Durkheim, *The Elementary Forms of the Religious Life* (1912; English trans., 1916).

88. Everett Dean Martin, *The Mystery of Religion* (1924).

89. J. G. Frazer, *The Golden Bough*, vol. i, " The Magic Art."

90. *R. R. Marett, *Faith, Hope and Charity in Primitive Religion* (1932).

91. Radin, *op. cit.*, pp. 50–51   92. *Ibid.*, pp. 42–43. Italics ours.

93. Howard Becker, "Process of Secularisation," *SR*, vol. xxiv (Apr.-July and Oct., 1932) pp. 138–54; 266–86.

94. *Ibid.*, p. 139. Cf. Wiese-Becker, *op. cit.*, pp. 21–22; and especially Chapter Twenty, pp. 779–81 *et passim*. The fact that we *construct* an *ideal-typical*

NOTES

epitome of isolated sacred societies should prevent the understanding reader from taking umbrage at " exceptions "; *nothing other than exceptions can be found.* When we say, for example, " there is no trade " (bottom of page 39), no useful purpose is served by pointing to the fact that many preliterate societies *do* have some trade. We are interested in the instrumental value of the ideal type.

95. Howard Becker, " Vicinal Isolation and Mental Immobility," *SF*, vol. ix (Mar., 1933), pp. 326–34.

96. Franz Boas, *Primitive Art* (Institutet for sammenlignende Kulturforskning, Series B, viii, Oslo, 1927), p. 150.

97. Howard Becker, "Process of Secularisation" (see above, note 93), pp. 140–42. Cf. Wiese-Becker, *op. cit.*, pp. 222–24.

98. *Ibid.*, pp. 142–44. Cf. Wiese-Becker, *op. cit.*, pp. 224–25.

CHAPTER II

1. P. A. Sorokin, *Contemporary Sociological Theories* (1928), pp. 197–98, 219–20, 435–36, 498, 681, 694–95, 697; *J. O. Hertzler, *The Social Thought of the Ancient Civilizations* (1936), chaps. vii and viii.

2. *K. S. Latourette, *The Chinese, Their History and Culture* (2 vols., 1923), chaps. i and ii, *passim.* This is one of the best books on the subject in English. Others are B. L. Putnam Weale, *The Vanished Empire* (1926, but a bit out of date); *Richard Wilhelm, *A Short History of Chinese Civilization* (1929); Herbert F. Rudd, *Chinese Social Origins* (1928); Friedrich Hirth, *The Ancient History of China* (1911); *Herbert A. Giles, *The Civilization of China* (1911), a good sketch; Marcel Granet, *La Civilisation chinoise: la vie publique et la vie privée* (1929), translated as *Chinese Civilisation* — this is probably superior to all others, but slights the presentation of generally known data in favor of interpretation. Original sources for this whole chapter are chiefly to be found (in translation, of course) in *The Chinese Classics* (7 vols.), and *The Sacred Books of the East*, vols. iii, xvi, xxvii, xxviii, xxix, and xl, all translated by James Legge.

3. Latourette, *op. cit.*, p. 34; Granet, *op. cit.*, p. 62.

4. E. H. Parker, *Ancient China Simplified* (1908), p. 387.

5. Granet, *op. cit.*, pp. 68–69, should be referred to in order to avoid the " hermetically sealed " conception of China.

6. James B. Pratt, *The Pilgrimage of Buddhism* (1928), p. 272. Cf. Granet, *op. cit.*, p. 72, and Max Weber, *Religionssoziologie* (3 vols.), vol. ii (1921),· p. 375.

7. *H. G. Creel, *Sinism: A Study of the Evolution of the Chinese World-View* (1929), p. 2. This is a valuable interpretation.

8. Granet, *op. cit.*, p. 139.   9. Creel, *op. cit.*, pp. 7–8.   10. *Ibid.*, p. 8.

11. Marcel Granet, *La Religion des Chinois* (1922), p. 22.   12. *Ibid.*, p. 26.

13. *Henri Maspero, *La Chine antique* (1927), p. 114.

14. *Ibid.*, p. 116; Granet, *op. cit.*, pp. 3–4. The Chinese *always* give *yin* and *yang* in the same order — the reverse of ours.

15. Creel, *op. cit.*, p. 13.   16. *Ibid.*, p. 17.

17. Granet, *Chinese Civilisation* (1929), p. 75.

18. *Ibid.*, pp. 178–79. Recent studies by Creel and others tend to show that there really was a Shang dynasty.

19. *Ibid.*   20. *Ibid.*   21. Weale, *op. cit.*, p. 11.

22. Granet, *op. cit.*, p. 14.   23. *Ibid.*

24. *G. Nye Steiger, *A History of the Far East* (1936), p. 16. This is a good textbook, with selected chapter references and a useful bibliography.

25. Granet, *op. cit.*, p. 149.

26. We say " apparently " because many scholars regard the *Chou-li*, on which these statements are based, as a forgery having the character of a retrospective utopia. Cf. Granet, *op. cit.*, p. 378. **27.** Steiger, *op. cit.*, pp. 17–18.

28. Granet, *op. cit.*, p. 234. **29.** *Ibid.*, pp. 258–60.

30. But see G. H. Mead, *Mind, Self, and Society* (1936), for a detailed demonstration of the importance of the " vocal gesture " for reflective thought.

31. *Granet, *La Pensée chinoise* (1934), pp. 32–43, " Les emblèmes vocaux." It is difficult to overestimate the importance of Granet's book. Nothing even remotely comparable to it, from the sociological standpoint, is to be found. Max Weber is outdistanced, although it is only fair to say that Weber was no Sinologist and dealt with a different problem. Cf. the review of Granet's book by E. Benoît-Smullyan, *ASR*, vol. i (June, 1936), pp. 487–92.

32. *Ibid.*, pp. 43–55, " Les emblèmes graphiques." See also Ernest Fenollosa, *The Chinese Written Character as a Medium for Poetry: An Ars Poetica*. With a Foreword and Notes by Ezra Pound (1936).

33. *Ibid.*, Bk. I, chap. ii, " Le Style."

34. *Ibid.*, Bk. I, chap. i, " Le Temps et l'espace." Cf. Pitirim A. Sorokin and Robert K. Merton, " Social Time: A Methodological and Functional Analysis," *AJS*, xlii (Mar., 1937), pp. 615–29. Exceedingly valuable also is volume ii of Sorokin's *Social and Cultural Dynamics* (1937).

35. *Ibid.*, Bk. II, chap. iii, " Les Nombres." Granet's analysis in this chapter is an amazing example of scholarly profundity. **36.** Creel, *op. cit.*, p. 36.

37. O. Z. Fang, *Complete Chinese-English Dictionary*, quoted in Creel, *op. cit.*, p. 28. **38.** Granet, *op. cit.*, Bk. II, chap. ii, " Le Yin et le Yang."

39. Creel, *op. cit.*, " Table of the five elements and their correlates," p. 34.

40. Granet, *op. cit.*, Bk. II, chap. iv, " Le Tao "; Creel, *op. cit.*, pp. 43–46.

41. Granet, *op. cit.*, Bk. III. **42.** *Ibid.*, pp. 415–18.

43. Wilhelm, *op. cit.*, p. 138; cf. Rudd, *op. cit.*, pp. 211–19. Wilhelm has a very good chapter (iv) on " Intellectual Currents in the Time of the Old Empire."

44. Hertzler, *op. cit.*, pp. 218–22.

45. Confucius, *The Analects*, 3, 26; Legge's translation in *The Chinese Classics*.

46. Creel, *op. cit.*, p. 72; Granet, *op. cit.*, pp. 473–90. " Confucius et l'esprit humaniste."

47. John K. Shryock, *The Origin and Development of the State Cult of Confucius* (1932), pp. 4–5.

48. This is the position taken, for example, by Hu Shih (Suh Hu), *The Development of the Logical Method in Ancient China* (1922), pp. 46–52, " The Rectification of Names and Judgments." **49.** Granet, *op. cit.*, p. 449.

50. *Ibid.* Cf. Moret and Davy, *From Tribe to Empire* (1926), p. 48.

51. *Analects*, 5, 20. **52.** *Ibid.*, 7, 35.

53. Creel, *op. cit.*, pp. 73–74; Hertzler, *op. cit.*, pp. 224–34.

54. *Max Weber, *Religionssoziologie* (3 vols., 1920), vol. i, p. 432. Weber's interpretation of Confucius is very important. See *ibid.*, pp. 396, 399, 400, 440.

55. *Ibid.*, p. 396. A full-length treatment of Confucius's social thought is offered by L. S. Hsü, *The Political Philosophy of Confucianism* (1932), but it is somewhat uncritical and " modernizing," in addition to being overloaded with pseudo-sociological jargon. See also W. S. A. Pott, *Chinese Political Philosophy* (1925). The article on Chinese law by Jean Escarra, *ESS*, vol. ix, pp. 249–54, is useful for its discussions of rectification of names, lack of abstractness, the Legists, etc. **56.** Creel, *op. cit.*, p. 40.

57. *E. D. Harvey, *The Mind of China* (1933), *passim*. This book is a splendid analysis of the mentality of the Chinese commoner of the present day, albeit somewhat too " Sumner-Kellerish."   58. Creel, *op. cit.*, p. 46.

59. Granet, *op. cit.*, p. 505; Creel, *op. cit.*, pp. 92–93.

60. *Ibid.*, p. 95; Hertzler, *op. cit.*, p. 209.

61. A. E. Haydon, quoted by Creel, *op. cit.*, p. 97.

62. Hertzler, *op. cit.*, pp. 213–14; Creel, *op. cit.*, p. 98.

63. *Ibid.*, pp. 98–99; *Tao Te King*, 3; 65.

64. *Ibid.*, 80; Creel, *op. cit.*, pp. 99–100.

65. Granet, *op. cit.*, pp. 506, 514, 544. Cf. E. D. Harvey, " Shamanism in China," in G. P. Murdock, ed., *Studies in the Science of Society Presented to Albert Galloway Keller* (1937), pp. 247–66.   66. *Ibid.*, pp. 507–18.

67. Kakuzo Okahura, *The Book of Tea* (1906), p. 46; Granet, *loc. cit.*

68. Creel, *op. cit.*, pp. 93–94.   69. *Ibid.*, p. 95.

70. Hertzler, *op. cit.*, p. 208; Pott, *op. cit.*, pp. 82–84.

71. Granet, *op. cit.*, pp. 542–44 *et passim*; A. Forke, trans., *Yang Chu's Garden of Pleasure* (1912), *passim*.   72. Yu-lan Fung, *Chuang-tzu* (1931), *passim*.

73. Creel, *op. cit.*, p. 101. Cf. Leon Wieger, *Taoisme*, vol. ii, p. 347. The sources for Yang Chu are *Lieh Tse*, vi and vii, and *Mencius* 3 (2), 9; 7 (1), 26; 7 (2), 26.

74. Creel, *op. cit.*, pp. 101–02; Granet, *op. cit.*, pp. 502–51. For a recent study of *yoga*, see K. T. Behanan, *Yoga, A Scientific Evaluation* (1937).

75. Wilhelm, *op. cit.*, pp. 102–03.

76. Cf. Harvey, *op. cit.*; Granet, *op. cit.*, *passim*; W. J. Clennell, *Historical Development of Religion in China* (1917), p. 76.

77. E. Faber, *The Mind of Mencius* (1882); Wen Kwei Liao, *The Individual and the Community* (1933) — this is also a useful survey of a number of other Chinese thinkers; *Andrew Chih-Yi Cheng, *Hsüntzu's Theory of Human Nature and Its Influence on Chinese Thought* (1928), pp. 21–28; Weber, *op. cit.*, pp. 455 ff.

78. Granet, *op. cit.*, pp. 425–71, has a fascinating chapter on " Les Recettes de gouvernement." See also his *Chinese Civilisation*, pp. 301, 308–09, *et passim*. For some of the competitors of Mencius, see A. Forke, " The Chinese Sophists," *JRAS*, vol. xxxiv, pp. 1 ff.   79. Granet, *La Pensée chinoise*, p. 498.

80. " Do not do unto others what you would not they should do unto you " (*Doctrine of the Mean*, 1, 32). See Hertzler, *op. cit.*, p. 227, for a discussion of this, and *ibid.*, pp. 344–46, of other " Silver Rules."

81. Hu Shih, *op. cit.*, pp. 53–82; Wen Kwei Liao, *op. cit.*, pp. 190–97.

82. See Hu Shih's discussion of the Neo-Mohists, *op. cit.*, pp. 83–130.

83. Creel, *op. cit.*, pp. 103–10. " The fundamental philosophy of Mo Tse is Sinism, simple, pure, and unmixed " (*ibid.*, p. 110).

84. *Ibid.*, pp. 80–84; Granet, *op. cit.*, pp. 554–61 *et passim*.

85. Quoted in Steiger, *op. cit.*, p. 32.   86. *Mencius* 6 (2), 13.

87. Creel, *op. cit.*, p. 83.   88. *Mencius* 2 (1), 6, 3.

89. Cheng, *op. cit.*, pp. 21–28; Granet, *op. cit.*, p. 557.

90. J. P. Bruce, *Chu Hsi and His Masters* (1933); *Frederick Starr, *Confucianism* (1930), pp. 121–40; Hu Shih, " Confucianism," *ESS*, vol. iv, pp. 198–201; Shryock, *op. cit.*, chap. x. But note Weber's remark: ". . . so war der Confuzianismus die Standessethik einer literarisch gebildeten weltlich-rationalistischen Pfründnerschaft " (*op. cit.*, vol. i, p. 239).

91. See H. H. Dubs, *Hsüntze, the Moulder of Ancient Confucianism, passim*; Cheng, *op. cit.*, p. 58.

92. Creel, *op. cit.*, pp. 85–90 — but cf. Granet, *op. cit.*, pp. 561–73.

93. Creel, *loc. cit.* **94.** *Ibid.* See also Cheng, *op. cit.*, especially chaps. iv and v.

95. Creel, *op. cit.*, p. 85.

96. Granet, *Chinese Civilisation*, pp. 96–125; Steiger, *op. cit.*, pp. 33–37.

97. Creel, *op. cit.*, p. 85.

98. Wen Kwei Liao, *op. cit.*, pp. 174–80; Cheng, pp. 54–56. But cf. Granet, *La Pensée chinoise*, pp. 561–73, " Siun tseu: le gouvernement par les rites." He concludes the section thus: [For Hsün Tse] . . . " le monde est régi par les rites, par le *li-yi* où s'expriment, ensemble, la *Civilisation* et la *Raison* " (p. 573). Not much absolutism here! It seems clear, however, that in this case Granet's interpretation, usually so trustworthy, is wrong, or at least too *zugespitzt*.

99. Liao, *op. cit.*, p. 180. **100.** Quoted in Creel, *op. cit.*, p. 125.

101. Granet, *op. cit.*, pp. 457–71. **102.** Wilhelm, *op. cit.*, p. 153.

103. Steiger, *op. cit.*, pp. 73–76; Granet, *Chinese Civilisation*, pp. 400–25.

104. For Tung Chung Shu, see Granet, *La Pensée chinoise*, pp. 573–76; Shryock, *op. cit.*, pp. 33–45 *et passim*; Kang Woo, *Les trois théories politiques du Tch-ouen Tsieou* (1932). For Wang Mang, see Steiger, *op. cit.*, pp. 77–78; Shryock, *op. cit.*, pp. 72–74; Hu Shih, " Wang Mang, the Socialist Emperor of Nineteen Centuries Ago," *JNCBRAS*, vol. xlix (1928), pp. 218–30. For Wang Chung, see Shryock, *op. cit.*, pp. 80–83; A. Forke, " Lun-Heng: Selected Essays of the Philosopher Wang Chung " (with an introduction), *MSOS*, 1923; Granet, *op. cit.*, pp. 580–82. For Han Yü, see Cheng, *op. cit.*, pp. 67–69, 73–74; Shryock, *op. cit.*, pp. 140–42; *ES*, p. 226. For Wang Yang-Ming, see *The Philosophy of Wang Yang-Ming* (Henke trans., 116); Starr, *op. cit.*, pp. 159, 164, 241; Shryock, *op. cit.*, p. 148; Cheng, *op. cit.*, pp. 73 ff., especially p. 74. For Chu Hsi, see his *The Philosophy of Human Nature* (J. B. Bruce trans., 1922); Shryock, *op. cit.*, pp. 149–52, 182–85, 200–02, *et passim*; Starr, *op. cit.*, pp. 121, 131, 133, 146; Weber, *op. cit.*, pp. 239, 440, 457; Cheng, *op. cit.*, pp. 73 ff.; Liao, *op. cit.*, pp. 259–67; Granet, *op. cit.*, pp. 351, 581.

In concluding this brief sketch of Chinese social thought, a suggestion about names seems pertinent. The writer's experience has convinced him that most persons cannot either pronounce or remember Chinese names, and that Latinization is sometimes a help. We already have the Latinized forms Confucius = Kung Fu-Tse and Mencius = Meng Tse; why not others like Laocius = Lao Tse; Siuncius = Hsün Tse; Micius = Moh Tse; Licius = Lieh Tse; Chusius = Chu Hsi; and the like?

105. The *Zwischenbetrachtung* in Max Weber's *Religionssoziologie*, vol. i, p. 536, begins thus: " Die Gebiet der indischen Religiosität . . . ist im *stärksten Kontrast* gegen China die Wiege der theoretisch und praktisch weltverneinendsten Formen von religiöser Ethik, welche die Erde hervorgebracht hat." Italics ours.

106. *Surendrenath Dasgupta, A History of Indian Philosophy (2 vols., 1922), vol. i, pp. ix, x, 3–6; Steiger, *op. cit.*, pp. 39–45; S. Radhakrishnan, " Indian Philosophy," *EB*, 14th ed., vol. xii, pp. 247 ff. The translations in *The Sacred Books of the East* series, edited by Max Müller, are accessible sources for us here as well. Translations in the *Harvard Oriental Series are also useful.

107. *Ibid.*, pp. 39–40; J. S. Meston, " India: Position and Shape," *EB*, 14th ed., vol. xii, pp. 150–51; Philip Lake, " India: Geology," *ibid.*, pp. 151–53; C. E. C. Fischer, " India: Climate," *ibid.*, pp. 153–55.

108. Meston, " India: Ethnology and Religion," *ibid.*, pp. 157–58; H. A. Rose, " India: Peoples, and Religion," *ibid.*, pp. 158–64; " Caste (Indian)," *ibid.*, vol. iv, pp. 976–86.

109. *Ibid.* Cf. F. E. Lumley, " Indo-Aryan Society," in G. P. Murdock, ed., *op. cit.*, pp. 411–22. **110.** *C. Bouglé, *Essai sur le régime des castes* (1908).
111. " Chinese Language," *EB,* 14th ed., vol. v, p. 568.
112. Ralph L. Turner, " Sanskrit Language and Literature," *ibid.*, vol. xix, p. 954. See Dasgupta, *op. cit.*, pp. 10–61, for a brief survey of the sacred writings; J. N. Farquhar, *An Outline of the Religious Literature of India* (1920), is full.
113. *Benoy Kumar Sarkar, *The Political Institutions and Theories of the Hindus* (1922), pp. 155–60. This book gives a good brief survey of the relevant secular writings. A useful conspectus is provided by Kewal Motwani, *Manu, A Study in Hindu Social Theory* (1934).
114. See Dasgupta, *op. cit.*, p. 63, for an illustration of the lengths to which this piling of commentaries upon commentaries has gone. **115.** *Ibid.*, p. 64.
116. *Max Weber entitles the second volume of his *Religionssoziologie* " Hinduismus und Buddhismus," i.e., he does not include the latter in the former. Creel, on the other hand, says that " Buddhism becomes, about the tenth century A.D., an organic part of Hinduism " (*op. cit.*, p. 40). We have chosen Creel's usage, largely for the sake of brevity. Hertzler, *op. cit.*, chap. vii, attempts no inclusive categorizations aside from those in current popular use.
117. *See Albert Schweitzer, *Indian Thought and Its Development* (1936).
118. Although Buddhism denies the existence of the self, it also teaches the doctrines of destiny and reincarnation. (See Lord Chalmers's translation of one of the earliest *corpi* of primitive Buddhism, the *Sutta-Nipata,* published as *Buddha's Teachings,* vol. xxxvii of Harvard Oriental Series.) There must be a kind of soul- or self-substitute to make reincarnation possible. Hence we shall use " soul " and " self " to apply only to the entity accumulating or casting off *karma* and thereby changing the nature of its *samsara* (thus making it possible to discuss Buddhism as part of Hinduism) when dealing with our inclusive concept, Hinduism. Cf. Weber, *op. cit.*, p. 117.
119. Dasgupta, *op. cit.*, pp. 71–72, " Some Fundamental Points of Agreement."
120. Weber, *op. cit.*, pp. 23–24. It hardly seems worth while to attempt to distinguish by spelling between the priestly Brahmin and other members of the Brahman caste, more especially as we shall frequently use " Brahman " to denote followers of the Brahman religion who are not members of the Brahman caste.
121. *Ibid.*, pp. 27–30.
122. *Ibid.*, p. 31. See H. Oldenberg, *Buddha, sein Leben, seine Lehre, seine Gemeinde* (5th ed., 1906).
123. Meston, *loc. cit.*; A. B. Keith, *The Religion and Philosophy of the Vedas and Upanishads* (2 vols., 1925), vol. ii, pp. 433–40; Weber, *op. cit.*, pp. 31–32.
124. Farquhar, *op. cit.*, pp. 1–32.
125. Even as late as the time of Buddha's birth (*c.* 563 B.C.) the Kshatriyas were superior in northeastern India. Cf. E. J. Thomas, *The Life of Buddha as Legend and History* (1927), pp. 21–23; Weber, *op. cit.*, pp. 124–25.
126. See Weber, *op. cit.*, pp. 31–56, and also his discussion of *den konkreten Kasten,* pp. 57–98. A good brief abstract of Weber's sociology of religion is to be found in English, in *Lowell L. Bennion, *Max Weber's Methodology,* doctoral dissertation, Strasbourg, 1933. Excellent, though difficult, are the chapters on Weber in Talcott Parsons's *The Structure of Social Action* (1937).
127. *V. A. Smith, *The Oxford History of India* (2nd ed., 1923), p. 37.
128. Steiger, *op. cit.*, p. 45; Dasgupta, *op. cit.*, p. 13.
129. Weber, *op. cit.*, pp. 125–33.
130. Sarkar, *op. cit.*, pp. 13–19, especially pp. 13–14.

131. "Brahmanism," *EB*, 14th ed., vol. iii, pp. 1013–17; "Hinduism," *ibid.*, xi, pp. 577–81.   132. Weber, *op. cit.*, pp. 351–58.

133. Dasgupta, *op. cit.*, pp. 25–26; Schweitzer, *op. cit.*, p. 30.

134. Schweitzer, *op. cit.*, pp. 35, 43, 262; Deussen, *The Philosophy of the Upanishads* (1906), pp. 148, 170.

135. Sarkar, *op. cit.*, p. 206; Weber, *op. cit.*, pp. 22–27, 144–46; *U. Ghoshal, *History of Hindu Political Theories* (1923), pp. 54–55.

136. Haridas T. Muzumdar, "Hindu Group Concepts," chap. i of unpublished M.A. thesis, Northwestern University, 1926; see also Ghoshal, *op. cit.*, p. 59; and *Matsya Purana*, cxlv, 27 — original Sanskrit text cited by Bhagavan Das, *The Science of Social Organisation* (1910), p. 34.

137. Weber, *op. cit.*, pp. 26–27, 142.   138. *Ibid.*, p. 26.

139. Helmuth von Glasenapp, *Der Hinduismus: Religion und Gesellschaft im heutigen Indien*, p. 239, quoted in Wiese-Becker, *Systematic Sociology* (1932), p. 258.   140. Weber, *op. cit.*, pp. 142 ff.

141. *Ibid.*, p. 143. But see footnote 1, same page.   142. *Ibid.*, pp. 142–47.

143. *Ibid.*, pp. 31–32.   144. Sarkar, *op. cit.*, pp. 2–5; Muzumdar, *loc. cit.*

145. Sarkar, *op. cit.*, p. 156.   146. *Ibid.* p. 157.

147. *Mahabharata*, Book of *Santi*, lix, 14, translated by Sarkar, *op. cit.*, p. 199.

148. 1st *ibid.*, lix, 15, 18–19, 20–21, translated in 2nd *ibid.*, p. 197.

149. Kamandaka, Kautilya, and Shukra, 2nd *ibid.*, pp. 193–99, *passim*.

150. Mahabharata, 2nd *ibid.*, pp. 194–200, *passim*.

151. 1st *ibid.*, translated in 2nd *ibid.*, pp. 197–203, *passim*.

152. 2nd *ibid.*, pp. 205–207.   153. 2nd *ibid.*, p. 201.

154. Laws of Manu, translated in 2nd *ibid.*, p. 181.

155. Shukra, translated in 2nd *ibid.*, p. 183.

156. Mahabharata, Manu, Shukra, and Kamandaka, translated in 2nd *ibid.*, pp. 183–86, 203–05.   157. Shukra, translated in 2nd *ibid.*, pp. 174–76.

158. Manu-smriti, ix, 296–97, in Max Müller, ed., *Sacred Books of the East* series, vol. xxv (1886), p. 395. There may be utterances equally explicit even earlier; the writer has not searched all the literature.

159. Sarkar, *The Positive Background of Hindu Sociology* (2 vols., 1914–21), vol. ii, pp. 34–39; *The Political Institutions and Theories of the Hindus* (1922), p. 166.

160. Kautilya, *Arthashastra*, quoted in Ghoshal, *op. cit.*, p. 140.

161. Shukra, *Shukra-niti*, quoted in Ghoshal, *op. cit.*, p. 252.

162. Manu-smriti, *loc. cit.* Ghoshal comments (*op. cit.*, p. 170): "Manu presents a completer conception of the organic unity of government than had occurred to his predecessors."

163. Weber, *op. cit.*, pp. 130–33; Sarkar, *op. cit.*, pp. 13–19.

164. Radhakamal Mukerjee, *Democracies of the East* (1917), provides a good description of these forms of social organization and their relation to Hindu sociological concepts. Wiser's *Behind Mud Walls* (1932) is an excellent study, as is also his *The Hindu Jajmani System* (1936). Cf. the bibliography in Sarkar, *op. cit.*, pp. xiii-xxiv.

165. The summary in Weber, *op. cit.*, pp. 363–78, is striking. We quote the opening sentences: "Fur Asien als Ganzes hat China etwa die Rolle Frankreichs im modernen Occident gespielt. Aller weltmännische 'Schliff' stammt von dort, von Tibet bis Japan und Hinterindien. Dagegen ist Indien etwa die Bedeutung des antiken Hellenentums zugefallen. Es gibt wenig über praktische Interessen hinausgehendes Denken in Asien, dessen Quelle nicht letztlich dort zu suchen wäre. . . ."

CHAPTER III

1. Even some fairly recent histories make no mention of the Indus culture, as all the important sites have been unearthed since the World War, and really thorough excavation dates only from the 1930's. See Marshall, Mackay, and others, *Mohenjo-Daro and the Indus Civilization* (1932); V. Gordon Childe, *New Light on the Most Ancient East* (1934); and the various accounts in *RASI* and *JRAI*. For a brief but excellent *textbook* treatment, see *Flenley and Weech, *World History* (1936), pp. 4–13.
This book provides a valuable historical auxiliary for all the chapters in case the time that can be devoted to supplementary reading is limited. The interrelations of geography and history in the Near East are dealt with in masterly fashion in *J. L. Myres's little book, *The Dawn of History* (1911). Other aids for the chapter as a whole are *BWC*, vol. i, chaps. iii-v; Albert A. Trever, *History of Ancient Civilization*, vol. i, chaps. i-ix (abreast of many recent discoveries); and Moret and Davy, *From Tribe to Empire* (1926), Parts II and III (henceforth cited as Davy and Moret to avoid confusion with another book).
The writer has been forced to keep qualification to a minimum; similarly, exposition and quotation have been slighted in favor of interpretation. If the result is an overpositive or dogmatic tone, we beg extenuating circumstances.

2. Flenley and Weech, *loc. cit.* See the map of the Near East in Childe, *op. cit.*, facing p. 1.   3. *Ibid.*, chap. ii, " The Setting of the Stage."

4. C. L. Wooley, *The Sumerians* (1929); *Ur of the Chaldees* (1923); S. H. Langdon, *CAH*, vol. i.

5. See L. Delaporte, *Mesopotamia: The Babylonian and Assyrian Civilization* (1925); *J. O. Hertzler, *The Social Thought of the Ancient Civilizations* (1936), chap. iv, especially pp. 75–84; *Will Durant, *The Story of Civilization* (1935), Part I, " Our Oriental Heritage," chap. vii.

6. Delaporte, *op. cit.*, p. 64, footnote 1.

7. Quoted in Flenley and Weech, *op. cit.*, p. 18.

8. See the article by Sidney Smith, *EB*, 14th ed., vol. ii, pp. 843–48, and related articles, *op. cit.*, on Babylonia and Assyria. *HERE* is also very valuable.

9. We follow Hertzler, *op. cit.*, in using the translation of the Code of Hammurabi provided by D. D. Luckenbill in Appendix II of *J. M. Powis Smith, *The Origin and History of Hebrew Law* (1931). Hertzler's book offers the only sociological discussion of the code, and quotes liberally from it. The treatment by C. J. Gadd, " Babylonian Law," *EB*, 14th ed., vol. ii, pp. 862–64, is very good, as is also that by Paul Koschaker in the somewhat complex and technical article on " Law: Cuneiform," *ESS*, vol. ix (1933), pp. 211–19.

10. J. H. Breasted, *The Dawn of Conscience* (1933), p. 10.

11. Hertzler has performed a signal service in collecting the scattered translations of the wisdom literature in his *op. cit.*, pp. 103–11.

12. Davy and Moret, *op. cit.*, pp. 234–35; Delaporte, *op. cit.*, pp. 43–49, 61. Richard A. Martin of the Field Museum has recently declared, however, that bones of the horse have been found in the tombs of Kish at a date not less than 3000 B.C. This would put the domestication of the horse in the Mesopotamian area much further back than has previously been assumed.   13. Myres, *op. cit.*, p. 127.

14. See the excellent discussions by C. J. Gadd, " Assyrian Law," *EB*, 14th ed., vol. ii, pp. 864–65, and Hertzler, *op. cit.*, pp. 118–35. Koschaker's treatment, *op. cit.*, is also useful, even though involved and overcondensed.

15. Hertzler, *op. cit.*, pp. 135–44.

16. *Alexandre Moret, *The Nile and Egyptian Civilization* (1927), chap. ii, " Country, Nile, and Sun."

17. Davy and Moret, *op. cit.*, pp. 125, 157–58; Moret, *op. cit.*, p. 38.

18. The sharpness of this transition has recently been somewhat mitigated by the discovery of the Badarian and related neolithic cultures, to say nothing of the even simpler Tasian, but a considerable gap still remains. However, see Childe, *op. cit.*, pp. 49–106, for a contrary opinion — and after all, the *Fachmann* decides.

19. Alexander Goldenweiser, " Totemism," *ESS*, vol. xiv (1934), pp. 657–61. Good bibliography. For a psycho-cultural analysis, by no means unobjectionable but perhaps suggestive, see Howard Becker and D. K. Bruner, " Some Aspects of Taboo and Totemism," *JSPS* (Aug., 1932), pp. 337–53.

20. Davy and Moret, *op. cit.*, p. 144.   **21.** Moret, *op. cit.*, p. 39.

22. We here follow English rather than American terminology; if we adopted the latter, we should have to use a term unfamiliar to the general reader, " sib," of which clan and gentes are the matrilineal and patrilineal divisions respectively. To be sure, the Egyptian kinship groups in the period we are here discussing *were* clans, in all probability, and continued to be such as long as they remained of any social significance; nevertheless, we should use the term even if they were patrilineal.

23. Moret, *op. cit.*, p. 40.   **24.** *Ibid.*, pp. 40–44.   **25.** *Ibid.*, p. 45.

26. *Ibid.*, p. 49.   **27.** *Ibid.*, p. 52.   **28.** Breasted, *op. cit.*, pp. 26–29.

29. We have followed Moret's chronology, *op. cit.*, p. 23. Cf. that given in Trever, *op. cit.*, pp. 76–77.   **30.** Moret, *op. cit.*, p. 91.

31. *Ibid.*, pp. 95–97. For the ethnology back of this, see Davy and Moret, *op. cit.*, pp. 20, 35–36, 66–67, 86 ff. We regard Davy's arguments as farfetched at times, and his evidence seems biased. Nevertheless, it is a most interesting treatment of the general problem of totemism.

32. Breasted, *op. cit.*, pp. 82–104; Moret, *op. cit.*, pp. 157–58.

33. Davy and Moret, *op. cit.*, p. 149.

34. This is clearly demonstrated in Moret, *op. cit.*, pp. 374–78.

35. *Ibid.* But see the conflicting statements by Erwin Seidl, " Law: Egyptian," *ESS*, vol. ix (1933), pp. 208–11.

36. *Ibid.*, p. 174. This forms part of *a marvelously vivid passage beginning on the preceding page.   **37.** Breasted, *op. cit.*, p. 144.

38. Moret, *op. cit.*, p. 214.   **39.** *Ibid.*, p. 220.   **40.** *Ibid.*, p. 219.

41. Davy and Moret, *op. cit.*, p. 218. Compare the following passage (p. 219) from the same treatise, discussing a somewhat later period:

" Attracted, perhaps, by the bait of easy and remunerative gains, the tribes of nomadic Semites from the isthmus and Palestine made their way into the disorganized country and stayed there till the day when the Theban Pharaohs had restored the Egyptian monarchy and cleansed her frontiers. It does not look as if this temporary occupation had the character of an armed expedition. The Biblical tradition, describing Abraham and his family quitting the town of Ur of the Chaldees, proceeding up the Euphrates by short stages, then descending by the Orontes and Jordan as far as Shechem, pushing on to Egypt to escape the famine, and then finally returning to Hebron, apparently accurately traces these tribal movements in the days of a King Amraphel, who is, perhaps, Hammurabi."

42. Breasted, *op. cit.*, pp. 156–57.

43. Hertzler, *op. cit.*, pp. 50–74, has an excellent chapter on " The Social Wisdom in the Egyptian Precepts."

44. Moret, *op. cit.*, p. 222. Compare Breasted's translation in *op. cit.*, p. 178: " Would that I had unknown utterances, sayings that are unfamiliar, even new

speech that has not occurred [before], free from repetitions, not the utterance of that which has long passed, which the ancestors spake. . . ."
  45. Moret, *loc. cit.*   46. Breasted, *op. cit.*, pp. 163–64.   47. *Ibid.*, p. 171.
  48. *Ibid.*, p. 176.   49. Moret, *op cit.*, p. 230.   50. Breasted, *op. cit.*, p. 199.
  51. *Ibid.*, p. 202.   52. *Ibid.*, p. 204.   53. *Ibid.*, p. 206.
  54. Moret, *op. cit.*, p. 259.   55. *Ibid.*, pp. 260–61.   56. *Ibid.*, p. 267.
  57. Gaston Maspero, *Les Contes populaires de l'ancienne Egypte* (4th ed., 1911), translated by C. H. W. Johns as *Popular Stories of Ancient Egypt* (1915). The reference, p. 70, is to the original.
  58. Hertzler, *op. cit.*, p. 41.   59. Moret, *op. cit.*, p. 268.   60. *Ibid.*, p. 270.
  61. Breasted, *op. cit.*, p. 210.   62. Davy and Moret, *op. cit.*, pp. 244–45.
  63. *Ibid.*, pp. 256–57.   64. *Ibid.*, pp. 269–75.   65. *Ibid.*, pp. 302–07.
  66. Moret, *op. cit.*, pp. 243–52; Davy and Moret, *op. cit.*, pp. 185–86; Breasted, *op. cit.*, pp. 272–73.   67. Davy and Moret, *op. cit.*, p. 297.
  68. Moret, *op. cit.*, p. 319; Davy and Moret, *op. cit.*, pp. 286–88, 290–91.
  69. Breasted, *op. cit.*, p. 275.   70. Davy and Moret, *op. cit.*, pp. 300–01.
  71. For all the period after the collapse of the New Kingdom, see Moret, *op. cit.*, pp. 327–52; *Breasted, *op. cit.*, pp. 303–35 (excellent); and Davy and Moret, *op. cit.*, pp. 302–54.
  72. T. G. Soares, *The Social Institutions and Ideals of the Bible* (1915), pp. 107–08. In addition to this book, these paragraphs are based on the following secondary sources: Louis Wallis, *Sociological Study of the Bible* (1912), chaps. v and vi (a revised edition of this, entitled *God and the Social Process*, appeared in 1934); George A. Barton, *The Religion of Israel* (1918), chap. i; Charles F. Kent, *The Social Teachings of the Prophets and Jesus* (1920), chap. ii; and Max Weber, *Religionssoziologie*, vol. iii, " Das antike Judentum," *passim*. The primary sources, being available in translation, have of course been extensively used. Recent treatises of which we have not been able to make effective use are: Salo Wittmayer Baron, *A Social and Religious History of the Jews* (3 vols., 1937); J. Garrow Duncan, *New Light on Hebrew Origins* (1936); and Charles L. Woolley, *Abraham: Recent Discoveries and Hebrew Origins* (1936).
  73. L. B. Paton, *The Early Religion of Israel* (1910), p. 4. Most of the material in these paragraphs is taken from this source and from Weber, *op. cit.*
  74. II Samuel, 6:6–7. Cf. the discussion of mana in Chapter One.
  75. E. D. Soper, *The Religions of Mankind* (1921), p. 259.
  76. I Samuel, 19:13–16.   77. Judges, 1:19; Joshua, 17:12.
  78. Judges, 3:5–6.   79. Paton, *op. cit.*, p. 59.
  80. *Ibid.*, pp. 70–74, 91–92. Cf. *Abingdon Bible Commentary* (1929), p. 776; Max Weber, *General Economic History*, translated by F. M. Knight (1927), p. 32.
  81. J. M. Powis Smith, *The Prophet and His Problems* (1914), pp. 49–50. Cf. Paton, *op. cit.*, pp. 91, 102.
  82. Kent, *op. cit.*, p. 14.   83. I Kings, 12:6–11.
  84. Exodus, 20:23–23:33.   85. Soares, *op. cit.*, p. 140.
  86. Exodus, 12:35–36.   87. Max Weber, *op. cit.*, p. 360.
  88. J. M. Powis Smith, *The Prophets and Their Times* (1925), p. 41. Cf. I Samuel, 9:1–10; 10:5–10; II Kings, 3:6–20.
  89. Isaiah, 20:3; Hosea, 1:2; Ezekiel, 12:7; Jeremiah, 13:7, 10.
  90. Cf. Max Weber, *Wirtschaft und Gesellschaft* (1920), pp. 140 ff.; Smith, *op. cit.*, pp. 3, 11; and *The Prophet and His Problems*, p. 4.
  91. Weber, *op. cit.*, pp. 142 ff.   92. Amos, 4:8.

93. Amos, 3:14–15; 4:4 ff.; 5:11, 21–22.
94. Amos, 2:7; 3:12; 5:7–12; 6:4–6, 12. **95.** Amos, 2:6–8; 5:11; 8:6.
96. Amos, 5:24. Cf. 4:1–2; 5:7, 10–13; 7:8.
97. Hosea, 4:2, 4, 9; 5:10, 13; 6:9; 7:1–11; 8:4; 10:3; 12:7.
98. Hosea, 8:8; 9:4, 6; 11:5. **99.** Hosea, 1:2; 2:16–17; 3:4–5; 4:14.
100. Hosea, 1:2, 4–9.
101. A. S. Peake, *A Commentary on the Bible* (1919), p. 559.
102. Micah, 3:11–12. **103.** Micah, 6:6.
104. Max Weber, *General Economic History*, pp. 360–61.
105. II Kings, 22:9–23:15. Cf. Soares, *op. cit.*, p. 32. The Deuteronomic Code
is preserved in our book of Deuteronomy, chaps. 12–19.
106. J. M. Powis Smith, *The Moral Life of the Hebrews* (1923), pp. 14–15.
107. II Samuel, 24:17.
108. I Kings, 19:18; Amos, 5:15; Micah, 2:12; Isaiah, 1:9; 46:3, etc.; Jeremiah, 23:3, etc., Ezekiel, 6:8, etc.
109. Jeremiah, 31:31–34. **110.** Ezekiel, 14:12–23; 18:4–28; 33:10–20.
111. Smith, *The Prophet and His Problems*, pp. 203–204. Cf. A. C. Knudson,
The Religious Teaching of the Old Testament (1918), p. 343.
112. Isaiah, 25:8. **113.** Job, 19:25–27. **114.** Psalms, 49:15.
115. Psalms, 73:24. **116.** Kuenan, quoted in Knudson, *op. cit.*, p. 407.
117. Jeremiah, 31:33–34. Cf. Amos, 5:18; Isaiah, 2:2–4; Hosea, 2:18;
Isaiah, 11:6–8; 45:22, 23; 19:23–25; Psalms, 22:27.
118. Isaiah, 9:6–7. **119.** Isaiah, 53:5.

CHAPTER IV

1. Gustave Glotz, *The Aegean Civilization* (1925), p. 8.
2. *Ibid.*, p. 49. **3.** *Ibid.*, p. 52.
4. *Gilbert Murray, *The Rise of the Greek Epic* (3rd ed.), p. 51.
5. Walter Pater, *Plato and Platonism* (3rd ed., 1925). Italics ours.
6. William Reginald Halliday, *The Growth of the City State* (1923), pp. 21–22. Italics ours.
7. Frederick J. Turner, *The Frontier in American History*, pp. 37–38.
8. Gilbert Murray, *The Rise of the Greek Epic*, pp. 57–58.
9. The relation of such processes to the rise of reflective thought — the Ionian school of philosophy! — has been sketched by Giddings. Cf. his *Studies in the Theory of Human Society*, pp. 264–65.
10. Murray, *op. cit.*, *passim.* **11.** *Ibid.*, pp. 57–58.
12. A. H. L. Heeren, *Researches into the Politics, Intercourse, and Trade of the Principal Nations of Antiquity*, vol. i, pp. 326–27.
13. In fact, some writers claim that the colonies never manifested release, individuation, etc. This is quite erroneous, but it makes plain the difference between frontier conditions and the slower processes of change in the commercial colonies; the changes were so much slower that the mistake has been made of assuming that there took place no change at all. See M. Croiset, *Hellenic Civilization*, p. 25, and *M. Rostovtzeff, *A History of the Ancient World*, translated from the Russian by J. D. Duff (1926), vol. i, p. 229.
14. Although to be construed only analogically, the comparison of Ionian with Western American characteristics is interesting. See F. J. Turner, " The Problem of the West," *op. cit.*, pp. 212–13.
15. Gustave Glotz, *Ancient Greece at Work* (1926), pp. 4–5.
16. Ferdinand Tönnies, *Soziologische Studien und Kritiken*, vol. ii, p. 7.

17. S. J. Altmann, " Simmel's Philosophy of Money," *AJS*, vol. ix, pp. 56–62.

18. John Burnet, *Greek Philosophy*, Part I, pp. 4–5. Italics ours.

19. Park, " Magic, Mentality and City Life," in Park and Burgess, *The City*, pp. 130–31.

20. Burnet, *op. cit.*, pp. 28–30. Italics ours.   **21.** *Ibid.*, p. 108.   **22.** *Ibid.*

23. Glotz, *op. cit.*, pp. 183–88. Italics ours.

24. Burnet, *op. cit.*, pp. 132–33.   **25.** *Ibid.*, p. 133.   **26.** *Ibid.*, pp. 132–33.

27. *Ibid.*, pp. 133–34.   **28.** *Ibid.*, p. 128.

29. L. Robin, *Greek Thought and the Origins of the Scientific Spirit*, pp. 131–33.

30. J. B. Bury, *A History of Greece to the Death of Alexander the Great*, p. 577.

31. In addition to the influences mentioned, the individuating effect of the plague that raged during the Peloponnesian War should also be noted, although Thucydides undoubtedly overemphasized it (Thucydides, *History of the Peloponnesian War*, II, liii).   **32.** Bury, *loc. cit.*   **33.** *Ibid.*

34. George Grote, *History of Greece* (London, 1830), vol. v, p. 541.

35. H. Mattingly, *Outlines of Ancient History*, p. 134.

36. Bury, *op. cit.*, p. 576.   **37.** Thucydides, I, vi.

38. Grote, *op. cit.*, vol. iv, pp. 251–52.

39. Walter Pater, *Plato and Platonism*, p. 24.

40. Grote, *op. cit.*, vol. vii, pp. 57, 250, footnote; cf. Thucydides, I, 144; VI, 7.

41. Bury, *op. cit.*, p. 581.   **42.** Glotz, *loc. cit.*

43. Pater, *op. cit.*, pp. 24–25. Italics ours.   **44.** *Ibid.*, pp. 21–22. Italics ours.

45. *Ibid.*, pp. 105–06. Italics ours.   **46.** *Ibid.*, p. 238.   **47.** *Ibid.*, p. 235.

48. Rostovtzeff, *op. cit.*, p. 319.   **49.** Bury, *op. cit.*, p. 384.

50. The Metics (of whom Aristotle was really one) continued to play a large part in Athenian philosophy. Cf. Glotz, *op. cit.*, pp. 183–88.

51. J. P. Mahaffy, *The Story of Alexander's Empire*, p. 92.   **52.** *Ibid.*, p. 94.

53. Quoted in J. P. Mahaffy, *Silver Age of the Greek World*, p. 165.

54. *Ibid.*, p. 169.

55. M. Rostovtzeff, *A History of the Ancient World*, vol. ii, p. 27.

56. *Ibid.*, p. 37.   **57.** *Ibid.*, pp. 242–43.   **58.** *Ibid.*, p. 291.

59. G. H. Stevenson, chapter on " Communication and Commerce " in *The Legacy of Rome*, pp. 160–61.   **60.** *Ibid.*, p. 302.

61. Rostovtzeff, *op. cit.*, p. 290.   **62.** *Ibid.*, p. 291.

63. Both the intellectual appeal and the emotional deficiencies of this type of rationalism have been most sympathetically portrayed in a pair of excellent historical novels: *Walter Pater's Marius the Epicurean* and *Dmitri Merejkowski's The Death of the Gods.*   **64.** Rostovtzeff, *op. cit.*, p. 340.

65. Henry P. Fairchild, *Immigration* (1920), pp. 1–2.

66. Hobhouse, Wheeler, and Ginsberg, *The Material Culture and Social Institutions of the Simpler Peoples: An Essay in Correlation* (1915), p. 28. See also R. Hennig's remarkable *Terrae Incognitae* (1936).

67. E. C. Semple, *Influences of Geographic Environment* (1911), p. 76.

68. Lyford P. Edwards, *The Natural History of Revolution* (1927), p. 1.

69. Herodotus, *History of the Persian Wars*, I, cxxxv.

70. *Ibid.*, IV, lxxvi.   **71.** *Ibid.*, IX, cxxii.   **72.** *Ibid.*, I, cxxxv.

73. Thucydides, I, ii, iii.

74. Floyd N. House, *The Range of Social Theory* (1929), pp. 54–55.

75. Thucydides, I, v.

76. *Ibid.*, I, vii.   **77.** *Ibid.*, I, xiii.

78. Plato, *The Laws*, in *The Dialogues of Plato* (Jowett trans.), IV.
79. F. H. Giddings, *Studies in the Theory of Human Society* (1922), p. 96.
80. Plato, *loc. cit.* 81. Aristotle, *Politics*, VII, vi, 1. 82. *Ibid.*, VII, iv.
83. Strabo, *The Geography* II, iii, 7. 84. *Ibid.*, II, vi, 20.
85. *Ibid.*, VII, XII, iii, 36. 86. *Ibid.*, XI, viii, 2 and 3.
87. *Ibid.*, VII, iv, 6. 88. *Ibid.*, VII, iv, 6. 89. *Ibid.*, III, iii, i.
90. Marcus Tullius Cicero, *The Treatise on the Republic*, I, 207–09.
91. Caesar, *Commentaries on the Gallic and Civil Wars*, I, i.
92. *Ibid.*, II, xv. 93. *Ibid.*, V, xiii.
94. Seneca, " Consolation to Helvia " in *Minor Dialogues*, XI, vi.

CHAPTER V

1. W. A. Dunning, *A History of Political Theories from Luther to Montesquieu*, p. 104.
2. J. W. Garner, *Introduction to Political Science*, p. 44. 3. *Ibid.*
4. W. W. Willoughby, *The Nature of the State*, p. 2. For precise and *strictly sociological* definitions and analyses of all the terms mentioned, see Wiese-Becker, *Systematic Sociology* (1932 — use index).
5. Dunning, *A History of Political Theories, Ancient and Medieval*, pp. 197–98; 310–15.
6. Dunning, *A History of Political Theories from Luther to Montesquieu*, p. 90.
7. T. D. Seymour, *Life in the Homeric Age*; A. G. Keller, *Homeric Society*. See also A. Moret and G. Davy, *From Tribe to Empire*.
8. Cf. Wiese-Becker, *op. cit.*, p. 306.
9. P. Janet, *Histoire de la science politique dans ses rapports avec la morale* (edition of 1872), vol. i, p. 72. 10. *Ibid.*
11. Botsford and Sihler, *Hellenic Civilization*, pp. 88–94.
12. Janet, *op. cit.*, p. 75.
13. Dunning, *A History of Political Theories, Ancient and Medieval*, pp. 21–23. 14. Janet, *op. cit.*, p. 91.
15. *Ibid.*, p. 102. For the suggestion of traces of the doctrine of a social contract among the Sophists, with whom Socrates is usually associated, see *Ernest Barker, *The Political Thought of Plato and Aristotle*, p. 36. For the same writer's acute analysis of the doctrines of Socrates, see pp. 46–60. For Willoughby's affirmation of the existence of the contract idea among the Sophists, see his *Political Theories of the Ancient World*, pp. 78–79. 16. Plato, *Laws*, V, 739.
17. Sir Frederick Pollock, *A History of the Science of Politics*, p. 14.
18. Richard Lewis Nettleship, *Lectures on the Republic of Plato*, p. 68.
19. Nettleship, *op. cit.*, p. 71.
20. Plato, *Republic*, II, 369–72. 21. *Ibid.*, 373–75.
22. Cf. J. Bonar, *Philosophy and Political Economy*, p. 15.
23. Nettleship, *op. cit.*, pp. 69–71.
24. P. Kropotkin, *Mutual Aid: A Factor in Evolution*, pp. 1–75.
25. F. H. Giddings, *Principles of Sociology*, pp. 5–8.
26. Adam Smith, *Wealth of Nations*, Bk. I, chaps. i–iii. Kropotkin, *op. cit.*, chaps. vii–viii; É. Durkheim, *De la division du travail social* (an English translation, occasionally inaccurate, by Simpson is available).
27. Barker, *op. cit.*, p. 113. For Barker's entire exposition of Plato's origin of the state in the *Republic*, see pp. 101–13.
28. Barker, *op. cit.*, pp. 183–86; Dunning, *A History of Political Theories, Ancient and Medieval*, p. 37.

29. *Laws*, III, 676–77. **30.** *Ibid.*, VI, 781. **31.** *Ibid.*, III, 678–83.
32. Barker, *op. cit.*, p. 191, note. For Barker's complete exposition of the evolution of the state in the *Laws*, see pp. 190–93. **33.** *Laws*, III, 684.
34. H. S. Maine, *Ancient Law, and Early Law and Custom*, chap. vii, where he defends the theory in opposition to critics; Zimmerman and Frampton, *Family and Society* (1935), *passim*. **35.** E. Jenks, *A Short History of Politics*, chap. iv.
36. Alexander Goldenweiser, " The Social Organization of the American Indians," *JAFL* (Oct.–Dec., 1914), pp. 417–18; R. H. Lowie, *Primitive Society* and *The Origin of the State*.
37. *Republic*, II, 369; IV, 433. **38.** *Ibid.*, III, 412–17; V, 458–62.
39. *Laws*, V, 739–40. For the history of the influences of the *Republic* of Plato, see Barker, *op. cit.*, Appendix B, pp. 525–30. For Janet's treatment of the political thought of Plato, see *op. cit.*, pp. 104–76.
40. J. H. Robinson, *The History of Western Europe*, p. 272.
41. Dunning, *op. cit.*, pp. 49–50. **42.** Pollock, *op. cit.*, p. 16.
43. *Politics*, II, 8. **44.** *Ibid.*, I, 1–2. **45.** *Ibid.*, VII, 16. **46.** *Ibid.*, II, 5.
47. *Ibid.*, I, 2.
48. *Ibid.*, I, 5. Cf. F. H. Hankins, " Individual Differences and Democratic Theory," in *PSQ* (Sept., 1923).
49. Cf. Wiese-Becker, *op. cit.*, pp. 292–302, " Genesis of Disparities."
50. See Adolf Menzel, *Griechische Soziologie* (1936), chaps. i, ii, and v, for an exhaustive survey and analysis of the *zoön politikon* and *zoön koinonikon* passages.
51. *Politics*, I, 2. Cf. G. H. Mead, *Mind, Self, and Society* (1935), *passim*.
52. *Politics, loc. cit.* For Barker's exposition of Aristotle's theory of the origin of the state, see *op. cit.*, pp. 269–76. Cf. on this question of " solitariness vs. associativeness " Wiese-Becker, *op. cit.* (use index).
53. *Politics* I, 1–2. **54.** Pollock, *op. cit.*, pp. 19–20.
55. J. B. Bury, in his *History of Greece*, pp. 834–35, has called attention to the lamentable failure of Aristotle to avail himself of the ethnographic discoveries made by Alexander on his conquest.
56. B. Jowett, *Politics*, Introduction, pp. xix–xx.
57. C. H. Cooley, *Social Organization*, chaps. i–ii; Wiese-Becker, *op. cit.*, chap. iv. **58.** Giddings, *Inductive Sociology*, p. 278.
59. Wiese-Becker, *op. cit.*, p. 33.
60. F. W. Coker, *Organismic Theories of the State*.
61. *Politics*, IV, 4. Cf. Spencer, *First Principles*, Part II; and *Principles of Sociology*, vol i, Part II. For exhaustive criticism of all organismic theories, see Wiese-Becker, *op. cit.* (use index, but especially chap. iv).
62. *Nicomachean Ethics*, VIII, i, ix; IX, xii. **63.** *Politics*, VII, 4–15.
64. Bury, *A History of Greece*, p. 835. For Janet's exposition of the political philosophy of Aristotle, see *op. cit.*, vol. i, pp. 177–255. For the later effect of the *Politics*, see Barker, *op. cit.*, pp. 525–30.
65. For the general character of Post-Aristotelian philosophy, see E. Zeller, *Stoics, Epicureans, and Sceptics*, chaps. i–iii.
66. Janet, *op. cit.*, pp. 256–70; Zeller, *op. cit.*, pp. 293–96; G. L. Scherger, *The Evolution of Modern Liberty*, pp. 18–19; Ludwig Stein, *Die Soziale Frage im Lichte der Philosophie*, pp. 222–24.
67. Franz Oppenheimer, *The State* (1912), p. 4. **68.** Pollock, *op. cit.*, p. 30.
69. Stein, *op. cit.*, p. 459. **70.** Zeller, *op. cit.*, p. 410; Stein, *op. cit.*, p. 228.
71. Zeller, *op. cit.*, pp. 427–28.
72. The Sophists are alleged by Barker to have had similar ideas.

73. Diogenes Laertius, *Lives and Opinions of Eminent Philosophers*, Bk. X, chap. xxi, secs., 33–35.

74. Zeller, *op. cit.*, pp. 462–63; Stein, *op. cit.*, pp. 228–30.

75. Giddings, *Studies in the Theory of Human Society*, pp. 103–104.

76. A. J. Todd, *Theories of Social Progress* (1918), p. 45.

77. J. T. Shotwell, *Introduction to the History of History*, chap. xvi. Cf. Menzel, *op. cit.*, pp. 195 ff. **78.** Polybius, *The Histories*, VI, 56.

79. *Ibid.*, VI, 7–9. Menzel, *loc. cit.*, has an interesting discussion of Polybius's cyclical theory. **80.** Polybius, *The Histories*, 11–15.

81. Dunning, *op. cit.*, p. 117.

82. David Hume, *Essays, Moral, Political, and Literary* (Green and Gross, eds.), vol. i, pp. 113–17.

83. See Howard Becker, "Some Forms of Sympathy: A Phenomenological Analysis," *JASP*, (Apr., 1931).

84. For Janet's excellent summary, see *op. cit.*, vol. i, pp. 270–74.

85. Cf. Bury, *The Ancient Greek Historians*, pp. 205 ff., 248.

86. Pollock, *op. cit.*, pp. 31–32.

87. Cf. Teuffel and Schwabe, *A History of Roman Literature*, vol. i, pp. 1–2, 77–87. **88.** See Masson's classic exposition of Lucretius.

89. A. C. Haddon, *A History of Anthropology*, pp. 122–24.

90. Lucretius, *De Rerum Natura*, V, 325–50. William Ellery Leonard's translation, in the Everyman's Library, is splendid. **91.** Lucretius, *op. cit.*, V, 838–68.

92. *Ibid.*, 920–56. Lucretius allowed no place for the primitive golden age later premised by Seneca and the Fathers, and recently revived by G. Elliot Smith and W. J. Perry. **93.** *Ibid.*, 970–1170. **94.** *Ibid.*, 1105–21.

95. Lucretius in this sentence shows his grasp of a fundamental principle of the psycho-sociology of revolution.

96. Lucretius, *op. cit.*, V, 1130–50. **97.** See *ibid.*, 1160–1207.

98. A. J. Carlyle, *A History of Medieval Political Theory in the West*, vol. i, p. 3.

99. Pollock, *op. cit.*, p. 32. Cf. Willoughby, *Political Theories of the Ancient World*, pp. 288–89.

100. Dunning, *op. cit.*, p. 121. **101.** Carlyle, *op. cit.*, pp. 3–4.

102. Ward Fowler has pointed out Cicero's similarly changing views of the nature of religion in his *Religious Experience of the Roman People*, p. 387.

103. Carlyle, *op. cit.*, p. 12. **104.** *Ibid.*, p. 13.

105. Cicero, *De officiis*, Bk. I, chap. xliv.

106. Cf. Rousseau, *Social Contract*, Bk. I, chap. v.

107. Carlyle, *op. cit.*, pp. 14–15.

108. Cicero, *De republica*, Bk. I, chaps. xxv–xxvi. **109.** *Ibid.*, I, xxv–xxvi. **110.** *Ibid.*, I, xlv. **111.** *De officiis*, Bk. I, chap. xvii.

112. Carlyle, *op. cit.*, p. 17. **113.** *Ibid.*, pp. 13–14.

114. Edmund Burke, *Reflections on the French Revolution*, especially the first few pages of Part II. **115.** Cicero, *De republica*, Bk. II, chap. i.

116. Carlyle, *op. cit.*, pp. 11–15. **117.** *Ibid.*, p. 19. **118.** *Ibid.*, p. 31.

119. *Ibid.*, p. 20. **120.** Cf. Rousseau, *op. cit.*, beginning of Part II.

121. Carlyle, *op. cit.*, pp. 23–24. **122.** *Ibid.*, p. 24. **123.** *Ibid.*, p. 31.

124. *Ibid.*, p. 25. **125.** *Ibid.*, p. 117. **126.** *Ibid.*, p. 127.

127. Stein, *op. cit.*, p. 459. **128.** Carlyle, *op. cit.*, pp. 43–44.

129. *Ibid.*, pp. 63–64. **130.** *Ibid.*, p. 70. **131.** *Ibid.*, pp. 68–70.

132. *Ibid.*, pp. 74–77.

133. Cf. Wiese-Becker, *op. cit.* (use index, but see especially pp. 43–48).

CHAPTER VI

1. This section is based largely on the following sources: J. S. Riggs, *A History of the Jewish People: Maccabean and Roman Periods* (1900); and *V. Simkhovitch, *Toward the Understanding of Jesus* (1921).

2. Most of the information in this section came from the following sources: J. Klausner, *Jesus of Nazareth* (1925), pp. 201–22; and *S. J. Case, *Jesus, A New Biography* (1927).

3. Cf. Klausner, *op. cit.*, pp. 398–400; and C. G. Montefiore, in Peake's *Commentary*, pp. 624–25.   **4.** Case, *op. cit.*, p. 198.

5. *Ibid.*, p. 371. See also *F. J. F. Jackson and Kirsopp Lake, *The Beginnings of Christianity*, vol. i (1920), pp. 282–83.   **6.** Matt. 23:23.

7. Matt. 22:36–40.   **8.** Matt. 5:44, 5:39, Luke 17:21.   **9.** Mark 12:17.

10. Cf. *Ernst Troeltsch, *The Social Teachings of the Christian Churches*, vol. i, translated by Olive Wyon (1931), pp. 52, 55–57.

11. *Ibid.*, p. 59; also T. G. Soares, *The Social Institutions and Ideals of the Bible* (1915), chap. xxxv.   **12.** Troeltsch, *op. cit.*, pp. 59–60.   **13.** *Ibid.*, p. 61.   **14.** *Ibid.*, pp. 61–62.

15. Seneca, *Ep.*, 41:2. Most of the information in this section was taken from Jackson and Lake, *op. cit.*, pp. 218–62; and *I. Edman, *The Mind of Paul* (1935), pp. 120–51.   **16.** I Cor. 9:16.

17. The following paragraphs are based on Troeltsch, *op. cit.*, pp. 39–69.

18. Romans 3:23.   **19.** Galatians 3:23.   **20.** Romans 13:1.

21. Troeltsch, *op. cit.*, p. 85.

22. Sir William Ramsay, *The Church in the Roman Empire* (1897), p. 208. Most of the present section was taken from this source.

23. A. J. Carlyle, *History of Mediaeval Political Theory*, vol. i, p. 102. The following paragraphs are based largely on Troeltsch, *op. cit.*, pp. 69–89.

24. Lactantius, *Divine Institutes*, Bk. VI, chap. x, in *Ante-Nicene Fathers*, vol. vii.   **25.** Matt. 19:6.

26. St. Jerome, *Letter to Eustochium*, sec. 16, in *Nicene and Post-Nicene Fathers*, vol. vi.

27. St. Ambrose, *Ep.* lxvii, 112, quoted in Carlyle, vol. i, p. 121.

28. St. Ambrose, *De Joseph patriarcha*, IV, quoted in Carlyle, vol. i, p. 114.

29. Irenaeus, *Against Heresies*, Bk. V, chap. xxiv, sec. 2, in *Ante-Nicene Fathers*, vol. i.   **30.** Troeltsch, *op. cit.*, p. 151.

31. Translated from a quotation in P. A. R. Janet, *Histoire de la science politique* (4th ed., 1913), vol. i, pp. 316–17.

32. St. Augustine, *De Civitate Dei*, xix, 24; cf. also sec. 21.

33. A. J. Carlyle, in F. J. C. Hearnshaw, ed., *The Social and Political Ideas of Some Great Medieval Thinkers* (1923), pp. 48–49.

34. A. Robertson, *Regnum Dei* (1901), p. 212.

35. Lynn Thorndike, *History of Medieval Europe*, p. 416.

36. Otto Seeck, *Geschichte des Untergangs der antiken Welt* (1897).

37. S. H. von Sybel, quoted in H. E. Barnes, "History, Its Rise and Development," in *EA* (1922 ed.), p. 217.

38. A. J. Carlyle, "Manegold of Lautenbach," in *ESS*, vol. x, pp. 94–95.

39. E. F. Jacob, in Hearnshaw, *op. cit.*, p. 67. Most of the present section is based on this source.   **40.** *Ibid.*, p. 64.

41. This section is based largely on the following sources: Troeltsch, *op. cit.*, pp. 280–328; and J. M. Littlejohn, *The Political Theory of the Schoolmen and Grotius*, Part II, Columbia dissertation (1895).   **42.** Troeltsch, *op. cit.*, p. 276.

43. St. Thomas, *Summa theologiae*, I, xciii, 4; II, 2, xxvi, 10; Supp. xxxix, 3, quoted from F. J. C. Hearnshaw, ed., *Mediaeval Contributions to Modern Civilization* (1921), pp. 222–23. 44. Littlejohn, *op. cit.*, pp. 79–83.

45. A. J. Carlyle, in *Property, Its Duties and Rights, Essays by Various Authors* (1913), pp. 128–31. 46. Troeltsch, *op. cit.*, p. 319.

47. St. Thomas, *De regimine principum*, in *Opuscula selecta S. Thomas Aquinatis*. 48. Littlejohn, *op. cit.*, Part II.

49. St. Thomas, *De regimine principum*, lib. i, c, 14; quoted in Hearnshaw, *Social and Political Ideas of Some Great Mediaeval Thinkers*, pp. 100–01.

50. *Ibid.*, p. 102.

51. F. Aveling, in Hearnshaw, *Social and Political Ideas of Some Great Mediaeval Thinkers*, p. 102.

CHAPTER VII

1. Ibn Battúta, *Travels in Asia and Africa, 1325–1354*, translated and selected by H. A. R. Gibb (1929).

2. Alfred von Kremer, " Ibn Chaldoun und seine Culturgeschichte des islamischen Reiches " in *SBKAWPH* (1879), Bd. 93, p. 620.

3. *Cf. Robert Briffault, *The Making of Humanity* (1919), *passim.*

4. " Social disorganization is not an exceptional phenomenon limited to certain periods or certain societies; some of it is found always and everywhere, since always and everywhere there are individual cases of breaking social rules, cases which exercise some disorganizing influence on group institutions and, if not counteracted, are apt to multiply and to lead to a complete decay of the latter. But during periods of social stability this continuous incipient disorganization is continuously neutralized by such activities of the group as reinforce with the help of social sanctions the power of existing rules. The stability of group institutions is thus simply a dynamic equilibrium of processes of disorganization and reorganization " (Thomas and Znaniecki, *The Polish Peasant in Europe and America* [1918], pp. 1129–30).

5. E. Pittard, *Race and History* (1924), pp. xiv–xv.

6. J. F. Dashiell, *JCP*, vol. v (June, 1925), pp. 205–08.

7. *L. P. Edwards, *The Natural History of Revolution* (1927).

8. Nels Anderson and E. C. Lindeman, *Urban Sociology* (1928), p. 325.

9. Robert E. Park and E. W. Burgess, *Introduction to the Science of Sociology* (1921), p. 866. 10. H. Prutz, *Kulturgeschichte der Kreuzzüge* (1883), p. 15.

11. *E. Barker, " Crusades," *EB*, 14th ed., p. 782.

12. B. Adams, *The Law of Civilization and Decay* (1895), p. 379.

13. Fr. Hertz, " Die Wanderungen und ihre geschichtliche Bedeutung," *KVS*, vol. viii (1929), chap. 1, pp. 36–52.

14. " Commerce presupposes the freedom of the individual to pursue his own profit, and commerce can take place only to the extent and degree that this freedom is permitted. Freedom of commerce is, however, limited on the one hand by the mores and on the other by formal law, so that the economic process takes place ordinarily within limitations that are defined by the cultural and the political processes. It is only where there is neither a cultural nor a political order that commerce is absolutely free " (Park and Burgess, *op. cit.*, p. 53).

15. *F. J. C. Hearnshaw, ed., *The Social and Political Ideas of Some Great Medieval Thinkers* (1923), p. 139. For a striking description of the later phases of the transition commonly called the Renaissance, see Ralph Roeder's *The Man of the Renaissance* (1933).

16. *F. J. Teggart, *The Processes of History* (1918), p. 109; A. N. Whitehead, *Science and the Modern World* (1925), pp. 86, 299.

17. Teggart, *op. cit.*, pp. 156–58.

18. J. Bryce, *Essays and Addresses in War Time*, pp. 84–102, as adapted and quoted in Park and Burgess, *op. cit.*, p. 988; F. C. Bartlett, " Psychology of Culture Contact," *EB*, 13th ed.; F. Boas, *Anthropology and Modern Life* (1928), pp. 162–63. Cf. also *F. S. Marvin, *The Living Past* (1913), chap. vii; *W. Cunningham, *Western Civilization* (1890–1900), vol. ii, pp. 162–224; *C. J. H. Hayes, *Political and Social History of Modern Europe* (1st ed., 1916), vol. i, pp. 27–73.

19. R. G. Latham, *Descriptive Ethnology* (1859), vol. ii, p. 502; *Alexander Goldenweiser, *Early Civilization* (1922), p. 27.

20. Ibn Khaldūn, *Les prolegomenes*, traduites en français et commentés par M. William MacGuckin (baron) de Slane (Paris: Imprimerie impériale, 1863), Extrait de la Tome XIX (trois parties) des Notices et extraits des manuscrits de la bibliothèque impériale.

21. Silvestre de Sacy, *Chrestomathie arabe* (1806), vol. ii, pp. 401–573; Joseph von Hammer-Purgstall, " Notice sur l'introduction à la connaissance de l'histoire, célèbre ouvrage arabe d'Ibn Khaldūn," in *JA*, 1. ser., vol. i, pp. 267–78; vol. iv, pp. 158–61 (Paris, 1822–24).

22. Jakob Grefve, " An Account of the Great Historical Work of the African Philosopher, Ibn Khaldūn," in *RAST* (London, 1835), vol. iii, pp. 387–404.

23. Ludwig Gumplowicz, *Sociologische Essays* (Innsbruck, 1899).

24. Gumplowicz, *Der Rassenkampf* (Innsbruck, 1909); *Grundriss der Soziologie* (Vienna, 1855), *translated by Moore as *Outlines of Sociology*.

25. Gustav Ratzenhofer, *Wesen und Zweck der Politik* (Leipzig, 1893); *Soziologie* (Leipzig, 1907).

26. *L. F. Ward, *Pure Sociology* (2nd ed., 1903), pp. 205 *et passim*.

27. Franz Oppenheimer, *System der Soziologie*, vol. ii, " Der Staat " (1926).

28. H. Lammens, *L'Islam: Croyances et Institutions* (1926), " Sciences having the traditions as their object," pp. 74–91. This discussion of Ibn Khaldūn owes much to a paper prepared for us by Richard Hays Williams of the University of Buffalo.

29. Ibn Khaldūn, *op. cit.*, i, p. 73.

30. *Ibid.*, i, p. 71. Freely translated from the French. **31.** *Ibid.*, i, pp. 84 ff.

32. Ibn Khaldūn, like Machiavelli and Hobbes, had a very clear conception of the problem of power in society. Anything analogous in the animal world he attributed to what we should term " instinct." This also suggests why Gumplowicz took such an interest in his work, and why Oppenheimer pays tribute to his thought. His conception of sovereignty, another example of the range and brilliance of his thought, as *a power and authority sufficiently strong to keep men within a given society from attacking each other*, foreshadows Hobbes.

33. In this section he shows very forcefully how interdependent human beings are for the very necessities of life, which may be summed up by saying, " *L'homme ne saurait se passer de la société* " (Ibn Khaldūn, *op. cit.*, i, p. 86).

34. *Ibid.*, i, p. 15. **35.** *Ibid.*, i, pp. 90–254.

36. These distinctions are the most explicitly developed in *ibid.*, i, pp. 255–57.

37. Ibn Khaldūn had a very clear idea of the nature and function of rural-urban migration. On this point see P. A. Sorokin, C. C. Zimmerman, and C. J. Galpin, *A Systematic Source Book in Rural Sociology*, vol. i, pp. 54–64.

38. See especially Ibn Khaldūn, *op. cit.*, i, pp. 277–78. Some of his critics, par-

ticularly Hussein, Gumplowicz, and Oppenheimer, seem to have overlooked this fact, which we feel is basic to the whole of the *Prolegomena*. **39.** *Ibid.*, i, p. 351.
40. See especially *ibid.*, ii, p. 313. **41.** *Ibid.*, ii, the entire 4th section.
42. For a good special treatment of this phase of his work see René Maunier, *Les Idées économiques d'un philosophe arabe au XIVᵉ siècle, RHES*, vol. vi (1913). **43.** See especially Ibn Khaldūn, *op. cit.*, i, pp. 292–93.
44. *Ibid.*, ii, pp. 342–44.
45. For an excellent discussion of Ibn Khaldūn's theories, see *Nathaniel Schmidt, *Ibn Khaldūn* (1930), chaps. entitled " The Historian," " The Sociologist," and " The Philosopher of History." Convenient summaries of some of his contributions may also be found in *Robert Flint, *History of the Philosophy of History* (1893), pp. 158 ff., and in G. DeGreef, *Le Transformisme social* (2nd ed., 1901), pp. 115–18. See also R. Altamira, " Notas sobre la doctrine historica de Abenjaldun," in memorial to Francesco Codera (1904).
46. Ibn Khaldūn, *op. cit.*, pp. 86, 90, 270 ff., 291 ff., 318 ff.
47. Erwin Rosenthal, *Ibn Khaldūn's Gedanken über den Staat* (1932), p. 113.
48. Schmidt, *op. cit.*, pp. 45–46. **49.** Hearnshaw, *op. cit.*, p. 107.
50. *Ibid.*, pp. 129, 142.
51. *Ibid.*, chap. vi, by *Eileen Power, " Pierre DuBois and the Domination of France."
52. J. N. Figgis, " A Forgotten Radical," *CR* (1899). Italics ours.
53. *Defensor pacis*, as translated in Hearnshaw, *op. cit.*, p. 154.
54. Hearnshaw, *op. cit.*, pp. 147–48. **55.** Figgis, *loc. cit.*
56. *De recuperatione terre sancte.* **57.** Hearnshaw, *op. cit.*, pp. 109, 165.
58. See Chapter Five.
59. W. A. Dunning, *A History of Political Theories, Ancient and Medieval* (1902), p. 403.
60. Hearnshaw, *op. cit.*, p. 107. See chap. v entire for an eminently just estimate of Dante: *E. Sharwood Smith, " Dante and World-Empire."
61. *Divine Basis of Political Authority.* See F. W. Coker, *Readings in Political Philosophy* (1914), pp. 154–55.
62. Hearnshaw, *op. cit.*, p. 177. See chap. vii entire, *J. W. Allen, " Marsilio of Padua and Mediaeval Secularism."
63. See Wiese-Becker, *Systematic Sociology* (1932), *passim.*
64. *Defensor pacis*, Bk. I, chap. iv. See Coker, *op. cit.*, pp. 160–62.
65. Hearnshaw, *op. cit.*, p. 181.
66. *Defensor pacis*, Bk. I, chap. xii. See Coker, *op. cit.*, pp. 164–65.
67. *Ibid.*, p. 166. **68.** *Ibid.*, p. 167. **69.** Hearnshaw, *op. cit.*, p. 184.
70. *Defensor pacis*, Bk. II, chap. i. See Coker, *op. cit.*, pp. 170–71.
71. *Ibid.*, pp. 172–74. **72.** Hearnshaw, *op. cit.*, p. 170.
73. E. F. Jacob, " Nicolas of Cusa " in F. J. C. Hearnshaw, ed., *The Social and Political Ideas of Some Great Thinkers of the Renaissance and Reformation* (1925), pp. 41–49.

CHAPTER VIII

1. *J. T. Shotwell, " Middle Ages," in *EB*, 11th ed.; *J. H. Robinson, *The New History* (1927), pp. 154–60; ——, *Petrarch* (2nd ed., 1914), Introduction; H. O. Taylor, *Thought and Expression in the Sixteenth Century* (1920), Preface and chap. i; K. Brandi, *Das Werden der Renaissance* (1908).
2. E. Emerton, *Beginnings of Modern Europe* (1917), chaps. ix–x; Taylor, *op. cit.*, Bk. I. **3.** J. H. Robinson, *op. cit.*, pp. 116–17, 157–58.

4. E. M. Hulme, *Renaissance and Reformation* (1915), chaps. i–xi; Paul Monroe, *Textbook in the History of Education* (1908), chap. vi.

5. K. Pearson, *The Ethic of Free Thought* (2nd ed., 1901), pp. 165–66.

6. Preserved Smith, *The Age of the Reformation* (1920), chap. i; *Erasmus* (1923), chaps. ix, xii, xv; E. Fueter, *L'Histoire de l'historiographie moderne*, Livre I (a new edition of Fueter's work — originally in German — is now [1937] available in English).

7. *F. J. C. Hearnshaw, " Nicolo Machiavelli," in F. J. C. Hearnshaw, ed., *The Social and Political Ideas of Some Great Thinkers of the Renaissance and Reformation* (1925), p. 97. An excellent literary treatment of Machiavelli and his work is to be found in *Ralph Roeder, *The Man of the Renaissance* (1933), pp. 131–312.

8. F. H. Giddings, *Readings in Descriptive and Historical Sociology* (1906), pp. 12–13.

9. W. A. Dunning, *History of Political Theories, Ancient and Medieval* (1923), p. 285.

10. *John Morley, " Machiavelli," *Roman Lectures* (1888), pp. 20–21.

11. Dunning, *op. cit.*, pp. 293, 306.

12. From Bks. I and II of *Discourses on the First Ten Books of Titus Livius*, translated by Christian E. Detmold in *The Historical, Political, and Diplomatic Writings of Niccolo Machiavelli*, vol. ii (1891), pp. 174, 225.

13. *The Prince, op. cit.*, pp. 55–56, 57–59.

14. Bk. III of *Discourses, op. cit.*, p. 421.   15. *Ibid.*, p. 376.

16. Bk. I of *Discourses, op. cit.*, p. 188.   17. *Ibid.*, p. 180.

18. Bk. III of *Discourses, op. cit.*, p. 422.

19. Bk. I of *Discourses, op. cit.*, p. 154.   20. *Ibid.*, p. 113.

21. Herbert Spencer, *First Principles* (1875), pp. 507 ff.

22. Bk. II of *Discourses, op. cit.*, p. 235.   23. *Ibid.*, pp. 237–41.

24. Bk. I of *Discourses, op. cit.*, pp. 129–31.   25. *Ibid.*, p. 214.

26. Bk. II of *Discourses, op. cit.*, p. 286.

27. Bk. I of *Discourses, op. cit.*, pp. 207–08.

28. Bk. III of *Discourses, op. cit.*, p. 396.

29. Cf. F. H. Giddings, *Sociology, A Lecture* (1908), pp. 19 ff.

30. *Thomas More, *Utopia*, in Henry Morley, ed., *Ideal Commonwealths* (1901), pp. 49–50. Italics ours.

31. Francis Bacon, *New Atlantis*, in Morley, *op. cit.*, pp. 117–20.

32. Bacon, *Essays* (1890), " Of Friendship."

33. *Thomas Campanella, *The City of the Sun*, in Morley, *op. cit.*, p. 166.

34. *Ibid.*, p. 168.   35. James Harrington, *Oceana*, in Morley, *op. cit.*, p. 316.

36. Thomas More, *Utopia*, in the Camelot Series, vol. xii, Maurice Adams, ed. (n. d.), pp. 89–90.   37. *Ibid.*, pp. 188–89.   38. *Ibid.*, pp. 125–26.

39. *Ibid.*, pp. 130–31. The quotation from Mims occurs at the end of his article on More in *ESS*, vol. xi.

40. *J. B. Bury, *History of the Freedom of Thought* (1913), chap. iv; K. Pearson, *op. cit.*, chaps. viii–ix.

41. Preserved Smith, *Erasmus* (1923), pp. 433–34; Pearson, *loc. cit.*; Charles Beard, *The Reformation in its Relation to Modern Thought and Culture, passim*.

42. J. H. Robinson, *op. cit.*, pp. 117–18.

43. J. H. Robinson, " The Study of the Lutheran Revolt," in *AHR* (Jan., 1903); ———, art. " Reformation," in *EB*, 11th ed.; *M. Weber, *The Protestant Ethic and the Spirit of Capitalism*, translated by Talcott Parsons (1930), Preserved Smith, *Age of the Reformation* (1920), chap. xiv; R. H. Tawney, " Six-

teenth Century Religious Thought," in *JPE* (1923), and *Religion and the Rise of Capitalism* (1927); *Ernst Troeltsch, *The Social Doctrines of the Christian Churches* (Eng. trans., 1931).

44. Pearson, *op. cit.*, chap. ix; Smith, *Age of the Reformation*, chaps. xii–xiii; *A. C. McGiffert, *Protestant Thought before Kant* (1929), chaps. i–v.

45. Fueter, *op. cit.*, pp. 329–31; *E. Gibbon, *Decline and Fall of the Roman Empire* (1891), chap. liv.; R. H. Tawney, *op. cit.*

46. Smith, *op. cit.*, chap. viii.

47. *Ibid.*, pp. 651–61; *W. E. H. Lecky (1865), *The Rise and Influence of Rationalism in Europe*, chap. i; C. Singer, *Studies in the History and Methods of Science* (1917), vol. i, pp. 189–224.

48. Cf. literature cited in footnote 43, and also Wiese-Becker, *Systematic Sociology* (1932), pp. 624–42.

49. *J. W. Allen, " Martin Luther," in F. J. C. Hearnshaw, ed., *The Social and Political Ideas of Some Great Thinkers of the Renaissance and the Reformation*, pp. 178–79.

50. Francis W. Coker, *Readings in Political Philosophy* (1914), pp. 193–200.

51. Dunning, *A History of Political Theories from Luther to Montesquieu* (1905), pp. 16–17.

52. Cf. J. G. Frazer, *Lectures on the Early History of the Kingship* (1905), pp. 111 ff.; John N. Figgis, *The Divine Right of Kings*, p. 2.

53. *J. G. Frazer, *The Golden Bough* (1890; 1 vol., abridged ed., 1924), chap. vii, " Incarnate Human Gods," pp. 91–106.

54. I Sam. 10:1; 16:13; II Sam. 5:3; Psalms 132:10. **55.** Rom. 13:1.

56. Cf. Dunning, *A History of Political Theories, Ancient and Medieval*, pp. 230 ff. **57.** *Ibid.*, pp. 228–29, 238 ff.

58. Figgis, *The Divine Right of Kings* (1914), pp. 5–263, *passim*.

59. *Ibid.*, pp. 199, 262–63. **60.** Coker, *op. cit.*, pp. 210, 211.

61. *Ibid.*, pp. 208–10. **62.** *Ibid.*, p. 213. **63.** *Ibid.*, pp. 219–20.

64. Dunning, *A History of Political Theories from Luther to Montesquieu* (1905), pp. 68–69.

CHAPTER IX

1. See A. E. Shipley, *The Revival of Science in the Seventeenth Century* (1913), *passim*.

2. *J. E. Gillespie, *The Influence of Oversea Expansion on England* (1920), chaps. vii–ix.

3. *Irene Cooper Willis, *Montaigne* (1927), pp. 10–12, 23–24.

4. *Ibid.*, p. 82. **5.** *Ibid.*, pp. 84–87.

6. *J. P. Lichtenberger, *The Development of Social Theory* (1923), pp. 184–85. **7.** *Ibid.*, p. 165.

8. Jean Bodin, *The Six Bookes of a Commonweale*, translated by Richard Knolles (1606), pp. 46–47. **9.** *Ibid.*, p. 406. **10.** *Ibid.*, pp. 564–68.

11. *Ibid.*, p. 361.

12. *F. W. Coker, *Readings in Political Philosophy* (1914), p. 226.

13. Bodin, *op. cit.*, p. 47.

14. Coker, *op. cit.*, p. 230; W. A. Dunning, *A History of Political Theories from Luther to Montesquieu* (1905), p. 96.

15. *J. W. Allen, " Jean Bodin," in F. J. C. Hearnshaw, ed., *Social and Political Ideas of Some Great Thinkers of the Sixteenth and Seventeenth Centuries* (1926), pp. 59–60. **16.** Bodin, *op. cit.*, p. 567. **17.** *Ibid.*, pp. 550, 561.

18. *Pitirim Sorokin, *Contemporary Sociological Theories* (1928), p. 5. Sorokin's chapter on " The Mechanistic School " should be read with reference to this period. Also of value is Franz Borkenau, *" Zur Soziologie des mechanistischen Weltbildes," ZSF, i, 3 (1932), pp. 311–35, as well as his *Der Übergang vom feudalen zum bürgerlichen Weltbild* (1933).

19. See O. F. Boucke, *The Development of Economics, 1750–1900* (1921), chaps. ii–iii.

20. Boucke, *loc. cit.*; *Gide and Rist, *History of Economic Doctrines* (2nd ed., 1913), Bks. I and II.

21. Cf. Herbert Spencer, *Principles of Sociology* (1875), vol. i, par. 271, as well as Part II of the *First Principles*.

22. *Bishop George Berkeley, *Works* (Fraser ed., 1901), vol. iv, pp. 186–90.

CHAPTER X

1. *F. J. C. Hearnshaw, " The Social and Political Problems of the Sixteenth and Seventeenth Centuries," in Hearnshaw, ed., *The Social and Political Ideas of Some Great Thinkers of the Sixteenth and Seventeenth Centuries* (1926), p. 27.

2. *A. J. Carlyle, " The Sources of Medieval Political Theory and its Connection with Medieval Politics," *AHR*, vol. xix (1913), pp. 6–8; *A History of Medieval Political Theory*, vol. iii, pp. 168, 185.

3. F. H. Giddings, " The Concepts and Methods of Sociology," *AJS*, vol. x (1904), pp. 169–70.

4. David G. Ritchie, " Contributions to the History of the Social Contract Theory," *PSQ*, vol. vi (1891), pp. 665–67.

5. For the fullest discussion of the environmental background of the social contract theory, see F. Atger, *L'Histoire des doctrines du contrat social* (1906), pp. 44–49, 91–94, 134–55, 226–52.

6. Cf. George Scherger, *Evolution of Modern Liberty* (1904), p. 41.

7. Richard Hooker, *Ecclesiastical Polity* (1594–1600), Bk. I, chap. x.

8. For a good discussion of the difference between these concepts, see Willoughby, *The Nature of the State* (1911), pp. 55–56; for the best historical treatment of the social contract theory, see F. Atger, *op. cit.*

9. Hooker, *loc. cit.* Cf. Willoughby, *op. cit.*, pp. 62–63; Tozer, *Rousseau's Social Contract* (1912), Introduction, p. 10; Ritchie, *op. cit.*, p. 666.

10. Hooker, *op. cit.*, Bk. I, chap. x.

11. *Ibid.*, Bk. I, chaps. v–vii; W. A. Dunning, *A History of Political Theories from Luther to Montesquieu* (1905), p. 210.

12. F. Suarez, *Tractatus de legibus ac deo legislatore* (1872), Bk. I, " On Law in General."

13. *A. L. Lilley, " Francisco Suarez," in Hearnshaw, *op. cit.*, p. 100.

14. *Ibid.*, pp. 101–02.

15. J. Mariana, *De rege et regis institutione* (edition of 1605), chap. i, " Homo natura est animal sociabile "; Dunning, *op. cit.*, pp. 68–69.

16. John Fiske, *Outlines of Cosmic Philosophy* (11th ed., 1890), pp. 340–44, 360–63, 369.

17. John N. Figgis, *Studies of Political Thought from Gerson to Grotius, 1414–1625* (2nd ed., 1907), pp. 230–36 *et passim*.

18. Althusius's chief work, *Politica Methodice Digesta*, was virtually unobtainable in this country (only two copies in reference libraries) until the appearance of *a splendid reprint, edited with an introduction by Carl Joachim Friedrich, *Politica Methodice Digesta of Johannes Althusius* (*Althaus*), reprinted from the third edition of 1614, augmented by the preface to the first edition of 1603 and by twenty-one hitherto unpublished letters of the author, with an introduction (Cambridge: Harvard University Press, 1932). The introduction is easily the most important secondary source of information about Althusius and his basic doctrines now extant. Although relatively brief, it definitely supersedes Gierke's treatise, *Johannes Althusius und die Entwicklung der naturrechtlichen Staatstheorien* (1880), vol. viii of his *Untersuchungen zur deutschen Staats- und Rechtsgeschichte*, and also invalidates the relevant portions of Figgis, *op. cit.*, pp. 229 ff.; C. F. Merriam, *A History of the Theory of Sovereignty since Rousseau* (1900), pp. 17–21; and Atger, *op. cit.*, pp. 121–27.

19. Friedrich, Introduction to Althusius, *op. cit.*, p. lxxxviii. Other passages from Friedrich quoted in the text are to be found on pp. lxviii, lxx, lxxxv, lxxxvii.

20. H. Grotius, *De jure belli et pacis* (abridged trans. by Whewell, 1853), "Prolegomena," particularly secs. 5–9, 15–16; Atger, *op. cit.*, pp. 155–62.

21. Dunning, *op. cit.*, pp. 160–61, 171 ff., 188.

22. *Ibid.*, pp. 179–87; Merriam, *op. cit.*, pp. 21–24.

23. "City of the Sun" in Henry Morley's *Ideal Commonwealths* (1885), pp. 217–63; Joyce O. Hertzler, *The History of Utopian Thought*, pp. 156–65. Cf. Guthrie, *Socialism before the French Revolution* (1907), chaps. iv–v; and Chapter Eight of this text.

24. "The New Atlantis," in Morley's *Ideal Commonwealths*, pp. 171–213; cf. Harald Höffding, *History of Modern Philosophy*, translated by B. E. Meyer (1900), pp. 184–206; Gooch, *Political Thought from Bacon to Halifax* (1914), pp. 22–34.

25. The contrary view is maintained by John N. Figgis, *The Divine Right of Kings* (1914), pp. 1–2. Figgis points out the important fact that Filmer's "patriarchal conception of society is far from being of the essence of the theory of the Divine Right of Kings; it is merely the best argument by which it is supported" (*op. cit.*, p. 150). For Filmer, see pp. 8, 146 ff., 252.

Figgis's above-mentioned work contains incomparably the ablest and most sympathetic interpretation of the divine right theory. While few are likely to be converted to Figgis's view, there can be no question but that one who has not read his exposition is unqualified to discuss the subject.

26. Cf. Dunning, *op. cit.*, chap. vii.

27. Cf. Masson, *Life of Milton* (1859–94); Gooch, *English Democratic Ideas in the Seventeenth Century* (2nd ed., 1927), pp. 177–83, 241–45, 314–19.

28. A. E. Levett, "James Harrington," in Hearnshaw, *op. cit.*, p. 188.

29. Thomas Hobbes, *Philosophical Rudiments concerning Government and Society* (Molesworth ed.), chap. i, secs. 11–12; *Leviathan* (A. R. Waller ed., 1904), chap. xiii. **30.** Hobbes, *Philosophical Rudiments*, chap. i, sec. 2.

31. Hobbes, *Leviathan*, chaps. xi, xvii.

32. Graham Wallas, *The Great Society* (1914), p. 191.

33. Hobbes, *op. cit.*, chap. xvii.

34. Atger's analysis of Hobbes's theory of the social contract is found in *op. cit.*, pp. 162–84; cf. also Leslie Stephens, *Hobbes*; Graham, *English Political Philosophy*, pp. 1–49; Dunning, *A History of Political Theories from Luther to Montesquieu* (1905), p. 290. **35.** Dunning, *op. cit.*, pp. 318–19.

36. Pufendorf, *The Law of Nature and of Nations*, translated by Basil Kennett, and annotated by Barbeyrac (London, 1729), Bk. I, chap. ii, pp. 102 ff.; Bk. VII, chap. i, pp. 629 ff.

37. *Merriam, *A History of the Theory of Sovereignty since Rousseau*, pp. 28–30.

38. Spinoza, "A Theological-Political Treatise," in *The Chief Works of Spinoza* (Elwes trans., 1889), chap. xvi.

39. *Ibid.*, chaps. v, xvi; *A Political Treatise*, chap. ii, sec. 15.

40. Spinoza, *op. cit.*, chap. xvi.

41. Cf. F. Pollock, *Spinoza* (2nd ed., 1899); Atger, *op. cit.*, pp. 184–93; Dunning, *op. cit.*, pp. 309–17.

42. Algernon Sidney, *Discourses concerning Government* (3rd ed., 1751), chap. ii, sec. 5, particularly pp. 75 ff.; Scherger, *Evolution of Modern Liberty*, pp. 144–47.

43. Locke, *Two Treatises of Government* (Morley ed., 1884), Bk. II, chap. ii, secs. 6–7; chap. iii, sec. 19; chap. vii, secs. 77, 87; chap. viii, *passim*; chap. ix, secs. 123–24, 127; chap. xi, secs. 135, 138.

44. Scherger, *Evolution of Modern Liberty*, pp. 148–49; cf. Graham, *English Political Philosophy*, pp. 50–87; Atger, *op. cit.*, pp. 204 ff.; and the exhaustive work of Bastide, *John Locke, ses théories politiques* (1907).

45. Even Lovejoy's excellent analysis does not wholly succeed in dispelling the fog in which Rousseau and some of his overeager critics have enfolded his doctrines. There can be little doubt, however, that Lovejoy is right in saying that Dunning misinterpreted Rousseau. A. O. Lovejoy, "The Supposed Primitivism of Rousseau's *Discourse on Inequality*," *MP*, vol. xxi (1923), pp. 165–86.

46. *Si le rétablissement des sciences et des arts a contribué à épurer les mœurs* (1750); *Sur l'origine de l'inégalité parmi les hommes* (1755). For a recent translation, see Cole, *Rousseau's Social Contract and Discourses*, pp. 129–238.

47. Rousseau, *Social Contract* (Tozer trans.), Bk. I, chap. vi.

48. *Ibid.*, Bk. III, chap. xvi.

49. *Ibid.*, Bk. I, chap. vi; Bk. II, chaps. iii–iv; Green, *The Principles of Political Obligation* (1917), p. 90.

50. Cf. Scherger, *Evolution of Modern Liberty*, Preface, chap. vii, and Part IV. The best recent collection of Rousseau's social and political philosophy in French is Vaughan's edition of *The Political Writings of Jean Jacques Rousseau* (1915); the *Discourses* and the *Social Contract* appear now in an excellent translation by Cole in the Everyman's Library series, the introduction of which contains a good bibliographic note; Tozer's translation of the *Social Contract* is a classic, as well as his excellent introduction; the *Émile* also appears in an English translation in the Everyman's Library series. Bosanquet's *Philosophical Theory of the State* contains one of the best critical analyses of Rousseau's political theories. Another critical analysis is Dunning's "The Political Theories of Jean Jacques Rousseau" in *PSQ* (1909), and Lovejoy's article (note 45) is a penetrating critique of Dunning as well as a great aid toward the understanding of many inconsistencies in Rousseau's writings. Atger's analysis of Rousseau's version of the social contract is to be found in *L'Histoire des doctrines du contrat social*, pp. 252–304. Morley's *Rousseau* remains the best biography.

51. Dunning, *op. cit.*, p. 345.

52. Locke, *Second Essay of Civil Government*, sec. 4.

53. *Ibid.*, secs. 124–26.   54. *Ibid.*, secs. 95, 99.   55. *Ibid.*, secs. 123, 124.

56. *Ibid.*, secs. 134–38.   57. *Ibid.*, sec. 211.   58. *Ibid.*, secs. 212, 221.

59. David Hume, *Treatise of Human Nature* (Selbu-Bigge ed., 1928), pp. 493, 494.

60. Hume, *Essays, Moral, Political, and Literary* (1904), vol. i, pp. 114, 115.

61. Dunning, *op. cit.*, pp. 381–82.   62. Hume, *op. cit.*, pp. 445–46.

63. *Ibid.*, pp. 447, 450.   64. *Ibid.*, p. 450.   65. *Ibid.*, p. 456.

CHAPTER XI

1. *Bernard Mandeville, *The Fable of the Bees: or Private Vices, Publick Benefits,* first appeared in 1714, with a Commentary, Critical, Historical and Explanatory, by F. B. Kaye (1924), vol. i, pp. 127–28. Italics ours.

2. *David Hume, " Of the Rise and Progress of the Arts and Sciences," and " Of National Characters," *Essays, Moral, Political and Literary* (first published in 1741 and 1742).

3. *Ibid.,* pp. 208–10.   4. *Ibid.,* p. 212.   5. *Ibid.,* pp. 120–22, 215.

6. *Baron de Montesquieu, *The Spirit of Laws,* translated by Thomas Nugent (1909), vol. i, Bk. XXI, chap. ii.

7. *Ibid.,* chap. v.   8. *Ibid.,* vol. i, Bk. XX, chap. i; Bk. VII, chap. i.

9. *McQuilkin DeGrange, introductory note in *Turgot on the Progress of the Human Mind* (1929), p. 3; Appendix, p. 21.

10. This is clearly indicated in the following fragment from the outline of his " Political Geography ":

" Digression sur les climats; combien leur influence est ignorée. Danger qu'il y aurait à faire usage du principe trop adopté sur cette influence. Fausses applications qu'on en a faites au caractère des peuples et de leurs langages; à la vivacité de l'imagination, à la pluralité des femmes, à la servitude des Asiatiques. Vraies causes de ces effets. Nécessité d'avoir epuisé les causes morales avant d'avoir droit d'assurer quelque chose de l'influence physique des climats . . ." (Turgot, *Oeuvres de Turgot* par M. Eugene Daire, ed. [1844], p. 616).

11. DeGrange, *op. cit.,* p. 6.   12. *Ibid.*   13. *Ibid.,* p. 10.

14. The passage in which this phrase occurs follows: " Tout obstacle qui diminue la communication, et par conséquent la distance qui est un de ces obstacles, fortifie les nuances qui séparent les nations; mais en général les peuples d'un continent se sont mêlés ensemble, du moins médiatement: les Gaulois avec les Germains, ceux-ci, avec les Sarmates, et ainsi jusqu'aux extrémités que de grandes mers ne séparent point. De là ces coûtumes et ces mots communs à des peuples fort eloignés et fort différents. Il semble que, m'imaginant comme des bandes colorées qui traversent en tout sens toutes les nations d'un continent, je vois les langues, les mœurs, les figures mêmes, former une suite de dégradations sensibles; chaque nation est la nuance entre les nations ses voisines. Tantôt toutes les nations se mêlent, tantôt l'une porte à l'autre ce qu'elle a elle-même reçu " (Turgot, *op. cit.,* p. 631).

15. DeGrange, *op. cit.,* pp. 5, 7, 10, 17. Italics ours.

16. Turgot, *Oeuvres,* p. 632.   17. DeGrange, *op. cit.,* p. 5.

18. Another passage bearing on this theme also shows Turgot's astonishing grasp of geographic factors:

". . . Causes du despotisme dans certains pays, tels que l'Asie, etc. 1 La nature du pays et la trop grand facilité des conquêtes par l'étendue des plaines et la distance trop grande des barrières que la nature a misés entre les nations. 2 Le progrès trop rapide de la société dans ces contrées et l'art de conquérir perfectionné avant que l'esprit humain fut assez avancé pour avoir perfectionné l'art de gouverner, avant que les petits États eussent un gouvernement fixe qu'un conquérant put laisser subsister, avant que les peuples eussent former des ligues et s'associer entre eux pour défendre leur liberté, avant que les conquérants trouvassent des peuples déjà policés dont ils fussent obliges d'adopter les mœurs et les lois " (Turgot, *op. cit.,* p. 616).

19. He discusses the relation of " lethargic repose " and conservatism in another passage:

". . . dans ces vastes États despotiques ils s'introduit . . . un despotisme qui s'étend sur les mœurs civiles, qui engourdit encore d'avantage les esprits . . . et met les membres de l'État dans un répos lethargique qui s'oppose à tout changement, par consequent à tout progrès " (*ibid*., p. 639). **20.** *Ibid.*, p. 636.

21. R. D. McKenzie, " The Concept of Dominance and World-Organization," *AJS*, vol. xxxiii, pp. 28–42. **22.** Turgot, *op. cit.*, p. 616.

23. Johann Gottfried von Herder, *Ideen zur Philosophie der Geschichte der Menschheit* (1792), translated by T. Churchill as *Outlines of a Philosophy of the History of Man* (1803), vol. i, Bk. I, chap. vi, p. 33. **24.** *Ibid.*, pp. 30–31.

25. Herder, *op. cit.*, p. 247. **26.** *Ibid.*, p. 441. **27.** *Ibid.*, p. 443.

28. *Ibid.*, p. 36.

29. Barnes, " History, Its Rise and Development," in *EA*, p. 231.

30. *A. H. L. Heeren, *Historical Researches into the Politics, Intercourse, and Trade of the Principal Nations of Antiquity* (1854), vol. i, p. 9.

31. Adam Smith has a valuable chapter on colonization in *The Wealth of Nations* (IV, vii), but he is more concerned with the strictly economic aspects of the process than is Heeren; we can learn from him little about the relation of migration to mental mobility and to social change. His discussions of the differences between Greek and Roman colonies, however, are enlightening.

32. Heeren, *op. cit.*, pp. 302–03.

Name Index for Volumes One and Two

Literary allusions, and names occurring on pages numbered in roman are not indexed. Volume One comprises pages 1 through 422, and Volume Two comprises pages 423 through 790.

Subject Index for Volumes One and Two

Volume One comprises pages 1 through 422, and Volume Two comprises pages 423 through 790.

Inasmuch as a very full Table of Contents has been provided, the Subject Index deals chiefly with matters not clearly recognizable in the section and chapter headings. For a full set of references, the Table of Contents, Name Index, and Subject Index should be used in conjunction.

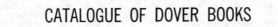
CATALOGUE OF DOVER BOOKS

Social Sciences

SOCIAL THOUGHT FROM LORE TO SCIENCE, H. E. Barnes and H. Becker. An immense survey of sociological thought and ways of viewing, studying, planning, and reforming society from earliest times to the present. Includes thought on society of preliterate peoples, ancient non-Western cultures, and every great movement in Europe, America, and modern Japan. Analyzes hundreds of great thinkers: Plato, Augustine, Bodin, Vico, Montesquieu, Herder, Comte, Marx, etc. Weighs the contributions of utopians, sophists, fascists and communists; economists, jurists, philosophers, ecclesiastics, and every 19th and 20th century school of scientific sociology, anthropology, and social psychology throughout the world. Combines topical, chronological, and regional approaches, treating the evolution of social thought as a process rather than as a series of mere topics. "Impressive accuracy, competence, and discrimination . . . easily the best single survey," Nation. Thoroughly revised, with new material up to 1960. 2 indexes. Over 2200 bibliographical notes. Three volume set. Total of 1586pp. 5⅜ x 8.

T901 Vol I Paperbound **$2.35**
T902 Vol II Paperbound **$2.35**
T903 Vol III Paperbound **$2.35**
The set **$7.05**

FOLKWAYS, William Graham Sumner. A classic of sociology, a searching and thorough examination of patterns of behaviour from primitive, ancient Greek and Judaic, Medieval Christian, African, Oriental, Melanesian, Australian, Islamic, to modern Western societies. Thousands of illustrations of social, sexual, and religious customs, mores, laws, and institutions. Hundreds of categories: Labor, Wealth, Abortion, Primitive Justice, Life Policy, Slavery, Cannibalism, Uncleanness and the Evil Eye, etc. Will extend the horizon of every reader by showing the relativism of his own culture. Prefatory note by A. G. Keller. Introduction by William Lyon Phelps. Bibliography. Index. xiii + 692pp. 5⅜ x 8. T508 Paperbound **$2.49**

PRIMITIVE RELIGION, P. Radin. A thorough treatment by a noted anthropologist of the nature and origin of man's belief in the supernatural and the influences that have shaped religious expression in primitive societies. Ranging from the Arunta, Ashanti, Aztec, Bushman, Crow, Fijian, etc., of Africa, Australia, Pacific Islands, the Arctic, North and South America, Prof. Radin integrates modern psychology, comparative religion, and economic thought with first-hand accounts gathered by himself and other scholars of primitive initiations, training of the shaman, and other fascinating topics. "Excellent," NATURE (London). Unabridged reissue of 1st edition. New author's preface. Bibliographic notes. Index. x + 322pp. 5⅜ x 8.
T393 Paperbound **$1.85**

PRIMITIVE MAN AS PHILOSOPHER, P. Radin. A standard anthropological work covering primitive thought on such topics as the purpose of life, marital relations, freedom of thought, symbolism, death, resignation, the nature of reality, personality, gods, and many others. Drawn from factual material gathered from the Winnebago, Oglala Sioux, Maori, Baganda, Batak, Zuni, among others, it does not distort ideas by removing them from context but interprets strictly within the original framework. Extensive selections of original primitive documents. Bibliography. Index. xviii + 402pp. 5⅜ x 8. T392 Paperbound **$2.25**

A TREATISE ON SOCIOLOGY, THE MIND AND SOCIETY, Vilfredo Pareto. This treatise on human society is one of the great classics of modern sociology. First published in 1916, its careful catalogue of the innumerable manifestations of non-logical human conduct (Book One); the theory of "residues," leading to the premise that sentiment not logic determines human behavior (Book Two), and of "derivations," beliefs derived from desires (Book Three); and the general description of society made up of non-elite and elite, consisting of "foxes" who live by cunning and "lions" who live by force, stirred great controversy. But Pareto's passion for isolation and classification of elements and factors, and his allegiance to scientific method as the key tool for scrutinizing the human situation made his a truly twentieth-century mind and his work a catalytic influence on certain later social commentators. These four volumes (bound as two) require no special training to be appreciated and any reader who wishes to gain a complete understanding of modern sociological theory, regardless of special field of interest, will find them a must. Reprint of revised (corrected) printing of original edition. Translated by Andrew Bongiorno and Arthur Livingston. Index. Bibliography. Appendix containing index-summary of theorems. 48 diagrams. Four volumes bound as two. Total of 2063pp. 5⅜ x 8½. The set Clothbound **$15.00**

THE POLISH PEASANT IN EUROPE AND AMERICA, William I. Thomas, Florian Znaniecki. A seminal sociological study of peasant primary groups (family and community) and the disruptions produced by a new industrial system and immigration to America. The peasant's family, class system, religious and aesthetic attitudes, and economic life are minutely examined and analyzed in hundreds of pages of primary documentation, particularly letters between family members. The disorientation caused by new environments is scrutinized in detail (a 312-page autobiography of an immigrant is especially valuable and revealing) in an attempt to find common experiences and reactions. The famous "Methodological Note" sets forth the principles which guided the authors. When out of print this set has sold for as much as $50. 2nd revised edition. 2 vols. Vol. 1: xv + 1115pp. Vol. 2: 1135pp. Index. 6 x 9.
T478 Clothbound 2 vol. set **$12.50**

Philosophy, Religion

GUIDE TO PHILOSOPHY, C. E. M. Joad. A modern classic which examines many crucial problems which man has pondered through the ages: Does free will exist? Is there plan in the universe? How do we know and validate our knowledge? Such opposed solutions as subjective idealism and realism, chance and teleology, vitalism and logical positivism, are evaluated and the contributions of the great philosophers from the Greeks to moderns like Russell, Whitehead, and others, are considered in the context of each problem. "The finest introduction," BOSTON TRANSCRIPT. Index. Classified bibliography. 592pp. 5⅜ x 8.
T297 Paperbound **$2.00**

HISTORY OF ANCIENT PHILOSOPHY, W. Windelband. One of the clearest, most accurate comprehensive surveys of Greek and Roman philosophy. Discusses ancient philosophy in general, intellectual life in Greece in the 7th and 6th centuries B.C., Thales, Anaximander, Anaximenes, Heraclitus, the Eleatics, Empedocles, Anaxagoras, Leucippus, the Pythagoreans, the Sophists, Socrates, Democritus (20 pages), Plato (50 pages), Aristotle (70 pages), the Peripatetics, Stoics, Epicureans, Sceptics, Neo-platonists, Christian Apologists, etc. 2nd German edition translated by H. E. Cushman. xv + 393pp. 5⅜ x 8.
T357 Paperbound **$1.85**

ILLUSTRATIONS OF THE HISTORY OF MEDIEVAL THOUGHT AND LEARNING, R. L. Poole. Basic analysis of the thought and lives of the leading philosophers and ecclesiastics from the 8th to the 14th century—Abailard, Ockham, Wycliffe, Marsiglio of Padua, and many other great thinkers who carried the torch of Western culture and learning through the "Dark Ages": political, religious, and metaphysical views. Long a standard work for scholars and one of the best introductions to medieval thought for beginners. Index. 10 Appendices. xiii + 327pp. 5⅜ x 8.
T674 Paperbound **$1.85**

PHILOSOPHY AND CIVILIZATION IN THE MIDDLE AGES, M. de Wulf. This semi-popular survey covers aspects of medieval intellectual life such as religion, philosophy, science, the arts, etc. It also covers feudalism vs. Catholicism, rise of the universities, mendicant orders, monastic centers, and similar topics. Unabridged. Bibliography. Index. viii + 320pp. 5⅜ x 8.
T284 Paperbound **$1.85**

AN INTRODUCTION TO SCHOLASTIC PHILOSOPHY, Prof. M. de Wulf. Formerly entitled SCHOLASTICISM OLD AND NEW, this volume examines the central scholastic tradition from St. Anselm, Albertus Magnus, Thomas Aquinas, up to Suarez in the 17th century. The relation of scholasticism to ancient and medieval philosophy and science in general is clear and easily followed. The second part of the book considers the modern revival of scholasticism, the Louvain position, relations with Kantianism and Positivism. Unabridged. xvi + 271pp. 5⅜ x 8.
T296 Clothbound **$3.50**
T283 Paperbound **$1.75**

A HISTORY OF MODERN PHILOSOPHY, H. Höffding. An exceptionally clear and detailed coverage of western philosophy from the Renaissance to the end of the 19th century. Major and minor men such as Pomponazzi, Bodin, Boehme, Telesius, Bruno, Copernicus, da Vinci, Kepler, Galileo, Bacon, Descartes, Hobbes, Spinoza, Leibniz, Wolff, Locke, Newton, Berkeley, Hume, Erasmus, Montesquieu, Voltaire, Diderot, Rousseau, Lessing, Kant, Herder, Fichte, Schelling, Hegel, Schopenhauer, Comte, Mill, Darwin, Spencer, Hartmann, Lange, and many others, are discussed in terms of theory of knowledge, logic, cosmology, and psychology. Index. 2 volumes, total of 1159pp. 5⅜ x 8.
T117 Vol. 1, Paperbound **$2.00**
T118 Vol. 2, Paperbound **$2.00**

ARISTOTLE, A. E. Taylor. A brilliant, searching non-technical account of Aristotle and his thought written by a foremost Platonist. It covers the life and works of Aristotle; classification of the sciences; logic; first philosophy; matter and form; causes; motion and eternity; God; physics; metaphysics; and similar topics. Bibliography. New Index compiled for this edition. 128pp. 5⅜ x 8.
T280 Paperbound **$1.00**

THE SYSTEM OF THOMAS AQUINAS, M. de Wulf. Leading Neo-Thomist, one of founders of University of Louvain, gives concise exposition to central doctrines of Aquinas, as a means toward determining his value to modern philosophy, religion. Formerly "Medieval Philosophy Illustrated from the System of Thomas Aquinas." Trans. by E. Messenger. Introduction. 151pp. 5⅜ x 8.
T568 Paperbound **$1.25**

LEIBNIZ, H. W. Carr. Most stimulating middle-level coverage of basic philosophical thought of Leibniz. Easily understood discussion, analysis of major works: "Theodicy," "Principles of Nature and Grace," "Monadology"; Leibniz's influence; intellectual growth; correspondence; disputes with Bayle, Malebranche, Newton; importance of his thought today, with reinterpretation in modern terminology. "Power and mastery," London Times. Bibliography. Index. 26pp. 5⅜ x 8.
T624 Paperbound **$1.35**

CATALOGUE OF DOVER BOOKS

AN ESSAY CONCERNING HUMAN UNDERSTANDING, John Locke. Edited by A. C. Fraser. Unabridged reprinting of definitive edition; only complete edition of "Essay" in print. Marginal analyses of almost every paragraph; hundreds of footnotes; authoritative 140-page biographical, critical, historical prolegomena. Indexes. 1170pp. 5⅜ x 8.
T530 Vol. 1 (Books 1, 2) Paperbound **$2.25**
T531 Vol. 2 (Books 3, 4) Paperbound **$2.25**
2 volume set **$4.50**

THE PHILOSOPHY OF HISTORY, G. W. F. Hegel. One of the great classics of western thought which reveals Hegel's basic principle: that history is not chance but a rational process, the realization of the Spirit of Freedom. Ranges from the oriental cultures of subjective thought to the classical subjective cultures, to the modern absolute synthesis where spiritual and secular may be reconciled. Translation and introduction by J. Sibree. Introduction by C. Hegel. Special introduction for this edition by Prof. Carl Friedrich. xxxix + 447pp. 5⅜ x 8.
T112 Paperbound **$2.00**

THE PHILOSOPHY OF HEGEL, W. T. Stace. The first detailed analysis of Hegel's thought in English, this is especially valuable since so many of Hegel's works are out of print. Dr. Stace examines Hegel's debt to Greek idealists and the 18th century and then proceeds to a careful description and analysis of Hegel's first principles, categories, reason, dialectic method, his logic, philosophy of nature and spirit, etc. Index. Special 14 x 20 chart of Hegelian system. x + 526pp. 5⅜ x 8.
T254 Paperbound **$2.25**

THE WILL TO BELIEVE and HUMAN IMMORTALITY, W. James. Two complete books bound as one. THE WILL TO BELIEVE discusses the interrelations of belief, will, and intellect in man; chance vs. determinism, free will vs. determinism, free will vs. fate, pluralism vs. monism; the philosophies of Hegel and Spencer, and more. HUMAN IMMORTALITY examines the question of survival after death and develops an unusual and powerful argument for immortality. Two prefaces. Index. Total of 429pp. 5⅜ x 8.
T291 Paperbound **$2.45**

THE WORLD AND THE INDIVIDUAL, Josiah Royce. Only major effort by an American philosopher to interpret nature of things in systematic, comprehensive manner. Royce's formulation of an absolute voluntarism remains one of the original and profound solutions to the problems involved. Part One, Four Historical Conceptions of Being, inquires into first principles, true meaning and place of individuality. Part Two, Nature, Man, and the Moral Order, is application of first principles to problems concerning religion, evil, moral order. Introduction by J. E. Smith, Yale Univ. Index. 1070pp. 5⅜ x 8.
T561 Vol. 1 Paperbound **$2.75**
T562 Vol. 2 Paperbound **$2.75**
Two volume set **$5.50**

THE PHILOSOPHICAL WRITINGS OF PEIRCE, edited by J. Buchler. This book (formerly THE PHILOSOPHY OF PEIRCE) is a carefully integrated exposition of Peirce's complete system composed of selections from his own work. Symbolic logic, scientific method, theory of signs, pragmatism, epistemology, chance, cosmology, ethics, and many other topics are treated by one of the greatest philosophers of modern times. This is the only inexpensive compilation of his key ideas. xvi + 386pp. 5⅜ x 8.
T217 Paperbound **$2.00**

EXPERIENCE AND NATURE, John Dewey. An enlarged, revised edition of the Paul Carus lectures which Dewey delivered in 1925. It covers Dewey's basic formulation of the problem of knowledge, with a full discussion of other systems, and a detailing of his own concepts of the relationship of external world, mind, and knowledge. Starts with a thorough examination of the philosophical method; examines the interrelationship of experience and nature; analyzes experience on basis of empirical naturalism, the formulation of law, role of language and social factors in knowledge; etc. Dewey's treatment of central problems in philosophy is profound but extremely easy to follow. ix + 448pp. 5⅜ x 8.
T471 Paperbound **$2.00**

THE PHILOSOPHICAL WORKS OF DESCARTES. The definitive English edition of all the major philosophical works and letters of René Descartes. All of his revolutionary insights, from his famous "Cogito ergo sum" to his detailed account of contemporary science and his astonishingly fruitful concept that all phenomena of the universe (except mind) could be reduced to clear laws by the use of mathematics. An excellent source for the thought of men like Hobbes, Arnauld, Gassendi, etc., who were Descarte's contemporaries. Translated by E. S. Haldane and G. Ross. Introductory notes. Index. Total of 842pp. 5⅜ x 8.
T71 Vol. 1, Paperbound **$2.00**
T72 Vol. 2, Paperbound **$2.00**

THE CHIEF WORKS OF SPINOZA. An unabridged reprint of the famous Bohn edition containing all of Spinoza's most important works: Vol. I: The Theologico-Political Treatise and the Political Treatise. Vol. II: On The Improvement of Understanding, The Ethics, Selected Letters. Profound and enduring ideas on God, the universe, pantheism, society, religion, the state, democracy, the mind, emotions, freedom and the nature of man, which influenced Goethe, Hegel, Schelling, Coleridge, Whitehead, and many others. Introduction. 2 volumes. 826pp. 5⅜ x 8.
T249 Vol. I, Paperbound **$1.50**
T250 Vol. II, Paperbound **$1.50**

CATALOGUE OF DOVER BOOKS

THE SENSE OF BEAUTY, G. Santayana. A revelation of the beauty of language as well as an important philosophic treatise, this work studies the "why, when, and how beauty appears, what conditions an object must fulfill to be beautiful, what elements of our nature make us sensible of beauty, and what the relation is between the constitution of the object and the excitement of our susceptibility." "It is doubtful if a better treatment of the subject has since been published," PEABODY JOURNAL. Index. ix + 275pp. 5⅜ x 8.
T238 Paperbound **$1.00**

PROBLEMS OF ETHICS, Moritz Schlick. The renowned leader of the "Vienna Circle" applies the logical positivist approach to a wide variety of ethical problems: the source and means of attaining knowledge, the formal and material characteristics of the good, moral norms and principles, absolute vs. relative values, free will and responsibility, comparative importance of pleasure and suffering as ethical values, etc. Disarmingly simple and straightforward despite complexity of subject. First English translation, authorized by author before his death, of a thirty-year old classic. Translated and with an introduction by David Rynin. Index. Foreword by Prof. George P. Adams. xxi + 209pp. 5⅜ x 8.   T946 Paperbound **$1.45**

AN INTRODUCTION TO EXISTENTIALISM, Robert G. Olson. A new and indispensable guide to one of the major thought systems of our century, the movement that is central to the thinking of some of the most creative figures of the past hundred years. Stresses Heidegger and Sartre, with careful and objective examination of the existentialist position, values—freedom of choice, individual dignity, personal love, creative effort—and answers to the eternal questions of the human condition. Scholarly, unbiased, analytic, unlike most studies of this difficult subject, Prof. Olson's book is aimed at the student of philosophy as well as at the reader with no formal training who is looking for an absorbing, accessible, and thorough introduction to the basic texts. Index. xv + 221pp. 5⅜ x 8½.   T55 Paperbound **$1.45**

SYMBOLIC LOGIC, C. I. Lewis and C. H. Langford. Since first publication in 1932, this has been among most frequently cited works on symbolic logic. Still one of the best introductions both for beginners and for mathematicians, philosophers. First part covers basic topics which easily lend themselves to beginning study. Second part is rigorous, thorough development of logistic method, examination of some of most difficult and abstract aspects of symbolic logic, including modal logic, logical paradoxes, many-valued logic, with Prof. Lewis' own contributions. 2nd revised (corrected) edition. 3 appendices, one new to this edition. 524pp. 5⅜ x 8.   S170 Paperbound **$2.00**

WHITEHEAD'S PHILOSOPHY OF CIVILIZATION, A. H. Johnson. A leading authority on Alfred North Whitehead synthesizes the great philosopher's thought on civilization, scattered throughout various writings, into unified whole. Analysis of Whitehead's general definition of civilization, his reflections on history and influences on its development, his religion, including his analysis of Christianity, concept of solitariness as first requirement of personal religion, and so on. Other chapters cover views on minority groups, society, civil liberties, education. Also critical comments on Whitehead's philosophy. Written with general reader in mind. A perceptive introduction to important area of the thought of a leading philosopher of our century. Revised index and bibliography. xii + 211pp. 5⅜ x 8½.
T996 Paperbound **$1.50**

WHITEHEAD'S THEORY OF REALITY, A. H. Johnson. Introductory outline of Whitehead's theory of actual entities, the heart of his philosophy of reality, followed by his views on nature of God, philosophy of mind, theory of value (truth, beauty, goodness and their opposites), analyses of other philosophers, attitude toward science. A perspicacious lucid introduction by author of dissertation on Whitehead, written under the subject's supervision at Harvard. Good basic view for beginning students of philosophy and for those who are simply interested in important contemporary ideas. Revised index and bibliography. xiii + 267pp. 5⅜ x 8½.
T989 Paperbound **$1.50**

MIND AND THE WORLD-ORDER, C. I. Lewis. Building upon the work of Peirce, James, and Dewey, Professor Lewis outlines a theory of knowledge in terms of "conceptual pragmatism." Dividing truth into abstract mathematical certainty and empirical truth, the author demonstrates that the traditional understanding of the a priori must be abandoned. Detailed analyses of philosophy, metaphysics, method, the "given" in experience, knowledge of objects, nature of the a priori, experience and order, and many others. Appendices. xiv + 446pp. 5⅜ x 8.   T359 Paperbound **$2.25**

SCEPTICISM AND ANIMAL FAITH, G. Santayana. To eliminate difficulties in the traditional theory of knowledge, Santayana distinguishes between the independent existence of objects and the essence our mind attributes to them. Scepticism is thereby established as a form of belief, and animal faith is shown to be a necessary condition of knowledge. Belief, classical idealism, intuition, memory, symbols, literary psychology, and much more, discussed with unusual clarity and depth. Index. xii + 314pp. 5⅜ x 8.   T235 Clothbound **$3.50**
T236 Paperbound **$1.50**

LANGUAGE AND MYTH, E. Cassirer. Analyzing the non-rational thought processes which go to make up culture, Cassirer demonstrates that beneath both language and myth there lies a dominant unconscious "grammar" of experience whose categories and canons are not those of logical thought. His analyses of seemingly diverse phenomena such as Indian metaphysics, the Melanesian "mana," the Naturphilosophie of Schelling, modern poetry, etc., are profound without being pedantic. Introduction and translation by Susanne Langer. Index. x + 103pp.
T51 Paperbound **$1.25**
⅜ x 8.

CATALOGUE OF DOVER BOOKS

THE ANALYSIS OF MATTER, Bertrand Russell. A classic which has retained its importance in understanding the relation between modern physical theory and human perception. Logical analysis of physics, prerelativity physics, causality, scientific inference, Weyl's theory, tensors, invariants and physical interpretations, periodicity, and much more is treated with Russell's usual brilliance. "Masterly piece of clear thinking and clear writing," NATION AND ATHENAEUM. "Most thorough treatment of the subject," THE NATION. Introduction. Index. 8 figures. viii + 408pp. 5⅜ x 8. S231 Paperbound **$1.95**

CONCEPTUAL THINKING (A LOGICAL INQUIRY), S. Körner. Discusses origin, use of general concepts on which language is based, and the light they shed on basic philosophical questions. Rigorously examines how different concepts are related; how they are linked to experience; problems in the field of contact between exact logical, mathematical, and scientific concepts, and the inexactness of everyday experience (studied at length). This work elaborates many new approaches to the traditional problems of philosophy—epistemology, value theories, metaphysics, aesthetics, morality. "Rare originality . . . brings a new rigour into philosophical argument," Philosophical Quarterly. New corrected second edition. Index. vii + 301pp. 5⅜ x 8. T516 Paperbound **$1.75**

INTRODUCTION TO SYMBOLIC LOGIC, S. Langer. No special knowledge of math required — probably the clearest book ever written on symbolic logic, suitable for the layman, general scientist, and philosopher. You start with simple symbols and advance to a knowledge of the Boole-Schroeder and Russell-Whitehead systems. Forms, logical structure, classes, the calculus of propositions, logic of the syllogism, etc., are all covered. "One of the clearest and simplest introductions," MATHEMATICS GAZETTE. Second enlarged, revised edition. 368pp. 5⅜ x 8. S164 Paperbound **$1.75**

LANGUAGE, TRUTH AND LOGIC, A. J. Ayer. A clear, careful analysis of the basic ideas of Logical Positivism. Building on the work of Schlick, Russell, Carnap, and the Viennese School, Mr. Ayer develops a detailed exposition of the nature of philosophy, science, and metaphysics; the Self and the World; logic and common sense, and other philosophic concepts. An aid to clarity of thought as well as the first full-length development of Logical Positivism in English. Introduction by Bertrand Russell. Index. 160pp. 5⅜ x 8. T10 Paperbound **$1.25**

ESSAYS IN EXPERIMENTAL LOGIC, J. Dewey. Based upon the theory that knowledge implies a judgment which in turn implies an inquiry, these papers consider the inquiry stage in terms of: the relationship of thought and subject matter, antecedents of thought, data and meanings. 3 papers examine Bertrand Russell's thought, while 2 others discuss pragmatism and a final essay presents a new theory of the logic of values. Index. viii + 444pp. 5⅜ x 8. T73 Paperbound **$1.95**

TRAGIC SENSE OF LIFE, M. de Unamuno. The acknowledged masterpiece of one of Spain's most influential thinkers. Between the despair at the inevitable death of man and all his works and the desire for something better, Unamuno finds that "saving incertitude" that alone can console us. This dynamic appraisal of man's faith in God and in himself has been called "a masterpiece" by the ENCYCLOPAEDIA BRITANNICA. xxx + 332pp. 5⅜ x 8. T257 Paperbound **$2.00**

HISTORY OF DOGMA, A. Harnack. Adolph Harnack, who died in 1930, was perhaps the greatest Church historian of all time. In this epoch-making history, which has never been surpassed in comprehensiveness and wealth of learning, he traces the development of the authoritative Christian doctrinal system from its first crystallization in the 4th century down through the Reformation, including also a brief survey of the later developments through the Infallibility decree of 1870. He reveals the enormous influence of Greek thought on the early Fathers, and discusses such topics as the Apologists, the great councils, Manichaeism, the historical position of Augustine, the medieval opposition to indulgences, the rise of Protestantism, the relations of Luther's doctrines with modern tendencies of thought, and much more. "Monumental work; still the most valuable history of dogma . . . luminous analysis of the problems . . . abounds in suggestion and stimulus and can be neglected by no one who desires to understand the history of thought in this most important field," Dutcher's Guide to Historical Literature. Translated by Neil Buchanan. Index. Unabridged reprint in 4 volumes. Vol I: Beginnings to the Gnostics and Marcion. Vol II & III: 2nd century to the 4th century Fathers. Vol IV & V: 4th century Councils to the Carlovingian Renaissance. Vol VI & VII: Period of Clugny (c. 1000) to the Reformation, and after. Total of cii + 2407pp. 5⅜ x 8.

T904 Vol I	Paperbound	**$2.50**
T905 Vol II & III	Paperbound	**$2.50**
T906 Vol IV & V	Paperbound	**$2.50**
T907 Vol VI & VII	Paperbound	**$2.50**
	The set	**$10.00**

THE GUIDE FOR THE PERPLEXED, Maimonides. One of the great philosophical works of all time and a necessity for everyone interested in the philosophy of the Middle Ages in the Jewish, Christian, and Moslem traditions. Maimonides develops a common meeting-point for the Old Testament and the Aristotelian thought which pervaded the medieval world. His ideas and methods predate such scholastics as Aquinas and Scotus and throw light on the entire problem of philosophy or science vs. religion. 2nd revised edition. Complete unabridged Friedländer translation. 55 page introduction to Maimonides's life, period, etc., with a important summary of the GUIDE. Index. lix + 414pp. 5⅜ x 8. T351 Paperbound **$2.**

Americana

THE EYES OF DISCOVERY, J. Bakeless. A vivid reconstruction of how unspoiled America appeared to the first white men. Authentic and enlightening accounts of Hudson's landing in New York, Coronado's trek through the Southwest; scores of explorers, settlers, trappers, soldiers. America's pristine flora, fauna, and Indians in every region and state in fresh and unusual new aspects. "A fascinating view of what the land was like before the first highway went through," Time. 68 contemporary illustrations, 39 newly added in this edition. Index. Bibliography. x + 500pp. 5⅜ x 8.   T761 Paperbound **$2.00**

AUDUBON AND HIS JOURNALS, J. J. Audubon. A collection of fascinating accounts of Europe and America in the early 1800's through Audubon's own eyes. Includes the Missouri River Journals —an eventful trip through America's untouched heartland, the Labrador Journals, the European Journals, the famous "Episodes", and other rare Audubon material, including the descriptive chapters from the original letterpress edition of the "Ornithological Studies", omitted in all later editions. Indispensable for ornithologists, naturalists, and all lovers of Americana and adventure. 70-page biography by Audubon's granddaughter. 38 illustrations. Index. Total of 1106pp. 5⅜ x 8.

T675 Vol I Paperbound **$2.25**
T676 Vol II Paperbound **$2.25**
The set **$4.50**

TRAVELS OF WILLIAM BARTRAM, edited by Mark Van Doren. The first inexpensive illustrated edition of one of the 18th century's most delightful books is an excellent source of first-hand material on American geography, anthropology, and natural history. Many descriptions of early Indian tribes are our only source of information on them prior to the infiltration of the white man. "The mind of a scientist with the soul of a poet," John Livingston Lowes. 13 original illustrations and maps. Edited with an introduction by Mark Van Doren. 448pp. 5⅜ x 8.

T13 Paperbound **$2.00**

GARRETS AND PRETENDERS: A HISTORY OF BOHEMIANISM IN AMERICA, A. Parry. The colorful and fantastic history of American Bohemianism from Poe to Kerouac. This is the only complete record of hoboes, cranks, starving poets, and suicides. Here are Pfaff, Whitman, Crane, Bierce, Pound, and many others. New chapters by the author and by H. T. Moore bring this thorough and well-documented history down to the Beatniks. "An excellent account," N. Y. Times. Scores of cartoons, drawings, and caricatures. Bibliography. Index. xxviii + 421pp. 5⅝ x 8⅜.   T708 Paperbound **$1.95**

THE EXPLORATION OF THE COLORADO RIVER AND ITS CANYONS, J. W. Powell. The thrilling first-hand account of the expedition that filled in the last white space on the map of the United States. Rapids, famine, hostile Indians, and mutiny are among the perils encountered as the unknown Colorado Valley reveals its secrets. This is the only uncut version of Major Powell's classic of exploration that has been printed in the last 60 years. Includes later reflections and subsequent expedition. 250 illustrations, new map. 400pp. 5⅝ x 8⅜.

T94 Paperbound **$2.00**

THE JOURNAL OF HENRY D. THOREAU, Edited by Bradford Torrey and Francis H. Allen. Henry Thoreau is not only one of the most important figures in American literature and social thought; his voluminous journals (from which his books emerged as selections and crystallizations) constitute both the longest, most sensitive record of personal internal development and a most penetrating description of a historical moment in American culture. This present set, which was first issued in fourteen volumes, contains Thoreau's entire Journals from 1837 to 1862, with the exception of the lost years which were found only recently. We are reissuing it, complete and unabridged, with a new introduction by Walter Harding, Secretary of the Thoreau Society. Fourteen volumes reissued in two volumes. Foreword by Henry Seidel Canby. Total of 1888pp. 8⅜ x 12¼.   T312-3 Two volume set, Clothbound **$20.00**

GAMES AND SONGS OF AMERICAN CHILDREN, collected by William Wells Newell. A remarkable collection of 190 games with songs that accompany many of them; cross references to show similarities, differences among them; variations; musical notation for 38 songs. Textual discussions show relations with folk-drama and other aspects of folk tradition. Grouped into categories for ready comparative study: Love-games, histories, playing at work, human life, bird and beast, mythology, guessing-games, etc. New introduction covers relations of songs and dances to timeless heritage of folklore, biographical sketch of Newell, other pertinent data. A good source of inspiration for those in charge of groups of children and a valuable reference for anthropologists, sociologists, psychiatrists. Introduction by Carl Withers. New indexes of first lines, games. 5⅜ x 8½. xii + 242pp.   T354 Paperbound **$1.65**

GARDNER'S PHOTOGRAPHIC SKETCH BOOK OF THE CIVIL WAR, Alexander Gardner. The first published collection of Civil War photographs, by one of the two or three most famous photographers of the era, outstandingly reproduced from the original positives. Scenes of crucial battles: Appomattox, Manassas, Mechanicsville, Bull Run, Yorktown, Fredericksburg, etc. Gettysburg immediately after retirement of forces. Battle ruins at Richmond, Petersburg, Gaines'Mill. Prisons, arsenals, a slave pen, fortifications, headquarters, pontoon bridges, soldiers, a field hospital. A unique glimpse into the realities of one of the bloodiest wars in history, with an introductory text to each picture by Gardner himself. Until this edition, there were only five known copies in libraries, and fewer in private hands, one of which sold at auction in 1952 for $425. Introduction by E. F. Bleiler. 100 full page 7 x 10 photographs (original size). 224pp. 8½ x 10¾.   T476 Clothbound **$6.00**

A BIBLIOGRAPHY OF NORTH AMERICAN FOLKLORE AND FOLKSONG, Charles Haywood, Ph.D. The only book that brings together bibliographic information on so wide a range of folklore material. Lists practically everything published about American folksongs, ballads, dances, folk beliefs and practices, popular music, tales, similar material—more than 35,000 titles of books, articles, periodicals, monographs, music publications, phonograph records. Each entry complete with author, title, date and place of publication, arranger and performer of particular examples of folk music, many with Dr. Haywood's valuable criticism, evaluation. Volume I, "The American People," is complete listing of general and regional studies, titles of tales and songs of Negro and non-English speaking groups and where to find them, Occupational Bibliography including sections listing sources of information, folk material on cowboys, riverboat men, 49ers, American characters like Mike Fink, Frankie and Johnnie, John Henry, many more. Volume II, "The American Indian," tells where to find information on dances, myths, songs, ritual of more than 250 tribes in U.S., Canada. A monumental product of 10 years' labor, carefully classified for easy use. "All students of this subject . . . will find themselves in debt to Professor Haywood," Stith Thompson, in American Anthropologist. ". . . a most useful and excellent work," Duncan Emrich, Chief Folklore Section, Library of Congress, in "Notes." Corrected, enlarged republication of 1951 edition. New Preface. New index of composers, arrangers, performers. General index of more than 15,000 items. Two volumes. Total of 1301pp. 6⅛ x 9¼.   T797-798 Clothbound **$12.50**

INCIDENTS OF TRAVEL IN YUCATAN, John L. Stephens. One of first white men to penetrate interior of Yucatan tells the thrilling story of his discoveries of 44 cities, remains of once-powerful Maya civilization. Compelling text combines narrative power with historical significance as it takes you through heat, dust, storms of Yucatan; native festivals with brutal bull fights; great ruined temples atop man-made mounds. Countless idols, sculptures, tombs, examples of Mayan taste for rich ornamentation, from gateways to personal trinkets, accurately illustrated, discussed in text. Will appeal to those interested in ancient civilizations, and those who like stories of exploration, discovery, adventure. Republication of last (1843) edition. 124 illustrations by English artist, F. Catherwood. Appendix on Mayan architecture, chronology. Two volume set. Total of xxviii + 927pp.

Vol I T926 Paperbound **$2.00**
Vol II T927 Paperbound **$2.00**
The set **$4.00**

A GENIUS IN THE FAMILY, Hiram Percy Maxim. Sir Hiram Stevens Maxim was known to the public as the inventive genius who created the Maxim gun, automatic sprinkler, and a heavier-than-air plane that got off the ground in 1894. Here, his son reminisces—this is by no means a formal biography—about the exciting and often downright scandalous private life of his brilliant, eccentric father. A warm and winning portrait of a prankish, mischievous, impious personality, a genuine character. The style is fresh and direct, the effect is unadulterated pleasure. "A book of charm and lasting humor . . . belongs on the 'must read' list of all fathers," New York Times. "A truly gorgeous affair," New Statesman and Nation. 17 illustrations, 16 specially for this edition. viii + 108pp. 5⅜ x 8½.   T948 Paperbound **$1.00**

HORSELESS CARRIAGE DAYS, Hiram P. Maxim. The best account of an important technological revolution by one of its leading figures. The delightful and rewarding story of the author's experiments with the exact combustibility of gasoline, stopping and starting mechanisms, carriage design, and engines. Captures remarkably well the flavor of an age of scoffers and rival inventors not above sabotage; of noisy, uncontrollable gasoline vehicles and incredible mobile steam kettles. ". . . historic information and light humor are combined to furnish highly entertaining reading," New York Times. 56 photographs, 12 specially for this edition. xi + 175pp. 5⅜ x 8½.   T964 Paperbound **$1.35**

BODY, BOOTS AND BRITCHES: FOLKTALES, BALLADS AND SPEECH FROM COUNTRY NEW YORK, Harold W. Thompson. A unique collection, discussion of songs, stories, anecdotes, proverbs handed down orally from Scotch-Irish grandfathers, German nurse-maids, Negro workmen, gathered from all over Upper New York State. Tall tales by and about lumbermen and pirates, canalers and injun-fighters, tragic and comic ballads, scores of sayings and proverbs all tied together by an informative, delightful narrative by former president of New York Historical Society. ". . . a sparkling homespun tapestry that every lover of Americana will want to have around the house," Carl Carmer, New York Times. Republication of 1939 edition. 20 line-drawings. Index. Appendix (Sources of material, bibliography). 530pp. 5⅜ x 8½.   T411 Paperbound **$2.0**

Art, History of Art, Antiques, Graphic Arts, Handcrafts

ART STUDENTS' ANATOMY, E. J. Farris. Outstanding art anatomy that uses chiefly living objects for its illustrations. 71 photos of undraped men, women, children are accompanied by carefully labeled matching sketches to illustrate the skeletal system, articulations and movements, bony landmarks, the muscular system, skin, fasciae, fat, etc. 9 x-ray photos show movement of joints. Undraped models are shown in such actions as serving in tennis, drawing a bow in archery, playing football, dancing, preparing to spring and to dive. Also discussed and illustrated are proportions, age and sex differences, the anatomy of the smile, etc. 8 plates by the great early 18th century anatomic illustrator Siegfried Albinus are also included. Glossary. 158 figures, 7 in color. x + 159pp. 5⅝ x 8⅜.   **T744 Paperbound $1.50**

AN ATLAS OF ANATOMY FOR ARTISTS, F Schider. A new 3rd edition of this standard text enlarged by 52 new illustrations of hands, anatomical studies by Cloquet, and expressive life studies of the body by Barcsay. 189 clear, detailed plates offer you precise information of impeccable accuracy. 29 plates show all aspects of the skeleton, with closeups of special areas, while 54 full-page plates, mostly in two colors, give human musculature as seen from four different points of view, with cutaways for important portions of the body. 14 full-page plates provide photographs of hand forms, eyelids, female breasts, and indicate the location of muscles upon models. 59 additional plates show how great artists of the past utilized human anatomy. They reproduce sketches and finished work by such artists as Michelangelo, Leonardo da Vinci, Goya, and 15 others. This is a lifetime reference work which will be one of the most important books in any artist's library. "The standard reference tool," AMERICAN LIBRARY ASSOCIATION. "Excellent," AMERICAN ARTIST. Third enlarged edition. 189 plates, 647 illustrations. xxvi + 192pp. 7⅞ x 10⅝.   **T241 Clothbound $6.00**

AN ATLAS OF ANIMAL ANATOMY FOR ARTISTS, W. Ellenberger, H. Baum, H. Dittrich. The largest, richest animal anatomy for artists available in English. 99 detailed anatomical plates of such animals as the horse, dog, cat, lion, deer, seal, kangaroo, flying squirrel, cow, bull, goat, monkey, hare, and bat. Surface features are clearly indicated, while progressive beneath-the-skin pictures show musculature, tendons, and bone structure. Rest and action are exhibited in terms of musculature and skeletal structure and detailed cross-sections are given for heads and important features. The animals chosen are representative of specific families so that a study of these anatomies will provide knowledge of hundreds of related species. "Highly recommended as one of the very few books on the subject worthy of being used as an authoritative guide," DESIGN. "Gives a fundamental knowledge," AMERICAN ARTIST. Second revised, enlarged edition with new plates from Cuvier, Stubbs, etc. 288 illustrations. 153pp. 11⅜ x 9.   **T82 Clothbound $6.00**

THE HUMAN FIGURE IN MOTION, Eadweard Muybridge. The largest selection in print of Muybridge's famous high-speed action photos of the human figure in motion. 4789 photographs illustrate 162 different actions: men, women, children—mostly undraped—are shown walking, running, carrying various objects, sitting, lying down, climbing, throwing, arising, and performing over 150 other actions. Some actions are shown in as many as 150 photographs each. All in all there are more than 500 action strips in this enormous volume, series shots taken at shutter speeds of as high as 1/6000th of a second! These are not posed shots, but true stopped motion. They show bone and muscle in situations that the human eye is not fast enough to capture. Earlier, smaller editions of these prints have brought $40 and more on the out-of-print market. "A must for artists," ART IN FOCUS. "An unparalleled dictionary of action for all artists," AMERICAN ARTIST. 390 full-page plates, with 4789 photographs. Printed on heavy glossy stock. Reinforced binding with headbands. xxi + 390pp. 7⅞ x 10⅝.   **T204 Clothbound $10.00**

ANIMALS IN MOTION, Eadweard Muybridge. This is the largest collection of animal action photos in print. 34 different animals (horses, mules, oxen, goats, camels, pigs, cats, guanacos, lions, gnus, deer, monkeys, eagles—and 21 others) in 132 characteristic actions. The horse alone is shown in more than 40 different actions. All 3919 photographs are taken in series at speeds up to 1/6000th of a second. The secrets of leg motion, spinal patterns, head movements, strains and contortions shown nowhere else are captured. You will see exactly how a lion sets his foot down; how an elephant's knees are like a human's—and how they differ; the position of a kangaroo's legs in mid-leap; how an ostrich's head bobs; details of the flight of birds—and thousands of facets of motion only the fastest cameras can catch. Photographed from domestic animals and animals in the Philadelphia zoo, it contains neither semiposed artificial shots nor distorted telephoto shots taken under adverse conditions. Artists, biologists, decorators, cartoonists, will find this book indispensable for understanding animals in motion. "A really marvelous series of plates," NATURE (London). "The dry plate's most spectacular early use was by Eadweard Muybridge," LIFE. 3919 photographs; 380 full pages of plates. 440pp. Printed on heavy glossy paper. Deluxe binding with headbands. 7⅞ x 10⅝.   **T203 Clothbound $10.00**

CATALOGUE OF DOVER BOOKS

THE HISTORY AND TECHNIQUE OF LETTERING, A. Nesbitt. The only thorough inexpensive history of letter forms from the point of view of the artist. Mr. Nesbitt covers every major development in lettering from the ancient Egyptians to the present and illustrates each development with a complete alphabet. Such masters as Baskerville, Bell, Bodoni, Caslon, Koch, Kilian, Morris, Garamont, Jenson, and dozens of others are analyzed in terms of artistry and historical development. The author also presents a 65-page practical course in lettering, besides the full historical text. 89 complete alphabets; 165 additional lettered specimens. xvii + 300pp. 5⅜ x 8. **T427 Paperbound $2.00**

FOOT-HIGH LETTERS: A GUIDE TO LETTERING (A PRACTICAL SYLLABUS FOR TEACHERS), M. Price. A complete alphabet of Classic Roman letters, each a foot high, each on a separate 16 x 22 plate—perfect for use in lettering classes. In addition to an accompanying description, each plate also contains 9 two-inch-high forms of letter in various type faces, such as "Caslon," "Empire," "Onyx," and "Neuland," illustrating the many possible derivations from the standard classical forms. One plate contains 21 additional forms of the letter A. The fully illustrated 16-page syllabus by Mr. Price, formerly of the Pratt Institute and the Rhode Island School of Design, contains dozens of useful suggestions for student and teacher alike. An indispensable teaching aid. Extensively revised. 16-page syllabus and 30 plates in slip cover, 16 x 22. **T239 Clothbound $6.00**

THE STYLES OF ORNAMENT, Alexander Speltz. Largest collection of ornaments in print— 3765 illustrations of prehistoric, Lombard, Gothic, Frank, Romanesque, Mohammedan, Renaissance, Polish, Swiss, Rococo, Sheraton, Empire, U. S. Colonial, etc., ornament. Gargoyles, dragons, columns, necklaces, urns, friezes, furniture, buildings, keyholes, tapestries, fantastic animals, armor, religious objects, much more, all in line. Reproduce any one free. Index. Bibliography. 400 plates. 656pp. 5⅝ x 8⅜. **T557 Paperbound $2.50**

HANDBOOK OF DESIGNS AND DEVICES, C. P. Hornung. This unique book is indispensable to the designer, commercial artist, and hobbyist. It is not a textbook but a working collection of 1836 basic designs and variations, carefully reproduced, which may be used without permission. Variations of circle, line, band, triangle, square, cross, diamond, swastika, pentagon, octagon, hexagon, star, scroll, interlacement, shields, etc. Supplementary notes on the background and symbolism of the figures. "A necessity to every designer who would be original without having to labor heavily," ARTIST AND ADVERTISER. 204 plates. 240pp. 5⅜ x 8. **T125 Paperbound $1.90**

THE UNIVERSAL PENMAN, George Bickham. This beautiful book, which first appeared in 1743, is the largest collection of calligraphic specimens, flourishes, alphabets, and calligraphic illustrations ever published. 212 full-page plates are drawn from the work of such 18th century masters of English roundhand as Dove, Champion, Bland, and 20 others. They contain 22 complete alphabets, over 2,000 flourishes, and 122 illustrations, each drawn with a stylistic grace impossible to describe. This book is invaluable to anyone interested in the beauties of calligraphy, or to any artist, hobbyist, or craftsman who wishes to use the very best ornamental handwriting and flourishes for decorative purposes. Commercial artists, advertising artists, have found it unexcelled as a source of material suggesting quality. "An essential part of any art library, and a book of permanent value," AMERICAN ARTIST. 212 plates. 224pp. 9 x 13¾. **T20 Clothbound $10.00**

1800 WOODCUTS BY THOMAS BEWICK AND HIS SCHOOL. Prepared by Dover's editorial staff, this is the largest collection of woodcuts by Bewick and his school ever compiled. Contains the complete engravings from all his major works and a wide range of illustrations from lesser-known collections, all photographed from clear copies of the original books and reproduced in line. Carefully and conveniently organized into sections on Nature (animals and birds, scenery and landscapes, plants, insects, etc.), People (love and courtship, social life, school and domestic scenes, misfortunes, costumes, etc.), Business and Trade, and illustrations from primers, fairytales, spelling books, frontispieces, borders, fables and allegories, etc. In addition to technical proficiency and simple beauty, Bewick's work is remarkable as a mode of pictorial symbolism, reflecting rustic tranquility, an atmosphere of rest, simplicity, idyllic contentment. A delight for the eye, an inexhaustible source of illustrative material for art studios, commercial artists, advertising agencies. Individual illustrations (up to 10 for any one use) are copyright free. Classified index. Bibliography and sources. Introduction by Robert Hutchinson. 1800 woodcuts. xiv + 247pp. 9 x 12. **T766 Clothbound $10.00**

A HANDBOOK OF EARLY ADVERTISING ART, C. P. Hornung. The largest collection of copyright-free early advertising art ever compiled. Vol. I contains some 2,000 illustrations of agricultural devices, animals, old automobiles, birds, buildings, Christmas decorations (with 7 Santa Clauses by Nast), allegorical figures, fire engines, horses and vehicles, Indians, portraits, sailing ships, trains, sports, trade cuts — and 30 other categories! Vol. II, devoted to typography, has over 4000 specimens: 600 different Roman, Gothic, Barnum, Old English faces; 630 ornamental type faces; 1115 initials, hundreds of scrolls, flourishes, etc. This third edition is enlarged by 78 additional plates containing all new material. "A remarkable collection," PRINTERS' INK. "A rich contribution to the history of American design," GRAPHIS Volume I, Pictorial. Over 2000 illustrations. xiv + 242pp. 9 x 12. T122 Clothbound $10.￼ Volume II, Typographical. Over 4000 specimens. vii + 312pp. 9 x 12. T123 Clothbound $10￼ Two volume set, T121 Clothbound, only $1￼

Miscellaneous

THE COMPLETE KANO JIU-JITSU (JUDO), H. I. Hancock and K. Higashi. Most comprehensive guide to judo, referred to as outstanding work by Encyclopaedia Britannica. Complete authentic Japanese system of 160 holds and throws, including the most spectacular, fully illustrated with 487 photos. Full text explains leverage, weight centers, pressure points, special tricks, etc.; shows how to protect yourself from almost any manner of attack though your attacker may have the initial advantage of strength and surprise. This authentic Kano system should not be confused with the many American imitations. xii + 500pp. 5⅜ x 8.
T639 Paperbound **$2.00**

THE MEMOIRS OF JACQUES CASANOVA. Splendid self-revelation by history's most engaging scoundrel—utterly dishonest with women and money, yet highly intelligent and observant. Here are all the famous duels, scandals, amours, banishments, thefts, treacheries, and imprisonments all over Europe: a life lived to the fullest and recounted with gusto in one of the greatest autobiographies of all time. What is more, these Memoirs are also one of the most trustworthy and valuable documents we have on the society and culture of the extravagant 18th century. Here are Voltaire, Louis XV, Catherine the Great, cardinals, castrati, pimps, and pawnbrokers—an entire glittering civilization unfolding before you with an unparalleled sense of actuality. Translated by Arthur Machen. Edited by F. A. Blossom. Introduction by Arthur Symons. Illustrated by Rockwell Kent. Total of xlviii + 2216pp. 5⅜ x 8.
T338 Vol I   Paperbound **$2.00**
T339 Vol II   Paperbound **$2.00**
T340 Vol III Paperbound **$2.00**
The set **$6.00**

BARNUM'S OWN STORY, P. T. Barnum. The astonishingly frank and gratifyingly well-written autobiography of the master showman and pioneer publicity man reveals the truth about his early career, his famous hoaxes (such as the Fejee Mermaid and the Woolly Horse), his amazing commercial ventures, his fling in politics, his feuds and friendships, his failures and surprising comebacks. A vast panorama of 19th century America's mores, amusements, and vitality. 66 new illustrations in this edition. xii + 500pp. 5⅜ x 8.
T764 Paperbound **$1.65**

THE STORY OF THE TITANIC AS TOLD BY ITS SURVIVORS, ed. by Jack Winocour. Most significant accounts of most overpowering naval disaster of modern times: all 4 authors were survivors. Includes 2 full-length, unabridged books: "The Loss of the S.S. Titanic," by Laurence Beesley, "The Truth about the Titanic," by Col. Archibald Gracie; 6 pertinent chapters from "Titanic and Other Ships," autobiography of only officer to survive, Second Officer Charles Lightoller; and a short, dramatic account by the Titanic's wireless operator, Harold Bride. 26 illus. 368pp. 5⅜ x 8.
T610 Paperbound **$1.50**

THE PHYSIOLOGY OF TASTE, Jean Anthelme Brillat-Savarin. Humorous, satirical, witty, and personal classic on joys of food and drink by 18th century French politician, litterateur. Treats the science of gastronomy, erotic value of truffles, Parisian restaurants, drinking contests; gives recipes for tunny omelette, pheasant, Swiss fondue, etc. Only modern translation of original French edition. Introduction. 41 illus. 346pp. 5⅝ x 8⅜.
T591 Paperbound **$1.50**

THE ART OF THE STORY-TELLER, M. L. Shedlock. This classic in the field of effective story-telling is regarded by librarians, story-tellers, and educators as the finest and most lucid book on the subject. The author considers the nature of the story, the difficulties of communicating stories to children, the artifices used in story-telling, how to obtain and maintain the effect of the story, and, of extreme importance, the elements to seek and those to avoid in selecting material. A 99-page selection of Miss Shedlock's most effective stories and an extensive bibliography of further material by Eulalie Steinmetz enhance the book's usefulness. xxi + 320pp. 5⅜ x 8.
T635 Paperbound **$1.50**

CREATIVE POWER: THE EDUCATION OF YOUTH IN THE CREATIVE ARTS, Hughes Mearns. In first printing considered revolutionary in its dynamic, progressive approach to teaching the creative arts; now accepted as one of the most effective and valuable approaches yet formulated. Based on the belief that every child has something to contribute, it provides in a stimulating manner invaluable and inspired teaching insights, to stimulate children's latent powers of creative expression in drama, poetry, music, writing, etc. Mearns's methods were developed in his famous experimental classes in creative education at the Lincoln School of Teachers College, Columbia Univ. Named one of the 20 foremost books on education in recent times by National Education Association. New enlarged revised 2nd edition. Introduction. 272pp. 5⅜ x 8.
T490 Paperbound **$1.75**

FREE AND INEXPENSIVE EDUCATIONAL AIDS, T. J. Pepe, Superintendent of Schools, Southbury, Connecticut. An up-to-date listing of over 1500 booklets, films, charts, etc. 5% costs less than 25¢; 1% costs more; 94% is yours for the asking. Use this material privately, or in schools from elementary to college, for discussion, vocational guidance, projects. 59 categories include health, trucking, textiles, language, weather, the blood, office practice, wild life, atomic energy, other important topics. Each item described according to contents, number of pages or running time, level. All material is educationally sound, and without political or company bias. 1st publication. Second, revised edition. Index. 244pp. 5⅜ x 8.
T663 Paperbound **$1.50**

CATALOGUE OF DOVER BOOKS

THE ROMANCE OF WORDS, E. Weekley. An entertaining collection of unusual word-histories that tracks down for the general reader the origins of more than 2000 common words and phrases in English (including British and American slang): discoveries often surprising, often humorous, that help trace vast chains of commerce in products and ideas. There are Arabic trade words, cowboy words, origins of family names, phonetic accidents, curious wanderings, folk-etymologies, etc. Index. xiii + 210pp. 5⅜ x 8. T710 Paperbound **$1.25**

PHRASE AND WORD ORIGINS: A STUDY OF FAMILIAR EXPRESSIONS, A. H. Holt. One of the most entertaining books on the unexpected origins and colorful histories of words and phrases, based on sound scholarship, but written primarily for the layman. Over 1200 phrases and 1000 separate words are covered, with many quotations, and the results of the most modern linguistic and historical researches. "A right jolly book Mr. Holt has made," N. Y. Times. v + 254pp. 5⅜ x 8. T758 Paperbound **$1.35**

AMATEUR WINE MAKING, S. M. Tritton. Now, with only modest equipment and no prior knowledge, you can make your own fine table wines. A practical handbook, this covers every type of grape wine, as well as fruit, flower, herb, vegetable, and cereal wines, and many kinds of mead, cider, and beer. Every question you might have is answered, and there is a valuable discussion of what can go wrong at various stages along the way. Special supplement of yeasts and American sources of supply. 13 tables. 32 illustrations. Glossary. Index. 239pp. 5½ x 8½. T514 Clothbound **$4.00**

SAILING ALONE AROUND THE WORLD. Captain Joshua Slocum. A great modern classic in a convenient inexpensive edition. Captain Slocum's account of his single-handed voyage around the world in a 34 foot boat which he rebuilt himself. A nearly unparalleled feat of seamanship told with vigor, wit, imagination, and great descriptive power. "A nautical equivalent of Thoreau's account," Van Wyck Brooks. 67 illustrations. 308pp. 5⅜ x 8. T326 Paperbound **$1.00**

FARES, PLEASE! by J. A. Miller. Authoritative, comprehensive, and entertaining history of local public transit from its inception to its most recent developments: trolleys, horsecars, streetcars, buses, elevateds, subways, along with monorails, "road-railers," and a host of other extraordinary vehicles. Here are all the flamboyant personalities involved, the vehement arguments, the unusual information, and all the nostalgia. "Interesting facts brought into especially vivid life," N. Y. Times. New preface. 152 illustrations, 4 new. Bibliography. xix + 204pp. 5⅜ x 8. T671 Paperbound **$1.50**

HOAXES, C. D. MacDougall. Shows how art, science, history, journalism can be perverted for private purposes. Hours of delightful entertainment and a work of scholarly value, this often shocking book tells of the deliberate creation of nonsense news, the Cardiff giant, Shakespeare forgeries, the Loch Ness monster, Biblical frauds, political schemes, literary hoaxers like Chatterton, Ossian, the disumbrationist school of painting, the lady in black at Valentino's tomb, and over 250 others. It will probably reveal the truth about a few things you've believed, and help you spot more readily the editorial "gander" and planted publicity release. "A stupendous colleotion . . . and shrewd analysis." New Yorker. New revised edition. 54 photographs. Index. 320pp. 5⅜ x 8. T465 Paperbound **$1.75**

A HISTORY OF THE WARFARE OF SCIENCE WITH THEOLOGY IN CHRISTENDOM, A. D. White. Most thorough account ever written of the great religious-scientific battles shows gradual victory of science over ignorant, harmful beliefs. Attacks on theory of evolution; attacks on Galileo; great medieval plagues caused by belief in devil-origin of disease; attacks on Franklin's experiments with electricity; the witches of Salem; scores more that will amaze you. Author, co-founder and first president of Cornell U., writes with vast scholarly background, but in clear, readable prose. Acclaimed as classic effort in America to do away with superstition. Index. Total of 928pp. 5⅜ x 8. T608 Vol I Paperbound **$1.85**
T609 Vol II Paperbound **$1.85**

THE SHIP OF FOOLS, Sebastian Brant. First printed in 1494 in Basel, this amusing book swept Europe, was translated into almost every important language, and was a best-seller for centuries. That it is still living and vital is shown by recent developments in publishing. This is the only English translation of this work, and it recaptures in lively, modern verse all the wit and insights of the original, in satirizations of foibles and vices: greed, adultery, envy, hatred, sloth, profiteering, etc. This will long remain the definitive English edition, for Professor Zeydel has provided biography of Brant, bibliography, publishing history, influences, etc. Complete reprint of 1944 edition. Translated by Professor E. Zeydel, University of Cincinnati. All 114 original woodcut illustrations. viii + 399pp. 5½ x 8⅝. T266 Paperbound **$2.00**

ERASMUS, A STUDY OF HIS LIFE, IDEALS AND PLACE IN HISTORY, Preserved Smith. This is the standard English biography and evaluation of the great Netherlands humanist Desiderius Erasmus. Written by one of the foremost American historians it covers all aspects of Erasmus's life, his influence in the religious quarrels of the Reformation, his overwhelming role in the field of letters, and his importance in the emergence of the new world view of the Northern Renaissance. This is not only a work of great scholarship, it is also an extremely interesting, vital portrait of a great man. 8 illustrations. xiv + 479pp. 5⅝ x 8½. T331 Paperbound **$2.00**

Dover Classical Records

Now available directly to the public exclusively from Dover: top-quality recordings of fine classical music for only $2 per record! Originally released by a major company (except for the previously unreleased Gimpel recording of Bach) to sell for $5 and $6, these records were issued under our imprint only after they had passed a severe critical test. We insisted upon:

First-rate music that is enjoyable, musically important and culturally significant.

First-rate performances, where the artists have carried out the composer's intentions, in which the music is alive, vigorous, played with understanding and sympathy.

First-rate sound—clear, sonorous, fully balanced, crackle-free, whir-free.

Have in your home music by major composers, performed by such gifted musicians as Elsner, Gitlis, Wührer, the Barchet Quartet, Gimpel. Enthusiastically received when first released, many of these performances are definitive. The records are not seconds or remainders, but brand new pressings made on pure vinyl from carefully chosen master tapes. "All purpose" 12" monaural 33⅓ rpm records, they play equally well on hi-fi and stereo equipment. Fine music for discriminating music lovers, superlatively played, flawlessly recorded: there is no better way to build your library of recorded classical music at remarkable savings. There are no strings; this is not a come-on, not a club, forcing you to buy records you may not want in order to get a few at a lower price. Buy whatever records you want in any quantity, and never pay more than $2 each. Your obligation ends with your first purchase. And that's when ours begins. Dover's money-back guarantee allows you to return any record for any reason, even if you don't like the music, for a full, immediate refund, no questions asked.

MOZART: STRING QUARTET IN A MAJOR (K.464); STRING QUARTET IN C MAJOR ("DISSONANT", K.465), Barchet Quartet. The final two of the famed Haydn Quartets, high-points in the history of music. The A Major was accepted with delight by Mozart's contemporaries, but the C Major, with its dissonant opening, aroused strong protest. Today, of course, the remarkable resolutions of the dissonances are recognized as major musical achievements. "Beautiful warm playing," MUSICAL AMERICA. "Two of Mozart's loveliest quartets in a distinguished performance," REV. OF RECORDED MUSIC. (Playing time 58 mins.) HCR 5200 **$2.00**

MOZART: QUARTETS IN G MAJOR (K.80); D MAJOR (K.155); G MAJOR (K.156); C MAJOR (K157), Barchet Quartet. The early chamber music of Mozart receives unfortunately little attention. First-rate music of the Italian school, it contains all the lightness and charm that belongs only to the youthful Mozart. This is currently the only separate source for the composer's work of this time period. "Excellent," HIGH FIDELITY. "Filled with sunshine and youthful joy; played with verve, recorded sound live and brilliant," CHRISTIAN SCI. MONITOR. (Playing time 51 mins.) HCR 5201 **$2.00**

MOZART: SERENADE #9 IN D MAJOR ("POSTHORN", K.320); SERENADE #6 IN D MAJOR ("SERENATA NOTTURNA", K.239), Pro Musica Orch. of Stuttgart, under Edouard van Remoortel. For Mozart, the serenade was a highly effective form, since he could bring to it the immediacy and intimacy of chamber music as well as the free fantasy of larger group music. Both these serenades are distinguished by a playful, mischievous quality, a spirit perfectly captured in this fine performance. "A triumph, polished playing from the orchestra," HI FI MUSIC AT HOME. "Sound is rich and resonant, fidelity is wonderful," REV. OF RECORDED MUSIC. (Playing time 51 mins.) HCR 5202 **$2.00**

MOZART: DIVERTIMENTO IN E FLAT MAJOR FOR STRING TRIO (K.563); ADAGIO AND FUGUE IN F MINOR FOR STRING TRIO (K.404a), Kehr Trio. The Divertimento is one of Mozart's most beloved pieces, called by Einstein "the finest, most perfect trio ever heard." It is difficult to imagine a music lover who will not be delighted by it. This is the only recording of the lesser known Adagio and Fugue, written in 1782 and influenced by Bach's Well-Tempered Clavichord. "Extremely beautiful recording, strongly recommended," THE OBSERVER. "Superior to rival editions," HIGH FIDELITY. (Playing time 51 mins.) HCR 5203 **$2.00**

SCHUMANN: KREISLERIANA (OP.16); FANTASY IN C MAJOR ("FANTASIE," OP.17), Vlado Perlemuter, Piano. The vigorous Romantic imagination and the remarkable emotional qualities of Schumann's piano music raise it to special eminence in 19th century creativity. Both these pieces are rooted to the composer's tortuous romance with his future wife, Clara, and both receive brilliant treatment at the hands of Vlado Perlemuter, Paris Conservatory, proclaimed by Alfred Cortot "not only a great virtuoso but also a great musician." "The best Kreisleriana to date," BILLBOARD. (Playing time 55 mins.) HCR 5204 **$2.00**

SCHUMANN: TRIO #1, D MINOR; TRIO #3, G MINOR, Trio di Bolzano. The fiery, romantic, melodic Trio #1, and the dramatic, seldom heard Trio #3 are both movingly played by a fine chamber ensemble. No one personified Romanticism to the general public of the 1840's more than did Robert Schumann, and among his most romantic works are these trios for cello, violin and piano. "Ensemble and overall interpretation leave little to be desired," HIGH FIDELITY. "An especially understanding performance," REV. OF RECORDED MUSIC. (Playing time 54 mins.) HCR 5205 **$2.00**

New Books

101 PATCHWORK PATTERNS, Ruby Short McKim. With no more ability than the fundamentals of ordinary sewing, you will learn to make over 100 beautiful quilts: flowers, rainbows, Irish chains, fish and bird designs, leaf designs, unusual geometric patterns, many others. Cutting designs carefully diagrammed and described, suggestions for materials, yardage estimates, step-by-step instructions, plus entertaining stories of origins of quilt names, other folklore. Revised 1962. 101 full-sized patterns. 140 illustrations. Index. 128pp. 7⅞ x 10¾.

T773 Paperbound **$1.85**

ESSENTIAL GRAMMAR SERIES
By concentrating on the essential core of material that constitutes the semantically most important forms and areas of a language and by stressing explanation (often bringing parallel English forms into the discussion) rather than rote memory, this new series of grammar books is among the handiest language aids ever devised. Designed by linguists and teachers for adults with limited learning objectives and learning time, these books omit nothing important, yet they teach more usable language material and do it more quickly and permanently than any other self-study material. Clear and rigidly economical, they concentrate upon immediately usable language material, logically organized so that related material is always presented together. Any reader of typical capability can use them to refresh his grasp of language, to supplement self-study language records or conventional grammars used in schools, or to begin language study on his own. Now available:

ESSENTIAL GERMAN GRAMMAR, Dr. Guy Stern & E. F. Bleiler. Index. Glossary of terms. 128pp. 4½ x 6⅜.

T422 Paperbound **75¢**

ESSENTIAL FRENCH GRAMMAR, Dr. Seymour Resnick. Index. Cognate list. Glossary. 159pp. 4½ x 6⅜.

T419 Paperbound **75¢**

ESSENTIAL ITALIAN GRAMMAR, Dr. Olga Ragusa. Index. Glossary. 111pp. 4½ x 6⅜.

T779 Paperbound **75¢**

ESSENTIAL SPANISH GRAMMAR, Dr. Seymour Resnick. Index. 50-page cognate list. Glossary. 138pp. 4½ x 6⅜.

T780 Paperbound **75¢**

PHILOSOPHIES OF MUSIC HISTORY: A Study of General Histories of Music, 1600-1960, Warren D. Allen. Unquestionably one of the most significant documents yet to appear in musicology, this thorough survey covers the entire field of historical research in music. An influential masterpiece of scholarship, it includes early music histories; theories on the ethos of music; lexicons, dictionaries and encyclopedias of music; musical historiography through the centuries; philosophies of music history; scores of related topics. Copiously documented. New preface brings work up to 1960. Index. 317-item bibliography. 9 illustrations; 3 full-page plates. 5⅜ x 8½. xxxiv + 382pp.

T282 Paperbound **$2.00**

MR. DOOLEY ON IVRYTHING AND IVRYBODY, Finley Peter Dunne. The largest collection in print of hilarious utterances by the irrepressible Irishman of Archey Street, one of the most vital characters in American fiction. Gathered from the half dozen books that appeared during the height of Mr. Dooley's popularity, these 102 pieces are all unaltered and uncut, and they are all remarkably fresh and pertinent even today. Selected and edited by Robert Hutchinson. 5⅜ x 8½. xii + 244p.

T626 Paperbound **$1.00**

TREATISE ON PHYSIOLOGICAL OPTICS, Hermann von Helmholtz. Despite new investigations, this important work will probably remain preeminent. Contains everything known about physiological optics up to 1925, covering scores of topics under the general headings of dioptrics of the eye, sensations of vision, and perecptions of vision. Von Helmholtz's voluminous data are all included, as are extensive supplementary matter incorporated into the third German edition, new material prepared for 1925 English edition, and copious textual annotations by J. P. C. Southall. The most exhaustive treatise ever prepared on the subject, it has behind it a list of contributors that will never again be duplicated. Translated and edited by J. P. C. Southall. Bibliography. Indexes. 312 illustrations. 3 volumes bound as 2. Total of 1749pp. 5⅜ x 8.

S15-16 Two volume set, Clothbound **$15.00**

THE ARTISTIC ANATOMY OF TREES, Rex Vicat Cole. Even the novice with but an elementary knowledge of drawing and none of the structure of trees can learn to draw, paint trees from this systematic, lucid instruction book. Copiously illustrated with the author's own sketches, diagrams, and 50 paintings from the early Renaissance to today, it covers composition; structure of twigs, boughs, buds, branch systems; outline forms of major species; how leaf is set on twig; flowers and fruit and their arrangement; etc. 500 illustrations. Bibliography. Indexes. 347pp. 5⅜ x 8.

T1016 Clothbound **$4.50**

CATALOGUE OF DOVER BOOKS

GEOMETRY OF FOUR DIMENSIONS, H. P. Manning. Unique in English as a clear, concise introduction to this fascinating subject. Treatment is primarily synthetic and Euclidean, although hyperplanes and hyperspheres at infinity are considered by non-Euclidean forms. Historical introduction and foundations of 4-dimensional geometry; perpendicularity; simple angles; angles of planes; higher order; symmetry; order, motion; hyperpyramids, hypercones, hyperspheres; figures with parallel elements; volume, hypervolume in space; regular polyhedroids. Glossary of terms. 74 illustrations. ix + 348pp. 5⅜ x 8.   S182 Paperbound **$2.00**

PAPER FOLDING FOR BEGINNERS, W. D. Murray and F. J. Rigney. A delightful introduction to the varied and entertaining Japanese art of origami (paper folding), with a full, crystal-clear text that anticipates every difficulty; over 275 clearly labeled diagrams of all important stages in creation. You get results at each stage, since complex figures are logically developed from simpler ones. 43 different pieces are explained: sailboats, frogs, roosters, etc. 6 photographic plates. 279 diagrams. 95pp. 5⅝ x 8⅜.   T713 Paperbound **$1.00**

SATELLITES AND SCIENTIFIC RESEARCH, D. King-Hele. An up-to-the-minute non-technical account of the man-made satellites and the discoveries they have yielded up to September of 1961. Brings together information hitherto published only in hard-to-get scientific journals. Includes the life history of a typical satellite, methods of tracking, new information on the shape of the earth, zones of radiation, etc. Over 60 diagrams and 6 photographs. Mathematical appendix. Bibliography of over 100 items. Index. xii + 180pp. 5⅜ x 8½.
                         T703 Paperbound **$2.00**

LOUIS PASTEUR, S. J. Holmes. A brief, very clear, and warmly understanding biography of the great French scientist by a former Professor of Zoology in the University of California. Traces his home life, the fortunate effects of his education, his early researches and first theses, and his constant struggle with superstition and institutionalism in his work on microorganisms, fermentation, anthrax, rabies, etc. New preface by the author. 159pp. 5⅜ x 8.
                         T197 Paperbound **$1.00**

THE ENJOYMENT OF CHESS PROBLEMS, K. S. Howard. A classic treatise on this minor art by an internationally recognized authority that gives a basic knowledge of terms and themes for the everyday chess player as well as the problem fan: 7 chapters on the two-mover; 7 more on 3- and 4-move problems; a chapter on selfmates; and much more. "The most important one-volume contribution originating solely in the U.S.A.," Alain White. 200 diagrams. Index. Solutions, viii + 212pp. 5⅜ x 8.   T742 Paperbound **$1.25**

SAM LOYD AND HIS CHESS PROBLEMS, Alain C. White. Loyd was (for all practical purposes) the father of the American chess problem and his protégé and successor presents here the diamonds of his production, chess problems embodying a whimsy and bizarre fancy entirely unique. More than 725 in all, ranging from two-move to extremely elaborate five-movers, including Loyd's contributions to chess oddities—problems in which pieces are arranged to form initials, figures, other by-paths of chess problem found nowhere else. Classified according to major concept, with full text analyzing problems, containing selections from Loyd's own writings. A classic to challenge your ingenuity, increase your skill. Corrected republication of 1913 edition. Over 750 diagrams and illustrations. 744 problems with solutions. 471pp. 5⅜ x 8½.   T928 Paperbound **$2.00**

FABLES IN SLANG & MORE FABLES IN SLANG, George Ade. 2 complete books of major American humorist in pungent colloquial tradition of Twain, Billings. 1st reprinting in over 30 years includes "The Two Mandolin Players and the Willing Performer," "The Base Ball Fan Who Took the Only Known Cure," "The Slim Girl Who Tried to Keep a Date that was Never Made," 42 other tales of eccentric, perverse, but always funny characters. "Touch of genius," H. L. Mencken. New introduction by E. F. Bleiler. 86 illus. 208pp. 5⅜ x 8.
                         T533 Paperbound **$1.00**

Prices subject to change without notice.

Dover publishes books on art, music, philosophy, literature, languages, history, social sciences, psychology, handcrafts, orientalia, puzzles and entertainments, chess, pets and gardens, books explaining science, intermediate and higher mathematics, mathematical physics, engineering, biological sciences, earth sciences, classics of science, etc. Write to:

Dept. catrr.
Dover Publications, Inc.
180 Varick Street, N.Y. 14, N.Y.